150
GLIMPSES
OF THE
BEATLES

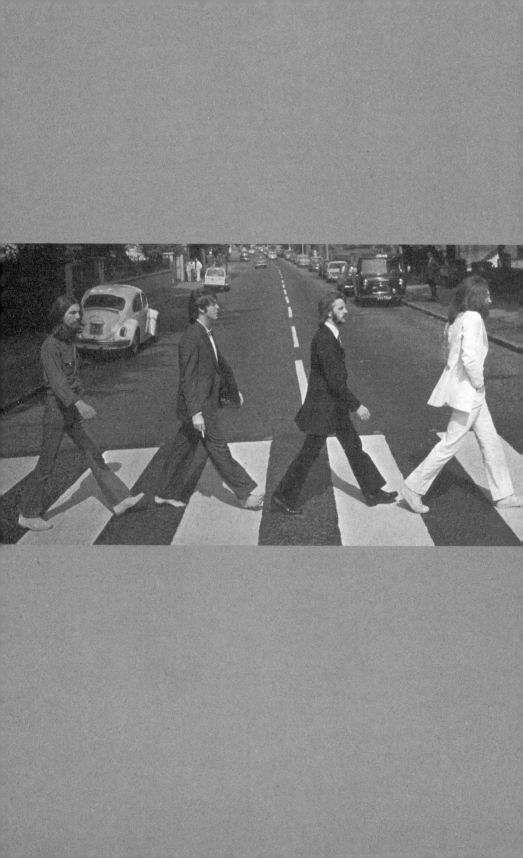

150

GLIMPSES

OF THE

BEATLES

CRAIG BROWN

FARRAR, STRAUS AND GIROUX
NEW YORK

Farrar, Straus and Giroux
120 Broadway, New York 10271

Copyright © 2020 by Craig Brown
All rights reserved
Printed in the United States of America
Originally published in 2020 by 4th Estate, Great Britain
Published in the United States by Farrar, Straus and Giroux
First American edition, 2020

Owing to limitations of space, illustration credits can be found on page 577.

Library of Congress Cataloging-in-Publication Data
Names: Brown, Craig, 1957– author.
Title: 150 glimpses of the Beatles / Craig Brown.
Other titles: One hundred and fifty glimpses of the Beatles
Description: First American edition. | New York : Farrar, Straus and Giroux, 2020. | Originally
    published in 2020 by 4th Estate, Great Britain. | Includes bibliographical references.
Identifiers: LCCN 2020022500 | ISBN 9780374109318 (hardcover)
Subjects: LCSH: Beatles. | Rock musicians—England—Biography.
Classification: LCC ML421.B4 B757 2020 | DDC 782.42166092/2 [B]—dc23
LC record available at https://lccn.loc.gov/2020022500

Designed by Gretchen Achilles

Our books may be purchased in bulk for promotional, educational, or business use.
Please contact your local bookseller or the Macmillan Corporate and Premium Sales Department at
1-800-221-7945, extension 5442, or by e-mail at MacmillanSpecialMarkets@macmillan.com.

www.fsgbooks.com
www.twitter.com/fsgbooks • www.facebook.com/fsgbooks

1   3   5   7   9   10   8   6   4   2

For Frances, Silas, Tallulah and Tom

In five-score summers! All new eyes,
New minds, new modes, new fools, new wise;
New woes to weep, new joys to prize;
With nothing left of me and you
In that live century's vivid view
Beyond a pinch of dust or two;
A century which, if not sublime,
Will show, I doubt not, at its prime,
A scope above this blinkered time.

—From '1967', by Thomas Hardy
(written in 1867)

What a remarkable fifty years they have been
for the world . . . Think what we would have
missed if we had never heard the Beatles.

—Queen Elizabeth II,
speaking in November 1997 at a celebration
of her golden wedding anniversary

150
GLIMPSES
OF THE
BEATLES

1.

One.

   Two.

      Three.

         Four.

In their neat black suits and ties, Brian Epstein and his personal assistant Alistair Taylor make their way down the eighteen steep steps into the sweaty basement on Mathew Street. Brian finds it 'as black as a deep grave, dank and damp and smelly'. He wishes he hadn't come. Both he and Taylor would prefer to be attending a classical concert at the Philharmonic, but curiosity got the better of them. Four young musicians saunter onto the stage. Brian recognises them from the family record shop he manages: they are the ones who lounge around in the booths, listening to the latest discs and chatting to the girls, with absolutely no intention whatsoever of buying a record.

Between songs, the three yobs with guitars start yelling and swearing, turning their backs on the audience and pretending to hit one another. Taylor notices Brian's eyes widen with amazement. Taylor himself is undergoing one of the most shocking experiences of his life – 'like someone thumping you' – and he is pretty sure Brian feels the same.

After the show, Taylor says, 'They're just AWFUL.'

'They ARE awful,' agrees Brian. 'But I also think they're fabulous. Let's just go and say hello.'

George is the first of the Beatles to spot the man from the record shop approaching.

'Hello there,' he says. 'What brings Mr Epstein here?'

2.

Other groups had a front man; your favourite was pre-selected for you. No one would ever pick Hank Marvin over Cliff Richard, say, or Mike Smith over Dave Clark.

But with the Beatles there was a choice, so you had to pick a favourite, and the one you picked said a lot about who you were. For their American fan Carolyn See, there was 'Paul, for those who preferred androgynous beauty; John, for those who prized intellect and wit; George because he possessed that ineffable something we would later recognize as spiritual life; and Ringo, patron saint of fuckups the world over.'

In Liverpool, the twelve-year-old Linda Grant favoured Ringo 'for reasons that are beyond me'. There was, she recalls, 'a real goody-two-shoes at school who liked Paul. George seemed a bit nothing. John seemed off-limits, too intimidating.'

Ringo was the Beatle for girls who lacked ambition. Picking him as your favourite suggested a touch of realism. It went without saying that the others were already taken, but you might just stand an outside chance with the drummer. 'If someone asked who my favorite was I always said, "Oh, I like Ringo,"' remembered Fran Lebowitz, who grew up in New Jersey. 'I liked the personality of Ringo Starr. I still do. He was not, of course, the favorite in my school among the girls. Paul McCartney was far and away the favorite. He was the cute Beatle. So it was probably just a contrarian position to choose Ringo Starr.'

Helen Shapiro was only sixteen but already a major star when the Beatles toured as one of her supporting acts at the start of 1963. Like any other girl, she had her favourite. 'John was married but nobody knew about it at the time so along with a few thousand other girls I had a crush on him . . . George was the most serious. He would occasionally talk about what he was going to do when he was rich, and try to pick my brains about the financial side of things. I couldn't have been a lot of help. I still wasn't interested in the money. Paul remained the spokesman. Ringo was the quiet one.'

Pattie Boyd met the four Beatles after being chosen to play one of the schoolgirls in *Hard Day's Night*. 'On first impressions, John seemed more cynical and brash than the others, Ringo the most endearing. Paul was cute, and George, with velvet brown eyes and dark chestnut hair, was the best-looking man I'd ever seen.' Unlike millions of other fans, Pattie was able to take her choice a stage further. Reader, she married him.

There was a Beatle to suit every taste. As a fan, you expressed yourself by picking one over the others. Each personified a different element: John fire, Paul water, George air, Ringo earth. Even their friends liked to paint them in primary colours, with sharply contrasting characters, like one of those jokes about the Englishman, the Welshman, the Irishman and the Scotsman. Carolyn See noted how, in *A Hard Day's Night*, they enacted their given personas: 'winsome Paul, witty John, thoughtful George, goofy Ringo'.

The actor Victor Spinetti once told this story about them. While filming *Help!* in Salzburg, he caught 'flu and was confined to bed. 'The Beatles came to my hotel room to visit. The first to arrive was George Harrison. He knocked, came in and said, "I've come to plump your pillows. Whenever anyone's ill in bed they have to have their pillows plumped." He then plumped my pillows and left. John Lennon came in next and marched up and down barking "*Sieg heil, Schweinhund!* The doctors are here. They're coming to experiment upon you. *Sieg heil! Heil Hitler!*" And he left. Ringo then came in, sat down by the bed, picked up the hotel menu and read out loud, as if to a child, "Once upon a time there were three bears. Mummy bear, Daddy bear and Baby bear." And then he left. Paul opened the door an inch, asked, "Is it catching?" "Yes," I said, on which he shut the door and I never saw him again.' Paul was being the pragmatist, as usual. He knew that if he or the others had caught 'flu, there'd be no filming.

Working alongside Brian Epstein, Alistair Taylor observed the different ways the Beatles dealt with their earnings. 'Every month, Brian would issue each of the boys with their financial statements, all neatly and accurately itemised, and sealed in a white manila envelope. They reacted very different. John would instantly crumple it up and stuff it in his pocket. George might have a look. Ringo certainly couldn't understand it and didn't waste any time trying. Paul was the one who opened it carefully and would sit in the corner of the office for hours going meticulously through it.'

As they grew older, the differences in their characters became sharper. It was as though the wind had changed, and each had been stuck with the face he last pulled. Asked to submit ideas for famous figures to include on the *Sgt. Pepper* album cover, George suggested a few Indian gurus, and Paul picked a broad variety of artists, from Stockhausen to Fred Astaire. John's suggestions were more macabre or offbeat: the Marquis de Sade, Edgar Allan Poe, Jesus, Hitler. And as for Ringo, he simply said he'd go along with what the others wanted.

Of course, the Beatles revolved around the contrasting characters of Paul and John. Their recording engineer Geoff Emerick watched the two of them at work. 'They couldn't have been two more different people. Paul was meticulous and organised, he always carried a notebook around with him, in which he methodically wrote down lyrics and chord changes in his neat handwriting. In contrast, John seemed to live in chaos: he was constantly searching for scraps of paper that he'd scribbled hurried ideas on. Paul was a natural communicator; John couldn't articulate his ideas well. Paul was the diplomat; John was the agitator. Paul was soft-spoken and almost unfailingly polite; John could be a right loudmouth and quite rude. Paul was willing to put in long hours to get a part right; John was impatient, always ready to move on to the next thing. Paul usually knew exactly what he wanted and would often take offence at criticism; John was much more thick-skinned and was open to hearing what others had to say.'

John was brittle, demanding and caustic; Paul emollient, engaging, agreeable. But there were those who detected something single-minded, perhaps even self-serving, beneath Paul's charm. Tony Barrow, who worked as the Beatles' press officer, felt that 'John made the most noise, especially with Epstein. But it was Paul who let John do the heavy lifting when there was a dispute with Brian. Then Paul would finish the persuasion. John would make Brian cry at times, but Paul, more of a politician, would use a quiet influence to get his way. John's bark was worse than his bite. He used the bark to cover up low self-esteem . . . Paul promised people everything, tickets, gifts, then left it to people like me to fulfil the promises. He wanted to look like a good benefactor, and he was long on promises, short on performance. He was a charmer who was a public relations delight, a man who was master of image-making. He is and was a sheer showman, from his bone marrow to his fingertips. He feeds on the approval of his public.'

Paul was baby-faced, meticulous, perky, diplomatic, energetic, tuneful, ingratiating, optimistic, outgoing, cheery, sentimental, solicitous. John was angular, slapdash, maudlin, difficult, lazy, dissonant, edgy, sardonic, pessimistic, solipsistic, sulky, cool, brutal. Paul considered himself lovable; John believed himself unlovable.

Paul once tried to explain how the two of them had become what they were. 'John, because of his upbringing and his unstable family life, had to be hard, witty, always ready for the cover-up, ready for the riposte, ready with the sharp little witticism. Whereas with my rather comfortable upbringing, a lot of family, a lot of people, very northern, "Cup of tea, love?", my surface grew to be easy-going. Put people at their ease. Chat to people, be nice, it's nice to be nice . . . Mentally, no one could say much to hurt me, whereas with John: his dad wasn't home, so it was "Where's yer dad, you bastard?" And his mother lived with somebody and that was called "living in sin" in those days, so there was another cheap shot against him. John had a lot to guard against, and it formed his personality; he was a very guarded person . . . He had massive hang-ups from his upbringing.'

The peculiar power of the Beatles' music, its magic and its beauty, lies in the intermingling of these opposites. Other groups were raucous or reflective, progressive or traditional, solemn or upbeat, folksy or sexy or aggressive. But when you hear a Beatles album, you feel that all human life is there. As John saw it, when they were composing together, Paul 'provided a lightness, an optimism, while I would always go for sadness, the discords, a certain bluesy edge'. It was this finely balanced push me/pull you tension that made their greatest music so expressive, capable of being both universal and particular at one and the same time.

Even as teenagers, they approached their songwriting with a sense of purpose. Paul would bunk off school, and John would join him in the McCartney house in Forthlin Road. Then Paul would open his school notebook, with its blue lines on white paper, and write, 'Another Lennon-McCartney original' on the next blank page, and the two of them would get straight down to composing their next song. Looking back, Paul struggled to recall a fruitless afternoon. 'We never had a dry session . . . In all the years, we never walked away from a session saying, "Fuck it, we can't write one."'

Sometimes their contributions to the same song were so keenly differentiated that they seemed to be playing up to their caricatures. Paul comes up with 'We can work it out', and John immediately undercuts it: 'Life is very short'. Paul sings 'It's getting better' and John butts in with 'Can't get much worse'. In 'A Day in the Life' it is John, compulsive reader of newspapers, who just has to laugh at the man who's blown his mind out in a car, while it is the happy-go-lucky Paul who wakes up, gets out of bed, drags a comb across his head.

Many of their songs have bright melodies but dark lyrics, or dark melodies but bright lyrics. The words of 'Help!', 'Run for Your Life', 'Misery' and 'Maxwell's Silver Hammer' are all about depression and psychosis, but they are set to jaunty tunes. Deprived of this tug-of-war between the two competing partners, their solo songs often lack that dimension of otherness, with John falling back on self-pity and Paul giving in to whimsy.*

As time went by, their collaboration dwindled, and they composed more and more of their songs separately. But they remained driven by a shared sense of competition; each sought the other's approval. 'It was an ideal match,' wrote the critic Ian MacDonald. 'They laughed at the same things, thought at the same speed, respected each other's talent, and knew that their unspoken urge to best and surprise each other was crucial to the continuing vitality of their music.'

---

* Fourteen years after the Beatles broke up, Paul told Steve Grant of *Time Out*: 'I know I've lost my edge . . . I need a kind of outside injection, stimulus, that's not there any more. And remember the edge came from all the Beatles – if Ringo or George didn't like anything, it was out. My stuff has got more poppy without that outside stimulus, but then I've always been more at home with love songs and anthems.' At the same time, John remained frustrated at the relative lack of take-up of his own songs. 'It would sometimes annoy him that Paul's songs were more covered than his,' Yoko told Philip Norman in 2008. 'He'd say, "They always cover Paul's songs – they never cover mine."' In 2019 Paul smiled as he told the BBC journalist Emily Maitlis how cross John would get when he walked into hotel lounges in New York and pianists, seeking to please him, would immediately launch into flowery renditions of 'Yesterday'.

3.

Mary Mohin is thirty years old, and still unmarried. Mary's mother died in 1919, while giving birth to her fifth child, who also died. At the time, Mary was ten years old. Perhaps influenced by this early tragedy, Mary set her heart on becoming a midwife. She achieved her ambition, and more: she is now not only a midwife, but a ward sister.

Jim McCartney is thirty-eight years old, and still unmarried. He was his mother's fifth child, but only the third to live beyond the age of two. He left school just before his fourteenth birthday, and got a good job at a cotton brokers. He is now a cotton salesman, on a decent wage. His main love, though, is playing trumpet with his own six-to-eight-piece ensemble – Jim Mac's Band. They perform all the latest dance tunes; Jim's favourite is 'I'll Build a Stairway to Paradise'.

Excused wartime service because he is deaf in one ear, Jim is attached to the Fazakerley Fire Unit. German bombs have been falling on Liverpool since August; London is the only city to have suffered more devastation.* Somehow, the deadpan Liverpudlian humour sees them through. Over in Arnold Grove, the Harrison family have had their windows blown out, and their leather sofa, which they reserved for special occasions, was shredded by the flying glass. 'If I'd known that was going to happen we could have been sitting on it all these years,' observes Mrs Harrison.

Mary lodges with Jim's sister Jin. Mary and Jim have known each other quite well for some years now, though they have never thought of each other in terms of romance.

---

* Over four thousand Liverpudlians were killed in the Blitz.

A

Tonight the Nazi bombers fly overhead. Jin and Mary are visiting Jim's mum in Scargreen Avenue when the sirens sound, so they have to stay over. As the bombs fall, Jim and Mary sit and chat for hours. By the time the all-clear is sounded, they feel they are meant for one another. After a brief engagement, they marry on 15 April 1941; just over a year later, Mary gives birth to their first child, a boy. They christen him James Paul McCartney.

B

Tonight is quiet. The sirens never sound. As it happens, they will tomorrow night, when Jin and Mary are planning on staying home. So Jim and Mary fail to have their heart-to-heart, and go their separate ways. James Paul McCartney is never born.

4.

We had been told to gather outside Liverpool at Speke Hall, described by the National Trust as 'a rare Tudor timber-framed manor house in a most unusual setting on the banks of the River Mersey'. The estate has, the guidebook advises, 'witnessed more than 400 years of turbulent history'.

I was early, so I hung around in the 'Visitor Complex' – a building, not a condition – looking at mugs and scarves and soaps and books about the Tudors. 'A bit of a bookworm? Thumb through our collection of adults' and children's books to find your next great read!'

Before long, a cheery driver called Joe shepherded us onto a minibus, then asked us where we were from. Three of us were from Spain, two from Italy, four from Australia, two from Austria, four from England. A couple of people who had bought tickets were missing, so we waited until two young women came running towards the bus, waving frantically. 'Let's give them a fright,' said Joe, turning on the ignition and setting off. They waved more frantically. 'And now let's see those tears turn to laughter,' said Joe, stopping the minibus and letting them in.

As the minibus left Speke Hall, Joe pressed a button and 'Love Me Do' came bursting from the speakers. 'Whassis rubbish then?' shouted an Australian at the back.

'I can see who'll be walkin' back!' said Joe. 'When he gets off the bus, let's jump 'im!' It was all very merry.

Soon we were in Forthlin Road, the kind of unassuming row of nondescript houses most National Trust members would normally drive through, rather than to.

The National Trust bought 20 Forthlin Road in 1995, on the suggestion of the then director-general of the BBC, a Liverpudlian called John

Birt,* who had noticed it was up for sale. Seven years later the Trust also acquired John Lennon's childhood home, 'Mendips', in Menlove Avenue, after it had been bought by Yoko Ono. In a statement around that time, she said: 'When I heard that Mendips was up for sale, I was worried that it might fall into the wrong hands and be commercially exploited. That's why I decided to buy the house, and donate it to the National Trust so it would be well looked after as a place for people to visit and see. I am thrilled that the National Trust has agreed to take it on.'

But it was a decision not welcomed by one and all. Tim Knox, at that time the National Trust's head curator,† declared himself 'furious'. The Trust's usual criterion for taking on a property – that the building should have intrinsic artistic merit – had, he felt, been abandoned in pursuit of shabby populism. 'They're publicity coups – not serious acquisitions,' he said, adding, only half-jokingly, 'Now we're going to take four properties on so Ringo doesn't feel left out.'

Others agreed. 'Architecturally, the house is no more or less interesting than any other arterial, pebble-dashed semi in any other middle-class suburb,' observed the design critic Stephen Bayley.‡ 'Its special value comes from the vicarious, mystical contact with genius. The problem for the Trust's architectural historians is that, since the house was pretty much denuded of its contents, there is no possibility of vicarious, mystical contact with the genius's telly set, kitchen unit or any other artefact that might

---

* John Birt, director-general of the BBC 1992–2000. In the summer of 1962 the seventeen-year-old Birt had a holiday job as a bouncer at Southport's Cambridge Hall, where the Beatles were playing two consecutive evenings with Joe Brown and the Bruvvers headlining. After the first concert he and a friend were told to guard the door of the Beatles' Green Room to keep out, in his words, 'a score of emotional and tearful girls of my own age'. One of these girls turned out to be 'the most beautiful girl in Formby. We saw her on the train to school each day. She was in a league of beauty of her own and paid no attention to any of us. No one in my circle had ever spoken to her.' She pleaded with Birt and his friend to let her in to see Paul McCartney. 'My friend said: "We'll let you in to see Paul if you let us have a snog and a feel." She immediately agreed and led us off to some backstairs [sic]. To my shame even at the time, I participated in the encounter despite her inert response. This unedifying experience was soon cut short and we led her back to the Green Room to find that the Beatles had gone. I rushed around in a guilty panic trying to locate Paul and, to my relief, found him at the bar. I retrieved the girl, and took her to Paul, who was with a crowd of admirers. He turned round, recognised me as the bouncer, realised I was there with a purpose and raised his eyebrows questioningly. I explained that I was with someone very keen to meet him and introduced Paul to the apparition at my side. He bowed graciously, and as I departed in embarrassment they were chatting politely to one another.'

† Now the director of the Royal Collection.

‡ Coincidentally, the very same Stephen Bayley who at the age of fifteen wrote the letter to John that spurred him to write 'I am the Walrus' (see page 374).

afford an insight into the inspiration that gave us such a torrent of brilliant words and music. So, they set about faking it.

'The National Trust . . . prides itself on its access to expertise. It has some of the world's leading architectural historians on its staff and they went out to buy the stuff to recreate Lennon's home. But when scholarly expertise is focused on junk, in a magical mystery tour of some dingy Liverpudlian dealers, scholarly expertise looks silly. A crap medicine cabinet is admired for its authenticity. The lino is subject to scrutiny worthy of a Donatello relief sculpture. They can find the conical legs of the television set, but not the set itself . . . If you are doing the long and winding road of fakery, where do you stop? In the dreamworld of folk memory and fantasy, is the answer.'

The National Trust remains undaunted. 'Imagine walking through the back door into the kitchen where John Lennon's Aunt Mimi would have cooked him his tea,' reads its awestruck introduction to Mendips. It treats the house as a religious shrine, a place of pilgrimage. 'Join our fascinating Custodian on a trip down memory lane . . . John's bedroom is a very atmospheric place in which to take a moment with your own thoughts about this incredible individual . . .'

Pilgrims to Mendips face rules and regulations stricter than those for the Sistine Chapel. 'Any photography inside Mendips or duplication of audio tour material is strictly prohibited. You will be asked to deposit all handbags, cameras and recording equipment at the entrance to the house.'

It can't be long, surely, before one of the faithful witnesses some sort of miracle at Mendips – a blind man sees, a crippled man rises up and walks, a little girl sees John's mother Julia in a vision – leading yet more pilgrims to flock to Menlove Avenue, forming orderly queues for the chance to see the exact spot where Julia met her end.

While our minibus was decanting its passengers, many more were pouring out of a 'Magical Mystery Tour' coach, and behind them, four Germans were stepping out of a black cab. The gateway to 20 Forthlin Road was pullulating with visitors from all over the world, wearing Beatles T-shirts and posing for selfies. The metal sign outside announces 'The proud family home of the McCartney family, Jim, Mary, Paul and Mike. Accessible via the National Trust.'

I started edging towards the front of the queue. I had booked way in advance and paid £31 (including guidebooks) for an official tour of both Beatles houses, and I was worried that people on unofficial tours would creep their way past the guide and elbow their way into Paul's house in my place. Luckily, Joe the driver was standing by, monitoring the chosen few. Our little group marched self-importantly into the front garden of 20 Forthlin Road, and the gates were then satisfyingly closed on everybody else.

Our National Trust guide introduced herself as Sylvia. She conducts 12,000 people a year around Paul's childhood home, twenty at a go, four times a day. Her voice has a hint of Hyacinth Bucket. Standing in the garden, she welcomed us to 20 Forthlin Road. This, she said, was where Paul lived for eight years: 'very important years musically. George Harrison was an early visitor. George would bring his guitar.'

A buzz went around. Stephen Bayley's promise of mystical contact seemed to be taking shape. 'And then when John Lennon started to come down to the house, John would take a short cut through the golf course to get here on his bicycle, taking less than ten minutes through the golf course. And in the room behind you there' – she gestured – 'that's where John and Paul sat down and began writing songs together. By the time Paul left here, it was right at the end of 1963, so the Beatles had already got hits in the charts, they were appearing on television. Paul was still coming back though, that was still his bedroom up there, right until the end of 1963. He was the last Beatle to move to London. So when the McCartneys came – sorry, are you recording?'

I froze. I had been covertly recording Sylvia on a mobile phone, but it turned out that she was talking to one of the Australians, standing closer to her. He assured her that, no, he wasn't recording. 'No?' she replied, suspiciously. 'I'm sorry, I just don't like it,' she muttered, before struggling to regain her thread. 'Erm. When. Erm. The McCartneys. So. Erm. When the McCartneys came to live here, erm, these were all council houses, so that means the McCartneys didn't own this house, it was social housing, everybody paid rent.'

Unbeknownst to Sylvia, I carried on recording, slyly holding my phone at a casual angle so as not to excite her attention. It made me feel on edge, as though I were pocketing household products within spitting distance of a store detective.

'Over the years, you can see what's happened. People have bought the houses, and they've changed the doors and windows. When the National Trust got this house, twenty-two years ago now, there were new windows at the front, but the Trust saw that a house across the street still had these original windows, so they did a deal, they got the new ones and we got the old ones back again. So now it looks exactly as it did when Paul and his family lived here.'

We all gazed dutifully at these front windows, marvelling that they now looked just like they would have looked before they looked different. Meanwhile, my phone was recording, and I was growing increasingly worried that Sylvia would notice, and denounce me.

'OK, so if anyone wants a photograph at the front of the house, just give me your phone or your camera. Move to the end of the window so I can fit you in, bunch up a bit for me.' Groups of visitors stood beaming in front of Paul's old front door, or what would have been Paul's old front door if it had been Paul's old front door, which it wasn't. 'Is that everyone? Is that it?'

Sylvia warned us that we were not allowed to take photographs in the house or the back garden. 'There's a special reason here. You'll see inside we've got Mike McCartney, Paul's younger brother's, copyright photographs all around the house. It's lovely to have them. And you'll enjoy them. But he'd take them away if people had photographs of them.'

We moved into the back garden. The National Trust blurb suggests '5 things to look out for at 20 Forthlin Road'. One is described as 'The Back Drainpipe: After Paul's mum died, his father would insist that the two boys were home in time for dinner, if not they were locked out. When this inevitably happened, Paul and Mike would run round the back of the house, climb up the drainpipe, and through the bathroom window, which they always left on the latch for such an eventuality.' Sylvia repeated this anecdote, almost word for word, as we all stared at the drainpipe – or, to be accurate, the replica drainpipe.

'So if when you come in you could hand me your bags and cameras, and if you've got a mobile phone can you switch it off and hand it in, so we don't want to see mobile phones in your pockets.'

With that, Sylvia ushered us inside. Everyone lined up to give her their phones and cameras, as though crossing the border of a particularly nervy country. She then locked them all in a cupboard under the stairs.

Disobediently, I kept my mobile phone in my pocket, and immediately regretted it. Throughout the rest of my visit I was terrified that someone would phone me, and the ringing would act as an alarm bell and I would be unmasked and shamed.

We all squeezed into the sitting room, decorated with three different types of wallpaper – 'the McCartney family bought end-of rolls' – none of them original. The brown armchair, chunky 1950s television and corner table were not original either, and nor were the rugs. 'This is the room the McCartneys called the front parlour. The National Trust has recreated it with the aid of photos and family memories,' said Sylvia. In response to a query she said that no, the piano was not original. 'Paul still owns his father's house, and he stays in it when he comes to Liverpool. And that's where the original McCartney piano is. Jim used to play "The Entertainer". Do you know that song – by Scott Joplin? If you think of Scott Joplin and "When I'm 64", you can really tell the influence . . . Father Jim was a good self-taught musician. Paul followed in his father's footsteps. After a few lessons, he said, "I'll be just like my Dad. I'll teach myself." . . . He composed "World Without Love" here, and the very beginnings of "Michelle" were written here. And "Love Me Do" – they were sitting here when they wrote it . . . Paul sat here and wrote "I'll Follow the Sun".' She pointed to a photo of John and Paul on the wall. 'The song they're finishing in this picture is "I Saw Her Standing There" . . . Another song they finished off was "Please Please Me".'

Every now and then, Sylvia tried to make things personal, beginning her sentences 'Paul told me' – as in, 'Paul told me, "We had some sad years but most of the time we were really happy."' Or, 'This was their dining room. Paul told me, "We never ate in here after Mum died."' She added, 'Paul told me, "A lot of people think 'Let it Be' is about the Virgin Mary, but it was about my mother, who would always say 'Let it be.'"' I had read these stories countless times over the years,* but it obviously afforded Sylvia satisfaction to say that she had heard them direct from Paul; and perhaps

---

* Most recently in the 2018 Paul McCartney *Carpool Karaoke* (50,000,000 views, 70,000 comments), in which Paul says, 'I had a dream in the sixties, where my mum, who'd died, came to me in the dream and was reassuring me, saying, "It's going to be okay, just let it be." And I felt so great, like, it's going to be great . . . So I wrote the song. But it was her positivity.'

  In the *New Yorker* in February 2020, James Corden, who chaperoned Paul around Liverpool for his *Carpool Karaoke*, revealed that Paul had initially been reluctant to return to his family home. 'He said, "I haven't been there since I left, when I was twenty. I just feel weird about it."'

in the coming years it would satisfy us, too, to say that we had heard them from someone who had heard them from Paul.

We shuffled into the kitchen. 'The quarry tiles have not been changed. All the Beatles have stood on those quarry tiles – though Ringo only twice, as he came late.' We peered down at the sacred tiles beneath our feet. 'The Trust found the original white sink in the garden with plants in it and returned it to its rightful position.' We gazed awestruck at the kitchen sink, imagining young Paul hard at work on the dishes.

Only the tiles and the sink are original to the kitchen, but the experts from the National Trust found feasible lookalikes for the rest: the packet of Lux soap flakes, the Stork margarine, the tea can, the biscuit tin, the wireless, the clothes horse. Photographs of all these items – the domestic equivalents of tribute bands – may be purchased on the National Trust website: photos of a 1950s record player, vacuum cleaner, bread bin, washing tongs, frying pan, kettle, clothes pegs, rolling pin. And everything has been diligently catalogued, like items from the Tower of London. A photograph of a wooden spoon (Date 1960–1962, 260mm; Materials: Wood) is described as 'Historic Services,/Food & drink preparation, Summary: Wooden spoon, kept in mixing bowl on dresser'.

Alternatively, you can buy a photo of a tea strainer or a doormat or a frying pan or a coat rack or 'Enamel bucket with black rim and handle with wooden grip, date unknown'.

The pride of the collection is surely 'Dustbin: Metalwork, Date 1940–1960, Summary: Metal dustbin with separate lid (plus spare lid in Coal Shed)'. If you were a battered old dustbin, circa 1940–1960, just imagine how proud you would be to end up as a key exhibit in a National Trust property, with 12,000 visitors a year admiring you for looking just like the dustbin into which the McCartney family used to throw its rubbish!

While we were still squeezed downstairs, I became so scared that my phone would ring that I surreptitiously switched it off, and began taking notes instead. 'The lino on the floors is just right,' Sylvia was saying, 'so we managed to track it down, and the cupboard where I put the bags, well, that was where Paul would hang up his jacket and sometimes his leather trousers. Excuse me, you're taking notes. Why are you taking notes?' With a start, I realised that Sylvia was talking to me. 'Who's it for?'

'Me,' I said.

'I'm just checking you're not a journalist.'

'I am. I'm writing a book.'

'Well, I don't like you taking notes.'

'Why not?'

'Well, it's just that a lot of what I say has been told to me by Mike, and it's private information.'

'But you've said you tell it to 12,000 people a year. It can't be all that private.'

'I'm sorry, it's making me uncomfortable. What did you say your name was?'

And so there we were, arguing away in the McCartney front parlour on a very hot day in August. We finally came to some sort of deal that I wouldn't write anything that Sylvia regarded as strictly private, but she kept throwing suspicious glances in my direction. I sensed my fellow visitors edging away from me, as though I had just broken wind.

Eventually we were permitted upstairs. Sylvia led us into Paul's bedroom. On his bed sat an acoustic guitar, strung for a left-hander. Inevitably, this was not the actual guitar. A few records were also on the bed, along with a sketch pad and a copy of the *New Musical Express*. 'We've collected all sorts of things he had in this room. For instance, the bird books – Paul was always a keen birdwatcher.'

'This is strictly private,' she added, looking daggers at me, 'but Paul told me he always liked looking out over these fields, which belonged to the police training college. He liked watching the police horses in the back field.'

It was only later, browsing through the National Trust's colour guide to 20 Forthlin Road, that I chanced upon this passage in Paul's introduction: 'The house looks onto a police training college, and we could sit on the roof of our shed and watch the annual police show without having to pay.'

5.

On 6 July 1957, Paul's school friend Ivan Vaughan suggested they go to the church fête at Woolton, where two of his mates would be playing in a skiffle group.

Paul and Ivan looked on as a carnival procession left the church – a brass band, followed by Girl Guides and Boy Scouts and a succession of decorated floats, all led by the Rose Queen and her attendants. At the tail end came the organisers' sole concession to modernity – a teenage skiffle group called the Quarrymen, playing on the back of an open lorry.

Once they had completed a circuit, the Quarrymen jumped off their lorry and set themselves up in a field just beyond the cemetery. Ivan and Paul paid threepence to see them. The first song they heard John sing was 'Come Go With Me' by the Del-Vikings. Paul looked on fascinated, not only by the chords John was playing, but by his ability to make things up as he went along: even then, he couldn't be bothered to learn the words. Using this improvisatory method, John sang his way through 'Maggie May', 'Putting on the Style' and 'Be-Bop-a-Lula'.

Between sets John wandered over to the Scout hut, where he knew his guitar would be safe. Elsewhere, crowds were enjoying a routine by the Liverpool City Police Dogs, while youngsters queued for balloons.

Paul wandered over to the hut with Ivan. He recognised John from the bus, but had never spoken to him: Paul had just turned fifteen, while John was nearly seventeen. Even at that age, John had an intimidating air about him: 'I wouldn't look at him too hard in case he hit me.' So Paul hovered shyly. The group then transferred to the church hall, where they were booked to play another set later. After a while Paul felt bold enough to ask John if he might have a go on his guitar.

Armed with the guitar, he grew bolder still. First, he asked to retune it, and then he launched into various songs, among them 'Twenty Flight Rock' and 'Be-Bop-a-Lula'. 'It was uncanny,' recalled another Quarryman,

Eric Griffiths. 'He had such confidence, he gave a *performance*. It was so natural.'

Ever more confident, Paul moved to the piano, and struck up a medley of Little Richard songs. John, too, was obsessed by Little Richard – when he first heard him singing 'Long Tall Sally', 'It was so great I couldn't speak.' And now here before him, a year later, was this kid who could holler just like his idol.

'WoooOOOOOOOOOOOOO!'

'I half thought to myself, "He's as good as me,"' said John, looking back on that singular moment. 'Now, I thought, if I take him on, what will happen? It went through my head that I'd have to keep him in line if I let him join. But he was good, so he was worth having. He also looked like Elvis.'

Another band member recalled the two of them circling each other 'like cats'. After a while Paul and Ivan drifted off home; the Quarrymen had another set to play.

Later, John asked his best friend Pete Shotton, who played washboard, what he thought of Paul. Pete said he liked him.

'So what would you think about having Paul in the group, then?'

'It's OK with me.'

Two weeks later, Paul was riding his bicycle when he spotted Pete Shotton walking along. He stopped to chat.

'By the way,' said Pete, 'I've been talking with John about it, and . . . we thought maybe you'd like to join the group.'

According to Pete, a minute ticked by while Paul pretended to give the matter careful thought.

'Oh, all right,' he replied with a shrug; and with that he cycled off home.

Everyone has a different version of this first meeting between John and Paul. No two accounts are the same. Some say they met in the hut, others in the hall; some are convinced Aunt Mimi was present, others are equally convinced she was not; of those who say she was, some think she enjoyed the concert, while others remember her tut-tutting all the way through. In 1967 Pete Shotton told the Beatles' first biographer, Hunter Davies, that he couldn't remember Paul making much of an impression on anyone: 'He seemed very quiet.' But sixteen years later, when he came to write his autobiography, his memory had changed: 'John was immediately impressed by what he heard and saw.'

6.

Back on the National Trust minibus, we were now on our way to Mendips, where John Lennon lived with his Aunt Mimi. The custodian of Mendips is Colin, who is, as it happens, married to Sylvia. He used to teach English and history, and had retired to Derbyshire. But in 2003 he answered an advertisement for a guide for Mendips, and he has been there ever since.

While I was on the bus between the two houses I worried that Sylvia might have phoned Colin to warn him of trouble ahead, but he appeared unruffled as he welcomed us to the front garden of Mendips. 'Also, welcome from Yoko Ono Lennon. It was Yoko who bought the house in 2002 and then immediately donated it to the National Trust . . . I hope you enjoy an insight into the formative years of John.'

He pointed to the blue plaque on the front of the house.

'You may have noticed there is no blue plaque on Paul's home. This is because you have to be twenty years dead before they give you a plaque.

'In your mind's eye, remember Paul's home. Well, this house was built in 1933. Paul's was twenty years younger. It was rented, not owned, what they used to call "social housing" – to live here, you would have

to have been working class. John's house was in one of the most sought-after neighbourhoods. Lawyers, doctors, bankers lived here. So he was the middle-class Beatle.

'Our researches show that its first owner was Mr Harrap, a banker, and we believe it was his family which called it "Mendips". These are the original windows – it has never been double-glazed. In 1938 George and Mary Smith bought the house; Mary's nephew John came to live with them in 1945. He was raised as an only child.

'Mary Smith – better known as Aunt Mimi – was known for her withering looks,' he continued, 'and she would cast these withering looks on the people who lived on the council estate. She'd call them "common" because they lived in social housing. And so did my mum. And that's because Mimi was a *snob*, and *so was my mum*! They were both SNOBS!'

I was taken aback by the note of anger he had injected into the word 'snobs'. It's not the sort of thing one usually hears from National Trust guides as they glide proprietorially around the stately homes of England. On the whole, they are tweedy types, well-adapted to the demands of snobbery. In fact, many of them would regard Aunt Mimi as something of a role model.

Colin informed us that Aunt Mimi did not like to get her front hall dirty, so she would direct people to the back door. Apparently there is an old Liverpool saying: 'Go round the back and save the carpet.'

'Paul said to me, "I arrived with a guitar on my back and forgot that John had said, 'Paul, don't go to the front door.'"' And, for you, too, it has to be the tradesman's entrance . . .'

With that, Colin shepherded us into the spacious garden behind the house. While we were shuffling through, I happened to turn round. The Beatles, in their smart grey suits, circa 1964, were leaning over the front gate, pointing at me and grinning.

I took a closer look: they were not the actual Beatles, but replicants, possibly one of the looky-likey groups who had come to Liverpool for that week's International Beatleweek Festival.

Colin led us through the back door, and into the kitchen. Mimi herself renovated it in the 1960s, introducing a shiny new yellow formica worktop and a double-drainer sink, and her refitting was itself refitted by subsequent owners. But with its determination to turn back the clock, the National Trust scoured the country for the type of kitchen items that might just possibly have been in Aunt Mimi's house back then: large jars of pick-

led onions, tins of baking powder and condensed milk, a bread bin with 'BREAD' on it, a wooden cutting board, PG Tips, Rinzo, Olive Green household soap, a –

'Are you taking notes?'

I looked up. Colin had stopped his spiel and was pointing at me.

'Are you taking notes? Because a lot of what I am talking about is private information.'

Once again I felt as if I had been caught shoplifting, and immediately turned defensive. How could it be private information if he was relaying it to 12,000 visitors a year? He said that he had already written one book about the Beatles, and was gathering material for another. He clearly wanted to ring-fence some of this information for himself. Yet so far he hadn't said anything that I hadn't read countless times.

'Well,' I said, attempting a conciliatory tone, 'tell me when there's something you don't want me to mention and I won't write it down.'

'OK,' he said. 'I don't want you to include anything I say from now on.'

This didn't seem fair. I had, after all, paid my £31 (including guidebooks) to go round the homes of Paul and John, and at no point was I told that I couldn't take notes. In the past I have taken notes on guided tours of Windsor Castle, Cliveden and Petworth House, and the guides have all looked on benignly.

By now I was bristling. Crammed into the little kitchen, everyone else started looking at the floor in embarrassment. It was ridiculous, I thundered, absolutely absurd: this was a public place, a National Trust tour, I had paid my way, the same restrictions didn't apply to any other National Trust house I knew of, and so on and so on. Colin hit back, asking if I'd applied to head office for permission to take notes, and if not, why not, and what he was saying was private information, etc. etc. As our arguments became increasingly circular and tormented, some of the other visitors began drifting off into the next room, forcing Colin to interrupt himself in order to corral them back. *'Could you please stay in this room until I tell you to go!'* he snapped.

Eventually he had no choice but to move on. Subversively, I placed myself at the back of the group and kept writing notes defiantly, but by now I had become so het up that they emerged as indecipherable squiggles. Meanwhile, Colin was prefacing even the most humdrum observations with phrases like 'Strictly between ourselves' and 'Between you, me and the gatepost'.

He told us that Aunt Mimi had taken lodgers (stale buns!) because she needed extra money to send John through art school. 'Considering she herself took in lodgers, it's ironic she called other people common,' he added, meanly. Once more, he called her a snob. Poor Aunt Mimi! I wondered how she would have felt in 1959 had she known that sixty years on, 12,000 visitors a year would be paying £25 a head (excluding guidebooks) to rootle around in her kitchen and be told that she was a snob.

It came as a relief when Colin suddenly announced that we could go upstairs unaccompanied. Free at last from his beady gaze, I poked my head around the door of the upstairs loo. Was this the actual seat that John himself had once sat on, or just a replica? I then went into his bedroom. Three magazine covers were stuck to the wall above the bed, each with Brigitte Bardot in an enticing pose.

Around the time when Mendips was first opened to the public, I watched a TV documentary about Yoko's involvement in the project. She emerged as a controlling figure, stating exactly how she wanted everything to be. Nothing would stop her getting her own way. In one scene, she had even objected to the colour of John's bedspread. 'It was definitely not pink. You know what? I remember John telling me it was green.'

I remember thinking this was one of the most improbable things I had ever heard. But, anxious to butter Yoko up, the National Trust operatives had taken pains to assure her that, yes, of course they would see to it that the bedspread was changed. So it made me very happy to see that the bedspread is still as pink as pink can be. I desperately wanted to point this out to Colin, just to show that I was on the case, but I was fearful that he would have me arrested. Instead, I studied the framed letter from Yoko propped up on the bed. She wrote of how John was 'always talking about Liverpool', and how, whenever they visited the city, they would drive along Menlove Avenue, and he would point at the house and say, 'Yoko, look, look. That's it!'

She went on to say that all of John's music and his 'message of peace . . . germinated from John's dreaming in his little bedroom at Mendips'. Characterising the young John as 'a quiet, sensitive introvert who was always dreaming', she said that he was 'an incredible dreamer, John made those dreams come true – for himself and for the world'.

She ended by saying that walking into this bedroom today still gave her 'goosebumps', and hoping that for the National Trust visitor it will 'make your dream come true, too'.

Every year, more pop stars pass from rebellion into heritage. In Bloomsbury, I live in a block of flats which bears a plaque saying that

ROBERT NESTA
MARLEY
1945–1981
SINGER, LYRICIST AND
RASTAFARIAN ICON
LIVED HERE
1972

Elsewhere in London there are plaques of one sort or another to, among many others, Jimi Hendrix, Tommy Steele, Dire Straits, Pink Floyd, the Small Faces, Don Arden, Spandau Ballet and the Bee Gees.

It turns out that Bob Dylan is an enthusiast for visiting sites associated with rock stars. In 2009 he visited Mendips, and was overheard saying, 'This kitchen, it's just like my mom's.' David Kinney, author of *The Dylanologists*, notes that Dylan has also visited Neil Young's childhood home in Winnipeg, as well as Sun Studios in Memphis, where he took the trouble to kneel down and kiss the spot where Elvis Presley first sang 'That's All Right'. Apparently, as Dylan left the studios, a man chased after him and told him how much he loved him. 'Well, son, we all have our heroes,' he replied.

Dylan's own hometown of Hibbing, Minnesota, now offers tours of his old family synagogue, his old school, his old house and the hotel where he had his bar mitzvah. The menu of a Dylan-themed bar called Zimmy's offers Hard Rain Hamburger, Slow Train Pizza, and Simple Twist of Sirloin.

7.

Something deeper than music linked John and Paul. Their mothers had died when they were in adolescence: Paul's when he was fourteen, John's when he was seventeen.

When he first met John, Paul had already lost his mother, but John's mother, Julia, was still alive. 'His mother lived right near where I lived. I had lost my mum, that's one thing, but for your mum to actually be living somewhere else and for you to be a teenage boy and not living with her is very sad. It's horrible. I remember him not liking it at all.'

Paul recalled 'a tinge of sadness' in John at being apart from Julia. 'She was a beautiful woman with long red hair. She was fun-loving and musical too; she taught him banjo chords, and any woman in those days who played a banjo was a special, artistic person . . . John and I were both in love with his mum. It knocked him for six when she died.'

It created a bond between them. Together, the two boys conspired to upend their grief, to turn the wound into a weapon. 'Once or twice when someone said, "Is your mother gonna come?" we'd say, in a sad voice, "She died." We actually used to put people through that. We could look at each other and know.'

There was something more peculiar that linked them, too. In 1997 Paul told his friend and biographer Barry Miles, 'At night there was one moment when she would pass our bedroom door in underwear, which was the only time I would ever see that, and I used to get sexually aroused. I mean, it never went beyond that but I was quite proud of it, I thought, "That's pretty good." It's not everyone's mum that's got the power to arouse.'

One afternoon John ventured into his mother's bedroom. Julia was taking a nap in a black angora sweater, over a tight dark-green-and-yellow mottled shirt. He remembered it exactly. He lay on the bed next to her, and happened to touch one of her breasts. It was a moment he would replay over and over again in his memory for the rest of his life: 'I was wondering if I should do anything else. It was a strange moment because at the time I had the hots, as they say, for a rather lower-class female who lived on the opposite side of the road. I always think I should have done it. Presumably, she would have allowed it.'

John's friends remember Julia as vivacious and flirtatious. The first time Pete Shotton met her, he found himself 'greeted with squeals of girlish laughter by a slim, attractive woman dancing through the doorway with a pair of old woollen knickers wrapped around her head'. John introduced him. 'Oh, *this* is Pete, is it? John's told me so much about you.' Pete held out his hand, but she bypassed it. 'Julia began stroking my hips. "Ooh, what lovely slim hips you have," she giggled.'

Twenty-four years later, in 1979, sitting in his apartment in the Dakota Building, John recorded a cassette tape. At the start he announced, 'Tape one in the ongoing life story of John Winston Ono Lennon.' After rushing through a variety of topics – his grandparents' house in Newcastle Road, Bob Dylan's recent Christian album *Slow Train Coming* ('pathetic . . . just embarrassing'), his love of the sound of the bagpipes at the Edinburgh Military Tattoo when he was a child – he returned, once more, to that recurring memory of the afternoon he lay on his mother's bed and touched her breast.

On *The White Album*,* the song 'Julia' sounds less like an elegy than a love song, full of yearning for someone unobtainable:

Julia, sleeping sand, silent cloud, touch me
So I sing a song of love – Julia.

---

* Officially titled *The Beatles*, it became popularly known as 'The White Album', or occasionally 'The Double White', but never 'The Beatles'. For the rest of this book I will call it *The White Album*.

8.

Julia's shifty forty-one-year-old boyfriend Bobby Dykins – 'a little waiter with a nervous cough and thinning margarine-coated hair', in John's words – had lost his driving licence, and his job. Driving drunk along Menlove Avenue at midnight, his erratic movements were clocked by a policeman, who signalled him to stop. But Dykins kept going, turning left when he should have turned right, then mounting the reservation. Asked to get out of the car, he fell to the ground and had to be helped to his feet. The policeman informed him he was under arrest, and made a note of his response: 'You fucking fool, you can't do this to me, I'm the press!'

Dykins was held overnight in a cell, taken to court the next morning, and then released on bail. A fortnight later, on 1 July 1958, he was disqualified from driving for a year and fined £25 – roughly three weeks' wages – plus costs.

Dykins decided that cuts to the household budget were in order; he centred them on the seventeen-year-old John. They could, he said, no longer afford his rapacious appetite; he would have to stay with Julia's sister Mimi. On Tuesday, 15 July, Julia popped round to Menlove Avenue to tell Mimi of these new developments.

Having sorted things out with Mimi, Julia set off for home at 9.45 p.m. Sometimes she would walk across the golf course, but on this occasion she opted for the no. 4 bus, due in a couple of minutes, a hundred yards along on the other side of the road.

As Julia was leaving, John's friend Nigel Walley dropped by, but Mimi told him John was out.

'Oh, Nigel, you've arrived just in time to escort me to the bus stop,' said Julia. Nigel walked her to Vale Road, where they said goodbye, and he turned off. As Julia crossed Menlove Avenue, Nigel heard 'a car skidding and a thump and I turned to see her body flying through the air'. He rushed over. 'It wasn't a gory mess but she must have had severe internal injuries. To my mind, she'd been killed instantly. I can still see her gingery hair fluttering in the breeze, blowing across her face.'

The impact of his mother's death on John was immediate. 'I know what a terrible effect it had on John,' Nigel said, decades later. 'He felt so lonely after it. His outlook changed completely. He hardened and his humour became more weird.' For months, John refused to speak to him. 'Inwardly, he was blaming me for the death. You know – "If Nige hadn't walked her to the bus stop, or if he'd have kept her occupied another five minutes, it would never have happened."'

9.

It is June 1957. Paul is a bright grammar-school boy; he has been encouraged to take two of his GCE O-Level exams – Spanish and Latin – a year early.

His father, Jim, keeps pointing out that it's not possible to do your homework and watch television at the same time. Paul argues that it makes no difference. His good marks at the Liverpool Institute seem to support this view. But in truth, his mind is on other things. All he wants to do is play records with his friend Ian James. The two of them go from record shop to record shop. Sometimes they play their guitars together. Revision takes a back seat.

At the end of August Paul's GCE results come through.

A

He has passed Spanish, but failed Latin. This means he will not be able to go up a year, as planned. Instead he must remain in the Remove, alongside boys a year younger. Jim is upset. He thinks Paul failed Latin deliberately, because he didn't want to go to university. Paul is also upset. When he goes back to school in September, he hates being in classes with his juniors.

Paul is now in the same year as a little boy he recognises from the bus as a fellow smoker. When he was in the year above, he never really spoke to him. But now that they are in the

B

He has passed both Spanish and Latin. This means he goes up a year, joining the Lower Sixth with his best friend Ian James. Now and then he sees George Harrison in the school corridors, but Little George is in the year below, and anyway, they don't have much in common. George and Paul occasionally bump into each other on the bus, but there is no reason why Paul would ever introduce him to John; so he never does.

same year, the two grow close. The boy is called George Harrison.

From the heights of the Lower Sixth, Paul's friend Ian James is baffled by the burgeoning friendship. To him, they have totally different personalities: 'George always seemed a bit moody, morose, whereas Paul was light-hearted – he probably could have been a comedian if he'd wanted, he can tell a tale so well. George was nothing like that. I found it really strange that they were friends.'

Paul is impressed by George's guitar-playing, and introduces him to John Lennon, who is seventeen and no longer at school. John doesn't want to be seen socialising with a fourteen-year-old. He is irritated by the way Little George, as he is known, follows him 'like a bloody kid, hanging round all the time'.

But one day, when John is on the same double-decker, Paul seizes the opportunity to get George into their new band. On the upper deck, Paul tells George to play the song 'Raunchy'. 'Go on, George, show him!' Little George, as they all call him, takes his guitar out of its case and starts to play. John is impressed. 'He's in, you're in, that's it!' The audition is over.

10.

On 21 May 1956, Léo Valentin, the Frenchman known as 'Birdman' and billed as 'The Most Daring Man in the World', was crouched in a plane above Liverpool Speke Airport. The author of *Je suis un homme-oiseau* was preparing to leap out wearing wings made from balsawood and alloy. He planned to retire after this one last leap: the £200 he was set to earn from the Liverpool Air Show would help fund his dream of owning a provincial cinema back in France.

'To see a man fling himself into space . . .' he once wrote. 'It is a mad action. You want to turn away, but you are fascinated, watching the man who takes pleasure in taunting death.'

An estimated 100,000 spectators were gathered on the airfield below; George Harrison, aged thirteen, and Paul McCartney, just shy of his fourteenth birthday, had cycled there together.

The two boys watched as Valentin hurled himself from the back of the plane. But as he leapt, one of his wings splintered against the plane's door frame. 'We watched him drop and went, "Uh-oh . . . I don't think that's right,"' recalled Paul.

Valentin spun around and around, out of control. His parachute failed to open, and then his backup parachute wrapped around him, like a shroud. This made it easier for the crowd below to see the plummeting figure.

'We thought, "Any second now his parachute's gonna open," and it never did. We went, "I don't think he's going to survive that." And he didn't.'

Valentin fell to the ground in a cornfield, 'spreadeagled like a bird', in the words of one spectator.

In 1964, John Lennon advised the Beatles' press officer, Derek Taylor, against eating the cheese sandwiches at Speke Airport. He had once been employed at Speke as a packer, he told him, and he used to spit in them.

In spring 2002, Speke Airport was renamed Liverpool John Lennon Airport. Along with John F. Kennedy, Leonardo da Vinci and Josef Strauss, John Lennon is one of very few people to have an airport named after them. A seven-foot-high statue of John overlooks the check-in hall, and a vast Yellow Submarine stands on a traffic island at the entrance. The airport's motto is taken from his song 'Imagine': 'Above Us Only Sky'.

II.

A Party:
22 Huskisson Street, Liverpool
8 May 1960

All-night parties have become so popular among art students in Liverpool that partygoers are expected to bring not just a bottle but also an egg, for breakfast.

John and his fellow Beatles band member Stu Sutcliffe have been invited to an all-night party at 22 Huskisson Street* by one of their art-school lecturers, Austin Davies. Stu occasionally babysits for Austin and his wife Beryl, who is an actress. John brings his girlfriend Cynthia, and his bandmates Paul and George, both seventeen, tag along, uninvited. The current name of their band is the Silver Beats, but it's still in a process of development.

The party is composed of an odd mixture of guests: in the upstairs room, musicians from the Royal Liverpool Philharmonic Orchestra, still in full evening dress, fresh from playing Tchaikovsky, chat with Fritz Spiegl, their principal flautist; downstairs, art students play Ray Charles's latest single 'What'd I Say' over and over again on the record player.

George can't hear enough of the song. He stands transfixed, knocking back glass after glass of wine and beer, slowly shedding his inhibitions. At one point he spots Spiegl, who has just ventured downstairs, and shouts, 'Hey, Geraldo – got any Elvis?'

Paul is beginning to enjoy these parties. Always keen to project the right image, he has begun to favour a black turtleneck sweater and to act

---

* By chance, the very same house in which John's mother Julia was living when she married Fred Lennon.

mysterious, like Jacques Brel. 'It was me trying to be enigmatic, to make girls think, "Who's that very interesting French guy over in the corner?"' He sometimes arrives at parties with his guitar, strumming a French song, singing 'rhurbarbe, rhubarbe'. He has composed a tune to sing along to, but for now it only has one word in French, and that just a name – 'Michelle'.* He can't think of anything to rhyme with it.

The party goes on way past the next morning. Later, Beryl estimates that it lasted three days and three nights. Halfway through the first night, John and his band get carried away, and start singing loudly. Beryl thinks they make a dreadful racket. 'They played almost for two nights. I said it was a disgusting noise. I took the children out.' She walks them down the road to a friend's house, and stays there herself. The next morning she returns to no. 22 to get some clothes, only to find her bedroom door locked. A partygoer tells her that her husband is in there, with a friend. 'That night we separated. We divorced amicably. I never saw the Beatles again.' But she harbours no grudge against the Beatles. In fact, quite the opposite. Forty-eight years later, the acclaimed novelist Dame Beryl Bainbridge talks of those early days with great affection, and picks 'Eleanor Rigby' as one of her Desert Island Discs.†

* Five years later, when Paul and John were harvesting songs for *Rubber Soul*, John suddenly remembered that Paul used to sing a French song at parties. Once again, Paul struggled to think of a rhyme for 'Michelle'. A visiting French teacher, Jan Vaughan, the wife of Paul's old schoolmate Ivan, suggested 'ma belle'. He then asked her to translate 'these are words that go together well' into French, and later sent her a cheque for her contribution. John supplied the 'I love you, I love you, I love you' interlude, after listening to Nina Simone's recently released 'I Put a Spell on You'.

† Bainbridge's other Desert Island Discs were characteristically eccentric, among them 'Two Little Boys' by Rolf Harris, 'Kiss Me Goodnight, Sergeant Major' by Vera Lynn and 'Bat Out of Hell' by Meatloaf.

12.

Already well-known as a journalist and editor, and rapidly becoming a household name as a television presenter, Malcolm Muggeridge took a flight from London to Hamburg on 7 June 1961. Two months earlier, he had recorded his distaste for the medium with which he would soon be identified.

> As always deeply distressed by seeing myself on television . . . Decided
> never to do it again. Something inferior, cheap, horrible about television
> as such: it's a prism through which words pass, energies distorted, false.
> The exact converse of what is commonly believed – not a searcher out of
> truth and sincerity, but rather only lies and insincerity will register on it.

Having visited the offices of *Stern* magazine, Muggeridge went out on the town. True to character, he took relish in finding it 'singularly joyless; Germans with stony faces wandering up and down, uniformed touts offering total nakedness, three Negresses and other attractions, including female wrestlers. Not many takers, it seemed, on a warm Tuesday evening.'

On a whim, he dropped into the Top Ten Club on the Reeperbahn, 'a teenage rock-and-roll joint'. A band was playing: 'ageless children, sexes indistinguishable, tight-trousered, stamping about, only the smell of sweat intimating animality'. They turned out to be English, and from Liverpool: 'Long-haired; weird feminine faces; bashing their instruments, and emitting nerveless sounds into microphones.'

As they came offstage, they recognised Muggeridge from the television, and started talking to him. One of them asked him if it was true he was a Communist. No, he replied; he was just in opposition. 'He nodded understandingly,' observed Muggeridge, 'in opposition himself in a way.'

'"You make money out of it?" he went on. I admitted that this was so. He, too, made money. He hoped to take back £200 to Liverpool.'

They parted on good terms. 'In conversation rather touching in a way,' Muggeridge recorded in his diary, 'their faces like Renaissance carvings of saints or Blessed Virgins.'

13.

POSTCARDS FROM HAMBURG

I   16 AUGUST 1960

George is just seventeen years old when he climbs into the cream and green Austin van owned by the band's tubby Welsh manager, Allan Williams. He holds a tin of scones baked by his mother. Before watching her son set off, Mrs Harrison takes Williams to one side. 'Look after him,' she says.

None of the Beatles has ever been abroad. Jim McCartney entertains misgivings, but doesn't feel he can stand in Paul's way. The contract they have just signed gives them 210 deutschmarks a week, or £17.10s; the average weekly wage in Britain is £14. 'He's being offered as much money as I make a week. How can I tell him not to go?'

II

The van is packed with a motley crew. George sits in the back with the other Beatles. Allan Williams is at the wheel, with his Chinese wife Beryl and Beryl's brother Barry sitting next to him. Also on board are Williams's business partner, 'Lord Woodbine', so-called in homage to his devotion to Woodbine cigarettes, and George Sterner, the second-in-command to Bruno Koschmider, the German club-owner with whom the boys have signed a contract.

III

It's the start of a long journey. There is a five-hour wait at Newhaven, and four hours at Hook of Holland while Williams insists that the Beatles don't require permits and visas because they are students. They stop off in

Amsterdam for a short break. John seizes the opportunity to shoplift two pieces of jewellery, several guitar strings, a couple of handkerchiefs and a harmonica. In his managerial role, Williams orders him to return them to the shops, but John refuses.

IV

As they drive through Germany, they sing songs – 'Rock Around the Clock', 'Maggie May' – but when they arrive at the Reeperbahn they are momentarily struck dumb, dazzled by so much neon, and so many open doors through which women can be glimpsed taking their clothes off. But they soon regain their natural ebullience, shouting 'Here come the scousers!' at the top of their voices.

V

Off the Reeperbahn runs Grosse Freiheit. The lights of the strip clubs are being switched on as they arrive, and the prostitutes are beginning to emerge. Still at the wheel, Allan Williams notes that the streets are 'swarming with all the rag-tag and bob-tail of human existence – dope fiends, pimps, hustlers for strip clubs and clip-joints, gangsters, musicians, transvestites, plain ordinary homosexuals, dirty old men, dirty young men, women looking for women'.

VI

Nevertheless, it seems like a dream destination for a band whose achievements in their homeland have bordered on the pitiful. In the autumn they failed to qualify for the talent show *TV Star Search*; in the first three months of this year they had no professional engagements at all; in May they failed an audition to be Billy Fury's backing group. So things are looking up. The people of Hamburg are bored by the lifeless efforts of their home-grown groups: Williams says Germans turn rock'n'roll into a death march. But British bands who have played in Hamburg – Dave Lee and the Staggerlees from Kent, the Shades Five from Kidderminster, the Billions from Worcestershire – have never looked back. The Germans seem to love them all, good, bad and indifferent.

VII

The Beatles are met at the Indra Club by Bruno Koschmider, an unprepossessing manager of an unprepossessing venue, cramped and clammy, with just two customers at the bar. Koschmider shows them to their lodgings. They haven't been expecting much, but what they see confounds even their most meagre expectations. Between the five of them, they are expected to occupy two dark, dank, tiny rooms around the back of Koschmider's grubby cinema, the Bambi Kino. There are no lightbulbs: they will have to make do with matches. The walls are concrete. The first room measures five feet by six. It is furnished with an army-surplus bunk bed and a threadbare couch.

VIII

'What the fucking hell!' says John, more used to Aunt Mimi's cosy interior décor. 'Fuck me!' chorus the others. 'Only temporary,' Koschmider reassures them; but he is lying.

This first bedroom is to be shared by John, Stu and George. John and Stu bag the bunk. George, being the youngest, has to make do with the couch.

The second bedroom is exactly the same size, but without a window. There is no means of telling if it is night or day. There are few blankets, and no heating.

Their rooms are a hair's breadth from being en-suite, because the wall is paper thin, and on the other side is a toilet, also used by customers of the cinema. The smells seep through into their rooms.

They have to wash and shave with the cold water from the basin next to the public urinals. George never has a bath or a shower during either of his first two seasons in Hamburg.

IX

It's all a far cry from Las Vegas. Understandably, their natural high spirits are deflated. Their first performance at the Indra is lacklustre. They stand still and chug their way through cover versions of popular hits, while half a dozen punters look glumly on. Koschmider is unimpressed. He hired the Beatles to provide energy; instead they just stand around looking woebegone.

'*Mach Schau*, boys! *Mach Schau!*' he demands. Make show! Make show! It does the trick, and becomes the catalyst for any amount of japes: from now on, the Beatles go all-out to enjoy themselves, strutting and dancing and screaming, hurling abuse at the audience and fighting among themselves.

X

They regularly play the same song for ten or twenty minutes at a time, just for the hell of it. One night, for a bet, they play a single song – 'What'd I Say', by Ray Charles – for over an hour. While the others rag about, Pete remains sombre, drumming as though it were a chore, a bit like washing up.

XI

Pete is also the only one who refuses stimulants. The others are helped in their high-jinks by a smorgasbord of cheap drugs – Purple Hearts and Black Bombers and Preludin, a slimming pill with an active ingredient* that charges up the metabolism, keeps you wide awake and ensures that you never stop talking. Stu's German girlfriend Astrid Kirchherr is blessed with an in-house supplier: her mother. 'They were fifty pfennigs each and my mummy used to get them for us from the chemist. You had to have a prescription for them, but my mummy knew someone at the chemist.' In time, they toss them back like Smarties, with beer chasers. They even talk of eating 'Prellie sandwiches'.

XII

Unsurprisingly, it is John who pops the poppermost, and to the greatest effect, yelling obscenities, rolling around on the stage, throwing food at other band members, pretending to be a hunchback, jumping on Paul's back, hurling himself into the audience, delighting in calling them 'fucking Krauts' or 'Nazis' or 'German spassies'.

* Phenmetrazine.

Diplomacy has never come naturally to him. One night he takes to the stage wearing nothing but his underpants, with a loo seat around his head, marching around with a broom in his hand, chanting *'Sieg heil! Sieg heil!'* On another, he appears in swimming trunks. Halfway through 'Long Tall Sally' he turns his back to the audience and pulls the trunks down, wiggling his bare bottom at the audience. Unversed in Liverpudlian manners, the Germans applaud politely.

XIII

Cynthia comes to Hamburg on a visit, and witnesses John so out of his mind on pills and alcohol that he falls about the stage in 'hysterical convulsions'. Offstage, he can be equally feral. He urinates from a balcony onto a group of nuns in the street below. Not that the others are models of sobriety: between numbers, Paul says something rude about Stu's beautiful girlfriend Astrid, who all the band fancy, and Stu duly punches him. Paul fights back, and before long they are grappling onstage in what Paul comes to remember as 'a sort of death grip'. But – *Mach Schau! Mach Schau!* – these spectacles prove popular. They begin to be known locally as the *benakked* Beatles – the crazy Beatles.

XIV

Hamburg audiences prefer to pick fights with each other, rather than with the band. The waiters – hired from the Hamburg Boxing Academy, so rusty on matters of etiquette – wear heavy boots, suitable for energetic kicking, and carry spring-loaded truncheons in the backs of their trousers, discreetly hidden beneath their jackets. Clubs keep tear-gas guns behind their counters, for use when a skirmish threatens to expand into a riot. In time, the Beatles are allotted the prefectorial duty of making the nightly announcement in German of a ten o'clock curfew for the under-eighteens: '*Es ist zweiundzwanzig Uhr. Wir mussen jetzt Ausweiskontrolle machen. Alle Jugendlichen unter achtzehn Jahren mussen dieses Lokal verlassen.*'*

XV

Bruno Koschmider is no jolly, thigh-slapping *Mein Host*. Kosch by name, Kosch by nature: he patrols his club brandishing the knotted leg of a hardwood German chair. If a customer proves unruly, or is too noisily dissatisfied, he will be bundled into Koschmider's office, pinned to the floor, and beaten black and blue with it.

XVI

In the early hours of the morning, Koschmider's fellow club-owners drop by for a nightcap. They like to send trays of schnapps up to the band, to be downed – '*Beng, beng – ja! Proost!*' – in one. They think it hilarious that this band from England is called the Beatles, which they pronounce 'Peadles', German slang for 'little willies'. 'Oh, zee Peadles! Ha ha ha!'

XVII

The band's japes are not confined to the stage. One afternoon they dare Paul to don a *Pickelhaube* and goose-step up and down the Reeperbahn with a broom for a rifle, while they yell '*Sieg heil!*' They also enjoy playing leapfrog in the street. These fun and games prove infectious: Pete Best re-members passers-by joining in, forming 'a long trail of Germans of varying ages all leapfrogging behind us . . . At some intersections, friendly cops would hold up the traffic to wave us through.'

---

* 'It is twenty-two hours. We must now make a passport control. All youth under eighteen years must now leave this club.'

XVIII

In the heart of the Reeperbahn, sex – 'almost limitless sex', in Pete's words – is freely available. 'How could we possibly invite a dame to our squalid digs alongside the cinema urinals, dark and damp as a sewer and about as attractive?' Pete asks, decades later, and then answers his own question. 'But we did, and not one girl ever said no.'

George Harrison loses his virginity at the Bambi Kino, while Paul, John and Pete look on. 'They couldn't really see anything because I was under the covers . . . After I'd finished they all applauded and cheered. At least they kept quiet whilst I was doing it.'

In these conditions, nothing is private. A fan from Liverpool, Sue Johnston,* receives a letter from Paul in Hamburg. He tells her that one night John ended up with 'a stunning, exotic-looking woman, only to discover on closer inspection that she was a he'. The other Beatles found it hilarious.

Perhaps, in years to come, Pete's description will be the subject of a question in a GCSE mathematics paper: 'For the nightly romp there were usually five or six girls between the four of us . . . We found ourselves having two or three girls a night each . . . the most memorable night of love in our dowdy billet was when eight birds gathered there to do the Beatles a favour. They managed to swap with all four of us – twice!' Many of the girls are prostitutes from Herbertstrasse, happy to waive their usual fees for these boisterous young Englishmen. Pete will never forget them: 'I still remember some of their names: Greta, Griselda, Hilde, Betsy, Ruth . . . The Beatles' first groupies.'

XIX

John is as avid as any of them, but, characteristically, will recall those days of sexual wonder with a mixture of disgust and disappointment.

'I used to dream that it would be great if you could just click your fingers and they would strip off and be ready for me,' he will tell Alistair

---

* At that time she was going out with Norman Kuhlke, drummer with the Swinging Blue Jeans. She later worked as a tax inspector, and then for Brian Epstein, before embarking on a successful acting career. In 2000 she received a BAFTA for Best TV Comedy Actress.

Taylor. 'I would spend most of my teenage years fantasising about having this kind of power over women. The weird thing is, when the fantasies came true, they were not nearly so much fun. One of my most frequent dreams was seducing two girls together, or even a mother and daughter. This happened in Hamburg a couple of times and the first time it was sensational. The second time it got to feel like I was giving a performance. The more women I had, the more that buzz would turn into a horrible feeling of rejection and revulsion.'

X X

Equally characteristically, Paul will look back on these sexual adventures largely in terms of self-advancement. 'It was a sexual awakening for us,' he tells Barry Miles in 1997. 'We didn't have much practical knowledge till we went to Hamburg. Of course, it was striptease girls and hookers . . . But it was all good practice, I suppose . . . So we came back from there reasonably initiated. It wasn't so much that we were experts, but that we were more expert than other people who hadn't had that opportunity.'

14.

We assemble by the Star-Club, or where the Star-Club used to be, before it was reduced to cinders in 1983. A tall black sign, like a shiny gravestone, announces 'Star-Club' in diagonal writing, with a picture of an electric guitar below. Beneath the guitar sits a scattering of names from long ago, each set at a jaunty angle, and in a different typeface: 'The Liverbirds Ray Charles The Pretty Things Gene Vincent Bo Diddley Remo Four Bill Haley King Size Taylor and the Dominoes Screaming Lord Sutch Little Richard Johnny Kidd and the Pirates Gerry and the Pacemakers The Rattles The Searchers Brenda Lee The V.I.P.s The Walker Brothers Ian and the Zodiacs Jerry Lee Lewis Tony Sheridan Chubby Checker Roy Young The Lords'.

And there, in the top left-hand corner: 'The Beatles'.

'OK, ze bend voss 300 days in Hemburg. Ze Feb Four in Hemburg only four weeks all other time we hev Pete Best on drums, 60–61 with Stuart, Stuart left ze bend 61 goes to art school dies April 62 in Hemburg 61 Paul change vrom guitar to bass.'

Our tour guide is Peter, a wiry, chain-smoking man in his seventies, his sparse grey hair bound in a ponytail. He rattles through the events and dates at breakneck speed, as though it were a summary of a summary, something he has recited hundreds of times before. Which, of course, he has: he has been guiding the same tour four days a week since 1970.

'Star-Club close 69, then ve hev cabaret for surteen years, in 83 everyzing burned down. One building was at ze front so they rebuild ze back one and where we hed the hall in sixties is beckyard today. Peadles play here April May then November and December 62.'

He has only been going a few minutes, but we are already finding it hard to keep up. It reminds me of a maths lesson, or perhaps a history lesson about the Wars of the Roses, a great jumble of dates and locations.

'Top ect in April, six weeks to May voss menly Gene Wincent, but

November Little Richard and December Johnny and ze Hurricanes. Peadles voss one of only four or five bends mostly supporting ze top ects.'

Every now and then he recites an anecdote, but they come unexpectedly, and are often hard to decipher.

'In Germany ve hev Tony Sheridan and the Beat Brothers on "My
Bonny" but in England it voss Tony Sheridan and ze Peadles so nobody
know Peadles voss sem bend as Tony Sheridan!!!! See some guys, I zink
who is zeez guys? I think who is deez English rockers? I sink, oh, shit, voss
ze Peadles!!!!!'

We do our best to smile in the right place. Peter leads us into a dingy
courtyard, full of litter, and hands around a postcard-sized black-and-
white photograph of what it used to look like. It seems to have been just as
dingy, but entirely different.

'Dis is picture after ze fire. Here voss stage, here voss hall, stage left to
right five metres. Voss a really goot fire!'

We pass the postcard around. Each of us gazes at it, then at the present-
day scene, then at the postcard again, as if attempting to work out a puzzle.
But nothing fits.

'Here voss zree steps, vun doo zree.'

We look down, pretending to spot three steps. 'OK, you hev your pictures here.' One or two people take photographs of where the three steps
would be, were they here, which they aren't.

Peter walks on, and we tag along behind him. As he walks, he zips
through another personal anecdote.

'I met John 66, in leather store on Reeperbahn. Zey buy cowboy boots,
leather jackets and I voz in ze store when he mek the movie *How I Von dur
Var*, I talk to him for ten minutes.'

Someone asks what they talked about.

'So long ago I cannot remember zet von.'

He rushes on, racing through all the bands that played in Hamburg,
back in the day.

'OK, so dur sixties was so amezin. Ve hev Jaybirds, voss complete line-
up of Ten Years After. Ve hev dur Small Faces. Ten weeks later ve hev Eric
Clepton and dur Cream. Ve hev bend called Mendrake Root vit Ritchie
Blackmore zey become Deep Purple. Ve hed really goot bend called Ze
Earth. On ze vay beck zey change name to Bleck Sabbath. Six months
later ve hed Jimi Hendrix here. 6 March 1967 Hendrix play zree days

here, Friday, Seturday, Sunday March 67. On ze Monday morning Jimi buy Fender Stratocaster, cost about eleven hundred. On Thursday, he play Monterey, he burn down ze new Stratocaster he buy in Hemburg. He hed not planned to burn down guitar but Ze Who kicked down zeir drums, yeah? So he thought, "Vot cen I do?"

'Now ve go Reeperbahn district.'

We walk towards the end of the street. On the way, he talks about the sort of people who come on his Beatles tours. 'Most English people. Most German not zo interested, maybe older people from East Germany. Ozzervise, Spain, Jepen, South Emerica. Hemburg people is not interested in Peadles. We have Peadlemania museum but after three years it closed. Now, all zey vont is Sex and Crime tours.'

He retains fond memories of the Beatlemania museum. It stretched across five floors, he says, but the exhibits consisted mainly of reproductions of the original items, rather than the items themselves. 'Only original voss contract from Bert Kaempfert with the Peadles, ze rest voss not original. Not original guitars, not original drums. But fifth floor zey hev original signs from ze Star-Club, Indra, all ze signs from the streets. Voss really good museum but not popular enough. I talk to zo many Hemburg people hev not been zere.'

We arrive at a circular paved area, where the street joins the Reeperbahn. It is called Beatles-Platz. Aluminium silhouettes of four figures with guitars and another on drums stand at one edge of the circle, looking rather like outsize pastry-cutters.

'Zis is ze line-up from 1960. We hev John, George, Paul, Pete and there's Stuart on ze right-hend side. On drums is Pete Best, not Ringo.'

He looks disconsolately at the circular area. It's draughty and lacklustre, as unglamorous as can be.

'I don't like zis place but is better zan nothing. We hev it about ten years. You see, it is record label.' We look again, and I can just about make out what he is getting at: in the centre of the circle is a smaller circle, in lighter stone, which could be the label of a giant LP, and two or three metal grooves run around what would be the disc itself, with various Beatles song titles written on them. It's all a bit makeshift.

Someone asks if Pete Best ever comes back. Of all the hundreds of names associated with the Beatles, his is the one that can still darken the atmosphere. 'Pete Best voss in Hamburg four five times, I see him many times, zum people say Pete he's earned nothing but, wideos, dee-wee-dees, they give him lot of money, he really heppy.'

We stare at the songs inscribed on the metal grooves, including 'She Loves You' and 'I Want to Hold Your Hand'. 'In 1964 ze bend voss one veek in Paris, they record two of zeir songs in German language – "Sie Liebt Dich" und "Komm Gib Mir Deine Hand" – you cen listen on YouTube.'

We cross the Reeperbahn. A shop called Tourist Center sports a huge Union Jack as a backdrop to its window display of novelty mugs and cats, dogs and penguins with wobbly heads. I can't spot any Beatles memorabilia, though. Apparently, this was the leather store where Peter encountered John, over half a century ago.

'I voss in the store ven John came in 66. He voss vith ze actor Michael Crarfood and Neil Espinall.' He brings himself up short, suddenly remembering that he has already told us about it. 'Jimi Hendrix stayed zree days in Hemburg in small hotel, March 67. You vont to see?'

He brings out his photographs and sifts through them. One, in black and white, is of Jimi Hendrix and Chas Chandler in a German street. 'All ze buildings are gone now. Jimi ask me, "Vare cen I find the Peadles' places?" and we walk around. I see six concerts with Jimi in March 67. I pick him up outside ze hotel. At end, Jimi give me autograph. He vrite, "To Peter stay kool Jimi Hendrix". Jimi gave me one of his cigarettes. It voss Kool with a K, so ze autograph says "stay kool" vith a K.'

He shows us a building where the Top 10 Club used to be, then whips through one of his hard-to-follow history lessons. 'Zet building voss Top 10 today id is discotheque. Before Top 10 voss a hippodrome, a little bit circus, donkey or a horse walk round – that voss showbiz in the fifties! Peadles played three months first April 61 to end of June six to eight hours every day 35 deutschmarks not a lod of money.' He points to the roof where John, George and Paul once posed for a photograph. '61, ze bend lived under ze roof, zey hev those rooms, one two. 61, Stuart left the bend, Paul changed vrom guitar to bass. Other bends play here – Elex Harvey, Rory Gellegher – but Top 10 Club close 88.'

There is nothing – no sign or statue or plaque – to show that this is where it once was. This makes him cross. 'Hemburg does nothing about Top 10 Club! Nothing about Peadles!'

Also on the Reeperbahn is the police station where Paul and Pete were held overnight, accused of starting a small fire in their apartment. 'Some say it voss con-domes on ze wall, others say it vos some sort of paper. Anyway, zey hev a fire, voss arrested, zen deported, from here ve valk to the Rock'n'Roll door, ten, fifteen minutes.'

On the way, Peter tells us again that since he first showed Jimi Hendrix round in March 1967, he has taken four tours a week, fifty weeks a year. 'Is a lod of tours.' Yet there is precious little to see. Nothing is as it was. Only the police station remains the same. Everywhere else is a memory of a memory, of interest only to the most dedicated Beatles archaeologist.

In 1967, when Hunter Davies first asked the Beatles about their time in Hamburg, they couldn't even remember how many times they had been there. Since then, Beatles historians regularly attempt to reconstruct their lives there, day by day, hour by hour. But in Beatles years, it's as distant as the Dark Ages.

At last we arrive at a vast gate off a street, with a sign in English saying 'Keep Out'. Pete tells us he is not allowed to take us in, but if we go in by ourselves, we should take a snap of the first doorway on the right. It is where John stood for the photo that was later used on the cover of his solo *Rock'n'Roll* album. 'I vish you good luck, ze first door behind the gate, not a problem for you, only for me.' We push the gate and find a gloomy five-storey red-brick building in a poor state of repair. We obediently take pictures of the doorway, but no one really knows why.

Finally, we end up by the Indra, which is still, miraculously, 'Musikeclub Live', but we're not allowed in. A plaque outside says, in German, 'On 17 August 1960 the Beatles performed on the stage of the Indra. It was their first German engagement and the beginning of a great career.'

And so to the Kaiserkeller, with a framed poster of Rory Storm and the Hurricanes outside. 'Von of those guys voss Ringo,' Peter says, and we all try to spot which one. He then shows us a photograph of the seventeen-year-old George with his guitar. 'Voss zold at Bonham auction for two hundred fifty thousand pound including tex and everyzing. Last week at Zotheby, one contrect from Brian Epstein viz ze bend, zet von sold for two hundred thirty-five thousand pound. Emezin!'

We sigh at the idea that so little could have mushroomed into so much.

'But in 62, zey close Kaiserkeller and it voss discothèque.'

15.

Their return to Liverpool after a stint of three and a half months in Hamburg was such a sorry affair that they avoided telling their families what had happened.

In brief, they had been tempted away from the Kaiserkeller by a rival club-owner. To exact revenge, the thuggish Koschmider reported George to the police for being under-age, and he was duly deported. On returning home, George felt 'ashamed, after all the big talk'. Koschmider subsequently reported Paul and Pete on the spurious grounds of setting fire to their lodgings, and they too were deported. On 1 December 1960, they arrived back in Liverpool disillusioned and penniless. Ten days later, John followed. Stu remained with Astrid in Germany, a Beatle no more.

The Beatles' fall from grace had been abrupt and painful. John woke Mimi in the middle of the night by throwing stones at her bedroom window. 'He just pushed past me and said, "Pay that taxi, Mimi." I shouted after him up the stairs, "Where's your £100 a week, John?"'

'Just like you, Mimi, to go on about £100 a week when you know I'm tired.'

'And you can get rid of those boots. You're not going out of this house in boots like that!'

Most of their equipment was stranded in Hamburg. They had nothing to show for their time away. Similar groups who had stayed in Liverpool were now several steps ahead of them. The Swinging Blue Jeans were clearly in the lead, headlining a regular 'Swinging Blue Jeans Night' at the Cavern in Mathew Street.

In the three months they had been away, fashions had moved on: everyone was now copying the Shadows, wearing slinky suits, playing instrumentals, performing synchronised dance routines. At first, the individual Beatles were so despondent that they didn't even bother to get in touch with one another: George was unaware that John and Paul had returned. John retired, depressed, to his bedroom at Mendips, refusing to see anyone.

While Aunt Mimi grudgingly indulged John's self-pity, Jim McCartney refused to have Paul slouching around the house. 'Satan makes work for idle hands,' he said, telling him to go out and get a proper job. 'This music thing is all right on the side, but Paul, it will never last.' Paul worked briefly for a delivery company, then did donkeywork at Massey & Coggins, a cable-winding firm. The moment his workmates discovered he was a musician, they nicknamed him 'Mantovani'. Being bright and personable, Paul was swiftly earmarked as management material. 'We'll give you an opportunity, lad,' declared the managing director, impressed by his exam results, 'and with your outlook on life you'll go a long way.'

Uncharacteristically, Paul was ready to throw in the towel. After a few weeks John and George turned up at Massey & Coggins. They had been booked for a lunchtime gig at the Cavern, they said, and they wanted Paul to join them. He told them he had a steady job, and was now on £7.10s a week. 'They are training me here. That's pretty good. I can't expect more.'

But they persisted, and Paul gave way, bunking off work on 9 February 1961 to play the Cavern at lunchtime. He did the same on 22 February, but it's possible that his employers issued a warning, because when another lunchtime gig at the Cavern was mooted for the following week, he ummed and erred. 'Either fucking turn up today or you're not in the band any more,' snapped John.

What to do? If he chose the Beatles, his father would be furious. If he obeyed his father, and stuck it out at Massey & Coggins, he would have to say goodbye to the Beatles, and any remaining chance of stardom. As usual, John was in no mood for compromise; his intransigence towards Paul may also have been a way of subcontracting his own Oedipal struggles: 'I was always saying, "Face up to your dad, tell him to fuck off. He can't hit you. He's an old man" . . . But Paul would always give in. His dad told him to get a job, he dropped the group and started working on the lorries, saying, "I need a steady career." We couldn't believe it. I told him on the phone, "Either come or you're out." So he had to make a decision between me and his dad . . .'

What would have happened had Paul chosen to stay at Massey & Coggins?* Looking back, he is adamant that he had been 'hopeless'

---

* A decade later, when pop music grew more solemn, Massey and Coggins might have been a winning name for a group, like Loggins and Messina, Gallagher and Lyle, or Crosby, Stills, Nash and Young.

at winding coils – 'Everybody else used to wind fourteen a day. I'd get through one and a half, and mine were the ones that never worked' – but it's hard to imagine he wouldn't have mastered the technique. And he had already been fast-tracked towards management. His subsequent career suggests that he possessed the drive, initiative and skills necessary for steering even the most troublesome company through rocky times.

Instead, he bunked off to rejoin the Beatles. A week later he received his wage packet through the post, along with his National Insurance card and his P45.

16.

A Party:
10 Admiral Grove, Liverpool
8 July 1961

Ritchie Starkey spent his seventh birthday in a coma, having been rushed by ambulance to the Royal Liverpool Children's Hospital. Doctors found he had a burst appendix, and was infected with peritonitis. As he was being wheeled into the operating theatre he asked the nurse for a cup of tea. 'We'll give you one when you come round,' she replied sweetly. But Ritchie failed to come round for another ten weeks. Three times during that first night, doctors told his mother Elsie that they did not expect him to survive. He was to remain in hospital for a year.

Ritchie was back in the same hospital for his fourteenth birthday, in 1954. This time he was admitted with pleurisy, and then developed TB. Convalescing in a hospital in the Wirral, he was taught to knit, to make baskets and to construct a toy farm out of papier-mâché. Every fortnight a music teacher arrived at the ward with a selection of percussion instruments – tambourines, maracas, triangles, tiny drums – and the children were expected to join in, playing 'Three Blind Mice' and 'London Bridge is Falling Down'. But Ritchie stubbornly refused to participate unless he could play a drum. When the teacher left, he would continue drumming on his bedside cabinet, in the absence of anything more drummable. This time he remained in hospital for two years.

But his twenty-first birthday is a much happier affair. Not only has he survived, but he has turned his percussive skills to advantage. He is now the drummer with Liverpool's top band, Rory Storm and the Hurricanes, and he even drives his own Ford Zodiac. Not long ago, he assumed the name Ringo Starr; his drum solos are billed as 'Starr Time'.

Rory Storm and the Hurricanes are playing a season at Butlin's holiday camp at Pwllheli in Wales, but they have one day a week off, so the day after his birthday Ringo drives home for a proper party. So many friends and family have packed into 10 Admiral Grove, his mother's tiny two-up, two-down – Ringo counts sixty-four people in all – that there is a continuous queue to get in. Guests include the Hurricanes, the Dominoes, the Big Three and the Pacemakers, as well as the young Priscilla White, who sometimes takes to the Cavern stage as 'Swinging Cilla', and regularly styles Elsie's hair in return for Spam and chips.*

Ringo is showered with presents, including two rings to add to the three he already wears, and a gold identity bracelet from Elsie, engraved with 'Ritchie' on one side and '21st birthday, love Mum' on the other. From his Auntie Nancy he receives a gold St Christopher medal. It depicts the patron saint of travellers carrying the Christ child on his shoulders across a river. Ringo hangs it around his neck, to keep him safe wherever he goes.

---

* Priscilla White is soon to become Cilla Black, and, under Brian Epstein's guidance, a big star. 'I always reckoned that if I wasn't going to be a singer, I'd be a hairdresser. Elsie was a real character, a surrogate mum to Pat and me and to the other Beatles, and we were forever bumping into each other there. She would cook us all delicious Spam, home-made chips and beans for tea, and she never seemed to mind how often we came round for more or how loud we played the latest records. I thought I did Elsie's hair really well, but, some thirty years later, Ritchie's stepdad Harry told me otherwise: "We didn't say anything at the time," he muttered, "but you used to make a right bloody mess of poor Elsie's hair!"'

17.

5 MORE POSTCARDS FROM HAMBURG

I

On their second stint in Hamburg the Beatles are working at a new venue, the Star Club, for a new manager, Manfred Weissleder, at new lodgings, a lovely clean flat in the Grosse Freiheit. Herr Weissleder tacks on one condition, though: 'I always want you should enjoy yourselves in the Star Club, but if you make shit I send you home.'

Within days, George has been sick on the floor by the side of his bed. The next morning, the unshapely pool is still there, glowering back at him.

The cleaning lady refuses to clear it up, arguing, not unreasonably, that it is not part of her duties. For reasons of his own, George refuses to dispose of it. He has always had this stubborn streak.

II

The next day, the pool remains doggedly present. The cleaning lady grumbles at the Beatles' general squalor: the smelly socks, the empty bottles, the clothes strewn all over the place. This latest infraction takes their misdemeanours to another level. She goes straight to Herr Weissleder and voices her complaints. Herr Weissleder lends a sympathetic ear. He will take a closer look.

III

Having examined the evidence, Herr Weissleder rules against George, charging his henchman and bouncer, Horst Fascher, with the job of forcing him to clean it up. Fascher is a former championship boxer. He has also spent time in prison for manslaughter, following a fracas with a sailor. Only the bravest of souls refuse to obey him. John has already fallen foul of him. When John called him a Nazi, Herr Fascher retaliated by marching him to the toilet and urinating over him.

But George, stubborn George, continues to put his foot down, or if not down, at least to one side. No, he says, he is definitely not going to clear it up. Why should he? It isn't his job. For all he cares, it can just stay there. When he needs to get in or out of bed, he simply climbs over it.

IV

The dispute has reached an impasse. The cleaning lady will not clean up the pool of vomit; nor will George. Over the next few days Pete Best observes its sluggish, odoriferous progress with a morbid fascination, watching it 'grow, and grow, mushrooming and taking on a life of its own. Cigarettes were crushed in it, bits of food fed to it, until it assumed the look of a hedgehog.'

The Beatles christen it 'The Thing', and treat it almost like a family pet. Before long, The Thing acquires a local reputation. Pete remembers how 'its fame spread, and people wanted to come and see it'. He estimates it measures roughly six inches in diameter, and it keeps growing upwards, 'like a miniature flower garden'.

As it blossoms, George harbours scary thoughts. 'I'm frightened to sleep in case it eats me,' he confesses.

V

One morning, Herr Fascher pays a return visit, unannounced. He takes one look at the ageing vomit before deciding that enough is enough. He returns with a shovel. 'Don't do it! That's our pet!' yell the Beatles. But their pleas fall on deaf ears. Fascher scoops it up and transports it down the stairs, through the front door and onto the Grosse Freiheit. The Beatles follow in a mock funeral procession. Fascher finds a bin on the street, and tips The Thing into it.

As for George, he feels he has won a small but significant victory. He kept his word, and refused to back down. Honour has been served.

18.

It's late August 1961. Rory Storm and the Hurricanes have come to the end of their summer season at Pwllheli. They were such a success that they have already been invited back next year.

Ringo loves to travel. The Hurricanes were promised tours on the Continent in the autumn, but somehow or other these failed to materialise. Ringo grows fidgety: now might be the time for a bold move, away from the group, away from Liverpool, away from Britain.

He has always been attracted to America, its large cars and country music and blues music and rock'n'roll and westerns. Why not live there? Inspired by Lightnin' Hopkins, he opts for Houston, Texas. Accordingly, he walks into the American Consulate in the Cunard Building in Liverpool and picks up the immigration forms. It turns out he will need to prove that he has money and the promise of a job. Undaunted, he writes to the Houston Chamber of Commerce; in return, he receives a list of local employment agencies. After more to-ing and fro-ing he picks out a job in a factory, thinking he can switch to something else once he gets there.

He's now all set, but what he later calls 'the really big forms' prove a stumbling block. The Americans want to know everything about his family, including their political affiliations. 'Was your grandfather's Great Dane a Commie?' is his way of describing it. These extra forms get the better of him: he simply can't face grappling with them, and eventually he calls it a day.

A few days later, Tony Sheridan asks him to join his backing band for a stint at the Top Ten Club in Hamburg. He doesn't hesitate. He gives Rory Storm twenty-four hours' notice, and sets off for Heathrow, a little nervous before boarding the aeroplane, as it's the first time he has ever flown. But for one or two forms, he might well have been flying on a different plane, in the opposite direction.

19.

Halfway through June 1962, Joe Flannery, the manager of Lee Curtis and the All Stars, drops by.

'When are you going to join us, Pete?' he asks.

Pete Best smiles. 'You must be joking. Why would I want to quit the Beatles when we're about to get our big break?'

Flannery stalls. 'Maybe I've jumped the gun. It's just a rumour going the rounds.'

'Why would anyone start a rumour like that?'

Pete is mystified. He has no intention of leaving the Beatles, not after drumming with them these past two years.

The conversation preys on his mind. What rumour? In mid-July he broaches the subject with Mr Epstein. Mr Epstein blushes and stammers. Pete cuts to the chase.

'Look, Brian. Are there any plans to replace me in the Beatles?'

Mr Epstein brushes away his fears. 'I'm telling you, as manager, there are no plans to replace you, Pete.'

That's good enough for Pete. Nothing more is said. Things carry on as usual: each morning, Pete and their road manager, Neil Aspinall, set off in Neil's van with all the Beatles' gear, which is still kept at Pete's mum's huge house in Hayman's Green. They pick up the other Beatles – John, Paul and George – along the way.

On 15 August the group plays two gigs at the Cavern, one at lunch-time, the other in the evening. 'Pick you up tomorrow, John!' calls Pete as he is leaving. 'No,' replies John. 'I've got other arrangements.'

They are to be the last words ever spoken to Pete by any member of the Beatles.

Before Pete leaves the Cavern that night, Mr Epstein says he'd like to see him in his office at ten o'clock the next morning. Nothing odd about that: they often meet to discuss arrangements. Neil drives him in, and

drops him off at the NEMS* office. Mr Epstein seems uneasy, blathering away about nothing at all. He asks Pete how he thinks the group is doing. Pete says, 'Fab,' a word not as fashionable as it will shortly become. He senses that something is on Mr Epstein's mind. Who can blame Epstein for his prevarication? He is still only twenty-seven years old, with a background in furniture sales.

Out of nowhere, Mr Epstein blurts out, 'I've got some bad news for you. The boys and myself have decided that they don't want you in the group any more, and that Ringo is replacing you.'

Pete finds it hard to speak. 'Why?'

'They don't think you're a good enough drummer, Pete,' he says. Then he adds: 'And George Martin doesn't think you're a good enough drummer.' George Martin is the producer from Parlophone who auditioned the Beatles. When Pete was out of earshot, he told Brian Epstein that Pete couldn't keep time, and that he planned on using a session drummer for the actual recording.

Pete says he thinks he's just as good as Ringo, if not better. 'Does Ringo know about this yet?' Ringo is a good friend.

* North End Music Stores, owned at that stage by Brian Epstein's father.

'He's joining on Sunday.'

Mr Epstein continues, briskly, with business. The phone rings. Mr Epstein picks up the receiver, and listens.

'I'm still with him at the moment,' he says, putting the receiver back down. He returns to their conversation. He says that while Pete is still under contract, he'll pay him his current wage – £50 or £60 a week – and he'll also put him in another group, and make him leader of it.

'There are still a couple of venues left before Ringo joins,' he adds, almost as an afterthought. 'Will you play?'

Pete doesn't know what to say, so he says yes. Then he leaves.

As Mr Epstein remembers it, the meeting lasted two hours. Pete thinks it lasted ten minutes.

Neil Aspinall is waiting for him downstairs. 'You look as if you've seen a ghost,' he says. 'They've kicked me out!' says Pete. Neil, who is going out with Pete's mum, says in that case he'll quit too. Pete talks him out of it. 'Don't be a fool – the Beatles are going places.'

Neil drops him home. The minute Pete closes the door, he bursts into tears. He feels like putting a stone round his neck and jumping off Pier Head. He can't face playing another two gigs with the Beatles, and doesn't turn up at the Riverpark Ballroom in Chester that night. 'I had been betrayed, and sitting up there onstage with the three people who had done it would be like having salt rubbed into a very deep wound.'

Only later does he discover that the Beatles were offered a contract with Parlophone a fortnight ago. No one told him about it.

His forthright mother Mona, who helped manage the group before Brian came on the scene, and always calls them 'Pete's group', immediately phones George Martin in London. The charming record producer assures her that, though he had wanted a different drummer for the recording session, it wasn't up to him whether or not the Beatles kept Pete.

Mona berates Brian Epstein: 'It's jealousy, Brian, jealousy all the way, because Peter is the one who has the terrific following – he has built up the following in Liverpool for the Beatles!' She is sure they got rid of Peter to stop him being the focus of attention, 'with the others just props'.

Whodunnit? As so often with the Beatles, everyone has a different story. In *The Beatles Anthology* – which is, in Biblical terms, the Authorised Version –

Paul recalls that after their audition at Abbey Road, George Martin took the other three to one side and said, 'I'm really unhappy with the drummer. Would you consider changing him?' 'We said, "No! We can't!" It was one of those terrible things you go through as kids. Can we betray him? No. But our career was on the line. Maybe they were going to cancel our contract.'

Yet George Martin always claimed to have been baffled by Pete's sacking. He was unimpressed by his drumming, and he had certainly noticed that he was out on a limb from the other three, who all liked larking around. 'But I never thought that Brian Epstein would let him go. He seemed to be the most saleable commodity as far as looks went. It was a surprise when later I learned that they had dropped Pete Best. The drums were important to me for a record, but they didn't matter much otherwise. Fans don't pay particular attention to the quality of drumming.'

But Pete Best always maintained that during his two years as a Beatle, not one of them ever complained about the quality of his drumming: 'Right to the end we were still drinking together and seemingly the best of friends.'

As time went by, John grew increasingly outspoken on this issue, as on so many others.

'We were pretty sick of Pete Best,' he said in 1967. 'He was a lousy drummer. He never improved. There was always this myth built up around him that he was great and Paul was jealous of him because he was pretty and all that crap . . . The only reason he was in the group in the first place was because the only way we could get to Hamburg, we had to have a drummer . . . we were always going to dump him when we could find a decent drummer.'

Ringo, too, showed his steel. Thirty years on, he was asked if he ever felt sorry for Pete. 'No. Why should I? I was a better player than him. That's how I got the job. It wasn't on my personality. It was that I was a better drummer, and I got the phone call. I never felt sorry for him. A lot of people have made careers out of knowing the Beatles.'

As in the dénouement of an Agatha Christie, it was the least likely suspect who finally confessed. Many years later, George – quiet, thoughtful young George – came clean. Pete kept calling in sick, he said, so they used to ask Ringo to take his place, 'and every time Ringo sat in, it seemed like "This is it." Eventually we realised, "We should get Ringo in the band full time." I was quite responsible for stirring things up. I conspired to get Ringo in for good. I talked to John until they came round to the idea . . . We weren't very good at telling Pete he had to go. But when it comes down to it, how do you tell somebody? . . . Brian Epstein was the manager so it was his job, and I don't think he could do it very well either. But that's the way it was and the way it is.'

BEATLES CHANGE DRUMMER!

Ringo Starr (former drummer with Rory Storm & the Hurricanes) has joined the Beatles, replacing Pete Best on drums. Ringo has admired the Beatles for years and is delighted with his new arrangement. Naturally he is tremendously excited about the future.

The Beatles comment, 'Pete left the group by mutual agreement. There were no arguments or difficulties, and this has been an entirely amicable decision.'

On Tuesday September 4th, the Beatles will fly to London to make recordings at EMI Studios. They will be recording numbers that have been specially written for the group.

Mersey Beat *front page, 23 August 1962*

When the news gets out, *Mersey Beat* receives a petition for Pete Best's reinstatement, signed by hundreds of fans. They descend on his family's home. Mo Best remembers her sitting room 'bulging with fans, sighing and sobbing'. These fans also picket Mr Epstein's offices in Whitechapel. The owner of the Cavern, Ray McFall, provides him with a bodyguard. Ringo receives a poison-pen letter.

The Beatles' next concert at the Cavern is a rocky affair. Pete's fans heckle them, chanting 'Pete is Best!' and 'Ringo never, Pete Best forever!' After half an hour of this, George loses his temper and snaps back. In reply, an aggrieved fan punches George, giving him a black eye. A Pete Best fan called Jenny writes a letter of complaint to George, who answers bullishly, 'Ringo is a much better drummer, and he can smile – which is a bit more than Pete could do. It will seem different for a few weeks, but I think that the majority of our fans will soon be taking Ringo for granted . . . lots of love from George.'

In time, George is proved right. Fans are fickle. 'I used to love Pete and was heartbroken when they sacked him,' one of them, Elsa Breden, tells the Beatles' biographer Mark Lewisohn over forty years later. 'But it soon passed and it was as if he'd never been there. They were *much* better with Ringo, without a doubt. He gave them that solid backbeat – he's a great rock'n'roll drummer – and he fitted in brilliantly.'

Just six days after Pete's dismissal, John, Paul, George and Ringo are filmed by Granada TV at a lunchtime concert in the Cavern. Pete goes along to watch them. On the way out, Paul's father Jim spots him and exclaims triumphantly, 'Great, isn't it? They're on TV!'

'Sorry, Mr McCartney,' replies Pete. 'I'm not the right person to ask.'

Over the next two years, the Beatles collectively gross £17 million.

For his part, Pete Best joins Lee Curtis and the All Stars. When Lee Curtis goes solo, they change their name to the Pete Best All-Stars. Then one of them leaves, and they become the Pete Best Four. Another leaves, and they become the Pete Best Combo. As the fame of the Beatles grows, interest in Pete fades. 'There was little or no revenue coming in, barely enough to pay my bills, and I reached the stage where I found myself scratching around for enough money to buy a packet of cigarettes. I just couldn't sit back and ignore the fact that I should have shared in the Beatles' success, which I considered to be part of my heritage.'

Pete's wife Kathy works on the biscuit counter at Woolworths. One day in 1967 he waits until she has left for work, goes up to the bedroom, locks the door, blocks any air gaps, places a pillow on the floor in front of the gas fire, and turns on the gas. He is fading away when his brother Rory arrives, smells gas, batters the door down and, screaming 'Bloody idiot!' saves his life.

That same year, Hunter Davies is finishing his pioneering biography of the Beatles. He often tells them tales from his travels, and they are always keen to know what old friends are up to. 'They were mostly interested to hear what had happened, except when the subject of Pete Best came up. They seemed to cut off, as if he had never touched their lives. They showed little reaction when I said he was now slicing bread for £18 a week, though Paul did make a face. John asked a few more questions, but then forgot about it, and they all went back to the song they were recording.'

In 1969 Pete embarks on a career as a civil servant, working in an employment office. For many years his two daughters, Beba and Bonita, have no idea that their dad was once a Beatle.

He is now retired, and, aged seventy-eight, fronts the Pete Best Band. His website, www.petebest.com, promises 'Right from the first beat, you'll be immersed in nostalgia, listening to "the best years" of the Beatles, 1960–62.' The website's tagline is 'The Man Who Put the Beat into the Beatles'.

In 2019 the *Sunday Times* estimates Ringo Starr's wealth at £240 million, which makes him the eighth-richest musician in the world. He is a knight of the realm, maintains homes in London, Los Angeles and Monte Carlo, and is married to Barbara Bach, a former Bond girl. Pete Best's old drum kit can be seen in Liverpool's The Beatles Story museum, sad and lonesome, a monument to loss; the tomb of the unknown drummer. On the audio guide, George Martin explains: 'He was probably the best-looking, but he didn't say much and he didn't have the charisma the others had. More importantly, his drumming was OK but it wasn't top-notch, in my opinion. I didn't realise that the boys were thinking much the same thing, and so they took that as the final word, a catalyst, and poor Pete got the boot. I've always felt a bit guilty about that. But I guess he survived.'

20.

I arrived at Pete Best's old house in Hayman's Green on the evening of day four of the annual Beatles Week. The basement recreated the old Casbah Club. A very basementy basement, dank, dark and sweaty, it was bursting at the seams with men in their seventies who looked like Bernie Sanders or Bernard Manning. Most wore Beatles T-shirts. A tribute band was tuning up in an authentically sixties manner, saying 'One-two, one-two' over and over again, with no indication that they would ever make it to three.

The Casbah is less a shrine to the Beatles than to Pete Best. Ringo is the great unmentionable. At the entrance, photographs of the Beatles – John, Paul, George and Pete, all autographed by Pete – were on sale for £15. A newspaper cutting with the headline '10,000 SUPPORTING PETE BEST STREET BID' was pinned to a red baize board. It posed an urgent question. In Liverpool, there's a Paul McCartney Way and a John Lennon Drive. So why not a Pete Best Avenue?

Out in the garden, a tribute band from Indonesia, the Indonesian Beat Club, composed of five 'die-hard Beatles lovers', were playing a spirited version of 'My Bonnie', just like Pete and the rest of his band used to do, back in the day. Queuing for a drink, I heard someone mention a Pete Best Fan Club. It is centred around Twitter, where it boasts fifty-three followers. Tweets include 'PETE is the BEST', 'I WANT PETE BEST SO BAAAAAD IT'S DRIVING ME MAD', 'Happiness Is Pete Best!' and the poignant 'MY PETE BEST GENTLY WEEEEEPSSS'.

Flyers near the entrance advertised The Magical Beatles Museum, run by Pete's half-brother Roag, the son of Mona Best and Neil Aspinall. Its collection includes Pete's Premier drum kit. History in the museum stops in June 1962: it is as though Ringo had never lived. Visitors are greeted by signs saying 'PETE, JOHN, PAUL, GEORGE, STUART'. Roag bills it as 'not just Liverpool's most authentic Beatles museum, but the world's most authentic Beatles museum. My oldest brother Pete Best was the original

Beatles drummer with the Beatles from 1960 to 1962. He performed over 1,000 shows and recorded 27 tracks as a Beatle.'

Pete Best's own website announces that 'When not undertaking a variety of celebrity duties, Pete has a busy schedule touring with the Pete Best Band. The Pete Best Band captures the sound of the Beatles in their formative years – the early years for many "was" the Beatles.'

21.

A Party:
Reece's Café
9–13 Parker Street, Liverpool
23 August 1962

In July 1962 Cynthia realises she is pregnant. She suspects John will take it badly, so puts off telling him for several days. Eventually, she plucks up the courage. 'As the news sank in he went pale and I saw the fear in his eyes. "There's only one thing for it, Cyn," he said. "We'll have to get married."'

She tells him he doesn't have to; he insists he wants to. The next day, John tells Brian Epstein, who says he doesn't have to go through with it. The Beatles have just signed their first recording contract, and Brian is worried the news will put the fans off. When John tells Aunt Mimi, she accuses Cynthia of wanting to trap him, and says she'll have nothing to do with the wedding.

Recognising that John is serious, Brian takes charge, applying for the emergency licence and booking the register office for the first available date, in a fortnight's time.

On 23 August, Brian, dapper in his pin-striped suit, picks up Cynthia from her bedsit. She is wearing a purple-and-black-checked two-piece suit over a frilly high-necked white blouse, with black shoes and a black bag. Brian takes her in a chauffeur-driven car to Mount Pleasant register office. On the way, he tells her she is looking lovely, and does his best to calm her nerves.

When they arrive, John, Paul and George are already pacing about in the waiting room, dressed in smart black suits. Cynthia thinks they all look 'horribly nervous'. Cynthia's brother Tony and his wife Marjorie are there too.

As the registrar begins to speak, a workman outside starts a pneumatic drill, but they struggle on. The ceremony takes a matter of minutes. They sign the register: John Winston Lennon, 21, Musician (Guitar) and Cynthia Powell, 22, Art Student (School). Now what? Brian suggests they all go to Reece's, round the corner, for lunch. They opt for the cheaper café on the ground floor rather than the more expensive Famous Grill Room on the top floor.

The bride and groom and their five guests queue for soup, chicken and trifle. Alcohol is not available, so they all toast the happy couple with water. John has a look of pride. Cynthia is over the moon: 'A full church wedding with all the extras couldn't have made me happier.'

Brian presents them with a silver-plated ashtray, engraved with the message 'Good luck JOHN & CYNTHIA. Brian, Paul & George 23 Aug 62', as well as a shaving kit in a leather pouch embossed 'JWL', which John will take everywhere. The lunch – fifteen shillings a head – is on Brian, who also announces that he has a bolt-hole in Falkner Street where John and Cynthia can live for as long as they want. Cynthia is so excited that she gives him a hug. Brian looks embarrassed.

That night the Beatles have a gig in Chester, so Cynthia takes the opportunity to make the flat nice. At the gig, John appears out of sorts, losing his temper with the support act and yelling, 'You're doing all our fucking numbers!' He doesn't tell anyone that he's just got married. Even the Beatles' new drummer, Ringo, is kept in the dark.

22.

In November 1962 a twenty-two-year-old Sheffield entrepreneur with the unusual name of Peter Stringfellow was casting around for an act for his new nightclub, the Black Cat. Though the Black Cat sounded with-it, it was just the name he gave St Aidan's church hall on the nights he hired it.

Searching through the *New Musical Express*, Stringfellow spotted an advertisement for a group called the Beatles. They seemed to be just what he wanted: at the beginning of October, their song 'Love Me Do' had been his very first record request from a punter; he had been playing it, on and off, ever since.

There was no phone at his parents' house, so he went to a public call box and was put through to the Beatles' manager, a Mr Epstein, who told him that the Beatles would cost £50.

'£50!' replied Stringfellow. 'Excuse me, I pay Screaming Lord Sutch £50, and nobody has heard of the Beatles!'

Epstein replied that, unlike Sutch, the Beatles had a record in the charts. Stringfellow knew that 'Love Me Do' was actually moving down the charts. He said he would think about it.

The next day he called Epstein back, saying he was prepared to pay £50. Epstein said the price had gone up to £65. Stringfellow felt that Epstein was as nervous as he was himself. He sensed that the Beatles were in real demand, and that their success was becoming more than Epstein could cope with. Once again, Stringfellow said he'd think about it.

True to his word, he called back two days later, and said, yes, he could manage £65. Mr Epstein replied that the price had now risen to £100. 'The Beatles have another single coming out and this will go to the top of the charts,' he said confidently. Stringfellow tried to haggle, but Mr Epstein said he wouldn't take anything less than £90. They finally agreed on £85. Stringfellow was shaken. 'I came out of the telephone in a sweat because I had never paid that amount of money to a band before.'

There was an eerie gap between 'Love Me Do' leaving the charts and the release of 'Please Please Me'. The Beatles seemed to go quiet. Stringfellow began to panic. Had he just wasted all his money?

He placed an advertisement in the *NME* announcing that the Beatles would be playing at the Black Cat in April, and ordered tickets from the printer, each priced at four shillings. Applications came pouring in, even from Scotland, so he went back to the printers and asked them to put up the price to five shillings. By January he had sold over 1,500 tickets, way beyond the capacity of the Black Cat.

He looked around for a larger venue, hit upon the Azena Ballroom, Sheffield's flashiest dance hall, and placed an advertisement in the *NME* announcing the change of venue. By 2 April he had sold two thousand tickets; on the night itself, a further thousand people turned up on the off-chance of getting in.

23.

I arrived too late at the International Beatles Week in Liverpool to catch the opening act, Les Sauterelles. They formed in 1962, and according to the brochure, 'soon became the most popular Swiss Beat Band of the sixties. In the hot summer of '68, their single "Heavenly Club" was number one for six weeks in the Swiss Charts.'

Next up were a Beatles tribute band from Hungary called the Bits, followed by the Norwegian Beatles, 'probably the world's northernmost Beatles tribute band', and then Clube Big Beatles from Brazil, who are apparently soon to open their own Cavern Club in São Paulo. Performers on the indoor stage included the Bertils from Sweden, the Fab Fourever ('Canada's Premiere Tribute to the Beatles'), Bestbeat from Serbia, crowned 'one of the thirty most prominent Beatles tribute bands on the planet' by *Newsweek* in 2012, and B.B. Cats, an all-female tribute band from Tokyo who specialise in playing the Beatles' Hamburg repertoire.

There are over a thousand Beatles tribute acts in the world today. Many of them – the Tefeatles from Guatemala, Rubber Soul from Brazil, the Nowhere Boys from Colombia, Abbey Road from Spain – have now been together longer than the Beatles themselves: Britain's Bootleg Beatles and Australia's Beatnix have both been going for forty years.

In the evening, I joined the long and winding queue outside the Grand Central Hall to see the Fab Four from California, one of the most successful Beatles tribute bands in the world. Most of those queuing were around the age of seventy, which would have made them fifteen or so at the height of Beatlemania. The men wore baggy jeans and Beatles T-shirts; the women slacks and generous tops. One or two people were in wheelchairs. At most rock concerts, fans rush to get close to the stage, but when the doors to the Grand Central Hall opened, most people rushed upstairs, to where the seats were.

A depressing man in jeans and a knitted bonnet opened the show,

moaning his way through John's passive-aggressive 'Don't Let Me Down', accompanying himself with jerky pyrotechnics on an acoustic guitar. What was I doing there, with these senior citizens togged up in their Beatles gear? With a change of clothes it might almost have been a reunion of Second World War veterans, gathered for a fly-past of Spitfires.

In the 1970s, my parents used to watch a TV programme called *The Good Old Days*. The audience would dress up as Edwardians, the men in straw boaters, fancy blazers and walrus moustaches, the women in feather-rimmed hats and voluminous dresses with high-boned collars. They would gasp adoringly as the high-camp Master of Ceremonies, Leonard Sachs, introduced each music-hall act – tap dancer, conjuror, barbershop quartet – with a stream of elaborate words: 'Prestidigitational!' ('Oooh!'), 'Plenitudinous!' ('Ahh!'), 'Sesquipedalianism!' ('Oooh!'), and then banged his gavel. At the curtain-call everyone would join in with a sing-song of 'Down at the Old Bull and Bush'. It was what was then known as a trip down memory lane, viewers at home happy to collude in the deception that time could be reversed, and the dead revived.

Was this Beatles revival another quest for the same old thing – dreams of blue remembered hills?

That is the land of lost content,
I see it shining plain,
The happy highways where I went
And cannot come again.

Such were my maudlin reflections as the Fab Four took to the stage. But then they started to play 'She Loves You', and they sounded just like the Beatles and, to my fading eyes, looked just like them too – Paul arching his eyebrows and rolling his eyes to the ceiling, George slightly dreamy and distant, Ringo rocking his head from side to side, John with his legs wide apart, as though astride a donkey. I was witnessing something closer to a wonderful conjuring trick. One half of your brain recognises that these are not the Beatles: how could they be? But the other half is happy to believe that they are. It is like watching a play: yes, of course you know that the couple onstage are actors, but on some other level you think they are Othello and Desdemona. The drama lies in the interplay of knowledge and imagination. And with the Fab Four, there is another illusion at work, equally convincing, equally transient: for as long as they play, we are all fifty years younger, gazing in wonder at the Beatles in their prime.

24.

Helen Shapiro had been asked to leave her school choir because she could never resist jazzing up the harmonies.

So, aged twelve, she formed a group, Suzie and the Hula-Hoops, with her schoolmates Mark Feld,* Stephen Gould and Susan Singer, but they disbanded soon afterwards. Helen liked to hang around the stage door of the Hackney Empire, up the road from her family home, spotting stars like Adam Faith, Billy Fury, Cliff Richard and Lord Rockingham's Eleven. Once, she even managed to get Marty Wilde's autograph.

Aged thirteen, she was determined to become either an air hostess or a singer. This choice was decided for her when her Uncle Harry happened to spot an advertisement for the Maurice Burman School of Modern Pop Singing, where Alma Cogan had once been a pupil. Burman himself had drummed with leading dance bands before the war, and now wrote a regular column for *Melody Maker*. Upon meeting little Helen, he was so excited by her deep, bluesy voice that he waived the fee. Every Saturday Helen attended his school, on the corner of Baker Street and Marylebone Road, and there she learned scales, diction, phrasing and microphone technique.

After six months Burman got in touch with his old friend, the conductor and producer Norrie Paramor. Paramor suggested Helen record a test tape at the EMI studios at Abbey Road. She sang 'Birth of the Blues'. Paramor found it hard to believe that these powerful, poised vocals sprang from a thirteen-year-old.

EMI gave Helen a contract. Instead of a percentage, they offered her a penny per single, and sixpence for each twelve-track LP. If she was a success, the amount would rise to three farthings per track, up to a maximum of tuppence a single. 'It all went totally over my head. The people from EMI were all clever businessmen while I was just a young girl who wanted

* Who later changed his name to Marc Bolan.

to sing. I never was interested in the financial side of things, until it was too late.'

Helen and her parents thought she should change her name: at that time Jewish performers tended to change their names to avoid anti-Semitism. But Norrie Paramor felt that most people wouldn't twig that Shapiro was a Jewish surname, and it sounded dashing, so they decided to stick with it.

Helen's first single, 'Don't Treat Me Like a Child', was released on 10 February 1961. It seemed to have peaked at a satisfactory number 28 in the charts, but then she appeared on the first edition of the new pop music show *Thank Your Lucky Stars*, and it zoomed to number 4. Helen began to be recognised in the streets.

Her next two songs, 'You Don't Know' and 'Walkin' Back to Happiness', both sold over a million copies, and reached number 1 in the charts. Helen was voted Best Female Act in 1961, and again the following year.

Towards the end of 1962, the promoter Arthur Howes told her about the line-up for her next British tour. 'We're going to put a nice package together for you. We've got Kenny Lynch, Danny Williams. Red Price will be backing you again. Dave Allen is compering, there's a girls' singing group, the Honeys, and a vocal group, the Kestrels. Then we've got this new group, the Beatles. I don't know whether you've heard their record, "Love Me Do"?'

Helen certainly did know about the Beatles: 'They were the funny fellows with the funny hair.'

Her tour kicked off at the Gaumont in Bradford on 2 February. The Red Price Band opened the show, then came the Honeys, the comedian (and compere) Dave Allen, and the Beatles, with Danny Williams ('Britain's Johnny Mathis') closing the first half. After the interval the Red Price Band appeared again, followed by the Kestrels, Kenny Lynch, Dave Allen again, and finally, topping the bill, Helen Shapiro.

During the sound checks in Bradford, Helen was introduced to the Beatles' bass player, Paul. 'I made some comment about liking "Love Me Do" and he introduced me to the rest of the guys who were really happy because this was their first major concert tour. They'd performed in clubs and ballrooms in Hamburg and Liverpool but never done anything like the pop package and were eager to be onstage.'

At this point, one of them mentioned that they had written a song called 'Misery' for Helen, but it had been turned down on her behalf by Norrie Paramor. Helen apologised, saying she hadn't known about it.

When the Beatles took to the stage, Helen was struck by quite how loud they were. They were used to a noisier crowd. 'They soon cottoned on to the fact that they didn't need to turn the sound up quite so much when people were sitting listening rather than dancing . . . They had a lot to learn.'

Her management encouraged Helen to travel by herself in a special limousine, to reflect her star status, but she preferred sitting in the coach with the supporting acts. 'I wouldn't have missed it for the world, especially while the Beatles were with us.' Together on the coach, the Beatles would bring out their guitars, and Helen would sing a song like 'The Locomotion'. She remembered how Paul would practise writing his autograph over and over again, and then ask her what she thought of it. On one of these coach rides John and Paul hit upon the idea of running up to the microphone together and singing 'Whoooo!', a routine that within a matter of weeks would be setting off explosions of ecstasy among their fans.

One night Helen let the Beatles into her changing room so they could watch themselves on television for the first time. John was surprised by the way he looked, particularly the odd, jockey-like stance he adopted onstage. They kept nudging one another and commenting. 'Eh, look at that.' 'You look awful.'

As the tour progressed, the Beatles' popularity grew and grew, while Helen's went into decline. By chance, both the Beatles and Helen had released new singles at roughly the same time – 'Please Please Me' on 17 January, 'Queen for Tonight' on 26 January. As the weeks went by, the status of the famous headliner and the lowly support act switched places. At the beginning of February 'Please Please Me' was at number 33, and 'Queen for Tonight' was nowhere to be seen. By 6 February 'Please Please Me' was number 16, and 'Queen for Tonight' was still nowhere to be seen. On 13 February 'Queen for Tonight' scraped in at 42, while 'Please Please Me' was number 3. By 23 February 'Please Please Me' was number 2 and 'Queen for Tonight' was 33, the highest position it would ever reach: the following week it had slipped to 35. Helen was only sixteen years old, and on the skids: 'I'd been a novelty at fourteen but I suffered from the Shirley Temple syndrome. I'd grown up. Suddenly I was beginning to look a little bit passé in spite of topping the bill.'

One day, reading a music paper on the tour coach, she saw the head-line 'Is Helen Shapiro a "Has-Been" at 16?' 'I felt just as if somebody had punched me in the stomach.' In the seat behind her, John Lennon, six years her senior, noticed that she was upset. They had always had a good relationship: like many girls her age, she had a crush on him. He in turn was uncharacteristically protective of her, treating her, in Helen's words, 'like some kind of kid sister'.

'What's up, Helly?'

She showed him the offending headline. John sought to reassure her. 'You don't want to be bothered with that rubbish. You're all right. You'll be going on for years.'

But no amount of reassurance could disguise the truth. Helen Shapiro was to look back on that moment as 'one of those milestones I would pinpoint as the beginning of change; not just for me but for a lot of solo singers. The Beatles were the beginning of a new era, a new wave of groups, the whole Merseyside thing.'

By the end of February, the Beatles had been promoted above Danny Williams on the tour, charged with closing the first half of the programme. For the first time, their music was being drowned out by screams. Helen continued to travel on the coach with the support acts, but, ever conscious of the Beatles' burgeoning star status, Brian Epstein made them travel in their own car, away from the others. They left the tour before the end, off to head their own shows. Helen missed the Beatles: 'Things were never quite the same afterwards.'

After the tour, she continued to record. 'My records were getting better, yet the sales were worse. All during '63 the whole Merseyside thing was growing and growing. London was out, along with solo artistes. The writing was on the wall for anyone who didn't belong to a group, preferably with drums, and lead, bass and rhythm guitars.'

Her next record, 'Woe is Me', peaked at number 35. By October 1963, when she came to release 'Look Who it Is', the Beatles had become the most famous act in Britain: 'She Loves You' was at number 1, and well on its way to selling a million copies.

To help Helen promote her single, the producer of *Ready Steady Go!* suggested she be filmed singing it to the Beatles, who were headlining. It was agreed that she would sing a verse to each Beatle in turn, but as there were only three verses, one of them had to stand aside. They tossed a coin, and the loser was Paul, who went off to a neighbouring studio, where he was charged with picking the winner of a competition in which four girls mimed to 'Let's Jump the Broomstick' by Brenda Lee.

Paul decided that the winner was girl number four, Melanie Coe, aged fourteen, from Stamford Hill in London.

25.

On previous shows, the prize had been a date with a pop star, but this time it was just the Beatles' LP, *Please Please Me*. Upon hearing this, Melanie Coe's face fell. 'I thought I was going to have a dinner date with the Beatles, so I was terribly disappointed.' Moreover, Paul McCartney's firm handshake caused her false nails to come loose. 'I don't think I'd ever worn them before, and I wanted to have everything perfect.' But her disappointment was assuaged when the producers, impressed by her natural exuberance, offered her a year's stint as a background dancer, which let her rub shoulders with stars like Stevie Wonder, Dusty Springfield, Cilla Black and Freddie and the Dreamers.

Had she not been picked out by Paul McCartney, might Melanie Coe have been more content with the life of a schoolgirl? Instead she grew restless, and as time went by she started venturing into central London, against her parents' wishes. 'In 1964, I'd say there were three or four discos in London, so you were likely to meet the same people wherever you went.'

On one of these secret excursions she went with a friend from Hamburg to the Bag o' Nails Club in Kingly Street, just off Carnaby Street. As in the Beatles song, she was just seventeen. Her friend had long boasted that she knew the Beatles very well, but Melanie didn't believe her. 'We were sitting down having a drink and in walks John Lennon with his entourage. And she waves to him and he comes over to us. "It's you! Come join us!" And before I knew it, I'm seventeen and I'm at a table with John Lennon! That's how it was!'

Touched by these two encounters, the first with Paul, the second with John, what young girl could have resisted the lure of adult life? Unfortunately, it wasn't long before Melanie became pregnant. One afternoon she left a note on the kitchen table that she hoped would say more, and left home, off to live with a croupier in Bayswater.

Melanie had been away from home for a week when on 27 February 1967 she saw her picture in the *Daily Mail*, alongside a headline saying:

'A-Level Girl Dumps Car and Vanishes'

On that same day, Paul McCartney also happened to be reading the *Daily Mail*, and his eye was caught by the same headline. The report began:

The father of 17-year-old Melanie Coe, the schoolgirl who seemed to have everything, spent yesterday searching for her in London and Brighton.

Melanie had her own car, an Austin 1100. It was left unlocked outside her home when she vanished.

She had a wardrobe full of clothes. She took only what she was wearing – a cinnamon trouser suit and black patent leather shoes.

She left her chequebook and drew no money from her account.

Melanie, who has blonde hair and is 5ft 1inch tall, was studying for her A-level examinations. She planned to go to university or drama school.

'I cannot imagine why she should run away,' her father told reporters. 'She has everything here. She is very keen on clothes, but she left them all, even her fur coat.'

Without realising that Melanie was the very same girl he had picked to win a prize over three years before, Paul was inspired to write 'She's Leaving Home'.

'I started to get the lyrics: she slips out and leaves a note and then the parents wake up and then . . . It was rather poignant,' he recalled. '. . . and when I showed it to John, he added the Greek chorus, long sustained notes, and one of the nice things about the structure of the song is that it stays on those chords endlessly.'

John found the Greek chorus – 'Sacrificed most of our lives', 'We gave her everything money could buy' – simple to write: these were the very same complaints he had heard so often from the lips of his Aunt Mimi.

The Beatles recorded 'She's Leaving Home' on the evening of 17 March 1967. By this time Melanie Coe was back home with her parents, who had managed to track her down. She first heard the song soon after it came out on the *Sgt. Pepper* album at the end of May. 'I didn't realise it was about me, but I remember thinking it *could* have been about me. I found the song extremely sad. It obviously struck a chord somewhere. It wasn't until later, when I was in my twenties, that my mother said, "You know, that song was about you."' She had seen an interview with Paul on television and he said he'd based the song on this newspaper article. She put two and two together.

'The most interesting thing in the song is what the father said: "We gave her everything money could buy." And in the newspaper article, my father actually says almost those words. He doesn't understand why I would have left home when they bought me or gave me everything. Which is true; they had bought me a car and they always bought me expensive clothes and things like that. But, as we know, that doesn't mean that you get on well with your parents, or even love them, just because they buy you material things.'

Quite by chance, McCartney had hit another nail on the head: before starting work as a croupier, her older boyfriend had worked in the motor trade.*

---

* The following year Melanie left home again, having married a Spaniard. They broke up after a year, and then she moved to California, intent on pursuing a career in acting and dancing. She enjoyed a brief romance with Burt Ward, the actor who played Batman's young sidekick Robin in the TV series. In 1981 she returned home to look after her mother, who was dying.

26.

The Beatles started 1963 playing modest gigs such as the Wolverham Welfare Association dance at the Civic Hall in Wirral (14 January) and a Baptist church youth club party at the Co-Operative Hall in Darwen (25 January). On 4 April, well into spring, they performed an afternoon concert for the boys of Stowe School in Buckinghamshire.

But their popularity was speedily growing. In March their second single, 'Please Please Me', had only been prevented from reaching number 1 in the UK charts by the continued popularity of Frank Ifield's 'Wayward Wind' and, latterly, Cliff Richard's 'Summer Holiday'. But in May 'From Me to You' became their first single to reach number 1, and their debut album, *Please Please Me*, also went to number 1, where it was set to remain for the next thirty weeks.

By the end of that month, they had appeared for a second time on national television, singing 'From Me to You' on the children's programme *Pops and Lenny*, accompanied by Lenny the Lion, the distinguished glove puppet. Furthermore, they had been given a new radio series on the BBC, *Pop Go the Beatles*. The corporation's Audience Research Department estimated that 5.3 per cent of the population, or 2.8 million people, had listened to the first episode, with audience comments ranging from 'an obnoxious noise' to 'really with-it'.

But fame comes with drawbacks. Paul had originally planned to celebrate his twenty-first birthday at the McCartney family home in Forthlin Road, but it soon became clear that fans might prove a hazard. So the McCartneys switched the party to his Auntie Jin's house, across the Mersey in Huyton, where there was plenty of room for a marquee in the large back garden, and privacy was assured.

The birthday party took place on 21 June 1963. Guests included the three other Beatles, John's wife Cynthia, Paul's brother Mike, Mike's two friends Roger McGough and John Gorman, John's friend Pete Shotton,

Ringo's girlfriend Maureen, the disc jockey Bob Wooler, Gerry Marsden, Billy J. Kramer and any number of musicians. Paul was particularly delighted when the Shadows came through the door. 'I can't believe it,' he said to Tony Bramwell, who worked for Brian Epstein. He then thought about it for a second, before adding, 'But we're sort of like one of them now, aren't we?'

'Yeah, only bigger,' replied Bramwell, who remembered Paul giving him a doubtful look, 'as if I was pulling his leg'.

Paul's new girlfriend, the seventeen-year-old actress Jane Asher, was also there. They had first met two months before. Cynthia was very taken with her: 'She was beautiful, with auburn hair and green eyes. Also, although she had been a successful actress since she was five, she was unaffected, easy to talk to and friendly.'

Paul's dad Jim played old-fashioned numbers on his piano, and, later, the up-and-coming band the Fourmost took to a makeshift stage. Their bass player Billy Hatton had struck the deal. 'Paul offered to pay us the usual rate for this kind of job, but as we were going to the party anyway, we said we would do it for just one and fourpence halfpenny each.'

As the party progressed, Pete Shotton spotted John in a corner, 'nursing a Scotch and Coke and looking glum as could be'. John seemed pleased to see Pete, and together they drifted into the garden. Over more drinks, John enjoyed pointing out the various pop stars present. 'Cliff Richard might even show up tonight,' he added, before going off to get yet another refill.

Pete set off to find a loo. On his return, everything had changed. 'When I emerged from the WC . . . the party seemed to have been somehow transformed from a celebration to a wake. Something, obviously, had gone terribly wrong.'

Bob Wooler, the Cavern MC, was lying on the floor, with blood everywhere. Apparently he had been teasing John about his recent holiday in Spain with Brian Epstein, and John had taken his revenge. 'A well-drunk John punched Wooler for taunting him,' recalled Tony Barrow in his autobiography. Another of Epstein's assistants, Peter Brown, added more detail, saying that 'in a mad rage and obviously very drunk', John had started 'pummelling' an unnamed guest; it had taken 'three men to pull John off, but not before he managed to break three of the man's ribs'.

Tony Bramwell remembered that 'John saw red. He assaulted Bob, breaking his ribs and ending up with a bloody nose himself.' Shotton took it a step further: 'John responded by knocking Bob to the ground and repeatedly clobbering him in the face with, I believe, a shovel. The damage to Bob's visage was so extensive that an ambulance had to be summoned to rush him to hospital.'

In her second autobiography, written forty-two years after the event (she failed to mention the incident in her first), Cynthia Lennon wrote: 'John, who'd had plenty to drink, exploded. He leapt on Bob, and by the time he was dragged off Bob had a black eye and badly bruised ribs. I took John home as fast as I could and Brian drove Bob to hospital.' Cynthia claimed to remember John telling her, 'He called me a queer.' Others, though, have suggested Wooler said something more insidious, like, 'Come on, John. Tell us about you and Brian in Spain. We all know.'

Thirty-six years later, Rex Makin, the Epstein family's solicitor,* gave an account in which he deftly avoided mentioning Brian Epstein or the Spanish holiday, and suggested that Wooler had come on to John: 'Everybody had a lot to drink and John Lennon thought or perceived that Wooler had made a pass at him, whereupon he socked him and broke his nose and gave him a black eye.'

The Beatles' biographers also offer radically different versions of the same event. Hunter Davies, who gave Epstein and the Beatles copy approval for his authorised 1968 biography, wrote that 'John picked a fight with a local disk [sic] jockey,' and quoted John saying, 'I broke his bloody ribs for him. I was pissed at the time. He called me a queer.'

Other biographers have tended to take it a stage further. 'Without warning, John exploded,' wrote Ray Connolly. 'Lashing out, he began to batter Wooler's face and body with both his fists and a stick . . . He went berserk, to the extent that when he was pulled off Wooler, the inoffensive and much older man had to be quickly driven to hospital by Brian, where he was treated for bruised ribs and a black eye.'

In his 1981 biography of the Beatles, *Shout!*, Philip Norman described the party as 'a typical Liverpool booze-up, riotous and noisy'. He mentioned that 'John Lennon got into a fight with another guest,' but didn't say who it was, or what the fight was about. Norman was more forthcoming

---

* In 1967, Makin was to make all the arrangements for Epstein's funeral. Some credit him with inventing the term 'Beatlemania'.

in his 2016 biography of Paul, disagreeing with Connolly that Wooler was inoffensive, and instead describing him as 'notoriously sharp-tongued'. In his account of the fight, Norman had John 'raining punches viciously on Wooler's head and body', but offered no assessment of the injuries. However, in his 2008 biography of John, he stated that Wooler 'suffered bruised ribs and a black eye'.

In his 2005 Beatles biography, Bob Spitz had John beating Wooler 'viciously, with tightly closed fists. When that didn't do enough damage, he grabbed a garden shovel that was left in the yard and whacked Bob once or twice with the handle. According to one observer, "Bob was holding his hands to his face and John was kicking all the skin off his fingers."' According to Spitz, Wooler was taken away in an ambulance with even more injuries: 'a broken nose, a cracked collar bone and three broken ribs'.

Do I hear any advance on a broken nose, a cracked collarbone and three broken ribs? Inevitably, the most excessive bid was submitted by Albert Goldman, the most merciless and hyperbolic of all John's biographers:* 'John doubled up his fist and smashed the little disc jockey in the nose. Then, seizing a shovel that was lying in the yard, Lennon began to beat Wooler to death. Blow after blow came smashing down on the defenseless man lying on the ground. It would have ended in murder if John had not suddenly realized: "If I hit him one more time, I'll kill him!" Making an enormous effort of will, Lennon restrained himself. At that instant three men seized him and disarmed him. An ambulance was called for Wooler, who had suffered a broken nose, a cracked collar-bone, and three broken ribs. Lennon had broken a finger.'

All in all, no other event in the lives of the Beatles illustrates more clearly the random, subjective nature of history, a form predicated on objectivity but reliant on the shifting sands of memory.

So a table of the final tally looks like this:

---

* Goldman (1927–94) wrote *The Lives of John Lennon* (1988), in which he portrayed John in a uniquely unflattering light, even going so far as to suggest he was a murderer. Goldman died of a heart attack in an aeroplane on the way to London, following a heated argument with flight attendants about having his seat upgraded. 'Goldman looked like Truman Capote and sounded like Bette Davis,' wrote his *Daily Telegraph* obituarist. 'He was not a modest man: "With the counter-culture," he declared, "I had found a great field that needed a great mind like mine to explore it."'

	ASSAULT	EXTENT OF INJURY
TONY BARROW	'Punched Wooler'	No mention
TONY BRAMWELL	'He assaulted Bob'	Broken ribs, bloody nose
PETER BROWN	'Pummelling'	Three broken ribs
RAY CONNOLLY	'He began to batter Wooler's face and body with both fists and a stick'	Bruised ribs, black eye
ALBERT GOODMAN	'. . . seizing a shovel . . . began to beat Wooler to death. It would have ended in murder . . .'	Broken nose, cracked collarbone, three broken ribs. Also, Lennon broke a finger
CYNTHIA LENNON	'He leapt on Bob'	Black eye, badly bruised ribs
JOHN LENNON (1963) to press	'I am terribly upset about this . . . too far gone to know what I was doing'	No mention of injuries
JOHN LENNON (1963) to Barrow	'He called me a bloody queer so I battered him'	Unspecific injuries: 'He got what he deserved'
JOHN LENNON (1968) to Hunter Davies	'I smashed him up'	'I broke his bloody ribs for him'
JOHN LENNON (1980)	'I was beating the shit out of him, and beating him with a big stick'	'I battered his bloody ribs for him'
REX MAKIN	'He socked him'	Broken nose, black eye
PHILIP NORMAN	'raining punches viciously on W's head and body'	Bruised ribs, black eye
PETE SHOTTON	'repeatedly clobbering him in the face with . . . a shovel'	Extensive damage to face
BOB SPITZ	'leapt on W, beating him viciously with tightly closed fists'	Broken nose, cracked collarbone, three broken ribs

No one seems to doubt, though, that the following day Wooler contacted Rex Makin, who decided to act for both parties, eventually negotiating a £200 payment to Wooler and an apology. Word soon reached the press about the incident. In charge of damage limitation, Tony Barrow got in touch with John, who was bullishly unrepentant. 'He told me gruffly, "Wooler was well out of fucking order. He called me a bloody queer so I battered him . . . I wasn't that pissed. The bastard had it coming. He teased me, I punched him. Of course I won't apologise."' Barrow then dutifully 'trimmed and toned and spun' this unpromising material, so that the next day's *Sunday Mirror* reported:

> Guitarist John Lennon, 22-year-old leader of the Beatles pop group, said last night, 'Why did I have to go and punch my best friend? . . . Bob is the last person in the world I would want to have a fight with. I can only hope he realises that I was too far gone to know what I was doing.'

Recuperating in hospital, Wooler received a conciliatory telegram from John: 'REALLY SORRY, BOB. TERRIBLY SORRY TO REALIZE WHAT I HAD DONE. WHAT MORE CAN I SAY?' As it happened, each word had been dictated by Brian Epstein.*

What exactly happened in Spain? Most people agree that when Julian was three weeks old, Brian took the unusual step of taking John on a Spanish holiday à deux. In her first autobiography (1978), Cynthia says that when John asked her if she would mind, 'I concealed my hurt and envy and gave him my blessing.' In her second (2005), her memories have altered; now, when John asks her if she would mind, there is no mention of hurt or envy. 'I said, truthfully, that I wouldn't.'

The implacable Albert Goldman, on the other hand, states that John only got round to seeing his newborn son a week after his birth, and then, 'turning to Cynthia, informed her bluntly that he was going off on a short holiday with Brian Epstein'. In the Goldman version, far from acquiescing,

---

* The telegram was sold at Sotheby's in 1984 for £550. In 1980, shortly before he died, John spoke of 'hitting him with a big stick, and for the first time I thought, I can kill this guy. I just saw it on a screen: if I hit him once more, that's going to be it. I really got shocked. That's when I gave up violence, because all my life I'd been like that.'

'Cynthia was outraged by his astonishing news.' Goldman adds that John was indifferent to Cynthia's feelings, saying: 'Being selfish again, aren't you?' He appears to have lifted this version of events from Peter Brown's waspish memoir *The Love You Make* (1983), though it seems unlikely that Brown himself was privy to John and Cynthia's discussion.

So, did they or didn't they? The simple truth is that no one knows, but everyone thinks they know, or at least they want everyone else to think they know. Cynthia covers the matter in two sentences. Pooh-poohing the gossip, she says that after John came back from Spain, 'He had to put up with sly digs, winks and innuendo that he was secretly gay. It infuriated him: all he'd wanted was a break with a friend, but it was turned into so much more.'

Of the Beatles' employees, Alistair Taylor and Tony Barrow agree with Cynthia that nothing sexual occurred. Taylor claims that 'in one of our frankest heart-to-hearts John denied it'. 'He never wanted me like that,' he told Taylor, adding, 'Even completely out of my head, I couldn't shag a bloke. And I certainly couldn't lie there and let one shag me. Even a nice guy like Brian. To be honest, the thought of it turns me over.' Barrow says, 'John made it abundantly clear to me that there was no two-way traffic along this route . . . I don't believe that the relationship between Brian and John became a physical one in Spain or elsewhere. I believe John's version, which was that he teased Brian to the limit but stopped short when they came to the brink.'

On the other hand, Tony Bramwell claims John told him that he finally allowed Brian to have sex with him just 'to get it out of the way'. But Bramwell adds that John may have been lying. 'Those who knew John well, who had known him for years, don't believe it for a moment.' However, Peter Brown begs to differ, painting an unfeasibly vivid picture, as though lifted from an airport novel: 'Drunk and sleepy from the sweet Spanish wine, Brian and John got undressed in silence. "It's OK, Eppy," John said, and lay down on his bed. Brian would have liked to have hugged him, but he was afraid. Instead, John lay there, tentative and still, and Brian fulfilled the fantasies he was so sure would bring him contentment, only to awake the next morning as hollow as before.'*

---

* The memoirs of former Beatles office staff share this strange quality of divine omniscience with the memoirs of royal housekeepers and valets.

Pete Shotton was closer to John than the others, and less given to speculation. He writes that when John and Brian went away 'tongues began wagging all over town'. On John's return, Shotton teased him – 'So you had a good time with Brian, then?' – only for John to respond quietly, 'Actually Pete, something did happen with him one night . . . Eppy just kept on and on at me. Until one night I finally just pulled me trousers down and said to him, "Oh, for Christ's sake, Brian, just stick it up me fucking arse then." And he said to me, "Actually, John, I don't do that kind of thing. That's not what I like to do." "Well," I said, "what is it you want to do then?" And he said, "I'd really just like to touch you, John." And so I let him toss me off . . . So what harm did it do, then, Pete, for fuck's sake? No harm at all. The poor fucking bastard, he can't help the way he is.'

So much for John's associates. Small wonder, then, that his biographers are also divided. Epstein's biographer Ray Coleman insists nothing sexual occurred: 'Since the death of Epstein and Lennon, many with no access to, or observation of, both men in their lifetime have peddled the assumption that Brian and John had a sexual liaison. This is despite the lack of any evidence, despite firm declarations of John's heterosexuality from Cynthia and many other women, and despite the statement by McCartney that he "slept in a million hotel rooms, as we all did, with John and there was never any hint that he was gay". Coleman argues that Epstein 'would never have risked so profoundly changing his relationship with them, individually or collectively'. He adds that 'Epstein was not a predator,' though there is in fact plenty of evidence to suggest that he was.*

In his biography of John, Ray Connolly judges Pete Shotton to be honest, so believes his claim that John said he had let Brian masturbate him. 'But was John telling the truth? It was well known to those around him that he was keenly heterosexual. But he loved to shock, too. Did he invent a homosexual experience for the fun of it, or, perhaps, did he just exaggerate the incident after Brian made a pass at him? Both are possible. But, equally, as all his life he would be eager to experience anything new, was he curious about homosexuality? When Brian came on to him, did he simply want to know what it was like to be touched by another man?'

---

* Those who have claimed Epstein made passes at them include Pete Shotton, Larry Kane, Pete Best and the Liverpudlian comedian Freddie Starr (1943–2019), who was then singing with a group called the Midniters. Given to exaggeration, Starr is the only one to talk of a struggle: 'I started punching his upper arms, which startled him, because it bloody hurt. He quickly backed off and composed himself.'

Bob Spitz is convinced 'something happened', but is unsure what: 'In the privacy of their room, after an evening of drinking and sporting about, Brian initiated something that led to physical contact.' Though Spitz peppers the relevant passage with conditionals – '*if* John participated in some sort of homosexual act, *it follows that* . . .' 'Curiosity *may well* have gotten the better of him . . .' 'He *may* have been experimenting . . .' – he concludes on a note of certainty: 'Away from home, in a beautiful resort with a man – certainly a father figure – who was devoted to taking care of him, John was relaxed and open enough to let it happen unconditionally.'

True to form, the relentless Goldman thinks there is no question about it: 'He and Brian had sex.' Quoting Shotton's book as evidence, he argues over the details: 'Brian told Peter Brown the real story: he had given John a blow job. Lennon couldn't afford to acknowledge that sort of intimacy because it would stigmatise him for life.' Yet, as we have seen, Peter Brown was in fact much more circumspect, saying only that Brian had 'fulfilled his fantasies'.

Having already gone too far, Goldman then goes miles further, asserting, on the basis of no evidence whatsoever, that 'John and Brian did not confine themselves to a single sexual experiment in Spain. They were sexually involved for the balance of Brian's life, and their relationship was a *controlling* one, with John playing the cruel master and Brian the submissive slave.'

Philip Norman labels Goldman's book, not unfairly, as both 'malevolent' and 'risibly ignorant'. In his biography of Paul, Norman judges the idea of a sexual encounter between John and Brian possible but not proven, adding that 'Years later, he told a close friend he'd had sex of some sort with Brian, "once to see what it was like, the second time to make sure I didn't like it".' But in his biography of John, Norman offers a different account, this one from Yoko Ono, with whom he had conducted a series of interviews over three years: 'Years later, John finally came clean about what had happened: not to anyone who'd been around at the time, but to the unshockable woman with whom he shared the last decade of his life. He said that one night during the trip, Brian had cast aside shyness and scruples and finally come on to him, but that he'd replied, "If you feel like that, go out and find a hustler."' Norman adds that 'Afterward, he had deliberately fed Pete Shotton the myth of his brief surrender, so that every-one would believe his power over Brian to be absolute.'*

Perhaps it is best to leave the last word to Paul. 'In an earthquake, you get many different versions of what happened by all the people that saw it,' he observed, decades later, of the Beatles phenomenon. 'And they're all true.'

* Yoko also told Philip Norman that 'from chance remarks' John made, she gathered that he had thought of having an affair with Paul, but Paul had not wanted it. 'Around Apple, in her hearing Paul would sometimes be called John's Princess,' writes Norman. Yoko also told him that she had once heard a rehearsal tape with John's voice calling out 'Paul . . . Paul . . .' in a strangely subservient, plead-ing way. 'I knew there was something going on there,' she remembered. 'From his point of view, not from Paul's. And he was so angry at Paul, I couldn't help wondering what it was really about.'

27.

The Beatles began 1963 in relative obscurity, and ended it the most famous group in the country. Within another six weeks, they were the most famous group in the world.

As we have seen, at the start of 1963 they were just another jobbing pop group. Their first single, 'Love Me Do', had peaked at number 17. Their first concert of 1963 was presented by the Elgin Folk Music Club at the Two Red Shoes Ballroom in Elgin, Scotland, and was attended by two hundred people. Driving in their van from Elgin to the town hall in Dingwall, they were so cold that they lay on top of one another to keep warm. 'When the one on top got so cold that hypothermia was setting in, it would be his turn to get on the bottom,' recalled Paul. 'We'd warm each other up that way.'

At the time, plenty of other British acts – Adam Faith, Mark Wynter, Jet Harris, and of course Cliff Richard and the Shadows – were doing much, much better.

But when success finally came, it came as a landslide, flattening those ahead. Bands and singers who a few months before might have agreed with some reluctance to employ the Beatles as their warm-up act now found themselves in the humiliating position of opening for them. Within the space of five days in September 1963 they were presented with the Top Vocal Group of the Year award at the Savoy Hotel and headed the bill of The Great Pop Prom at the Royal Albert Hall. Meanwhile, 'She Loves You' was at number 1 in the charts. As they stood in their smart new suits at the top of the steps behind the Albert Hall, Paul felt the sunshine on his face. 'We looked at each other, and we were thinking, "This is it! London! The Albert Hall!" We felt like gods! We felt like fucking gods!'

And this was just the beginning. In October, their appearance on *Sunday Night at the London Palladium* attracted fifteen million viewers. On 4 November they played the Royal Command Performance. Later that month their new single, 'I Want to Hold Your Hand', sold a million copies in the UK before it had even been released – roughly one copy for every fifty people in the country.

By the end of 1964 they had become the most famous young men on earth. In Madame Tussauds, their wax effigies took their place alongside world leaders, mass murderers and members of the royal family. In West Bridgford, Nottinghamshire, four brainy pupils of the Becket Grammar School closed their school concert with a spirited rendition of 'From Me to You' in Latin.* The students of Leeds University elected Ringo Starr their vice-president in preference to a former Lord Chief Justice. Visiting the EMI studios, Sir Malcolm Sargent, the most celebrated British conductor of the day, asked George Martin if he might effect an introduction ('Chaps, Sir Malcolm would like to say "Hello"').

Everyone wanted to meet them. In Hollywood, top movie stars – Edward G. Robinson, Dean Martin, Lloyd Bridges, Kirk Douglas, Shelley Winters, Jack Palance, Jack Lemmon – donated money to charity in order to queue for their autographs. In exile in France, the Duchess of Windsor sang their songs to herself. 'Oh, the Beatles. Don't you just love 'em?' she said to the up-and-coming young interior designer Nicky Haslam, over on a visit. '"I give her all my love, that's all I do-ooo!" Adore 'em. Do you know them? Oh, you are lucky!'

Where did this leave their rivals? For groups like Peter Jay and the Jaywalkers, it must have been hard to stomach. A year before, the Beatles had looked up to them. From the back of the hall, George would gaze at the Jaywalkers as they set up their flashing coloured lights, their flashing drum kit and their exploding cymbals, and he would think of them as 'real big shots'. But now those days were past.

Groups that just a short time before had been on level pegging now found it impossible to keep up. The Hollies had formed in 1962, and were having hits by 1963, but by 1964 their achievements seemed minuscule beside the Beatles'. It's not hard to spot a note of resentment in Graham Nash's reminiscences, published half a century later:

In those days, tweaking a Beatle was like blaspheming the pope. But who the fuck cared? I was getting sick and tired of their holy status, the

---

* 'A Me ad Vos'.

way they said whatever was on their minds, no matter whom it affected, right or wrong. All of London was in their thrall. And if you didn't know Popes John or Paul, or at least drop their names in conversation, you might as well take the next train back to the provinces, over and out. Keith Richards said it best in *Life:* 'The Beatles are all over the place like a fucking bag of fleas.' They were a great band and I loved their records. Every English group owed them a huge debt, but I had no intention of kissing their asses. Besides, last I looked, the Hollies were holding down places on the same top 10 as the Beatles, so pardon me if you don't like our fucking record but keep it to yourself, if you please.

28.

At the close of 1963 the Beatles starred in their own Christmas variety show at the Astoria in Finsbury Park, playing twice a day for fifteen days. In all, a hundred thousand people bought tickets. The show's compere was Rolf Harris, the chummy Australian entertainer whose novelty singles 'Tie Me Kangaroo Down, Sport' and 'Sun Arise', both produced by George Martin, had been top 10 hits. Ten years older than the Beatles, Harris belonged to an older showbusiness tradition, in which professionalism was paramount.

One night, while Harris expounded on the Aboriginal setting of 'Sun Arise' to a restless young audience, John began larking around with a microphone backstage. As Rolf was explaining how some tribes regarded the sun as a goddess, John's grating voice boomed harshly over the speakers: 'I dunno about that, Rolf.'

The audience laughed uproariously. Rolf looked around, but couldn't see where the interruption was coming from. So he persevered, describing how, every morning, the tribes thought the sun's skirts of light were covering the earth.

'Well, of course, you could say that,' John piped up. 'But, then again, I dunno, Rolf! Maybe you're just making it up!'

Ever the pro, Rolf put on a brave face, and emitted a laugh of forbearance. 'But inside,' he later admitted, 'I was seething.'

When the show was over, he barged his way into the Beatles' dressing room and shouted, 'If you want to fuck up your own act, do it! But don't fuck up mine!'

But the Beatles remained unbowed. 'Oooh, Rolfie's lost his rag,' said John, and George joined in: 'Yeah, Rolfie's upset.'

Harris tells the story in his 2001 autobiography *Can You Tell What it is Yet?*, and affects good cheer. 'They started laughing and so did I,' he writes.

'They had such charm that I couldn't be angry with them. At least I'd made my point and they didn't do it again.'

But was he really so conciliatory? In an unguarded moment in 1994, he offered a much less merry version of the event: 'The Beatles mucked about with me. At that Christmas show, they stood off in the wings with a microphone and made silly comments during one of my songs and I came storming off the stage and shouted, "Get some bloody professionalism into you! Jesus! You don't muck around with somebody else's act. Don't ever bloody do that again." I was so angry. And after that they didn't bloody do it again, I can tell you!'

29.

Just five days separated the births of John Lennon (9 October 1940) and Cliff Richard (14 October 1940).

By the winter of 1958 Cliff had become a big star, number 2 in the charts with 'Move It'. Meanwhile, John remained a no-hoper, scuttling around Liverpool with his Quarrymen, playing the odd village hall or private function, often for no more payment than a beer and a sandwich.

'Is this boy too sexy for television?' gasped the *Daily Sketch* after Cliff had gyrated a little too suggestively on television's *Oh Boy*. The critic on the *New Musical Express* was even more perturbed: 'His violent hip-swinging was revolting, hardly the performance any parent could wish her children to see.' Before 1963 it was Cliff, not John, who was the rebel, the firebrand, the threat to civilisation. The same evening when Cliff and the Shadows were causing a stir on national television, the Quarrymen were playing skiffle standards at George Harrison's brother Harry's wedding reception in Upton Green.

From 1958 to 1962 Cliff had twenty songs in the top 20, including six number ones. He also starred in two films, *Expresso Bongo* and *The Young Ones*. Small wonder then that John, no stranger to envy, entertained mixed feelings towards him. When the Beatles finally squeezed into the charts with 'Love Me Do' in December 1962, reaching a high point of number 17, Cliff was looking down at them from number 2 with 'Bachelor Boy'. The following month, the *New Musical Express* published its annual readers' survey. In 'Top Acts' Cliff Richard came second to Elvis Presley, with the Beatles a lowly joint 111th. They did better in the more specialist 'British Small Group' category, coming eighth with 735 votes; but the Shadows came first, with 45,951 votes.

Three months later, in March 1963, the Beatles reached number 2 with 'Please Please Me', but they were prevented from reaching number 1 by Cliff, who was already there with 'Summer Holiday'.

But as 1963 rolled on, the tables turned. By the end of that year the Beatles were making Cliff seem old hat. For George Melly, Cliff's erotic twitching was now no more than 'a bent-kneed shuffle, not so much a sexual courtship dance as a suggestion that he'd wet himself'. The Beatles were the future, and Cliff the past. Try as Cliff might, it niggled. In a rare fit of candour, he grumbled about the Beatles' primitivism to a reporter from the *Daily Mirror*: 'All they've done is revert to rock'n'roll. We've played the whole thing down, the screaming and the raving. The Beatles have stoked the whole thing up again.'

That Christmas, the Beatles occupied the number 1 and number 2 slots in the UK charts with 'I Want to Hold Your Hand' and 'She Loves You', while Cliff languished at number 8 with 'Don't Talk to Him'. By now, his fans were drifting off in search of brighter, brasher idols. In the New Year it was revealed that Cliff's own sisters had recently formed a Dave Clark Five fan club.

For five years Cliff had struggled to crack the American market, but without success. In fact, it was Cliff's failure that spurred Brian Epstein to plot the Beatles' American campaign with such meticulous care. 'Cliff went there and he died,' John told the American journalist Michael Braun with pitiless relish as they boarded their plane to Kennedy Airport. 'He was fourteenth on a bill with Frankie Avalon.'

Cliff was in the Canary Isles, completing his third movie, *Wonderful Life*, when he heard the news that the Beatles had achieved the success in America that still eluded him. *Wonderful Life* was released on 2 July 1964, but was overshadowed by *A Hard Day's Night*, released four days later. *A Hard Day's Night* broke box-office records, and was hailed by critics on both sides of the Atlantic for its freshness and originality. In contrast, *Wonderful Life* was called 'a sad little picture' by *Films and Filming*, while the *Sunday Times* described it as 'this bloodsome bore of a film' and 'drivel'. The film was retitled *Swingers' Paradise* for the American market, but to no avail. At the age of twenty-three, Cliff's film career was over.

Soon after the release of both films, *Melody Maker* published a feature on the shifting tastes of youth. 'I grew out of my Cliff Richard days a couple of years ago,' said a twenty-year-old man. 'When I look back I think how soppy I must have been. Groups now like the Beatles and the Stones have really got something and I can't see me getting tired of them. Not until I'm old, anyway.'

From then on, John occupied such a peak of fame and fortune that he rarely bothered to glance down at Cliff Richard. On the other hand, the slightest allusion to the Beatles played havoc with Cliff's composure. From the mid-sixties he was an 'all-round family entertainer', wholesome and unthreatening, performing in cabaret, in pantomime* and on Saturday-evening television. Deep in his bones, he knew he was no longer 'with-it': 'The success of the Beatles and the Stones had shelved me and the Shadows. We were now the oldsters.' On Saturday, 6 April 1968, while John Lennon was staying with the Maharishi Mahesh Yogi in India, composing songs for *The White Album*, Cliff was bouncing his way through 'Congratulations' in the Eurovision Song Contest, dressed in a light-blue double-breasted suit with frothy white ruffles around the neck and wrists. When the final scores were totted up, it emerged that Cliff had come second to Spain's Massiel singing 'La La La'.

Though he was known for his pleasant, can-do persona and his Christianity, Cliff never quite managed to stifle his indignation towards the Beatles. On Sunday, 19 January 1969 he was singing hymns in an Edinburgh church and talking about his religious beliefs when he snapped, 'The Beatles are very successful artists, and yet they are not successful in life. The Beatles do nothing but chase around the world after a dream, and they must now realise that their Maharishi just doesn't help them at all. I think they are looking for what Christians have found.'

Almost a quarter of a century later, Cliff could still be rattled by a mention of the Beatles. Interviewing him for *Q* magazine in 1992, Tom Hibbert† asked if he had ever felt jealousy towards them. The vehemence of his reply suggests he had never stopped brooding.

'There was a certain amount of jealousy. It was hurtful to be overlooked so dramatically by the media. But I still sold records by the million, so

---

* I myself greatly enjoyed Cliff Richard's performance as Buttons in *Cinderella* at the London Palladium in 1966, with Terry Scott and Hugh Lloyd as the Ugly Sisters, Tudor Davies as Dandini, and Jack Douglas as Baron Hardup. The Brokers' Men were played by the Shadows. The speciality act was a baby elephant called 'The Adorable Tonya'. During this same period, the Beatles were recording 'Strawberry Fields Forever' and 'Penny Lane'.

† Tom Hibbert (1952–2011) wrote very funny interviews with, among many others, Robert Maxwell, Bernard Manning, Yoko Ono and Sir Jimmy Savile for *Smash Hits* and *Q* magazine. In his obituary of him in the *Guardian*, Mark Ellen wrote: 'Tom was unafraid of silence. He would give his subjects the impression that, despite their obvious successes, they were still somehow shameful underachievers, and then sit back quietly with a cigarette to enjoy the panicked response.'

what the heck? And look at me now. The Beatles don't exist any more, and I was going five years before the Beatles, so no one's ever going to catch me up. I'll always be ahead of everybody. I've just done my thousandth week in the chart and my nearest competitor hasn't reached five hundred weeks in the chart, which means that if that person is to catch me up, I would have to stop recording now and they'd have to have a record in the charts every week for the next five years. It's not possible. I'm well ahead . . . And another thing: when it came to rebellion, we were far more the rebellious crowd. The Beatles were accepted by royalty, they were accepted by all the high society. The Shadows and I never were. So we had one up on them.'

30.

One day, it struck Ringo Starr that he would never be able to go back to being plain Ritchie Starkey.

He was with his family at his auntie's house in Liverpool, when some of Ringo's tea spilt into his saucer. He was shocked by what happened next.

'Everyone's reaction was, "He can't have that! We have to tidy up!"'

In the old days, he would have been left to clear up his own mess. But not any more. Now they were treating him differently, as though he were a superior outsider, and not one of them. It felt, he said, 'like an arrow in the brain': 'Suddenly I was "one of those", even within my family, and it was very difficult to get used to. I'd grown up and lived with these people and now I found myself in weirdland . . . Once we'd become big and famous, we soon learnt that people were with us only because of the vague notoriety of being a "Beatle". And when this happened in the family, it was quite a blow.'

There was no way back. Any complaint would serve only to reinforce their attitude. 'I couldn't stand up and say, "Treat me like you used to," because that would be acting big-time.'

31.

A Party:
King's Road, London SW3
18 April 1963

'Please Please Me' is going down in the charts, crossing paths with 'From Me to You' on the way up. Meanwhile, the Beatles are appearing in a variety concert at the Royal Albert Hall, 'Swinging Sound '63', along with Del Shannon, Lance Percival, Rolf Harris, Shane Fenton and the Fentones, the Springfields and George Melly.

In an interval between rehearsals, they meet Jane Asher in the Green Room. At the age of sixteen, Jane is already something of a showbiz veteran: her first starring role was *Mandy* in 1952, and then she starred opposite Jack Warner as the Little Girl in Hammer Horror's *The Quatermass Xperiment.* Since then she has appeared in *Alice in Wonderland, The Prince and the Pauper, The Adventures of Robin Hood.* In the theatre, she was the youngest ever Wendy in *Peter Pan.* Recently she has become a household name as a regular panellist on TV's *Juke Box Jury.*

Jane is attending the variety concert on behalf of the *Radio Times*: a reporter and a photographer are there to record her reactions. The Beatles are in awe of her, perhaps Paul most of all: 'We had a photo taken with her and we all fancied her. We'd thought she was blonde, because we've only ever seen her on black-and-white telly doing *Juke Box Jury*, but she turned out to be a redhead. So it was: "Wow, you're a redhead."'

Their Royal Albert Hall concert proves to be a milestone, the first time an audience has screamed with quite such abandon. Later, fans climb on the roof of their car and block its way. The police eventually manage to clear a path, and the Beatles and their friends drive off, without really knowing where they are going. They usually end up at the Ad Lib

Club, just off Leicester Square, but George, the shyest of the four, worries that hundreds of fans will already be on their way there. Accompanying them, the journalist Chris Hutchins suggests they all go to his place on the King's Road. He then immediately regrets it, wondering how the four Beatles, Shane Fenton* and Jane Asher will all be able to squeeze into the tiny bedsit, and where they will sit, given that there aren't enough chairs.

The problem is solved by everyone sitting on the carpet. But then another problem presents itself: John finds a bottle of amphetamines and starts swallowing them, washing them down with the Mateus rosé provided by Hutchins. Charged up, he becomes aggressive towards Jane. For John, thwarted sexual attraction can sometimes shrivel into spite. First, he talks about their adoring fans.

JOHN: Yeah, the group the fans love so much they want to tear us to pieces.

JANE: (laughing) Oh, John. You're such a cynic. Admit it, you adore the attention!

JOHN: Sure I'm a cynic. What we play is rock'n'roll under a new name. Rock music is war, hostility, conquest. We sing about love, but we mean sex, and the fans know it.

HUTCHINS: The fans think you're decent, clean-living chaps.

JOHN: It's just an image, and it's the wrong one. Look at the Rolling Stones. Rough as guts. We did that first and now they've pinched it.

RINGO: You can't blame them for that.

JANE: The fans have to dream that one day they might marry a Beatle.

JOHN: Yeah, but only those who haven't reached the age of puberty. I give some girl an autograph and she wants my tie or some hair. Then she wants to have sex. Then she tells me she's only fifteen. Jailbait. Is there any more booze?

HUTCHINS: (pouring the last of the wine into John's empty glass) That's the last of it. I wasn't expecting company.

JOHN: OK, there's no more booze. Let's talk about sex. Jane, how do girls play with themselves?

JANE: (shocked but cool) I'm not going to talk about that!

* Born Bernard Jewry, he changed his name to Shane Fenton, and later to Alvin Stardust.

JOHN: You're the only girl here and I want to know. How do you jerk off?

HUTCHINS: There's only one jerk here.

JOHN: Oh fab! No booze, no birds, insults from the host . . . what kind of rave is this? Bleedin' marvellous. I'm going in search of some crumpet. Call me a taxi.

JANE: (crying, comforted by George) You know, John, you can be very cruel sometimes.

JOHN: (standing at the front door) It's the beast in me.

Around this point, Paul ushers Jane out of the room, and away from John. They sit on a bed together, and chat about food and books. They get on to Chaucer's *Canterbury Tales*, which they were both taught at their respective schools. Off the cuff, Paul quotes from 'The Prioress's Tale': 'Ful semly hir wympul pynched was.' Jane, a former pupil at the sophisticated Queen's College in Harley Street, seems much more impressed by this than by Paul's status as a pop idol, and Paul is equally impressed by her order of priorities. As the evening draws to a close, Paul volunteers to drop Jane home. Before they say goodbye, he has decided that this is the girl for him. On the doorstep of the Asher family home in Wimpole Street he asks for her phone number, and Jane happily gives it to him.

32.

They became boyfriend and girlfriend, and Jane's parents gave Paul his own little bedroom on the top floor of 57 Wimpole Street, next to Jane's brother Peter's room. Paul was to live there, as part of the Asher family, for the next three years, his bedroom filling up with the fruits of his extraordinary career: eventually he was to stow his gold records under his bed, and his MBE on a shelf, alongside two drawings by Jean Cocteau. It was at Wimpole Street that Paul received a letter from the Beatles' accountant in 1965 informing him that, at the age of twenty-three, he had become a millionaire.

The Ashers were a remarkable family in every way: remarkably accomplished, remarkably civilised, remarkably welcoming. At the age of eight, Peter Asher had appeared opposite Claudette Colbert and Jack Hawkins in the film *The Planter's Wife*, and at ten, opposite Cecil Parker and Donald Wolfit in *Isn't Life Wonderful*. Jane's younger sister Claire had acted in the BBC's long-running radio soap opera *Mrs Dale's Diary*. Their mother Margaret was a professor at the Guildhall: back in 1948 she had tutored George Martin in the oboe.

Just like Paul fifteen years later, Martin had relished his visits to the Asher home, with all its comfort and erudition. Despite his upper-class persona (the legacy of wartime service with the RAF, during which 'we were taught important military details like how to hold a knife and fork correctly') he had been brought up in a three-room flat in Drayton Park with no kitchen, no bathroom and a toilet shared with three other families. Coming from such an impoverished background, he had been tantalised by the glimpse of a more agreeable life offered by the Ashers of Wimpole Street. And now, Paul, in his turn, was to be tantalised. Everything seemed touched by culture. In the hall of no. 57 hung an engraved portrait of Alfred, Lord Tennyson, a distant relative of Margaret Asher; the glass-fronted bookcase in the dining room contained a rare 1926 first edition of *Seven*

Pillars of Wisdom, brought into the family by Margaret's father, the Hon. Edward Granville Eliot, who had been Lawrence of Arabia's solicitor.

Jane's father, Dr Richard Asher, was a pioneering endocrinologist who in 1951 had named and identified Munchausen's Syndrome, the mental disorder that drives individuals to fabricate symptoms of illness. He was also a skilled and witty writer: an article by him in the *Lancet* in February 1951 begins: 'Here is described a common syndrome which most doctors have seen, but about which little has been written. Like the famous Baron von Munchausen, the persons affected have always travelled widely; and their stories, like those attributed to him, are both dramatic and untruthful. Accordingly, the syndrome is respectfully dedicated to the Baron, and named after him.' Inevitably, the title 'Munchausen's Syndrome' was criticised by the po-faced for being inappropriately light-hearted.

Dr Asher's articles in the *British Medical Journal* remain a joy to read – funny, alert, aphoristic, self-deprecatory, sparklingly clear – and they indicate the breadth of education Paul would have received in his conversations with him. In 'The Dangers of Going to Bed', Asher argues against the medical consensus that staying in bed was the surest route to recovery: 'Look at a patient lying long in bed. What a pathetic picture he makes! The blood clotting in his veins, the lime draining from his bones, the scybala stacking up in his colon, the flesh rotting from his seat, the urine leaking from his distended bladder, and the spirit evaporating from his soul.' He then undercuts himself by saying, 'I have painted a gloomy and unfair picture: it is not as bad as all that.' Later in the same article, he speculated as to the reasons why confinement caught on: 'Too often a sister puts all her patients back to bed as a housewife puts all her plates back in the plate-rack – to make a generally tidy appearance.'

Another of his articles in the *BMJ*, carrying the incendiary title 'Why are Medical Journals so Dull?', argues against stodginess and obscurity in favour of lucidity and precision: 'A poor title dulls the clinical appetite, whereas a good title whets it. I have called this article "Why are Medical Journals so Dull?". I do not claim this title is specially good, but it is better than "A Study of the Negativistic Psychomotor Reactions induced by Perusal of Verbalized Clinical Material".'

It's easy to see how Paul would have revelled in such cheery cut-and-thrust. The whole Asher family involved themselves in discussions around the table, alive with erudition and curiosity and fun. 'They would do things that I'd never seen before, like at dinner there would be word games,' Paul told Barry Miles. 'Now, I'm bright enough, but mine is an intuitive brightness. I could just about keep up with that, and I could always say, "I don't know that word."' He remembered an argument over dinner between Dr Asher and his son Peter, Paul's contemporary, over when the tomato was first introduced to England. This was not the sort of topic they discussed in Forthlin Road. Throughout his years with the Ashers, Paul was treated not as a pop star, but as one of the family: 'It was very good for me, because in their eyes I wasn't just the Beatle.' The atmosphere at Wimpole Street also appealed to his competitive spirit: 'I often felt the guys were sort of partying, whereas I was learning a lot; learning an awful lot.' In her music room in the basement, Margaret Asher taught Paul how to play the recorder – he plays it on 'Fool on the Hill' – though her attempts to teach him how to read music were soon abandoned.

His intellectual curiosity was stimulated. 'I don't want to sound like Jonathan Miller going on, but I'm trying to cram everything in, all the things I've missed,' he told the journalist Maureen Cleave in 1966. 'People are saying things and painting things that are great, and I must know what people are doing . . . I vaguely mind people knowing anything I don't know.' He read Jung and Huxley, watched plays by Alfred Jarry and Harold Pinter and listened to avant-garde composers like Stockhausen and Luciano Berio.

Sometimes Jane would take Paul to stay with family friends out of town. 'This was another rather upper-class thing: going for the weekend to the country . . . It was the first time I'd seen people leaving a book by your bedside for you to read. I was quite impressed by their choice of books. It was the assumption that you were reasonably intelligent that I liked. They didn't talk down.'

Inevitably, Beatles fans would linger outside the house, ready to pounce. While Paul was away filming *Help!*, Jane's father set himself the task of plotting an escape route for him. He climbed out of a back window and scaled his way along to the house next door, then tapped on a window to explain Paul's peculiar problem to the occupier of the neighbouring flat. On Paul's return to London, Dr Asher was thus able to present him with a secret route through to New Cavendish Street. 'I used to go out of the window of my garret bedroom, onto a little parapet. You had to be pretty careful, it wasn't that wide, it was only a foot or so, so you had to have

something of a head for heights. You'd go along to the right, which was to the next house in Wimpole Street, number 56, and there was a colonel living there, an old ex-army gentleman. He had this little top-floor flat, and he was very charming. "Uh! Coming through, Colonel!" "Oh, oh, OK, hush-hush and all that!" and he'd see me into the lift and I'd go right downstairs to the basement of that house. There was a young couple living down there and they'd see me out through the kitchen and into the garage.'

If I could be any Beatle, at any time, I would be Paul in his Wimpole Street years, living with Jane, cosseted by her family, blessed by luck, happy with life, alive to culture, adored by the world, and with wonderful songs flowing, as if by magic, from my brain and out through the piano: 'I Want to Hold Your Hand', 'I'm Looking Through You', 'The Things We Said Today', 'And I Love Her', 'We Can Work it Out', 'Here, There and Everywhere', 'Yesterday'.

But nothing lasts. On Christmas Day 1967, Paul and Jane announced their engagement; seven months later, in reply to a chance question from the TV chat-show host Simon Dee, Jane announced that it was all over: 'I haven't broken it off, but it is broken off, finished. I know it sounds corny, but we still see each other and love each other, but it hasn't worked out.

Perhaps we'll be childhood sweethearts and meet again when we're about seventy.'

Over fifty years on, they both remain discreet about the break-up, speaking about it in nothing but the most general terms, leaving others to speculate. Some suggest Jane caught Paul in bed with an American woman called Francie Schwartz.* While Jane was away acting, Paul and Francie had been together in his new house in St John's Wood. 'There were fans waiting at the gate as usual and they tried to warn Paul that Jane was approaching. But Paul thought they were joking,' recalled Alistair Taylor. According to Taylor, Jane broke up with Paul, rather than vice-versa, and refused to take him back. Though Paul, a master of self-possession, has said 'I don't remember the break-up as traumatic really,' and 'I got cold feet,' elsewhere he has admitted, 'It was shattering to be without her.' Others remember the shock he suffered. Taylor, who thought Jane 'the most adorable woman you could expect to meet', recalled Paul being 'absolutely devastated . . . he went completely off the rails. "I had everything and I threw it away," he would say.' His hairdresser, Leslie Cavendish, noted that 'he seemed heartbroken to me. He'd stopped shaving his beard, hardly ever left the house and began taking more drugs.'

One or two of their acquaintances claim to have seen it coming. Marianne Faithfull never felt they were a natural fit: 'I always thought Jane and Paul were very tense. I do remember very clearly an evening at Cavendish Avenue where she wanted the window shut and he wanted the window open. That really was like a Joe Orton play. It was fucking great. I sat there all night watching Jane get up and open it, and Paul close it, and . . . nothing was said. And quite soon after they split up, which of course I could have told anyone they would.' But she fails to offer a reason why Jane would have wanted the window open. Might it have been to release the fumes of marijuana that were the necessary accompaniment to any visit by Mick and Marianne?

* Who later wrote a kiss-and-tell book called *Body Count*.

33.

Before going onstage at the Majestic Ballroom, Newcastle upon Tyne, John and Paul seized the time to write a song.

On 26 June 1963 the two of them were sharing a twin-bedded room at the Royal Turk's Head Hotel.* Paul reached for his cigarettes. 'We must have had a few hours before the show, so we said, "Oh, great! Let's have a ciggy and write a song!"'

The lyrics of their previous singles – 'Love Me Do', 'Please Please Me', 'From Me to You', 'I Saw Her Standing There' – all revolved around a single person, but Paul now resolved to do something different.

'It was Paul's idea,' recalled John. 'Instead of singing "I love you", we'd have a third party.' This signalled the way their different approaches to songwriting were to develop: Paul's towards a third-person narrative, rather like a miniature short story, and John's more autobiographical.

> You think you've lost your love
> Well I saw her yesterday-ay

One young man is talking to another about a girl who may or may not have left him. The two men are, consciously or unconsciously, versions of the two composers – Paul optimistic, self-confident, never short of advice, and John, primed to cause hurt – 'she said you hurt her so' – while in retreat from his own sense of guilt. Like so many subsequent Lennon/McCartney songs, its energy comes from this intermingling of the dark and the sunny.

The Beatles had the next day free, so John and Paul went back to Liverpool. This gave them the chance to complete their new song in Forthlin Road, while Paul's dad Jim sat in the next room, smoking and watching television.

---

* Later renamed the Rainbow.

At this stage John and Paul were both magpies, lifting whatever took their fancy from other people's songs: the 'woo woo' came from the Isley Brothers' 'Twist and Shout'. John, in particular, was fond of these whoops and hollers, noises below or beyond words: when he heard Elvis Presley singing 'All Shook Up', his first thought was that he had never heard 'uh huh', 'oh yeah' and 'yeah, yeah' all in the same song before.

After a while, the two of them burst into the living room. 'Dad, listen to this. What do you think?' Then they sang him their new song: 'She Loves You'.

'That's very nice, son,' said Jim, one of the old school. 'But there's enough of these Americanisms around. Couldn't you sing, "She loves you, yes, yes, yes"?' John and Paul failed to take this advice seriously. 'We collapsed in a heap and said, "No, Dad, you don't quite get it."'

Four days later, the Beatles went to the EMI studios in Abbey Road to record their new song. They arrived early, in order to pose for a new set of pictures in the alleyway behind the studio. By now, wherever they went they were attracting fans. One thing led to another: the fans who were already waiting outside telephoned their friends to tip them off, and those friends told more friends, and so forth. Before long, this mass of girls somehow managed to break through the front door and to rush around the building in search of their idols. 'It's a bloody madhouse out there,' said Neil Aspinall as he entered the studio.

Meanwhile, placing the song sheets on the music stands, the EMI recording engineer Norman Smith* glanced at the lyrics. 'I thought, "I'll just have a quick look. 'She loves you, yeah, yeah, yeah; She loves you, yeah, yeah, yeah; She loves you, yeah, yeah, yeah.'" I thought, "Oh my God, what a lyric. This is going to be one that I do not like."'

George Martin, calm as ever, ran John and Paul through their new song, with George Harrison joining in on the choruses. 'I thought it was great, but was intrigued by the final chord, an odd sort of major sixth, with George doing the sixth and John and Paul the third and fifths, like a Glenn Miller arrangement. They were saying, "It's a great chord! Nobody's ever heard it before!" Of course, that wasn't quite true.'

---

* While working at EMI, Norman Smith (1923–2008) produced Pink Floyd's 'See Emily Play', as well as their first four albums. He later became briefly famous as the gravelly-voiced Hurricane Smith, whose single 'Don't Let it Die' reached number 2 in the charts in 1971.

In fact, much of John and Paul's early inventiveness as songwriters sprang from a kind of blissful ignorance. Neither could read music, or had ever had formal lessons. This meant they tended to come across chords by chance. Their early songs reflect the innocent wonder with which they chanced upon the source of all music, as if for the very first time.

With the marauding fans dispersed from the building, the recording session could begin. It occurred to recording engineer Geoff Emerick that the excitement generated by the invading fans helped to spark a new level of energy and invention in the band's playing, not least from Ringo and George. Hearing the song performed, Norman Smith, having been sceptical, immediately got the point of it: 'When they started to sing it – bang, wow, terrific. I was up at the mixer jogging around.'

Emerick, too, was enthralled: 'There was a level of intensity in that performance that I had not heard before and have rarely heard since. I still judge that single to be one of the most exciting performances of the Beatles' entire career.'

'She Loves You' was released on 23 August 1963. Within a month it had sold three quarters of a million copies in Britain, making it the fastest-selling record ever. It was to remain in the top three for eighteen weeks, and in the charts for thirty-one weeks. For many, fans and foes alike, it remains the quintessential Beatles song. The words to which Jim McCartney had objected – Yeah! Yeah! Yeah! – have become emblematic of the Beatles phenomenon: either callow and inarticulate, or fresh and liberating, depending on your outlook. In Europe, the Beatles were commonly referred to as 'the Yeah-Yeahs'.

For conservatives who preferred the world to stay the same, 'She Loves You' acted as an alarm call; for Marxists, it symbolised Western decadence. 'Is it truly the case that we have to copy all the dirt that comes from the West?' asked the East German leader Walter Ulbricht in a speech to his party. 'I think, Comrades, with the monotony of the yeah yeah yeah or whatever it is called we should make a stop.'

For once, America was slow to pick up on a new trend. Released in the States on 16 September, 'She Loves You' sold barely a thousand copies in its first few weeks, and failed to hit the charts. At the cutting-edge Cafe Wha? in Greenwich Village, the hard-boiled folk singer Steve De Naut first heard it in October. His then girlfriend, Vicky Tiel, remembers him marching into her apartment and – 'Listen to this, baby' – placing it on the record player. 'Steve and I started to make love. At the point where it changes beats, he stopped in the middle of having sex. "Listen to this!" he said. The music went down to another beat. He said, "Nobody fucking *does* that! That's *no*! And the 'yeah, yeah, yeah'? That's fucking *no*! Nobody *does* that!"'

Vicky couldn't understand what Steve was getting at. 'It's a new type of music,' he explained. 'I've never heard anything like it. And it's fantastic.' He then added, more despondently: 'I'm finished. It's over. It's over for all of us.'

34.

John Lennon and Ringo Starr were born in 1940, when the words *blitz, paratroops, call-up* and *quisling* came into being, as well as the verb *to scramble* in its new meaning of 'to make a speedy take-off'.

Other neologisms of 1940 heralded a bold new unstuffy age of American goods and trends: *beefburger, crew-cut, holiday camp, mobile home, nylons, telly, super-duper, youth club*. Many were born of inventions: *jeep, plutonium, radar*. Some, like *telly*, were chummy abbreviations for recent inventions now so widespread that they felt like old friends. Others, like *extra-sensory perception*, emerged from a closer study of what had always been there, or – viewed from another angle – what had always been not there.

The following year, 1941, the term *welfare state* was coined, as were *disc jockey, boogie, cheesed-off, Terylene, sunbathe, straight*, in its meaning of 'conformist', and *knockers* meaning breasts. It was also in this year – the year between the births of John and Paul – that the word *teenager* made its first appearance.

Paul McCartney was born in 1942, when *spaceman, office block, napalm* and *sixty-four-dollar question* first appeared, along with the abbreviations *PR* and *preggers*. George, the youngest Beatle, was born in 1943, when *bobby socks, disposable, paper towel, pizzeria, double glazing* and *falsies* were coined. *Squarebashing* also made its debut that year, and, perhaps as a sort of cosmic counterbalance, so did *group therapy* and *free expression*. In England, Barnes Wallis invented the *bouncing bomb*, and in Switzerland, Dr Albert Hofmann combined Lysergic Acid with Diethylamine to create *Lysergic Acid Diethylamide*, later to become known as *LSD*.

Most people date the origin of the Beatles to 1957, when the fifteen-year-old Paul introduced himself to the sixteen-year-old John. Many of that year's new words and expressions were centred around youth: *Frisbee, skiffle, sexpot, scooter, pop art, bonkers, backlash, Hell's Angel, flick knife, diminished responsibility, consenting adult, role model, angry young man*. A

long-playing record began to be known as an *album*. In the USA, female traffic wardens were nicknamed *meter maids*. The adjective *fab*, an abbreviation of fabulous, was first heard that year, though it wasn't to become widespread until 1963, more often than not preceding the number four.

It was also in 1963 that another word associated with the Fab Four came into being. On 5 October 1963 a young concert promoter called Andi Lothian was in Glasgow's Carnegie Hall when onto the stage came the young group he had booked. For him, the audience reaction called to mind the relief of Mafeking: 'absolute pandemonium. Girls fainting, screaming, wet seats. The whole hall went into some kind of state, almost like collective hypnotism.' Amidst the mayhem, a startled reporter from Radio Scotland yelled, 'For God's sake, Andi, what's happening?' From out of nowhere, a new word popped into his head. 'Don't worry,' he yelled back, 'It's only . . . *Beatlemania!*'

35.

Towards the end of 1963, the sanity of the younger generation was being called into question. 'Many young people these days complain that adults tend to condemn them,' wrote one irate newspaper reader. 'But when one sees the disgusting behaviour now occurring up and down the country under the name of "Beatlemania" it is impossible not to draw certain conclusions.'

A columnist in York's *Evening Press* echoed this sentiment: 'Ask any teenager in York and they could name the four Beatles. Now ask those same teenagers for the names of a few other well-known personalities. The Secretary General of the United Nations, for example, or even our own Prime Minister. The answers, in many cases, will not slip so easily off the tongue. Such is fame. Such is our sense of values in the modern world.' That same columnist, the aptly-named John Blunt, decried 'the howling, screaming, bustling, shoving, fighting mobs which collect whenever they make an appearance'.

Throughout the Beatles' tour of the UK, reporters struggled to de-scribe the sound of thousands of adolescents screaming at the top of their voices. 'I have not attended the mass torture or execution of 5000 assorted farmyard animals,' wrote the *Newcastle Journal*'s reporter Rodney Pybus. 'But I imagine the noise they would make would be very similar to that which forced my fingertips deep into my ears.' Other newspapers roped in tame psychologists to dig deeper in the hope of uncovering the source of this mayhem. 'This is not really hysteria. Hysteria is pathological. It is a disease,' concluded Professor John Cohen, the head of the Psychology Department at Manchester University. To the central question – why do the girls scream? – he drew a blank: 'You might as well ask a flock of geese why they fly and flap their wings.' At the Beatles' concert in the Southend Odeon on 9 December, a policeman armed with a noise meter recorded the screaming at 110 decibels, the equal of a sustained artillery barrage.

The American journalist Michael Braun accompanied the Beatles to the Cambridge Regal on 26 November. At that same venue the previous March the group had supported 'America's Exciting' Chris Montez and 'America's Fabulous' Tommy Roe. But now it was they who were being supported by others. Fans had been queuing in the streets outside the Regal since 10.30 a.m. By 6 p.m. the line was already half a mile long. Hours before the show, the Beatles had met the police at an agreed spot a mile away, to be smuggled into the theatre in the back of a police van.

When I was a child, whenever we went to the cinema in Dorking, or the pantomime in Leatherhead, 'God Save the Queen' would be played before and after each show. As if by magic, the audience would rise from their seats and stand to attention until the patriotic strains were finally exhausted. When the National Anthem was played at the start of the Beatles' Cambridge show, Michael Braun witnessed not a hint of rebellion. But then again, there were plenty of unscream-at-able support acts to get through before the Beatles were due on, among them Peter Jay and the Jaywalkers, the Vernon Girls and the Brook Brothers. But the second the Beatles were announced the audience burst into high-pitched screams that continued right up to the strumming of the final chord of 'Twist and Shout'. 'Some girls are now waving handkerchiefs,' wrote Braun. 'Others are sitting in a foetal position: back arched, legs folded under, and hands alternately punching their thighs and covering their ears. Most of the boys just keep their hands over their ears.'

Braun watched a girl in an aisle seat crying every time the lights went up and down. At the end, after 'Twist and Shout', she stood on her seat screaming and crying until the National Anthem began to play over the house speakers. At that moment, in common with all the other girls, she stopped screaming and stood stock-still. But the second it drew to a close – Gar-aar-ard Say-aay-aayve the Quee-eee-eeen! – they all started screaming again.*

This peculiar pattern was repeated throughout the Beatles' tour of Britain. Stewards at these shows tended to be middle-aged and hard-done-by,

---

* While writing this book, I have had nights when I have been kept awake as this or that Beatles song played over and over again in my brain. When it has been some particularly repetitive song – 'Yellow Submarine', say, or 'All Together Now' – I found that singing an opposing 'God Save the Queen' in some other part of my head proved the only way to drown it out. The trouble with this method, though, is that you are left with a song even more annoying than those it has replaced.

temperamentally ill-suited to extracting enjoyment from youthful exuberance. At the show in Leicester's De Montfort Hall on 1 December, police and stewards were supplied with cotton wool to protect their ears. The fifty-nine-year-old Ray Millward complained that he had been kicked and punched by a delirious female fan: 'We used to get a lot of hysteria with Cliff Richard, but this beats everything. I had a shoe and an umbrella thrown at me. One girl fought like a wildcat. I had to force her arm behind her back to get her to sit down. She was scratching, kicking and screaming.' Jelly babies – which, in an offhand moment, the Beatles had said they enjoyed – were now being hurled at them from every corner, even though the group had publicly protested that they would prefer it if they weren't. Misunderstanding them, some girls started throwing full boxes of chocolates instead. Autograph books, a doll and a giant panda were also hurled. Despite this pandemonium, the fans still stood stock-still for the National Anthem, a godsend from the Beatles' point of view, as it gave them plenty of time to make a speedy getaway through the stage door to their waiting Austin Princess. Meanwhile their fans remained inside, rooted to the spot out of respect for Her Majesty.

That November, as the Queen Mother, Princess Margaret and Lord Snowdon arrived at the Prince of Wales theatre for the Royal Command Performance, they were greeted by crowds chanting 'We want the Beatles!' At that moment, it must have dawned on them that, like so many other long-established groups that year, they too had just been downgraded to a support act.

Taking his seat in the audience, Brian Epstein was nervous. Could he trust John to behave? The day before, John had worked out a cheeky joke for introducing their final song, 'Twist and Shout': 'For our last number, I'd like to ask your help. Would the people in the cheaper seats clap your hands. And the rest of you, if you'd just rattle your jewellery.' It was already slightly edgy, but in the dress rehearsal John had made it a good deal edgier by saying 'rattle your *fucking* jewellery'. To Epstein's relief, when the big moment came John omitted the expletive, and even added a chummy thumbs-up to show it was only a joke. In their black ties and evening dresses, the audience burst into laughter and applause.

After the show, the Beatles were presented to the Queen Mother. Or – given society's new priorities – was it the Queen Mother who was presented to the Beatles? She had, she said, very much enjoyed herself. And where would they be performing next? Slough, came the answer. 'Oh, that's near us,' she replied.

The next day's newspapers were full of the Beatles. Devoting an editorial to their triumph, the working-class *Daily Mirror* welcomed the revolution:

> Fact is that Beatle People are everywhere. From Wapping to Windsor. Aged seven to seventy. And it's plain to see why these four cheeky, energetic lads from Liverpool go down so big.
>
> They're young, new. They're high-spirited, cheerful. What a change from the self-pitying moaners, crooning their lovelorn tunes from the tortured shallows of lukewarm hearts.
>
> The Beatles are whacky. They wear their hair like a mop – but it's WASHED, it's super clean. So is their fresh young act. They don't have to rely on off-colour jokes about homos for their fun . . .
>
> Youngsters like the Beatles are doing a good turn for show business – and the rest of us – with their new sounds, new looks.
>
> *Good luck Beatles!*

On perpetual guard against the new and unseemly, the *Daily Telegraph* condemned the delirium. 'This hysteria presumably fills heads and hearts otherwise empty,' argued the author of an anonymous editorial. 'Is there not something a bit frightening in whole masses of young people, all apparently so suggestible, so volatile and rudderless? What material here for a maniac's shaping! Hitler would have disapproved, but he could have seen what in other circumstances might be made of it.'

On their return to Leicester a year later, in October 1964, the Beatles attempted to execute their usual trick, rushing offstage and into their car while the National Anthem was playing. But in that brief period, the mores of society had changed: this time, a group of sixty or seventy fans failed to stand to attention, preferring to run out of the theatre and swarm around the Beatles in their car, hammering on the roof and windows. Discombobulated, the driver lost his nerve and careered into another car, but still the fans hammered away, forcing the Beatles to wait for the police to come and free them.

36.

The sudden arrival of the Beatles came as a shock to many in the old guard of showbusiness.

Marlene Dietrich, star of *The Blue Angel* (1930) and *Blonde Venus* (1932), was sixty-one years old when she agreed to appear in the 1963 Royal Variety Performance. Her international stature seemed to guarantee her the role of star of the evening.

In July 1963 the impresario Bernard Delfont was asked by his sixteen-year-old daughter Susan to book the Beatles for the show. Delfont was nonplussed: 'I had never heard of them . . . when I asked what they did, she said they were somehow – well, you know – different.'

Soon afterwards, he heard that someone in his organisation had booked them for a Sunday performance at the Princess Theatre, Torquay. He immediately phoned the theatre manager.

'How's business?' I asked the manager.

'We've sold out,' he said. 'There are fans sleeping on the street, waiting for returns.'

That was good enough for me. I made the booking.

By November, the Beatles' fame had eclipsed Dietrich's. As the big day drew closer, Delfont noticed how much this upset Dietrich, who felt that all the kudos should be hers. 'I anticipated a clash of temperament, but I should have known that Miss Dietrich would not stoop to a vulgar brawl,' he recalled. 'Instead, she fought back with all the subtle ruthlessness of Lady Macbeth.'

During rehearsals, Delfont's sister Rita noticed Dietrich behaving 'petulantly and selfishly', hogging more than her fair share of the time available. When she had finished, all the photographers swept down to the front of the stalls. 'Not now, darling!' she ordered. 'Come back in an hour

when I've got my make-up on!' It had simply not occurred to her that they were there for the Beatles.

The cameras flashed away as the Beatles rehearsed for their allotted period. 'By the time Marlene returned, now resplendent in a sequined gown and wearing full make-up, there wasn't a photographer in sight,' recalled Rita Delfont.

The photographers returned for photocalls just before the show. Once again, the Beatles were the centre of attention, but each time they struck a new pose Dietrich would miraculously appear, elbowing her way into the frame. 'The boys, who were still a little unsure of themselves, accepted the intrusion as a compliment. Not so the production team, who recognised scene-stealing when they saw it.'

Nevertheless, she made quite an impression on Ringo: 'I remember staring at her legs, which were great, as she slouched against a chair. I'm a leg-man. "Look at those pins!"'

Dietrich herself finally warmed to the group. 'They are so SEXY!' she remarked to Brian Epstein after the curtain went down. 'It was a joy to be with them. I adore these Beatles. They have the girls so frantic for them. They must have quite a time!'

Four years later, the Beatles repaid the compliment by placing Marlene Dietrich among the chosen few on the cover of *Sgt. Pepper*.

37.

In the basement of the Ashers' house in Wimpole Street was a little room where Margaret Asher would teach her pupils how to play the oboe. It contained a sofa, an upright piano and a music stand. When Margaret wasn't in need of the room she let Paul use it to write his pop songs.

One day in mid-October 1963 John dropped by. The two of them went down to the little room in the basement and sat together on Mrs Asher's piano stool. Brian Epstein had told them that their next, most important task was to compose a song to crack the elusive American market. Up to now, their hit singles in Britain – 'From Me to You', 'She Loves You', 'Please Please Me' – had all flopped over there.

Doodling about, they came up with the line 'Oh, you-ou-ou got that something'. Paul hit a chord to accompany it. 'That's it!' said John. 'Do that again!'

After an hour or so, Paul went upstairs and put his head around the door of Peter Asher's bedroom. 'Do you want to come and hear something we've just written?' he asked. Peter accompanied him back downstairs, and together Paul and John played him their new song, 'I Want to Hold Your Hand'.

'What do you think?' asked Paul.

'Oh, my God! Can you play that again?' said Peter. As he listened to it for a second time, he thought: 'Am I losing my mind, or is this the greatest song I ever heard in my life?'

A day or two later, John and Paul took 'I Want to Hold Your Hand' along to the Abbey Road studios. They were speedy workers: in the same session they recorded 'I Want to Hold Your Hand', its B-side, 'This Boy', their first Christmas message for their fan club, and half of 'You Really Got a Hold on Me'. As if this were not enough, Paul left halfway through to go out to lunch with a girl who had won first prize in a 'Why I Like the Beatles' essay competition.

These were busy days. Over the next three weeks they packed in an appearance on *Thank Your Lucky Stars*, a tour of Scandinavia, the Royal Command Performance ('rattle yer jewellery'), concerts in Cheltenham, Sheffield, Slough, Leeds and Northampton, and a trip to Dublin.

On 9 November they were driven in their Austin Princess to East Ham, where the crowds outside the Granada cinema were so wild that even the Beatles' food had its own police escort.

Before they went onstage, George Martin put his head round the door and called for silence.

'Listen, everybody, I've got something important to tell you all. I have just heard the news from EMI that the advance sales of "I Want to Hold Your Hand" have topped a million.'

Everyone cheered. 'Yeah, great,' said John, never slow to spot the cloud blocking a silver lining. 'But that means it'll only be at number 1 for about a week.'

'I Want to Hold Your Hand' was released in Britain on 29 November 1963, little more than six weeks after John and Paul had composed it in an hour in Margaret Asher's basement room. Two weeks later it reached number 1, knocking 'She Loves You' down to number 2. Contrary to John's prediction, it was to remain at number 1 for another four weeks, and was in the charts until the end of April, by which time their follow-up single, 'Can't Buy Me Love', had already topped the charts for three weeks.*

'I Want to Hold Your Hand' was not released in America for another month, and then only after a notably random chain of events. A Washington disc jockey had been given a British copy by an air hostess, and played it over and over again on his show, prompting top-forty stations in Chicago and St Louis to follow suit. At this point, Capitol Records recognised its potential, and released it as a single on Boxing Day 1963. Within a week it had reached number 43 in the US charts; it seemed likely to climb higher.

---

* 'Can't Buy Me Love' surrendered its number 1 slot to another Lennon/McCartney composition, 'World Without Love', sung by Peter Asher and his friend Gordon Waller, jointly known as Peter and Gordon.

38.

At three in the morning on 17 January 1964, the Beatles were in their palatial suite at the George V Hotel in Paris, having just played the first of a series of concerts at the Olympia Theatre. As they sat around in their pyjamas and dressing gowns, Brian Epstein came in, clutching a telegram.

'Boys,' he said, 'you're number 1 in America!' For once, even John was thrilled. Their road manager, Mal Evans, witnessed their elation. To him they were 'just a bunch of kids, jumping up and down with sheer delight'.

Ringo was cock-a-hoop: 'We couldn't believe it. We all started acting like people from Texas, hollering and shouting Ya-hoo.' Paul climbed onto Mal's shoulders and demanded a piggyback ride. There to cover their tour, the photographer Harry Benson suggested they stage a celebratory pillow-fight. 'That's the stupidest thing I've ever heard,' said

John. A second later he picked up a pillow and whacked Paul on the back of the head, and then all four of them leapt onto the vast Empire bed and started walloping one another with pillows. In their pyjamas and dressing gowns, they continued their merry japes, picking Ringo up and – 'One, two, three, four!' – throwing him into the air. Would they ever again be so deliriously happy?

39.

It had all happened so fast. Exactly a year before, on 17 January 1963, they had been playing the Cavern and the Majestic Ballroom, Birkenhead. A year before that, on 1 January 1962, they had been turned down by Dick Rowe of Decca Records, on the grounds that 'groups of guitars are on their way out'.

And now they had cracked America. In the first three days of its US release, 'I Want to Hold Your Hand' sold a quarter of a million copies. It went on to sell five million.

The poet Allen Ginsberg was in the Dom, a 'hip hangout' in New York's East Village, when he first heard the song: 'I heard that high, yodelling alto sound of the OOOH that went right through my skull, and I realised it was going to go through the skull of Western civilisation.' To the amazement of his fellow intellectuals, the portly Ginsberg got up and danced around.

When Brian Wilson of the Beach Boys heard it, 'I flipped. It was like a shock went through my system.' The current Beach Boys single, 'Be True to Your School', had the chorus:

Be true to your school now
Just like you would to your girl or guy
Be true to your school now
And let your colors fly.

In that instant, Wilson realised that the Beatles had rendered him antique. He was two days younger than Paul, but now felt like an old-timer: 'I immediately knew that everything had changed.'

For the past six months the Beach Boys had been the most popular group in America. But from now on they would be obliged to live in the shadow of the Beatles. To make matters worse, the Beatles were signed to Capitol, the same label as the Beach Boys. The very same executives who had been giving the Beach Boys all their attention now couldn't stop talking about the Fab Four. 'The Beach Boys had been it for two years, but now people thought the Beatles were the future. And loyalties ran thin at Capitol,' recalled their promoter, Fred Vail.

The following April they recorded 'Don't Back Down'. Unlike their other songs, it had an air of doom about it: 'The girls dig the way the guys get all wiped out . . . When a twenty-footer sneaks up like a ton of lead'. It was to be the Beach Boys' very last surfing song.

In Freehold, New Jersey, a fourteen-year-old boy was sitting in the front seat of his mother's car when the song came on the radio. He felt time stop, and his hair standing on end. 'Some strange and voodoolike effect' took hold of him, 'the radio burning brighter before my eyes as it strained to contain the sound'. They reached home, but he didn't go in. Instead, he ran straight to the bowling alley on Main Street, rushed to the phone booth and called his girlfriend Jan.

'Have you heard the Beatles?' he asked.

'Yeah, they're cool,' she replied. He then rushed to Newbury's, a store with a minimal record section. 'I Want to Hold Your Hand' wasn't in stock, so instead he bought a single called 'My Bonnie', apparently by 'The Beatles with Tony Sheridan and Guests'. 'It was a rip-off. The Beatles backing some singer I'd never heard of . . . I bought it. And listened to it. It wasn't great but it was as close as I could get.'

He instantly set his heart on a guitar displayed in the window of the West Auto store on Main Street. When the summer came, his Aunt Dora paid him to paint her house, and he bought the guitar with the money he earned: 'That summer, time moved slowly.' He lived for every release by the Beatles. 'I searched the newsstands for every magazine with a photo I hadn't seen and I dreamed . . . dreamed . . . dreamed . . . that it was me . . . I didn't want to *meet* the Beatles. I wanted to *be* the Beatles.'

Over half a century on, Bruce Springsteen still believes that hearing 'I

Want to Hold Your Hand' that day in his mother's car changed the course of his life.

In Chicago, the ten-year-old Ruby Wax was standing in a record shop when the B-side of 'I Want to Hold Your Hand' came blasting out.

'Over the speakers the Beatles were singing "Well, she was just seventeen", and all of my organs lit up into red alert. This was the most exciting sound I had ever heard – it was a Big Moment. No one man since then has ever switched the "on" button like they did.'

Over the next few weeks, Ruby plastered her bedroom wall with Beatles posters, which she then ritually licked. She collected Beatles magazines, pens, records, sunglasses, clocks, socks and stickers. 'I would turn up the sound of my Beatles records to eardrum-shattering levels and weep and moan and scream out my love.' She would even call the telephone operator in Liverpool just to hear her say 'Hello' in a Scouse accent. 'Then I'd become so overwhelmed I'd have to hang up.'

Serving a ten-year sentence in McNeil Island Corrections Center, Washington State, the petty criminal Charlie Manson kept hearing 'I Want to Hold Your Hand' playing on the radios circulating among the inmates.

According to his biographer, Manson was impressed by the music, but far more impressed by the adulation the Beatles were receiving: 'Charlie always yearned for attention; now he decided that fame was what he really wanted. If these four Beatles could have it, why couldn't he? . . . Charlie started telling anyone willing to listen and also those who weren't that he was going to be bigger than the Beatles.'

From that point on, Manson spent his time in McNeil hunched over a guitar. Whenever his mother Kathleen came visiting he would tell her, with an almost manic insistence, that one day soon he too would be famous.

40.

In January 1964 the Ronettes came to London to headline their first British tour, supported by a local group, the Rolling Stones.

On their first night a party was thrown for them by the Radio Luxembourg disc jockey Tony Hall at his home in Green Street, Mayfair, just down the road from where George and Ringo were living.

John, George and Ringo were already there when the Ronettes came in. The Ronettes were aware of the fame of the Beatles – since their arrival they had heard of little else – but had still not heard their music. For their part, the three Beatles were mustard-keen on the Ronettes, with their lusty, yearning voices and shapely bodies.

As the Ronettes entered, John, George and Ringo made a beeline for them, and showered them with praise. 'You've got the greatest voice,' George told Ronnie Bennett, the lead singer. 'We loved it the first time we heard you.' Generally thrifty with his compliments, John was similarly effusive. 'Fuckin' great,' he said.

'They kept telling us how much they loved our long black hair, and how our whole look blew them away,' remembered Ronnie. 'And we weren't exactly having a bad time ourselves.'

They all started dancing to records by the Ronettes – 'Be My Baby', 'Baby, I Love You', 'I Saw Mommy Kissing Santa Claus'. Over the course of the evening the three girls enjoyed teaching the Beatles the latest dance moves from America: the Pony, the Jerk, the Nitty-Gritty. Usually a reluctant dancer, John proved eager for tuition from Ronnie. 'Every time we'd start to dance, John would come over and say, "I don't know if I've got this one yet, Ronnie. I may need some extra instruction." It didn't take me long to figure out that he liked me.'

At the same time, George was making it clear that he was similarly taken with Ronnie's elder sister, Estelle. 'We were young and in a foreign country, so we decided to forget our boyfriends back home and have some fun,' recalled Ronnie, whose highly-strung boyfriend, the record producer Phil Spector, was safely back in America.

As the night wore on, George and Estelle disappeared from the dance floor, and Ronnie agreed to let John take her on a tour of the house. She was impressed: 'There were antique vases and fine art in every room.' Upstairs, John began trying all the door handles. It dawned on Ronnie that he was after a hidey-hole. 'John finally found one door open, so we walked in, but it was so dark we didn't even notice that George and Estelle were already in there, sitting on the bed. "Oops! Sorry guys!" I said.' They eventually found an empty room. Together they sat on a window seat, gazing out over a view of 'this fairy-tale land of lights and towers that seemed to go on forever' as the mood became more intimate.

'What's all this like for you?' asked Ronnie.

'Well, there's a draught, and this window seat is killing my bum.'

'That's not what I meant. I mean being famous.'

'Oh, I see. Serious stuff. I'll need a smoke for this, then.'

They talked about fame. John remembered sitting in cafés with the other Beatles, fantasising about the future. 'We'd sit there with our jam butties and tea, saying, "When we get our record contract, everything's going to change. We'll have limousines and chauffeurs, and we'll never have to eat another jam butty as long as we live!" Then we got our record contract, and you know what's 'appened?'

'Nothing really changed?'

'Nope. Turns out we were right – everything did change. We got our limousines and our drivers, and now we've gone right off jam butties. If I even think of them I want to heave up.'

All this talk made Ronnie wonder whether John was 'one of these heavy brain people, just like Phil'. She could also tell that John liked her 'for more than just my voice. When he leaned over and started kissing me, I have to admit he made me forget about Phil for a few seconds.'

Professionally, Ronnie had often sung about kissing – 'I'll make you happy, baby, just wait and see. For every kiss you give me, I'll give you three' – but so far she had taken things no further. 'I know it might seem hard to believe now, but I hadn't done much more than kiss a guy on the lips until then, and that included Phil. Romance was everything, and sex was still a mystery. But the way things were going on that window seat, it didn't look like it was going to stay that way for long.' As they kissed, John

started 'moving his hands around in places I didn't even know I had'. He then put them around her waist, and tried to edge her towards the king-sized bed, but at that moment Ronnie's thoughts turned to Phil, and she suddenly dug her feet into the rug, causing John to topple over onto the floor. 'Do you think we could go back down to the party?' she asked.

Estelle and Ronnie embarked on a series of double dates with George and John. Ronnie was intrigued by how starstruck the two Beatles were, always wanting to know more about American singers and musicians: 'Tell us about the Temptations! . . . What's Ben E. King really like?'

One night, George and John collected Estelle and Ronnie from the lobby of the Strand Palace Hotel. Caught off-guard, John made the mis-take of asking their mother, who was accompanying the girls, if she would like to come too. Her enthusiastic response came as a bitter disappoint-ment. 'Dinner? Oh, that sounds fun. Let me get my purse.'

The evening proved awkward, not least for Ronnie. 'How can you say any-thing with your mother sitting around? And the worst part was that she didn't say a word the whole time. She just kept staring at us through the whole meal.'

Decades later, her mother confessed to Ronnie that she didn't care for the way 'these big grown men were really liking my little girls . . . I thought, "Well, what kind of a life am I going to have now?"' It was, she thought, 'the most hurtingest night of my life'.

Towards the end of the month, Phil Spector arrived in town. Ronnie knew his presence would spell the end of their fun: he was bound to refuse to go clubbing, and would certainly never let her go out without him. Phil never said anything, but Ronnie sensed that he didn't like the way she had been spending so much time with the Beatles: Phil could be tricky that way.* At the same time, on their UK tour Keith Richards of the Rolling Stones had fallen in love with Ronnie: 'Keith used to say, "Oh, we would have great babies because you have that black, thick hair and I have black, thick hair."'

On 5 February Tony Hall threw another party at his Green Street flat, this time for the Beatles, who were set to embark on their first US tour. 'It was a very sweet evening,' recalls one person there that night, 'because the Beatles, as big as they were at that time, had no idea what was about to hit them when they went to America, so they were very apprehensive.' Everyone danced along to Martha and the Vandellas' 'Heat Wave', and Ronnie joined in the singing at the top of her voice.

'Ronnie was the bird everyone wanted to shag' remembered Tony Calder, a music PR. 'Everybody was salivating over this incredible little thing.' Meanwhile, he saw Phil Spector 'getting very wound up about the attention everybody was paying to Ronnie. You could feel the sexual tension, every guy in the place looking at her. Because she was exotic. And she was American!'

Phil's jealousy rocketed still further when he heard from Ronnie's mother that John had invited the Ronettes to fly to America with the Beatles. Ronnie hadn't had the nerve to tell Phil about their generous offer, so she had asked her mother to broach the topic.

'You know, Phil, it might be good publicity if the girls went back on the jet with the Beatles.'

'No, I've already bought their tickets.'

The Ronettes flew back to New York the next day, without the Beatles. Phil told Ronnie he would make his own way back.

---

* And how! In 1968, soon after their marriage, he gave her a car for her twenty-fifth birthday, but insisted she drive it only when accompanied by him – or if he was unavailable, by a life-sized inflatable plastic replica of him, with its knees bent in a permanent sitting position. 'Now nobody will fuck with you when you're driving alone,' he explained triumphantly. Year upon year, Phil's jealousy increased. He trapped Ronnie in their house, surrounding it with barbed wire and guard dogs, and confiscating her shoes to prevent her from running away. Furthermore, he threatened to have her murdered if ever she tried to escape. 'I'm completely prepared for that day,' he told her mother. 'I've already got her coffin. It's solid gold. And it's got a glass top, so I can keep my eye on her after she's dead.'

41.

Ronnie was back home with her mother and sister in Spanish Harlem, watching TV coverage of the Beatles arriving at JFK, when she happened to recognise a familiar figure on the screen: 'I almost fainted when I looked at the TV and saw Phil Spector following the Beatles out of their plane. I wanted to strangle him!'

Having wheedled his way on board the Beatles' plane, Spector had proved a tricky passenger. 'He's as mad as a hatter,' observed Ringo. '. . . We realised how crazy he was because he "walked to America". He was so nervous of flying he couldn't sit down, so we watched him walk up and down the length of the plane all the way.'

By the time their plane touched down in New York, 'I Want to Hold Your Hand' was number 1 in the *Billboard* charts. And the pre-orders for merchandise were rolling in: half a ton of Beatles wigs were following them to America, as well as 24,000 rolls of Beatles wallpaper.

After a press conference at the airport the Beatles were driven to the Plaza Hotel,* and shepherded past thousands of fans who were screaming 'We want the Beatles!'

John and George took the trouble to leave the names of the Ronettes with hotel security. Ronnie and Estelle were ushered upstairs, together with their cousin Nedra, the third member of the group, and Nedra's boyfriend Scott. For once, Phil Spector had taken his eye off the ball: while Ronnie was out having fun, he was busy in the studio.

The Beatles had an entire floor of the hotel to themselves. Every surface

* In her autobiography Ronnie states that it was the Warwick Hotel, but on their first visit to the US the Beatles stayed at the Plaza, transferring to the Delmonico on their next visit, in August of that same year, after the Plaza, upset by the mayhem, refused to have them back. Nor does she mention the presence of John's wife Cynthia, even though Cynthia had flown out with him. Albert Goldman, one of John's least reliable biographers, states boldly that 'As soon as Cynthia's back was turned, he hustled Ronnie into an adjoining bedroom.' It is possible that Ronnie has got her dates muddled, and John's failed seduction took place at the Delmonico. The Beatles didn't stay at the Warwick until 1966.

groaned with sandwiches and alcohol. 'We're prisoners up here, so they have to feed us well,' explained John. In every room there was a television switched on, but with the sound turned down. Record players were dotted about, with singles scattered all over the floor. 'I love America,' said John. 'People here just bring you anything you want.'

Estelle and Ronnie sat on the floor with George and John, playing records and chatting. As it grew dark, Ronnie noticed that many of the original visitors had started to leave, and a whole lot of new guests were arriving, most of them young ladies with very short skirts: 'You didn't have to be a genius to figure out that a whole new kind of scene was about to start.'

Mal Evans was going around the remainder of the first batch of guests telling them that it was time to go. 'Don't worry, Scott's with us,' said Ronnie. 'We don't know him, Ronnie,' replied John. 'He's got to leave.'

In that case, said Estelle, she was leaving too. She tried to encourage Ronnie to come with her, but, as the group's name suggests, Ronnie was always the most forward of the Ronettes: 'If weird things were going to happen up there, I didn't want to miss them.'

The remaining guests started flocking into one of the bedrooms. John grabbed Ronnie's hand. 'C'mon, don't you want to see what's so interesting?'

The bedroom was, to Ronnie's eyes, abnormally crowded. Everyone had gathered around in a circle; a man was standing on a chair taking photographs of whatever was going on in the centre. When people spotted John with Ronnie, they made way for them.

Ronnie looked on aghast. 'It was the most amazing thing I'd ever seen. This girl was lying on the bed, and one of the guys in the Beatles' entourage was having sex with her – right in front of all these people . . . And from the look on her face, she didn't seem to mind being used as entertainment at a Beatles party, even though none of them were even taking part. I guess it was enough to just be in the same hotel suite as them, as if that gave her something to tell her grandchildren.'

The man and woman kept at it, 'having sex every which way', while the photographer snapped away. For Ronnie, it was an education. She was still a virgin, and furthermore, she always made a point of keeping her underwear on in bed, just to be on the safe side. Though she knew the basic details, 'I didn't know the first thing about doing sixty-nine, or any of these other variations. This was 1964, when you couldn't even get films with that stuff on them – and here was an actual girl having naked sex in every different position! That was a scene I'll never forget.'

She was so nonplussed by the goings-on in front of her that she couldn't help emitting – 'Oh my God!' – involuntary exclamations. Before long, John leaned over and whispered, 'Ronnie, could you do that a little quieter, please.'

As the floorshow continued, John helped himself to the only armchair in the room, and encouraged Ronnie to sit on his lap. His excitement was all too tangible: 'I may have been dumb back then, but I knew when it was time to get up off a guy's lap.' She left the room.

John followed her, and they went into his bedroom. He pointed to the Manhattan skyline, and asked if she remembered the time they looked out of the window in London. Then Ronnie sat down, and John stood behind her, rubbing her neck with his hands.

Ronnie said she had to tell him something. Not now, he said. She said she must. He said he knew all about her and Phil – 'I just thought you and I might have something too.' Ronnie stood up. She loved talking to him about music, she said, 'but sometimes a guy can seem more like a brother than a boyfriend. And that's the way I think of you. I adore you, John. But not the way you want.'

As she left the room, John slammed the door behind her. But when he phoned her the next day, he behaved as though nothing had happened. Was she free that evening? The Beatles wanted to get away from it all, and to try some real New York food.

And so the three Ronettes enjoyed a quiet night out with the four Beatles at Sherman's Barbecue in Harlem, on 151st and Amsterdam. In future, whenever Ronnie dropped by Sherman's, the manager would greet her with a smile. 'I remember you! You're the little girl that brought the Beatles!'

42.

In Britain, the success of the Beatles was comparatively gradual: they hoved into view. But in America, they arrived with the sudden impact of a tidal wave. One minute, silence; the next, everywhere the Beatles.

For most of 1963 the Beatles were famous in Britain, but unknown in America. Both Brian Epstein and the group themselves were wary of mis-timing their first appearance there. Having seen what happened to Cliff Richard, they were determined not to make the same mistake. 'Lots of British artists had been across the Atlantic and died a death,' noted Ep-stein's personal assistant, Alistair Taylor. 'Cliff Richard invaded the United States and nobody noticed.'

It so happened that on the morning of 31 October the lugubrious chat-show host Ed Sullivan touched down at Heathrow Airport, following a talent-scouting tour of Europe. He was immediately struck by thousands of screaming girls crowded onto the roof of the Queen's Building. Might it be the royal family? He put this suggestion to one of the girls, but she just burst out laughing. Finally he asked an airport official, who replied, 'It's the Beatles.'

Sullivan was quick off the mark. He contacted Brian Epstein with a view to getting them on his show. With the spectre of Cliff fresh in his mind, Epstein had already planned to make his American campaign invin-cible: everything – marketing and record deals, concerts and promotion, press and TV – would be in place before the band arrived. So at the begin-ning of November he flew to New York for a series of business meetings, one of them with Ed Sullivan's producer and son-in-law, Bob Precht.

Precht definitely wanted the Beatles, but only as a novelty item, a curi-osity from England. Epstein, on the other hand, was determined that they should appear as stars, topping the bill. The deal Epstein finally negoti-ated was a brilliant compromise – the Beatles would top the bill on two consecutive shows, but for the negligible payment of $7,000. Precht saved money – they both knew that Epstein would be making an operating loss of about $50,000 – and the Beatles would get the platform they craved: two weeks headlining America's most popular show. And by the beginning of 1964 the deal was looking good for Ed Sullivan too: when the Beatles finally touched down in America on Friday, 7 February, 'I Want to Hold Your Hand' was already number 1 in the charts, with 'She Loves You' at number 21 and rising.

Their screaming fans precede them, pressed five deep against the windows of the terminal building at Kennedy Airport. As the plane door is opened, the screams drown out the sound of the jet engines. After their press conference at the airport the Beatles are escorted to the Plaza Hotel by four New York City Police cars and two motorcycle outriders, sirens wailing. At the Grand Army Plaza they are greeted by fans ten feet deep, many of whom have been waiting since dawn.

In a housing complex in Philadelphia, the fitfully employed Joe Queenan Sr learns from the *Catholic Standard and Times* that the Beatles are wholly unsuitable for children. To his thirteen-year-old son, Joe Jr, it is as though his father believed that 'their sole purpose in life was to corrupt the youth of America and lead them down the road to rack and ruin'.

Joe Sr refuses to let Joe Jr and his three sisters watch the group's appearance on *The Ed Sullivan Show*. He gives all four children advance warning that he will be commandeering the family's tiny black-and-white television on each of the nights on which the Beatles are due to appear. 'It was as if he were inviting us, nay, encouraging us, to slip rat poison into his lager,' recalls Joe Jr.

At the Beatles' rehearsal in the afternoon, the audience, mainly teenage girls, are reasonably quiet as they sit gazing at the empty stage; but when Ringo's drums are rolled onstage, they all start to scream.

The rehearsal starts with Ed Sullivan instructing the audience to pay attention to all the other fine performers, not just the Beatles. 'Because if you don't, I'll call in a barber.' After this little quip, he returns to his usual portentous self. 'Our city – indeed, the country – has never seen anything like these four young men from Liverpool. Ladies and gentlemen – the Beatles!'

A reporter from the *New York Herald-Tribune* compares the noise that erupts from the audience to 'that terrible screech the BMT Astoria train makes as it turns east near 59th Street and Seventh Avenue'.

Backstage, Brian Epstein corners Sullivan. 'I would like to know the exact wording of your introduction,' he says.

Sullivan replies, 'I would like you to get lost.'

An hour later, Sullivan returns to the stage to practise his warm-up. 'Listen, kids,' he says, 'there are other talented performers on this show, so clap for them too.' Just to be sure, he makes them rehearse their clapping. They are obedient. And so they should be: though the theatre seats seven hundred, over 50,000 requests for tickets were received for tonight's show.

'We'll be going on in eight minutes,' he announces, to low groans: eight minutes is an eternity.

Eight minutes later – a trumpet fanfare. The glossy curtain rises to form an arch. 'Good evening, ladies and gentlemen! Tonight, live from New York – *The Ed Sullivan Show*! Tonight, *The Ed Sullivan Show* is brought to you by Anacin, the headache remedy with a special combination of in-gredients to relieve pain, to relax tension, soothe irritability – *Anacin!* And by Pillsbury, makers of light, fluffy Pillsbury refrigerated biscuits and a complete line of fresh foods in the dairy case. And now' – a roll of drums – 'here he is – Ed Sullivan!'

Head down, eyes darting to and fro, Sullivan enters, sombre and shifty, looking like the shady brother of Humphrey Bogart. 'Thank you very much,' he says, putting his hands up and then swiftly bringing them back down, to make the audience stop applauding. He takes a nervous look to his left, then scratches his nose with the back of his hand. Once again he signals the audience to shut up; he shows no trace of a smile.

Finally, hush descends. 'You know, something very nice happened and the Beatles got a great kick out of it,' he says, in an oddly offhand way. His hands are in his pockets. 'We just received a wire, *they* did, from Elvis Presley and Colonel Tom Parker, wishing them a tremendous success in our country, and I think that was very nice.' In fact, this is not strictly true: Colonel Parker sent the telegram without Elvis's knowledge.

There is yelling. 'Now this –' Sullivan clears his throat. 'Now this –' he clears his throat again. More yelling. He holds up a forefinger, shakes it, the irate headmaster, then looks down at his shoes. 'Now this, this particular series, we've had many exciting acts on the stage. Thanks to our little Italian cook, Topo Gigio. Thanks to Belgian Singing Nun, Sister Soeur Sourire. To Milton Berle . . . and last Sunday, of course, the never-to-be-forgotten teaming on our stage of Sammy Davis and Ella Fitzgerald. Now tonight the whole country is waiting to hear England's Beatles. And you're gonna hear them – and they're tremendous ambassadors of goodwill – after this commercial. Now, if you're a person who has to be shown, here's a really big brute from all-new Aero Shave!'

After the commercial break, we return to Ed Sullivan, who looks as if he's going to announce a fatal car accident. 'Now, yesterday and today our theatre has been jammed with newspaper men and hundreds of photographers from all over the nation, and these veterans agree with me that the city has never witnessed the excitement stirred by these youngsters from Liverpool who call themselves the Beatles. Now, tonight you're gonna twice be entertained by them – right now, and again in the second half of our show. Ladies and gentlemen' – an extravagant wave of his arms – 'the Beatles!'

Screaming, screaming and yet more screaming. The camera cuts to the audience – virtually all girls between twelve and fifteen years old.

'Close your eyes and I'll kiss you,' sings Paul, waggling his head, raising his eyes to the ceiling. Next to him, George taps his toes. Ringo looks happy. John, to the right, appears detached, perhaps even slightly bored.

Close-ups show tearful girls, screaming and holding their heads as if they might otherwise fall off. They all remain firmly seated: perhaps they are obeying pre-show instructions from the fearsome Mr Sullivan.

Paul seems at home – jigging about, shaking his head from side to side. Throughout the show, it is clear that he is the Beatle in the driving seat.

The camera moves in on Ringo, who can obviously see a monitor, because he now smiles even harder, prompting a huge yell from the audience.

'All my loving, I will send to you-ou-ou!' When George and John go 'ooo' everyone screams some more. John permits himself a quick smile. The most abrasive of the Beatles, he is also their most nervous performer.

George, who was suffering from a high temperature this morning, launches into a twangy country-and-western guitar solo. What big eyebrows he has!

A girl of twelve bounces up and down in her seat, clapping, screaming, running her hands through her hair, up and down, up and down.

The song comes to an end; they all take deep bows, and then Paul launches straight into 'There were bells, on a hill, but I never heard them ringing' – the cheesy ballad from *The Music Man* – 'till there was you.' A subtitle appears on-screen beneath his head saying 'PAUL'. Then – to more screams – a close-up of Ringo ('RINGO'). Ringo grins, seems to say something to himself, and laughs. And then George, who bursts into his first big smile. Finally John, whose close-up comes with the caption 'SORRY GIRLS, HE'S MARRIED'. The screams for him are more subdued, but he smiles nonetheless.

The song ends. Another deep bow, and then straight into: 'She loves you, yeah, yeah, yeah!' Everything comes alive. There is scarcely a child who isn't screaming and clutching her head, as though on a particularly scary rollercoaster.

'She said she loves you' – a close-up of Ringo, grinning and nodding his head – 'and you know that can't be ba-ad. WOOOOOOH!'

The four of them shake their heads with amazing vigour, the starting pistol for the most frantic screams so far. John, legs wide apart and arched, jogs up and down. His microphone is on the blink, so his voice is barely heard throughout the evening, which makes him seem more of a backing singer, even when he is singing lead.

By now, everyone in the audience is clapping along. Most of the girls are sporting old-fashioned side partings and sweaters topped with strappy dresses.

'YEAH, YEAH, YEAH, YEAH, YEAH, YEAH, YEEEEAAAAAH!'

It's over. Screams galore. Cut to Ed Sullivan applauding. He is smiling, or very nearly smiling, but with the ends of his mouth turned down. He puts his hand up for silence.

'Now, you promised!' he barks, reminding the girls of his talking-to before the show began. They hush, but not entirely; there is excited chatter in the background as he continues, in his eat-your-greens tone: 'They'll be back in the second half of the show after you've enjoyed Georgia Brown, the star of *Oliver!*, Tessie O'Shea, one of the stars of *The Girl Who Came to Supper* – but right now, a word about Anacin.'

A hundred miles away, the thirteen-year-old Joe Queenan Jr has managed to bypass his father, slipping around the corner of the block to the television of his more merciful Uncle Jerry. He is amazed by what he has just seen: 'To this day I believe my life as a sentient human being, and not merely as my parents' chattel, began at that moment.'

In El Cerrito, California, the Fogerty brothers, Tom and John, are watching *The Ed Sullivan Show* with their friends Doug Clifford and Stu Cook. They immediately think of forming a quartet, just like the Beatles. 'Wow, we can do that. If these guys from England can come out and play rock'n'roll, we can do it.' They can't lay their hands on Beatle wigs, so they wear Three Stooges wigs instead.*

The thirteen-year-old Tom Petty, watching the show on the family television in Gainesville, Florida, thinks, 'There is a way out . . . You get your friends and you're a self-contained unit. And you make the music.' Within weeks, groups are playing in garages all over his neighbourhood.

Chrissie Hynde, aged twelve, is the daughter of a Yellow Pages manager. She watches *The Ed Sullivan Show* on her family television in Akron, Ohio. She will never forget it: 'It was like sex, but without the sex. I remember exactly where I was sitting. It was amazing. It was like the axis shifted . . .

---

* The Fogerty brothers' band was to develop into Creedence Clearwater Revival.

It was like an alien invasion. If you were a little virgin and didn't want to grow up like I didn't, didn't want to enter the adult world like I didn't, it gave you some kind of new avenue of sexuality. It could be more cerebral. You didn't have to actually touch the person's acne.' Going into Harvey S. Firestone High School the next day, Chrissie notices that all the boys have combed their hair down over their foreheads, so she does the same: 'I could never set my hair in rollers again. I combed it out straight and cut my bangs.'

In Baltimore, thirteen-year-old Greg Kihn follows suit. On the Friday he'd left school looking like Dion. On the Monday he returns to class with his hair ungreased and brushed forward: 'That's how quickly it happened.'

For the little Wilson sisters in Bellevue, Washington – Ann, thirteen, and Nancy, nine – it's as if a lightning bolt has struck them: 'It was a huge event, like the lunar landing . . . Right away, we started doing air-guitar shows in the living room, faking English accents and studying all the fanzines.'*

Billy Joel, fourteen, is watching with his family on Long Island: 'They looked like these working-class kids, like kids we all knew. And John Lennon had this look when he was on Ed Sullivan like: *Fuck all of you. This is total bullshit to me.*' Billy knew his destiny then and there: 'I said at that moment, "I know these guys. I can relate to these guys. I am these guys. That's what I want to do. I want to do that. I want to be like those guys. This is what I'm going to do – play in a rock band."'

Ed Sullivan reappears, looking as though he might benefit from a couple of Anacin himself. 'Now here . . .' There is a buzz of chatter from the audience. Ed drops his voice to a bass. '*Quiet!*' he snaps, then, perhaps surprised at his own irritability, flashes a quick lizardy smile. 'Here's a very amusing magician we saw in Europe and signed last summer – Fred Kaps!'

In white tie and tails, the Dutch magician doggedly goes through his routine. When Kaps finishes his act, Sullivan fails to signal his approval by inviting him over for a congratulatory handshake. Instead, he waves

---

* The Wilson sisters later rose to fame with the band Heart.

in his general direction. Next come the cast of the Broadway production of *Oliver!*, headed by Georgia Brown, singing 'As Long as He Needs Me', then 'I'd Do Anything', accompanied by the seventeen-year-old English actor Davy Jones.*

They are followed by an impressionist, Frank Gorshin, who rattles through Dean Martin, Marlon Brando and Burt Lancaster to effortful laughter. And so to another ad break, for New Pillsbury Quick Refrigerated Dinner Rolls. 'Nothing says lovin' like something from the oven – and Pillsbury says it best!'

'England's wonderful Tessie O'Shea' takes to the stage, a plump, chirpy, white-haired lady, rather full of herself, in a long sparkly dress and white fur stole. 'Oh hello, good people, how do you do?' she sings in her introduction. 'It's wonderful to be here to sing to you, but darlings, please don't ask me what the songs will be – I like a bit of everything, well, you know me!'

The young audience, having patiently sat through the Dutch conjuror, the cast of *Oliver!*, the impressionist and the fat lady on the banjo, have never been more desperate for the Beatles. Instead, Sullivan introduces comedy duo McCall and Brill, who perform a wordy sketch involving a series of aspirant actresses trying to impress a Hollywood agent. The only real laugh they get is from a topical joke they added just before they came on: 'My little girl is waiting outside. You know, she used to be one of the Beatles.' 'What happened?' 'Somebody stepped on her!'

Sullivan fails to thank them. At last, after a commercial for Pineapple Lemon Parfait from Pillsbury, the moment has arrived. 'Ladies and gentlemen, once again – THE BEATLES!' For the first time, Sullivan's smile seems wholehearted.

'She was just seventeen – you know what I mean!' sings Paul, to an audience largely composed of young girls who probably have no idea what he means. But they couldn't care less: by now they are all screaming their heads off.

George looks much more cheerful, but it is Ringo whose close-up seems to prompt the loudest cries. Perhaps through a trick of perspective, John looks a bit too wide and chunky, as though he is in a hall of mirrors.

---

* Hearing the screams that greeted the Beatles, Davy Jones thought to himself, 'I'd like a little bit of this action.' Two years later, he successfully auditioned to become the lead vocalist of the Monkees.

'Woooh!' The four of them all shake their heads at once, prompting the girls to go berserk. 'Oh yeah, I'll tell you somethin', I think you'll understand . . .' The camera zooms in on a girl in winged glasses, chewing gum, bouncing up and down in her seat, clasping her hands together, as if in prayer, while radiating pure delight. 'I can't hide! I can't hide! I can't hide!' Behind her, a portly grey-haired man in horn-rimmed specs and a bow tie manages a pained smile, but you can tell he wishes it were over.

And it is. Screams pile upon screams. Paul, George and John are joined by Ringo, who jumps down from his elevated platform and skips behind them. Ed Sullivan shakes each of them by the hand. You can see George saying 'Thank you!' He waves to the back row, and the others join in. Even Sullivan is smiling. They mouth 'Thank you' as they leave the stage. Sullivan wants to say something, and signals for silence. 'All of us –' he begins, but the screaming continues. 'All of us. All of us –' He holds up his hands. 'All of us on this show want to express our deep appreciation to the New York Police Department for its superb handling of thousands of youngsters who cluttered Broadway and 53rd Street ready to greet the Beatles under the command of Deputy Chief Standford, and our deep appreciation of the newspapermen, magazine writers and photographers who have been so darned kind to the Beatles and to us.'

It should be over, but for some reason it isn't. 'And now, ladies and gentlemen, a very fine novelty act – Wells and the Four Fays!' An all-singing, all-dancing troupe of acrobats trot on, performing cartwheels and contortions in time to the music.

And it's still not over. 'Before I tell you about next Sunday's show starring Mitzi Gaynor and the Beatles, right now – here's a real treat from the folks at Pillsbury!'

Sullivan, the severe headmaster, permits himself just a hint of goodwill. 'You've been a fine audience, despite severe provocation.' A quick lizard smile. 'Next Sunday, our show originates at Miami Beach from the Deauville Hotel . . . Next Sunday's show stars Hollywood's Mitzi Gaynor, the Beatles –' More screams, which continue at such a pitch that they drown out his announcement of the other acts. 'We'll also have the winner of the Liston/Clay fight at Miami Beach, which plays host to President Johnson on February 27th.' And, in closing: 'Now I'm delighted, all of us are delighted, and I know the Beatles on their first appearance here have been very deeply thrilled by their reception here. You've been fine. Now get home safely – good night!'

Then, as the closing credits roll: 'Tonight *The Ed Sullivan Show* has been brought to you by Pillsbury, where the good things you bake always begin with the best – Pillsbury's best. And by new Aero Shave – Keeps Drenching Your Beard Through the Shave.'

43.

Many American teenagers watch the Beatles on *The Ed Sullivan Show* against a noisy backdrop of snorts and harrumphs. In New York, twelve-year-old Sigrid Nunez has to contend with her mean uncle mocking their looks, their voices, their every movement. Some parents call them faggots. Others take the ultimate stand and switch their televisions off. 'You call that music?' Sigrid's friend's father shouts. 'And when do you think was the last time those creeps had a bath?'

But not every member of the older generation is against them. Billy Graham watches *The Ed Sullivan Show* in order to, as he puts it, 'gain a better understanding of the youth of today'. For the first time, America's most celebrated evangelist breaks his own rule to avoid television on the Sabbath. After all, he has to know what is going on. He concludes, not unfairly, that 'The Beatles are a product of our time. They represent the restlessness and the longing of young people today for something off-beat, something different.' Later, in Omaha, he advises a packed audience: 'Watch the kids' reaction to the Beatles and you'll know that man is an emotional creature.'

In New York, Jamie, Alexander and Nina Bernstein, aged from twelve to two, keep an eye on their forty-five-year-old father Leonard. Barely three months ago, on the day after the assassination of President Kennedy, he conducted the New York Philharmonic playing Mahler's Resurrection Symphony for a televised memorial. For Leonard, as, in a different way, for Billy Graham, the Beatles represent a vision of the future: 'I fell in love with the Beatles' music (and simultaneously, of course, with their four faces-cum-personae) along with my children, two girls and a boy, in whom I discovered the frabjous falsetto shriek-cum-croon, the ineluctable beat, the flawless intonation, the utterly fresh lyrics, the Schubert-like flow of musical invention and the Fuck-You coolness of these Four Horsemen of Our Apocalypse . . . Together we saw it, the Vision, and heard the same Dawn-Bird, Elephant-Trump, Fanfare of the Future.'

The following morning, over breakfast in their suite at the Plaza Hotel, the Beatles sift through their reviews. Conservative commentators compete with one another to voice the most vehement disdain. The *New York Times* carries two reviews, neither appreciative. 'The Beatles' vocal quality can be described as hoarsely incoherent, with the minimal enunciation necessary to communicate the schematic texts,' writes the music critic Theodore Strongin. The TV critic, Jack Gould, calls their performance both 'a sedate anti-climax' and 'a fine mass placebo'.

Under a front-page headline, 'Beatles Bomb on TV', the *Herald-Tribune* says: 'The Beatles apparently could not carry a tune across the Atlantic but were saved by the belles in the audience.' Their reviewer condemns them as '75 per cent publicity, 20 per cent haircut, and 5 per cent lilting lament', and 'a magic act that owed less to Britain than to Barnum'.

The *New York Daily News* offers a mixed response: admiration, stupefaction, incomprehension. 'Not even Elvis Presley ever incited such laughable lunacy among the screaming generation. The Presleyan gyrations and caterwauling, in fact, were but luke-warm dandelion tea compared to the 100-proof elixir served by the Beatles.'

'Just thinking about the Beatles seems to induce mental disturbance,' notes George Dixon in the *Washington Post* a week later. Like many other commentators, he can't stop going on about how they aren't worth going on about. 'They have a commonplace, rather dull act that hardly seems to merit mentioning,' he writes, 'yet people hereabouts have mentioned scarcely anything else for a couple of days.'

The viewing figures offer no comfort to the critics. Seventy-three million Americans tuned in, the second-largest viewing figure in the history of commercial television. The first came eleven weeks earlier, following the chilling words 'News just in of shots fired in Dallas.'

In many people's minds, the two events will always be linked: the assassination of JFK was winter; the Beatles are spring. Years later, Joe Queenan Jr, now a successful writer, is convinced the link is valid: 'I have always believed that the Beatles' stupendous success in America was directly related to JFK's death. I remember reading this theory years and years after the fact and thinking, "Yes. Here is one theory about pop culture that is not stupid or obvious." The Beatles helped heal America . . . Some musicians heal ethnic groups. Some musicians heal nations. The Beatles healed an entire planet.'

44.

From the *Billboard* Hot 100 for the week of 4 April 1964:

1. 'Can't Buy Me Love' – The Beatles
2. 'Twist and Shout' – The Beatles
3. 'She Loves You' – The Beatles
4. 'I Want to Hold Your Hand' – The Beatles
5. 'Please Please Me' – The Beatles

Also:

31. 'I Saw Her Standing There' – The Beatles
41. 'From Me to You' – The Beatles
46. 'Do You Want to Know a Secret' – The Beatles
58. 'All My Loving' – The Beatles
65. 'You Can't Do That' – The Beatles
68. 'Roll Over Beethoven' – The Beatles
79. 'Thank You Girl' – The Beatles

Two songs about the Beatles also made the Hot 100 that week: 'We Love You Beatles' by the Carefrees, and 'A Letter to the Beatles' by the Four Preps.

45.

Once the Beatles' *Ed Sullivan Show* was all over, one or two of the performers couldn't bear to remember it.

For Charlie Brill and Mitzi McCall, it had all started so well. They were a sophisticated young comedy duo, striving to make their mark. They had, in their own words, been 'sitting at home, starving' in Los Angeles, when their manager called. 'Guess what?' he said. 'I got you on *The Ed Sullivan Show*.'

They let out a yell. This was the biggest show in America, miraculously able to transform jobbing performers into national stars.

They immediately set to work honing a routine. 'We rehearsed and rehearsed and we fine-tuned it . . . and we told everybody, in fact I think I sky-wrote it over Hollywood: "We're on *The Ed Sullivan Show*. Yippeeee!" We were on our way!' They were excited, too, by the chance to meet some of their idols: they had been tipped off that two big musical theatre stars, 'Two Ton' Tessie O'Shea and Georgia Brown were on the same bill, along with the impressionist Frank Gorshin. Someone also mentioned this new pop group they'd never heard of, from England.

On the way to the studio, Charlie and Mitzi were still finessing their routine when their cab came to a halt. The streets had been cordoned off, with thousands of people queuing around the block. They couldn't understand why.

Low on the bill, they were shown to the worst dressing room. In the corner was a soda machine for the use of one and all. Presently, they were called for a dress rehearsal. After it, a voice came over the loudspeaker: 'McCall and Brill, Mr Sullivan's office, please!' So they went downstairs, and were shown in. 'And there he was! Ed Sullivan! He was sitting on the chair getting made up and I looked at the man who could make our entire careers!' Sullivan had been observing their rehearsal, and he was not pleased. 'The piece of material you're doing is too sophisticated for this audience,' he said. 'It's going to be mainly fourteen-, fifteen-, sixteen-year-old girls in the audience tonight, and kids.'

In an hour's time they were going to be live on television, and here was Mr Sullivan ordering them to change a routine they had been fine-tuning for weeks! Determined not to panic, they got down to work.

Suddenly, there was a knock at the door. 'And there was this guy standing there with funny hair and granny glasses,' recalled Charlie, 'and he said, "Givvuzza coagluv." And I said, "This guy wants a glove or something, I'm not sure what he wants." And he started to laugh, and he said, "No – *givv uzz a coag luv*," and he pointed to the Coke machine. And I said, "Oh – *yeah*! Come in!" And he said, "Can you give me a dime, 10 cents?" And I said, "Oh, I gotta buy you the Coke as well. Whaddya think, we're made out of money, kid?"'

The young man took the Coca-Cola, then sat down on the sofa in their dressing room and started chatting away. 'While he's talking to us, he takes out a pen and a napkin and he's drawing me. He's looking at me and he's drawing some pictures of me and Mitzi on napkins.'

Eventually the show began, and the young man was onstage with his group. They were singing 'Close your eyes and I'll kiss you', but neither Charlie nor Mitzi could hear them. 'Honest to God, the screams all through were so loud I never got a chance to hear what they sounded like. I never heard or saw such bedlam in my life! And when they finish, the screams keep going on!'

McCall and Brill were the last act before the reappearance of the Beatles in the second half of the show. Before they came on, there were screams from the audience, who thought the Beatles were next. Undaunted, the two of them launched into a jaunty satirical routine in which Charlie played a casting director while Mitzi, an energetic mimic, played a succession of different women, from a stage mom to a method actor. Each of their gags was met with silence.

'We were up there for two years . . . We didn't know what we were doing. We didn't know if we'd finished the act or not finished the act. The band leader had the punchline, and he played it – Ta-da!'

They now reckon it was the worst three minutes of their lives. In fact, they had bombed so badly that when they came offstage the other performers looked away. Meanwhile, the Beatles were singing 'I Saw Her Standing There' and 'I Want to Hold Your Hand', and the screams were unabated.

After the show, Frank Gorshin took the couple out to Sardi's and tried to comfort them. 'Don't worry,' he said. 'This is not the end of your lives.' But they were so downhearted and embarrassed that they couldn't face returning home to California. Instead they headed south to Florida, for a week's break.

In Miami, they were walking to their car one night when a limousine pulled up alongside them. Inside were the Beatles, there for a second appearance on *The Ed Sullivan Show*, which was being recorded at the Deauville Hotel. John Lennon remembered them from their dressing room, and cheerfully introduced them to Paul, George and Ringo.

'What are you doing here?' he asked.

'Escaping from you,' they replied.

Back in Los Angeles, their agent failed to call them for six months. Eventually their careers got back on track, but they would never forget the day that had held such promise, and delivered such disappointment. 'We were in the midst of greatness. We didn't know it,' says Charlie. For the rest of the sixties they couldn't help but wince every time they heard the Beatles. And it was still only 1964: an awful lot of wincing lay ahead.

46.

And there were other, more grievous casualties too. In the eleven-week period between the Kennedy assassination and the Beatles' appearance on *The Ed Sullivan Show*, the *Billboard* chart had been dominated by a most unlikely record: a young Catholic nun from Belgium, singing a hymn to St Dominic in French.

In September 1959, twenty-five-year-old Jeanne-Paule Marie Deckers, the daughter of a *patissière*, entered the convent of the Missionary Dominican Sisters of Our Lady of Fichermont, to become Sister Luc-Gabrielle.

Permitted an acoustic guitar, she would occasionally perform her own songs to her fellow nuns. Her superiors were so taken with her singing that they encouraged her to record an album, to be sold as a souvenir to visitors to the convent.

Sister Luc-Gabrielle recorded it at the Philips studios in Brussels in 1961. The studio engineers passed the album to the record company executives, who persuaded the convent to release the track 'Dominique' as a single, and Sister Luc-Gabrielle to change her name to 'Soeur Sourire', or 'Sister Smile'.

The song became a hit in Belgium, then in Europe, then in the United States. The charts have always been a mixed bag, but 'Dominique' is without doubt the first and only single about the thirteenth-century founder of the Dominican order, sung in French, to have become an international hit.

> Dominique-nique-nique went about simply,
> A poor singing traveller.
> On every road, in every place,
> He talks only of the Good Lord,
> He talks only of the Good Lord.

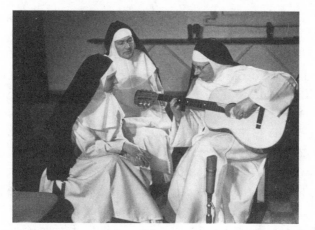

Sister Luc-Gabrielle, now nicknamed 'the Singing Nun', was an unlikely pop star. The money she earned from the records went straight to her convent: 'My superiors wanted to protect my personal religious life, and I was kept away from the whole world of the song, the spectacle, and so on. In a way it was good. My superiors feared that I would become haughty.'

On his talent-scouting trip to Europe, Ed Sullivan had visited the convent at Fichermont, filming the heavily bespectacled Sister Luc-Gabrielle strumming her acoustic guitar and singing 'Dominique'. She became one of his most popular novelty acts ever, more popular even than the cheeky puppet Topo Gigio and the dancing bear from the Moscow State Circus.

After the assassination of President Kennedy, the American public took to the innocent, hopeful sound of the Singing Nun. Within a week her album, *Her Joys, Her Songs*, elbowed 'Louie Louie' by the Kingsmen out of the way to reach number 1 in the charts. There it remained from December through January.

But with the arrival of the Beatles, and the release of *With the Beatles*, the chart career of Sister Luc-Gabrielle ground to a halt. After a world tour, she retreated to the convent, where she heard the news that 'Dominique' had won a Grammy for Best Gospel or Religious Song, and that her album had sold two million copies.

In 1966 Debbie Reynolds starred in the title role of a feature film called *The Singing Nun*, but by now Sister Luc-Gabrielle had grown notably less docile, describing the film as 'absolutely idiotic'. Around this time she left the convent and reverted to her old nickname, 'Jeannine' Deckers. Set on pursuing a singing career, she released a succession of singles, but they were too radical for her fans to swallow. The first, a protest song against the Roman Catholic Church's attitude to birth control, was called 'Glory be to God for the Golden Pill'; the next was the unusually morose 'Sister Smile is Dead'. Neither played to her strengths.

Later, in the 1970s, her similarly downbeat album *I Am Not a Star in Heaven* also flopped. By now she was living with a woman, though they shared a vow of celibacy, and had transformed their living room into a chapel. Realising that her career as a chart-topper was over, Deckers became a teacher of handicapped children. In the early 1980s she was pursued by the Belgian authorities for $63,000 of back taxes earned on her records. But she had nothing: not unreasonably, she argued that the convent, having taken most of her royalties, was liable for any tax. In an attempt to raise money she re-recorded 'Dominique', this time to a heavy disco beat, but it failed to catch on.

In April 1985 Deckers and her companion Annie Pécher, or 'Sister Annie', committed suicide together in their shared flat in Wavre, near Brussels. 'We are going together to meet God our Father,' read their joint suicide note. 'He alone can save us from this financial disaster.'

47.

Staying in Miami for their second *Ed Sullivan Show* appearance, the Beatles were approached by Harold Conrad, the publicist for the World Heavyweight Boxing Championship. He wanted photographs of them with either the champ, Sonny Liston, or the upstart no-hoper Cassius Clay, who would be challenging him in Miami in a week's time. Bookies were quoting odds of 7–1 against Clay; the *New York Post* was predicting the fight would be over in eighteen seconds.

John showed no hesitation: 'Clay's not going to win. He's a big mouth. The other one is going to kill him. We want him.'

But Liston had no interest in being photographed with what he called 'those skinny little bums'. He'd gone with Harold Conrad and Joe Louis to watch the Beatles recording *The Ed Sullivan Show*. Halfway through, he'd turned to Conrad and said, sniffily, 'Are these motherfuckers what all the people are screaming about? My *dog* plays drums better than that kid with the big nose!'

It was the British photographer Harry Benson, desperate for a shot combining the two biggest news stories of the moment, who persuaded the Beatles to court the no-hoper: 'I go to the Beatles and I say, "This man's very colourful and he's young and good-looking and I'll see what I can do."'

Clay agreed to meet the Beatles at the Fifth Street Gym on 18 February. The Beatles were joined by Robert Lipsyte, a twenty-six-year-old cub reporter from the *New York Times* who was covering the fight because the veteran sports reporters considered it beneath them: they were convinced they would have to spend their time hanging around outside Mount Sinai Hospital, waiting for the latest report from Intensive Care. Nor did they like the loudmouth Clay; they were irritated by his cockiness, his verbosity, the way he danced about in the ring.

The Beatles arrived on time, annoyed that they had been cajoled into the project. Lipsyte witnessed their surly entrance: 'These four little guys were being herded up the stairs and they were cursing with British accents, and apparently these were the Beatles. They were very angry – they didn't want to pose with Clay, he was a loser.'

Ringo, in particular, felt they were wasting their time. 'Let's get the fuck out of here,' he said. Lipsyte heard one of them saying, 'That stupid wanker is going to get knocked out in the first round.'

The contempt flowed in both directions. When Ferdie Pacheco, Ali's personal physician, set eyes on the Beatles, he was equally dismissive: 'They were street kids from Liverpool, sunburnt like lobsters. They looked so small and pitiful.'

Clay was nowhere to be seen, but suddenly the dressing-room door burst open. His frame filled the doorway. 'Hello, Beatles!' he said. 'Let's go and make some money!'

Benson persuaded them all into a boxing ring as Clay took control: 'The four couldn't get a word in edgeways. They were like little lambs.' They pretended to fight, four against one. Clay held Ringo in the air, called Paul 'pretty boy', and lined them up, tapping Ringo on the chin and making them collapse like dominoes. They did whatever he told them to do. At one point he made them pose lying flat on the floor. Then he said, 'Who's the greatest?' and they chorused 'You are!' All the photographs make them look weak and tiddly next to Cassius Clay: they barely come up to his shoulder.

After a while, Clay and the Beatles started chatting about music and boxing, as well as the money they were all going to make.

'You're not as dumb as you look,' said Clay.

'No,' replied John. 'But you are.'

It was a risky reply. Clay checked to see John was smiling, and decided it was only a joke.

After a few minutes they said their goodbyes, and the Beatles were led away. Once they had gone, Clay turned to Lipsyte and said, 'Who were those little sissies?'

On 25 February 1964, Cassius Clay beat Sonny Liston in six rounds. Liston left the hall in tears, his arm in a sling, while Clay hollered, 'I want everybody to bear witness! I am the greatest! I shook up the world! I am the greatest thing that ever lived!'

Clay was twenty-two years old, a little younger than Paul, a little older than George. Veteran sports writers smelled something unpleasant in the air. The gruff columnist Jimmy Cannon was particularly steamed up. 'Clay is part of the Beatle movement,' he wrote. 'He fits in with the famous singers no one can hear and the punks riding motorcycles with iron crosses pinned to their leather jackets and Batman and the boys with their long dirty hair and the girls with the unwashed look and the college kids dancing naked at secret proms held in apartments and the revolt of students who get a check from Dad every first of the month and the painters who copy the labels off soup cans and the surf bums who refuse to work and the whole pampered style-making cult of the bored young.'

For many of the older generation, Cassius Clay and the Beatles were auguries of impertinence, dirtiness, disrespect, and everything else that was dragging the world downhill. Yeah, yeah, yeah: what kind of language was that?

48.

Yeah, yeah, yeah: a *Newsweek* critic focused on those three little words – or rather, one little half-word, repeated – to convey everything he hated about the Beatles: 'Musically they are a near disaster, guitars and drums slamming out a merciless beat that does away with secondary rhythms, harmony and melody. Their lyrics (punctuated by nutty shouts of "yeah, yeah, yeah") are a catastrophe, a preposterous farrago of Valentine-card romantic sentiments.'

In the *National Review*, the conservative iconoclast William F. Buckley penned a diatribe under the title 'Yeah, Yeah, Yeah, They Stink': 'Let me say it, as evidence of my final measure of devotion to the truth: The Beatles are not merely awful, I would consider it sacrilegious to say anything less than that they are godawful. They are so unbelievably horrible, so appallingly unmusical, so dogmatically insensitive to the magic of the art that they qualify as crowned heads of anti-music, even as the imposter popes went down in history as "anti-popes".'

But young people felt differently. Roz Chast was coming up to her ninth birthday when she first heard it. 'That song provided my first inkling that there was another world out there, one that did not include my parents, my relatives, my neighbours, my teachers or my classmates – a world of carefree and attractive young people who did not worry about illness or money, and who did not care about homework or why one was not popular . . . What was it about "She Loves You" that felt like an anthem of liberation? Perhaps it was that chorus of "Yeah, yeah, yeah", or maybe it was that thrilling "Wooooo!", or maybe it was the Beatles themselves. I'd never seen anything like them.'

Later that spring, Roz was staying with her parents at a hotel in Puerto Rico when she paired up with another little girl. One day the two families went out driving together. While the parents chatted away, the two girls began to sing 'She Loves You' as loud as they possibly could, though they were shaky on most of the words, except for 'Yeah, yeah, yeah!' and 'Wooooo!'.

'More than fifty years later, I still remember how thrilling that was. I don't recall any of the grown-ups getting particularly mad at us. They were just baffled. This was us, this kind of music. Not for them. And that was OK with us.'

In the third grade, Roz found herself close to the bottom of the social pecking order. The four most popular girls in the school dressed up in Beatle suits, Beatle boots and Beatle wigs, and played cardboard guitars. They sang 'She Loves You' and went 'Woooo!' and shook their heads.

'When I think about "She Loves You", and how much I loved that song, how new it sounded, and how happy it made me feel to hear it, I think about how much it represented the mirage of a possible future, one that was more joyful and more interesting than my lonely and borderline-grim childhood with its homework and tests and mean girls and stupid boys and parents who worried about everything and got angry over nothing.'

Joe Queenan had never heard anything like it. Before 'She Loves You' came blaring through his sister's transistor radio in Philadelphia, 'I had no interest in music, period. Until that moment, I viewed music as an annoyance at best, and at worst as a punitive child-rearing device.' His parents played Frank Sinatra, Tony Bennett and Perry Como. 'When the Beatles showed up, we felt the way the French must have felt when the GIs swarmed into Paris in August 1944 . . . The Beatles held out hope that life might actually be worth living, that popular culture need not be gray, predictable, sappy, lethal.' For him, that moment he first heard 'She Loves You' signalled 'the first time in my life I heard a song that seemed to speak directly to me and not to adults . . . I still think it is the greatest song ever written. For me, it is and always will be the song that changed the world. I love that song. I absolutely love it. And with a love like that, you know you should be glad.'

49.

In Reseda, California, sixteen-year-old Pam Miller was so besotted with the new arrivals that within the privacy of her schoolgirl diary she turned herself into a Liverpudlian. On 10 February 1964 she wrote: 'Paul you are gear. Really Fab. Say chum, why are you so marvellous, luv? The most bloomin' idiot on earth is me, cause I'm wild over you chap.'

From then on she posted Paul a poem every day, sealed with a kiss. As February rolled into March, her diary entries grew more intimate:

2 March 1964: It is 2:21 am at Paul's house. He's sleeping. I'm glad. I wish I could see him sleeping, I really do. I wish I could be *with him* sleeping (just kidding). I hope he read my poem before he closed his beautiful brown eyes.

Pam was perhaps rather more forward than other Beatles fans of her age. One of her particular treasures was a bubble-gum card of Paul – a photograph of him playing his bass guitar on a hotel bed, with his legs apart. She studied it close-up: 'You could actually see the shape of his balls being crushed by the tightness of his trousers. I carried that card around with me in a little gold box with cotton covering it like it was a precious jewel.'

Virtually every day, on her local radio station KRLA the disc jockey Dave Hull, 'the Hullabalooer', would deliver an update on the state of Paul's relationship with his new girlfriend. Pam listened with growing resentment of the young lady she came to call 'the creepy freckle-faced bow-wow, Jane Asher', or simply 'Pig-Face'.

Pam covered her bedroom with Beatles merchandise. Her three best friends were also Beatles fans. Each had her own favourite. Stevie loved Ringo: 'I've got to meet Ringo or my whole life will be completely empty. Oh, I'm suffering so. He's my love and I love him. Oh, God, please don't let my Ringo be taken away!'

Linda loved John. Together, Pam and Linda would *be* Paul and John. They spoke to each other in Liverpudlian accents, pretending to go to parties and to eat in expensive restaurants. Pam had a reel-to-reel tape-recorder, and would make up little plays, taking all the parts herself. In all of them, Jane Asher would die. But in her letters to Paul, she was the soul of tact:

> Dear Paul, Your fans will always love you. Personally, I will never stop. Since hearing about your engagement to Jane Asher, I'll have to love you in another way, all of my own.

Pam's friend Kathy was in love with George. It so happened that Kathy's father had a pal who worked at the Hollywood Bowl, where the Beatles were due to play in August. Luckily, this pal managed to wangle them four tickets. Pam framed hers, hung it on her bedroom wall and started counting down. In her diary entry for 3 June she wrote: 'There's an actual day this year that is called August 23rd! It comes in 83 days!!'

With twenty-one days to go, the four girls went to see *A Hard Day's Night*. It was everything Pamela hoped it would be. 'The Beatles are the greatest actors alive,' she told her diary.

On 23 August she wrote: 'Day Of All!! Tonight I saw Paul. I actually looked at his lean slender body and unique too-long legs. I saw his dimples and his pearly white teeth. I saw his wavy, yet straight lengthy hair, I saw his doe-like eyes . . . and they saw me. Maybe it's fate that brought him to our sunny shores . . . for I am here too.'

50.

Dear George.

Lots of people ask me if I think the Beatles will become American citizens after their stay but I know you well enough to say that you love your home (Liverpool) best, don't you, George? But of course! Oh well . . . I hope I can come to your birthday party as I must talk to you, George, before I go bonkers. My friend at school went to your party last year. You came with the others to pick her up at her house. It was funny, really, 'cause Paul used her 'lav' and she would'nt [*sic*] let her mum clean the 'lav' out until – months later, it was. It started to smell so it had to be cleaned after long last. But it was funny, 'cause she was always up in that toilet.

Emma P.

Harrisburg, Pennsylvania

Dear, darling Beatles,

To think that I, Harriet Watts, live on the same planet with the Beatles, breathe the same air as the Beatles, see the same sun, moon, and stars as the Beatles.

Oh! It's just too much!!

Fondly and Forever,

Harriet W.

Atlanta, Georgia

Dear Beatles,

I told my Mother that I can't imagine a world without the Beatles, and she said she could easily.

Loyal forever,

Lillie K.

Fairbanks, Alaska

Dear Beatles,

I have 826 pictures of the Beatles, and am just beginning.

All my love,

Diana A.

New York City

Dear Beatles,

We have started a Beatle fan club.

So far we have two members. I am club President and Winifred is Vice President in charge of new members.

Your fans,

Gloria J. and Winifred Z.

Oakland, California

Dear Beatles,

Please dedicate your next song to me.

If you do, it will be a terrific seller, because I have loads of friends, and they will all buy the record.

Your fan,

Irma S.

Raleigh, North Carolina

Dear Beatles,

Please call me on the Telephone. My # is 629-7834

If my mother answers, hang up. She is not much of a Beatle fan.

With love from,

Maxine M.

Cleveland, Ohio

Dear Beatles,

I am a loyal fan. I have every one of your records and I don't even have a record player.

Love, Donna J.

Portland, Maine.

Dearest, sweetest Beatles,

I have Beatle pictures all over my room. I have Beatle pictures over my bed. I have Beatle pictures over my desk. I have Beatle pictures in my closet. I have Beatle pictures over my bookcase.

My mother hopes you are just a fad.

Love from a Beatle fan – all the way!

Stella J.

Chicago, Illinois

DEAR BEATLES

DO YOU THINK THAT YOU COULD SING AT OUR SCHOOL DANCE ON MAY 15?

THE REASON IS NOBODY EVER SANG AT OUR SCHOOL DANCE, EXCEPT MARSHA GOLDMAN, WHO IS IN GRADE 10.

MARSHA SINGS OK BUT SHE ALWAYS FORGETS THE WORDS.

PLEASE SAY YES.

LOVE,

JOAN G.

ST. PAUL, MINNESOTA

Dearest John,

I would like a lock of your hair. Also, a lock of hair from George, Paul, and Ringo. You know you have plenty of hair, so you can spare one lock each for me.

With love,

Sylvia M.

New York City

P.S. Please write the name of the person on each lock, so I will know who the lock of hair belongs to, as it is hard to tell when it is not on a person's head.

51.

At their first American concert, at the Washington Coliseum, the screaming was so piercing that a police officer was driven to block his ears with bullets. Straight afterwards, the Beatles were guests of honour at a reception at the British embassy, where the hysteria took on a different form.

They were welcomed by the ambassador, Sir David Ormsby-Gore.

'Hello John,' he said, as he put out his hand.

This gave rise to a standard piece of Beatles horseplay. 'I'm not John,' said John. 'I'm Charlie. That's John.'

'Hello John.'

'I'm not John,' said George. 'I'm Frank. That's John.'

'Oh dear. I'll never get these names right. My wife is much better at remembering names.'

Ormsby-Gore then led them through into the embassy's ballroom, heaving with men in dinner jackets and women in evening gowns, all peering at the Beatles with a peculiar mixture of excitement, curiosity and disdain.

'There were a lot of Hooray Henrys there, and we had never really met that kind before,' recalled Paul. John escaped into a neighbouring room in search of a drink, only to find himself buttonholed by a British diplomat: 'We were wondering whether we might prevail upon our guests to participate in our rather small but not insignificant raffle?'

John hesitated.

'Come along now! Come and do your stuff!' snapped someone else from the embassy. Always the least biddable Beatle, John insisted on finishing his drink first, adding, 'I'm not going back into that crowd.'

'Oh yes you are! Come on, come on!'

'Come along now!' chorused a young woman in a ballgown.

John turned to Ringo. 'I'm getting out of here.'

Ringo calmed him down. 'Let's get it over with.'

Presently, the Beatles pulled the winning raffle tickets out of a hat. Afterwards, a tipsy lady put her arms around Paul. 'And which one are YOU?'

'Roger.'

'Roger what?'

'Roger McCluskey the Fifth.'

Later, asked what she thought of the Beatles, she replied, 'Monstrous.'

The Beatles were soon surrounded by yet more guests asking for autographs for their children or grandchildren. Watching John, one said in a stage whisper, 'Look, he can actually write!'

It was a remark designed to be heard by its victim. The other Beatles froze, and so did Brian Epstein: it seemed to them perfectly possible that John would reply with his fists. Instead, he simply refused to sign, even when an embassy official pressed a piece of paper into his hand and barked, 'You'll sign this and like it!'

Ringo, being more compliant, kept signing away. While he was signing, a mystery assailant took out a pair of scissors and began to snip away at his hair.

With each new telling, the incident was to take on the texture of a parable.

Ringo was convinced the offender was a man. As he remembered it, when challenged, the man had replied, 'Oh, it's OK, old chap . . . bullshit, bullshit.' Peter Brown, on the other hand, was convinced that 'a woman in an evening gown produced a pair of cuticle scissors from her evening bag and before he could stop her, snipped off a lock of his hair as a souvenir for her daughter'. This version was confirmed by a reporter from *Newsweek*, who claimed that 'a matron whipped out scissors, snipped off a lock of Ringo's hair', adding that she then 'disappeared in the crowd'.

John thought 'some bloody animal cut Ringo's hair. I walked out of that swearing at all of them, I just left in the middle of it.' But Paul was pretty sure that there was more than one perpetrator, and all four Beatles had been targeted: 'I remember girls wanting to cut bits off our hair, which was not entirely on – so there were a few elbows in gobs.'

In his autobiography George Martin blamed 'the full quota of chinless wonders', saying they 'behaved abominably. They would approach the boys with an off-hand, "Oh, which one are you?" and one actually got a pair of scissors and snipped off a piece of Ringo's hair while he was talking to someone else.'

The American journalist Michael Braun, trailing the Beatles around for a book, was sure it was 'a British debutante' who had withdrawn 'a pair of nail scissors from her purse'. Their authorised biographer, Hunter Davies, claimed that 'Several elderly ladies, with glasses of drink in their hands, accosted the Beatles and demanded autographs.' But Davies thought it was a single 'young lady guest' who 'started snipping off locks of Ringo's hair'. In *The Beatles Diary: An Intimate Day by Day History*, Barry Miles added extra colour: 'The British community, arrogant debutantes and aristocrats, disgraced themselves, and one woman even snipped off a lock of Ringo's hair just behind his left ear. John pushed all the autograph seekers away saying, "These people have no bloody manners."'

It was Cynthia Lennon whose memory proved the least forgiving. In her first autobiography, *A Twist of Lennon* (1978), she described the episode in terms of class warfare: 'The true-blue British high society abroad treated them like freaks, as only the upper-class British at their worst could do. Scissors were produced by their hosts. "Oh which one are you? I'm sure you won't mind will you, darling, if I cut a little of your hair to send home to my daughter in boarding school." Not bloody likely, Missus. That was it. They left. Protocol or no protocol they weren't going to stand for that.'

It was a man, or a woman, or women, either young or old. At any rate, most of the witnesses agreed that whoever did it was British, and posh.

Epstein led the Beatles away, with John swearing. As they were leaving, Lady Ormsby-Gore said, 'Thank you so much for coming. I'm sorry about all that down there. It can't have been much fun for you.'

Ringo turned to Sir David and asked, 'And what do you do?'

In the car back to their hotel, Epstein assured the Beatles that he would never again force them into attending an official function.

Foreign Office officials publicly denied that any such manhandling had taken place, repeating Sir David's assurances that 'The suggestion they were manhandled by anyone is untrue.' Back in London, a Conservative MP, Joan Quennell, wrote to the Foreign Secretary, Rab Butler, asking if it was true that 'the young British entertainers known as the Beatles were manhandled by British officials'. Mr Butler replied stating that, on the contrary, the Beatles' manager had written to Lady Ormsby-Gore 'thanking her for a delightful evening'.

52.

The mystery was solved forty years later, when a fifty-eight-year-old Canadian woman named Beverly Markowitz confessed to the *Oshawa Times*.

In 1964 Beverly had been living with her parents in Silver Spring, Maryland, and dating a local disc jockey. Though she had heard 'I Want to Hold Your Hand' a couple of times on the radio, it had made little impression: 'I just thought it was another rock'n'roll band with a cool hairdo. They were all cute, though.'

Beverly's boyfriend had managed to buy tickets to the Beatles' first American concert, at the Washington Coliseum, and she had agreed to come along: 'He told me that the Beatles were going to be really big.' After the show he told Beverly that the Beatles would be at a party at the British embassy. Why didn't they try to crash it? Beverly was reluctant: 'We were in the parking lot. It was cold. It was snowy. It was late and dark and everything, and I had to get home or my dad was going to kill me.' But her boyfriend wouldn't take no for an answer. After all, they looked the part: 'I had a dress and heels on. My hair was all done up, and my date was in a suit.' Finally, she agreed.

It was much easier to get into the embassy than they had imagined: 'This white-haired drunk guy walked out, and when he went back in, we just walked right in with him. We got to go past the press and the velvet rope and right into the party.'

But the Beatles were upstairs, in a roped-off area. It was getting late. Beverly asked her boyfriend to take her home, but 'he said we weren't going anywhere until the Beatles came down'.

So they waited, and soon the Beatles came downstairs. Beverly approached them and asked for their autographs. 'They were all very nice, except for John. He wouldn't sign anything for anybody at all. I kept saying to him, "What is the matter with you?" Very arrogant.'

Her boyfriend still refused to take her home, even though she insisted her father would be furious. 'I kept saying, "Let's go, let's go, let's go," and my boyfriend just didn't want to leave. I couldn't figure how to get out, so I thought we'd just get thrown out.'

She worked out that the quickest way to be ejected was to cut some hair off a Beatle. She picked Ringo: 'He's kinda short, and I had on heels, so I could kind of get to him easier than the taller ones . . . I pulled out those little scissors from my purse. I just went clip, clip, clip, clip, clip all around the side, and he didn't feel it at first.'

Beverly remembered Ringo turning round and grabbing her by the shoulder. Just as she planned, she was immediately thrown out of the embassy, and returned home bearing a lock of Beatle hair.

Shortly afterwards she taped Ringo's hair into her autograph book, where it remains to this day, alongside his autograph.

Others were to find the process of harvesting Ringo's hair less irksome. Back in England, a thirteen-year-old Beatles fan, Katie Riggins, and a friend wrote letters to the mothers of Ringo and George asking for something belonging to their boys. Nearly a year later, Katie received a lock of Ringo's hair through the post, accompanied by a letter from Freda Kelly, the Beatles' Northern Fan Club secretary, saying that Mrs Starr wanted her to have it. Her friend received a similar envelope, containing George Harrison's old toothbrush.

53.

For Christmas 1964, when I was seven, my brothers and I were given Beatles wigs by our parents. At that time, a factory in Bethnal Green was manufacturing 30,000 Beatles wigs a week, to be sold in shops for 30 shillings a head. But those were quality wigs, made of fabric: ours were 7/6d, and made of the same thin, moulded plastic as cheap masks, so brittle and sharp-edged that they were painful to wear: if you tilted your head upwards, the bottom edge would cut into the crook of your neck, and if you turned your head to the side, it would scrape the skin behind your ears.

Nor did these 'wigs' look at all like hair. In fact, they could have doubled as Frisbees. That same year, Santa also put a Beatles Magnetic Hair Game in my Christmas stocking. It turned out that it wasn't really a game at all, in that it had no rules or even instructions. It simply consisted of four outlines of the Beatles' heads, a magnet, and hundreds of little black iron filings. What little game there was involved using the magnet to move the iron filings into place, so that each Beatle would be left with something vaguely approaching a Beatles haircut, or what a Beatles haircut might have looked like if the Beatles had been stricken with alopecia. Fifty-five years later, in the spring of 2019, I noticed the very same Beatles Magnetic Hair Game, in good condition, advertised for £1,250.

Before I ever heard their music, all I knew about the Beatles was their hair; that, and their 'yeah, yeah, yeahs'. Everyone talked about their hair, and in families these talks would often end in rows, the younger generation being strongly for, and the older generation just as strongly against. The rows even brewed in the Beatles' own families. 'That hair, it was the very limit, the absolute end,' John's Aunt Mimi complained after watching one of their first TV appearances, on *Thank Your Lucky Stars* on 13 January 1963.

At the end of that year, Field Marshal Montgomery, 'Monty', became the first person to mention the Beatles' hair in a parliamentary debate.

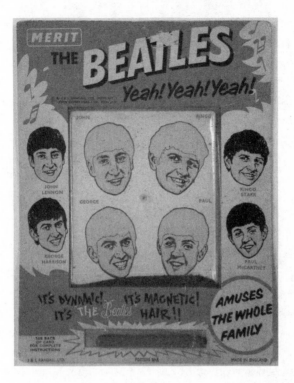

Speaking in the House of Lords in support of young men undergoing National Service – 'Look how well they fought in Malaya, in Korea and against the Mau-Mau' – he ended his speech with the words, 'In closing, I should like to say one thing: that if it is decided to have National Service, it may even result in the Beatles having to get their hair cut.' A few weeks later, on 9 December, the Labour MP Emrys Hughes answered Montgomery's point.

MR EMRYS HUGHES: I do not know why they should get their hair cut. I do not understand that that argument is likely to bring young men into the Army at present. Why should a soldier need to have his hair cut in a certain way? Why should not soldiers be allowed to wear beards? [Laughter.] My hon. and learned Friend the Member for Northampton (Mr. Paget) laughs. I have myself been asked why the young man who wants to join the Army is told that, if he goes into the Army, he will have to cut off his beard, whereas if he joins the Navy he can keep his beard.

Not for the first or last time, an argument about the Beatles' hair reeled off into an argument about everything else:

LORD ROBERT GROSVENOR (Fermanagh and South Tyrone, Ulster Unionist): Is the Hon. Gentleman aware that some soldiers are allowed to wear beards?

MR EMRYS HUGHES: I was not aware of that. If the Hon. Member wishes to develop that point later, I shall be very pleased indeed to have expert information upon this point.

MR REGINALD PAGET (Northampton, Labour spokesman for the Royal Navy and Army): If my Hon. Friend is interested in a reason, the traditional reason why soldiers are precluded from wearing beards is that a beard is a convenient thing to get hold of when you are cutting somebody's head off, and that occurs much more rarely in ships.

The origin of the Beatles' haircut is generally dated to the afternoon of 12 or 13 October 1961 at 29, rue de Beaune, Paris. John, the most well-to-do of the group, had been given £100 – £2,000 or more in today's terms – for his twenty-first birthday by his Aunt Mater. He had decided to spend it on a holiday in Paris with Paul. At this time both of them wore their hair slicked back, with quiffs, in the manner of Elvis.

Arriving in Paris, they looked up an old friend from Hamburg, Jurgen Vollmer, and hung around with him. Vollmer wore his hair in a fringe, as a reaction to, in his words, 'the bourgeois horrors in Hamburg'. Calculating that it might give them more pulling power with the fast girls of the Left Bank, John and Paul wanted their hair like Vollmer's, though 'his was actually more coming over to one side', recalled Paul. 'A kind of long-haired Hitler thing.' In his garret room at the Hôtel de Beaune, Jurgen agreed to style it. First he cut Paul's hair, then John's. The next day, when the concierge spotted all the hair clippings on the floor, he let out a yell.

This may have been the first time that John and Paul adopted their 'moptop' hairdos, but where did the style itself originate? Stu Sutcliffe's exotic German girlfriend Astrid Kirchherr has sometimes claimed the credit, though on other occasions she has denied it: 'All that shit people said, that I created their hairstyle, that's rubbish! Lots of German boys had that hairstyle!'

She had certainly cut Stu's hair into a fringe six months earlier in Hamburg. Pete Best remembered both John and Paul poking fun at it. 'This was going too far, we all thought, and fell about, pointing to the fringe.' Suitably embarrassed, Stu combed it out, but according to Best he let it reappear over the course of the next few days, at which point George copied it.

Astrid herself traced its origin back two thousand years or more, claiming to have copied it from Jean Marais' haircut in Jean Cocteau's *Le Testament d'Orphée* of 1960, 'which I am certain was inspired by the ancient Greeks'. But the most dogged of all Beatles sleuths, Mark Lewisohn, casts doubt on this claim, having unearthed a photo of Jurgen Vollmer with the very same haircut in 1957, nearly three years before the release of Cocteau's film.

Though the hairstyle's lineage may be lost in time, its impact on the world is undeniable. As Pete Best asked, 'Who would ever have foreseen that Astrid's simple experiment with Stu would eventually result in half the male population of the world getting in on the act, and some worried nations like Indonesia even going so far as to pass laws making Beatle cuts illegal?'

John and Paul arrived back in Liverpool on 15 October. Neil Aspinall was in charge of picking them up for their next gig: 'We went to collect John, and his hair was down. But it was when we went to collect Paul that we realised something was going on, because not only was Paul's hair down as well, but he *skipped* out of his house – in that way he does – pointing at his hair and generally unable to be subtle about it. His hair was different and we had to notice it.' Paul remembered everyone saying, 'Eh, your hair's gone funny,' to which he and John replied, 'No, this is the new style.'

And so it turned out to be: in the fifties, young men in Britain wore their hair swept back, larded with hair cream, thinking it looked moody and metropolitan. The Beatles' hair, combed forward and unsculpted, was boyish, cocky and bright. Within two years their hairstyle had become a symbol of a new decade of freedom and youth, with the result that, in certain institutions, it was outlawed. In November 1963 the headmaster of Clarks Grammar School in Guildford issued a ban on Beatle haircuts. 'This ridiculous style brings out the worst in boys,' he thundered. 'It makes them look like morons. If I find the ban is being disregarded I shall write to all the parents asking them to support me.' But an anonymous 'senior boy' reacted grumpily to the injunction. 'The ban will not go down well with most boys,' he told the *Surrey Advertiser*. 'I think it is stupid. The Beatles are great and I see nothing wrong with their style of haircut.'

Within a few months the craze had spread to America. On 7 February 1964 the writer Tom Wolfe witnessed the arrival of the Beatles in the US: 'When they arrived at Kennedy, I could see all the boys running down the halls combing their hair forward. That's when the sixties really began.' George Martin remembered watching fully grown men walking down 5th Avenue in Beatles wigs: 'It was just madness.' Twenty thousand Beatles wigs a day were being sold in New York alone, costing $2.98 each.

Around that time, the fourteen-year-old Bruce Springsteen entered the record section of Newbury's store in Freehold, New Jersey, and clapped eyes on *Meet the Beatles*. It was, he still believes, 'the greatest album cover of all time . . . All it said was *Meet the Beatles*. That was exactly what I wanted to do. Those four half-shadowed faces, rock'n'roll's Mount Rushmore, and . . . THE HAIR . . . THE HAIR. What did it mean? It was a surprise, a shock. You couldn't see them on the radio. It is almost impossible to explain today the effect of . . . THE HAIR.'

Bruce's immediate reaction was to have his hair styled like the Beatles'. He knew the consequences: 'The ass-whippings, insults, risks, rejections and outsider status you would have to accept to wear it.' When his father saw what he had done, 'his first response was laughter. It was funny. Then, not so funny. Then, he got angry. Then, finally, he popped his burning question: "Bruce, are you queer?"'

Most of Bruce's contemporaries proved every bit as unforgiving. But one or two others were, like him, prepared to brave the taunts of the world for the sake of the Beatles. And so they soldiered on, ships against the storm: 'I ignored the insults, avoided the physical confrontations as best I could and did what I had to do . . . each sunrise held the possibility of a showdown.'

Twenty years earlier, Frank Sinatra had attracted his own 'Sinatramania'. Girls had gone crazy at his concerts, screaming the house down. Back in 1962, the composer Jule Styne had declared that Sinatra had 'defeated rock'n'roll', but this prediction now seemed premature. Aged forty-nine, Sinatra had no single in the charts, and just the one album, at number 10. In contrast, the Beatles had the top five singles, and the top two albums.

Sinatra found it hard to stomach. 'He genuinely hated rock'n'roll, hated the Beatles . . . He had nothing but contempt,' noted the Sinatra family friend Rock Brynner, then aged seventeen.* Whenever the Beatles came on the radio or television, Sinatra would make his children switch them off. 'Long hair drove him batty,' recalled his valet George Jacobs. 'He didn't care how good the new music was . . . to him it was all one big excuse to take drugs.'†

By the end of 1964, all but the most stalwart British opponents of the Beatles' hairdos had run up the white flag. In December of that year, Earl Mountbatten of Burma, Chief of the Defence Staff, former First Sea Lord, last Viceroy of India, asked the head of his private staff, William Evans, to obtain a box of Beatles wigs for his grandchildren. The managing director of the manufacturing company drove to Mountbatten's Hampshire home, Broadlands, with a special presentation set. 'Mountbatten pranced around in a wig throughout Christmas Day,' recalled Evans. A year after criticising their hairdos in the House of Lords, Field Marshal Montgomery performed an about-turn, declaring that he looked forward to inviting them down to his country house 'to see what kind of fellas they are'.

But more oppressive regimes sought to outlaw Beatles hairstyles. In July 1964 President Sukarno of Indonesia announced that his government would no longer permit 'a hair style a la Beatles' on the heads of the country's youth: 'A few days ago there came to these parts some confused young men from England called "the Beatles",' he declared at an assembly. 'Their hair reaches down to their eyebrows . . . Young men, if there are any among you who imitate them, beware! I will issue an order to the police throughout Indonesia, if there is an Indonesian youth who imitates, has

---

* Rock Brynner (1946–), son of Yul Brynner. Historian, academic, co-founder of the Hard Rock Café.

† Whether out of familiarity or expediency, Sinatra eventually came round to the Beatles, recording both 'Yesterday' and 'Something', which he described as 'the greatest love song of the last fifty years' (though he misattributed it to Lennon and McCartney). In the summer of 1968 he also agreed to perform a one-off recording of 'The Lady is a Tramp' for Maureen Starkey's twenty-second birthday. The revised lyrics included the lines 'She married Ringo, and she could have had Paul/That's why the lady is a champ.' The master recording of the single was destroyed, and only one copy now exists, though its whereabouts are unknown. It has since been described by Daniel Finkelstein in *The Times* as 'the rarest and most valuable record ever made'.

his hair "Beatled", hold him, shave him completely bald . . . Are the police here or not? Make a note, make a note of my order!'

In the Soviet Union, Beatles records were banned, long hair on men was outlawed, and anti-Beatle propaganda was rife. In 1966 a news programme on the lone, state-run TV channel featured a series of grotesque photographs of the group and their screaming fans, backed by a commentary that mixed horror with sarcasm:

> Pop quartet the Beatles – look how elegant they are! But when they started their career they were performing onstage just wearing swimming trunks with toilet seats on their necks! Then they met a kind fairy – London dealer Brian Epstein. This London fairy understood that these gifted guys could be real cash earners. Struck down with psychosis, the fans don't hear anything any more. Hysterics, screams, people fainting! Demolished concert halls and fights are the usual finale of a concert. It's a world consisting of four walls covered with the photos of four singers with long hair.

There followed images of extreme poverty in the Deep South, of teenagers dancing wildly and of members of the Ku Klux Klan with burning crosses, all contributing to a portrait of Western indifference to social injustice.

> Keep on dancing, lads, don't look around! You don't really want to know what's happening! Keep on going, louder and faster! You don't care about anyone else!

Mikhail Safonov was a schoolboy in Leningrad when Soviet radio played 'A Hard Day's Night' as an example of a capitalist song about the relentless pursuit of money. It was the first time he had ever heard the Beatles. Initially, he was unmoved, but before the end of 1965 he had become caught up in a particularly perilous form of Beatlemania. He and his school friends would copy Beatles records and exchange them on the black market. All over the Soviet Union, young fans like Mikhail would write out Beatle lyrics and pass them around, learning English from them. The most rebellious liked to switch the names of Lenin and Lennon, even though discovery could cost them any hope of further education. One school staged and broadcast a show trial of the Beatles, with a prosecutor railing against them as 'Bugs'. At the end of the trial they were found guilty, in their absence, of antisocial behaviour. But this verdict was set to backfire: 'The more the state persecuted the Beatles,' recalls Mikhail, 'the more they exposed the falsehood and hypocrisy of Soviet ideology. And in attacking something the whole world had fallen in love with, they isolated themselves even more. It made us more doubtful that our beloved country was right after all.'

Mikhail's nickname at school was 'Ringo', because he aped his hairstyle. Having won a silver medal at school, he was obliged to go to the Palace of Culture to collect it, his banned Beatle hair glued down and parted with sugar and water to replicate an approved cut. But as he was leaving, a group of policemen spotted its true length and chastised him for being a long-haired deviant, setting him free only after he had shown them his silver medal.

As an adult, Mikhail became a senior researcher at the Institute of Russian History in St Petersburg. Looking back, he believes that 'Beatlemania washed away the foundations of Soviet society . . . One could argue they did more for the destruction of totalitarianism in the USSR than Solzhenitsyn and Sakharov.'

Strange though it may seem, this view has been confirmed by both Mikhail Gorbachev and Vladimir Putin. When Paul visited Moscow in May 2003, to perform a concert in Red Square, he had an audience with President Putin, who told him that hearing the Beatles as a boy growing up in the Soviet Union was 'like a gulp of freedom'. On the same visit, former president Gorbachev told Paul: 'I do believe the music of the Beatles taught the young people of the Soviet Union that there is another life.'

As the Beatles' hair inched downwards, past their collars, across their ears and over their shoulders, hair on other heads followed suit. For young people, long hair came to symbolise freedom, even happiness. 'If my hair seems a little on the long side it's because the idea became implanted in my brain at a very early age: long hair equals happiness. And that's from the Beatles,' says the cellist Steven Isserlis, who turned nine years old at the end of 1967.

When 'Penny Lane' was released at the beginning of that year, many of his regular customers expected Harry Bioletti, whose barber shop it immortalised, to be filled with delight. 'Oh dear me no!' he protested. 'I did the Beatles' haircuts when they started up and became the Quarrymen. But I've taken their pictures down. Such hair is bad for trade. I'm not disloyal, but business is business. I encourage plenty off the top in my shop.'

Our village barber in Surrey had a cartoon stuck on the wall next to his mirror. It showed two men standing next to each other in a public urinal, one with long hair, the other with short hair.

'Blimey! You gave me a start!' exclaims the short-haired man. 'I thought you was a girl!'

A popular joke of that time involved a young man going into his local barber shop and saying that he'd like a Beatles haircut. The barber then gives him a short-back-and-sides.

'But the Beatles don't have their hair cut like that!' protests the young man.

'They would do if they came in here,' comes the reply.

During the mid to late sixties it was hard to keep up with the Beatles and their hair, particularly if one took their moustaches, beards and sideburns into account. September 1968 marked the fifth time in four years that the technicians at Madame Tussauds felt obliged to update the Beatles' waxworks to allow for their ever-changing appearances; three months later Paul grew a beard, and they had to start the process all over again.

By then the Beatles' personal hairdresser, Leslie Cavendish, had become a celebrity in his own right. Having started off in the trade washing hair for Vidal Sassoon, he was now photographed and interviewed in fashionable magazines, and invited to all the best parties. He went on to write an autobiography, *The Cutting Edge*, full of details about the way each of the four would react to his styling. Oddly enough, it was Ringo he found the least approachable, 'the only Beatle . . . who didn't want you to forget that he *was* a Beatle', whereas Paul was always easy-going and appreciative. George had the thickest head of hair, 'at least twice as thick as Paul's', but barely spoke while it was being cut, beyond offering 'a polite word of thanks' when it was over. John was tricky – 'perhaps the worst client I ever had to handle' – because he was a terrible fidget. '"Could you please keep your head still, John?" I'd ask, again and again, as patiently as I could. John would briefly acknowledge me, nodding his head as if he'd understood, but the mere fact of nodding demonstrated he hadn't quite got the message.'

Latterly, John would have his haircuts supervised by Yoko Ono:

Frankly, I couldn't grasp half of what Yoko was going on about, but then again, neither could John. In fact, he was becoming increasingly exasperated by her:

'I don't understand what you're trying to say!' he'd complain, shaking his head dangerously. 'I just don't understand!'

'You don't understand because you don't listen,' Yoko would answer playfully, as if he were a stuck-up little boy – which perhaps he was. Amazingly, this only seemed to turn him on more. John was normally the dominant character in any conversation. And yet here, for the first time, I saw this fierce little lady completely in control of their dialogue.

Being the only part of the Beatles' bodies that could be chopped off and removed without causing alarm, their hair was particularly coveted by fans and collectors. In 1966 a German barber, Klaus Baruch, gave John a short-back-and-sides in preparation for his role as a soldier in the film *How I Won the War*. It made headlines around the world: 'LENNON ACTS WITHOUT LOCKS'. 'BEATLE SEVERS MOP TOP'. 'SHORN LENNON: TOP CHOPPED'. So determined was Brian Epstein to prevent the precious hair clippings falling into the hands of souvenir-hunters that he deputed Neil Aspinall to supervise its incineration.

But it now appears that Mr Baruch retained a few locks as a nest-egg for his retirement. Fifty years on, a four-inch lock of Lennon's hair from this trim was placed on sale by Heritage Auctions of Dallas. 'This is the largest lock of John Lennon's hair ever offered at auction,' said the auctioneer, Gary Shrum. It eventually sold to Paul Fraser from Bristol for £35,000, three times the estimate. At the time of writing, Paul Fraser Collectibles is offering 'a guaranteed genuine half-inch strand of John Lennon's hair – exceptional provenance – acquired from barber Klaus Baruck in Berlin' for £399. The brochure adds that this single strand of hair is 'presented on a display sheet ready for framing'.

54.

Dear Ringo,

There is only one Ringo, and there is only one Winifred Henderson.

Isn't it about time that the one and only Ringo and the one and only Winifred Henderson got two — gether at last!

Love and stuff,

Winifred H.

Bayonne, New Jersey

Dear Ringo,

what did you do before you were a Beatle? were you an ordinary person?

love,

Janet L.

Miami, Florida

Dear Ringo,

You have the nicest smile of all the Beatles. Are those your real teeth?

I hope you don't mind my asking.

Sincerely,

Evelyn M.

Salt Lake City, Utah

Dear Ringo:

I named my new dog after you, and he is the proudest dog on the block.

with love,

Susie P.

Winston-Salem

North Carolina

Dear Ringo,

YOU ARE THE HANDSOMEST MAN IN THE WORLD, EXCEPT FOR MY
FATHER.

MY FATHER IS HANDSOME TOO, IN AN OLD WAY.

Love,

Norma A.

Denver, Colorado

55.

These days, Ringo is a byword for good luck, but his early life was riddled with misfortune. The Starkey house was a two-up, two-down in a very rough part of the Dingle, where they are traditionally rumoured to 'play rag-tag with hatchets'. The house had no bathroom, and an outside toilet. His father left home when Ringo was three years old. 'We were working-class, and in Liverpool when your dad left you suddenly became lower working-class.' At school he was placed in the C-stream, where he was regarded as unexceptional – or, to quote one of his reports, 'honest, cheerful, and willing and quite capable of making a satisfactory employee'. But he was in hospital for two years from the age of thirteen, so his education effectively stopped then: had it not been for the efforts of the daughter of a neighbour who taught him to read, he would have been functionally illiterate.

Aged fifteen, young Ritchie Starkey went straight from hospital to a job as a messenger with British Railways, but after six weeks he was sacked for failing his medical. For a while he worked as a waiter, and then his step-father found him a job as an apprentice pipe-fitter: 'I started to be an engineer but I banged my thumb the first day. I became a drummer because it was the only thing I could do.' He lacked both vanity and any trace of self-pity. Despite all his misfortunes, he refused to believe that as soon as you're born, they make you feel small. In a radio interview in 1966, Brian Matthew breezily asked him: 'Would you say on the whole that you've had a fairly easy life?'

> RINGO: I've had an easy life. Never been hungry. Never been cold. Y'know, I've had a good life. I wouldn't change any of it. This bit's much better, but still it wouldn't bother me to go through all the rest again.
>
> MATTHEW: Are you from a big family or a small family?

RINGO: I'm the only child.

MATTHEW: Oh, well, there you go.

RINGO: People say, 'Oh, you're an only child, you must've been spoilt,'
but my mother went out to work and she was the only one getting
any money, so I suppose that's why I only asked for little things, not
big things. They may have seemed big but they weren't really.

It was always rumoured that Pete Best was sacked from the Beatles because
the others were jealous of his good looks. If so, what someone once referred
to as a bus-driver's face was Ringo's passport to fame and fortune.

He was not the best-looking or most charismatic or most musical or
most interesting of the Beatles, but somehow this made him an essential
part of the group's mix. He was the Horatio figure, the Dr Watson, the
Tommy Atkins who in his plodding, selfless, reliable way may be a few
steps behind the rest, but is always there to stop them going over the edge.

'Why don't you ever say anything except "I'm the drummer"?' John asked
him irritably, in front of a journalist, as they were touring Britain in 1963.
'I don't like talking. It's how I'm built,' replied Ringo. '. . . I don't mind
talking or smiling, it's just I don't do it very much. I haven't got a smiling
face or a talking mouth.'

In narrative terms, he serves as a workhorse among prize ponies, the
honest-to-goodness, plain-speaking character to whom others can relate.
Of the four Beatles, he is the only one who could be described as a bloke.
'Ringo is not the world's most inventive drummer,' observed George
Melly, 'but he IS lovably plain, a bit "thick" as a public persona, and decidedly ordinary in his tastes. He acts as a bridge, a reassuring proof that
the Beatles bear some relation to ordinary people.'

In May 1963, when the Beatles were just taking off, Ringo went into
their fan club's office and asked the secretary, Freda Kelly, if she would deal
with his fan mail. Freda was reluctant: 'Get your mum and dad to do it.
All the other parents do,' she said.

'Me mum doesn't know what to put,' Ringo replied, adding, 'Anyway,
I don't get a lot.'

Feeling sorry for him, Freda said, 'All right, bring it in, but just this once.'
She remembers him arriving the next day 'with one of those small poly bags
that tights come in – that was all his mail, stuffed inside. Paul got two feet of
mail, but Ritchie only had that small sack, with ten letters in it.'

To this day, jokes are made about his lowly position as the runt of the Beatles litter. In an episode of the cartoon *Family Guy*, three girls sit in a bedroom talking about their favourite Beatle. The first two declare their love for Paul and for John. 'You know what? I'm in love with Ringo!' says the third girl. At this point, Ringo appears outside the bedroom window, at the top of a ladder, and asks her to repeat what she said. The girl suddenly becomes hesitant: 'I don't know what I said.' But Ringo is not to be deflected. 'It sounded like you said you were in love with Ringo,' he says.

'Um. Um. I don't think so.'

'I'm pretty sure you said "I'm in love with Ringo." Well, here I am!'

He opens his arms wide and beams.

At this point the first girl asks, hopefully, 'Are John and Paul out there?' Ringo replies, 'No, just Ringo!' and all three girls look downcast.

But over the years Ringo has had the last laugh. In America, more so than in Britain, he gathered a sizeable following of his own fans. Characteristics that appeared run-of-the-mill in Britain seemed to strike Americans as remarkable, even exotic. Phil Spector wrote and produced a song, 'Ringo, I Love You', for the singer Bonnie Jo Mason,* who sang of dreaming about Ringo holding her hand, and running her fingers through his hair. A single by the Young World Singers, released during the 1964 US presidential elections, was called 'Ringo for President'.† As Brian Epstein once noted: 'America discovered Ringo.'

And Ringo continues to pop up in the intimate reminiscences of models, singers and actresses. A few years ago I was browsing through the memoirs of Christine Keeler‡ when I came across this passage in her chapter 'Lust and Marriage':

> I kept going to the Ad Lib and one night ended up dancing with Ringo Starr. The Fab Four were the biggest thing in the world and we were great curiosities on the dance floor. Which is why we ended up in bed

---

* A pseudonym disguising the sixteen-year-old Cheryl LaPiere: Spector favoured all-American names for his female singers. LaPiere was shortly to become more famous as Cher. 'Ringo, I Love You' failed to chart. Some attributed its failure to Cher's deep voice: apparently, many radio producers feared that the person yearning to hold Ringo tight was a man.

† In Britain, a raucous cover version by Rolf Harris failed to chart.

‡ The call girl whose affair with the Secretary of State for War John Profumo was said to have led to the downfall of the Conservative government in 1964.

together the next morning, the morning Freddy turned up unexpectedly for a reconciliation. If it had been anyone else but a Beatle I think he might have bashed Ringo about. As it was, he was so taken aback when he saw it was Ringo in bed with me that he did nothing, just stood there gawping. Ringo made a break for it – and broke my banister as he went. He got married for the first time a week later.

In his memoirs, the NEMS director Peter Brown notes that Ringo was the 'last Beatle to settle down with one girl', and furthermore, that 'with his big puppy eyes and self-effacement, he seemed an easy target for every blonde bombshell who could get near to him', among them the glamour model Vicki Hodge.* In the memoirs of Chris O'Dell ('the remarkable story of an ordinary woman who lived the dream of millions'), several pages are devoted to the former Apple employee's affair with Ringo in the early 1970s: 'It was as if two wires suddenly connected, sending an electrical jolt of attraction right through me. In that instant, Ringo wasn't just a friend, he wasn't just a Beatle – he was a man. A very desirable man . . . We comforted each other at a time when we both needed comforting. He was good to me, and always, always kind, and just being with him made me happy. I wanted it to last, but I knew it wouldn't . . .' In 1981 Ringo married the former Bond girl Barbara Bach.

Somehow he possessed the happy knack of turning misfortune to advantage. He had been born left-handed, but his grandmother – his father's mother – had forced him to use his right hand. Such brutal coercion can lead to lifelong problems, but in Ringo's case it meant that he tackled a right-hand drum kit with the thwarted instincts of a left-hander, which gives his drumming the idiosyncratic style that countless Beatles tribute acts still find hard to duplicate.

His drumming was never flash: he was content to let it pass unnoticed, at the service of the song. In all his years as the Beatles' recording engineer, Geoff Emerick found his character dull – 'I honestly don't remember having one memorable conversation with Ringo' – but he was often struck by the galvanising effect his drumming had on the group's creativity: 'It could get incredibly boring and depressing hearing them play the same

* Who also boasted of flings with, in alphabetical order, Prince Andrew, David Bailey, John Bentley, John Bindon, Yul Brynner, Elliott Gould and George Lazenby.

song for nine or ten hours at a stretch, especially if it was getting worse and worse as they got more drugged and went off into tangents. Interestingly, during those long jam sessions Ringo would most often be the one to take them in new directions – he'd get fed up doing the same beat all the time and he'd change it, which sometimes sparked a musical change from one of the others.'

Like many musicians, Graham Nash feels that Ringo's drumming is undervalued: 'Ringo plays a heartbeat, which is a sound I love. It's one of the secrets of great drumming, because, in life, everything starts with a heartbeat. Your mother's heartbeat is the very first thing you hear when you are conceived, and that sets the rhythm for the rest of your life . . . The heartbeat is the most important part of music if you want to connect on a personal level. And it's very subtle . . . He's an incredible drummer, one of the most underrated. And the Beatles were very lucky to get him.'

He was always unassuming. 'Ringo is a lovely boy,' Brian Epstein said to his solicitor, Nat Weiss. 'One of the great assets of him is that even though he's the least talented he's not uptight about it.' This may sound patronising, but it was undoubtedly well-meant: with three competitive songwriters, the group grew increasingly combustible – a fourth might have created an explosion.

Alone of all the Beatles, Ringo possessed no talent for composing. But one day, in a sudden flash of inspiration, the germs of a song entered his head, as if from nowhere. He worked on the song for three hours, and presented it to the other three the next day. After an awkward silence, they felt obliged to point out that it had already been written and recorded by Bob Dylan.

Nor was he much of a vocalist, though the others were happy to maintain a touching tradition of giving him one song to sing per album. During the recording of *Sgt. Pepper*, Emerick watched as Ringo struggled through 'With a Little Help from My Friends'. Appropriately, given that it was a song about friends helping you hit the right notes, John, Paul and George gathered round him, 'silently conducting and cheering him on as he gamely tackled his vocal duties'. But when it came to sustaining the final high note he grew self-conscious, and lost his nerve. 'It's OK, just put your mind to it. You can do it,' said George. 'Just throw yer head back and let 'er rip!' Finally he succeeded, and the others all cheered, toasting him with their

Scotch and Cokes. The next day, as the rest of them added their backing vocals, 'Ringo sat up in the control room . . . beaming like a proud papa.'

He is the personification of the adage 'Dogged as does it.' Against all the odds, he carries on, come what may. Before playing to 10,000 people at the Forum in Montreal in 1964, the Beatles received news of a plot by anti-Semites to kill Ringo. Ringo reacted by pointing to a gap in their logic: 'The one major fault is that I'm not Jewish.' However, the authorities took the threat seriously, and feared that behind his drums onstage he was, quite literally, a sitting target. For his part, Ringo faced the threat with his usual sang-froid, his only concession being to adjust his cymbals to a 45-degree angle, in the hope that they might deflect a bullet. Throughout the concert a plain-clothes policeman sat beside him. Drumming away, Ringo couldn't stop thinking about this bodyguard: 'If someone in the audience has a pop at me, what is this guy going to do? Is he going to catch the bullet?' Before long, he couldn't stop smiling. 'I found this was getting funnier and funnier all the time, and the guy just sat there.'

Ringo is buoyant; no matter what happens, he bobs back up. He is the common man for whom providence keeps coming up roses, the triumphantly untragic hero, raised higher and higher by his flaws. There is a scene in *Help!* in which he escapes from a yacht by diving overboard into the ocean. It was filmed in the Bahamas with a camera mounted on a raft positioned a hundred yards away. Meanwhile, the area was surrounded by nets to keep sharks at bay. Victor Spinetti watched as Ringo kept leaping overboard for take after take, only to be picked up and hoisted back onto the yacht, shivering.

'Oh V-vi-vic,' he said as, once more, the hairdresser dried his hair, 'd-d-do I have to do this a-g-gain?'

'Why?' I asked him. His answer stunned me.

'I c-c-can't swim.'

56.

On page 598 of James Boswell's *Life of Johnson*, an unnamed clergyman puts in the briefest of appearances. Boswell and Dr Johnson are in the middle of an argument about the best sermons in English when 'a Clergyman, whose name I do not recollect' pipes up with a suggestion. Johnson slaps him down – 'They were nothing, Sir . . .' – and the unnamed clergyman is never mentioned again.

One hundred and twenty-five years after Boswell recorded the incident, the essayist Max Beerbohm lamented the way this curt dismissal by Dr Johnson was now all that anyone would ever know of this anonymous clergyman: 'Fragmentary, pale, momentary; almost nothing; glimpsed and gone; as it were, a faint human hand thrust up, never to reappear, from beneath the rolling waters of time . . .'

Jimmie Nicol makes the same sort of fleeting appearance in the story of the Beatles. In the 420 pages of Hunter Davies's pioneering biography of the group he appears nowhere at all, and he pops up just twice in Bob Spitz's 983-page biography, on pages 506 and 507, his Christian name mis-spelled as 'Jimmy'. The Beatles' own vast *Anthology* allots him a single entry, on page 139. In Philip Norman's 400-page *Shout! The True Story of the Beatles*, he merits three passing mentions, all in the same brief paragraph:

> In June they toured Scandinavia, Holland, the Far East and Australasia. Ringo Starr was having his tonsils out and missed three-quarters of the journey; in his place sat Jimmy Nicol, a session drummer small and obscure enough to scotch any rumour of permanent change. Nicol drummed with them until Melbourne, where Ringo rejoined: history from then on relates nothing further on Jimmy Nicol.

Fragmentary, pale, momentary; almost nothing; glimpsed and gone: such is the fate of Jimmie Nicol. Until June 1964, his career had been up and down, but largely down. He had drummed on 'Giddy-Up-a-Ding-Dong' by Colin Hicks & His Cabin Boys,* but it had failed to chart. He then briefly joined Tony Sheridan and the Wreckers, before leaving them to play with Vince Eager and the Quiet Three.† They toured Britain in 1960, on the same bill as Eddie Cochran and Gene Vincent. Cochran took a shine to them and promised to take them back to Los Angeles at the end of the tour; but on 17 April 1960 Cochran was killed when his taxi crashed on the outskirts of Chippenham.‡ Having lost their mentor, Vince Eager and the Quiet Three were forced to stay in Britain, playing a summer season in Great Yarmouth instead of flying out to Los Angeles. Subsequently, after a row over money with their manager/promoter Larry Parnes, Eager and the band broke up, leaving Jimmie once more high and dry.

Going it alone, he formed Jimmie Nicol and the Shubdubs, but their ska version of 'Humpty Dumpty' failed to take off. In early 1964 he drummed on *Beatlemania*, a cut-price album of Beatles cover versions, and then he drummed for Georgie Fame's backing band, the Blue Flames, by night, and worked in a music store during the day.

On the afternoon of 4 June 1964 he was sitting at home in Barnes, south-west London, when the telephone rang. 'Hello, is Jimmie Nicol in please? This is George Martin calling. What are you doing for the next four days? Ringo is ill, and we want you to take his place on the Beatles' tour. Would you mind going to Australia?'

---

* Colin Hicks was the younger brother of Tommy Steele. He had been a cabin boy on a Cunard cruise, returning in autumn 1957 to find his elder brother famous. Colin looked like Tommy, and sounded like him too: he would later ascribe his failure to crack the charts to this insuperable resemblance.

† Vince Eager was born Roy Taylor, but was given a fresh name by his manager, Larry Parnes. Known by some as 'Parnes, Shillings and Pence', Larry Parnes made it a rule to select stage names for his protégés, among them Billy Fury (born Ron Wycherley), Marty Wilde (Reginald Smith), Dickie Pride (Richard Knellar), Lance Fortune (Chris Morris), Johnny Gentle (John Askew), Georgie Fame (Clive Powell) and Tommy Steele (Thomas Hicks). One of the few to mount a successful resistance to Parnes's compulsive name-changing was Joe Brown, who refused to go by the name Parnes had allotted him: Elmer Twitch.

‡ The first policeman on the scene of the crash was a young cadet called Dave Harman. Back at the station, he began strumming on Cochran's Gretsch guitar, which he had rescued from the wreckage, and found he had an aptitude for music. Consequently he left the police force, changed his name to Dave Dee and formed Dave Dee, Dozy, Beaky, Mick and Tich. Between 1965 and 1969 the group spent more weeks in the UK singles chart than the Beatles.

Who would have said no? Martin told Jimmie to come to the EMI studios at 3 p.m., adding, 'The Beatles want to run through some numbers with you.'

Earlier that day the Beatles had been posing for photographs to mark the beginning of their first world tour when Ringo had begun to vomit. Rushed to University College Hospital, he was diagnosed with tonsillitis and pharyngitis. Brian Epstein told the other three that they would need a replacement. George, never the most pliable of the Beatles, put his foot down: 'If Ringo's not part of the group, it's not the Beatles. I don't see why we should do it. I'm not going to go.'

Epstein talked them through the economics of cancelling a world tour, whereupon George, always beady about money, immediately changed his mind. They now had twenty-four hours to find someone who could drum, and who looked, however fleetingly, like a Beatle. As it happened, their first two choices – Raye Du-Val of the Blue Notes and Bobby Graham of Marty Wilde's Wildcats – had prior commitments, but after a friendly phone call from Paul, Georgie Fame agreed to release his new drummer.

At Abbey Road, Jimmie successfully drummed his way through 'I Want to Hold Your Hand', 'She Loves You', 'I Saw Her Standing There', 'This Boy', 'Can't Buy Me Love' and 'Long Tall Sally'.

'Right then, you're in,' said John.

That evening, two women arrived at Jimmie's house: a hairdresser, ready to give him a new Beatle fringe, and a wardrobe lady, carrying Ringo's Beatle suit, which would need to be altered overnight for this taller, burlier new Beatle.

The following day, John, Paul, George and Jimmie flew to Copenhagen, where they were booked into the Royal Hotel, staying in the same suite of rooms President Khrushchev had occupied a fortnight before. Meanwhile, Ringo lay in his bed at University College Hospital, feeling sorry for himself: 'It was very strange because I wasn't well and they'd taken Jimmie Nicol and I thought they didn't love me any more. All that stuff went through my head.'

But Ringo's cloud was Jimmie's silver lining. 'The day before I was a Beatle, not one girl would even look me over. The day after, when I was suited up and riding in the back of a limo with John Lennon and Paul McCartney, they were just dying to get a touch of me.'

His first concert as the Beatles' new drummer got off to a shaky start.

'He was sitting up on this rostrum, just eyeing up all the women,' recalled Paul. 'We'd start "She Loves You" – "1, 2," and nothing. "1, 2," still nothing.' But he soon got the hang of it.

For the next ten days Jimmie was treated as a full member of the Beatles, appearing alongside John, Paul and George at press conferences, grinning broadly and laughing at all their jokes. However, film footage shows that he himself contributed little in the way of banter. Asked in Holland how he feels about his first two shows with the group, he replies, 'Sweat was rolling off my cheeks in buckets.' But the rest of the questions – 'Do you wear something on your head when you go swimming?' 'Do you do it for the money?' are directed at the others, with George struggling to explain the pun within the name of the Beatles through a Dutch interpreter.

In Hong Kong, the Beatles' press officer, Derek Taylor, introduced them as 'John, Paul, George and Jimmie Nicol', at which the first three hooted and whistled in his support.

'Mr Nicol, how do you feel being rushed into this vast world of publicity all at once?' asks a reporter.

'It's a most exciting experience,' replies Jimmie.

'Correct!' chorus John and George.

Even now, photographs of the Beatles taken during their ten-day tour can bring the viewer up with a jolt: it is as if a random tourist has thrust his head through the hole of a 'Picture Yourself as a Beatle' stand at a funfair. He leaps out at you, an intruder in a family album.

On their flight from Hong Kong via Darwin to Sydney, Jimmie sat next to John. The two of them seemed to hit it off, and it even crossed Jimmie's mind that if he played his cards right, he could be in with a chance of replacing Ringo on a permanent basis.

At their first press conference in Sydney, the three regular Beatles batted away questions with their usual chirpy banter.

'What do you expect to find here in Australia?'

'Australians.'

'Have you been practising up your Australian accents?'

'No, cobber, not at all.'

As the conference progressed, the chain-smoking Jimmie was put on the spot.

'How about you, Jimmie? You haven't said anything. How do you feel, Jimmie, being in with the Beatles – a new talent – standing in for Ringo?'

'It's a good experience, man.'

'How is Ringo?'

'Erm, he's much better. He joins them on Sunday.'

'What do you do then?'

'Erm, I go back to London and they're fixing up a band for me, and I do some television.'

The spotlight swung back on John, Paul and George, who were better equipped to answer the more general questions. But, noticing Jimmie's silence, one reporter asked, 'Have you got an agreement that Jimmie mustn't speak?'

'Ask him a question,' said George.

'I can't answer questions that, erm, I don't know anything about.'

'What's the group you play with in England, Jimmie?'

'Well, I've played with a lot of groups in England. Just before I left, I was playing with a rhythm and blues band . . .'

'Does Brian Epstein manage you?'

Jimmie thought for a few seconds. 'Nobody . . . No, he doesn't.'

The other three all laughed at his hesitant response.

'You'd know it if he did!' said John.

Three hundred thousand people packed the streets to welcome John, Paul, George and Jimmie to Adelaide, where they were greeted by the lord mayor and honoured with a civic reception in the town hall. Out on the balcony in front of the cheering crowds, each of the Beatles was introduced in turn. A noticeable drop in temperature came when Jimmie's name was called, and even one or two boos.

At the press conference, one reporter observed: 'There's more people here than came to see the Queen.'

'I should think so,' said George. 'She didn't have any hit records.'

'Jimmie, do you think that Brian Epstein is going to wave his magic wand at you sometime and include you as a fifth Beatle?'

'That I don't know.'

'What's it like being thrust in with the Beatles?'

'It's the end, you know!' By this he meant 'It couldn't be better,' though it now carries a hint of doom.

Throughout his time as a Beatle, Jimmie was in two minds about the man he had been hired to replace: 'Until Ringo joined us in Melbourne, I was praying he would get well. At the same time, I was hoping he would not come back. I was having a ball.' But in public, he remained sunny.

'Jimmie, you've got your final performances tonight and then Ringo arrives tomorrow.'

'Yeah, that's right. I'm looking forward to meeting him.'

'And then it's all over for you. What's going to happen? I hear you may not be going back to England?'

'Not for a little while, no. I fancy going back to Sydney.'

At the end of the Beatles' final concert in Adelaide, Jimmie's very last show as a Beatle, Paul publicly thanked him for standing in as their drummer. He then added that Ringo would be returning the next day, and the audience burst into rapturous applause.

Ringo and Brian Epstein flew from London to Melbourne, arriving just before the others, who were flying from Adelaide. Up to a quarter of a million fans surrounded their hotel, screaming 'We want the Beatles! We want the Beatles!' The police called in the armed services, but they failed to prevent Ringo having clumps of hair pulled from his head as he rushed from his car to the hotel. The other three Beatles were then smuggled into the hotel through the back door, along with Jimmie. Once they were all inside, John, Paul and George were reunited with Ringo, and Ringo and Jimmie shook hands.

The five Beatles were escorted onto the hotel balcony. 'Hello everybody, how are you?' Paul said over a loudspeaker. 'Hello, hey!' added Ringo, and the crowd went wild. Jimmie joined in the waving, but said nothing. Sensing a bit of comical argy-bargy was in order, Ringo grabbed Jimmie's neck and performed a mock-strangling for the camera.

At the press conference in the hotel ballroom, Jimmie sat at one end of the table. He was asked if he would be forming a new band, but no one seemed particularly interested in his reply. 'I don't know yet,' he began. 'Until I get back . . .' Then John started to interrupt and Ringo signalled for Jimmie to be quiet. Feeling unwanted, Jimmie began drumming his fingers on the table. It was to be the last time he ever drummed with the Beatles.

That evening, Brian Epstein issued strict instructions that no one was to leave the hotel: if they wanted to have fun, they must have it in their suite. While John, Paul, George and Ringo had a party, Jimmie disobeyed orders and slipped out onto the streets. Realising he had absconded, Epstein despatched Mal Evans and Derek Taylor to look for him; they eventually tracked him down to a bar.

'You mustn't be on the streets,' said Taylor. 'You can't come into a bar.'

'What are you talking about? I'm not a Beatle any more.'

'You're a Beatle until we put you on the plane.'

Evans and Taylor settled his bill, and marched him back to the hotel.

The next morning, before his former bandmates had woken up, Jimmie was escorted to the airport by Brian Epstein. The atmosphere in their car was, he felt, a little testy. Was Epstein still cross about his behaviour the night before?

There were no fans at the airport, and no press or television. Sitting alone, he was spotted by a journalist who happened to be passing through. The journalist asked him what his plans were.

'Well, I hope to do something that I want to do,' he replied. 'Now there's a possibility that I might be able to do something.'

Before bidding him farewell, Epstein presented him with a gold watch, inscribed 'To Jimmie, with appreciation and gratitude – Brian Epstein and the Beatles'. He also gave him an envelope containing £500 for ten days' work. Jimmie then climbed the steps of the plane, giving a parting wave to a solitary cameraman. As the plane left the runway, he ceased to be a Beatle. He never spoke to any of the Beatles again: 'After my part of the Beatles' tour ended, I went back to England on my own. None of the Beatles ever phoned me after that. No phone call.'

For a few weeks, he felt the warm afterglow of celebrity: one or two people recognised him in the street, and when he went to watch Shirley Bassey performing at the Talk of the Town, she told the audience he was there, and asked him to stand and take a bow.

What next? In his position, which of us would not have felt, deep down, that, with a little bit of luck, all this fame and fortune, fun and adoration, might last forever?

At first, Jimmie seemed to have the wind behind him. Alert to his new-found fame, Pye Records re-released his ska version of 'Humpty Dumpty', slyly crediting it on the label to 'Jimmy Nicol now with the Beatles'. The *Daily Mirror* ran headline 'Jim Plans to Rival Beatles', on top of a story in which he was quoted as saying he wanted to make Brian Epstein wish he'd made him a permanent Beatle. Georgie Fame had kindly kept his place in the Blue Flames open, but, bucked by his new celebrity, Jimmie felt he could do better, and told him he was moving on.

Luck seemed to be on his side. It so happened that, three days after Jimmie's return, Dave Clark, the vocalist-drummer of the Dave Clark Five, was rushed to hospital with a duodenal ulcer, just when his band had been booked to top the bill for a three-week summer season at the Winter Gardens in Blackpool. This time, rather than simply step in for the drummer, Jimmie was invited to replace the entire band with one of his own. Understandably, he felt glad all over. 'I just can't find words to describe how I feel about taking Dave's place,' he told the *Daily Mirror*. 'One week, you're drumming away with the biggest group in the world. Then you hear they want you to take over from the second-biggest group.'

Within two days he had re-formed his earlier group, the Shubdubs, and they were on their way to Blackpool. Needless to say, a few of the supporting acts at the Winter Gardens – among them comedian Dick Emery and trumpeter Eddie Calvert – were put out by the news that Jimmie was now topping the bill. 'Most of the cast were bemused that we had come from nowhere to top the bill, due to Jimmie's sudden leap to fame,' recalled a Shubdub.

It was while Jimmie Nicol was in Blackpool that things began to go wrong. A rush-released follow-up single, 'Husky', failed to make the charts, despite an appearance by the band on *Ready Steady Go!*. Jimmie had a three-single contract with Pye; after the failures of 'Humpty Dumpty' and 'Husky', it was vital that his next single was a hit, or he would be dropped.

For this crucial record, Jimmie chose to revive an old blues song from the 1930s, 'Baby Please Don't Go'. Little did he know that another band, Them, had recorded the very same track for Decca, with two unknowns – Van Morrison and Jimmy Page – on vocals and lead guitar, and a song called 'Gloria' on the B-side.

The version by Them went to number 10; the Shubdubs' vanished without trace. From that point on, Jimmie's life seemed to go into freefall. Pye refused to renew his contract; his wife filed for divorce. Undaunted, he bought himself a brand-new Jaguar, but within a fortnight the police had issued him with court summonses for four motoring offences.

He continued to pay each of the other five Shubdubs £26 a week, even though they were getting little work, and he himself was playing solo in bars for only £10 a week: 'I borrowed everywhere because I believed that one day there would be a turning point.' But the turning point never came. At the beginning of 1965 the Shubdubs' trumpet player decided to call it a day; soon the others followed suit.

Jimmie then formed a seven-piece group – the Sound of Jimmie Nicol – and somehow managed to convince Decca that an upbeat version of 'Oh My Darling Clementine', renamed 'Sweet Clementine', had all the ingredients of a hit. In pursuit of this dream he borrowed £3,000 to equip his band. They made their debut at the Chelmsford Corn Exchange on 3 April 1965, but failed to attract a single review.

Failure craves a reason. Jimmie developed a theory to explain his fall from grace: obviously, Brian Epstein had turned against him, punishing him for his rebellious behaviour on that last night in Australia; Epstein had clearly put pressure on promoters to blacklist him. No one could see the logic behind this theory – why would Epstein do such a thing? – but the scepticism of others served only to fuel Jimmie's burgeoning sense of conspiracy.

In April, George Harrison took the trouble to come to a performance by the Sound of Jimmie Nicol. Between sets, he asked a waiter to take a drink to Jimmie, but Jimmie sent it back. 'I declined the offer,' he explained later. 'I do have my self-respect. I will not be bought by anyone.' By now, he was finding hurt everywhere.

'Sweet Clementine' proved a flop, and Decca dropped Jimmie. He could no longer afford to pay the band. At the same time, he split up with his manager. On 30 April 1965, while the Beatles were filming *Help!*, he was declared bankrupt, his debts of £4,066 far surpassing the £50 in his bank account.

The *Daily Mail* ran the headline 'The Rise and Fall of the Fifth Beatle'. In the accompanying interview, Jimmie complained that 'standing in for Ringo was the worst thing that ever happened to me. Up to then I was feeling quite happy, turning over 30 to 40 pounds a week. I didn't realise that it would change my whole life. Everyone in show business said I couldn't miss. I was the hottest name there was. But after the headlines died, I began dying too. No one wanted to know me any more.' Quizzed about his future, he replied, 'The future? Nothing. There's nothing for me now.'

Ringo Starr read this maudlin interview while he was filming the scene in *Help!* in which he fails to notice someone cutting out the floor around his drum kit, and tumbles through the hole. 'I didn't think he could fail,' he said. 'No one did.' The following week Jimmie was taken to court by his ex-wife, who was seeking £30 in maintenance arrears.

For his part, Paul McCartney tried to lend a helping hand, persuading Peter Asher, brother of Jane, to hire Jimmie for a brief tour with his duet Peter and Gordon. Jimmie then moved to Gothenburg, where he played with a Swedish band, the Spotniks. He eventually went with them to Mexico City, where they were employed as the house band at the Alameda Hotel. Like the Beatles, Jimmie experimented with drugs in the second half of the sixties, though with notably less aplomb: one night he fell off his seat while attempting to play drums for the Spotniks, and was asked to leave.

Teaming up with a musician called Eddie Quinn, he then formed Los Nicolquinn, an awkward combination of their two surnames. Together they performed one of his songs, 'I'm Lost', which came with a gloomy lyric about being 'badly beaten up'. The chorus consisted of the title, sung over and over again.

He remarried in Mexico, but his new wife soon grew tired of his end-less complaints that Brian Epstein had ruined his life. One day he took off his Beatles commemorative watch and smashed it to bits. The marriage was to last barely a year.

And so the decades rolled by. Jimmie made an experimental movie called *Gas*, in which he can be seen drumming his hands on a naked woman; he formed a band called Blue Rain; he recorded a version of 'Jumpin' Jack Flash'. Returning to London in the mid-1970s, he aban-doned music for the building trade. By now he had become too forgotten a figure even to feature in round-ups of forgotten figures.

Philip Norman's book *Shout!*, with its single disobliging reference to Jimmie, was published in 1981. Three years later, the Official Beatles Fan Club of the Netherlands tracked him down and persuaded him to attend their convention in Amsterdam. During a question-and-answer session, Jimmie claimed that the Beatles had forced him to pretend he was Ringo Starr: 'They did not want to admit, even though it was black and white in the press, that there was anybody else playing drums except Ringo.'

Since then, sightings of Jimmie Nicol have been few and far between. In 1988 there were unconfirmed rumours that he had died, but it emerged that they had been put about by Jimmie himself. In 2005 a reporter from the *Daily Mail* caught up with him in London, but he refused to say a word. In Mexico, his former wife continues to believe that he never recov-ered from his ten days as a Beatle: 'Jimmie was affected for his entire life because of his experience with the Beatles. He didn't get to stay with the Beatles. He thinks he failed because of that time with them. He was frus-trated. So maybe his whole life has been frustrating, from being the Fifth Beatle. I think it affected his mental health.'

At a record convention in Utrecht in 2011, a Dutch record collector spotted Jimmie Nicol, or someone who looked like him. 'I went up to the man and said, "Are you Jimmie Nicol? The drummer?" . . . He signed his name – Jimmie Nicol – on a piece of paper, but then headed off without saying a word.'

57.

Eric Clague was a postman. Every day throughout 1964 he used to deliver a sack of fan letters to 20 Forthlin Road, Liverpool, where Paul McCartney was brought up, and where his father still lived.

'At the height of the Beatles' fame, I used to deliver hundreds of cards and letters to the house,' Clague recalled thirty-four years later. 'I remember struggling up the path with them all. But of course they just reminded me of John Lennon and his mother.'

Six years before, Clague had been a junior constable in the Liverpool Police Force. On 15 July 1958, while off-duty, he was driving a Standard Vanguard sedan along Menlove Avenue when a forty-four-year-old woman stepped into his path. He braked, but too late: his car hit the woman, hurling her into the air.

In the kitchen of her home in Menlove Avenue, Mimi Smith and her lodger Michael Fishwick heard a screech of brakes and a thud. They looked at each other, but didn't say a word. In Fishwick's words, they 'just ran like hell'.

An ambulance arrived, but there was nothing to be done. Mimi's younger sister Julia was dead. 'When I ran across the road and saw her, I knew there was no hope,' Mimi remembered.

At that time Eric Clague was a learner driver, and was not supposed to be driving alone. An internal police inquiry was followed by an inquest. Clague insisted he had been driving at 28 mph in a 30 mph zone. Though this was contradicted by an onlooker, the jury chose to believe him. Mimi was furious: 'The coroner seemed to be bending over backwards to help this man who'd killed Julia.' A verdict of misadventure was returned, and Eric Clague was exonerated.

Mimi waved her walking stick at him. 'I got so mad . . . that swine . . . If I could have got my hands on him, I would have killed him.' John's friend Nigel Walley, who was present at the inquest, remembers Mimi screaming 'Murderer!' at Clague, before being hushed by the ushers.

Clague was suspended from duty, and resigned from the police force shortly after. He then took a job as a postman, which is how he came to be making daily deliveries to the Allerton district of the city.

His identity remained a secret until February 1998, when he was tracked down by a reporter from the *Sunday Mirror*. Up until that moment he had told no one of his involvement in the death of Julia Lennon.

'I have been haunted by this for all these years,' Clague told the reporter. 'Hardly a week goes by when I don't think about it. Ever since the Beatles became famous I have been expecting this to come out. To be honest I've been dreading it. It's not something I like to think about. At the time, I thought of sending the family my condolences, but I thought it would only make matters worse. They were very angry and upset by what had happened, naturally so, I suppose. I remembered how the family had blamed me and I wanted to tell them that there was really nothing I could have done. Mrs Lennon just ran straight out in front of me. I just couldn't avoid her. I was not speeding, I swear it. It was just one of those terrible things that happen. I read later how his mother's death had affected John Lennon terribly. I feel desperately sorry about that. But, as I say, it was just an accident.'

After the Beatles became world famous, Clague had read in a newspaper that John's mother had been killed by a car in Menlove Avenue. 'I put two and two together and realised that it was his mum that I had killed. Everything came back to me and I felt absolutely terrible. It had the most awful effect on me. The Beatles were everywhere, especially in Liverpool, and I couldn't get away from it. My postman's round took me to Forthlin Road, where Paul McCartney used to live. At the height of the Beatles' fame I used to deliver hundreds of cards and letters to the house. I remember struggling up the path with them all. But of course they just reminded me of John Lennon and his mother. It is something I have always kept deep inside. I haven't even told my wife and children. I suppose I will have to now.'

58.

The dislikes of Noël Coward were legion, spanning most of the twentieth century and much of the nineteenth. They included Gilbert and Sullivan ('I HATE Gilbert and Sullivan'), Tallulah Bankhead ('a conceited slut'), Marilyn Monroe ('silly bitch'), Arthur Miller ('lacking humour to an alarming degree'), Mrs Alexander Woolcott ('that dreadful blouse she wore made me feel quite ill and she squinted vilely'), Oscar Wilde ('a silly, conceited, inadequate creature'), Neville Chamberlain ('bloody conceited old sod'), the Duke of Windsor ('I've known for years that he had a common mind and liked second-rate people'), Mandy Rice-Davies ('squalid, conceited nasty little slut') and Samuel Beckett ('I would rather play bingo every night for a year than pay a return visit to *Waiting for Godot*'). So it should come as no surprise that 'the Master', as he was known, had little time for the Beatles.

When the Beatles first met Coward, on Saturday, 6 June 1964, it all seemed to go swimmingly. They were introduced by the flamboyant bouffant-haired singer Alma Cogan, famous for her novelty records 'I Can't Tell a Waltz from a Tango' and 'Never Do a Tango with an Eskimo', who had, in turn, first encountered them backstage at the London Palladium. Alma had taken a particular shine to Brian Epstein; there was even talk of marriage. So it was perfectly natural that she should invite Brian and the boys along to the frequent showbiz parties she threw at her swish apartment in Stafford Court, on Kensington High Street.

There the Beatles mixed with mainstream showbiz types, most of them top-of-the-range family entertainers: Danny Kaye, Frankie Vaughan, Ethel Merman, Sammy Davis Jr. Paul, in particular, thrived in such company: 'We were on the cusp of the change-over between showbiz styles . . . They were all a little older than us, probably ten, twelve years older than us, but they were great fun, very confident showbiz people who welcomed us into their circle.'

He regarded these parties, like so much else in his life, as an education: 'I saw a documentary about John Betjeman, who said that when he got out of college there was a country house to which he was invited. And he said, "There I learned to be a guest." And that's what was happening to us at Alma's flat. There we learned to play charades, and we started to do it at our own parties. It was just a little learning curve.'

6 June 1964 was a typically hectic day for Noël Coward. He lunched with Vivien Leigh ('she was fine and gay') at her home, Tickerage Mill in Sussex, and from there he motored to Brighton to pop in on Vivien's former husband, Sir Laurence Olivier, and his new wife Joan Plowright. In the evening it was back to London to dine with Terence Rattigan and Robin Maugham, and then on to Alma Cogan's birthday party, shortly after midnight.

Alma introduced Coward to John and Paul. He found them 'pleasant young men, quite well behaved and with an amusing way of speaking'. But he thought no more about them: his social whirl scarcely allowed time for cogitation. The next day he lunched with 'the dear Queen Mother at Clarence House. She was more enchanting than ever.'

Did he, perhaps, feel threatened by the Beatles? By 1964, Coward was part of the old guard. He was born in 1899, and took his first role on the West End stage back in 1911, at the age of eleven. Though his background was not so very different from the Beatles' – his father was an impoverished piano salesman – he swiftly assimilated into high society, readily adopting the mannerisms and accents of the English upper classes. Small wonder, then, that the

current rise of working-class culture held so little appeal for him. 'I wonder how long this trend of dreariness for dreariness' sake will last?' he sniffed after emerging from John Osborne's play *Look Back in Anger* in 1956.

In his style and outlook, Coward was a far cry from the Beatles. His singing voice was clipped and refined, his songs crisp, witty, knowing and polished. The three words least likely to emerge from his mouth were yeah, yeah and yeah.

Coward made the mistake of relaying his encounter with John and Paul, in derogatory terms, to David Lewin of the *Daily Mail*. It never occurred to him that Lewin would quote him in print complaining that the Beatles were 'totally devoid of talent. There is a great deal of noise. In my day, the young were taught to be seen but not heard – which is no bad thing.'

A year later, on 11 June 1965, Coward was upset to read that there were MBEs for the Beatles in the Queen's Birthday Honours List. 'It is, of course, a tactless and major blunder on the part of the Prime Minister,' he confided to his diary. 'And also I don't think the Queen should have agreed. Some other decoration should have been selected to reward them for their talentless but considerable contributions to the Exchequer.'

A fortnight later, he happened to be in Rome for the wedding of the Italian Princess Torlonia, which he attended with Merle Oberon. Finding himself with time on his hands, he went to the Teatra Adriano, where the Beatles were playing. It seems more than likely that he was the only sixty-six-year-old man in the audience.

It proved to be an unusually raucous and ramshackle concert, possibly owing to the fact that the theatre was half empty, giving the Beatles licence to fool around. While Ringo was singing 'I Wanna Be Your Man' Paul contracted a fit of the giggles and had to leave the stage; George, unamused, scowled in his direction. On his return to the stage Paul's microphone toppled over, which set John laughing, though George remained irritated.

But not half so irritated as Noël Coward, who spent most of his time with his fingers in his ears. 'I had never seen them in the flesh before,' he wrote in his diary. 'The noise was deafening throughout and I couldn't hear a word they sang or a note they played, just one long ear-splitting din.' Nevertheless, he decided to go backstage to see them afterwards, only to be met by Brian Epstein, 'who told me they had gone back to the hotel and would I go there'.

Coward was duly received at the hotel by Epstein and the band's publicist Wendy Hanson, who gave him a drink then scurried off to get them, but returned saying they had been upset by his remarks in the *Daily Mail* a year before.

'I thought this graceless in the extreme, but decided to play it with firmness and dignity,' recalled Coward. 'I was told that the Beatles refused to see me because that ass David Lewin had quoted me saying unflattering things about them.' At this point, either Epstein or Wendy Hanson – the memories of Coward and McCartney differ on this – decided to try them again.

'Brian came and said, "Noël Coward would like to meet you boys,"' remembered Paul. 'We all said, "Oh, fucking hell, no! No, no, no. I'm going to bed." . . . Brian said, "You can't! You just can't!"' Ringo also remembers that it was Epstein who tried to persuade them: 'Brian came to us and said, "Noël Coward is downstairs and he wants to say 'hi'."' Ringo captures the general mood of the group: '"Fuck off!" We wouldn't see him. I mean, "Sod off, Noël."'

But Epstein persisted. Finally Paul, ever the diplomat, agreed to appear as their representative.

'I asked Wendy to go and fetch one of them and she finally reappeared with Paul McCartney,' wrote Coward, 'and I explained gently but firmly that one did *not* pay much attention to the statements of newspaper reporters. The poor boy was quite amiable and I sent messages of congratulation to his colleagues, although the message I would have liked to send them was that they were bad-mannered little shits.'

Coward died in 1973; his private diaries, containing these reminiscences, were not published until 1982. 'He said some not too pleasant things about us . . .' Paul observed to Barry Miles in 1997, 'so fuck him anyway.'

But Coward had reserved even harsher words for the Beatles' fans there that night: 'It was like a mass masturbation orgy, although apparently mild compared with what it usually is. The whole thing is to me an unpleasant phenomenon. Mob hysteria when commercially promoted, or in whatever way promoted, always sickens me. To realise that the majority of the modern adolescent world goes ritualistically mad over those four innocuous, rather silly-looking young men is a disturbing thought. Perhaps we are whirling more swiftly into extinction than we know. Personally I should have liked to take some of those squealing young maniacs and cracked their heads together.'

59.

How else to describe the sound of Coward's 'squealing young maniacs'? In February 1965 Eleanor Bron travelled back with the Beatles from Nassau to Heathrow, having completed the Bahamian shoot for *Help!*: 'I was not prepared for the noise when we walked out onto the tarmac. It was Trafalgar Square with the volume up, beyond imagination – the sound of millions of starlings startled into the air. But the starlings were girls, when I looked back, very very young ones, who covered the airport buildings. Wherever you could see, wherever they could see, wherever they were allowed, and elsewhere, oozing and easing themselves in where they were not; waving banners and arms, pushing and heaving, in great danger I imagine of falling over the edges, wriggling and ceaselessly squealing – a high sighing hopeless poignant sound, unrequitable.'

From a film-maker's point of view, there were some advantages to the screaming. Clive Reed, the first assistant director of *Help!*, was responsible for making sure the Beatles got to the set on time. He found he was able to monitor how far away their car was by the decibels of the screams. 'He'd say, "They're just by the roundabout," or "They're just coming over the bridge,"' remembered the director of photography, David Watkin.

Ronnie Spector and her cousin Nedra were in the audience at Shea Stadium. Afterwards, they were climbing into their companion's Bentley when a group of fans recognised them and assumed that the Beatles were in there too. 'We had just enough time to slam the doors shut before the kids were climbing all over our car, screaming and yelling and bouncing it back and forth . . . There were at least a hundred teenagers screaming outside our car. They were pounding on the windows with their fists, and the ones on top of the car were kicking at the glass with their heels. Being trapped in a car while a mob of kids tries to beat their way in is about the most terrifying thing you can imagine. We looked out the window and all we could see were fists and feet. It reminded me of the little sparrows who kept throwing themselves against the door in that Alfred Hitchcock movie *The Birds*.'

The screaming was uncontrolled, and uncontrollable. In November 1963, two hundred women working at a cotton mill in Accrington went on strike after their foreman banned them from listening to the radio programme *Housewives' Choice*: he was sick of the way they would start to scream the moment a Beatles song came on.

But other fans, less flighty, were able to locate their inner off-switch. The jazz singer George Melly took his little daughter to the Beatles' Christmas show at Hammersmith in 1964. Before it began, he heard two girls behind him discussing whether to scream at the supporting acts, or to save it up for the Beatles. 'They decided to save it, and then, when the Beatles did come on, they quite calculatedly covered their ears and let rip.' The forceful sixty-nine-year-old Lady Christabel Ampthill, escorting a grandchild to the same concert, couldn't contain her irritation with a screamer.

Prodding at her with her umbrella, she bellowed, 'You know, my dear, it's only the plain girls who scream.'

The twelve-year-old Linda Grant couldn't stop screaming, though she didn't know why: 'I didn't understand why you had to scream, but it was what you did. It was mandatory. There was this cult-like element to it.' At the Seattle Center Coliseum in August 1964, the screaming kicked off well before the Beatles appeared. The reporter Larry Kane noted that by the time Jackie DeShannon was launching into her final song, 'The screams were at such a pitch that for the first time on the tour I had to hold my hands over my ears and grasp my tape recorder between my elbows. Actual pain had set in. And it was just beginning . . . I could see abject fear in the eyes of Paul McCartney. Paul always had an upbeat look, but his lips pursed and his brows tightened in signs of obvious tension . . . The combination of noise, onrushing fans, and jellybeans flying randomly about the small stage made me feel that I was in the middle of a psychotic ward with fourteen thousand crazies.'

Dr Bernard Saibel, supervisor of the Washington State Division of Community Services, was stationed in the same audience, an unlikely figure in horn-rimmed spectacles, studiously jotting his psychological observations in a notebook, ready to write a report. 'BEATLEMANIA ANALYZED – Frightening, Says Child Expert' ran the headline in the next day's *Seattle Daily Times*.

The experience of being with 14,000 teenagers to see the Beatles is unbelievable and frightening . . . The hysteria and loss of control go far beyond the impact of the music. Many of those present became frantic, hostile, uncontrolled, screaming, unrecognizable human beings.

. . . The externals are terrifying. Normally recognizable girls behaved as if possessed by some demonic urge, defying in emotional ecstasy the restraints which authorities try to place on them.

. . . The music is loud, primitive, insistent, strongly rhythmic and releases in a disguised way (can it be called sublimation?) the all too tenuously controlled, newly acquired impulses of the teen-ager.

Mix this up with the phenomena of mass hypnosis, contagious hysteria and the blissful feeling of being mixed up in an all embracing, orgiastic experience and every kid can become 'Lord of the Flies' or the Beatles.

Later, in Vancouver, Larry Kane witnessed 'a riot, pure and simple', with girls trampled in the rampage, and medical crews racing around in all directions. 'When the victims were retrieved, they bore the signs of Beatles-induced combat – bloody lips and noses, bruises, welts, abrasions and contusions.' By the end of the evening 135 people had been treated for injuries, including broken limbs and trauma to the head.

Touching down in Houston the following year, the Beatles' plane was surrounded by fans while its engines were still running. Some managed to climb onto the wings, and crawled towards the portholes, waving at those inside. In Dallas, young fans walked from the airport to the Beatles' hotel, many of them in tears. One clutched a bunch of grass in her hands, screaming: 'Ringo! Ringo walked on this grass!'

At their concert the following night, when they started playing 'I Saw Her Standing There' one young fan, Carol Bedford, 'lost control completely. My hands were stretched over my head.' Hoping to calm the crowd down, the Beatles played the slower 'This Boy', but to little effect: 'During this song, a policeman nearly lost his life. He was blocking my view of Ringo and I raced to push him over the balcony.' Fortunately, Carol's boyfriend managed to hold her back.

When the Beatles came to Chicago in August 1965, twelve-year-old Ruby Wax's mother bought tickets for both the afternoon and evening shows at the White Sox Stadium: 'I loved Paul the most – I was ready to give myself to him but first I had to look like Jane Asher. I had to straighten my hair, so I plugged in the iron. No one told me you were supposed to put a cloth between the iron and your hair – most of my crispy hairs dropped out, leaving a couple of burnt knots on my scalp. In the end, four remaining hairs jutted out from beneath my plastic John Lennon hat.'

At the afternoon concert she screamed along with all the other girls, but for the evening concert she hatched a cunning plan to meet the Beatles in person. Having noticed that they exited through a dugout in the stadium, she calculated that it was the route to their dressing room. So she waited until they finished their first song, then nipped into the dugout. Ruby arrived in a shower area, but to her annoyance 'four other fat, sad, hairless, girdled girls' were already there. Together, they found somewhere to hide. 'Before getting into the shower stall, I went around touching the toilet lids because I believed they had Beatles germs on them. Then I joined the fat losers, and we stood in that shower stall for God knows how long – we didn't know how much time went by, as we were panting with excitement.'

After a while, they noticed that the screaming had stopped. Hesitantly, they emerged from the shower and looked around for the Beatles, but they were nowhere to be seen. 'The stadium was empty and dark, there was silence only broken by my mother's voice shouting, "Vooby, vooby ver are you?"'

Newspapers of all stripes employed psychiatrists to come up with theories to explain this curious phenomenon. In Britain, Dr David Holbrook reported to readers of the *New Statesman* that 'The Beatles are a masturbation fantasy, such as a girl presumably has during the onanistic act – the genial smiling young male images, the music like a buzzing of the blood in the head, the rhythm, the cries, the shouted names, the climax.' In the more racy *News of the World*, the newspaper's 'resident psychologist' declared, 'the girls are subconsciously preparing for motherhood. Their frenzied screams are a rehearsal for that moment.' Holbrook felt that the craze for hurling jelly babies at the Beatles was probably symbolic too.

Driving with the Beatles to the premiere of *Help!* in Piccadilly Circus, Victor Spinetti was taken aback by the screaming maelstrom. As their limousine edged through the crowds, John said, 'Push Paul out first! He's the prettiest!' But George's was the first door to open. A girl reached in and tore madly at his hair. Spinetti compared it to a scene from *The Bacchae*: 'Two thousand years ago, its author, Euripides, could tell you all about Beatles fans, only his hero had not just his hair but his arms and legs pulled off.'

In Panama City, Florida, a fundamentalist preacher detected the devil at work. 'What can we learn from the Beatles in the light of the Bible?' he asked his congregants. He suggested that the group had emerged from 'the slums of Liverpool' as 'the apocalyptic minions of Satan'. Furthermore, 'demonic, evil powers' were at work in their music, as described in 1 Timothy 4:1: 'Now the Spirit speaketh expressing, that in the latter times some shall depart from the faith, giving heed to seducing spirits, and doctrines of devils.' He reported that his own daughter had fallen under Satan's spell: 'I watched my Christian daughter dance, frenzied, to Beatle music and rock'n'roll records for five months,' he declared. Her frenzy came to an end only when 'the Lord condemned her in a still voice'.

Even the most sophisticated found themselves succumbing to the general hysteria. In February 1964, George Martin and his wife Judy were sitting with the audience to watch the Beatles' first US concert, in Washington, DC. In the seat next to him, a teenage girl was busy bouncing up and down.

'Aren't they just great?' she said. 'Aren't they just fabulous?'

'Yes,' Martin replied, in his understated way. 'Yes, they certainly are.'

'Do you like them too, sir?'

'Yes, I do rather.' All the while, he thought she must be wondering what this old gentleman was doing there. Then, as the Beatles started to play 'I Want to Hold Your Hand', Martin surprised himself: 'Judy and I just found ourselves standing up and screaming along with the rest. This may sound daft, but it was exactly the same screaming that adults do at football matches . . . it was all too easy to scream, to be swept up in that tremendous current of buoyant happiness and exhilaration.'

60.

At that same Washington concert, a thirteen-year-old girl called Jamie stood close to the stage, clutching a plastic bag containing jellybeans, ready to throw at the Beatles.

Jamie was hanging around in the auditorium after the show when a friendly policeman handed her a crumpled piece of paper he had picked up from the stage: a set list scribbled by John, beginning with 'Roll Over Beethoven' and ending with 'Long Tall Sally'.

Without thinking, Jamie tucked the piece of paper into her plastic bag, where it joined a handful of jellybeans still unthrown. For the next thirty-odd years the bag mouldered in a cupboard, but in 1995 Jamie, now a mother, needed money to help pay for her teenage daughter's education, and remembered the smeary set list. Accordingly, she sent it to auction, where it was bought by a collector for $5,000, though it would now be worth something closer to $40,000.

The price of Beatles relics, even the least noteworthy, continues to soar. In 2016, an unused ticket for that Washington concert fetched $30,000. Even a set of four tiny squares of white bedlinen, each square measuring half a centimetre by half a centimetre, cut from sheets slept in by the Beatles when they stayed at the Whittier Hotel in Detroit on the night of 6 September 1964, sold for £595.

A single red brick mounted on a silver plaque with the inscription 'This is to certify that this is one of 5,000 bricks which Royal Life have salvaged from the original Cavern Club, Mathew Street, Liverpool England' was sold in Los Angeles for £896 in 2019. Item 83 in the same auction was billed as 'an overtime requisition form for G.T.H. Hipson, who was employed at Ringo Starr's Sunny Heights, Weybridge, home, with the last week ending on April 30, 1967. Starr signed the form "R. Starkey" when it was passed for payment on May 4, 1967. Attached is a The Beatles Limited petty cash claim form that is also dated May 4, 1967.' The pleasure afforded by the ownership of this wonderfully obscure item may be hard to pin down, but a collector was nevertheless prepared to pay £384 for it. Other items included a sheet of paper listing John's high-school detention records from 28 October 1954 to 9 January 1955 – 'Reasons for detention include "chatter ad nauseam", "talking repeatedly", "noise" and "eating again"' (£3,125), a June 1967 quarterly telephone bill totalling £12.91, addressed to Mrs M.E. Smith (Aunt Mimi) and signed 'in blue pen' by John (£1,024), and a ticket stub for the 7 December 1963 BBC recording of *Juke Box Jury* on which the Beatles appeared (£437).

These were some of the more affordable lots. An early, smudged draft of John's letter to the Queen announcing the return of his MBE sold for £19,200; a baseball signed by all four Beatles before their last US concert for £56,250; a New Zealand autograph book containing the autographs of all four Beatles as well as Brian Epstein, Jane Asher, Pattie Boyd and Helen Shapiro for £10,240; and a modest 1964 announcement (17×22 inches) declaring that the Blenheim Lounge of Liverpool Airport 'will be closed in the interest of public safety' for a Beatles press conference, signed by the group, sold for £31,250.

Over the years, grander items of Beatles memorabilia have fetched infinitely more: in 2005, Madame Tussauds discovered the wax heads of John, George and Ringo featured on the *Sgt. Pepper* album cover, which had been lost for nearly two decades, and auctioned them for £81,500. In 2018, Sotheby's sold the 'Apple Corps Ltd Dissolution of Contract, signed by all four Beatles' for $118,750. John's copy of the abandoned 'butcher' cover for the album *Yesterday and Today*, featuring the band in butchers' smocks with dismembered dolls, signed by John, Paul and Ringo, sold for £179,200. But these were a snip compared to the $790,000 paid in 2015 for copy 0000001 of *The White Album* ('very clean and fresh with very minor abrasions').

Musical instruments associated with the Beatles are perhaps the most valuable relics of all: at that same sale in 2015, a skin from the drum kit played by Ringo on *The Ed Sullivan Show* sold for $2.1 million, while a guitar played by John fetched $2.4 million. At Bonham's in 1997 a guitar commissioned by Paul but never played by him was sold to a bidder from Tokyo for £126,000.

A group photograph signed by all four Beatles would currently fetch £29,500. By comparison, a colour photograph of all three members of the

Apollo 11 space crew – Neil Armstrong, Buzz Aldrin and Michael Collins – would fetch only £10,000, roughly the same as a signed photograph of John Lennon. A signed photograph of Neil Armstrong, the first man on the moon, might go for £3,000; signed photographs of Winston Churchill and John F. Kennedy are currently on sale for £1,750 and £3,000 respectively. Signed photographs of President Trump go for around $1,000. Paul McCartney's autograph is £2,950, which makes it currently the most valuable of any living person.*

When someone dies, their autograph gains in value, death having limited the stock. It is in the macabre nature of idolatry that an autograph associated with the death of the idol is the most valuable of all: in 2011, the *Double Fantasy* album cover signed by John Lennon for his killer, Mark Chapman, sold at auction for $532,000.

---

* Annoyingly, I have lost the autograph Paul gave me circa 1972. I spotted him and Linda sitting towards the back of the auditorium before a concert at the Victoria Palace theatre by the group Grimms, of which his brother was a member. The only item I could find for him to sign was a photograph of Roxy Music, signed by the group, which I was carrying from the previous day. Paul obligingly wrote 'And me too – Paul McCartney' on the top right-hand corner.

61.

From *Fabulous* magazine, 1965

1. John flew to Hong Kong wearing pyjamas.
2. John is a cat-lover.
3. Ringo spent much of his childhood in a Cheshire hospital.
4. John used to envy his cousin Stanley's Meccano set.
5. Brian Epstein hesitated a long time before taking Ringo as a replacement for Pete Best.
6. George is afraid of flying.
7. George has bought a bow and arrow.
8. Pattie Boyd didn't like the Beatles before she met them on the set of *A Hard Day's Night*.
9. John's father was a singer on pre-war Atlantic liners.
10. Ringo's stepfather, Harry Graves, sings Beatles songs at family parties.
11. The Beatles never visit a barber.
12. Paul washes his hair every day.
13. The Beatles turned down the offer of an appearance on the 1964 Royal Variety Show.
14. Ringo cannot swim, except for brief doggie paddle.
15. Brian Epstein made the Beatles have their hair cut short after he signed them in 1962.
16. They are never photographed with their hair 'up'.
17. Paul ate corn flakes and bacon and eggs at a champagne and caviar luncheon in London. Music publisher Dick James was host.
18. The Beatles didn't want to go to Australia without Ringo when he was ill. But Brian persuaded them to change their minds.

19. Paul has a mini as well as an Aston Martin DB4.

20. George's personal Christmas card was a photograph of him scowling at a cameraman.

21. John never saw an audience properly until Dundee in Scotland. Then he wore contact lenses.

22. An American firm wrote to the Beatles asking if they could market the Beatles' bathwater at a dollar a bottle.

23. They refused the offer.

24. Their road manager, Mal Evans, was once a bouncer at the Liverpool Cavern Club.

25. Neil Aspinall, their other road manager, was given a Jaguar last Christmas – a present from the Beatles.

26. Paul drinks coffee for breakfast. The other three drink tea – even in America.

27. Ringo had his new clothes designed by a woman, Caroline Charles.

28. Jane Asher bought Paul a record player for his Aston Martin.

29. Brian Epstein says, 'America discovered Ringo.'

30. Paul believes he is not a very good guitarist.

31. None of the Beatles drinks Scotch and Coke. They now dilute the occasional spirit with lemonade.

32. John told an American journalist that US fashions were five years behind the UK.

33. The Beatles never really liked jelly babies. They just said they did for a joke.

34. They carry a crate of pop in the trunk of their Austin Princess.

35. Their new chauffeur, Alf Bicknell, used to drive for David Niven and Cary Grant.

36. Burt Lancaster has sent Ringo a set of pistols. They became friends in Hollywood.

37. Burt let them use his home for a showing of *A Shot in the Dark*.

38. Edward G. Robinson and his grandchild twice joined the queue to shake hands with the Beatles at their Hollywood garden party.

39. So did Mrs Dean Martin and her five children.

40. The Beatles have no pockets in their trousers and only two side pockets in their jackets. Paul designed them.

41. All they carry on them in the way of money is a few banknotes.
42. John has bought his mother-in-law a house near his own in Surrey.
43. None of the Beatles wears undershirts.
44. Paul wants to buy a farm.

62.

I was about eleven years old when the Beatles came to power. We lived in Larne in Northern Ireland. One of the pop magazines was very big – twice the size of A4 – and had full-page headshots of the Beatles. I didn't particularly like the shots of John, Ringo and George, but I pinned them up anyway, as I felt it would be disloyal to Paul if I didn't. Paul's face was right next to my head when I was in bed. I cherished it, but then I cut it around the face and sellotaped it onto my teddy bear's face so it could sleep next to me. Before long, it started crumbling to dust.

The Beatles were a game-changer as regards what type of men one fancied. It was simply that they had long hair. Other men in those times all had short hair – moreover, short hair with dandruff. The longer, softer style was just more flattering. I suppose they were girly men.

And that was the point. Recently, someone told me that there is a period of latency when a young girl just daydreams about men but doesn't actually want to have sex with them, and that's why so many boyband members are effeminate. It's a 'moony adolescent' period where you think about romance and idealise the object of your passion, but don't actually want the fantasy spoiled by the reality of going on a date with them.

My father was a doctor, a GP. My dream was that Paul, somehow, would have a minor injury and would have to call at our house for my father to stitch it up. My father would decree it would be best if he went to bed for a couple of days to recover, and since he would be recognised if he went to a hotel, he should stay in our house, in a pop-up hospital ward for one. I would help to nurse him. So then it would only be a matter of time before we got engaged.

The trouble was that Paul didn't come to Northern Ireland very often. But in November 1964 he came and my Aunt Sheila bought tickets for me and my sister and our cousins and we went to the King's Hall in Belfast. The four Beatles came onstage and they held their instruments but any tunes would have been totally drowned out by the mass hysteria of the audience. The hall erupted into screaming and moaning. I just mimed screaming, to fit in. Have you tried screaming? It's not at all easy to do for more than two ten-second bursts. You don't get anywhere and it just wears out your voice. You should try it. We couldn't hear a word anyway, and I don't know if the Beatles were even bothering to play or just miming.

One thing put me off Paul, though. He was pouring with sweat and he wiped the sweat on his clothes. Despite this I genuinely, at the back of my mind, thought I was going to marry him. I felt it in every fibre of my being. It was the reason I didn't work for my A-Levels. I reckoned that anyway I wouldn't have time to go to university or have a career as I would be constantly on tour with Paul. The fact that I was going to marry Paul informed my behaviour in general, but I didn't tell anyone, obviously, because it was a kind of religious thing, a secret between me and God.

The day I turned eighteen I got on a plane to London. I had left school and done my A-Levels. I got bad grades. I knew Paul lived in St John's Wood, so I went to the nearest tube station. I thought it would require some sleuthing, but no, the man behind the counter of the tube station told me the exact address, and, armed with an *A to Z*, I walked towards it.

I had imagined that I would just stand outside his house and sooner or later Paul would come out and, seeing me, invite me in, and then he would fall in love with me and the engagement would be announced within a few days and that would show my parents that I knew best about my life plans. That would put them in their place.

But when I got to the house I was amazed that there were about twenty to thirty other girls there. How come there was a sense of camaraderie when we were all competing for the same prize? I don't know. Perhaps it was part of that moony adolescent thing, and we didn't actually want to set up home with Paul, we were just in love with the idea of it.

The other girls said that Paul wasn't even inside the house anyway. So why were they standing outside crying and moaning and pushing letters through the railings? I think there were railings.

Shortly after that he got married to Linda, and I was genuinely thrown, like one of those men who go to Cirencester Agricultural College to train to run their estate, and then the estate is sold and they are left washed-up without a role in life, fit for purpose but with no ability to demonstrate their fitness. So I had been cheated of my destiny by Linda.

63.

The Rolling Stones were among those attending the premiere of *A Hard Day's Night* on 6 July 1964, in the gracious presence of HRH Princess Margaret and Lord Snowdon.

Outside the London Pavilion, two hundred policemen were restraining 12,000 fans chanting 'Beatles! Beatles! Beatles!' The band had still not grown accustomed to such hullabaloo. Approaching Leicester Square in the back of their chauffeur-driven car, John looked out of the window and asked Brian Epstein, in all innocence, 'Is it a Cup final or something?'

The Beatles' arrival was accompanied by what one onlooker called 'an immense throaty roar', followed by a massed chorus of 'Happy Birthday to You'. Ringo, the oldest Beatle, would be celebrating his twenty-fourth birthday the following day.

Once the Beatles were safely inside the cinema, a clean red carpet was rolled out by the theatre manager and his staff, just in time for the arrival of the royal party. On the day of their wedding, in May 1960, Princess Margaret and Lord Snowdon were possibly the most adored people in Britain, perhaps even the world. At that time, up in Liverpool, the Silver Beetles had just failed their audition to support Billy Fury on his northern tour.

But four years on, the crowds made it quite clear which of them inspired the most adoration. After all the mayhem surrounding the Beatles, the arrival of the royal couple seemed a terrible anti-climax, the cheers for the princess and her husband pitiful compared to those that had greeted the band.

As Princess Margaret and Lord Snowdon walked into the auditorium, a detachment of trumpeters heralded their arrival with a fanfare, and the Metropolitan Police Band launched into a stately rendition of 'God Save the Queen'. The audience stood keenly to attention, and so did the Beatles. But Mick Jagger and the Rolling Stones, sitting in the seats immediately behind the Beatles, refused to budge. Alistair Taylor, Brian Epstein's personal assistant, was appalled. 'Of course, John is seen as the great rebel but he wasn't really like that. In fact, he was the first on his feet when the first bars of the National Anthem were played, and all the other boys stood up. So did everyone else, except for the Rolling Stones. They sat sprawled out as an arrogant gesture of defiance. John was definitely not impressed.' Forty years on, Taylor still found it hard to contain his outrage. 'I suppose they thought they were making a point, but they were guests of the Beatles that night and I believe they should have shown more respect.'

After the film, the Beatles were presented to Princess Margaret. Cynthia Lennon had made a special effort. She was wearing a full-length sleeveless dress in black and beige silk from Fenwicks, along with a black Mary Quant chiffon coat, bordered with black feathers. At John's urging she wore her hair up, to make herself more like Brigitte Bardot. In common with the other Beatles, John wore a dinner jacket and black bow tie. In his first book, *In His Own Write*, published just three months before, he had referred to the royal couple in his punning way as 'Priceless Margarine and Bony Armstrove', but he now seemed cowed in their presence. 'When it came to meeting royalty in the flesh John was as much in awe as the rest of us,' Cynthia was to recall. 'He was so pleased and proud that the princess had come to see the film that his anti-establishment views flew out of the window and he stood red-faced as she spoke to him.'

'How are you coping with all the adulation?' asked the princess. Cynthia was unimpressed by such a drab question, and found the princess's conversation 'clipped and superficial'. Attempting to draw his wife in, John said, 'Ma'am, this is my wife Cynthia,' but the princess offered her only the most cursory of glances. 'Oh, how nice.'

The reception at the Dorchester was attended by the princess and her husband, though they were due to leave before dinner for another appointment. Brian Jones and Keith Richards of the Rolling Stones had not been invited, but had somehow got in, provocatively underdressed in turtleneck shirts. 'Isn't this the greatest party crash of all time?' smirked Jones. The night before, they had appeared on *Juke Box Jury*: the morning's newspapers described them as 'rude', 'anthropoid', 'boorish' and 'charmless'.

The party was an uneasy mix of the old and the new, the young and the old. As a creaky dance orchestra struggled through a selection of tunes from the top 10, an elderly woman in a ballgown buttonholed John.

'You're simply darling,' she said.

'Can't say the same for you, love,' he replied.

Meanwhile, Princess Margaret and Lord Snowdon were clearly enjoying themselves, and stayed much later than planned. This, in turn, meant that dinner had to be postponed. Unaware of the protocol, George Harrison approached the film's producer, Walter Shenson, and asked, 'When do we eat?' Shenson told him that dinner could not be served until the departure of the royal couple. At this, George strode across to the princess and said bluntly, 'Ma'am, we're starved, and Walter says we can't eat until you leave.'

'Come on, Tony. We're in the way,' replied the princess, taking orders from the youngest of the Beatles. This might be seen as a pivotal occasion in British social life, the moment a princess scuttled away on the orders of a Beatle; for the first time, but not the last, royalty deferred to celebrity.

As the reception drew to an end, everyone grew more relaxed. Brian Jones and Keith Richards were surrounded by begowned and bejewelled autograph-hunters, and Jones was happily signing away. At this point, the orchestra struck up the National Anthem. True to form, Jones ignored it, and carried on signing. 'Stop it! Stop it!' hissed an elderly woman in a diamond necklace. In reply, Jones stopped signing, picked up a woman's scarf from a nearby table, wrapped it around his neck and, in time to the slow drudge of the music, executed a pastiche of a burlesque dancer.

When the orchestra reached the final chorus, John Lennon found his anti-establishment attitudes boosted by champagne and shrieked 'Go-o-d save the Cream!' On the way out, he spotted the old woman in the ballgown to whom he had been so terse earlier in the evening. 'Good night, Mrs Haitch! We'll dance again some Somerset Maugham!' he yelled, punningly. Nothing like this had ever happened at the Dorchester before; the times they were a-changin'.

64.

Afterwards, John, Paul and Ringo went with Brian and Keith to the Ad Lib Club, just around the corner in Leicester Place. Paul left comparatively early – they had to mime on the next day's *Top of the Pops* – and Ringo, now the Birthday Boy, left shortly after 4 a.m., having stayed up to look at the film's reviews in the early editions of the newspapers: 'I got all the papers at four in the morning, drunk out of my mind trying to read them. But I couldn't focus.' This was a shame, as the reviews were full of superlatives, with the *Daily Mail* comparing them to the Marx Brothers.

John was clearly in for the long haul, draining Scotch and Cokes one after the other. 'His hand gripped his glass as if he were trying to crush it,' noted one observer. 'His eyes seemed hard, sharp and unsmiling. His upper lip sometimes curled as he talked, displaying hard white teeth.'

The more the night wore on, the fonder John grew of the two Rolling Stones present. 'I love you. I loved you the first time I heard you,' he said. But, even when drunk, he never plunged so deeply into sentimentality that he was unable to haul himself back out. 'But there's something wrong with you, isn't there? There's one of you in the group that isn't as good as the others. Find out who he is and get rid of 'im.'

The talk turned to music: Jones and Richards argued that the Stones played genuine rhythm and blues, while the Beatles just played commercial pop. This was a sore spot for John; he abruptly changed the subject.

First, he looked at Jones. 'Your hair makes it,' he said. Then he looked at Richards. 'Your hair makes it,' he said. Then he turned to absent friends. 'But Mick Jagger. You know as well as I do that his hair doesn't make it.'

And so it went on.

John said, 'In another year, I'll have me money and I'll be out of it.'

'In another year,' said Brian, 'we'll be there.'

John took a philosophic drag on his cigarette. 'Yeah,' he said, 'but what's *there*?'

The Beatles and the Rolling Stones were always being treated as rivals. They had first met just over a year before, at the Station Hotel in Richmond, Surrey. At that point the Beatles were far ahead, topping the bill on a nationwide tour, while the Stones were still playing in pubs.

In the first week of May 1963 George Harrison was judging a talent contest at the Liverpool Philharmonic Hall, and found himself on a panel with Dick Rowe, who was already widely known as The Man Who Turned Down the Beatles. Rowe told George that he was still kicking himself for that mistake. Graciously, George replied that he had probably been right, as they'd done a terrible audition.

Sensing Rowe's disappointment with the talent on show at the Philharmonic, George tipped him off about a great new group who played every Sunday in Richmond. Within days, Rowe had offered them a contract. Ever competitive, the Beatles were distressed that the Stones had negotiated a better deal with Decca than they themselves had with EMI. They soon began to worry that the underdog was becoming the overdog. From then on, there was always an edge to their friendship. One day, John and Paul were emerging from Dick James's* office on Charing Cross Road when they heard Mick and Keith shouting at them from a passing taxi. The two Beatles cadged a lift, and as the four of them travelled along, Mick said, 'We're recording. Got any songs?' John and Paul thought of one straight away. 'How about Ringo's song? You could do it as a single.' And so, from this chance encounter, the Rolling Stones gained their first top 20 single, 'I Wanna Be Your Man'.

In some ways, John helped to fuel his own fears that the Stones were a more authentic version of the Beatles, the Beatles freed from Sunday best. Mick Jagger sang 'wanna', while John sang 'want to'; the Beatles were happy to settle for holding hands; the Stones aimed to go the whole hog. The rough, bluesy insolence of the Stones reminded John of the Beatles before they had been buffed and polished by Brian Epstein. In hip circles it

---

* Dick James (1920–86), music publisher of the Beatles. Originally a singer with Henry Hall's Dance Band, his most celebrated performance was the theme to the popular TV series *Robin Hood*, with its rousing chorus, 'Raarbin Hood, Raarbin Hood, riding through the glen, Raarbin Hood, Raarbin Hood, with his band of men . . .' James was known for his stinginess. For Christmas 1964 he gave the Beatles a bottle of Brut aftershave each.

had become fashionable to regard the Beatles as soft, pretty and artificial, and the Stones as tough, bullish and real.

John was increasingly riled by the comparison. 'John went bananas about all the publicity the Stones were getting for being rough,' recalled Bill Harry, editor of *Mersey Beat*. 'He knew the Stones were middle-class boys from the Home Counties, not leather-jacketed Teds at all. While the Beatles had been swearing and whoring it in Hamburg, they had been attending trendy schools. John hated it. He really hated it.'

Before long, music fans felt they had to support either the Beatles or the Stones, as though they were rival football teams, or warring countries. It made men feel more manly to prefer the Stones, and women more raunchy. Somehow, the Beatles' most vociferous supporters only made matters worse. 'This horrible lot are not quite what they seem,' Maureen Cleave wrote of the Stones in the *Evening Standard* in March 1964. '. . . They've done terrible things to the music scene, set it back, I would say, about eight years.' But some of her complaints against the Stones seemed closer to compliments: 'Just when we'd got our pop singers looking neat and tidy and, above all, *cheerful*, along come the Rolling Stones, looking almost like what we used to call beatniks . . . They've wrecked the image of the pop singer of the sixties.'

A couple of days later, in a bold headline, *Melody Maker* asked, 'WOULD YOU LET YOUR SISTER GO WITH A ROLLING STONE?' To which Maureen Cleave replied, a week later: 'But would you let your daughter marry one? Parents do not like the Rolling Stones. They do not want their sons to grow up like them; they do not want their daughters to marry them.'

She went on to associate the Beatles with the very same mores John had striven so hard to reject: 'Never have the middle-class virtues of neatness, obedience and punctuality been so conspicuously lacking as they are in The Rolling Stones. The Rolling Stones are not the people you build empires with: they are not the people who always remember to wash their hands before lunch.'

The divide continues to this day. Men and women now in their seventies and eighties proudly declare, 'Actually, I always preferred the Rolling Stones,' as though it were proof of their raw integrity.

John's fixation with the Rolling Stones lasted for years to come, not least because people like him tended to prefer groups like them. At the same time, he resented them as copycats who stole ideas from the Beatles. After the Beatles released 'Yesterday', the Stones recorded 'As Tears Go By'. Hearing from their shared engineer, Glyn Johns, that one of the Beatles' new songs was to be called 'Let it Be', the Stones decided to call their new album *Let it Bleed*, and so forth. Shortly before the Beatles split up, John was still complaining of their plagiarism: 'I would just like to list what we did and what the Stones did two months after on every fucking album and every fucking thing we did. And Mick does exactly the same. He imitates us. You know, *Satanic Majesties* is *Pepper!*' "We Love You", man, it's fucking bullshit! That's "All You Need is Love".'

Like rival Elizabethan households, Britain's two most illustrious groups operated a delicate rivalry, its wheels oiled by deference from the upstart towards the grandee. From George Harrison's perspective, 'Mick Jagger was always lurking around in the background, trying to find out what was happening. Mick never wanted to miss out on what the Fabs were doing.'

Jagger lived in Marylebone Road, a walk across Regent's Park from Paul's house in St John's Wood. They would meet from time to time, but it was Jagger who would always come to McCartney, not vice versa. 'I don't remember him coming to us,' Marianne Faithfull, Jagger's then girlfriend, says of Paul. 'Mick always had to come to his house, because he was Paul McCartney, and you went to him. Paul never came to us. I was always very curious about how Mick saw him, how Mick felt about him. It was always fun to watch. There was always rivalry there. Not from Paul, none at all. Paul was oblivious, but there was something from Mick. It was good fun. It was like watching a game on the television.'

In some ways, the two bands were mirror images of one another: Paul and Mick the savvy front men, always with an eye on the prize; Ringo and Charlie the older, unflappable blokes on drums; John and Keith the rogues, the hard men, the undeceived; and Brian and George the otherworldly ones, nursing resentment at their exclusion by the top dogs.

Beneath his brittle façade, John was scared by life. Nicky Haslam, who knew him and liked him, describes him as 'a wuss'. Sensing this vulnerability, Keith Richards would goad him. Like many bullies, John dreaded being bullied. He would try to get his dig in first, but unlike him, Richards was impregnable. On one occasion John told Keith that his guitar solo in the middle of 'It's All Over Now' was 'crap'. Keith remained unruffled:

'Maybe he got out the wrong side of the bed that day. OK, it certainly could have been better. But you disarmed the man. "Yeah, it wasn't one of my best, John. Sorry. Sorry it jars, old boy. You can play it any fucking way you like."'

In the early days, Richards enjoyed telling John that he wore his guitar too high. 'Got your fucking guitar under your fucking chin, for Christ's sake. It ain't a violin.' 'Try a longer strap, John. The longer the strap, the better you play.' 'No wonder you don't swing, you know? No wonder you only rock, no wonder you can't roll.' As time went by, he would note with satisfaction the furtive but steady descent of John's strap.

65.

We last encountered sixteen-year-old Pamela Miller* in 1964, when she saw the Beatles at the Hollywood Bowl. In her diary, she wondered if fate had brought Paul to America 'for I am here too'. But within a year she had met a boy called Bob, who converted her to the Rolling Stones. When Pamela told her old Beatle friends Kathy and Stevie of her new passion, they reacted badly:

5—9—65

Dear Pam, I suppose you are wondering why Linda, Stevie and I acted the way we did after school yesterday. The main reason is because you are a phony person. You better watch out before you become completely friendless. Why on earth could you even start to like Mick over Paul? . . . Pam, you try to be strange, but you aren't. You are just being a loser. Nobody likes you when you act the way you do . . . You were always so enthusiastic about the Beatles and now you're a Rolling Stones fan. I don't see how you could pick them over the Beatles unless . . . you were being a phony all that time. The Stones are dirty and sloppy and they repugnate me. When I think back to how you used to sign your name 'Paul n Pam', I can't believe you're the same girl. I don't hate you, but frankly, I don't like you much.

Kathy 'n' Stevie

---

* From this point on she would style herself Pamela, not Pam. Her tastes broadened still further: her future conquests were to include, in alphabetical order, Woody Allen, Chris Hillman, Mick Jagger, Waylon Jennings, Don Johnson, Keith Moon, Jim Morrison, Jimmy Page, Gram Parsons and Noel Redding. Under her married name, Pamela Des Barres, she wrote two entertaining memoirs, *I'm With the Band: Confessions of a Groupie* (1987), from which this letter is taken, and *Take Another Little Piece of My Heart: A Groupie Grows Up* (1992).

66.

The greater their success, the more the Beatles fell prey to chancers and charlatans.

Six months older than John Lennon, Jeffrey Archer arrived in Oxford in October 1963, having enrolled on a one-year course for a diploma from the Oxford Department of Education. In later years he was happy to be described as a graduate of Oxford University, though his qualifications for enrolment consisted only of three O-Levels and a diploma from the International Federation of Physical Culture, a bodybuilding club run from an office block in Chancery Lane.

By now, he had embarked on a lifelong career in self-promotion. On his arrival at the offices of the Oxford student magazine *Cherwell*, he announced that, with its aid, he would raise £500,000 for Oxfam. 'It will be the biggest story you've ever had. But I need your help.'

The editor of *Cherwell* arranged for Archer to meet the universities correspondent of the *Daily Mail*. Over a drink at the Union, Archer ran through his plan, and asked if the *Daily Mail* would back it. 'Very unlikely,' came the reply.

'Would it help if I managed to bring in the Beatles?' added Archer.

According to Archer, he then telegrammed Brian Epstein 'and asked for an interview, and signed it on behalf of eight thousand students at Oxford, having of course had the blessing of the Vice-Chancellor and the Proctors'.

Epstein was wary of allowing the Beatles to give their blessing to this sort of charitable fund-raising, believing it would make it harder to refuse anyone else. Though they had received no reply from him, *Cherwell* ran a front-page headline, 'A Million Pound Beatle Drive', which the national press duly covered. Archer then elbowed his way backstage at a Beatles concert, and persuaded them to pose for a photo putting money into collection tins while they held a poster saying 'WANTED £1,000,000'.

On seeing the photograph, Epstein was livid. 'He was absolutely spitting blood about it,' recalled Pat Davidson, Oxfam's press officer. 'He didn't want to speak to anyone from Oxfam. He was furious.'

At this point, Archer explained to Epstein that it might gravely damage the Beatles' reputation if they withdrew from the project. At the same time, he promised Epstein that he would arrange an agreeable lunch for the Beatles to meet the new university chancellor, the former prime minister Harold Macmillan. Impressed by the idea of such a get-together, Epstein was, however reluctantly, persuaded. 'It's not clear, however, that Archer had actually booked Macmillan when he made the promise to Epstein,' writes Archer's canny biographer Michael Crick. 'But he was certainly confident that he could.'

Such is the power of PR, or myth, or both, that many people continue to believe that, thanks to Jeffrey Archer, the Beatles once had lunch with Harold Macmillan. But such a meeting never took place. Archer claimed to have arranged this lunch in late February 1964, but when he rang to confirm, he discovered that they were in Florida, and all set to meet Cassius Clay. So Macmillan had lunch alone with Jeffrey Archer, gloomily

complaining that, without the Beatles, the event was like '*Hamlet* without the ghost'. Or the ghost without Hamlet, he might more accurately have said.

On the Beatles' return, Archer fixed a date for them to be photographed at Oxford University alongside their autographed poster. This time it was Harold Macmillan who cried off. But on 5 March 1964, John, Paul, George and Ringo dined at Brasenose College. The dean remembered John being 'asleep most of the time' and Ringo 'monosyllabic', but on the other hand George and Paul were full of beans. In fact, the dean considered Paul so 'quick and intelligent that he could easily have been an Oxford undergraduate'. Over dinner, George turned his nose up at the smoked salmon, and asked a waiter, 'Have you any jam butties?' 'I'll trade you an autograph for a jam butty,' replied the waiter, and the deal was done.

After dinner, Sheridan Morley, a student at Merton College,* found himself standing next to Ringo Starr in the Brasenose urinals. 'He asked if I knew this Jeffrey Archer bloke. I said everyone in Oxford was trying to work out who he was. Ringo said: "He strikes me as a nice enough fella, but he's the kind of bloke who would bottle your piss and sell it."'

---

* Later a theatre critic.

67.

As 1963 drew to a close, the *Evening Standard* concluded, '1963 has been the Beatles' year. An examination of the heart of the nation at this moment would reveal the name Beatles engraved upon it.' By now, politicians of all parties were recognising the importance of mentioning the Beatles. It proved they were modern, democratic and on-the-ball. In February 1964, while the Beatles were away on their first US tour, the Conservative prime minister Sir Alec Douglas-Home told the annual conference of the Young Conservatives that they were 'our best exports'. He praised their 'useful contribution to the balance of payments', adding, 'If any country is in deficit with us I only have to say the Beatles are coming . . . Let me tell you why they have had a success in the United States – it is because they are a band of very natural, very funny, young men.'

Soon politicians were vying with each other to garland the Beatles with superlatives. As the general election loomed, Conservative parliamentary candidates were advised to drop the Beatles into their speeches as often as possible. It was almost as if their name had become a spell, with magical powers to transform the old into the young, and the fuddy-duddy into the with-it.

The Labour Party leader, Harold Wilson, was not to be outdone. A crusader for the modern, the classless and the go-ahead, he pooh-poohed Douglas-Home's elderly, aristocratic attempts to appear young and trendy, poking fun at 'these apostles of a bygone age trying to pretend they are with-it by claiming the Beatles as a Tory secret weapon'. Wilson insisted that the Conservative government 'would not hesitate, if there were votes in it, to appoint Paul and George, Ringo and John, collectively to Washington to run the embassy'.

Knowing that the Beatles would be receiving the Variety Club 'Show Business Personalities of 1963' award, Wilson telephoned Sir Joseph Lock-

wood, the chairman of EMI, to suggest that 'as a fellow Merseysider', he would be the ideal person to make the presentation.

And so it happened that, on 19 March 1964, at a packed luncheon at the Dorchester Hotel, the leader of the opposition delivered a speech in praise of the Beatles.

This is a non-political occasion so I'll stay non-political. Unless I'm tempted. I said that yesterday, and I was. But there were attempts recently by a certain leader of a certain party – and wild horses wouldn't drag his name from me – to involve our friends the Beatles in politics. And all I could say, with great sadness as a Merseyside Member of Parliament, which I am, was that whatever other arguments there may be, I must ask, is nothing sacred, when this sort of thing can happen? So to keep out of politics, I just repeat to you what the *Times* musical correspondent said referring to this music as distinctly indigenous in character, most imaginative and inventive examples, and I'm sure the *Times* music correspondent spoke for all of us when he said of our friends the Beatles that harmonically it is one of their most intriguing, with its 'chains of pandiatonic clusters' (laughter).

Wilson then bustled about with a proprietorial air as the Beatles came up for their awards.

WILSON: One at a time! There's yours! And there's yours!

GEORGE: Ladies and gentlemen, Mr Barker, Mr Dobson (laughter), and the press, I'd just like to say it's very nice indeed, especially to get one each, because we usually have a bit of trouble cutting them in four.

WILSON: (keen to nose in, and to show he knows which Beatle was which) And now Paul.

PAUL: Thank you very much for giving us this silver heart. But I still think you should have given one to good old Mr Wilson.

WILSON: Ringo . . .

RINGO: Anyone who knows us knows that I'm the one who never speaks, so I'd just like to say thanks a lot.

JOHN: I'd just like to say the same as the others – thanks for the Purple Hearts.

RINGO: Silver! Silver!

JOHN: Sorry about that, Harold! We'd like to sincerely thank you all, and we've got to go now because the fella on the film wants us and he says it's costing him a fortune.

Some weeks later, Edward Heath, recently promoted to President of the Board of Trade, joked that the Beatles were now making so much money that they were 'propping up the entire national economy'.

Wilson's Labour Party entered the October 1964 general election under the self-consciously 'pop' campaign slogan 'Let's Go with Labour'. On polling day the Beatles were filmed for the TV news programme *North-East Newsview* sitting around a table in a hotel in Stockton-on-Tees, smoking cigarettes and pouring themselves tea from a silver pot. They were, as usual, light-hearted and wisecracking. The only comments to border on the political came from George, who was upset by the demands of the taxman.

Q: Have you in actual fact had time to vote yourselves?

PAUL: No, we missed it actually. We . . .

JOHN: We were having dinner at the time.

JOHN AND PAUL: (laugh)

Q: I think Paul has aspirations to become prime minister. Have you still got those ideas?

PAUL: No. Not a politician. It's a hard life, you see. It's a hard day's grind.

RINGO: (narrating) . . . he said, in a merry voice.

PAUL: (to the interviewer) Like a cigarette?

Q: No, I don't smoke at all. Thank you.

RINGO: They're [cigarette prices] going up, you know.

GEORGE: We'll have to give those up soon.

PAUL: We'll have to give these up.

RINGO: (lights Paul's cigarette) Aye! None of these luxuries!

JOHN: Don't tax THEM, Harold.

RINGO: It's bad enough as it is.

. . .

Q: During the last few weeks, the Grimond group and the Home group and the Wilson group have been edging you off the papers. Have you been envious of all these groups?

GEORGE AND JOHN: No.

PAUL: No. We sell more records and things than they do.

GEORGE: The situation looks pretty Grimmond, doesn't it!

BEATLES: (laugh)

RINGO: That's a good'n.

PAUL: No, you know. Good luck to 'em.

Q: Have any political parties contacted you and said, 'Would you say publicly you'd vote for us?'

JOHN: Oh, no.

GEORGE: No, 'cuz then the others don't buy the records.

Harold Wilson led Labour to victory at the election, becoming the youngest prime minister in 150 years. Decades later, another Labour prime minister, Gordon Brown, contended that 'the Beatles helped Labour win in 1964'. As an exceptionally young history undergraduate at Edinburgh University in the late sixties, he had argued with his lecturers that 'the 1964 and 1966 elections were won on a wave of enthusiasm for change and that no one illustrated this mood better than the Beatles. Without their fame, Harold Wilson might have struggled to popularise his theme: creating a vibrant, dynamic Britain free from the stuffy establishment living in the past . . . There was no better example of his theme that Britain was changing than the Beatles, who I and millions of other teenagers first followed from 1962 – young, unconventional, from the north, and awash with new energy.'

The president of the United States took more convincing. On the Beatles' first American tour, at the start of 1964, Lyndon Johnson's sixteen-year-old daughter Luci pleaded with her father to invite them to the White House.

'All our country was just peppered with pain,' she recalled half a century later, 'and so it occurred to me that, being the daughter of the president of the United States, I might be able to have every adolescent's dream come true: the Beatles to my house. So I got extremely excited about it and went to my father and asked if we could have the Beatles come. I was dumbfounded by his response. He said that this was the time for our family to be getting down to work. We couldn't be all about "yeah, yeah, yeah". He didn't tell me not to play their records and he didn't tell me not to dance to them. But he sure as heck said they weren't coming to the White House. Period. End. Closed subject.'

But by the summer of that year, President Johnson had changed his mind. Like everyone else, he craved their light. Before the Beatles' second American tour the White House press office put out feelers to Brian Epstein: would they consent to being photographed laying a wreath on President Kennedy's grave in Washington, alongside President Johnson? On behalf of the Beatles, Epstein politely but firmly declined.

68.

As the years rolled by, even politicians with the most meagre interest in the Beatles felt obliged to drop their names, just to show they were in touch. On 11 October 1969, celebrating her tenth anniversary as an MP, Margaret Thatcher spoke at her Finchley Conservative Association Ball. Over the past ten years there had, she said, been many changes in society: 'In 1959 we had not heard of the Beatles or David Frost, there was no permissive society and no hippies.' Though she was probably unaware of it, the previous week John and Yoko had been recording 'Don't Worry Kyoko (Mummy's Only Looking for Her Hand in the Snow)', the B-side of the Plastic Ono Band's 'Cold Turkey', just a few miles away, in Abbey Road.

'But some things have not changed,' she continued. 'Right is still right and wrong is wrong . . . It is the good news which should be broadcast, and in Finchley there is a lot of good news.' She then paid tribute to the Finchley Chrysanthemum Society for 'producing bigger and better blooms'.

Eighteen years later, Mrs Thatcher was preparing to fight her second general election as prime minister. Keen to harness the skittish youth vote, her aides lined up an interview with *Smash Hits*, a magazine with an estimated readership of 3.3 million, its average reader being fifteen years old.

A week before the interview, Mrs Thatcher's aide Christine Wall wrote her a briefing note, suggesting topics that the interviewer, Tom Hibbert, might raise. They included 'any pop star/film star heroes you had as a youngster', 'your feeling about today's stars' and 'your position on drugs'.

Under the heading Points to Make, Ms Wall advised: 'It is worth mentioning that a degree of teenage rebellion is part of growing up,' and 'Teenagers have long been anti-establishment whatever the political persuasion of the Government of the day,' adding that 'You may not enjoy the interview. Mr Hibbert may ask superficial questions which betray a lack of

understanding. The challenge of the interview will be for you to demonstrate that just because you are not part of the pop scene, you are still in
touch with youngsters and understand their needs . . .'

On the morning of the interview, she handed Mrs Thatcher a further
memo:

PRIME MINISTER
YOUR INTERVIEW WITH SMASH HITS
You asked for some examples of contemporary and past popular music.
Here are some suggestions:

CURRENT POP CHARTS
At Number 1 and 2 in the singles charts at the moment are two Ameri-
can 'soul' songs both hits in the sixties and now hits again 20 years later.
At No. 1 is 'STAND BY ME' by BEN E. KING. At No. 2 is 'WHEN A
MAN LOVES A WOMAN' by PERCY SLEDGE . . . I attach the latest
Top Ten chart list.
    Music from the Andrew Lloyd Webber musical 'PHANTOM OF
THE OPERA' continues to do well in the charts. The soundtrack album
is at No 1 in the LP charts and the single 'MUSIC OF THE NIGHT'
sung by MICHAEL CRAWFORD is now at No 34 in the singles charts
after being in the top ten . . .

A bizarre paragraph reminded Mrs Thatcher that 'Two of the most recent
BIG BAND HITS are "PASADENA" by the TEMPERANCE SEVEN in
the 1960s and "THE FLORAL DANCE" by THE BRIGHOUSE AND
RASTRICK BRASS BAND in the 1970s.' Punk was also mentioned. The
only other musical phenomenon to be accorded its own briefing note, seventeen years after they had split up, was:

THE BEATLES
Probably the two most famous BEATLES songs amongst many hits are
YESTERDAY which has been recorded by hundreds of people including
FRANK SINATRA AND ELVIS PRESLEY and ALL YOU NEED IS
LOVE which was performed live in front of 64,000,000 people on TV
in 1968.

When the big day came, Mrs Thatcher did her best to show that her finger was on the pulse of youth. Having offered Hibbert a glass of water ('It's Malvern Water. British! We only serve British!'), she rattled through most of the points on the memo, even mentioning 'When a Man Loves a Woman', big bands, and punk ('I know we have got the punks. The punks spend a lot of time and money on their appearance').

When Hibbert asked if she would have been very upset if her children had formed a pop group, she replied, 'No, I should not have been at all upset . . . I would have been much more concerned if they did not do anything. Mark did, as a matter of fact learn the guitar.' He was not particularly good at it, she added, 'but he had quite a musical sense, and they all listened to – heaven knows, we had all the latest pop records – there were the Beatles in our time you see, and they are very interesting and they are just coming back because their songs were tuneful. I remember "Telstar", lovely song, I absolutely loved it.'

'Telstar', Hibbert politely pointed out, was not by the Beatles but by the Tornados.

'The Tornados, yes, then we had Dusty Springfield, but the Beatles I remember most of all. They had to have this thing on all day, I said [to her children], "The pair of you, did you have to listen to that?" but it became part of the background.'

On 31 May 1990, six months before being squeezed from office, Margaret Thatcher paid a visit to Abbey Road, to celebrate the eightieth anniversary of the EMI studios. While there, she posed for photographs, playing the drums in the studio and walking across the famous zebra crossing on the road outside. 'I loved the songs of the Beatles,' she told journalists. 'They were sheer genius both in the way they performed and in some of the songs they wrote.'

But five years into her retirement, she had grown less enamoured of the Beatles' influence. In her autobiography she complained of 'a whole "youth culture" of misunderstood Eastern mysticism, bizarre clothing and indulgence in hallucinatory drugs'.

'I found Chelsea a very different place when we moved back to London in 1970,' she continued. 'I had mixed feelings about what was happening.

There was vibrancy and talent, but this was also in large degree a world of make-believe. A perverse pride was taken in Britain about our contribution to these trends. Carnaby Street in Soho, the Beatles, the mini-skirt and the maxi-skirt were the new symbols of "Swinging Britain". And they did indeed prove good export earners. Harold Wilson was adept at taking maximum political credit for them. The trouble was that they concealed the real economic weaknesses which even a talented fashion industry and entrepreneurial recording companies could not counter-balance. As Desmond Donnelly remarked, "My greatest fear is that Britain will sink giggling into the sea."'

69.

A Party:
Mr Brian Epstein. At Home.
Buffet Supper 9.30 p.m. Informal Dress.
15 Whaddon House, William Mews
Knightsbridge, London SW1
12 August 1964

Brian Epstein is throwing a party to launch the Beatles' second tour of the United States: thirty performances in twenty-four cities in thirty-two days, covering 22,441 miles.

Invitations have been posted to a variety of stars, including Cilla Black, Peter and Gordon, the Searchers, Tommy Steele, Mick Jagger, Keith Richards, Lionel Bart, Dusty Springfield and Alma Cogan. Three cutting-edge disc jockeys have also been invited: Alan Freeman, Pete Murray and Brian Matthew.

Epstein has roped in his interior decorator, Ken Partridge, to help with the ambience. Partridge erects a marquee on the roof, complete with french windows, so guests can look out over the city. The floor is raised, and covered in cherry-red sisal carpeting. There is a bandstand big enough for a small orchestra, plus a dance floor. The centre pole of the marquee is covered in Spanish moss, and intertwined with seven hundred carnations in the shape of a palm tree. The entire structure has taken five days to erect.

Brian is determined to keep it tasteful. 'I don't want any gimmicks,' he says.

'You mean you want white tablecloths, silver candelabra, white flowers?' says Partridge.

'Perfect.'

'Pink-and-white-striped?'

'Yes, I want all that.'

On the big day, Partridge is adamant that no one goes up on the roof before the party. But, late in the afternoon, Brian tells him his mother is downstairs. 'She's just back from the hairdresser, and she'd love to come and see it.'

'No,' says Partridge.

'Please.'

'Well, all right. Just this once.'

Queenie Epstein is ushered upstairs. She takes one look at all the carnations, half red and half white, and is horrified. Combining red and white is unlucky, she insists. This is one of a number of superstitions she harbours: she is also convinced that birds pictured on curtains will bring bad luck.

'What are we going to do?' Brian asks Partridge, adding, 'It must be changed! We can't have any bad luck just before the boys leave on tour!'

'What are we going to do? Nothing,' replies Partridge. But then he asks Pam Foster, who is in charge of the flowers, to come up with a solution. She nips down to Harrods, a few hundred yards away, to buy a quantity of red ink. Back at the flat, she pours the ink into a bucket, then removes the white carnations from the various displays and dips them all in it.

The guests arrive. The rooftop dinner is sumptuous. Tony Barrow considers the word 'buffet' inadequate to describe 'the spectacular display of food on offer, from fillets of beef to slices of duck, from chilled lobster to all manner of other seafood delicacies and baskets laden with exotic fruits'.

Everything is going swimmingly when there is a small commotion at the front door. A woman in a mink coat insists that she and her escort have been invited, yet they are not on the guest list. 'This is awful,' she tells the doorman.

Upstairs, Ken Partridge is told of the commotion below. 'Who is this woman?' he asks. He goes downstairs, to be confronted by 'this little woman in a pink coat'. She tells him, 'We met Brian with Li in a restaurant and he asked us to come along.' Partridge recognises her. 'Judy Garland!' he exclaims delightedly. 'Please come in! You're my guest!'

Like many fractured souls, Brian Epstein is a big fan of Judy Garland. He ran into her the previous night at the Caprice with Lionel Bart, or 'Li', and asked her to come and meet the Beatles. Stupidly, he forgot to add her name to the guest list.

Judy passes through the downstairs room, which is now deserted, and according to Partridge looks as if a bomb has hit it: 'Everybody had gone upstairs and there were hundreds of dirty glasses, cigarette butts, everything around.'

'Oh my God, I'm late,' says Judy.

'No, they're on the roof.'

'What are they doing on the roof?'

'Well, they're not jumping off. They're having dinner.'

Partridge ushers her upstairs, and places her next to Lionel Bart. Cilla Black notices that Judy has made no attempt to disguise her recent injuries: 'The first thing we all noticed was that both her wrists were covered in white bandages.'

'Hold my hand,' Judy tells Partridge. 'I'm so frightened.' As he moves his hand in her direction, she stubs out her cigarette on the back of it.

'I've never burned anybody before,' insists Judy.

'I shall treasure it for the rest of my life,' Partridge replies stoically.

Brian comes over to greet her, and the older members of the party gather round admiringly. Judy begins to relax, and after dinner is over, seems happy to mix with the other guests. The younger types – the Stones, the Searchers – don't really know, or care, who she is. She encountered the Beatles three weeks ago, when she joined them in *The Night of a Thousand Stars* at the London Palladium, alongside Gloria Swanson, Merle Oberon, Laurence Olivier and Zsa Zsa Gabor. She had gone to the Palladium straight from a nursing home to which she had been admitted after having suffered cuts to her arms and wrists – sustained, or so she insisted to the press, while struggling to open a metal trunk with a pair of scissors. The actress Hayley Mills, aged sixteen, had been standing backstage next to the Beatles when Garland took to the stage in a red sequined sheath dress with long sleeves: 'There was tremendous applause and then there was a lull before she started to speak or sing. And in that lull, you suddenly heard John's voice yelling out, "Show us your wrists, Judy!" I don't think she heard. I do hope she didn't hear.'

Tonight, John makes no attempt to renew his brief acquaintance, but Paul engages Judy in a conversation about Lionel Bart's new show, *Maggie May*. Looking across the room, Tony Barrow considers that Judy looks 'pale, weak, ill at ease and a million miles from the effervescent personality we'd seen so many times on the cinema screen'. Nevertheless, amidst the general melee, he observes her 'bouncing off the walls and gabbling away to her host'.

At one point, Brian spots his grandmother buttonholing Judy. After Judy has moved on, Brian asks what they were talking about. 'How to make chocolate cake,' replies Judy.

Judy potters off in search of the lavatory, and fails to reappear. Cilla Black is just leaving when Brian approaches in a panic.

'Judy's been in the bathroom for at least fifteen minutes.'

'So? Women are not like guys, Brian,' she replies. 'They take a while in there.'

Five minutes later, Cilla is saying goodnight to Ringo when Brian hurtles over again. 'She's still in there,' he hisses. 'We can't have her committing suicide here. Go in and get her, Cilla.'

'Oh God!' replies Cilla, who is beginning to worry. 'You want me to go in there and see if she's slashed her wrists again?'

'*Please*, Cilla.'

Outside the lavatory, concern is growing. One or two guests have tried rapping on the door, but to no avail. At last, Judy emerges. Tony Barrow notes that she is 'perspiring profusely', but otherwise perky.

Around midnight, the police arrive: neighbours have been complaining about the noise. Summoned to deal with them, Alistair Taylor picks up an unopened bottle of champagne. Brian asks him what he is doing with it. He explains that it is a peace offering for the police. 'Oh no you don't,' says Brian. 'If anybody's going to give away my wine it's going to be me.' He snatches the bottle from Taylor's hands and stomps off. But then he thinks better of it.

'Alistair,' he says, 'give this champagne to the police with my compliments, and in future please make sure you ask me personally before you shower my hospitality on outsiders.'

Later, after Judy has left, Brian and Lionel Bart hatch a plan to present her in the West End, but nothing comes of it.

At this moment, Judy Garland has a little under five years left to live, and Brian Epstein exactly three years, two weeks.

70.

On 28 August 1964, as the Beatles struggled to make their way through the crush in the lobby of the Delmonico Hotel on Park Avenue, Ringo found himself trapped in a crowd of girls. One of them tore his shirt open; another grabbed at the gold St Christopher medal he had been given by his Auntie Nancy.

Ringo only realised it had disappeared once he had extracted himself from the scrum, and by then it was too late. When the Beatles arrived at their suite at the Warwick Hotel for a live interview, it was clear that Ringo was upset. 'What's the matter?' asked the WABC disc jockey 'Cousin Brucie' Morrow, who was to conduct the interview. 'You don't look too good.'

'Somebody grabbed me St Christopher's medal,' said Ringo mournfully. He had worn it, night and day, ever since his twenty-first birthday, a year before he joined the Beatles; small wonder he associated it with good luck.

The interview was being broadcast live. Outside in the street, six thousand fans were glued to their transistor radios to hear what was being said in the room above.

Cousin Brucie had a bright idea. 'I went on the air and said to the kids: "Look, somebody must have found Ringo Starr's St Christopher medal." I didn't say "took it" or "stole it", I said, "Somebody must have found it." I said, "Look, if you return it you will not be in trouble and you'll come up here with Cousin Brucie and you'll meet Ringo and he'll give you a kiss." Well, of course, the place went crazy, and you heard them outside – WAAAGH! – through the windows. There were thousands of them.'

Other radio interviews repeated the sad tale of the lost St Christopher, along with Ringo's promise to reward whoever found it with a kiss. The fans proved wily. Within an hour, the shops of Manhattan had sold out of St Christopher medals, and an equal number of calls had been received from girls claiming to have found Ringo's. One of them was answered by

Cousin Brucie himself. 'Cousin Brucie, my name is Mrs McGowan, and my daughter Angela found Ringo's St Christopher medal. Is she in any trouble?'

But was she telling the truth? Her fear that her daughter might be in trouble suggested she was. When Angela said it had come loose from Ringo's neck when she tore his shirt in the Delmonico Hotel, Cousin Brucie knew he had found the culprit.

'I knew right away that I had a tremendous news piece, and I didn't want anybody else to get it. "Stay right where you are," I said. "I'm going to send a car for you."'

The next day, with television cameras whirring, Ringo was interviewed by three different reporters, who towered over him with their microphones. Then Angie McGowan was introduced to him by Cousin Brucie.

'Angie, sweetheart, this is your idol, this is Ringo.'

Angie, a pretty brunette, stepped forward, gave a little curtsey, and returned the St Christopher to its owner.

'It's very small,' said Ringo, 'but it means a lot.'

'Sorry about your shirt,' said Angie.

'I can buy another shirt, but I can't buy another one of these.'

Ringo gave Angie the promised kiss, whereupon three of her friends stepped forward, and he kissed them too. Angie kissed him again, with her hand to his head, and Ringo signed an autograph for her. Cousin Brucie reported that the girls were kissing him again, off camera. 'He's still kissing Angie; what is going on over there!?'

Meanwhile, Ringo tucked his St Christopher into his jacket pocket, just to be on the safe side.

71.

Penelope Fitzgerald identified the social message Evelyn Waugh wished to convey as: *I am bored; you are frightened.*

The same might be said of Bob Dylan. Though unlike Waugh in most other respects, his presence can be intimidating, his disdain curbed only by indifference.

This was never more true than in the summer of 1964. Dylan had recently established himself as the most hip, most gritty, most forceful performer on the planet. Yet the title of most popular belonged elsewhere.

Like most people in America, Dylan first heard the Beatles in January 1964. They had soon become unavoidable. 'We were driving through Colorado, we had the radio on, and eight of the top 10 songs were Beatles songs . . . "I Wanna Hold Your Hand", all those early ones,' he recalled.

Dylan immediately recognised that they were not purely a commercial phenomenon, bound up with screaming girls: 'They were doing things nobody was doing. Their chords were outrageous, just outrageous, and their harmonies made it all valid . . . I knew they were pointing the direction of where music had to go.'

The meeting between these two musical superpowers was brokered by a journalist called Al Aronowitz. While the Beatles were staying at the Delmonico, Dylan was at home in Woodstock, in upstate New York. Aronowitz took a call from John Lennon, with whom he had become chummy.

'Where is he?'

'Who?'

'Dylan.'

'Oh, he's up in Woodstock, but I can get him to come down.'

'Do it!'

That evening, Dylan and Aronowitz dutifully pushed their way through the fans outside the hotel, accompanied by Dylan's tour manager Victor Maymudes, who doubled as his dope-carrier. In the hospitality suite on the

Beatles' floor, Derek Taylor was busy entertaining some lesser celebrities, including the disc jockey Murray 'The K' Kaufman, the Kingston Trio and Peter, Paul and Mary, but Dylan and his entourage were a cut above, so they were ushered into the Beatles' suite without further ado.

They had just finished their room-service dinner when Dylan arrived. Brian Epstein acted as greeter: 'I'm afraid we can only offer champagne.' Dylan said he'd prefer cheap wine, but having established his no-nonsense credentials, gruffly agreed to make do with champagne.

The introductions were tentative. 'Bob and the Beatles all needed room to swashbuckle,' Aronowitz recalled, 'but nobody wanted to step on anybody else's ego.'

At once, the talk turned to drugs. The Beatles offered Purple Hearts, but Dylan declined, suggesting marijuana.

'We've never smoked marijuana before,' confessed Epstein.

'But what about your song? The one about getting high?' said Dylan.

'Which song?' asked John.

'You know – "I get high! I get high!"'

John was driven to correct him, pointing out that the chorus to 'I Want to Hold Your Hand' is not 'I get high', but 'I can't hide'. How, John wondered, would marijuana make them feel?

'Good,' said Dylan. He began to roll a joint, but was unexpectedly cack-handed.

Aronowitz looked on in despair. 'Bob hovered unsteadily over the bowl as he stood at the table while he tried to lift the grass from the baggie with the fingertips of one hand so he could crush it into the leaf of rolling paper which he held in his other hand. In addition to the fact that Bob was a sloppy roller to begin with, what Bob had started drinking had already gotten to him.'

There were roughly twenty policemen stationed in the corridor outside, while waiters kept popping in and out. Dylan, Aronowitz and Maymudes felt that somewhere more discreet was required, so everyone crammed into one of the bedrooms.

Dylan lit the first joint, and passed it to John, who, always more cautious than he liked to appear, passed it on – 'You try it!' – to Ringo. It was, Aronowitz noted, an act that 'instantly revealed the Beatles' pecking order. Obviously Ringo was the low man on the totem pole.'

'He's my royal taster,' explained John, confirming Aronowitz's suspicions.

Ringo was unsure what to do, so Aronowitz talked him through the correct procedure: inhale deeply, hold it in your lungs for as long as possible, exhale. But he failed to add, 'then pass it on'. As it became clear that Ringo considered the joint his to keep, Maymudes got down to rolling some more. Within minutes they had one each, and everybody was puffing away.

Paul was underwhelmed. 'For about five minutes we went, "This isn't doing anything," so we kept having more.' Suddenly, Ringo started giggling. It proved infectious. 'His laughing looked so funny that the rest of us started laughing hysterically at the way Ringo was laughing hysterically. Soon, Ringo pointed at the way Brian Epstein was laughing, and we all started laughing hysterically at the way Brian was laughing.'

Aronowitz remembered Epstein saying, 'I'm so high I'm on the ceiling,' over and over again. Then he started looking at himself in the mirror, saying 'Jew, Jew . . .' It was, thought Paul, 'as if he was finally sort of talking about the fact – "Oh, I'm Jewish. I forgot."'

Later that evening, the British journalist Chris Hutchins returned from an evening out with Neil Aspinall. He was unlocking the door to his bedroom when Aspinall whispered, 'Come and look at this.'

The two of them crept into the Beatles' suite. 'Seated on five chairs arranged in a line were the Fab Four and their manager Brian Epstein, all stoned. Every now and again, a man standing at one end of the line would push the closest Beatle off his chair and, in domino effect, each would knock the next one off, ending with Brian, who would collapse to the floor laughing helplessly, setting the others off. It was a surreal scene, made more bizarre by the fact that the man doing the pushing was Bob Dylan.'

Presently, Paul convinced himself that he had discovered the meaning of life, and started bustling around the suite looking for a pencil and paper to jot it down before he forgot. 'I suddenly felt like a reporter, on behalf of my local newspaper in Liverpool. I wanted to tell people what it was.' He instructed Mal Evans to follow him around the suite with a notebook, to inscribe his words of wisdom. Whenever the telephone rang, Dylan would answer it with the words, 'This is Beatlemania here.'

The Beatles rang through to Derek Taylor in the suite next door, telling him to join them. Taylor found Epstein 'reeling around, holding a flower', telling him that 'I MUST try it, this wonderful stuff that made everything seem to float upwards'.

'We've been turned on,' explained George. For the next quarter of an hour Taylor encountered 'a smoky, murky muddle of unfamiliar expressions' – 'turned on', 'stoned', 'way out' – peppered with the more commonplace 'incredible', 'wow', 'man', 'fab' and 'gear'. It was clear to him that Bob Dylan was top dog, 'thin and beaked, with the beady-eyed gaze of a little bird'.

The effect of Dylan's visit on the Beatles was deep and long-lasting. Two months later they recorded 'She's a Woman', which included John's line 'Turn me on when I get lonely'. By the time they came to film *Help!* in February 1965 they were, according to John, 'smoking marijuana for breakfast . . . it was all glazed eyes and giggling all the time'. The following June they recorded 'It's Only Love', which included the very words Dylan had misheard: 'I get high'.

From then on, drugs references in their songs kept tumbling out – 'riding so high', 'find me in my field of grass', 'because the wind is high, it blows my mind'. Most of them passed unnoticed at the time: only years later did Paul confess that his jaunty, upbeat 'Got to Get You Into My Life', with its tender, loving lyrics 'I need you every single day of my life' and 'When I'm with you I want to stay there', was in fact an ode to pot. By the time they came to record *Sgt. Pepper*, tracks free of drugs references were thin on the ground.

Like so many fans, John took steps to turn into his hero. His voice grew more rasping, his attitude more sarky, his lyrics more opaque. Years later, he told the photographer David Bailey about these replicant instincts. 'He said to me, "Y'know, when I've discovered someone new, I tend to become that person. I want to soak myself in their stuff to such an extent that I have to be them." When he first found Dylan, he said, he would dress like Dylan and only play his kind of music, till he kind of understood how it worked.' During one recording session, George Martin had to ask John if he could try to sound less like Bob Dylan. 'He wasn't doing it deliberately. It was subconscious more than anything.'

Dylan seems to have enjoyed the Beatles' company. Their friendship blossomed in a haze of dope. But there was never any question as to who was the master, and who the servants. Marianne Faithfull witnessed the Beatles greeting Dylan after they watched him perform at the Royal Albert Hall on 27 May 1966.

'Dylan went into the room where the Beatles were sitting all scrunched up on the couch, all of them fantastically nervous. Lennon, Ringo, George and Paul, Lennon's wife Cynthia and one or two roadies. Nobody said anything. They were waiting for the oracle to speak. But Dylan just sat down and looked at them as if they were all total strangers at a railway station. They were frozen in each other's company. It wasn't so much a matter of them being so cool as the fact that they were too young to be genuinely cool. Like teenagers, they were afraid of what others might think.'

Their subservience surprised her. 'I thought, Jesus, how could anyone ever have thought these scared little boys were gods?'

72.

The Beatles phenomenon came as a surprise to composers still working in the classical tradition. What to make of it all?

Some tried to grin and bear it. 'I don't think the Beatles are by *any* means a wholly *bad* influence,' said Benjamin Britten, retreating into litotes for an interview with Radio Finland in 1965. 'I think they're charming creatures. I don't happen to like their music very much, but that's just me. I think it's very natural that light music should exist; but if a person likes the Beatles, it doesn't by any means preclude their love of Beethoven. Everything I read about the Beatles gives me great pleasure. I also think they're *frightfully* funny.'

Aaron Copland, sixty-three years old when the Beatles burst on America, approved of them, though in a slightly mystified sort of way. Their music, he said, 'has an unanalyzable charm. It's very hard to say what they do, but the result has a fascination about it. It is immediately recognizable and it sticks in the mind.' Later, he came to recognise their unearthly grip on the zeitgeist. 'If you want to know about the sixties, play the music of the Beatles.'

By and large, classical music critics were just as keen to prove they were not fuddy-duddy. In the *Sunday Times*, Richard Buckle called the Beatles the greatest composers since Beethoven; in the *New York Review of Books*, Ned Rorem compared them to Schubert; in *The Listener*, Deryck Cooke attempted to convey the full majesty of 'Strawberry Fields Forever' by elevating it to a branch of Higher Mathematics: 'It has a first nine-bar section divided into one-and-a-half, two, two, one-and-a-half and two, the penultimate bar being in 6/8 instead of 4/4, quaver equalling quaver. After a delaying six-beat major phrase harmonised by the tonic chord ("Let me take you down, 'cos I'm going") the tune plunges fiercely on to the flat seventh, harmonised by the minor seventh on the dominant, for a solidly rhythmic beat phrase ("*to* Strawberry Fields").'

Writing in *The Times* on 27 December 1963, William Mann had famously praised a song he misnamed 'That Boy' for its 'chains of pandiatonic clusters'. He went on to note that 'they think simultaneously of harmony and melody, so firmly are the major tonic sevenths and ninths built into their tunes, and the flat submediant key switches, so natural is the Aeolian cadence at the end of "Not a Second Time" (the chord progression which ends Mahler's Song of the Earth'.

By now, Mann had the wind behind him. 'Those submediant switches from C major into A flat major,' he continued, 'and to a lesser extent mediant ones (e.g. the octave ascent in the famous "I Want to Hold Your Hand") are a trademark of Lennon–McCartney songs . . . The autocratic but not by any means ungrammatical attitude to tonality (closer to, say, Peter Maxwell Davies's carols in "O Magnum Mysterium" than to Gershwin or Loewe or even Lionel Bart); the exhilarating and often quasi-instrumental vocal duetting, sometimes in scat or in falsetto, behind the melodic line; the melismas with altered vowels ("I saw her yesterday-ee-ay") which have not quite become mannered, and the discreet, sometimes subtle, varieties of instrumentation – a suspicion of piano or organ, a few bars of mouth-organ obbligato, an excursion on the claves or maracas . . .'

Ever the ingrate, John refused to thank Mann for his appreciation. 'He uses a whole lot of musical terminology,' he complained to an interviewer. 'And he's a twit.'

It was left to the wayward Canadian classical pianist Glenn Gould to mount a full-blown counterattack on the Beatles. Gould refused to go along with the prevailing notion that they were a breath of fresh air, the natural heirs to Schubert, and so forth.* Instead, he described their music as 'a happy, cocky, belligerently resourceless brand of harmonic primitivism'.

As the Beatles' music developed, Gould disapproved of their pretension

---

* Gould was a non-conformist in other ways too; he made many a rock star appear strait-laced. As a child, he kept a pet skunk. He refused to wear tails for public performances, preferring to appear in scruffy clothes and mismatched socks, with his shoes often held together by rubber bands. He liked to play on a low chair, sitting just fourteen inches from the ground, so that his knees were higher than his buttocks. On many of his recordings of Bach he can be heard humming along and making odd clucking sounds. He gave up concert performances at the age of thirty-one, describing live audiences as 'a force for evil'. He also disliked bright colours, sunny weather, shaking hands, Mozart and Italian opera. On the road, his motoring skills were particularly quirky: he liked to drive with his legs crossed, dummy-conducting from a score open on the passenger seat. He couldn't see anything wrong with it. 'It's true that I've driven through a number of red lights on occasion,' he once protested. 'But on the other hand, I've stopped at a lot of green ones and never gotten credit for it.'

more than their primitivism – or rather, he saw the one as a cover-up for the other: 'After all of the pretension has been cut away and after all the faddish admiration . . . has been removed, what you really have left is three chords.' To him, these three chords were 'ultrasimplistic', but the group counterfeited complexity by topping off their little ditties with what he called 'piles of garbage'. For Gould, 'The Beatles seem to want to say, "We are going to show you that it is possible to work with a minimal harmonic structure and to so becloud the issue that that's what we're doing that you're going to think it's new and it's different and whoopee!" And all of this electric garbage – I mean, you don't necessarily get it good by adding a sitar.' It was this sense of a cover-up that made Gould particularly dislike those Beatles songs that others regarded as their most advanced. For him, their apparent sophistication was no more than an elaborate deceit, artificially manufactured with knobs and switches; he even went so far as to liken 'Strawberry Fields Forever' to 'a mountain wedding between Claudio Monteverdi and a jug band'.

Those in search of true simplicity would be better off looking elsewhere: 'Now, if what you want is an extended exercise in how to mangle three chords, then obviously the Beatles are for you; but, on the other hand, if you prefer to have the same three chords unmangled – just played nicely – then Tony Hatch* is your man.'

The music critic Fritz Spiegl – who we last encountered bumping into a tipsy George at Beryl Bainbridge's Liverpool party in May 1960 – went even further. He argued that the Beatles had done more damage to music than any other four people in history. They did this, he said, by offering instant bliss without effort. Their music lacked the reserve that characterises all good art; it held nothing back.

Within the literary world, opinions on the Beatles were also divided – largely, though not exclusively, along lines of age. The buttoned-up English poet Philip Larkin (1922–85) recognised the Beatles' sociological importance, while not particularly enjoying their music. In one of his most quoted poems, 'Annus Mirabilis', he declares that:

---

* Born 1939. Composer of hits like 'Downtown' and 'Don't Sleep in the Subway' for Petula Clark, and later the catchy theme tunes for, among others, *Emmerdale Farm*, *Crossroads* and *Neighbours*.

Sexual intercourse began
In nineteen sixty-three
(which was rather late for me) –
Between the end of the 'Chatterley' ban
And the Beatles' first LP.

Larkin's attitude to the Beatles changed with the years. By nature a fan of trad jazz, he was always feeling left behind. In December 1963 he noted that their second LP, *With the Beatles*, 'suggests that their jazz content is nil, but that, like certain sweets, they seem wonderful until you are finally sick'. After his death in 1985 it emerged that he had once nursed a craving for at least one of their sweets, having bought his lady friend Maeve Brennan a copy of 'Yesterday' before playing it over and over again to himself, in a fashion verging on the obsessive.

By 1967 Larkin was feeling a pang of nostalgia for their early records. What had all that wealth and acclaim done to them in the meantime? Listening to 'A Collection of Beatles' Oldies', in March 1967, he thought it would 'prove admirable demonstration material for Marx's theory of artistic degeneration: WEA lecturers please note'. Four months later, the release of *Sgt. Pepper's Lonely Hearts Club Band* confirmed that they had taken off in the wrong direction. 'The Beatles, having made their name in the narrow emotional and harmonic world of teenage pop, are now floating away on their own cloud. I doubt whether their own fancies and imagination are strong enough to command an audience instead of collaborating with it.'

Larkin's curmudgeonly friend Kingsley Amis was less mealy-mouthed. 'Oh fuck the Beatles,' he wrote to Larkin on 19 April 1969. 'I'd like to push my bum into John L's face for forty-eight hours or so, as a protest against all the war and violence in the world.' Amis had personal reasons for his dislike. 'I met Lennon a couple of times. The first time he was being nasty to his wife, the English one not the Nip, the second time she wasn't there and he was just generally offensive. No breeding, what?'

The most furious condemnation of the Beatles came from Paul Johnson, writing in the *New Statesman* in February 1964. 'The Menace of Beatlism' was a bracing riposte to a speech made by the Conservative government's minister of information, William Deedes, to the City of London Young Conservatives. Deedes had cannily noted that the Beatles 'herald a cultural movement among the young which may become part of the history of our time . . . For those with eyes to see it, something important and heartening is happening here. The young are rejecting some of the sloppy standards of their elders . . . they have discerned dimly that in a world of automation, declining craftsmanship and increased leisure, something of this kind is essential to restore the human instinct to excel at something and the human faculty of discrimination.'

That these remarks should have passed unchallenged by Young Conservatives infuriated the thirty-five-year-old Johnson. 'Not a voice was raised to point out that the Emperor wasn't wearing a stitch,' he thundered. He felt that it was only because the Beatles were earning over £6 million a year that they had gained the approval of the moneyed classes: overnight, they had become part of the export trade, and electorally valuable.

Johnson had seen the signs coming: 'Of course, our society has long been brainwashed in preparation for this apotheosis of inanity.' Writers of distinction could now be spotted 'squatting on the bare boards of malodorous caverns, while through the haze of smoke, sweat and cheap cosmetics comes the monotonous braying of savage instruments'.

Johnson compared the teenagers of 1964 with his own generation twenty years before: 'At sixteen, I and my friends heard our first performance of Beethoven's Ninth Symphony; I can remember the excitement even today. We would not have wasted 30 seconds of our precious time on the Beatles and their ilk.'

He ended his piece on a note of optimism. Cells of resistance were springing up. Teenagers 'who flock around the Beatles, who scream themselves into hysteria, whose vacant faces flicker over the TV screen, are the least fortunate of their generation, the dull, the idle, the failures . . .'

'The Menace of Beatlism' prompted more letters of complaint than any other article ever published in the *New Statesman*. Many readers worried that Johnson had grown old before his time; one even suggested he try ingesting monkey glands.

73.

Q: What will you do when the bubble bursts?
JOHN: Get jobs.

Press conference, Los Angeles, 23 August 1964

Q: What will you do when the bubble bursts?
JOHN: Count the money.

Press conference, Cincinnati, 27 August 1964

Q: Have you fellas given any thought to what you're going to do when the bubble breaks, so to speak?
PAUL AND GEORGE: (laugh)
JOHN: Well, we're gonna have a good time.
GEORGE: We never plan ahead.
Q: How about your retirement or buying into a big business . . .
JOHN: We already are a big business, so we don't have to buy into another one.
Q: Well, I'm talking about if this business should wane slightly.
GEORGE: We'll start planning when it starts to wane, but at the moment we'll just let it go on as it is.
PAUL: Anyway, yeah. We've never made plans for anything, so there's no real reason to make plans now.

Press conference, Chicago, 5 September 1964

Q: It's assumed that you will sing for quite some time yet, but what do you plan to do after . . .
GEORGE: . . . the bubble bursts.
PAUL: Nobody's made any plans, but John and I will probably . . . (laughs) Ooo, we have this one every day, you know. John and I

will probably carry on songwriting. And then George will go into basketball.

GEORGE: Or rollerskating. I haven't decided yet.

Press conference, Kansas City, 17 September 1964

Q: Fred Paul from KAXK. First of all I'd like to say Hi to you all again, it's really good to see you. I'd like to ask a question that you've never been asked before.

JOHN: Oh no.

Q: What are you going to do when the bubble bursts?

Press conference, Los Angeles, 24 August 1966

I came back to my publisher and told him that I had the exclusive contract to be the Beatles' biographer, and he said, despondently, 'Oh . . . the bubble's going to burst. This is 1967, we know everything that we could possibly want to know about the Beatles, and they'll disappear soon.'

Hunter Davies, new introduction to his 1968
authorised Beatles biography (1996)

74.

At 10 p.m. on Saturday, 21 August 1965, a week into their second full North American tour, the Beatles set off from Minneapolis to Portland, Oregon, in an Electra plane.

Among those travelling with them was Larry Kane, covering the tour for the top 40 music station WFUN Miami. After he had eaten, Kane pushed his seat back and dozed off, only to wake up with a start. 'My eyelids popped open in reaction to what appeared to be a bright light off the wing. Was I dreaming? I looked and looked again. My adrenaline surged. I swallowed hard. There, in front of my eyes, was a fire, racing out of the right engine on the wing.'

Kane ran to the front of the plane and thumped on the door to the flight deck, but was met with no response. The plane was on autopilot, and the pilot and his co-pilot were at the back of the cabin, hobnobbing with Paul and John. Kane rushed towards them, screaming, 'There's a fire in the right engine!' Immediately, everyone on the plane began to panic.

Each of the Beatles acted in his own different way. Ringo simply stared at the fire. Paul tried to act cool, but Kane noticed that he was biting his lip. George ran to the back, saying, 'Beatles and children first.'

John, on the other hand, could not hide his terror. He looked at the fire, said, 'Oh shit, oh shit, oh shit,' ran to the emergency door at the back, and began tugging at the handle. Kane grappled with him, pulling his hands off and pushing him away, saying 'Are you crazy? You'll get us all killed.' At that point they were flying at a height of 22,000 feet.

But John was not to be put off by logic. He charged at the door again, but the burly Mal Evans stood in his way.

By now the pilots had returned to the cockpit. Over the intercom came the announcement that they were close to Portland, and that they could rely on the remaining engines to get them there safely. 'What a bunch of rubbish!' yelled John, with his eyes tight shut.

Half an hour later the plane landed at Portland, to be greeted by fire-fighters, who covered it in a sea of foam. Kane remembered everyone on board sighing 'Oh God' and 'I'll never fly again.' But two days later they had to board another plane to take them to Los Angeles, where they were due to meet Elvis Presley. As they boarded, Ringo chirped up, 'Let's stay alive in '65.'

Eight months later, an Electra plane operated by the same charter service crashed in Ardmore, Oklahoma, killing seventy-eight soldiers on their way home from training, and five crew members, three of whom – the pilot and two engineers – had been with the Beatles on their hazardous flight to Portland.

75.

A Party:
525 Perugia Way
Beverly Hills, Los Angeles
27 August 1965

The party arrangements have been lengthy and fraught; almost closer, in their withdrawals, stand-offs and concessions, to negotiations for a peace settlement.

Which is, in a way, what it is. The brash young Beatles are in the ascendant. Elvis Presley was once the talk of America, but now it is all Beatles, Beatles, Beatles. They have stolen his thunder. Until the spring, Elvis's career was in the doldrums, with no top 10 single since 1963. His movie career, too, is adrift: his last, *Tickle Me*, set in a beauty parlour, was barely noticed. But the Beatles can do no wrong. They have just premiered *Help!*, which seems set to repeat the success of *A Hard Day's Night*. Three days ago, Hollywood's crème de la crème – Rock Hudson, Jack Benny, Jane Fonda, Groucho Marx, James Stewart – attended a party in their honour, and even queued for autographs.

At the beginning of the month, Elvis's manager, Colonel Tom Parker, invites Brian Epstein to his New York office to hammer out a deal. They sit on chairs made from elephants' feet and finalise arrangements over pastrami sandwiches and root beer. The colonel calls the shots. The Beatles will come to Elvis, not the other way round; no cameras or tape-recorders will be permitted; and no publicity of any sort. In turn, Epstein insists that there must be extra security on the gates.

John makes his own demands, saying he doesn't even want the colonel or Epstein to be at the meeting: 'If both sides start lining up teams of supporters it will turn into a contest to see who can field the most players.' But

over another business lunch, beside the pool of the Beverly Hills Hotel, Parker insists he will attend, so Epstein demands parity. Before long, the numbers have increased: as Elvis invites more of his self-styled 'Memphis Mafia', the Beatles invite their roadies Neil and Mal, their press officer Tony Barrow, and their driver Alf Bicknell, as well as Chris Hutchins from the *NME*, who helped Epstein gain an entrée with the colonel.

When the big day comes, there are nerves on both sides. 'Before the Beatles arrived that night, Elvis and I were in his bathroom doing his hair,' recalls one member of his entourage, Larry Geller. 'Elvis was unusually quiet, even pensive, as he drummed his fingers on the marble ledge.' In their limousine on the way there, Barrow notices the Beatles growing tense. They are, after all, about to meet the man who has long been their idol. 'Do you think the colonel has bothered to tell Elvis we're coming?' asks John.

The Beatles and their entourage are led into a vast circular room, lit in red and blue. In a red shirt with bolero sleeves, Elvis stands in the centre of a ring of twenty people. His wife Priscilla stands beside him. 'Her black bouffant towered above her head and she was heavily made up with thick black mascara, midnight-blue eyeliner, red blusher and Heartbreak Pink lipstick,' noted Chris Hutchins. 'She was wearing a figure-hugging cream jacket with long pants and there was a jewelled tiara on her head.'*

---

* Or so Hutchins wrote in the notes he secretly maintained over several visits to the loo. Others remembered differently: Paul had Priscilla wearing 'a purple gingham dress and a gingham bow in her very beehive hair'; Neil thought it was 'a long dress and a tiara'; George was convinced it was 'some sort of tight cream top with long flimsy trousers to match'; and Tony Barrow was equally sure that it was 'a full-length lime-coloured gown'.

For a few seconds, silence falls as the English and American gangs face each other. Priscilla Presley senses their nervousness: 'You could hear a pin drop when they walked in . . . I was amazed at how shy they were . . . they were speechless, totally speechless, truly like kids, meeting their idol. Especially John – John was shy, timid, looking at him. I mean, I really believe he just couldn't believe he was actually there with Elvis Presley.'

Priscilla finds the atmosphere 'a little bit awkward because they kept looking at him, not really saying anything and not really sitting down, just staring at him'. She remembers Elvis saying, 'Guys, if you're gonna just stand around and stare at me, I may as well do my own thing.' He sits down, and the Beatles sit cross-legged on the floor around him. 'A chair for Mr Epstein,' says the colonel, and people rush forward with a selection of them.

They talk about touring; George tells Elvis about their plane catching fire on their flight to Portland on Monday. Elvis says one of his aircraft engines once gave out over Atlanta. Meanwhile, the two managers huddle in a corner; Brian is keen to organise UK concert dates for Elvis, but the colonel has a rule not to mix business with pleasure. Instead, he announces to the room, 'Ladies and gentlemen, Elvis's private casino is now open for your pleasure. Brian, let's play roulette.'

The two managers go through to the casino as Elvis picks up a bass guitar and starts playing along to songs on his jukebox. A television is on, with its sound turned down. Occasionally he picks up a remote control to switch channels. It is the first remote control Paul has ever seen. 'He was switching channels and we were like, "Wow! How are you doing that?"'

Elvis calls for more guitars for the Beatles, and they join in. Paul chats to him about playing bass. The conversation is a little desultory, until John sharpens it up. 'Why have you dropped the old rock stuff?' he asks Elvis, adding that he'd loved his early records, but didn't like the more recent ones. Elvis says he'll soon be making rock records again. 'Oh, good,' says John. 'We'll buy them when you do.' Elvis is nonplussed: he has grown accustomed to everyone telling him what he wants to hear. Later, John says he spotted a slogan saying 'All the Way with LBJ'. John regards LBJ as a warmonger. Was this what prompted his putdown of Elvis?

They all go back to their jamming, this time 'I Feel Fine'. Ringo has no drums, and feels under-used drumming on a table with his fingers, so he drifts off to play pool with the roadies.

John puts on a comical Clouseau voice, saying, 'Zis is ze way it should be . . . ze small homely gathering wiz a few friends and a leetle muzic.' Elvis looks baffled. After a while, the songs run dry and they all join the others in the games room. The colonel is more forthcoming than his client. John is amused by his swashbuckling stories of his early life as a carnival show-man: how he wrestled with a lion, how the dancing chickens danced only when he placed them on an electric plate. 'He's an amazing character, a real hustling showman,' John tells Hutchins later. 'But Elvis – what a total anti-climax HE was. He seemed to be completely out of his head. Either he was on pills or dope . . . whatever it was, he was just totally uninterested and uncommunicative.'

Colonel Parker signals the end of the party by handing out presents of Elvis records to one and all. He also gives the four Beatles little covered wagons that light up when you push a button. He tells Brian Epstein he is going to buy him a cocktail cabinet. Brian says he is going to ask Harrods to send the colonel a Shetland pony, as a memento of his days in the circus.

As they are ushered out the front door, Elvis says, 'Don't forget to come and see us again in Memphis if you're ever in Tennessee.'

Still adopting a comical voice, John shouts back, 'Zanks for ze music, Elvis! Long live ze King!' Then he asks Elvis to join the Beatles at their place in Benedict Canyon the following night.

'Well, I'll see. I'm not sure I'll be able to make it or not,' replies Elvis.

On the way back, John describes the party as a total non-event: 'I can't decide who's more full of shit, me or Elvis Presley.'

Once the Beatles are safely out of sight, Elvis goes back into the house and draws Larry Geller to one side. What really blew his mind, he says, is the state of their teeth. He can't understand why, with all their money, they haven't had them fixed.*

---

* Five years later, on 30 December 1970, on an impromptu visit to the White House, Elvis tells Presi-dent Nixon that 'The Beatles had been a real force for anti-American spirit . . . The Beatles came to this country, made their money, and then returned to England where they promoted an anti-American theme.' Present at the meeting, the White House counsel Egil 'Bud' Krogh noted that, while the presi-dent nodded in agreement, he also 'expressed some surprise'. Early the following year, Elvis expresses similar misgivings on a tour of the FBI building in Washington: 'Presley indicated that he is of the opinion that the Beatles laid the groundwork for many of the problems we are having with young people by their filthy unkempt appearances and suggestive music,' reads an official memo.

76.

Even Beatles need dentists. To become the Fab Four, their teeth needed as much tweaking as their hair and clothes, perhaps more.

John Riley was the son of an upstanding south London police constable. He had studied cosmetic dentistry at Northwestern University Dental School in Chicago before setting up a practice in Harley Street. He is said to have possessed a quality rare, and perhaps dangerous, in a dentist: charisma. 'He was the sort of man that if he walked in the room, you'd feel his presence even before you saw him,' observed one of his clients. By the early 1960s he had become one of the most fashionable dentists in town, much sought after by figures in showbusiness and the arts, including all four Beatles.

George's teeth needed particular attention: photographs from the Cavern days reveal them as uneven and rickety. Through the latter part of 1963 and into 1964 he became such a frequent visitor to Riley's clinic that the two men struck up a friendship of sorts, sometimes going out clubbing together. In February 1965 the Beatles even invited Riley to the Bahamas to keep them company while they were filming *Help!*. Yet Pattie Boyd never felt entirely comfortable in his presence, particularly when lying back on his dental chair with her mouth wide open. To be a dentist in Swinging London may have seemed like an anomaly, but it was the ideal profession for someone who regarded teeth as mere stepping stones to other, more potent, areas of the human body. Pattie wondered if he might have taken advantage: 'No matter what he was going to do in our mouths, he would give us intravenous Valium. All of the Beatles went to him and we took it for granted that this was what happened – no one questioned it. We would go into a deep sleep and wake up not knowing what he had done. I watched him trying to revive George once by slapping his face. It was sinister – he could have been doing anything to us while we were out.'

In April 1965 Riley and his girlfriend Cyndy, whose job was to hire the bunny girls for the Playboy Club, invited John and Cynthia and George and Pattie over for dinner at his home in Bayswater. 'We had a lovely meal, plenty to drink,' Pattie recalled.

As dinner came to an end, George and Pattie got up to leave, explaining that they were planning to see Klaus Voorman and his new band playing at the Pickwick Club, just off Leicester Square.

As Pattie remembers it, Cyndy then said, 'You haven't had any coffee yet. I've made it – and it's delicious.' So they sat down and drank their coffee. Then John made another move to leave, explaining that Klaus was due on soon.

'You can't leave,' said John Riley.

'What are you talking about?'

'You've just had LSD.'

'No we haven't.'

'Yes you have. It was in the coffee.'

According to Pattie, John was 'absolutely furious'. He had read about this comparatively new drug in *Playboy* magazine. 'How dare you fucking do this to us!'

In great waves, the LSD took effect. Cyndy thought time had stopped, and as if this weren't bad enough, that they were all going to drown. 'The *Bismarck* is sinking! The *Bismarck* is sinking!' she shouted, over and over again. Pattie felt strongly that she didn't want to stay there: 'I wondered if the dentist, who hadn't had any coffee, had given it to us hoping the evening might end in an orgy.' George entertained similar suspicions: 'I'm sure he thought it was an aphrodisiac. I remember his girlfriend had enormous breasts and I think he thought that there was going to be a big gang-bang and that he was going to get to shag everybody. I really think that was his motive.'

The four guests insisted on leaving. Riley said they shouldn't drive, and offered to drive them himself. They refused, and the four of them squeezed into Pattie's Mini and set off. Pattie was convinced it was shrinking: 'All the way the car felt smaller and smaller, and by the time we arrived we were completely out of it.'

They stumbled into the lift at the Pickwick Club, then became convinced that the little red light in it was a raging fire. When the doors opened they emerged screaming into the club. John Riley had followed them in his car. He sat at their table, and turned into a pig.

Pattie was discombobulated: 'People kept recognising George and coming up to him. They were moving in and out of focus, then looked like animals.' They left the Pickwick and walked to the Ad Lib, in Leicester Place: 'On the way I remember trying to break a shop window.' As the lift doors opened there, they crawled out and bumped into Mick Jagger, Marianne Faithfull and Ringo. 'John told them we'd been spiked. The effect of the drug was getting stronger and stronger, and we were all in hysterics and crazy. When we sat down, the table elongated.'

After heaven knows how long, they made their way home, with George driving 'at no more than ten miles an hour' all the way back to Esher. John couldn't stop cracking jokes; LSD is the ideal drug for those addicted to puns, as it turns everything into something else, then back again.

The LSD took eight hours to wear off. Cynthia remembered the four of them sitting up for the rest of the night 'as the walls moved, the plants talked, other people looked like ghouls and time stood still'. For her, it was 'horrific, I hated the lack of control and not knowing what was going on or what would happen next'.

George and Pattie vowed never again to visit John Riley. No one wants a groovy dentist, any more than they want a sybaritic bank manager or a butter-fingered brain surgeon. But while Pattie and Cynthia felt that the whole experience had been very frightening, George saw it as a revelation: 'It was if I had never tasted, talked, seen, thought or heard properly before. For the first time in my whole life I wasn't conscious of ego.' And John loved exactly what Cynthia loathed: the lack of control, the unexpected weirdness of everything. Within weeks of that first trip, he would be dropping acid every day.

77.

On a pretty regular basis, Omega Auctions – 'proud to be one of the top auction houses worldwide for music memorabilia' – auction items associated with the Beatles. In March 2019, for instance, they took £3,600 at auction for a Quarrymen business card, £2,640 for a programme for the 1963 Northwich Carnival and Gala ('where the Beatles crowned the Carnival Queen') and £48,800 for Paul McCartney's English Literature schoolbook.

The catalogue for their sale on 5 November 2011 included a more peculiar item:

> JOHN LENNON TOOTH – this truly unique piece of memorabilia, a tooth of John Lennon's, was given to his housekeeper, Dorothy (Dot) Jarlett during her employment as housekeeper at his Kenwood home in Weybridge, Surrey. Dot was employed at Kenwood approximately between 1964 and 1968. John had a warm relationship with Dot and her family, often referring to her as 'Aunty Dot' and even naming his dog Bernard after Dot's husband. John was to give many gifts to Dot and her family over the years, some of which have previously been sold by the family through Sotheby's. The tooth, being such a rare item, has been kept in the family until now and comes with a sworn legal affidavit by Dot Jarlett attesting to the authenticity of the item. The tooth was given to Dot as a souvenir for her daughter who was a huge Beatles fan. The tooth is discoloured and contains an obvious cavity.
> Estimate: £10,000–£20,000

'It was by far the most weird and wonderful item we have ever had submitted to us,' recalled the auctioneer, Paul Fairweather. 'It was a very tense bid towards the end, and a huge cheer rang out when the final bid was made.'

The successful bidder was Dr Michael Zuk, a dentist from Alberta,

Canada, who paid £19,000.* At the time, Dr Zuk said he planned to display the tooth in his surgery, before taking it on a tour of dental schools.

It might seem strange, or at any rate unusually zealous, for any dentist to spend so much money on a discoloured tooth in order to take it on tour. But in fact Dr Zuk had another, more crafty, plan in mind.

'I am looking for people who believe they are John Lennon's child and have a claim to his estate and hopefully I can legitimise their claim,' he announced seven years later. 'John was a very popular guy who was having sex with lots of women, and I doubt birth control was on his mind. I would ask anyone who is participating to sign a commission agreement which would mean if they were related they would pay my company a percentage of their inheritance, like a finder's fee.'

Dr Zuk said he planned to extract DNA from the discoloured tooth; in the event of a match he would seek a settlement from Lennon Inc., which had recently recorded an annual income of £10 million from holdings of £400 million. He recognised that Yoko Ono Lennon would, in all likelihood, express 'huge concern' at any such claim. On an earlier occasion, when he publicly suggested cloning John Lennon from the tooth, he had received a stiff letter from her solicitor.

He added that he was searching for men or women in their fifties, born at a time 'when young women were throwing themselves at the Fab Four'. He had, he explained, already been contacted by a woman who claimed to be the daughter of John Lennon, but her claim had been based only on anecdotal evidence. 'I want to hold off testing until I have a small group of hopefuls, or one with a very high supporting story.'

Now based in New York, Dr Zuk confessed to purchasing the tooth as a businessman rather than as a fan. It was, he said, 'a business opportunity. I bought the tooth not because it's a stinky rotten tooth. I was thinking, "How can I turn this into something which pays for itself?"'

* By chance, a year earlier Sir Winston Churchill's set of false teeth had sold for £15,200.

78.

On the morning of Saturday, 12 June 1965, Tony Benn, the radical Postmaster General, picked up his *Daily Mirror*. The headline read: 'Now They've Got Into the Topmost Chart of All'.

It seemed that the Beatles were to be appointed Members of the British Empire in the Queen's Birthday Honours. Never before had any pop star come close to such an award.* A truffle-hound for conspiracies, Benn could sniff an establishment plot: 'No doubt Harold [Wilson] did this to be popular and I expect it *was* popular – though it may have been unpopular with some people too . . . But the plain truth is that the Beatles have done more for the royal family by accepting MBEs than the royal family have done for the Beatles by giving them.'

Benn's cabinet colleague Barbara Castle was similarly sceptical. 'Over coffee at the Welsh table I sounded out the boys about the Beatles' MBEs,' she wrote in her diary. 'The reaction was wholly unfavourable, the word "gimmick" being prominent. The ploy of Harold's seems to have boomeranged . . . He seems to have a streak of vulgarity which is also part of his strength.'

The Beatles themselves had received the news by post. 'Paul was looking through the pile of fan mail in our dressing room a few weeks back and he came across this envelope that had "From the Prime Minister" written on it,' George told a press conference on the day of the announcement. 'It must have been there at least a couple of days. He opened it and the letter said that he was being considered for an award and would he sign the enclosed form. We all said, "We wish we had one," then dived through the rest of the mail and found that we did have one – one each!'

---

* Awards for popular entertainers were at that time few and far between: George Robey, 'the Prime Minister of Mirth', was appointed a CBE for his charity work in 1919. Gracie Fields (1938), George Formby (1946) and Stanley Holloway (1960) all received OBEs.

When a reporter asked what they were planning to do with their medals, they each reacted according to character.

'Hang it on the wall,' said George.

'Tuck it around my neck,' said Ringo.

'Keep it in a safe place,' said Paul.

'I think I'll have mine made into a bell push so that people have to press it when they come to the house. Or I'll take it to an antique dealer and find out what it is,' said John.

The other 182 recipients of MBEs that year were not natural bedfellows of the Beatles. They included Thomas Arthur Bish, executive engineer in the Telephone Manager's Office at the Nottingham General Post Office; William Boggon, manager of the Ravensworth Ann Colliery; Edwin Cuthbert Cory Crapp, head of the Supply Section in the Conference, Services and Supply Department of the Diplomatic Administration Office; and Charles Edwin Puddle, the aptly-named head gardener at Bodnant Garden in Denbighshire. Apart from the Beatles, the only MBE for anyone in the public eye was awarded to Louis George Martin, an Olympic weightlifter.

It was perhaps inevitable that a number of previous recipients of honours were to take personal offence. Hector Dupuis, a Canadian MP, complained that he was being placed 'on the same level as vulgar nincompoops'. Richard Pape, a wartime escapee, returned his Military Medal to the Queen, protesting that 'The Beatles' MBE reeks of mawkish, bizarre effrontery to our wartime endeavours.'*

Most aggrieved of all was Colonel Frederick Wagg, who had served in the armed forces during both world wars. Colonel Wagg returned no fewer than twelve military decorations and cancelled a £12,000 bequest to the Labour Party, declaring that 'Decorating the Beatles makes a mockery of everything this country stands for. I've heard them sing and play and I think they're terrible.' His outspoken comments gave rise to a mountain of counter-complaints sent to him by Beatles fans. A message on one envelope

* In 1953 Pape had published a book about his wartime exploits, *Boldness Be My Friend*. 'Unique among the escapers of the Second World War, Richard Pape was neither an officer nor a gentleman,' wrote his literary agent Anthony Blond in Pape's obituary, following his death in 1995. 'A red-headed Yorkshireman, his frame bulged with unofficer-like qualities; he was brutally drunk, murderous, treacherous and sly.' Blond successfully negotiated a contract for Pape's memoirs: 'When we sent the contract to Pape in South Africa – he was a natural unreconstructed hard-line Boer, who regarded me as a nigger-loving, wimpish Jew – he got out of his car and went to shoot his wife. Luckily, he missed.'

saying 'WAGGY WILL PAY THE POSTAGE' did nothing to calm Colonel Wagg's temper.

Before the ceremony itself, the Beatles were surrounded by their fellow MBE recipients asking for autographs. 'They were all nice,' observed Paul. 'But one fellow said, "I want it for my daughter, but I don't know what she sees in you!"' During the ceremony, he recalled, 'The man shouted out, "George Harrison, John Lennon, Paul McCartney and Ringo Starr!" The word "Starr" was the cue for us to walk forward, left foot forward. It was just like a show.'

The Queen asked John, 'Have you been working hard recently?' Like many of her subjects when confronted by Her Majesty, John went blank. 'I couldn't think what we've been doing, so I said, "No, we've been having a holiday," when actually we've been recording.'

She then asked them all, 'Have you been together long?' Ringo replied, 'Yes, many years. Forty years.' And together, Ringo and Paul chorused: 'We've been together now for forty years and it don't seem a day too much.'

According to Ringo, at this moment a 'strange, quizzical look' came over Her Majesty's face.

'Did you start it all?' she continued.

'No, they did,' replied Ringo. 'I joined last. I'm the little fellow.'

'It's a pleasure giving it to you,' she said.

'But that's what she said to everybody,' George told the press conference afterwards. 'Then we bowed and we walked towards the Queen, then we walked back and bowed, and then we walked away.'

'She was just like a mum to us,' added John.* 'She was so warm and sweet. She really put us at ease.'

Over the years, Paul's memories of his visit to the Palace remained much the same: a mixture of amazement and amusement, in roughly equal measure. 'For four Liverpool lads it was, "Wow, hey man!" It was quite funny. But she was sweet. I think she seemed a bit mumsy to us because we were young boys and she was a bit older.' George and Paul both wore their MBEs on the *Sgt. Pepper* album cover. Ringo, being more conservative, obeyed the instruction that came with the medal, which specified that it was on no account to be worn in public.

---

* In fact the Queen was only fourteen years older than Ringo and John: thirty-nine compared to their twenty-five.

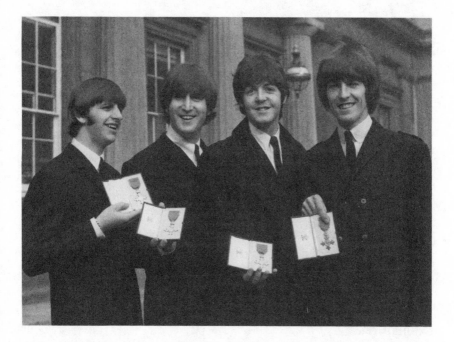

A photograph taken immediately after the ceremony shows John holding up his medal. There is a guileless smile on his face, and not a trace of his usual ironic detachment. Pete Shotton remembers him as 'genuinely thrilled'. When John next visited his Aunt Mimi, he pinned the medal to her chest, saying she deserved it more than he did. For the next four years it was to take pride of place on her mantelpiece.

79.

A short, blurry black-and-white newsclip shows the Beatles climbing the steps of an aeroplane through an arch emblazoned with the message 'BOAC welcomes the BEATLES'.

Two oddities date it to 7 June 1964. First, the Beatle at the back is taller than Ringo, but he is definitely not George, who is three steps up, or John, two steps up, or Paul, who is alongside him. When this unidentified Beatle turns round to wave to the crowds, it turns out to be our poor old friend Jimmie Nicol, who stood in for Ringo when Ringo went down with tonsillitis.

But there is also another person walking up those steps with the group: a matronly figure in an old-fashioned hat, like a figure out of a Giles cartoon. For a split-second she half-turns, beaming. It is Aunt Mimi, who had been invited by John to join them on their flight to the Antipodes, where she had relations.

George judged this trip his favourite. 'I remember them saying, "Return to your seats because we're approaching Hong Kong," and I thought, "We can't be there already." We'd been sitting on the floor drinking and taking Preludins for about thirty hours and so it seemed like a ten-minute flight.'

Aunt Mimi would have known nothing of this particular variety of in-flight entertainment. Had she got wind of it, she would not have been amused, but John was clearly on best behaviour. Interviewed during the flight by an Australian journalist called Bob Rogers, he is a little sleepy and tongue-tied, but unusually polite.

'John, have you ever been interviewed 34,000 feet above sea level before?'

'Er . . . no. Definitely not.'

'How are you enjoying the trip?'

'Not bad. It's a bit long, y'know. But they're looking after us well.'

'Is this the longest trip you've made?'

'I don't know.' He scrunches up his eyes, as if trying to work it out. 'Yes. It is, isn't it?'

In a voiceover, Rogers says, 'John Lennon's famous Aunt Mimi, who brought him up in Liverpool, was also on board. It was Lennon's way of saying Thank You.'

Aunt Mimi is much more outgoing than John. She has made an effort, with a string of pearls around her neck and an elaborate hat consisting of lots of flowers bunched together. She is a good-looking woman, with high cheekbones, and, despite her sourpuss reputation, merry almost to the point of bubbliness.

Rogers introduces her. 'Mrs Mary Elizabeth Smith of Woolton, just outside of Liverpool, better known as Aunt Mimi, the lady who brought John Lennon up from a boy.'

'Yes, that's right.' She looks very proud.

'What sort of boy was he?'

'A lovable rebel.' She laughs out loud, and grins.

'A lovable rebel. Did he get into trouble?'

'Not real trouble, just mischievous, you know.'

'Did you think he was going to become a star such as this in the music world when he was a boy?'

'No. Not in the music world at all. But I always felt he would do something with his writing and drawing.'

The only other filmed interview with Aunt Mimi was to take place seventeen years later, in 1981, a year after John's death. Southern TV's James Montgomery* conducted it at Mimi's seaside house, 'Harbour's Edge', which John bought for her in 1965.

'. . . now, for the first time, his aunt Mimi Smith has opened the door of her home in Dorset to talk of an extraordinary friendship that existed between them and lasted until his death just a year ago. John Lennon bought this house, which looks over Sandbanks Bay, for his Aunt Mimi sixteen years ago . . .'

Montgomery and Aunt Mimi are seen sorting through old snapshots of the young John. Mimi is wearing a smart black suit with a white silk shirt, and a silver brooch.

---

* Later to marry model, actress and *Men Only* columnist Fiona Richmond, star of, among others, *Let's Get Laid* (1977), *From Here to Virginity* (1981) and *Tell Tale Tits* (1987).

Now aged seventy-five, she remembers buying John his first guitar. 'Well I battled against it for quite a long time. I didn't want him wasting his college time and missing lectures by *wasting his time playing the guitar*.'

Exasperation creeps into her voice, as though, in some parallel universe, her feckless nephew is still nagging her for his first guitar, and she is still trying to steer him onto the straight and narrow.

'Whereas his training would last, these things *come and go*, they're playing their guitar one week, everyone's clamouring for them – then they disappear, and *nobody ever hears of them again*. And then what was I going to do if I had a boy of twenty-one thrown back on my hands, *qualified for nothing*?!?!' Her voice rises and trembles on the word 'nothing'.

Montgomery asks Aunt Mimi if she can remember when John got his first guitar.

'He was a bit like yourself, a soft-soaper.' A flash of her nephew's combative flintiness. 'And he picks me up, and, you know' – here she performs kissing gestures and noises – 'kisses me on the cheek. "Mimi, can I have a guitar?" And he *hadn't any money to get a guitar*. There was only me who could buy him one! And I remember we went to Liverpool and we went into a guitar shop and they were all over the place, and I didn't know anything about them so he chose one and it was *seventeen pounds*!'

'How surprised were you that the Beatles went on to achieve worldwide fame and success?'

'I knew they had something – but *nobody expected this*. It was a shock to them, too.'

She talks of the days when John would come to visit her at her new house by the seaside. 'He'd nip down weekends. Suddenly there'd be a whirlwind, and he'd come in. It was usually when the pressure was getting a bit much and he'd come down here and do cartwheels on the beach.' She laughs and smiles. 'By himself, nobody else there.'

After he'd gone to live in America, they would talk on the telephone once or twice a week, 'about current affairs, how the pound was going up and down, that sort of thing. Another time, he'd be reminiscing about his childhood. The funny things – I was always chasing him, you know.' She gives a throaty chuckle. 'I knew what he was up to before –' She pauses, clearly visualising the young John. 'What he could *not* make out was how I knew when he was up to something!' She carries on laughing, obviously enjoying the memory.

'What about the antics he got up to – the famous love-in with Yoko Ono? Did you talk to him about that?'

'I certainly did. I just found him, telephoned him, and said, "That's enough! Thank you! We've had enough! Keep that lot for the music hall!"' She giggles. 'And that was the end of it.'

'So he listened to you, then?'

'Well, though he rebelled, and said, "I'm not going to do as you tell me," he always did! . . . When he'd been naughty, I'd ring him up and I'd say, "Don't have me come to New York!" And then he'd say, "You're just being grumpy." So as soon as he said that, down goes the phone, you see. And then I'd wait for about half an hour and he'd get friendly with me again.' She puts on John's voice: '"Hello, is that you, Gertie? Never mind, Gertie."' She roars with laughter.

'Did he give you many presents?'

'Honestly, the place is full of presents – beads, pearls, *everything*! I could have had anything in the world. But I'm just one of those people who's rather spartan, and I don't want anything.'

The camera focuses on John's framed Silver Heart from the Variety Club of Great Britain sitting on the mantelpiece, presented to him by Harold Wilson in 1964.

'What do you think of all these stories that have been published about him since his death? . . . Stories about his private life, his sex life?'

'I've never heard anything like it in my life! . . . I think they're sick, depraved people, obsessed with sex, craving for attention.'

'When was the last time he phoned you?'

'The night before he was murdered. Two hours. And he would say, "I'll be seeing you soon Mimi, I can't wait to see you," and then of course at five o'clock the next morning it came over the overseas news, and honestly, if I thought he was dead I don't think I could go on. I don't think of him as dead.'

'Of all the songs that John played and sang, was there a favourite one that you enjoyed?'

'Well I don't know. I think "A Hard Day's Night" is not so bad at the present time!' Once again, she laughs her throaty laugh.

80.

On YouTube, that brief interview has attracted over half a million views, and over a thousand comments, almost all of them fond: 'What a grand lady.' 'National treasure Rest in peace.' 'What a caring, grounded soul. She gave a legend love and a bit of discipline and wings to grow. Heaven bless the Mums and Aunties of the world.' 'I believe if there had been no Mimi there would not have been the John Lennon who we came to love and therefore no Beatles.' 'Aww, a lovely lady. I know he had difficulties during childhood, but he was lucky to have someone so kind-hearted RIP.'

Yet two women who knew her well – John's first wife Cynthia, and his half-sister Julia Baird – have written damning portraits of Aunt Mimi. Julia – the daughter of John's mother (also called Julia) and her waiter boyfriend Bobby Dykins – nurses a particular antipathy to her mother's elder sister. Aunt Mimi had, says Julia, an 'obsessive need to control the lives and actions of those around her'. In her memoir, *Imagine This: Growing Up with My Brother John Lennon* (2007), she accuses Aunt Mimi of 'the greatest possible hypocrisy', claiming that in 1956, at the age of fifty, this prim, upstanding woman embarked on an affair with a lodger twenty-six years her junior. The accusation of hypocrisy is due to Mimi's appearance of propriety and the apparently sly means by which she eased John away from his mother, complaining to social services that a couple living in sin were not to be trusted with a child. According to Julia, Aunt Mimi's last words, spoken to a nurse, were 'I'm terrified of dying. I've been so wicked.' Though, to be fair, the same nurse has been reported elsewhere as saying they were much sunnier: 'Hello, John.'

Cynthia Lennon was no more forgiving. 'She loved to fuel the image of the stern but loving aunt who provided the secure backdrop to John's success,' she writes of Aunt Mimi in one of her two autobiographies. 'But that wasn't the Mimi I knew. She battered away at John's self-confidence and left him angry and hurt.' Cynthia portrays Mimi as very la-di-da:

'Mimi's manner was almost regal. She spoke without a hint of Scouse and I thought John must have adopted his working-class Liverpool accent as a rebellion against her. Early on it became apparent to me that Mimi was something of a snob; she was middle-class with upper-class aspirations, and one of her favourite words was "common". She used it to condemn most of John's interests and friends – including, I suspect, me.'

Far from accepting the idea that Aunt Mimi gave John 'wings to grow', Cynthia portrays her as trying to clip them: while the other families encouraged the Beatles to go to Hamburg, Mimi 'did everything she could think of to stop John going'.

On John's arrival back from Germany, he presented Cynthia with a chocolate-brown leather coat from C&A Modes: 'I felt so gorgeous in it I couldn't wait to show it off.' They both dropped round to Aunt Mimi's with a chicken for lunch, but she showed no gratitude: 'Mimi saw the coat and heard that John had bought it for me and she hit the roof. She screamed at John that he'd spent his money on a "gangster's moll" and hurled first the chicken, which she grabbed from me, then a hand-mirror, at John. "Do you think you can butter me up with a chicken when you've spent all your money on this?" she screamed.' Cynthia remembered John leaving by the back door. '"All she cares about is fucking money and cats," he said.'

During the Beatles' residencies at the Cavern, Jim McCartney often dropped by to hear them, and George's mum, Louise, was also a frequent visitor, cheering them along. But it was definitely not Aunt Mimi's scene. According to Cynthia, she put her head round the door only once, to see where John had been wasting his time. Louise Harrison called over to her, 'Aren't they great?'

'I'm glad someone thinks so,' Mimi shouted back. 'We'd all have had lovely peaceful lives but for you encouraging them!'

She was filled with horror at the smell and the noise. 'Try as I might, I just couldn't get near the stage,' she complained to Hunter Davies. 'If I could, I would have pulled him off it.'

After the show, she forced her way into the Cavern's squalid dressing room. 'Very nice, John,' she said sarcastically, leaving soon afterwards. 'Her abrupt departure hurt John,' recalled Cynthia. 'He'd have loved her to be proud of him.'

In 1962, John played Aunt Mimi the Beatles' first single, 'Love Me

Do'. Her reaction was uncompromising: 'If you think you're going to make your fortune with that, then you've got another think coming.'

When John finally plucked up the courage to tell Aunt Mimi that he and Cynthia were getting married, 'She screamed, raged and threatened never to speak to him again if he went ahead with it.'

Everyone is agreed that Aunt Mimi was a snob. They take note of her collection of Royal Worcester dinner plates, her leather-bound collected works of Sir Winston Churchill, and the gardener she employed. Mimi objected to George's thick Scouse accent, but she didn't approve of Paul either, blaming him for tempting John into the unseemly world of rock'n'roll. 'She would always refer to me as "Your little friend",' says Paul. 'I'd look at her, she'd smile. I'd know what she'd done. I would ignore it. It was very patronising, but she secretly quite liked me, she sort of twinkled, but she was very aware that John's friends were lower-class. She was the kind of woman who would put you down with a glint in her eye, with a smile, but she'd put you down all the same.'

In those early days, Aunt Mimi refused to allow George or Paul to cross her threshold. 'He [Paul] used to come to my front door. He'd be on his bike, which he'd lean against the fence. He would look over at me with his sheep eyes and say, "Hello, Mimi. Can I come in?" "No, you certainly cannot," I'd say.' One day Aunt Mimi appeared to relent, telling John that

if George came round, she would be prepared to let him in. 'He arrived with a crewcut and a pink shirt. I threw him out. Well, it wasn't done. I might have been a bit old-fashioned, but schoolboys dressing like that! Up till John was sixteen, I always made sure he wore his regulation school blazer and shirt.'

After the Beatles became world famous she would rail against John for assuming an exaggerated Scouse accent. After all, she had brought him up to speak the Queen's English. To a thirteen-year-old Beatles fan who wrote saying she had seen John on television, she replied, 'When he came home, I said, "John, what's all this about, what's happened to your voice?" . . . He didn't really talk like that. I brought him up properly, not to talk like a ruffian.' While the other Beatles' relatives remained awestruck by their celebrity, Aunt Mimi always treated John as Brian's mother treats her son in *Monty Python's Life of Brian*: 'He's not the Messiah. He's a very naughty boy!' On the release of *Two Virgins*, with its cover photograph of John and Yoko naked, she made her feelings all too clear: 'It would have been all right, John, but you're both so ugly. Why don't you get somebody attractive on the cover if you've got to have someone completely naked?'

Soon after embarking on his relationship with Yoko, John took her to meet Aunt Mimi in Poole. It was never going to be the easiest of introductions. Aunt Mimi told James Montgomery about the encounter: 'He came in all bright and breezy – typical John – and she followed behind. I took one look at her and thought, "My God, what is that?"

'Well, I didn't like the look of her right from the start. She had long black hair, all over the place, and she was small – she looked just like a dwarf to me. I told John what I felt while she was outside, looking across the bay. I said to him, "Who's the poison dwarf, John?"

'. . . Well, I didn't know what it was all about. I wondered who it was. And he said, "It's Yoko." I didn't think anything of it, you know. But I did say, "What do *you* do for a living?" She said, "I'm an *artist*." I said, "That's very funny, *I've* never heard of you!"'

While John was in the loo, Aunt Mimi informed Yoko that she had always brought him up to have good manners, and that was why he always stood up when a woman came into the room. On his return, she warned him of what happened to the Duke of Windsor, the former King Edward VIII. The duke had been remarkably popular, she said, but the public had gone off him when he married Mrs Simpson. 'He lost his popularity, and John, you'd better know that.'

Mimi remembered John brushing her little homily away. 'He laughed it off, but he knew I didn't like her and he knew I was a good judge of character. I couldn't see what he saw in her and I thought it was wrong and nothing good would come of it.'

81.

But another argument, equally strong, can be made in favour of Aunt Mimi. After all, she lies in the grand tradition of Great British Aunts: bossy, demanding and fearsome, unabashed upholders of the social fabric, capable of reducing even the most recalcitrant nephews to jelly. 'It is no use telling me that there are bad aunts and good aunts. At core, they are all alike,' observes Bertie Wooster. 'Sooner or later, out pops the cloven hoof.'

Pete Shotton recalled John's childhood obsession with Richmal Crompton's *Just William* books, which are choc-a-bloc with aunts, most of them forbidding, in both senses of the word. They range from Aunt Jane, 'tall and prim and what she called "house proud"', to Great-Aunt Augusta, who lives by the adage 'There's no joy like the joy of duty done.' With his pals Ivan Vaughan and Nigel Whalley in tow, John led a gang called the Outlaws, just like William's. 'I used to live *Alice* and *Just William*,' he recalled. 'I wrote my own William stories, with me doing all the things . . . After I'd read a book, I'd relive it all again. That was one reason why I wanted to be the gang leader at school. I'd want them all to play the games that I wanted them to play, the ones I'd just been reading.'

His Outlaws would get up to all sorts of pranks and japes, some playful, others verging on the delinquent. They would pinch apples, ride up Penny Lane on the bumpers of the tram cars, spend money intended for the church collection on bubblegum, smash street lamps with stones, shoplift cigarettes, and pull girls' knickers down. At the school fête, John and Pete set up a dartboard decorated with their teachers' faces. On another occasion, they made dog collars out of old cereal packets and dressed up their classmates as vicars. To make money, they stole school-dinner tickets and sold them around school.

The influence of William is tangible, and may well have infected the Beatles. 'The Beatles made me laugh immoderately, the way I used to laugh as a child at the *Just William* books,' recalled Maureen Cleave, the journalist who knew them best in their early days of fame. 'Their wit was just so keen and sharp – John Lennon's especially. They all had this wonderful quality – it wasn't innocence, but everything was new to them. They were like William, finding out about the world and trying to make sense of it.' William's Outlaws, like John's, were always on the lookout for fishy ways to make their fortunes. In *William's Double Life* (1929), when the Outlaws try to raise money, they are disappointed by the poor response from their various aunts and uncles:

> 'I went round to them ALL,' said Ginger mournfully, 'an' my Aunt Emma she said, "Certainly not, after your ball comin' in through my landin' window like it did last week," an' my Uncle John said, "Cert'nly not after you goin' over my lawn with your scooter the way you did yesterday," an' my Aunt Jane said, "Cert'nly not after you chasin' my dear Pussy as I saw you last week," an' my Uncle George said, "Cert'nly not after you throwin' stones up at my walnut tree like I saw you doin' yesterday," an' my Uncle John said, "Cert'nly not after you climbin' my rose pole an' breakin' it" . . .'

In *Just William* (1922), William puts one of his scariest aunts to good use. He arrives in her room to find his imposing Aunt Emily has fallen asleep, and that 'She lay in her immense stature in a blouse and striped petticoat, while from her open mouth issued the fascinating sounds.' Seizing an opportunity for commerce, William then places a sign on her door saying:

FAT WILD WOMAN
TORKIN NATIF
LANGWIDGE

and charges the neighbouring children tuppence to see her. 'They stood in a hushed, delighted group around her bed. The sounds never ceased, never abated. William allowed them two minutes in the room. They came out reluctantly, paid more money, joined the end of the queue and re-entered.'

William extends the exhibit to incorporate Aunt Emily's dressing table, posting notices such as 'FAT WILD WOMAN'S TEETH' and 'FAT WILD WOMAN'S HARE'. But suddenly Aunt Emily comes to life.

She sprang up and, seizing him by the shoulders, shook him till his teeth chattered, the tinsel crown fell down, encircling ears and nose, and one of his moustaches fell limply at his feet.

'You wicked boy!' she said as she shook him. 'You WICKED, WICKED, WICKED BOY!'

John and his gang once constructed a makeshift raft from old planks, but it tipped over, casting them into a murky pond teeming with frogs. In an attempt to dry his clothes so Aunt Mimi wouldn't know what they had been up to, John built a bonfire, but it got out of hand and the fire brigade arrived with sirens blaring. It could just as well have happened to William.

Called to see the deputy head, Mr Gallaway, on charges of mis-behaviour, John and Pete were told to stand behind him while he got out the Headmaster's Punishment Book. To amuse Pete, John put out a hand and tickled Mr Gallaway's bald pate. Thinking it was a fly, Mr Gallaway kept swatting his head. 'This subtle play of hands continued for several minutes,' Pete recalled, 'until both of us were doubled up with suppressed laughter – to the point that John (as was his wont in such desperate situ-ations) literally pissed himself.' When Mr Gallaway asked what the pud-dle was, John replied, 'I think the roof's leaking, sir.' Pete exploded with laughter, but once again John saved the day. 'Bless you, Pete!' he exclaimed, adding, for Mr Gallaway's benefit, 'He's been sneezing all day, sir. He has a dreadful cold.'

Mimi was strict with John. Whenever word got back to her about his bad behaviour, she would send him to his bedroom without any supper. Only once did she beat him, having caught him stealing money from her handbag. But these punishments had little effect. 'I was coming down Penny Lane one day and I saw this crowd of boys in a ring, watching two boys fighting,' Aunt Mimi recalled. '"Just like those common Rose Lane scruffs," I said . . . Then they parted and out came this awful boy with his coat hanging off. To my horror it was John. John always liked me telling him that story. "Just like you, Mimi. Everybody else is always common."'

To the end of his life, John stayed in constant touch with Aunt Mimi, perhaps because she was the only person on the planet who could see through his nonsense. In 1968 Hunter Davies observed that of all the Beatle parents, 'Mimi is probably the only one whose relationship has not really changed. She still in many ways treats John as she's always done, whereas with the others there is a hint of hero worship, almost reverence. Mimi still criticizes John's clothes and how he looks, as she did when he was a teenager. She tells him when he's looking fat and not to spend too much. Mimi even doesn't care for the way John speaks. She says he won't speak properly, never finishing sentences. "John's always been a bad speaker. And he's getting worse all the time. I often can't understand what he's talking about. His mind's jumping all over the place."'

In turn, John's devotion to Aunt Mimi transcended all his fads and his failings, and all her rantings against them, justified and unjustified. As a child he could bear her reprimands, and even her occasional praise, but he hated it when she ignored him. 'Don't 'nore me, Mimi,' he would say. When he grew up, and all the rest of the world started paying him attention, he still needed to be sure that Mimi wasn't ignoring him. To the end of her days, Mimi kept a plaque in pride of place on her mantelpiece, given to her by John, and engraved with one of her grumbles from his adolescence: 'The guitar's all very well, John, but you'll never make a living out of it.' For both of them, her admonishment had become a source of pride. To the end of his days, John wrote a long letter to her once a week, signed 'Himself'. In their monthly phone conversations he liked to tease her into a furious response by exaggerating his Scouse accent. In New York he developed a craving for items that reminded him of his childhood with his Aunt Mimi. She dutifully posted him her Royal Worcester tea service, along with his Quarry Bank school blazer and stripy school tie: 'I sent him parcel after parcel of stuff.'

John kept urging Aunt Mimi to abandon Dorset for an apartment in the Dakota. The uncompromising tone of her reply must surely have pleased him, as it was so entirely in character: 'You'll never catch me over there. I have never liked Americans. And you shouldn't be there either, it's no good for you.'

'He comes to see me as often as he can,' she told Davies in 1968. 'He sat up on the roof for four days in the summer. I ran up and down getting drinks for him. He never shows much emotion. He finds it hard to say sorry. But one night he said that even if he didn't come down to see me every day, or every month, he always thought about me at some time every day, wherever he was. That meant a great deal to me.'

In 1979 John wrote a long, nostalgic letter to his cousin Leila – 'I thought of you a lot this Xmas – the shadows on the ceiling as the cars went by at night – putting up the paper chains . . .' He ended it with a reference to Aunt Mimi: 'I'm almost scared to go to England, 'coz I know it would be the last time I saw Mimi – I'm a coward about Goodbyes.' For her part, Yoko thought that when John sat down with a cup of tea in their apartment at the Dakota, stroking a cat, 'he always looked just like Mimi'.

Every Christmas when John was little, Mimi would take him to *Puss in Boots* at the Liverpool Empire. One year it was snowing, and John went in his Wellington boots. When Puss first came onstage, John stood and piped up, 'Mimi, he's got his Wellington boots on! So have I!' Everyone in the audience turned to him and smiled.

In December 1963, after a year in which the Beatles had, in the words of the TV host Alexander Kendrick, transformed the country into 'Beatle-land, formerly known as Britain', they brought their Christmas show to the Liverpool Empire. Aunt Mimi stood at the back, having turned down John's offer of a seat in the front row.

'I was very proud of course to see him playing on the stage at the Empire. It was the first time I realised what an effect they had. They had mounted police to keep the crowds back . . . It was very exciting. But I couldn't help thinking all the time: "No, he's not really a Beatle. He's the little fellow who once sat upstairs with me and shouted, 'Mimi, he's got his Wellington boots on!'"'

82.

Compared to the other three, John was Lord Snooty. In 1950s Liverpool, his family was regarded as posh by the teenage George and Paul. Unlike them, John lived in a privately-owned semi-detached house that had a name – 'Mendips' – not a number. As if this were not smart enough, it overlooked a golf course. John had an aunt not an auntie, and not just any old cat but a Siamese cat, as well as one relative who was a dentist in Edinburgh and another who worked for the BBC. He also had an uncle who taught Paul handwriting and English at the Liverpool Institute.

Paul was impressed. 'John had an Aunt Harriet, and Harriet was not a name we came across, especially when they called her Harrie! We never knew women called Mimi, which is very sophisticated, very twenties and thirties, very jazz era. So it was Harriet and Mimi. I can imagine them with long cigarette-holders. It was like Richmal Crompton's *Just William* books to me . . . So John was a particularly attractive character in that kind of world.' Even now, when Paul speaks of John's comparatively well-to-do childhood, there is a slight element – 'So there!' – of reverse snobbery about it. It is as if, after all these years, he still feels the need to counter John's claims of poverty. 'John lived just the other side of the golf course, literally and metaphorically. People don't realise how middle-class he was. It's a very fancy neighbourhood . . . In fact, John once told me that the family had once owned Woolton, the whole village.' In *The Beatles Anthology* he goes a few steps further, saying, 'To us, John was *upper* class . . . It's ironic, he was always very "Fuck you!", and he wrote the song "Working Class Hero" – in fact, he wasn't at all working class.'

In an interview John gave shortly before his death, he acknowledged that he had never really been a Working-Class Hero: 'I was a nice clean-cut suburban boy, and in the class system that was about half a niche higher-class than Paul, George and Ringo, who lived in council houses. We owned our own house, had our own garden, they didn't have anything like that.

So I was a bit of a fruit compared to them, in a way. Ringo was the only real city kid. I think he came from the lousiest area . . . I was always well dressed, well fed, well schooled, and brought up to be a nice lower-middle-class English boy, you know?' In middle age he had come to think that it was being middle class, not working class, that had made the Beatles different. After all, George, Paul and John were all grammar-school boys. 'Up until then all rock'n'rollers . . . had been black and poor: rural South, city slums. And the whites had been truckers, like Elvis. But the thing about the Beatles was that we were pretty well educated and not truckers. Paul could have gone to university. He was always a good boy. He passed his exams. He could have become, I don't know – Dr McCartney. I could have done it myself if I had worked. I never worked.'

On first becoming famous, both Paul and John took care to overplay their Scouse accents. When Paul arrived home after the Beatles' first TV appearance, his younger brother Michael asked him, 'Why did you talk like that on the TV? It sounded like George gone wrong.' Among his Liverpudlian contemporaries, Paul was teased for having risen a notch up the social scale by passing his 11-Plus and going to the Liverpool Institute. 'There weren't many other kids from the Institute living round our way. I was called "college pudding". "Fucking college pudding" they said.'

This did little to staunch the flow of snobbery that greeted their early success. While the Beatles were away on a brief tour of Scandinavia in October 1963, the Lord Privy Seal, Edward Heath MP, was heard to say that he found it hard to recognise what they said as 'the Queen's

English'.* On their return to London, the group were asked to comment on this hoity-toity remark. John put on a theatrically posh accent: 'Ay can't understand Teddy saying thet et awl, reyaleh, I can't understand Teddy!' Then he smiled, looked at the camera and said, in a rather more menacing way, 'I'm not going to vote for Ted.'

PAUL: Oooh!

Q: But you're not going to change your accent for the Lord Privy Seal?

JOHN: (swinging into an exaggerated Scouse accent) Ah, no lak will keep lak the same kand of thing like, won't we? Yeah thaz right.

PAUL: Oh, aye! Yes!

To another reporter, Paul said, 'And I bet half the people who voted for him didn't speak the Queen's English either.' Later, Heath tried to make amends, bafflingly hailing the group as 'the saviours of the corduroy industry'. Who knows? Perhaps corduroy represented Mr Heath's outer limit of modishness.

Six months later, the Beatles were filming *A Hard Day's Night*. The American director Richard Lester, who had lived in England for a decade, was intrigued by their impact on the British class system. 'I think they were the first to give a confidence to the youth of the country, which led to the disappearance of the Angry Young Man with a defensive mien,' he told his biographer. 'The Beatles sent the class thing sky-high; they laughed it out of existence and, I think, introduced a tone of equality more successfully than any other single factor I know. Eventually it became taken for granted that they were single-handedly breaking Britain's class system without the benefit of an education or family background.' Yet even he couldn't resist adding a corrective: 'They were, of course, much more middle-class than most people admitted.'

Filming *Help!* in the Bahamas in February 1965, Eleanor Bron went with the Beatles to a smart party in Nassau, ostensibly held in their honour.

---

* The son of a Kent builder, Heath had altered his own accent, and was teased for his idiosyncratic vowels, not least by Monty Python's Flying Circus, who released a spoof educational disc called 'Teach Yourself Heath'.

She was put off by what she saw. The Beatles were, she felt, simul-taneously patronised and scorned. The 'swells of the island' were 'able to contain neither their curiosity nor their middle-aged spleen at seeing these four "uneducated", "lower-class" youngsters (products of the Welfare State) succeed. Who knows what manoeuvres they must have gone through for the privilege of being able to assemble at this scandal of a dinner given in honour of these mere boys, just so that they could turn their noses up at them; or – if they could thrust themselves close enough – to insult them personally, down their noses, with snide remarks; requesting autographs for "demented" granddaughters. And if they could not get close, watching from afar with pouchy eyes for proofs of callowness, social solecisms and unacceptable accents, so that they could relay these to the world, and their sense that they have been cheated – the shockingness of what the world is coming to.'

Her fellow actor Victor Spinetti took a similar view. 'We were driven to the home of the minister of finance. The guests, Government House officials and their wives, sipped at their drinks and milled about in a group, carefully preserving, I noticed, a gap between themselves and the Beatles. From their vantage point, they stared at the boys and talked, not to them but about them. "Which one is Ringo?" I heard a voice call out.

'"I think it's that one, the one with the big nose," came a drawled an-swer as they all continued to stare. One of them, a woman, left the group and wandered across to George.

'"Is that hair real?" she asked, and, without waiting for an invitation, tugged it. "Oh yes," she said, turning in astonishment to the others. "It is." These people were looking at the Beatles as if they were prize polo ponies, except that for them, prize polo ponies would have been more interesting.'

They were all led into dinner. Each place setting was laid with row upon row of gold cutlery and a variety of glasses. Ever mischievous, the Beatles played up to the roles assigned to them by the dignitaries. 'Oooh, what are those?' they asked. The po-faced wife of the governor turned to her husband and murmured, 'They don't know their knives and forks.'

Such was the all-pervasive nature of the British class system that there were booby traps even within the bosom of the family. Forty years after his mother's death, Paul told Barry Miles of a moment in his childhood that continued to be 'a strange little awkwardness for me'. He had, he said, once chastised his mother for saying the word 'ask' with a long 'a'. 'She pronounced it posh. And I made fun of her and it slightly embarrassed her. Years later I've never forgiven myself. It's a terrible little thing. I wish I could go back and say, "I was only kidding, Mum."'

As we have seen, John's Aunt Mimi looked down on the young George Harrison for having what she referred to as a 'low Liverpool voice'. 'You always seem to like lower-class types, don't you, John?' she said.

With the Beatles' fame came status. They entered the celebrity class, which has long maintained a sort of non-aggression pact with the upper class. At the height of their success, George spoke proudly of what he had learned from his privately-educated wife, Pattie Boyd. 'The natural thing when you get money is that you acquire taste,' he told Maureen Cleave in 1966. 'I've got a lot of taste off Pattie. You get taste in food as well. Instead of eggs and beans and steak you branch out into the avocado scene. I never dreamt I would like avocado pears. I thought it was like eating bits of wax – fake pears out of a bowl – when I saw people shoving it down.'

In their journey up the social ladder, the Beatles were sometimes obliged to learn the ropes. Looking back on her marriage, Pattie remembered that George's family 'held their knives like pens, and "tea" consisted of cold ham or pork pie, tomatoes cut in half, pickled beetroot and salad cream, with sliced white bread. They had it at six o'clock, and later in the evening there was tea and biscuits.'

Some credited the Beatles with fracturing the class system. In her novel *A Word Child* (1975), Iris Murdoch – a tremendous Beatles fan – pictured her narrator listening to four young men from disparate backgrounds chatting around a kitchen table. 'Here at any rate class no longer existed,' he reflects. 'The Beatles, like Empedocles, had thrown all things about.'

The Beatles arrived on the scene after a series of plays and novels – *Look Back in Anger* (1956), *Room at the Top* (1957), *Saturday Night and Sunday Morning* (1958), *The Loneliness of the Long Distance Runner* (1959) – had focused on English working-class youth. But while these works portrayed young men stuck at the bottom of a merciless hierarchy, or forced to adapt if they want to rise, in *A Hard Day's Night* and *Help!* the Beatles threw off any such shackles to create a world of their own; they are cheerful and self-confident, scorning any pressure to conform.

In both films they subvert expectations of how working-class lads should behave. One scene in *Help!* shows the four Beatles arriving at a traditional working-class terrace in a chauffeur-driven Rolls-Royce. Two old dears, played by Dandy Nichols and Gretchen Franklin, wave at them from the other side of the street.

'Lovely lads, and so natural. I mean, adoration hasn't gone to their heads one jot, has it?'

'Just so natural, and still the same as they was before they was.'

Each Beatle enters a different front door. The camera follows them inside, only to reveal not four little houses but one big luxurious pad, filled with all the fashionable accoutrements of the sixties high life – sliding bookshelves, fitted carpets, leather sofas, trendy lighting, even a Wurlitzer organ that rises from the ground. It's a sweet joke, and one that gleefully subverts the dictum that the proper way to deal with success is to not let it change you. The Beatles stand for fun and enjoyment, for doing whatever you want, regardless of your background. Unlike Jimmy Porter and Joe Lampton, they are neither angry nor cowed: they are free.

83.

When we talk about the Beatles, we talk about ourselves.

At the end of August 1966 the *Saturday Evening Post* published 'The Monarchs of the Beatle Empire', a piece by the British journalist James Morris.* In it, Morris saluted the Beatles for liberating Britain from class. To twenty-first-century ears its tone may hint of Lady Bracknell, but its sentiments remain radical. First, he described the arrival of these 'four young roosters from the north' into 'a country so long hag-ridden by class'. When Morris had been to Liverpool, somebody had complained that 'They're all grammar-school boys really,' but for Morris this was by the way: 'the point is that they have managed to make the whole subject of personal origins, so long an obsession of the English, irrelevant to themselves'. In the past, the regional character in England was always exploited for comic purposes, but the Beatles had just carried on regardless: 'They have simply ignored the old English social divisions and effortlessly stormed the barricades of custom.'

Morris confessed that he was not their biggest fan: 'I still, to be honest, don't awfully like the look of them – which is to say, I don't like their faces, just as I don't happen to like caraway seeds or Rubens.' But he was attracted to the Beatles for their 'absolute aloofness to old prejudices and preconceptions, their brand of festive iconoclasm'. Their glory lay in their detachment from Britain's imperial grandeur. They are New Men, 'the British emancipated at last from the White Man's burden'. Morris proclaimed 'an inescapable sense of holiday in England today – a springy, frothy sense of release'.

He then touched on what many people thought of as their androgyny, the product of long hair, pretty faces and skinny frames. They had thrown aside all the old tenets of manliness: 'Children are said to love them because

* Educated at Evelyn Waugh's old school, Lancing College, and Christ Church, Oxford.

they don't know whether they are boys or girls.' They were, he said, 'minstrels of . . . emancipation' who had 'expressed something that most of us in England have instinctively felt – that the old values really did need a cheerful dust-down. Why *should* we be manly? Why *should* life be quite so real, quite so earnest? Why should we stiffen our upper lips? Who says so? *Why?*'

Though he never mentioned it in the piece, two years before, James Morris had embarked on a prolonged course of pills derived from the urine of pregnant mares. In his autobiography, *Conundrum*, written many years later, he chronicled his transformation 'gradually from a person who looked like a healthy male of orthodox sexual tendencies, approaching middle age, into something perilously close to a hermaphrodite, apparently neither of one sex nor the other, and more or less ageless'. This initial treatment led him to full sex reassignment surgery in 1972, at which point James became Jan.

84.

A week after the Beatles' civic reception in Liverpool Town Hall on 10 July 1964, John bought his first property. From now on, he too had somewhere to rattle his jewellery.

'Kenwood' is a mock-Tudor mansion situated on the St George's Hill estate in Weybridge, Surrey, bang next to the golf course. It cost the twenty-three-year-old John £20,000, at a time when the average house in Britain sold for £3,400. He added a swimming pool – 'Nothing like I ordered,' he complained – and countless luxuries and further embellishments – two eighteen-foot sofas, a marble fireplace, a sunken bathtub, a jacuzzi in the master bathroom. These cost a further £40,000. For all its eccentricities, this was the bourgeois dream.

Each day, vans from the smartest stores delivered unimaginable quantities of merchandise: telephones and tape-recorders, a gorilla fancy-dress costume, a suit of armour, a jukebox, a pinball machine, a vast altar crucifix and five televisions, which John liked to keep turned on, but with the sound down.

He had two large attic rooms knocked together to make room for twenty different Scalextric model racing car sets, complete with landscaping. 'If you're going to do something, you might as well do it properly,' he told a friend.

He bought books galore, including leather-bound editions of Tolstoy and Oscar Wilde, and the complete *Just William* series, along with more specialist and unexpected works such as *Forty-One Years in India* by Field Marshal Lord Roberts and *Curiosities of Natural History* by Francis T. Buckland.

The dining room, covered in purple velvet wallpaper, sported a long white table surrounded by a dozen antique chairs. The kitchen contained any number of cutting-edge gadgets, none of which John was able to operate. Cynthia was similarly bamboozled, but managed to master the waffle machine. Tired of eating just waffles, John asked his interior designer, Ken

Partridge, to send someone down to teach Cynthia how to work the other appliances, though he himself never bothered to learn.

The garden was filled with furniture and statuary, much of it covered in psychedelic colours after John and his friend Terry went wild with the spray paints. Later, a giant boot, eight feet high, from the film *Help!* stood at the bottom of the garden. Four garages, all in a row, provided shelter for three shiny new cars – a Rolls-Royce, a Mini Cooper and a Ferrari.

For most of his life, the only space John had had to himself was his cosy little bedroom in Mendips. It is understandable, then, that rather than expanding into Kenwood's twenty-seven rooms, or parading around its impressive gardens, he spent most his time confined to the modest sun-room, scrunched up like an embryo on a tiny yellow sofa which had, naturally enough, been a gift from Aunt Mimi.

In those days, John only had to imagine more possessions and – Hey presto! – they would appear overnight. A standing order with Hamley's toy shop supplied him with every new board game the moment it was issued.

He found his staff harder to manage. He liked his amiable daily, Dot Jarlett, but she got on badly with the cook, whose handyman husband wouldn't stop flirting with the guests. Before long, the cook's daughter left her husband and moved into the staff flat with her parents, but she then started making passes at John. Meanwhile, household items kept disappearing. The never-ending episodes of pilferage and squabbling upstairs and downstairs gave Kenwood something of a psychedelic Swinging Sixties Downton Abbey feel. In a later episode, Cynthia was informed by a nosy neighbour that John's smelly, chain-smoking chauffeur Jock was living in the back of the Rolls-Royce. 'I was hopeless when it came to standing up to people,' admitted Cynthia. Eventually, Brian Epstein took control, sacking the cook, her husband and the chauffeur.

Though decorated and furnished as a fun palace, Kenwood soon became the setting for an Ibsen drama, forgotten figures emerging from the fog of the past, set on sabotaging the future. By now, John was one of the four richest and most famous and most liberated young men in the world; but he was also a husband, a father, a nephew and a son. And a son-in-law, too: from the start, he was at daggers drawn with his forceful mother-in-law, Lillian, who had moved down from Liverpool to live in nearby Esher. Lillian liked to spend her days busying herself at Kenwood, or rootling around antique shops and auction houses for bits and pieces she judged would contribute to the interior decoration. Though the beneficiary of John's largesse – he had not only bought her a house, but also paid for its upkeep, and gave her an allowance – Lillian remained convinced that her daughter had married beneath her. For his part, John found it easier to pretend that Lillian wasn't there. One visitor remembered seeing her 'flopped on a couch, stuffing glacé fruits into her mouth', while John 'passed through without comment'.

And ghostlier figures than Lillian would also come knocking. One day, when Cynthia was alone in Kenwood, she opened the door to a stranger, 'a tiny man with lank grey hair, balding on top'. The man introduced himself as John's long-lost father, Fred, a claim confirmed at first sight: 'He looked as unkempt and down-at-heel as a tramp – but, alarmingly, with John's face.'

Cynthia said she was expecting John back in an hour or two. She told Fred he was welcome to wait, introduced him to his grandson, Julian, and gave him a cup of tea and cheese on toast. Their conversation proved stilted, but they soon found a shared pursuit: when the fifty-two-year-old Fred mentioned that his hair was a mess, Cynthia offered to cut it for him.

For some reason John had failed to tell Cynthia that, just a few weeks before, he had met his father for the first time in seventeen years. John had been six years old when Fred had tussled with Julia over which of them would look after him. Fred had been gone to sea for four years, working as a ship's steward. On his return to England he had smashed a shop window and stolen a mannequin. Having been arrested while waltzing with the mannequin, he had been imprisoned for six months.

From prison he wrote to Julia's sister, John's Aunt Mimi, asking her to help him regain a role in John's life. Mimi's response had been severe: 'You have made an absolute shambles of your life and have brought shame and scandal upon your family. If you have a shred of decency left in you I advise you to go to New Zealand alone and put your past life behind you. Surely you don't want your son to know you've been in jail?'

By 1963, Fred was working as an itinerant washer-up in hotels and restaurants. He had given up any hope of seeing his son again until a fellow worker at the Moore Place Hotel in Esher pointed out that the leader of the Beatles was called Lennon, and looked just like Fred.

Fred despatched a series of letters to John, but they went unanswered. In time he contacted a reporter from the *Daily Sketch*, who, sensing a cracking story, engaged in negotiations with Brian Epstein for a meeting between long-lost father and famous son. At last, on 1 April 1964, the two met at the NEMS offices in Monmouth Street.

John's first words to Fred were testy, to say the least: 'What do you want, then?'

Fred replied that he didn't want anything. 'I told him that he got his talent from me,' he told the *Daily Sketch*, adding, with familial tactlessness, 'I don't want to sound boastful, but I was doing what John is doing twenty-five years ago – and better!' In his seafaring days, Fred had entertained his fellow crew members with selections from the musicals: for his showpiece, he would black up his face to deliver a tearful rendering of Al Jolson's 'Little Pal'.

After fifteen minutes or so, Fred and John were interrupted by Epstein, on the pretext of an engagement at the BBC. The meeting had been awkward, but not disastrous.

John can surely be forgiven for harbouring mixed feelings towards his father. From that moment on, his relationship with Fred would swing between love and hate, interspersed by long periods of surliness. He seems to have recognised similarities in their characters which, had providence worked in a different way, might have set him on a similar path. 'I don't really hate him now, the way I used to,' he told Hunter Davies. 'It was probably Julia's fault as much as his that they parted. If it hadn't been for the Beatles, I would probably have ended up like Freddie.' At the time, Davies thought this an unlikely scenario, but he came to recognise the truth in it: 'It is hard to imagine John fitting in with a proper job, or office hierarchy, or even managing to make a living as an artist or designer, not of course that he had passed any of his art college exams. He would have become bored far too quickly. So he might well have ended up as a bum.'

Fred managed to establish some sort of patchy relationship with John, who appreciated his cocky, rackety, rebellious side, and recognised in his more forgiving moments that Fred – who had himself been brought up in an orphanage – was the victim of circumstances. 'He's all right. He's a bit wacky – just like me,' John told Cynthia; and he said much the same to Pete Shotton: 'He's good news. A real funny guy – a loony just like me.'

Their future relationship was fitful and explosive, their reconciliations often ending in arguments, requiring fresh reconciliations. When things were going swimmingly, Fred made a habit of putting his foot in it. Chatting about music one day, John asked Fred which of his own compositions was his favourite. 'I think all your songs are bloody great,' he said. 'But I've always had a special affection for "Penny Lane".'

Fred's interest in John was not wholly paternal. 'Now, it's back to finding some work. John has his thousands and I've got four shillings,' he told a reporter after their first meeting. 'But I'm still the happiest bloke alive.' But the temptation to capitalise on their relationship proved irresistible. First, he sold his life story to *Titbits* magazine for £200, and then in 1965 he recorded a dreadful single, half-sung, half-spoken, 'That's My Life'. 'I've been an entertainer all my life,' he explained to the press.

He had high hopes for the song, but it failed to sell. Like many unsuccessful artistes before him, Fred looked around for someone to blame, and found Brian Epstein. There may even have been some truth in this: in her autobiography, Cynthia says that John 'was furious at his father's blatant jump on the bandwagon of his own success', and 'asked Brian to do anything he could to stop it. Whether Brian did or not I don't know, but the record never made it into the charts.' Together with his new-found manager, Fred dropped round at Kenwood at eleven o'clock one evening, ready to demand an explanation, but John was not in a welcoming mood. 'Fuck off!' he shouted, before slamming the door in his father's face.

Yet the two continued to keep in touch, and John financed Fred's existence, albeit on a modest level, giving him a one-bedroom flat in Kew and £10 a week. While employed washing dishes at the Toby Jug Hotel in Tolworth, Surrey, Fred became engaged to a student called Pauline, thirty-five years his junior. He then turned up at the door of Kenwood with Pauline, asking if John and Cynthia might give her a job and somewhere to live. Once again, Kenwood became a setting for family melodrama. 'She lived with us for a few months, but it was a nightmare,' recalled Cynthia. 'She was constantly in tears and arguing with her mother over Alf [Fred]. She slept in the attic, and we'd hear her screaming down the phone and sobbing up there.'

For her part, Pauline did not take to John: 'His table manners were the most atrocious I had ever witnessed. He said little, but as he munched

I noticed him sizing me up with those penetratingly suspicious eyes that were to become quite familiar to me during my stay at Kenwood.'

One evening, Pauline and Fred went out to a nightclub in Kew, where they bumped into Cynthia, all by herself. According to Pauline, 'Freddie was deeply shocked to find John's wife clubbing without a suitable escort, and he treated her to a lecture on the subject of wifely duties . . . I was furious with him for offending Cynthia.' But perhaps he had also offended Cynthia in another, less seemly way. Pete Shotton remembered that 'Freddie exhausted the limits of even John's tolerance when he attempted to seduce his daughter-in-law. Cyn was so distraught that John threw his father out of the house, and refused ever to see him again.'*

With so much drama going on, it is perhaps not surprising that John sought refuge in 'Sunny Heights', just down the hill.

---

* John's relationship with his father finally came to an end in 1970, when Fred wrote to him mentioning that he was planning to write his autobiography. An Apple secretary asked Fred and Pauline to come to Tittenhurst Park on John's thirtieth birthday, 9 October. Kept waiting in the kitchen, they were greeted by an irate John, saying, 'I'm cutting off your money and kicking you out of the house . . . Get out of my life – get off my back!'

It emerged that John's post-Beatles 'primal scream' therapy had triggered violent feelings against his father. 'Have you any idea of what I've been through because of you? Day after day in therapy, screaming for my daddy, sobbing for you to come home!' According to Pauline, John also repeatedly described his mother as a 'whore'. Grabbing his father's lapel, he said, 'As for your life story, you're never to write *anything* without my approval. And if you tell anyone what happened here today . . . I'll have you killed.' This threat worried Fred so much that he gave a statement of their conversation to a solicitor, with instructions that it be made public if he should 'disappear or die an unnatural death'.

85.

Ringo had bought his very own mock-Tudor residence on the same swish estate a year after John bought Kenwood. He then hired a building company to undertake extensive renovations. These soon got out of control. Thinking to reduce costs, and hoping for a sound investment to fall back on when the famous bubble burst, Ringo then bought the building company. But he was no businessman: he bought the property for £37,000, spent a further £53,000 on it, and then sold it four years later for £47,000. Neither did his new building company ever get off the ground. When asked what went wrong, he replied, 'No one wanted to buy the houses we put up.'

But it was all good fun while it lasted, and John and Cynthia would pop by whenever they needed cheering up, which was most of the time. Unlike Kenwood, which rapidly became a museum for exhausted enthusiasms, Sunny Heights* was, as its name suggests, a fun palace, its jollity undimmed by angst or self-pity. As well as adding a whole new wing, a workroom and a home cinema, Ringo installed his own pub, the Flying Cow, in the front room, complete with mirrored walls, sporting prints and a psychedelic light show. He relished playing mine host from behind the bar, pulling the beer taps and pressing the buttons on the fully operational till. The Flying Cow also boasted a dartboard, and a pool table specially flown over from America. 'It was always party time at the Starkeys', recalled Cynthia. 'Ringo was gregarious and fun-loving, a clown and a joker with an infectious laugh. Together, he and Maureen made an irresistible double act, both extrovert and uninhibited.'

Sunny Heights was, in many ways, more lavish and luxurious than

* The original owner of the house had called it 'Haleakala', the name of the massive volcano that forms the larger part of the Hawaiian island of Maui. 'Haleakala' means 'House of the Sun', so when a Mr Pope bought the property in 1948 and changed its name to 'Sunny Heights', he wasn't being quite as radical as it might appear. So now you know.

Kenwood. Finding John's five televisions a little meagre, Ringo installed a television and two telephones in every single room. For some reason he hated seams, so he ordered a chocolate-brown Wilton carpet to be woven in one huge stretch for the main living room. But he was soon to discover that there is no clear correlation between luxury and happiness, and that, more often than not, the one is a substitute for the other. Drawing Ringo's portrait on a spare wall, the caricaturist Gerald Scarfe* noticed that many of the rooms in Sunny Heights were completely empty: 'I thought coming from a two-up-two-down house he didn't know what to do with them.' When Ray Connolly visited Ringo there in March 1968, he found him bewildered by choice. 'I've got a friend in Liverpool called Roy,' Ringo told

---

* Later to marry Jane Asher.

him. 'You know, he's a joiner, and he's only got about thirty records, but he gets so much pleasure from them. Yet I've got a cupboard here with about five hundred LPs, and when I want to play one I have to close the cupboard again because I don't know which one to put on any more . . . I suppose I get bored like anyone else, but instead of having three hours a night, I have all day to get bored in. Even this house was a toy. In Liverpool, I'd always lived in a four-roomed house and the height of my ambitions was a semi in Aigburth. Sometimes I feel like I'd like to stop being famous and get back to where I was in Liverpool. There don't seem to be so many worries in that sort of life, although I thought there were at the time. But I had to come here to realise that they counted for very little'.

86.

A Party:
Studio Two, EMI
Abbey Road, London NW8
1 June 1966

The Beatles have already taped a rhythm track for 'Yellow Submarine', along with Ringo's unsteady vocals and his meandering, mock-poetic introduction* ('And we will march to free the day to see them gathered there, from Land o'Groats to John o'Green . . .'). But it is essentially a singalong song, so in the evening they invite a few party-loving friends to join them in Studio Two, among them Pattie Boyd, Mick Jagger, Brian Jones, Marianne Faithfull, and the Beatles' faithful chauffeur Alf Bicknell.

As they enter, the Beatles' engineer, Geoff Emerick, realises that they are all what he euphemistically describes as 'distinctly in a party mood'. From the look of them, he suspects that at their dinner beforehand 'more than food was being ingested'. Though he himself has never tried pot, he has been around enough musicians to recognise its aroma: 'We were sometimes aware of the funny smell in the studio after the Beatles and their roadies snuck a joint off in the corner, though I doubt very much if the straitlaced George Martin knew what was going on.'

The studio rapidly transforms into the ultimate Swinging Sixties party, with women in mini-skirts and flowing blouses, and men in purple bell-bottoms and fur jackets. Emerick suspects they are unlikely to stay still – 'There was no way I was going to try to contain that lot!' – so he gives them all handheld microphones on long leads.

John says he wants to sound as though he's singing underwater. He

---

* Later junked.

tries gargling and singing at the same time, but ends up choking. So he changes tack, insisting on a tank being brought into the studio so he can stick his head in it.

By now, George Martin is adept at dealing with John's excesses, and tries to dissuade him. But John is insistent. Emerick suggests a compromise: why not get John to put the microphone underwater? George Martin is worried that the microphone will be wrecked, and warns Emerick that any damage will be paid for by him.

They look for something with which to waterproof the microphone. Mal Evans finds a condom in his bag. Emerick wraps it around the microphone, and then dips the finished product into a milk bottle filled with water. They are about to start recording when the bossy studio manager, Mr Fowler, puts his head around the door to check that nothing is amiss.

Emerick knows that if Mr Fowler spots the microphone in the milk bottle he will be sacked on the spot. But John is quick-witted: the second he sees Mr Fowler, he grabs the apparatus and hides it behind his back.

'Everything all right, lads?' asks Mr Fowler.

'Yes, sir, Mr Studio Manager, sir, absolutely smashing, sir,' says John, to the sound of suppressed giggling from everyone, including George Martin.

The recording goes ahead, but the underwater sound is unsatisfactory, and is soon abandoned. On with the party!

The Beatles raid an oversized cupboard in the studio, known as the Trap Room, a treasure trove of odds and ends: thunderstorm gadgets, old hosepipes, a football rattle, wartime hand bells, chains, gongs, wind machines, whistles and hooters. The beautiful people grab what they can, and amidst much merriment and clinking of glasses, the sing-song begins. You can hear the yelps and hollers of the partygoers on the record, during the second verse, the most voluble coming from the previously softly-spoken Pattie Boyd.

Soon everyone squeezes into the tiny echo-chamber at the back of the studio. Once again, Emerick detects 'the faint smell of "incense"'. While the partygoers clank and giggle and rattle and hoot, John puts on a Goon-style voice and says, 'Full steam ahead, Mr Bo'sun! Full steam ahead!' The evening ends with Mal Evans marching around the studio, banging on the big bass drum strapped to his chest, and everybody else straggling behind him, whooping and hollering and dancing the conga.

87.

A 'Pre-Opening Celebration' for Sibylla's discothèque in Swallow Street, Mayfair, was thrown at the club's premises on 21 June 1966. In a feature in *Queen* magazine, Cathy McGowan, the presenter of *Ready Steady Go!*, enthused that 'a more glittering line-up of guests could hardly be imagined'.

The discothèque's prospectus stated that membership would not be based on the old class divisions of 'breeding, schooling and wealth'; the new requirement was more modern, though just as inexact: 'hipness'.

Interviewed by Jonathan Aitken,* the co-owner Kevin Macdonald said that he and his partners had brought together 'the new aristocracy in Britain . . . the current young meritocracy of style, taste and sensitivity . . . the top creative people; the top exporters; the top brains; the top artists; the top social people'.

The guest list† was published in the next issue of *Queen*, under the heading 'How Many Swinging Londoners Do You Know?'

David Bailey, photographer
John Barry, composer
Jane Birkin, actress, wife of John Barry
Jacqueline Bisset, actress
Pattie Boyd, Beatle wife
Michael Caine, actor
Leslie Caron, actress
Julie Christie, actress

---

* Aitken (1942–) is the author of, among many other works, *The Young Meteors* (1967), a collection of profiles of the young and fashionable, and *Nixon: A Life* (1993), a sympathetic portrait of the former US president. He became a Conservative MP in 1974. In 1999 he was convicted of perjury and perverting the course of justice, and sentenced to eighteen months in prison. Twenty years later, in June 2019, he was ordained as an Anglican priest.

† Here abbreviated.

Mike d'Abo, singer, soon to join Manfred Mann

Nigel Dempster, gossip columnist

Terry Donovan, photographer

Peregrine Eliot, aristocrat

Alan Freeman, disc jockey (shareholder)

Nicholas Gormanston, Anglo-Irish aristocrat

Celia Hammond, model

Anita Harris, singer

Bruce Higham, property developer (major shareholder)

Terry Howard, photographer (major shareholder)

Mick Jagger, Rolling Stone

Brian Jones, Rolling Stone

John Lennon, Beatle

Paul McCartney, Beatle

Kevin Macdonald, copywriter (major shareholder)

Cathy McGowan, presenter, *Ready Steady Go!*

David Mlinaric, designer

Andrew Loog Oldham, Rolling Stones manager

Jane Ormsby-Gore, daughter of UK ambassador to the USA

Sir Mark Palmer, founder, 'English Boy' model agency

Lance Percival, entertainer

Sir William Pigott-Brown, National Hunt jockey, principal shareholder

Alexander Plunket Greene, fashion entrepreneur, husband of Mary
    Quant

Mary Quant, fashion designer

Michael Rainey, fashion designer, 'Hung On You', husband of Jane
    Ormsby-Gore

Keith Richards, Rolling Stone

Edina Ronay, designer and actress

Maureen Starkey, Beatle wife

Eric Swayne, photographer, former boyfriend of Pattie Boyd

Gordon Waller, singer, Peter and Gordon

Writing in the *Daily Express* that year, Robin Douglas-Home, a Scottish aristocrat, recognised that London's 'privileged class' was now 'actors, pop singers, hairdressers, and models'. Times, he said, had changed. 'If a 14th Earl with a grouse moor and George Harrison with Pattie Boyd walked together into a restaurant and there was only one table left, who would be given the table? Well – if the head waiter had any sense – obviously George and Pattie.'

But pockets of resistance remained. On New Year's Eve 1966, George was refused admission to Annabel's, the smart nightclub in Mayfair, for not wearing a tie. In her autobiography, Lady Annabel Goldsmith, after whom the club had been named, recalled the incident with thinly-disguised relish: 'On 31 December 1967' (she was in fact a year out) 'the Beatle George Harrison arrived at the blue and gold canopy, intending to see in the New Year in style. With him were his wife, Pattie Boyd, his manager Brian Epstein and his friend, the rock star Eric Clapton. Heavily bearded, wearing a polo-necked sweater and a thick scarf, he was astonished to be refused entry by the doorman. Insulted at being offered a shirt and tie when the dress code was not being met, Mr Harrison reminded the doorman that in his opinion Annabel's needed the Beatles rather more than the Beatles needed Annabel's. "I don't think this is the case nowadays or ever was in the past," was the doorman's reply, and the Harrison party saw in the New Year at the nearby Lyon's Corner House.'

88.

We are on the Mop Tops Tour of Liverpool. 'So that's the Roman Catholic cathedral. It has four bells – Matthew, Mark, Luke and John. But Beatles fans call them John, Paul, George and Ringo! When I told that to an American tourist the other day he said, "Ringo? That's a good name for a bell!" I said, "I make the jokes, mate!"'

We walk around the corner to what was once the Oxford Street Maternity Hospital, but is now part of the university. A rival guide has beaten us to it.

'Good day, Sunshine!' says the rival guide to our guide, and then adds, 'Here comes the sun!' Our guide, Stevie T, chuckles effortfully, then waits for his rival to go away before walking us to the plaque by the front door.

TO JULIA LENNON, NÉE STANLEY, A SON
JOHN LENNON
(1940–1980)
BORN HERE IN THE FORMER
LIVERPOOL MATERNITY HOSPITAL
6.30 P.M. 9 OCTOBER 1940

He tells us of the Nazi bombing of Liverpool that took place that same week. 'But there was no bombing on 9 October. John must have been singing "Give peace a chance"!' In Liverpool, everything returns to the Beatles.

He drives us to the other end of Hope Street, to Gambier Terrace, a beautiful 1830s terrace close to the Anglican cathedral.

'Now, you all know your Beatles. Rod Murray – does that name ring a bell?'

We act as though it's on the tip of our tongues.

'Well, it's impossible to remember everything, isn't it?' he says, with an air of forbearance. It's Beatles Week in Liverpool, and levels of Beatles expertise are disarmingly high. I've been reading about the Beatles non-stop for a year, but compared to most of the fans I've barely reached inter-mediate level.

Rod Murray was, it turns out, one of the Dissenters, an arty group distinguished by its refusal to play any music. John and Stu Sutcliffe lived in Murray's scruffy first-floor flat in Gambier Terrace in early 1960. John said it was just like a rubbish dump. Stevie T allows time for photographs of the front door that John used to walk in and out of.

Back in the minibus, Stevie T talks of the various Beatles tours he has been on. 'I went with the Beatles team to Manchester. The trouble was – nothing there. None of the places they went to exist any more. There's a lovely fellow there who does rock'n'roll tours of Manchester – Stone Roses, Oasis, all the rest of 'em. Now, what's 'is name? Wilde. Paul Wilde. That's it!'

I ask him whether his children are keen on the Beatles. 'They're not all that interested in music, to be honest. Mind you, the other day I heard my younger son playing music in his room. So I went in, and do you know what he was playing? Barry White! BARRY WHITE!' I shake my head sympathetically.

We drive to Toxteth. Stevie T parks near no. 9 Madryn Street, Ringo's grandparents' house, where Ringo was born. In 2005, Liverpool City Council ruled that Madryn Street and ten neighbouring streets were to be demolished. Following an outcry from Beatles fans, it was announced that no. 9 would be saved. It was to be dismantled brick by brick and stored until a suitable site could be found. There were even plans to reconstruct it in the Museum of Liverpool, but they fell through.

We walk round the corner to 10 Admiral Grove, where Ringo lived with his mother from the age of six. I ask Stevie T if Ringo bought his mother a smarter house when he became rich and famous. 'He bought her a lovely bungalow in Gateacre. She stayed there to her dying day, but she never liked it. Too posh for her.'

No. 10 is painted pink and white, like a party cake. A middle-aged businesswoman, Jackie Holmes, bought it recently for £70,000. She also owns 9 Newcastle Road, Julia Lennon's old home, and 25 Upton Green, where George once lived. No one seems to know what she plans to do with her purchases.

A rival tour is busy peering through the windows of no. 10, so we have to wait our turn for a snoop. There is not much to see: the front room is entirely bare. Stevie T fills in the hiatus with an anecdote. 'The house only had an outside toilet, by that wall at the back. The only place for Ringo's fans to sit was on the wall. When he walked to the outside toilet, they'd all scream, so whenever he wanted to go to the toilet, the whole of Liverpool would know.'

'And so on to our next moptop-tabulous tour destination!' It's the lake in Sefton Park. We gaze at it from the road. This, says Stevie T, is where Fred Lennon first met Julia. In the distance, we can just about make out the top of the Palm House. 'It was in a terrible condition. George gave them half a million towards restoring it, but he didn't want anyone to know.'

Clearly, a Liverpool by-law requires any building associated with the Beatles, however tangentially, to display a statue or plaque. There is a Beatles statue at Pier Head, and a further eight Beatles statues are in the Cavern Quarter, including one of John Lennon outside the club itself and one of Eleanor Rigby – by Tommy Steele, of all people – in Stanley Street.

The statue of John at Liverpool John Lennon Airport was unveiled by Yoko Ono in 2002. Plaques abound, too. You can find plaques to Bob Wooler, their first manager; to Mal Evans, their roadie; to the Quarrymen and to the Dissenters. A plaque between a tattoo parlour and a tattoo removal parlour on Rodney Street reads: 'THIS PLAQUE COMMEMORATES THE BIRTH HERE OF BRIAN SAMUEL EPSTEIN BORN 19 SEPTEMBER 1934 + DIED LONDON 27 AUGUST 1967'. There are further plaques on the Cavern Club, the Casbah Coffee Club, the Grapes pub, all the Beatles' individual homes, and the Grosvenor Ballroom, where they used to play. With the benefit of hindsight, it might have been less time-consuming to place plaques on the handful of buildings in Liverpool with no Beatles associations.

Stevie T walks us to the Sefton Park Hotel, billed as 'located in a former Beatle's home, offering comfortable accommodation, a warm welcome and great food and drink'. The plaque by the entrance reads:

STUART SUTCLIFFE
THE
FAMILY HOME OF
STUART SUTCLIFFE
1961–1970

This claim seems a little fanciful, as everyone knows that Stu died very young, before the Beatles took off. Later, I check out the dates. Stuart Sutcliffe died from a cerebral haemorrhage in Hamburg on 10 April 1962, having been in Germany for most of 1961 and 1962. Admittedly, he was in Liverpool from 20 January to 27 March 1961, but that was before his family moved to Sefton Park. This leaves just a handful of days in August 1961, when he returned from Hamburg for hospital tests, and a few more days in February 1962, when he came back to see his mother, who was recovering from an operation.

Not to worry! The hotel dining room is decorated with photos of Stu and the Beatles, Stu and Astrid, Stu and John. The wordy inscription above a framed copy of Stu's birth certificate reads: 'Stuart's sudden death in Hamburg is part of Beatles folklore, a poignant story of a young man whose promising career as an artist/musician was tragically cut short, but Stuart's importance to the Beatles as one of the founding members and a close friend of John Lennon is legendary.'

Back in the minibus, Stevie T announces that next week he is off to Bangor in Wales with a group of Beatles fans from Sweden. They plan to look round places visited by the Beatles when they stayed in Bangor for two nights in August 1967, for a seminar by the Maharishi. 'I'm just going for the ride, not for work. Should be a lorra fun.'

'Guess where we're going next?' he says, pressing a button on the dashboard. Out through the speakers comes 'Penny Lane'. We halt by a street sign saying 'Penny Lane' and wait for other tours to move on before taking a closer look. This sign, says Stevie T, is not original. 'The minute the song came out, they were all stolen. Eventually the council stopped replacing them. This meant there were Penny Lane signs everywhere in the world – except for Penny Lane!' The current sign, firmly affixed to the wall, is covered in fans' signatures. A sheet of Perspex has been stuck over it ever since Paul McCartney came up to Liverpool with James Corden for his *Carpool Karaoke* in 2018 and added his modestly-sized autograph.

We stop off at St Barnabas church hall, where Paul served as a chorister, and the Beatles used to play from time to time. It's now a pub. 'Make a lovely photo, them hanging baskets. Fun question: what famous musician once lived in that flat up there? You'll never guess! No? No? Put you out of your misery – Freddie Mercury! Yes, Freddie Mercury! Unbelievable!' As we set off, Stevie T points at an elderly man in the car park. 'Look! Over there! That's LEN GARRY! And that woman next to him, that's his wife!' We try to look excited. Sensing that we haven't a clue who he's on about, Stevie T informs us that Len Garry was one of the original Quarrymen.

Penny Lane is rich in buildings mentioned in the song – the barber shop, the bank, the shelter in the middle of the roundabout – but they are drabber than expected. The barber shop is still there, now called Tony Slavin, but instead of the barber showing photographs, he is subject to them: every tourist in the city is busy snapping a selfie against the shop-front. 'John, Paul and George all had their hair cut here,' says Stevie T proudly. I think of asking him why Ringo never did, but the question evaporates in my mouth. The famous 'shelter in the middle of the round-about' now has a sign saying 'Sgt Pepper Bistro', but it is boarded up, with no bistro in sight. It emerges that a Mr Ray Maatook bought the former tram stop in 2004, with exciting plans to develop it as a 'Beatles-inspired bistro', but it has remained empty ever since.

What about the banker who never wears a mac in the pouring rain? Where's the bank? 'There used to be three banks claiming the title,' says Stevie T. 'But there's only one left, the TSB. D'y'see it over there? So they have the claim to fame.'

We talk about Len Garry. Surely some of those Quarrymen wish they'd stuck it out, and become Beatles? If the group had been John, Paul, George and Craig, and I'd decided to leave them for a proper job, I would still be bristling with envy and resentment. 'No, no, I don't think so,' says Stevie T thoughtfully. 'Well, maybe Chas Newby. You see, Chas was good-looking – just like Paul. He played bass – just like Paul. He was left-handed – just like Paul.' I try to nod knowingly, hoping that Stevie T won't twig that I have no idea who Chas Newby is.

Later, I look him up. Chas Newby was not, as I had imagined, an actual Quarryman, but he filled in for Stu Sutcliffe for four gigs in December 1960. John then asked Chas to go back to Hamburg with them, but he opted for university instead. He went on to become a maths teacher in Droitwich. In retirement, at the age of seventy-five, he joined the Quarrymen for the very first time, having missed the bus well over half a century earlier.

'Here's a question for you. Great final question for *Who Wants to Be a Millionaire?*! What name did George Harrison sometimes use as a pseudonym?' We look blank. 'Wanna know the answer?' Stevie T parks his minibus and points at the street sign. 'Arnold Grove!' We are standing out-side no. 12, the birthplace of George Harrison. 'Two up, two down. Six in the house, no bathroom. When they wanted a bath, they got the tin bath off its peg, and put the kettle on.'

We stare at the front door. We stare at the top windows. We stare at the bottom windows. We take photographs. I feel a little sheepish. 12 Arnold Grove is not operated by the National Trust: it is the home of Kathleen Hughes, a retired carer. Mrs Hughes complained to the *Daily Telegraph* in 2015 that she was 'sick to death' of tourists: 'The tour taxis come zooming up the street and in the summer there are hundreds of them every day. At the weekend, they are turning up constantly, even as late as two o'clock in the morning. I live on my own . . . It's horrible having strangers sticking their faces in my window and knocking at all times of the day . . . I'm re-ally fed up of it and so are my neighbours, especially with these cruise ships coming into Liverpool bringing hundreds of coaches of tourists outside my door. The whole Bayern Munich football team came to see the house once, and they were all sticking their faces in the window. Frankly, it's getting out of hand.'

We steal away. Next stop Woolton, and Strawberry Field, where once again Stevie T vents his irritation with his rivals. 'You'll find some tour guides pointing to that tree over there, or that one, or that one, and they say, "That's the tree in the song, where John says, 'No one I think is in my tree'." Well, it drives me mad! They're daft! I mean, he's not talking about an ACTUAL tree! He said he always felt special and different growing up. That's what "no one else is in my tree" means! Yet they still go on pointing to this tree or that! Drives me hopping mad!'

In 2000 the original wrought-iron gates were stolen, and sold to a scrap-metal dealer. Two days later the dealer started entertaining suspicions, and went to the police. The originals are now in storage, and the present gates are replicas.

We drive on to St Peter's church. The churchyard is pullulating with other guides, so Stevie T walks us across the road to St Peter's church hall, which has yet another plaque:

IN THIS HALL ON 6TH JULY 1957
JOHN & PAUL
FIRST MET

This plaque comes with a plaque of its own, the second one in metal, and much more wordy than the first, suggesting it had been dictated in a pub towards closing time:

> The Quarrymen featuring Eric Griffiths, Colin Hanton, Rod Davies, John Lennon, Pete Shotton and Len Garry performed on the afternoon of 6th July at St Peter's Church Fete. In the evening before their performance in this hall, Ivan Vaughan, who sometimes played in the group, introduced his friend Paul McCartney to John Lennon. As John recalled . . . 'that was the day, the day that I met Paul, that it started moving'.

We take photographs of the hall, and the plaque, and the plaque's plaque. As we walk back towards the churchyard, I notice that Stevie T is taking care to avoid the other guides.

'Do you have a friendly rivalry with them?' I ask him.

'Not friendly,' he replies. Tension creeps into his voice. 'A lot of them don't know what they're talking about.' He takes us into the churchyard. 'See, come over here. Look at this!' We gaze at a gravestone to John Mackenzie, 'who died September 16th 1915, aged 73 years'.

'These other guides, they just stand there spouting rubbish. They say that's Father Mackenzie from "Eleanor Rigby", and then they encourage everyone to take photographs of the gravestone. And you ask me why I don't like them! Do you want to know the true story? Do you? Well, I'll tell you the true story. The true story is that the real Father Mackenzie had nothing to do with that Father Mackenzie. The real person wasn't called John, he was called Tom. And he wasn't a priest, but a guy who used to introduce the Beatles onstage who they nicknamed "Father Mackenzie". In fact, he was ex-army, and they say he was always darning socks. Does that remind you of something – yes, "darning his socks in the night when there's nobody there" – are you with me? So please, please, I beg of you, don't tell me that John Mackenzie was the original Father Mackenzie. Drives me hopping mad!'

89.

Doctrinal differences have led to schisms among Beatles historians quite as fierce as those that beset the early Christian Church. Behind and a bit to the left of John Mackenzie's gravestone another gravestone commemorates various other members of the Rigby family, including, roughly halfway down, Eleanor Rigby. Stevie T complains that rival guides encourage people to believe that this is the famous Eleanor Rigby. 'It's a lovely romantic story. Only trouble is – it's just not true!'

Stevie T has faith in those Beatles theologians who believe that Paul took the name 'Rigby' from a wine-shippers in Bristol, and 'Eleanor' from Eleanor Bron. Paul himself has confirmed this version of events on a number of occasions, but that has done nothing to stifle the voices of the dissenters.

Lionel Bart once declared that 'Paul always thought he came up with the name Eleanor because of having worked with Eleanor Bron in the film *Help!*, but I am convinced he took the name from a gravestone in a cemetery close to Wimbledon Common where we were both walking. The name on the gravestone was Eleanor Bygraves. He then came back to my office and began playing it on my clavichord.'

The nominative etymology of Father Mackenzie has been subject to similar schisms. Pete Shotton remembered being in the room when Paul named the priest in his new song 'Father McCartney'. Shotton recalled saying, 'Hang on a minute, Paul. People are going to think that's your poor old dad, left all alone in Liverpool to darn his own socks.' He then said, or claimed to have said, 'Give us that phone book, then, and I'll have a look through the Macs.' First he suggested 'McVicar', and then, when that didn't fit, 'Mackenzie'.

However, in a 1966 interview with Hunter Davies in the *Sunday Times*, Paul, who suffers from a forgivable tendency to place himself centre-stage, recalled that it was he, not Pete, who looked through the telephone directory in search of an alternative Mac: 'I went through the phone book and got the name Mackenzie.'

Thirty-one years later, in 1997, Paul told Barry Miles of false Father Mackenzies popping up in his life, along the lines of false Anastasias. 'A man appeared, who died a few years ago, who said, "I'm Father Mackenzie." Anyone who was called Father Mackenzie and had any slim contact with the Beatles quite naturally would think, "Well, I spoke to Paul and he might easily have written that about me."'

There are divisions, too, over who composed the song – Paul or John or both of them. In *Melody Maker* in 1971, John claimed to have written 'at least 50 per cent' of it. By 1972, in an interview with *Hit Parader*, this had risen to '70 per cent'. Later that same year, talking to Ray Connolly, he increased it to '80 per cent'. A week before he died in 1980, he was less specific about percentages but equally proprietorial, claiming to an interviewer from *Playboy* that 'The first verse is his [Paul's] and the rest are basically mine.'

But those who were present when the song was composed remember John's contributions as negligible. Even his most loyal friend, Pete Shotton, reckoned they were 'virtually nil'. When Paul couldn't think of an ending, Pete had been 'seized by a brainwave. "Why don't you have Eleanor Rigby dying?" I said, "and have Father Mackenzie doing the burial service for her? That way you'd have the two lonely people coming together in the end – but too late."'

Then John spoke up for the very first time, just to put his friend down: 'I don't think you understand what we're trying to get at, Pete.' Pete felt humiliated. 'All I could think of to say was "Fuck you, John."' With that, the composing session came to an end. But when Pete heard the record for the first time, he felt 'over the moon' that Paul had gone along with his suggestion. 'Perhaps, I reflected, it was *John* who hadn't understood what we were getting at.'

Why would John have so exaggerated his contribution to 'Eleanor Rigby'? Perhaps it was simple envy. Of all the Beatles' songs, its lyrics have been the most extravagantly praised, and by all the right people. On its release, George Melly said, 'Pop has come of age,' and Jerry Leiber said, 'I don't think there's ever been a better song written.' 'Eleanor Rigby' was taken up by poets, including Allen Ginsberg, who claimed to have played it to Ezra Pound, who, he said, 'smiled lightly'. Thom Gunn compared it to Auden's ballad 'Miss Gee'. Karl Miller included it in his anthology *Writing in England Today*. James Fenton remembers Auden listening to it 'in search of something to be influenced by'. More recently, the novelist and critic A.S. Byatt praised the lyric for displaying 'the minimalist perfection of a Beckett story'. Its appeal is wide-ranging: over the years it has been chosen as a Desert Island Disc by, among others, the cosmologoist Professor Carlos Frank, the actress Patricia Hayes, the American mezzo-soprano Cathy Berberian, the Armenian balladeer Charles Aznavour and the former Chancellor of the Exchequer Geoffrey Howe.

One Beatles theologian, Erin Torkelson Weber, author of *The Beatles and the Historians* (2016), offers another reason for John's dubious claims. In an interview with *Playboy* in 1971, the Beatles' dodgy business manager, Allen Klein, admitted that, in his attempts to cultivate John through flattery, he had taken care to 'remind' him of his authorship of 'Eleanor Rigby', assuring him that he wrote 60 or 70 per cent of the lyric. 'He just didn't remember until I sat him down and had him sort through it all.'

Torkelson pins John's misattribution to Klein's persuasiveness. 'It appears that in his efforts to become Beatles manager and gain Lennon's approval, Klein may have convinced the songwriter that he had written lyrics actually by McCartney.'

90.

Fame came with advantages. One quiet Sunday, the singer songwriter Donovan was sitting in his flat in Maida Vale when the doorbell rang. Paul had arrived, with his acoustic guitar.

They smoked a joint or two. Paul played Donovan two songs he was working on. One of them was about a yellow submarine, and the other went:

Ola Na Tungee,
Blowing his mind in the dark with a pipe full of clay –
No one can say . . .

In time, Ola Na Tungee would transmute into Eleanor Rigby, and his mind in the dark with a pipe full of clay would turn to rice in the church where the wedding had been. But for the moment, Paul was just fiddling around.

Before long, the doorbell rang again. Donovan went to answer it. A young policeman told him that there was a car outside; it was parked illegally, at an odd angle, the doors open, with its radio still on.

Paul joined them at the door.

The policeman's eyes lit up. 'Oh, it's you, Mr McCartney. Is it your car, sir? A sports car?'

Anyone else would have been faced with a reprimand and a parking fine. Instead, the policeman offered to park Paul's car in a more suitable spot. Paul thanked him, and handed over the keys. A few minutes later the policeman returned, to tell him that everything was now in order. As he handed over the keys he saluted, allowing Paul to return to his guitar, and Ola Na Tungee.

91.

Paul changed 'Ola Na Tungee' to 'Daisy Hawkins', but it didn't scan properly, so he changed it again, this time to 'Eleanor Rigby'. Half a century on, Colin Campbell, Professor of Sociology at York University, was to devote an entire book to an analysis of the lyrics of 'Eleanor Rigby':

> As we have seen, Paul seemed to envisage Eleanor Rigby as picking up rice after the wedding was over, having 'missed the wedding'. In other words she turned up for the wedding but was too late to take part in the celebrations. This suggests that the reason she picked up the rice was in order to have something to connect her not just with weddings in general, but this wedding in particular, one in which she had intended to participate. So should we really think of her as a wedding guest? In which case presumably this picking up rice is not something that she does on a regular basis. It is simply that she wishes to have something to remind her of this wedding. But then if she is a guest but has missed the service would she not now be on her way to the reception? Or has she missed that as well?

. . . And so on. But, as with many Beatles songs, the lyrics have been misheard as well as misinterpreted. Some hear 'all the homely people'. Later in the song, the words after 'Father Mackenzie' are sometimes taken to be 'Darling it sucks in the night when there's nobody there'. At the same time, Eleanor Rigby 'picks up her eyes from the church where the wedding has been'.

And what's this song? 'Take the back right turn!' 'Pay per bag right turn!' When the songwriter Bobby Hart first heard it in 1966, he imagined the Beatles were singing 'Take the last train!' By the time he realised it was 'Paperback Writer', it was too late: the wrong words had lodged in his brain. Three months later, he was trying to write a debut single for the

Monkees. Asked by their management for something that sounded like the Beatles, he composed a song from the misheard line. 'Take the last train to Clarksville', it began, and it took the Monkees to number 1 in the US charts.

Everyone has a different Beatles songbook nestling in their heads, because everyone hears different words to different songs. Deep down, I still think that John is singing 'Kangaroo days, ah!' in 'Across the Universe'. Maybe it's because I first heard the track on the World Wildlife Fund charity album, *No One's Gonna Change Our World*, which had a photograph of a panda on the cover, and liner notes by, of all people, the Duke of Edinburgh.* In fact John was singing the no less obscure 'Jai Guru Deva'.†

When 'Penny Lane' was released, many American fans, ignorant of Britain's charity Poppy Day, were left wondering why a pretty nurse would be selling puppies from a tray. The other side of the single was also subject to misinterpretation. Elvis Costello's manager, Jake Rivera, long thought that on 'Strawberry Fields Forever' John sang 'Living is easy with nice clothes'. Additionally, he thought Paul liked the girl in 'And I Love Her' because 'She gives me everything, and tender veal'. Others heard it as 'And I love fur' because 'She gives me everything, internally'. And what of the orthodontist? 'And in my orthodontist, she is standing right in front me'.

Even the simplest Beatles lyric is open to mishearing. 'And when I get home to you, I find a broken canoe'. 'I don't care to march for money'. 'Friday night arrives without a fruitcake'. 'Michelle, ma belle, Sunday monk, he wants to ban odd socks, to ban odd socks'. 'There beneath the goose and bourbon skies'. 'But if you go carrying picture of German cows'.

From sense to nonsense; from nonsense to sense. For years, I thought I was mishearing the words of 'Come Together'. They seemed like nonsense, from the first line – 'You come all flat up' – to the last. When I finally got round to reading the lyrics, it turned out that the first line was 'Here come old flat top', which really makes no more sense than 'You come all flat up', and perhaps rather less. Two lines on, I was relieved to find that what I had always taken to be 'Jew Jew eyeballs' – John was no stranger

---

* It was an unlikely location for a Beatles premiere. The album was subtitled 'The Stars Sing for the World Wildlife Fund'. Other tracks included 'Cuddly Old Koala' by Rolf Harris, 'When I See an Elephant Fly' by Bruce Forsyth, 'I'm a Tiger' by Lulu, 'Wings' by the Hollies, 'The Python' by Spike Milligan and 'Land of My Fathers' by Harry Secombe.

† Literally, 'Glory to the shining remover of darkness.'

to anti-Semitism – was written as 'joo joo eyeballs', though heaven knows what *they* are. Other lyrics that I had always imagined I had misheard – 'Joe jam football', 'walking finger', 'he back production', 'oh, no sideboard' – weren't all that off-track: they're actually 'toe jam football', 'monkey finger', 'he bad production' and 'Ono sideboard'.

Like searching for human faces in a cloud, those who look hard enough for a particular meaning will eventually find it. Some were convinced that each verse of 'Come Together' contained a description of a different Beatle – George, the holy roller; Ringo, the shooter of Coca-Cola; Paul, the good-looking one who's so hard to see. But, as was so often the case, this interpretation never occurred to the song's composer.

John's love of nonsense can be traced back to the time he learned to read and write. Aunt Mimi remembered that from an early age his spelling had been notably offbeat: 'Chicken pox was always chicken pots. He went on holiday to my sister's in Edinburgh once and wrote me a card saying *Funs are getting low.*' As a child he was captivated by the works of Edward Lear and Lewis Carroll, reciting 'Jabberwocky' over and over again to his friends: *"Twas brillig, and the slithy toves/Did gyre and gimble in the wabe . . .'* For the rest of his life John responded gleefully to puns and wordplay, relishing the way that, through the simple act of altering a letter, sense could so easily be nudged into nonsense.

'You should say what you mean,' the March Hare went on.

'I do,' Alice hastily replied; 'at least – at least I mean what I say – that's the same thing, you know.'

'Not the same thing a bit!' said the Hatter. 'Why, you might just as well say that "I see what I eat" is the same thing as "I eat what I see"!' . . .

Alice felt dreadfully puzzled. The Hatter's remark seemed to her to have no sort of meaning in it, and yet it was certainly English.

Paul reckons that 'Strawberry Fields Forever' and 'I am the Walrus' both sprang from John's obsession with 'Jabberwocky': '"I am he as you are he . . ." It's thanks to "Jabberwocky" that he could do that . . .' His childhood friend Pete Shotton remembered that 'From a very early age, John's ultimate ambition was to one day "write an *Alice*" himself.'

Every evening the twelve-year-old John would work furiously at pastiches of Carroll and Lear, scribbling them into an exercise book before transferring them to a hand-written newspaper he called 'The Daily Howl'. Items included a weather report – 'Tomorrow will be Muggy, followed by Tuggy, Wuggy and Thuggy' – and a parody of *Davy Crockett*, 'The Story of Davy Crutch-Head'. He was also clearly influenced by *1066 and All That*, the popular mock-history book by two schoolmasters, W.C. Sellar and R.J. Yeatman, in which half-remembered facts are tossed and turned, replicating the internal muddle of a schoolboy's mind, so that past and present, fact and fiction, the silly and the solemn are transformed into a jumbled version of the truth: 'The gun powder plot was an awful thing it is still done on the 5th Nov. Guy Fawkes chose the 5th Nov because it was Fireworks Day. Guy Mitchell, the singer, claims direct descent from Guy Fawkes.' Reading this, Sellar and Yeatman would have recognised John as one of their own.

John loved to listen to the relentless, unstoppable punning of the Goons on the wireless, imitating them in class the next day. He spent the money he had been given for his sixteenth birthday on two 78rpm records. One was Elvis Presley's 'Hound Dog'; the other 'The Ying-Tong Song' by the Goons, with its B-side of 'Bloodnok's Rock'n'Roll Call', 'featuring Major Denis Bloodnok, Roland Rockcake and His Wholly Rollers'.

The Goon scripts were all written at a frenzied pace by Spike Milligan, a manic depressive who lived his life at the mercy of puns, the willing victim of the twisted logic they both reflected and fanned. At the height of his success, Milligan was writing the third series of the Goons when he experienced a complete mental breakdown: 'The madness built up gradually. I found I was disliking more and more people. Then I got to hating them. Even my wife and baby.' Soon, he began to believe that only by killing his fellow Goon Peter Sellers would his mind correct itself. Accordingly, he went round to Sellers' house and walked straight through a glass door, cutting himself all over and ending up in the isolation ward of a mental hospital, bound in a straitjacket.

'Before becoming the Beatles' producer, George Martin, who had never recorded rock-n-roll, had previously recorded with Milligan and Sellers, which made him all the more acceptable,' John reminisced in the *New York Times* in 1973, while reviewing *The Goon Show Scripts*. 'Our studio sessions were full of the cries of Neddie Seagoon, etc., etc., as were most places in Britain.' In the same piece he argued, accurately, that *The Goon Show* was more original and revolutionary than John Osborne's *Look Back in Anger.* Looking back on his schoolboy newspaper 'The Daily Howl', he acknowledged that 'it seems strangely similar to *The Goon Show*'.

Were the jokes Milligan cracked – those manic, relentless, unstoppable jokes – an escape from the trap of depression? Or were they part of that trap – the little lumps of cheese beneath the coiled spring? Whenever he sensed the world was not mad enough, his brain found ways to make it madder. And there was a degree of megalomania to his comedy: he wanted the world, and everyone in it, to bow before his jokes. If they refused, he gave them hell. Performing onstage with the Goons in Coventry in 1954, he grew increasingly furious at the lacklustre response of the audience. Finally he snapped, screamed 'I hope you all get bombed again!', left the stage and locked himself in his dressing room. When his fellow Goons finally managed to prise the door open they found Milligan standing on a chair with a noose around his head, trying to hook the other end of the rope around a pipe overhead.

The pun is a kind of verbal schizophrenia, in which a word points in two ways at once, meaning two entirely different things at the same time. Shakespearian characters tumble into a world of puns when they begin their descents into madness. In his *New York Times* review John described the *Goon Show* scripts as 'a conspiracy against reality. A coup d'état of the mind.' The same might be said of his own incessant punning.

A psychological phenomenon known as Forster's Syndrome is named after the German surgeon who first described it. Dr Forster had been removing a brain tumour when he observed a singular phenomenon. As he manipulated certain areas of the brain, his patient would burst into a manic flight of puns, the sound of one word echoing but also distorting that of its predecessor, turning it into something more savage and brutal. All the words the patient uttered had something to do with knives and butchery – and this black humour came, as Arthur Koestler put it, 'from a man tied face down on the operating table with his skull open'.

The pun can also arise from aggression, a revenge for being mocked or patronised. It is a covert way of establishing superiority in a hostile environment, of ordering the world according to one's own whim. The pun slips madness into language: what is the Freudian slip, if not a pun?

Lennon had a facility, bordering on a compulsion, for puns. Perhaps being asked to choose between your mother and your father splits your mind and your emotions in a pun-like way. The pun allows you to say two things at once. Like the Freudian slip, of which it is a more conscious variant, it might be defined as saying one thing when you mean a mother.

When he first became friends with Paul, John would show him the pun-based jokes he had typed out the night before, many of which he was later to include in his pun-titled book *In His Own Write*.* 'We would sit around giggling, just saying puns really, that's basically what it was. In the early owls of the Morecambe. I remember "a cup-o-teeth" was one section that was in the typewriter when I was around there.'

The name of the Beatles now passes unquestioned. Even though beetles established themselves on this planet roughly 300 million years before their Liverpudlian counterparts, it is beetles, not Beatles, whose spelling we instinctively query. The group's name is itself a pun, 'the worst and most glorious band name in all of rock'n'roll history', as Bruce Springsteen once put it. John and Stuart Sutcliffe had been trying to think of an animal name, along the lines of Phil Spector's Teddy Bears or Buddy Holly's Crickets. They came up with 'the Lions' or 'the Tigers', before hitting upon 'the Beetles'. With characteristic perversity, John liked the idea of naming his band after such a low life-form, and then he converted it into a pun, to incorporate 'beat'.

From the early days of the Beatles, his long letters to fans are riddled with puns, many impenetrable. One, written in 1961 or 1962 to a Norwegian girl called Lindy Ness, begins, 'I am typing this one fingered lettuce to you,' and goes on to warn her of 'the evil temptations which confront a jung girl in a forrid country'. Other puns in the same letter include 'condiment' for continent, 'debb and duff' for deaf and dumb, 'thy kingdom come thy Wilbur Dunn', and 'suffer little chilblains to come over me'. What can Lindy Ness – who he calls Sad Ness – have thought?

After a show at the Rialto cinema in York in November 1963, the American journalist Michael Braun recorded the banter between the four Beatles. 'One more ciggy and I'm gonna hit the sack, "hit the sack" being an American thing we got off Gary Coople as he struggled along with a clock in *Hi, Goons*,' says John, adding, 'But I never really liked "sack", it's, uh, something you put potatoes in over here.'

'The whole thought of hitting the sack,' says Paul. 'It's so – so dirty, and it can mean a lot of things.'

* One copy of which he inscribed to a fan, 'To Sheila, with love and dressed fishes'.

'You can sack Rome,' says John, 'or you can sack cloth – or you can sacrilege, or saxophone, if you like, or saccharine.'

Five years later, Victor Spinetti worked with John on the stage adaptation of *In His Own Write*. He was amazed by John's facility with puns: 'During work on the play at the Mamounia, I noticed that something was missing. Over my shoulder I said, "I need a Queen's speech here, John." Without hesitating, he grabbed a sheet of cardboard from a shirt Cynthia had just bought and wrote:

> My housebound and eyeball take great pressure in denouncing this loyal ship in the blue corner, two stone three ounches, and he was sitting on the lav at the time.

'"Will that do?" he said, shoving it over to me. He hadn't paused. He hadn't crossed anything out.'

The Beatles albums *Revolver* and *Rubber Soul* had punning titles, and so did John's first two books, *In His Own Write* and *Spaniard in the Works*. In some passages, the puns are so ubiquitous as to be claustrophobic:

> Azue orl gnome, Harrassed Wilsod won the General Erection, with a very small marjorie over the Torchies. Thus pudding the Laboring Partly back into powell after a large abscess.

Authority figures of the time have their names fed into the pun machine, only to emerge eviscerated: Selwyn Lloyd, Harold Macmillan, Ted Heath, LBJ, Emmanuel Shinwell and Princess Margaret are transformed into 'Seldom Loyal', 'Harrassed Macmillion', 'Head Teeth', 'LBW', 'Emmanuel Shitwell' and 'Priceless Margarine'.

Once the Beatles had finished recording *Sgt. Pepper*, they gathered in Studio Two of Abbey Road to listen to the end result, right up to the final thunderous piano chord of 'A Day in the Life'. All four of them were delighted, but then John and Paul had the idea of squeezing in something extra, on the inner part of the disc where the needle ends up going round and round.

The engineer, Geoff Emerick, remembered John saying, 'Let's just put on some gobbledegook, then bifurcate it, splange it, and loop it.' They then nipped back into the studio, and spoke whatever nonsense came into their heads. Emerick played the tape back to them, and they chose a snippet of Paul saying, 'Never needed any other way.' This meant that listeners with primitive record-players would hear 'never-needed-any-other-way-never-needed-any-other-way-never-needed-any-other-way' ad nauseam, until they were driven to reach out and turn it off.

In those days of few distractions, some Beatles fans liked to place the stylus at the end of side two, then turn the record anti-clockwise by hand, in order to hear the same words in reverse. To many people, 'never-needed-any-other-way' backwards sounded just like 'Will-Paul-be-back-as-Superman,' a phrase that offered further encouragement to those who were already convinced that Paul was dead. But other people heard other things. Some heard 'The corned beef there is super, man,' or 'We're parking our Kings Super van,' while others were convinced that the original message was not 'Never needed any other way' but the saucier 'Never could see Annie's u'. These issues continue to engage Beatles fans with time on their hands. On YouTube, a film of the *Sgt. Pepper* LP going round and round on a turntable, first clockwise, then anti-clockwise, has attracted more than 200,000 views, and seven hundred comments, most of them arguing, with varying degrees of passion, for their own interpretation of the words, forwards and backwards, backwards and forwards, sense into noise, noise into sense.

92.

On 29 August 1966, the Beatles closed their set at the Candlestick Park baseball stadium in San Francisco with 'Long Tall Sally', an old Little Richard number that had been part of their repertoire from the very start. 'See you again next year,' said John as they left the stage. The group then clambered into an armoured car and were driven away. It was to be their last proper concert.

Their American tour had been exhausting, sporadically frightening, and unrewarding. Their brief tour of the Philippines the previous month had been even more gruesome. The haughty first lady, Imelda Marcos, felt that the Beatles had snubbed her by failing to attend a party in their honour, and had consequently instructed thugs to jostle and kick them as they tried to navigate the departure lounge at Manila Airport. 'I have never been so terrified in my life,' said George. 'We will never go back there.'

By this stage their delight in their own fame had worn off. They were fed up with all the hassle of touring, and tired of the way the screaming continued to drown out the music, so that even they were unable to hear it. Having been shepherded into an empty, windowless truck after a particularly miserable show in a rainy St Louis, Paul said to the others, 'I really fucking agree with you. I've fucking had it up to here too.'

'We've been telling you for weeks!' came the reply.

On their flight back to England, George told Tony Barrow, 'That's it. I'm not a Beatle any more.' Like the others, but perhaps more so, after 1,400 shows he was sick to death of playing live: at the age of twenty-three, he had had enough.

John, too, was despondent. 'He was very depressed about everything,' said a journalist who sat with him on the plane. 'He felt there was no point in doing anything, since it wouldn't last very long anyway.' As the years rolled by, John allowed his view of these days of touring to curdle into self-pity. Five years on, he was to describe them to Eric Clapton as 'night after night of torture'.

For the first time in years, the four of them were able to take a break from being Beatles. With three months free, they could do what they liked. Ringo chose to relax at home with his wife and new baby. John went to Europe to play Private Gripweed in Richard Lester's film *How I Won the War*. George flew to Bombay to study yoga and to be taught to play the sitar by Ravi Shankar. This left Paul to his own devices.

For a while, he enjoyed himself in London, immersing himself in the counter-culture, as the avant-garde was then briefly known. By now he was one of the most famous men in the world. Even as a member of an audience, or a visitor to a gallery, he was always the centre of attention. So at the beginning of November he decided to conduct a little experiment: what would it be like to be normal?

Paul's pursuit of anonymity had its showy aspect. It was almost as if he were acting not acting, or being ostentatiously incognito. His first stop was a company called Wig Creations, who dutifully measured his upper lip and gauged the exact colour of his hair in order to produce a false moustache, and provided him with two pairs of fake spectacles fitted with clear lenses. By slicking his hair back with Vaseline and donning a long overcoat, Paul found he could wander unrecognised.

Suitably togged up, he set off on a solo motoring holiday in France. Looking back on that jaunt, he pictured himself as just another humble traveller. 'I was a lonely little poet on the road,' he said, though few poets in history have been able to cruise around the Continent in a brand-new Aston Martin DB6.

Paul and his Aston Martin were transported to France by an exclusive air-ferry service operating from a little airport in Kent. On arrival he glued on his moustache, donned his overcoat and his glasses, jumped into his sports car, and headed off for Paris.

Once there, he wandered around by himself, filming bits and pieces, employing experimental filming techniques he had picked up from New Wave cinema and Andy Warhol. Sometimes he stayed in his hotel room writing a journal. At dinner he sat by himself, jotting down notes. He wanted to 'retaste anonymity. Just sit on my own and think all sorts of artistic thoughts like, I'm on my own here, I could be writing a novel, easily.

What about these characters here in this room?' It's easy to forget that he was still only twenty-four years old, with his life ahead of him.

After Paris he embarked on a leisurely drive towards the Loire, filming as he went. 'I was looking out of the hotel window in one French city and there was a gendarme on traffic duty. There was a lot of traffic coming this way, then he'd stop 'em, and let them all go. So the action for ten minutes was a gendarme directing the traffic.' After shooting this scene he rewound the film and shot more footage, so that the one was superimposed over the other, the cars appearing to pass through the gendarme like ghosts.

Upon reaching Bordeaux, he felt a hankering for the night life. Still in disguise, he turned up at a local discothèque, but was refused entry. 'I looked like old jerko. "No, no, monsieur, *non*" – you schmuck, we can't let you in!' So he went back to his hotel and took off his scruffy overcoat, his moustache and his glasses. Then he returned to the disco, where he was welcomed with open arms.

By now, he had begun to recognise the shortcomings of anonymity. 'It was kind of therapeutic, but I'd had enough. It was nice, because I remembered what it was like to not be famous, and it wasn't necessarily any better than being famous. It made me remember why we all wanted to be famous; to get that thing.' Reflecting on his brief retreat from celebrity, he felt happier with his lot. Fame, success and money may well have their shortcomings, but they are still a lot better than their alternatives.

Before setting off on his jaunt, Paul had arranged to meet Mal Evans under the Grosse Horloge in the centre of Bordeaux, reckoning that by then he would be in need of company. The two of them drove to Madrid, then down to Cordoba and Málaga, vaguely thinking they would hook up with John. But when Paul discovered that John had already left Spain he abandoned his plans, phoning Brian Epstein to send someone from London to drive his car home. Epstein also booked Paul and Mal Evans flights to Rome, then on to Kenya, where they went on safari, with a night at Treetops Lodge in Aberdare National Park.

Paul flew from Nairobi to London on 19 November, ready to record the Beatles' new album on the 24th. On the flight back with Mal, he was thinking about his recent assumption of another persona, and wondering if the Beatles might benefit from something similar. 'With this alter-ego band, it won't be us making all that sound, it won't be the Beatles, it'll be this other band, so we'll be able to lose our identities in them.' But what would they call themselves? While he was wondering, their in-flight meals arrived, complete with packets marked 'S' and 'P'.

'What's that mean?' asked Mal, before answering his own question: 'Oh, salt and pepper.'

'Sergeant Pepper,' said Paul, without thinking.

93.

In the early hours of the morning, John, Paul and George were working on 'It's Getting Better' in Abbey Road. Looking down from the control room, George Martin noticed something wrong. John was sitting down, and George and Paul had their hands on his shoulders.

Martin pressed the intercom button. 'What's the matter, John? Is it something you ate?'

George and Paul laughed. John said, 'No, it's not that. I'm just having trouble focusing.'

'Do you want to be driven home?'

'No.'

'OK. Come up here.'

Slowly, John climbed the stairs to the control room. Then he looked up at the ceiling.

'Cor, look at the stars, George.'

Martin looked up, but saw only ceiling.

A few minutes before, John had dipped into his discreet little art-nouveau Liberty pillbox. Meaning to take some uppers, he had taken a tab of LSD by mistake. George Martin was from another generation; he had no idea about hallucinogens. 'How about a spot of fresh air, John?'

But where to go? Outside, the usual array of fans were hanging around, ready to pounce. Martin thought that the roof would be the best place. 'Come on, John, I know a way up the back stairs.'

Paul and George began clowning around, singing old numbers in silly voices, unaware that Martin was taking John up to the roof.

Martin and John walked around for a while. It was a lovely night, with very bright stars. 'Aren't they fantastic?' said John.

John sensed that Martin was looking at him in a funny way. At that moment he realised that he had accidentally taken LSD.

'Don't go too near the edge, there's no rail there, John,' said Martin. There was a drop of ninety feet to the pavement below.

After a while, Martin returned to the control room alone.

Paul asked, 'Where's John?'

'I left him up on the roof, looking at the stars.'

'Ah, you mean like Vince Hill?' joked Paul – Vince Hill's rendition of 'Edelweiss', from *The Sound of Music*, was challenging their 'Penny Lane'/'Strawberry Fields Forever' single for the number 2 slot in the charts.* Paul and George started singing 'Edelweiss' at the top of their voices.

'Edelweiss! E-del-weiss! You look happy to gree-ee-!'

Suddenly it struck them that John, high on LSD, was in great peril. Together, they hurtled up the stairs and brought him back down. Then they all decided that this was a good time to end the session, and Paul took John back to his house, close by.

For some time John had been badgering Paul to try LSD, but Paul, naturally cautious, had kept putting it off. But now he made a snap decision to take some. 'John's on it already, so I'll sort of catch up.'

The pair of them stayed up all night, hallucinating together. 'And we looked into each other's eyes, the eye-contact thing we used to do, which is fairly mind-boggling. You dissolve into each other . . . And it was amazing. You're looking into each other's eyes and you would want to look away but you wouldn't, and you could see yourself in the other person. It was a very freaky experience and I was totally blown away. John had been sitting around very enigmatically and I had a big vision of him as king, the absolute Emperor of Eternity. It was a good trip.'

---

* 'Release Me' by Engelbert Humperdinck remained, resolutely, at number 1.

94.

At 8 p.m. on 10 February 1967, forty-two classical musicians, most of them middle-aged, assembled in Studio One at Abbey Road. On the instructions of the Beatles, they had donned full evening dress, for which they were to be paid a little extra.

The musicians included the violinists Henry Datyner, forty-four, who had won first prize in the 1944 Geneva International Music Competition, and Erich Gruenberg, forty-three, who had been the leader of the Palestine Broadcasting Corporation Orchestra from 1938 to 1945, and had since led the Stockholm Philharmonic Orchestra, the London Symphony Orchestra and the Royal Philharmonic Orchestra. The leader of that evening's orchestra was David McCallum, sixty-nine, who had led the London Philharmonic Orchestra.

On arrival, the musicians found the studio decked out in brightly coloured balloons. They were then ordered to don a selection of comical masks, party hats, rubber noses, bald wigs, clip-on breasts and gorilla paws. 'Here you go, mate, have one of these,' said Mal Evans, handing them out.

'Most of the musicians seemed taken aback,' recalled Geoff Emerick. 'One of them even rudely slapped Mal's hand aside.'

David McCallum sat motionless in his clown's nose, while Erich Gruenberg held his bow in a gorilla's paw.

Next to arrive were a hand-picked selection of beautiful people, or the Beatles' 'way-out friends', as George Martin, also decked in evening dress, preferred to dub them. They included Mick Jagger and Marianne Faithfull, Keith Richards, Donovan, Pattie Boyd, Mike Nesmith of the Monkees, and Graham Nash of the Hollies. Having drifted in, they wandered around the orchestra handing out party novelties, sparklers, joints and, as Martin put it, 'God knows what'. As was customary on such occasions, pretty bubbles filled the air. Unusually, Brian Epstein was in the studio too, nervously surveying this bizarre clash of cultures. For Geoff Emerick, the session marked a transition:

'The lines between classical and pop music were blurring, and even though many of the orchestral players were disdainful of contemporary music, they could see the writing on the wall.'

The four Beatles arrived last of all, Paul in a tweed overcoat, John in a smart blue velvet suit and bright red tie, his face adorned with a Zapata moustache and extravagant sideburns. They were all, noted Emerick, 'in a decidedly jolly mood . . . as if they had started the party several hours earlier'. Like royalty, they 'wandered around bestowing their attention on one subject, then the next'.

Already discombobulated by the fancy dress and party novelties, the orchestra were now obliged to take instructions on how to play their own instruments. Between them, Paul and George Martin had decided that the twenty-four-bar bridge between John's 'I read the news today, oh boy' section and Paul's 'Woke up, got out of bed' section should be filled by individual orchestra members playing the lowest to the highest notes in an unsynchronised slide.

Apart from a shared start and finish, there was to be no coordination, no sense of unity, none of the usual orchestra teamwork. 'I want everyone to be individual,' Martin told them. 'It's every man for himself. Don't listen to the fellow next to you. If he's a third away from you, and you think he's going too fast, let him go.'

Gruenberg, who had delivered the first Russian performance of Benjamin Britten's violin concerto in Moscow, appeared disgruntled. 'All we want you to do is some free-form improvisation,' Paul chipped in.

'Not completely free-form, Erich,' said Martin, encouragingly. 'I'll be conducting, and there is a score of sorts. But we need each musician to play on his own, without listening to those around him.'

Emerick wandered around adjusting the microphones as Gruenberg passed on these outlandish instructions to his baffled colleagues. 'For a moment you could hear a pin drop. Then the murmuring began. "Do *what*??" "What the bloody hell . . . ?"'

'They all looked at me as though I were completely mad,' recalled Martin. Emerick sensed that 'The general response wasn't so much outrage as dismay. The musicians knew they were there to do a job; they just didn't like what they were being asked to do. These were forty of the top classical musicians in England, and they certainly hadn't spent decades honing their craft in order to be told to improvise from their lowest note to their highest . . . It wasn't exactly dignified, and they resented it.'

But Martin, a natural optimist, felt that they eventually came round to it. At first they 'thought it was all a stupid giggle and a waste of time', but in the end 'they were carried into the spirit of the party just because it was so ludicrous'. The session ended, unexpectedly, with a spontaneous burst of applause from everyone in the studio, including the orchestra. Had it dawned on them that they had just participated in the creation of something extraordinary? Perhaps they were simply relieved.

Twelve days later, the Beatles recorded the long, booming piano chord that ends 'A Day in the Life'. For this, EMI dogsbodies moved five different keyboards into Studio Two: two Steinway grand pianos, a Steinway upright piano, a Wurlitzer electric piano and a spinet. John, Paul, Ringo, Mal Evans and George Martin each stood by a keyboard, and when Martin called out 'One, two, three – go!' they hit the chords as hard as possible. Soon after they had finished, George Harrison arrived with Dave Crosby of the Byrds. 'Nice of you to turn up, George,' said John shirtily. 'You only missed the most important overdub we've ever done.'

'A Day in the Life' lasts 5 minutes 34 seconds. It had taken, in all, thirty-four hours to record. Four years earlier, the entire recording of the Beatles' first album, *Please Please Me*, was all done and dusted in a day.

95.

During that same week in January in which the Beatles began recording 'A Day in the Life', Joe Orton was contacted by Walter Shenson, the producer of *A Hard Day's Night* and *Help!*. Would he be interested in rewriting a script for the Beatles?

Orton – the most fashionable, witty and shameless young playwright of the day – tried to play it cool. 'Well, I'm frightfully up to my eyes in it at the moment. I'm writing my third play.'

'I'd certainly love to have you take a look at this draft,' said Shenson. 'I've discussed it with the boys, I mean I mentioned your name to them. They didn't react too much, I must say. But I think I can persuade them to have you.'

Orton had just been taken down a peg or two. 'Yes,' he replied. 'Please send the script over and I'll read it.'

He found it dreary, but with scope for improvement, particularly as Shenson had said that the Beatles wanted to make it more challenging. In his diary Orton wrote: 'Already have the idea that the end should be a church with four bridegrooms and one bride . . . but albeit in such a way that no one would object. Lots of opportunities for sexual ambiguities . . .' He felt there were opportunities, too, for rehashing old material from a rejected novel he had written with his boyfriend, Kenneth Halliwell.

Over lunch, Walter Shenson told him that the Beatles had been thinking of doing a remake of *The Three Musketeers*.

'"Oh, no," I said. "That's been done to death."

'"Brigitte Bardot wanted to play Lady de Winter," he said.

'"She's been done to death as well," I said.

'"Oh, heh, heh, heh, boy!!" he said. "You certainly are quick."'

Orton got to work on a new script, with the provisional title of 'Up Against It'. By the end of the day he had completed the first two pages. He was ruthless in offloading a lot of old material onto the Beatles. 'I'm not

bothering to write characters for them,' he confided to his diary. 'I shall just do all my box of tricks – Sloane and Hal – on them. After all, if I repeat myself in this film it doesn't matter. Nobody who sees the film will have seen Sloane or Loot.'

The next day, Walter Shenson phoned to say that Brian Epstein was 'delighted' he was on board. 'You'll be hearing either from Brian or Paul McCartney. So don't be surprised if a Beatle rings you up.'

'What an experience. I shall feel as nervous as I would if St Michael, or God was on the line.'

'Oh, there's not any need to be worried, Joe. I can say, from my heart, that the boys are very respectful of talent. I mean, most respectful of any-one they feel has talent. I can really say that, Joe.'

A week later, someone from Epstein's office invited him to 'meet the boys' the following Wednesday. Orton's report of his visit is characteris-tically comical: 'a youngish man with a hair-style which was way out in 1958, short, college boy, came up and said, ". . . I'm Brian Epstein's per-sonal assistant." It crossed my mind to wonder why the English have never got around to finding a perfectly respectable word for "boy-friend". "I'm afraid there's been a most awful mix-up. And all the boys' appointments have been put back an hour and a half." I was a bit chilly in my man-ner after that. "Do you want me to come back at six?" I said. "Well, no. Couldn't we make another appointment?" "What guarantee is there that you won't break that?" I said. "I think you'd better find yourself a different writer." This said with indifferent success, though the effect was startling.

He asked me to wait a minute and went away to return with Brian Epstein himself.

'Somehow I'd expected something like Michael Codron.* I'd imagined Epstein to be florid, Jewish, dark-haired and overbearing. Instead I was face to face with a mousey-haired, slight young man. Washed-out in a way. He had a suburban accent. I went into his office. "Could you meet Paul and me for dinner tonight?" he said. "We do want to have the pleasure of talking to you." "I've a theatre engagement tonight," I replied, by now sulky and unhelpful. "Could I send the car to fetch you after the show?"'

Orton arrived at Epstein's Belgravia house ten minutes early, and walked around to kill time. When he rang the bell, an old man appeared. 'He seemed surprised to see me. "Is this Brian Epstein's house?" I said. "Yes, sir," he said, and led the way to the hall. I suddenly realised that the man was the butler. I've never seen one before . . . He took me into a room and said in a loud voice, "Mr Orton." Everybody looked up and stood to their feet. I was just introduced to one or two people. And Paul Mc-Cartney. He was just as the photographs. Only he'd grown a moustache. His hair was shorter too. He was playing the latest Beatles record "Penny Lane". I liked it very much. Then he played the other side – Strawberry something. I didn't like this as much.'

They chatted, and agreed that the film should not be set in the 1930s. Later, they went down to dinner. 'The trusted old retainer – looking too much like a butler to be good casting – busied himself in the corner. "The only thing I get from the theatre," Paul M. said, "is a sore arse."' Paul added that *Loot* was the only play he hadn't wanted to leave before the end.

'"I'd've liked a bit more," he said. We talked of the theatre. I said that compared with the pop-scene the theatre was square. "The theatre started going downhill when Queen Victoria knighted Henry Irving," I said. "Too fucking respectable."'

The two men talked of drugs, magic mushrooms and LSD. '"The drug not the money," I said. We talked of tattoos. And after one or two veiled references, marijuana. I said I'd smoked it in Morocco. The atmosphere relaxed a little.'

After dinner, they watched a television programme. 'It had phrases in it like "the in crowd" and "swinging London". There was a little scratching at

* Theatre producer (b.1930), knighted in 2014.

the door. I thought it was the old retainer, but someone got up to open the door and about five very young and pretty boys trooped in. I rather hoped this was the evening's entertainment. It wasn't, though. It was a pop group called the Easybeats. I'd seen them on TV. I liked them very much then.'

At this point the French photographer Jean-Marie Périer arrived, bearing a set of photographs for the cover of *Strawberry Fields Forever*. 'Excellent photograph,' judged Orton. 'The four Beatles look different in their moustaches. Like anarchists in the early years of the century.'

Orton engaged an Easybeat in conversation, 'feeling slightly like an Edwardian masher with a Gaiety girl', before deciding it was time to go home. 'I had a last word with Paul M. "Well," I said, "I'd like to do the film. There's only one thing we've got to fix up." "You mean the bread?" "Yes." We smiled and parted. I got a cab home.'

The next day Orton spoke to his agent, Peggy Ramsay. '"We should ask 15,000 pounds," I said, "and then if they beat us down, remember no lower than 10,000. After all whether I do it or not is a matter of indifference to me." Peggy agreed. She said she'd ask 15 and try to get 12 and a percentage. "If they won't pay us 10 they can fuck themselves," I said. "Of course, darling," Peggy said.'

Leaving Ramsay to sort out the contract, Orton got down to the writing, unashamedly plundering his unpublished novel *Head to Toe* for most of the action. He thought it 'might have been designed with the Beatles in mind', though even in 1967 he was probably overestimating their appetite for decadence.

Within a fortnight he had almost completed his script. After a vague suggestion from Epstein that they might get Antonioni to direct the film, Orton heard nothing more from either Shenson or Epstein; both failed to return his calls. A livid Peggy Ramsay described Epstein as 'an amateur and a fool'. In his diary, Orton condemned him as 'a thoroughly weak, flaccid type'.

After some time, he was informed that 'Up Against It' was being returned to him. 'No explanation why. No criticism of the script. And apparently, Brian had no comment to make either. Fuck them.' But in his heart, he knew full well why they had turned it down. 'By page 25, they [the Beatles] had committed adultery, murder, dressed in drag, been in prison, seduced the niece of a priest, blown up a war memorial and all sorts of things like that. I can't really blame them, but it would have been marvellous.'

Within a week, the producer Oscar Lewenstein purchased Orton's rejected script for £10,000. On 9 August a chauffeur arrived at Orton's Islington flat to drive him to Twickenham Studios for a meeting with Lewenstein and the Beatles' old film director, Richard Lester. When there was no answer he telephoned Lewenstein, who told him to try again. Finally he looked through the letterbox, and saw the naked body of a bald man lying flat on the hallway floor.

The police found two corpses: Kenneth Halliwell on the floor, and Joe Orton on the bed, bludgeoned to death with a hammer. Orton's brilliant success had exacerbated Halliwell's already heightened sense of failure. After killing Orton, he had swallowed twenty-two Nembutals, washed down with a can of grapefruit juice.

At Joe Orton's funeral in the West Chapel of Golders Green Crematorium they played 'A Day in the Life', which had been Joe's favourite track. Some thought it too quiet; others disapproved of the way all the psychedelic references had been spliced out, on the un-Ortonesque grounds of good taste. On the way out of the chapel, one of the mourners pointed out that the booming piano chord at the end sounded just like the lid of a coffin being banged shut.

96.

The further they travelled, the more they looked back. They were Pied Pipers, leading their generation in a conga along untrodden paths; but they were also the little boys at the end of the line, filled with longing for the world they had left behind.

After the Beatles finished playing the Liverpool Empire in December 1963, John went to his Aunt Harrie's house, and rootled through his old bits and pieces. His school friend Pete Shotton looked on in amazement as John sorted through old books and drawings: 'It seemed to me that John, at a glittering crossroads of his life and career, was grasping instinctively for the mementoes of his childhood – as if these reassuringly familiar objects might somehow ease his transition into an unknowable future.'

At the age of twenty-four, John was perplexed by the complexities of adulthood, and yearning for days gone by. 'When I was younger, so much younger than today'. Aged twenty-five, he sang wistfully of the 'places I'll remember all my life'. At twenty-six, his great eulogy to childhood, 'Strawberry Fields Forever', juxtaposed the hallucinogenic and the nostalgic, like an acid trip in a nursery. Paul has described the Salvation Army garden on which it was based as a form of utopia, John's 'secret garden . . . there was a wall you could bunk over and it was a rather wild garden, it wasn't manicured at all, so it was easy to hide in. The bit he went into was a secret garden like in *The Lion, the Witch and the Wardrobe*, and he thought of it like that, it was a little hideaway for him where he could maybe have a smoke, living his dreams a little, a getaway. It was an escape.'

Some of Lennon and McCartney's darkest songs exhibit the ruthlessly jaunty quality of nursery rhymes. Bungalow Bill goes into the jungle with his gun and kills animals; Maxwell murders his victims with a silver hammer. John's solo song 'My Mummy's Dead' has the same tune as 'Three Blind Mice', whose tails are chopped off with a carving knife.

When Kenneth Tynan was working on the stage version of two of John's books for the National Theatre, he set himself the tricky task of trying to explain what they meant to a bemused Laurence Olivier. 'John's poems are all about the beginning of things,' he said. 'The first awareness of cinema, of books, or poetry. Through that, we get a whole picture of his childhood in Liverpool.' He then remembered something the Maharishi had said about 'that absorption that comes when children are playing and they're nowhere else'.

For his part, Paul had been brought up on family sing-songs. It gave him pleasure to write music that his father might have played 'a long, long time ago'. The Beatles' surreal TV film *Magical Mystery Tour* was regarded as almost incomprehensibly adult by most viewers at the time, but it was largely formed of random memories of childhood. 'I've had this idea,' Paul told his assistant Alistair Taylor when he was wondering what to film. 'Do they still do mystery tours on buses?' For all its progressive wackiness, it was a trip into the past, dotted with scenes from the Beatles' childhoods – brass bands, sing-songs on coaches, Busby Berkeley dance routines, men with knotted hankies on their heads, tug-of-wars at village fêtes – all viewed through the distorting mirrors of dreams or LSD or both. The Beatles embarked on the filming with the capriciousness of children. Paul once phoned Taylor at two in the morning saying, 'I want a dozen midget wrestlers by tomorrow.' The film looks ramshackle because that's what it was: ideas that had occurred overnight would be filmed the next day. One morning John said to Paul, 'God, I had the strangest dream.' 'Come on, then,' replied Paul. 'Remember it and we'll film it.' John said he had turned into a waiter and had been shovelling spaghetti over someone. 'Fantastic!' said Paul. 'That's on!'

On its release in May 1967, *Sgt. Pepper's Lonely Hearts Club Band* was hailed as a vision from the future. Timothy Leary, allergic to understatement, declared, 'John Lennon, George Harrison, Paul McCartney and Ringo Starr are mutants. Evolutionary agents sent by gods, endowed with mysterious powers to create a new human species.' Even the more nuanced Kenneth Tynan considered it 'a decisive moment in the history of Western civilisation'.

But it is as much an exercise in playing about with the past: a wallow in nostalgia, embroidered with quaint brass bands and fairground paraphernalia. Hippies loved to spot references to dope and LSD in the album, but

Paul's grandfather Joe, the tuba-player in his workplace* company band, would have spotted just as many allusions to Edwardian circuses and music halls. The title track looks back twenty years to when 'Sgt. Pepper taught the band to play'; 'Getting Better' is based in school; in 'She's Leaving Home', the runaway girl's parents 'sacrificed most of our lives'; 'Being for the Benefit of Mr Kite' celebrates the good old days, when a splendid time was guaranteed for all; in 'Good Morning Good Morning', John decides to 'take a walk by the old school', and finds 'nothing has changed it's still the same'. Even in the most outwardly progressive of the tracks, 'A Day in the Life', John sees a film in which 'the English army had just won the war'; and 'When I'm Sixty-Four' extends the reach of nostalgia into the future, with Paul looking forward to the time when he can look back on a golden past.

* Cope Bros & Co. They manufactured tobacco products – snuff, cigarettes, pipe tobacco, cigars.

97.

Figures on the cover of *Sgt. Pepper's Lonely Hearts Club Band*:

Fred Astaire, dancer
Mahavatara Babaji, guru
Aubrey Beardsley, artist
The Beatles, in person and in waxwork
Larry Bell, sculptor
Wallace Berman, artist
Issy Bonn, comedian
Marlon Brando, film star
Bobby Breen, singer
Lenny Bruce, comedian
William S. Burroughs, author
Lewis Carroll, author
Stephen Crane, author
Aleister Crowley, author, occultist
Tony Curtis, film star
Marlene Dietrich, singer, film star
Dion, singer
Diana Dors, actress
Bob Dylan, singer songwriter
Albert Einstein, physicist
W.C. Fields, comedian
Sri Yukteswar Giri, guru
Huntz Hall, actor
Tommy Handley, comedian
Oliver Hardy, comedian
Aldous Huxley, novelist and philosopher

James Joyce, author

Carl Jung, psychologist

Stan Laurel, comedian

T.E. Lawrence (Lawrence of Arabia)

Richard Lindner, artist

Sonny Liston, boxer

Dr David Livingstone, explorer

Karl Marx, economist and philosopher

Richard Merkin, artist

Max Miller, comedian

Tom Mix, film star

Marilyn Monroe, film star

Sir Robert Peel, prime minister, founder of the police

Edgar Allan Poe, author

Tyrone Power, film star

Simon Rodia, sculptor

George Bernard Shaw, playwright

Terry Southern, author

Karlheinz Stockhausen, composer

Albert Stubbins, footballer

Stuart Sutcliffe, former Beatle

Shirley Temple, child film star

Dylan Thomas, poet

Johnny Weissmuller, actor

H.G. Wells, author

Mae West, film star

H.C. Westermann, sculptor

Oscar Wilde, author and playwright

Sri Paramahansa Yogananda, guru

Timothy Carey, actor (obscured by George Harrison)

Sophia Loren, actress (invisible behind the Beatles' waxworks)

Marcello Mastroianni, actor (invisible behind the Beatles' waxworks
but for his hat)

Proposed but not used:

Mahatma Gandhi, political activist (dropped following pressure from
   Sir Joseph Lockwood, head of EMI)
Leo Gorcey, actor (dropped after asking $400 for his image)
Adolf Hitler (requested by John, but dropped as too controversial)
Jesus Christ (requested by John, but dropped as too controversial)

98.

If you were twenty in the summer of 1967, San Francisco was the only place to be. But I was ten, and boarding at a Roman Catholic prep school called Farleigh House, in Farleigh Wallop, a few miles from Basingstoke. My friend Miller tried wearing a flower in his hair, only to be told by Major Watt to take it out at once. Major Watt was rumoured to be a Nazi spy. Someone had seen him in the school grounds late at night flashing secret messages to the Germans with a torch.

Gentle people were few and far between. Our new history master, Mr Wall, wore pink socks and had a slapdash, bohemian air about him, but he left under a cloud after dropping his trousers when someone enquired as to what colour his pants were. Gentleness, flowers, and even hair were in short supply.

I was studying hard for my confirmation. Why did God make me? God made me to know him, love him and serve him in this world and be happy with him forever in the next. In our confirmation classes we took a peculiar delight in cross-questioning Mr Callaghan on the fine points of Roman Catholic theology. It always came back to the same old desert island. 'Sir, sir, sir! But what if you were stuck on a desert island, and there was a baby who was dying, and the baby hadn't been christened, sir, and there was no water about, sir. Would you be allowed to use your spit, sir? Would you be allowed to use your *pee*, sir?'

We had two Masses a week, on Wednesdays and Sundays, and two Benedictions, on Tuesdays and Fridays. Every Benediction, we would sing a hymn called 'Tantum Ergo':

Tantum ergo
Sacramento
Veneremur cernui
Et antique

Documentum
Novo cedat ritui

I sang it twice a week for five years. None of us ever asked what it meant, and I still don't know. Sacraments, venerate, antique, documents . . . but its meaning didn't matter. Its sound was its meaning; its absence of meaning was its meaning. Latin was God's first language, and its meaning floated direct to heaven on a cloud of incense pouring out of a thurible swung with such vigour by the seniors that the new boys in the front row would often disappear, coughing and spluttering, in an unholy fog.

'Lady Madonna' came out halfway through the next spring term. I have a vivid memory of hearing it coming from a radio belonging to builders who were patching up the school swimming pool. Its title represented the perfect amalgam of the two essentials of a private Catholic education in Britain, suggesting that the Virgin herself was an aristocrat.

But what did it all mean? Why would Lady Madonna have to worry about making ends meet?

'Lady Madonna' was followed by 'Hey Jude' and 'Instant Karma'. Pop music was moving away from meaning, and closer to the language of 'Tantum Ergo', forcing sense to make way for something more mysterious.

At Boy Scout camp we sang 'Gin gan gooly-gooly-gooly-gooly watch-a, gin gan goo, gin gan goo'. In maths, we drew Venn diagrams. The Beatles sang 'I am the Walrus' ('goo-goo-ga-joo'). On Ash Wednesday we heard the priest repeat, 'Remember man that thou art dust and unto dust thou shalt return' over and over again as he rubbed ash onto our foreheads. On holy days of obligation we all went to visit priests' hidey-holes in Catholic stately homes. I often wondered whether groups with Latin names, like Procul Harum and Status Quo, were Catholic too. And behind it all, 'Tantum Ergo' was our soundtrack.

My reverence for the faraway heaven of San Francisco was never at odds with my reverence for what in another hymn we called 'Faith of Our Fathers'. I remember feeling a sharp sense of shock on first glimpsing the heading at the top of the music master's sheet music for 'While Shepherds Watched Their Flocks'. It simply said, 'Sox'.

Fifty or more years on, I make my living from parody, easing sense into nonsense, translating the words of others back into their original gibberish. I find 'Tantum Ergo' has lodged in my head, a dissident group of my brain cells forming a chapel choir, singing it at full blast at impromptu moments. And at other times I find the choir in my head singing,

> Friday night arrives without a suitcase
> Sunday morning creeping like a nun

or

> Semolina pilchard
> Climbing up the Eiffel Tower
> Elementary penguin singing Hare Krishna . . .

or

> There's nowhere you can be that isn't where you're meant to be

and my imagination keeps returning to Farleigh House, Farleigh Wallop, Basingstoke, Hampshire. Or perhaps it has always been stranded there, and I am the boarder who never came home.

99.

At the dawn of the Summer of Love, Brian Epstein informed George Martin of his bold plans for the Beatles' biggest audience ever. 'He came to me and said, "Look, there's an international hook-up with all nations and the Beatles have been chosen to represent it. We'd be doing a live broadcast to 200, 300 million people in every part of the globe."'

A 'party atmosphere' was required, so, with time running out, Epstein instructed Tony Bramwell to gather suitably groovy stars for the next day's live broadcast. Bramwell decided to trawl the most fashionable clubs: the Speakeasy, the Cromwellian, the Bag o'Nails, the Scotch of St James. In the Speakeasy he found Keith Moon hurling peanuts around, 'absolutely stonkers'. Moon eagerly accepted the invitation, but turned down Bramwell's suggestion that he should first get some rest: 'If it's all the same to you, I'll just keep going.'

Bramwell found Mick Jagger in the Scotch of St James, and explained that the broadcast would be transmitted worldwide. Jagger's casual acceptance – 'No hassle' – possibly concealed a degree of envy. 'You couldn't *buy* that kind of publicity,' he said. Other clubs proved equally fruitful, with Eric Clapton and various Small Faces agreeing to turn up.

And so, on the afternoon of 25 June 1967, the beautiful people flowed into Studio One at Abbey Road: Jagger and Richards, Marianne Faithfull, Graham Nash of the Hollies, Gary Leeds of the Walker Brothers. In line with Royal Ascot, which was running simultaneously, many attendees had gone to some fuss with their clothes, not least Paul, who had stayed up all night applying psychedelic patterns to his shirt. Ringo wore a suit tailored for him by Simon and Marijke from the Dutch design group The Fool, while Eric Clapton arrived with his hair freshly permed, a striking new advance in male grooming.

Watching film of the broadcast of 'All You Need is Love' is like finding the Summer of Love in a grain of sand. It starts with trumpeters from the thirteen-strong orchestra, in regulation dinner jacket and black tie, blasting out 'La Marseillaise'. Paul choruses 'Love, love, love' sitting cross-legged on a high stool, a red flower sticking out of the headphone on his left ear. The cellists have their eyes glued to their sheet music. How do they feel about being plunged into this brave new world of free love, its music so different from their own? Do these serious musicians, these men of gravitas, resent having to kowtow to a bunch of stoned hippies, or are they exhilarated at being allowed into this magical universe where there's nothing you can do that can't be done?

John has one hand pressed on the headphone over his left ear, his eyes closed, his glasses a third of the way down his nose, two flowers sprouting from the top of his head with another popping up from his forehead like a miner's torch. He offhandedly chews gum as he sings 'Nothing you can say but you can learn how to play the game'. He appears unruffled by the idea of singing to 350 million viewers worldwide, but at the same time intent on the job in hand: he doesn't look around, or acknowledge the audience. Tony Bramwell said later that John was 'wired and speeding', but he gives a good impression of insouciance.

And so to the violin quartet, sitting in a circle, bespectacled and studious, one with a bald head bobbing in a sea of hair. The lead violinist, Sidney Sax, is fifty-four in a roomful of twenty-somethings; he also played on 'Yesterday' and 'Eleanor Rigby'.

The camera moves to a tape-machine, whirling around, then to a wider shot of the studio, decorated with flowers galore and, to add to the illusion of a children's party, hundreds of brightly coloured balloons. Aha! There's Paul's brother Mike, sitting on the floor close to John's knees, looking bored, or stoned, or possibly a bit of both. We see George for the first time, in red flares, fur coat and moustache, and there at the back the reassuring figure of Ringo, dependable as a bookend, chugging away on his drums, acting the hippy in a purple silk jacket with beads all over the place, but, despite the effort, still the obliging bus conductor.

Back to the beefy brass section, and the olden days. They are led by David Mason, forty-one, a professor at the Royal College of Music. Back in 1958 he played the flugelhorn at the premiere of Ralph Vaughan Williams's Ninth Symphony, conducted by Malcolm Sargent, in the presence of the composer.* Vaughan Williams – pupil of Ravel, friend of Holst – was then eighty-five years old, and just three weeks from death. For the first ten years of his life he had known his great-uncle, Charles Darwin. When the young Ralph had asked his mother about *On the Origin of Species*, she told him: 'The Bible says that God made the world in six days. Great-Uncle Charles thinks it took longer; but we need not worry about it, for it is equally wonderful either way.' From Charles Darwin to John Lennon in just three handshakes: the Beatles concertina time in the most extraordinary way.†

The studio is packed with so much stuff that it has an air of the set of *Steptoe and Son*: people remember the cameramen puncturing the spirit of love and peace with curses as they got caught up in all the odds and ends. In the background, a string puppet has four lettered balloons – L, O, V and E – attached to its head.

Many members of the audience stare into space, looking either bored or cool: in those days, it was hard to tell the difference. Mick Jagger sits to the front, facing away from the camera, two huge embroidered eyes staring out of the back of his jacket. Throughout, there are glimpses of oddities: as John sings 'All you need is love' for the umpteenth time, the camera floats to a bald man in a white shirt and black trousers, looking mildly cheesed-off, as though he's waiting to lock up. Seconds later, as John sings 'It's eea-seey!' someone who looks like Princess Margaret spins into view. *Might* she have been there? This was the Summer of Love, when the world went topsy-turvy: anything was possible.‡ In August, the EMI chairman Sir Joseph Lockwood was received by the Queen at Buckingham Palace. 'The Beatles are turning awfully *funny*, aren't they?' she said to him.

For some reason, George barely merits a look-in, and is not filmed at

---

* He also played the flugelhorn on 'Penny Lane'.

† Around this time Paul discussed Vietnam with Bertrand Russell, who remembered childhood meetings with William Gladstone; Gladstone himself used to breakfast with the elderly William Wordsworth (b.1770). So it's 'Blackbird' to 'Daffodils' in three meetings. Russell's grandfather, the Victorian prime minister Lord John Russell, visited Napoleon in exile on Elba. So, if you'd prefer, you can leap from Paul McCartney to Bertrand Russell to Lord John Russell to the Emperor Napoleon in just three bounds.

‡ In April 1969 Princess Anne, wearing a navy-blue trouser suit, joined other audience members to dance onstage at the hippy musical *Hair*. 'The eighteen-year-old Princess broke into a hipswinging routine, flinging her arms in abandon,' observed the *Daily Telegraph*.

all during his brief guitar solo, once voted the fifth-worst of all time. Then the coda gets under way, the orchestra zipping through George Martin's masterly mish-mash of Bach, 'Greensleeves' and 'In the Mood', and the audience claps sluggishly along; Mick Jagger gives up halfway between claps. Where are the other members of the Rolling Stones, the Who, the Small Faces, the Walker Brothers, who were said to be there? I must have watched the video twenty-five times or more, but I still haven't caught sight of them.

Towards the end, five Beatle apparatchiks parade on, sandwich boards bearing the slogan 'All You Need is Love' in different languages hanging from their necks. They form a small, uncomfortable circle, like children forced into an Easter Parade. Tony Bramwell's board reads 'LOVE LOVE LOVE', and Alistair Taylor's 'LOVE ЛЮБОV AMOR AMORE'. Earlier in the day Taylor had been forced into a psychedelic shirt by Paul Mc-Cartney, who thought his usual office attire too square. Towards the back, someone holds a sign saying 'COME BACK MILLY', a personal message to one of Paul's aunts, away in Australia visiting her son and grandchildren.

As the song draws to a close, John and Paul start singing 'She loves you yeah, yeah, yeah,' which they first released just four years earlier, but which now breaks through the hippy fog like a hymn to lost youth.

And what of 'All You Need is Love'? Some Beatles purists find it too banal, its lyrics an odd mix of truisms – 'Nothing you can sing that can't be sung' – and untruisms – 'nowhere you can be that isn't where you're meant to be', the whole thing too mushy and meaningless and contradictory to be taken seriously.

Ian MacDonald describes it as 'one of the Beatles' less deserving hits', adding that it 'owes more of its standing to its local historical associations than to its inspiration'. For him, it was sloppy and slapdash: 'Drug-sodden laziness was half the problem.' His argument was as much with the zeitgeist as with the song that expressed it: the idea that anything worthwhile can be attained without effort – it's *ea-seey* – and that every single person, however dull and droopy, can count himself an artist.

Yet at the same time, 'All You Need is Love' captures the zeitgeist like no other song, which is perhaps why it is loved by such a wide range of people: the boxer George Foreman, the comedy actress Penelope Keith, the dancer Wayne Sleep and the racing driver Jackie Stewart all chose it as a Desert Island Disc. When he was Home Secretary in the mid-

1990s, Michael Howard used to play the Beatles in his government car. He considers 'All You Need is Love' 'perhaps the quintessential record of the sixties'. On the other side of the Atlantic, Al and Tipper Gore played it at their 1970 wedding. In 2005 John's transcription of the verse, which he used as a crib at the recording, sold for $1 million at auction.

Brian Epstein seemed at his happiest and most relaxed that day. It was, he declared, the best thing the Beatles had ever done: 'It's a wonderful, beautiful, spine-chilling song.' He attended the session in an open-necked shirt and black velvet suit, looking unusually carefree. Maybe the song said everything he was too tortured to express. He could look through the window at the utopia beyond, but the window itself remained firmly closed. No one you can save that can't be saved; except for Brian. On that day, he had nine weeks left to live.

IOO.

A month before his death, Brian Epstein wrote to his American business partner Nat Weiss, thanking him for his kind words following the recent death of his father.

He went on: 'The week of Shiva is up tonight and I feel a bit strange. Probably been good for me in a way. Time to think and note that at least I'm really needed by Mother. Also time to note that the unworldly Jewish circle of my parents' and brother's friends are not so bad. Provincial maybe, but warm, sincere and basic.'

He moved on, as always, to the Beatles: 'The boys have gone to Greece to buy an island . . . a dotty idea but they're no longer children and must have their own sweet way'.

The idea of buying a Greek island had been popped into John's head by his new best friend, 'Magic Alex' Mardas, perhaps the most fraudulent of all the Beatles' hangers-on.

Alexis Mardas was the son of a major in the Greek secret police. Arriving in London in 1965 on a student visa, he worked briefly as a television repairman before a chance meeting with Marianne Faithfull's husband, John Dunbar. Handy with a screwdriver, Mardas had constructed a box with small lights which flashed on and off at random. This was enough to convince Dunbar of his genius. The box served no practical purpose, which only added to its wonder.

Dunbar introduced him to the Rolling Stones, and Mardas seized the opportunity to pitch them a system of spotlights designed to go on and off to the beat of live music. The Stones employed the system on their next tour, though with mixed results. In Mardas's defence, Dunbar claimed the system had worked 'some of the time' – possibly during the 'off' moments.

Having failed to convince the Stones, Mardas concentrated his energies on John Lennon. Cynthia watched as John succumbed to his charms: 'John was knocked out by Magic Alex . . . He was a truly plausible person, and had the face of an innocent. His hair was as blond and as angelic as his smile. To John, who was totally ignorant of the tricks one can make with electricity, he believed that Alex really had something magic about him. He believed every word that he said.'

One morning John brought him along to Paul's house. 'This is my new guru – Magic Alex,' he said. Paul was a little taken aback, but made no comment. These were happy-go-lucky times, when scepticism was outlawed. 'We didn't really call anyone's bluff, it would have been a bit too aggressive,' says Paul. 'So we just let him get on with it.'

John regarded Mardas as a genius, and sought to reward him accordingly. On 1 May 1966 he was at Kenwood with his old friend Pete Shotton when he suddenly remembered that the following day was Mardas's birthday. 'Fuck me,' he said. 'Magic Alex is coming round tomorrow and I haven't even got anything for him. What can I give him, Pete?'

Shotton had no idea. John remembered that Mardas had purred appreciatively over the expensive Iso Grifo Italian sports car he had bought at the Earl's Court Motor Show a week before. At that time it was the only Iso Grifo in the UK. 'Let's give him the fucking Iso then!'

Pete and John wound great spools of ribbon around the car, rounding

it all off with a big bow. 'The birthday boy was suitably impressed,' recalled Pete.

Mardas's adoption by the Beatles was perfectly timed. At the end of 1966 the group had been advised by their accountants to avoid an excessive tax bill by investing their money in freehold property and retail trading. They duly set up a number of companies under the umbrella of Apple Corps, among them Apple Records, Apple Films and Apple Retail (which ran their boutique on Baker Street). With the promise of far-reaching, mind-blowing inventions, Apple Electronics was given to Alex Mardas to run.

By now John was taking daily doses of LSD, which perhaps left him better equipped to appreciate the full glory he called 'one of those massive, big, sort of computerised laboratories they've been trying to invent for years'. In the months ahead, he allowed himself to be convinced by Magic Alex that generous sums of money were all that was needed to usher in a golden age of electronic wizardry.

Sitting in the studio one night, the Beatles were complaining to each other about their lack of privacy when John suggested they should create their own little kingdom, like an island, where they could build houses, and a studio, and even a school. Julian could be taught alongside the children of Bob Dylan, who would be sure to join them. At this point, Mardas's ears pricked up. There were, he volunteered, thousands of islands off the coast of Greece, and moreover they were 'dirt cheap'.

Mardas was summarily despatched to Greece to pick the perfect island. Within forty-eight hours he phoned to say he had found a cluster of Aegean islands, one of eighty acres, with a sixteen-acre olive grove and four secluded beaches, surrounded by four smaller islands, one for each Beatle. The asking price was £90,000. Mardas added that in his estimation the profits from the olive groves would pay back the total cost within seven years.

All four Beatles flew out to Greece, unfazed by the new ruling military junta's ban on both long hair and rock music, and its declarations that drug offences were to be punished with possible life sentences.

Through family connections, Mardas seems to have struck some sort of deal with the junta: in return for a form of diplomatic immunity, the

Beatles would agree to pose for a series of pictures for the Ministry of Tourism. John was warned not to criticise the junta, and to behave himself. 'All I remember about the holiday is that some of us took acid, and we didn't have to go through passport control because Alex's father was so important,' recalled Pattie Boyd. As it happened, the moment he landed at Athens airport, John realised to his horror that he had left his drugs at home. 'What good is the Parthenon without LSD?' he complained. After a frantic call to the NEMS office, their willing dogsbody Mal Evans was on board the next flight with the mislaid package.

'It was a great trip,' recalled George. 'John and I were on acid all the time, sitting on the front of the ship playing ukuleles. Greece was on the left; a big island on the right. The sun was shining and we sang "Hare Krishna" for hours and hours.'

They went ahead with the purchase, against the advice of their accountants, who insisted it would place their already precarious finances in further jeopardy. Arrangements for transferring the money were made directly with the Chancellor of the Exchequer, James Callaghan. At one point the avuncular Callaghan wrote to the Beatles informing them that £95,000 was 'the absolute limit' he would allow to flow out of Britain, adding in his own hand at the foot of the letter, 'But not a penny more . . . I wonder how you're going to furnish it?'

This particular problem was solved by indifference. Having bought the islands, the Beatles immediately lost interest, forgot to build their utopia, and never visited them again. A year later they sold them for a profit of £11,400. Looking back, George noted approvingly that 'It was about the only time the Beatles ever made any money on a business venture.'

101.

George and Pattie flew from Greece to California, where they attended a recording session by the Mamas and the Papas, dropped in on Ravi Shankar's music school, and dined out on Sunset Strip. On 7 August 1967 they flew to San Francisco in a private Learjet with Derek Taylor and Neil Aspinall to see Pattie's sister Jenny, who was living there. It is probably no coincidence that the B-side to 'All You Need is Love' is 'Baby, You're a Rich Man'.

After lunch with Jenny, George and his gang thought it would be fun to drive to Haight-Ashbury, the hippy district, where the grooviest musicians – Jefferson Airplane, the Grateful Dead, Janis Joplin – were known to hang out. On their way there, Derek passed around LSD. 'Since we were going to Haight-Ashbury, it seemed silly not to,' recalled Jenny. As they got out of the car, 'the acid kicked in and everything was just whoah, psychedelic and very . . . I mean, it was just *completely fine*.'

George hoped to wander around unrecognised in his blue denim jacket, psychedelic jeans, heart-shaped shades and moccasins: after all, most people in Haight-Ashbury were trying to look just like him, so who could tell the difference? Moreover, San Francisco was famous for being mellow: even if the hippies did recognise him, they would surely be too laid-back to give him any hassle.

So it came as a surprise when George and Pattie drifted into a shop, and found it immediately filling with new customers. As they left the shop and walked along the street, a crowd of people trailed behind them. Pattie could even hear them muttering, 'The Beatles are here, the Beatles are in town . . .'

It wasn't what George had expected. 'We walked down the street, and I was being treated like the Messiah.' How did it feel to be one of the beautiful people? At that very moment, most uncomfortable. Pattie was shaken: 'We were expecting Haight-Ashbury to be special, a creative and artistic place, filled with beautiful people, but it was horrible – full of ghastly drop-outs, bums and spotty youths, all out of their brains. Everybody looked stoned – even mothers and babies – and they were so close behind us they were treading on the backs of our heels. It got to the point where we couldn't stop for fear of being trampled.'

Hoping to shake off these hangers-on, they set off for Golden Gate Park, to the area that had recently become known as Hippie Hill. But George had become an unwitting Pied Piper. As the five of them sat down on the grass, a stream of hippies followed suit, to be joined by many more.

From the back of the gathering a guitar was produced, and passed from hand to hand to the front, before finally reaching George. It then dawned on Pattie that they wanted more from him than he was either willing or able to give. 'I had the feeling that they'd listened to the Beatles' records, analysed them, learnt what they thought they should learn, and taken every drug they'd thought the Beatles were singing about. Now they wanted to know where to go next. And George was there, obviously, to give them the answer.'

George made an attempt to give them a little of what they wanted, demonstrating the guitar's chords – 'This is G, this is E, this is D' – rather than singing a song. A girl started yelling, 'Hey! That's George Harrison!

That's George Harrison!' Hearing the cry, more hippies began to edge towards him; the crowd grew bigger and bigger.

They all started calling for a song, but George, increasingly frightened, politely handed back the guitar, saying, 'Sorry, man, we've got to go now.'

As he and his friends stood up to walk away, a hippy approached him saying, 'Hey, George, do you want some STP?' George hesitated. A week or two before, five thousand tabs of STP had been distributed at the Summer Solstice Celebration, and a large number of people had ended up in hospital. 'No, thanks, I'm cool, man,' he said, and carried on walking.

The hippy was affronted, saying, 'Hey, man – you put me down,' then turning to the crowd of followers and complaining, 'George Harrison turned me down!' The easy-going, hippy-dippy mood suddenly altered. 'The crowd became hostile,' recalled Pattie. 'We sensed it because when you're that high you're very aware of vibes.'

George and the others began to walk away slowly, before it dawned on them that their car was parked a mile away, so they picked up their pace. But as they walked faster, so did the crowd. George experienced some form of panic attack, accelerated by the LSD: 'It was like the manifestation of a scene from a Hieronymus Bosch painting getting bigger and bigger, fish with heads, faces like vacuum cleaners.'

Neil Aspinall remembered them growing ever more frantic. The drugs had made them lower their guard, putting them in the same situation they'd always taken such pains to avoid. By now, a thousand people or so were chasing them. 'In the end, we were running for our lives.'

At last they spotted their limousine, and jumped into it, slamming the doors. The crowd of hippies circled the car. 'The windows were full of these faces, flattened against the glass, looking at us.' They began rocking the car. Adulation had turned to menace, and menace to attack. Somehow, George and his friends managed to inch the car forward, and then shot away.

It was the last time George ever took LSD; never again would he place his faith in followers. 'It certainly showed me what was really happening in the drug culture. It wasn't what I'd thought – spiritual awakening and being artistic – it was like alcoholism, like any addiction. That was the turning point for me – that's when I went right off the whole drug cult and stopped taking the dreaded lysergic acid.'

102.

Another guitar-playing Messiah figure on Hippie Hill that Summer of Love was also attracting a flock of devotees.

Earlier in the year, Charlie Manson had come to the end of seven years in prison for forging checks and jumping parole. During that time he had read up on the Bible, and Scientology. With his high IQ he had been fast-tracked by the authorities onto a special course studying *How to Win Friends and Influence People* by Dale Carnegie, in the hope that it would help him forge a better, more productive life. Carnegie's book certainly chimed with his key beliefs. 'Everything you or I do springs from two motives: the sex urge and the desire to be great,' wrote Carnegie.

On his release that March, Manson had headed for Haight-Ashbury, fuelled by his faith in himself as a musician, and his mission to recruit followers from the 75,000-odd youngsters set to gravitate there during the Summer of Love. Unlike Manson, most of them were in search of something – or someone – greater than themselves.

Though his time in prison lasted from June 1960, when the Beatles were still the Silver Beetles, to March 1967, when they were recording *Sgt. Pepper*, Manson had managed to imbibe their songs on prison radios, and was in the habit of telling his fellow jailbirds that one day he would outshine them.

Coloured by his paranoia, the Beatles' lyrics formed a vital part of Manson's philosophy. By combining them with passages from the Book of Revelation, he constructed an urgent message of revolution and destruction. In Haight-Ashbury he passed on his findings to the starry-eyed youngsters who gathered around him, some of them sixteen years old, barely half his age.

103.

During that same period, the Beatles were in search of a guru of their own. It was Pattie Boyd who first had the idea. Browsing through the Sunday newspapers in February 1967, she chanced upon an advertisement for a Transcendental Meditation course in central London. 'Perfect. Off we went to Caxton Hall and enrolled in the Spiritual Regeneration Movement. In the course of a long weekend we were initiated and given our mantras.'

The leader of the Spiritual Regeneration Movement, Maharishi Mahesh Yogi, was a somewhat mysterious figure, either fifty or sixty years old, or somewhere in between: it was his belief that such personal considerations distracted from the universality of his message. The son of a civil servant, Mahesh Prasad Varma grew up in the central Indian city of Jabalpur, going on to take a degree in physics and mathematics at the University of Allahabad. In 1940 – the year John and Ringo were born – he became a disciple of a swami known as Shri Guru Deva, who, alone among Indian mystics, was to crop up in a Beatles song, 'Across the Universe'.

On the death of Guru Deva in 1953, Mahesh Prasad Varma restyled himself Maharishi ('great seer') and carved out a career of his own. By 1958 he had developed a ten-year plan for 'the regeneration of the whole world through meditation'. To this end he developed spiritual techniques such as levitation, or 'yogic flying', in which participants either fly, hop or bounce, depending upon their relationship with gravity. The Maharishi's promise of 'the positive experience of Heavenly Bliss' proved especially attractive to well-heeled Westerners, and in 1959 he set up a base for his Spiritual Regeneration Movement in Hollywood, from where he embarked upon an annual worldwide tour, taking in Hong Kong and Hawaii. Far from timid, he called for a new Spiritual Regeneration Movement Centre for every million people on the planet: each of these centres would then train a thousand initiators, who would each initiate a thousand more, and so on, until all mankind had been cured of suffering.

For Pattie, his classes were 'life-changing. I couldn't wait to tell George. As soon as he came home I bombarded him with what I had been doing, and he was really interested. Then, joy of joys, I discovered that Maharishi was coming to London in August to give a lecture at the Hilton Hotel. I was desperate to go, and George said he would come too. Paul had already heard of him and was interested, and in the end we all went – George, John, Paul, Ringo, Jane and I.' The session went well. 'We were spellbound.'

The next day, Friday, 25 August 1967, the Beatles cancelled a recording session and boarded a train to Bangor, where the Spiritual Regeneration Movement was holding its ten-day summer conference. Cynthia Lennon came too, along with Mick Jagger and Marianne Faithfull and Pattie's sister Jenny. Brian Epstein had been tempted, but was already committed to hosting a house party in Sussex. To be without Brian's guiding hand made the Beatles uneasy. It was, complained John, 'like going somewhere without your trousers on'. Within hours, they realised how much they re-lied on him: that evening they ate in a Chinese restaurant in Bangor, only to discover that they had no money to pay the bill. Over the past few years they had grown as demanding and defenceless as infants.

That Sunday morning, they heard of the sudden death of Brian Ep-stein. John, Paul, George and Ringo immediately went to the Mahari-shi for guidance. Marianne Faithfull looked on as the Maharishi told the Beatles, 'Brian Epstein is dead. He was taking care of you. He was like your father. I will be your father now.' It struck her that the Maharishi was exploiting their grief, and she found it creepy: 'These poor bastards just didn't know. It was the most terrible thing.'

The Beatles were soon surrounded by press and TV crews, anxious to gauge their reactions. John had never been more subdued. He seemed punctured: 'I can't find words to pay tribute to him. It is just that he was lovable, and it is those lovable things we think about now.'

Paul said: 'This is a terrible shock. I am terribly upset.'

104.

GEORGE MARTIN: No one could have conceived that it would happen, and the boys were completely broken up by it. They were like a ship without a rudder. One of the awful things is that, if Brian had lived, he would have lost the Beatles. He wouldn't have survived as their manager. Because they would have split up anyway. They would probably have sought their own, younger, different people to look after their affairs. Brian, by his own design, had become too fragmented, and the Beatles were too selfish to ever have someone like that. They wanted someone who did nothing else but the Beatles. Even more than that: by that time, Paul wanted someone who did nothing but Paul, John wanted someone exclusively, and so on. So it would have become an impossible situation.

JOANNE PETERSEN, PERSONAL ASSISTANT TO BRIAN EPSTEIN: Things started to unhinge pretty quickly, almost immediately. It seemed to me that things became unstable very quickly. Brian was the glue. He held it all together, and the moment he wasn't there it was like a rudderless ship. There was no one steering the ship.

DEREK TAYLOR: Had he lived, Brian might have been more decisive and more tenacious and seen the Beatles through a lot of the things that no one else could. John had a famous quote, 'We've fucking had it now,' and to the extent that they did break up, that's true.

MARIANNE FAITHFULL: The Beatles were just fucking around, really, with the Maharishi, that's all. Brian was much more than a brilliant businessman. He was a spiritual centre. So I think what happened with the Maharishi was a betrayal of spiritual values, that's how it must have appeared to Brian. If he had met the Maharishi, he would have seen immediately that this idiotic little guy wasn't going to be able to take his place. I think everybody realised that from the minute they met him.

Here's what would have happened if he hadn't taken the overdose. They would have come back to London and Brian would have said, 'How was it?' and they would have all cracked up laughing as if it was the most ridiculous thing. The trouble with him dying at that moment was that it actually pushed them into the arms of the Maharishi, whereas if he hadn't died, it would have blown over. The Maharishi was the most ludicrous little man you could imagine. Everybody realised this, and we were all embarrassed.

Brian had an incredible antenna for sensing things. If he had been there in London when they got back from Wales and answered the phone in his silk dressing gown when John or Paul rang, the Beatles would not have gone to India and all these things would not have happened.

PAUL: Brian's death kind of opened the floodgates. It gave other people the possibility to come in whereas there had been no possibility before.

It would be too glib to suggest that the Beatles looked to the Maharishi to fill the gap left by Brian Epstein. Compared to Epstein, he was a fly-by-night. But by now the pace they had set themselves had become so rapid, their needs and quests and fads so random and restless, that perhaps they were bound to look for another hand to guide them.

John and George left Bangor so full of the benefits of Transcendental Meditation that a month later they appeared on *The Frost Report* to extol its virtues. The following week, they were invited back on the same show. Unusually, George was by far the more talkative of the two, rattling on about levels of consciousness:

. . . Transcendental Meditation takes you to that transcendental level of pure consciousness, but by going there often enough, you bring that level of consciousness out onto this level, or you bring this level onto that level. But the relative plus that level becomes cosmic consciousness, and that means that you're able to hold on to the full bliss consciousness in the relative field, so you can go on about your actions all the time with bliss consciousness . . .

And so on; and on; and on. It says much for the awe in which the Beatles were held that the usually snappy David Frost let him drone on at such length, and on such an abstruse topic, leaving even his wildest claims unchallenged. At one point George mentioned that he had been reading a book about a yogi who lived to be 136, 'and there's another one, living in the Himalayas at this very moment . . . It seems pretty far out, you know, to the average person, who doesn't know anything about it. But this fellow has been there since before Jesus Christ, and he's still here now in the same physical body. They have control over life and death. They have control in everything, having attained that higher state of consciousness . . .'

105.

On 23 August 1967, Brian Epstein had looked in on the second day of recording 'Your Mother Should Know'. Four days later he was dead. The Beatles hoped to attend his funeral in Liverpool two days later, but his family asked them to stay away, as they wanted to avoid any turmoil.

A week later, on the evening of 5 September, the four of them assembled at Abbey Road, determined to press on with the recording of *Magical Mystery Tour*. The mood was sombre. 'There was a pallor across the session that day,' recalled Geoff Emerick. 'We were all distracted, thinking about Brian.'

On his acoustic guitar, John went through a new song. 'I am he as you are he as you are me and we are all together,' he began.

Geoff Emerick wondered what on earth he was on about: 'Everyone seemed bewildered. The melody consisted largely of just two notes, and the lyrics were pretty much nonsense.'

Some of the lyrics seemed to stray beyond nonsense. When John sang 'pornographic priestess' and 'let your knickers down', George Martin turned to Emerick and whispered, '*What* did he just say?'

John finally reached the end. There was silence. John looked up at the sound box for George Martin's reaction. 'That one was called "I am the Walrus",' he said. 'So, what do you think?'

Martin was lost for words, but hesitation soon gave way to irritation. 'Well, John, to be honest, I have only one question. What the hell do you expect me to do with that?'

Nervous laughter ensued. It was evident to Emerick that John 'was clearly not amused'.

The impetus to write the nonsensical words of 'I am the Walrus' had sprung from a letter John was sent at the end of August by Stephen Bayley,* a fifteen-year-old pupil at John's old school Quarry Bank. Bayley explained that his English teacher was in the habit of playing Beatles songs in class, and getting the boys to analyse the lyrics, before weighing in with his own interpretation.

Pete Shotton, who was with John when he first read the letter, remembers John howling with laughter at the notion that his old school, which had once written him off as a failure, was now elevating his output to a set text. Shotton noticed how he saw it as a challenge. 'Inspired by the picture of that Quarry Bank literature master pontificating about the symbolism of Lennon–McCartney, John threw in the most ludicrous images his imagination could conjure.'

Trying to think of the daftest rhymes, John remembered a playground jingle. 'Pete, what's that "Dead Dog's Eye" song we used to sing at Quarry Bank?'

Pete thought for a moment, then remembered:

Yellow matter custard, green slop pie
All mixed together with a dead dog's eye,
Slap it on a butty, ten foot thick
Then wash it all down with a cup of cold sick.

Versions of this ditty were chanted by schoolchildren the length and breadth of the country in the 1950s.† It is included in *The Lore and Language of Schoolchildren* by Iona and Peter Opie, first published in 1959, alongside many regional variants. In Manchester the custard was 'splish splashy' and the pie was made of giblets; in the Forest of Dean it was 'scab and matter', and came with 'green snot pies'; in Ipswich the pie was at its least tempting – it was made of bogie, and served with hard-boiled snails and a dead man's eye.

John was delighted by Pete's recital. 'That's it!' he said, reaching for a pen. 'Fantastic!' He duly wrote down 'Yellow matter custard', before adding

---

* Bayley (1951–) grew up to be an iconoclastic cultural critic, and the author of books about cars, sex, and the Albert Memorial.

† And well into the sixties: I remember chanting it in the playground of Grove House School in Effingham, Surrey, circa 1964.

other bits and pieces retrieved randomly from childhood memories. 'He thought of semolina (an insipid pudding we'd been forced to eat as kids) and pilchard (a sardine we often fed to our cats). "Semolina pilchard climbing up the Eiffel Tower . . ." John intoned, writing it down with considerable relish.' He was clearly amused by the idea that teachers would spend their time clawing away at an inner meaning. 'Let the fuckers work *that* one out, Pete,' he said.

The song was further filtered through John's childhood fascination with the topsy-turvy world of Lewis Carroll, and in particular the poem 'The Walrus and the Carpenter', which is told to Alice by Tweedledee in *Through the Looking-Glass*. Beneath its merry rhythm lies a Hannibal Lecterish tale of two exquisite psychopaths. It starts with the Walrus encouraging a crowd of young oysters to join him and the Carpenter as they walk along the shore. But once they get to their destination:

'A loaf of bread,' the Walrus said,
'Is what we chiefly need:
Pepper and vinegar besides
Are very good indeed –
Now if you're ready, Oysters dear,
We can begin to feed!'

'But not on us!' the Oysters cried,
Turning a little blue.
'After such kindness, that would be
A dismal thing to do!'

The Walrus and the Carpenter immediately change the subject, complimenting the oysters and pointing out the lovely view. The Walrus then grows sentimental:

'I weep for you,' the Walrus said:
'I deeply sympathize.'
With sobs and tears he sorted out
Those of the largest size,
Holding his pocket-handkerchief
Before his streaming eyes.

'O Oysters,' said the Carpenter,
'You've had a pleasant run!
Shall we be trotting home again?'
But answer came there none –
And this was scarcely odd, because
They'd eaten every one.

It is, as the psychoanalyst Paul Schilder pointed out some time ago, a poem of 'astonishing cruelty'. This cruelty, shielded by nonsense, clearly struck a chord with John.

As John predicted, his hotchpotch of words has indeed been subjected to all kinds of analysis – in fact, almost as much as *Alice in Wonderland* itself. Is it anti-capitalist ('pigs in a sty'), anti-academia ('expert texperts') or anti-bureaucracy ('corporation T-shirt')? You can find in it whatever you want. 'I was writing obscurely, à la Dylan, never saying what you mean, but giving the *impression* of something, where more *or* less can be read into it. It's a good game,' John confessed years later. He had, he added, written the entire song on LSD.

His dismissal of any serious intent has done nothing to staunch the flow of interpretations. And why should it? Some regard it as an attack on the police (imagining 'pilchard' to be John's near-homonymic pursuer Det. Sgt Pilcher*), while others see it as a defence of drug culture. The I-am-he-as-he passage has been interpreted as both a satirical attack on Eastern religion and an impassioned defence of it. For the Beatles' biographer Jonathan Gould, the Walrus is 'a potent symbol of John's contempt for the Beatles' idealized image as popular heroes of youth'. Ian MacDonald, who considered it the high point of Lennon's songwriting oeuvre, believed the song was 'its author's ultimate anti-institutional rant – a damn-you-England tirade that blasts education, art, culture, law, order, class, religion, and even sense itself'. John's actor friend Victor Spinetti thought it an encrypted protest against family life.

Some have been keen to stake their claim to central roles in the story. 'I was the Egg Man,' wrote John's drinking partner Eric Burdon of the Animals in his autobiography. 'Or, as some pals called me, "Eggs". The nick-

---

* See pages 445–453.

name stuck after a wild experience I'd had at the time with a Jamaican girlfriend named Sylvia. I was up early one morning cooking breakfast, naked except for my socks, and she slid up behind me and cracked an amyl nitrate capsule under my nose. As the fumes set my brain alight, and I slid to the kitchen floor, she reached to the counter and grabbed an egg, which she broke into the pit of my belly. The white and yellow of the egg ran down my naked front, and Sylvia slipped my egg-bathed cock into her mouth and began to show me one Jamaican trick after another. I shared the story with John at a party at a Mayfair flat one night with a handful of blondes and a little Asian girl.

'"Go on, go get it, Egg Man," Lennon laughed over the little round glasses perched on the end of his hooklike nose as we tried the all-too-willing girls on for size.'

As it happens, Eric Burdon's claim has been subject to the vagaries of history, or at least historians, with many muddling up his role and making him the egger, not the egged.

John took a particular pride in 'I am the Walrus': 'It's one of those that has enough little bitties going to keep you interested even a hundred years later.' This may seem boastful, but fifty years on, it is also halfway to being true. Nevertheless, he came to think that he had made a mistake in casting himself as Carroll's Walrus. 'Later I went back and looked at it and realised that the Walrus was the bad guy in the story, and the Carpenter was the good guy. I thought, "Oh, shit. I've picked the wrong guy."' Hence, when it came to writing his self-referential song 'Glass Onion', he came up with the line, 'Here's another clue for you all – the Walrus was Paul.' But he was a slapdash reader. In the original poem there is little to choose between the Walrus and the Carpenter: both use their charm to lure the oysters away, before gobbling them up without a hint of remorse.

'What the hell do you expect me to do with that?' The answer to Martin's question was that John didn't have a clue, and nor did the others. Epstein's death had left them bewildered. At the start of the session Ringo had been

close to tears, and John himself appeared to be in a state of shock. George looked beyond the here and now. 'Mr Epstein's body may be gone,' he said, 'but his spirit remains.' Not for the first time, Paul was the pragmatist: 'We just have to carry on, I suppose.'

'I distinctly remember the look of emptiness on all their faces while they were playing "I am the Walrus",' remembered Geoff Emerick. 'It's one of the saddest memories I have of my time with the Beatles.'

John told Martin and Emerick that he wanted his voice to sound as though it were coming from the moon. This left them none the wiser. Emerick set about distorting the amps to make John's voice sound both edgier and more ethereal. 'I had no idea what a man on the moon might sound like – or even what John was really hearing in his head – but, as usual, no amount of discussion with him could shed a lot of light on the matter.' The next day, John insisted on adding random sounds from the radio. George Martin rolled his eyes.

The completed mish-mash includes a snatch of dialogue from *King Lear*, and the Mike Sammes Singers* chanting 'Everybody's got one,

---

* The Mike Sammes Singers, easy-listening doyens of *Sing Something Simple*, had one of the most varied and least trumpeted careers in the history of popular music. Their voices can be heard on 'Let it Be' and 'Good Night', and they also provided backing for, among many others, Tom Jones on 'Delilah', Ken Dodd on 'Tears' and Olivia Newton-John on 'Banks of the Ohio'. They also sang the memorable theme song for Gerry Anderson's *Stingray*. The day after their 'I am the Walrus' session, they recorded a session with Kathy Kirby, and then went straight to the ATV studios to record *The Benny Hill Show*. In his days as a session musician, Elton John would occasionally work alongside them: 'Frightening isn't an adjective you would normally associate with the Mike Sammes Singers, who did backing vocals for everyone – they looked like middle-aged aunties and uncles who'd arrived at the studio direct

everybody's got one', along with the playground ditty 'Oompah, oom-pah, stick it up your jumper.' It is both everything and nothing. It may derive, in George Martin's words, from 'organised chaos', but, like Coleridge's 'Kubla Khan', it somehow transcends interpretation to touch upon the sublime.

---

from a golf-club dinner-dance. But if you had to sing alongside them, they suddenly struck the fear of God into you, because they were so good at what they did.'

106.

A Party:
Westbourne Suite, Royal Lancaster Hotel
Lancaster Terrace, Bayswater, London W2
21 December 1967

On 8 December 1967, the elaborately neurotic comic actor Kenneth Williams picks up his fountain pen and, in his perfect italic script, writes an enraged letter to a friend. 'Do you know those Beatles gave a private party recently at the new Royal Lancaster Hotel and their manager rang and asked if I would go along and compere their cabaret? – have you ever heard such impudence. Just cos you do it on the Telly don't mean you are available for functions does it? – the nerve of it.'

In fact, the party in question, to celebrate the completion of filming the *Magical Mystery Tour*, is not due to be held until 21 December, five days before its television transmission on Boxing Day.

Echoing the pantomime nature of *Magical Mystery Tour*, the party has a fancy-dress theme. Paul and Jane Asher come as a Pearly King and Queen, Derek Taylor as Adolf Hitler, Alistair Taylor as a matador, Tony Bramwell as a court jester, and Peter Brown as King Louis XIV, while George Martin and his wife Judy come as Prince Philip and Queen Elizabeth II. As though to emphasise their differences, John comes as a teddy boy, while Cynthia is a Regency lady in bonnet, crinoline and bows. She immediately feels overdressed, 'like the lady on the Quality Street tin'.

The party happens to coincide with one of John's brief reconciliations with his ne'er-do-well father, Fred, who dresses, appropriately enough, as 'My Old Man's a Dustman'. Earlier in the day Fred paid a real dustman £5 to swap clothes with him. Pete Shotton can't bear to be in his vicinity: 'He

literally reeked of garbage, and all the other partygoers did their utmost to keep him at a safe distance.'

Even allowing for the bizarre freemasonry of showbiz, an unexpected guest is the portly comic actor Robert Morley, who arrives as Father Christmas. 'He was really sweating,' observes one guest. 'Perhaps it was a fault in the hotel's air conditioning, but he looked so uncomfortable, I couldn't believe he was doing it. I felt that perhaps his agent made him.'

Dinner is followed by a screening of *Magical Mystery Tour*. John sits at a table with his smelly father and Fred's young fiancée Pauline, dressed, just as appropriately, as a schoolgirl. At the same table are Cilla Black, dressed as a labourer, and her husband Bobby, as a nun.

There is a hiatus between the end of dinner and the beginning of the screening. 'Come on, John – do a number while we're waiting!' suggests Lulu, who is dressed as Shirley Temple, in white ankle-socks, carrying a giant lollipop, with her hair in ringlets, topped off with a bow.

'Not bloody likely,' replies John. 'How about you, Fred?'

This is a mistake. Alistair Taylor, who has organised the party, notes that Fred is 'pissed out of his head'. Consequently, when Fred leaps onto the stage he falls flat on his face.

After the screening the Bonzo Dog Doo-Dah Band take to the stage, and everybody starts to dance. John has always hated dancing, but is enticed onto the floor by the alluring sight of Pattie Harrison, who has come as a belly-dancer. Cynthia is the gooseberry, 'left sitting primly and stiffly, very much out in the cold'. Pete Shotton, dressed, like John, as a teddy boy, looks on as an unpleasant scene develops: "Though Pattie had, undeniably, made herself especially desirable as a scantily clad belly-dancer, neither Cyn nor George were the least bit amused by John's open flirtation with her.' Upset by what is happening, Lulu, still clutching her giant lollipop, gives John a good telling-off.

At last Cynthia is asked to dance by Billy J. Kramer, who is dressed, by happy coincidence, as a Regency soldier. 'We made a lovely couple,' she recalls, 'until we tried to jive instead of waltz.' Catching her foot on her dress, Cynthia falls over, 'masses of material billowing out like a huge lavender balloon around my crumpled body'.

When John glances over in her direction, Cynthia catches his eye. 'His looks on that occasion were not of love or admiration, but pure embarrassment. I was letting him down yet again.'

107.

The Beatles failed to attend the first Apple board meeting. Those who managed to make it included John's childhood friend Pete Shotton, who had been appointed even though his only previous experience of business was owning a newsagent's shop on Hayling Island, given him by John.

Shotton kicked off the meeting by saying that he didn't know anything about Apple: could the other members of the board fill him in? His request was met with silence: no one else knew anything either. Presently Clive Epstein, brother of the late Brian, piped up. 'Well, it was my impression,' he began, 'that Apple would manufacture greetings cards and the boys have agreed to write the little poems for them.'

As each board member spoke, it became increasingly clear that everyone present had a different notion of Apple's aims. Eventually, Terry Doran,* who had co-owned Brydor Cars with Brian, turned to Shotton. 'Thank God you're here, Pete. As you can see, nobody else really has much of a clue. We desperately need someone like you who can get this whole thing organised.' The meeting broke up shortly afterwards, each member saying 'Best of luck, Pete,' and 'Congratulations, Pete,' as they left.

Pete then drove straight to John's house to find out what on earth was going on. John laid out his business plan. 'In a nutshell, what's going on is this,' he said. 'The Beatles have been told that we have £3 million, which will have to be paid off in tax if we don't put it into a business. All we've really got to do, then, is just fucking spend it! So why not have a go at business and have a few laughs while we're at it?'

As it happened, the laughs were few and far between. The business unrolled, and then, just as swiftly, unravelled. Early on, the music paper

---

* Sometimes credited as the 'man from the motor trade' in 'She's Leaving Home'.

Disc and Music Echo got together with Apple to announce a nationwide
hunt for new stars: 'There are hundreds of unheard-of groups who, with
the right handling, could be every bit as big as today's top pop names.'
Readers were asked to vote for the best groups in their area, on the understanding that Apple would despatch talent scouts to check out the winners.
The six 'lucky readers' who had nominated the winning group were to
be presented with vouchers for £25 to spend on clothes at the brand-new
Apple Boutique.

Thousands of readers sent in nominations; almost as many posted music tapes and novels and poems. No more than a handful were ever heard or
read or even opened. Instead, they were piled into cardboard boxes which
were then stacked in a dark nook at the Apple headquarters that came to
be known as the Black Room. Pete Shotton didn't like to think about it.
'It was really quite a heartbreaking sight, when one stopped to consider all
those starry-eyed kids who had been left sitting on the edge, waiting to
hear from the Beatles and to claim their Bentleys.'

In no time at all, every nutter and chancer in town was making a beeline for Apple, ready to be showered with fame and fortune. One young
American who worked there, Richard DiLello, compared the office hallway to 'the waiting room at a VD clinic in Haight-Ashbury at the height of
the Acid Madness of '67'. One day he was summoned to deal with a man
who claimed to be able to communicate with animals, and vice versa. As
proof, he produced from his pocket a poem he had transcribed at London
Zoo, with alternate verses composed by himself and his friends the animals. Perhaps the only real surprise is that he was not immediately given
his own department to supervise.

One of the first beneficiaries of the Apple munificence was the indomi-
table Japanese artist Yoko Ono, whose relationship with John was still essentially one-sided. Ono had put in an application for £5,000 to finance an
exhibition at the Lisson Gallery of white objects – a chair, a table, a shoe,
a hat – all cut in half. Having failed to receive the go-ahead, she waylaid
John at Apple headquarters. 'I feel like only half,' she told him. 'You are my
other half, and I am yours. We have been lost in space searching, and now
we have found each other.'

John gave her the money, on condition that his name would not be associated with her exhibition. Tony Bramwell remembered asking him why

he had agreed to it. 'To get rid of her,' John had replied. 'With women like that you have to pay them off, or they never stop pestering you.'

In this, Yoko was to prove him wrong. She immediately sent out a press release announcing a joint exhibition: 'Half a Wind by Yoko Ono and John Lennon'.

108.

Parallels with the childhood of Yoko Ono may be found in that of Queen Victoria, who was said never to have looked over her shoulder before sitting down, as she knew a footman would always be there, ready with a chair. The Ono family kept thirty servants, all of whom would approach the young Yoko on their knees, and then leave on their knees, shuffling backwards. Whenever Yoko ventured beyond her family home, she was forbidden from sitting down until a servant had cleaned the seat with cotton wool soaked in disinfectant.

Yoko Ono was born on 18 February 1933 (barely thirty-two years after the death of Queen Victoria), the product of a union between two of the wealthiest families in Japan. Her maternal great-grandfather, Zenjiro Yasuda, had made his fortune in currency-dealing, going on to found the Third National Bank of Japan. Her father, Eisuke Ono, was also a banker, rising to become director of the New York office of the Bank of Tokyo.

On a trans-Pacific ship from Japan to see her father in San Francisco, little Yoko took part in a fancy-dress competition. Electing to go as Shirley Temple, she walked away with the first prize. Who knows? This early triumph may have had a lasting impact, ensuring that, for the rest of her long life, she would draw on the simple utopian messages, laced with occasional silliness, characteristic of Shirley Temple's most celebrated songs, such as 'Tra-la-la-la':

Tra-la-la-la, what a merry world we live in
Tra-la-la-la, all of it is yours and mine
So wear a smile, sing a little while it's raining
And through the clouds, ev'ry little star will shine

Clouds were also to be a mainstay of Yoko Ono's maxims for the next eighty years or so. For instance, in 'Cloud Piece', from her 1964 volume *Grapefruit*, she writes:

Imagine the clouds dripping. Dig a hole in your garden to put them in.

Four years later, bombarding John in Rishikesh with letters, she advised him:

I'm a cloud. Watch for me in the sky.

Over the decades that followed, she seemed unable to spot a cloud without drawing a moral from it. In 2019, now aged eighty-six, she put this cloud-based question to her 4.78 million Twitter followers:

When I look at clouds, I see our beauty and transcience [*sic*]. What do you see?

In 'Polly Wolly Doodle', Shirley Temple sang:

I came to a river and couldn't get across
Sing Polly Wolly Doodle all the day
I jumped on a gator and thought he was a hoss
Sing Polly Wolly Doodle all the day.

Similar themes of happiness gained through impossible feats are threaded throughout Ono's entire oeuvre. In one of her maxims, she advises the reader to 'Carry a heavy object on your back'; once it is in place, you should 'Dance as swiftly as you can.' In another she tells us to sit at a dock, watch the seagulls dance and 'dance with them in your mind'. We must then 'Keep dancing until you can feel their heartbeats.'
    Certainly these Ono maxims:

Carry a bag of peas. Leave a pea wherever you go.

and:

Imagine letting a goldfish swim across the sky. Let it swim from the West to the East. Drink a liter of water.

clearly echo Temple's most celebrated song:

On the good ship *Lollipop*
It's a sweet trip to a candy shop
Where bon-bons play
On the sunny beach of Peppermint Bay

Most days, Yoko still takes the trouble to share her words of wisdom on Twitter. Their cosy optimism makes little Shirley Temple seem jaded: 'All animals feel love', 'You have infinite wisdom', 'Start by imagining a world where all of us are having good fun'.

Sometimes she is political: 'The prospect of making big money always dulls the senses of some people, even if it is very bad for the health of all living things on the planet,' she tweeted on 22 May 2019. 'We have to keep communicating the reality until these people wake up.' Her own net worth is currently estimated at $600 million.

Occasionally she stops dispensing advice, and asks for it instead. At 5.18 p.m. on 2 February 2019 she tweeted this request: 'Give us some advice that will make our lives heal and shine.'

A flood of advice followed, much of it more straightforward than she might have anticipated:

'Put marmite on your cheese on toast before you put it under the grill.'

'The quickest way to change lines at Green Park is to ignore all the (very circuitous) directions and head up the escalator to the ticket hall and down the relevant escalator to your chosen line. You're welcome.'

'Open a pesky bin liner with ease by giving the top of it a slight stretch.'

'Put a splash of fizzy water in your Yorkshire pudding batter.'

'Turn your tins of beans upside down when you put them in the cupboard, that way none get stuck in the bottom when you open them.'

'A decent pair of oven gloves is worth 1000 towels.'

'Avoid Tesco Value rice crispies. They're really horrible.'

'If you're commuting from Barnsley to Sheffield a McDonald's coffee is now 10p cheaper at Tankersley than at Meadowhall Retail Park.'

And:

'Don't split up the Beatles when they have a few more albums in them.'

Yoko Ono was educated at Gakushin, the most distinguished private school in Japan; the Crown Prince Akihito was a contemporary. At the age of eighteen she moved with the rest of her family to New York, to join her father, who had been appointed president of the Bank of Tokyo in the US. There, she entered Sarah Lawrence College in Bronxville; Barbara Walters and Princess Lee Radziwill (*née* Bouvier) were among her fellow students. In 1956, while John Lennon was struggling with his homework at Quarry Bank School, Yoko Ono left home to live with a young composer-pianist, Toshi Ichiyanagi, who was studying at Juilliard. The two shared a loft in Greenwich Village, and soon married. During this time she began wearing black, a habit to which she was to adhere for the rest of her life. She was always the most conservative of experimentalists.

In 1958, Toshi Ichiyanagi enrolled on a course in experimental composition. His tutor was John Cage, who introduced Toshi to Merce Cunningham, who in turn employed him as a rehearsal pianist with his dance company. Through her talented husband, Yoko met not only Cage and Cunningham but a wider group of experimentalists, including Allan Kaprow and Jim Dine. But among this bohemian set, she failed to make her mark. Her husband could play the piano, and compose, but her own particular talents were less easy to pinpoint: 'It was very hard to make people understand that I was an artist too. My husband was famous in his own circle around Juilliard and John Cage and those people . . . I was having affairs and things like that to compensate, so our relationship deteriorated.'

In the winter of 1960–61 she organised a series of events in their shared loft, and managed to attract some of the key movers in the avant-garde, among them the minimalist composers La Monte Young and Terry Riley, and the Beat poet Diane Wakoski. The audience perched on orange crates. Every now and then, Yoko squeezed her way into someone else's performance, or performed something of her own. On one occasion she took a bowl of Jell-O and hurled it at a large piece of paper tacked to the wall. Having exhausted the Jell-O, she threw two eggs at the paper. She then picked up an inkpot and started finger-painting around the mess already created by the Jell-O and the eggs. Finally, she lit the paper with a match. Despite such effort, some remained unconvinced of her genius. 'I resented her calling her very bad and silly writing "poetry",' said Diane Wakoski. 'And I thought she was hustler, not artist . . . because she earned her living as a model, seemed to go to bed with all the men around, and in fact never seemed to sacrifice much for her "art" as all the other avant-garders that I knew did.'

In 1961, Toshi returned to Japan to pursue a musical career. Meanwhile, Yoko remained in New York, conducting an affair with a gallery owner called George Maciunas, who subsequently – or consequently – put on her first show. By this time she had nimbly embraced a form of art that centred around self-assertion bound to a single idea, no matter how pedestrian that idea might be. Her first show included a scrap of canvas laid on the floor, titled *Painting to be Stepped On*, and another scrap of canvas with a peephole called *Painting to See the Room Through*. She applied a similarly minimal technique when she staged a 'performance' at a small recital theatre adjoining Carnegie Hall, in which melody took a back seat to a medley of silence and shrieks.

Neither event proved successful, however, so she returned to Japan, where her husband was willing to take her back. She staged further conceptual events in her homeland, but they too drew reviews ranging from the lukewarm to the dismissive. Distressed by the refusal of the Japanese to acknowledge her art, she suffered some sort of breakdown, and checked into a clinic. There she was visited by Tony Cox, a young American filmmaker who had grown attached to her. In 1962 she divorced Toshi and married Cox. The couple had a daughter, Kyoko.

Yoko's strength lay in perseverance. She was unbudgeable in her in-stinct that in the world of art, skill would soon be edged out by audacity. In 1964 she performed *Cut Piece*, in which she sat onstage and invited members of the audience to cut pieces off her clothes. She also produced *Grapefruit*, a book of 'instructional poems' that resembled haikus, but jet-tisoned their rules:

Eat your soup with a fork.
Treasure eternity.

Drop a pebble in the ocean.
The pebble is wet.
But the ocean is not dry.

Neither of these are by her, but they might just as well be. Her poems, to which she has devoted so much of her creative life, can be replicated in a matter of seconds:

Cut a hole in a bag filled with seeds
of any kind and place the bag where
there is wind.

Actually, that one was by her.

Empty your head.
Pour water into your ear.
You have become a bucket.
Open your mouth.
Water a flower.

Whereas that one was not.

Tony Cox devoted himself to managing and promoting Yoko's career; he also took on the responsibility of looking after Kyoko, thus leaving his wife free to pursue her art. 'I always thought of him as my assistant,' Yoko recalled years later. Gradually, she built up a reputation in avant-garde circles. In September 1966, after an English magazine published an enthusiastic piece about her – written, as it happened, by Cox – she accepted an invitation to appear at a London symposium, 'The Destruction of Art'.

Yoko performed *Cut Piece*; other artistes included a nihilist who burned a tower of art books outside the British Museum, and an Australian who mutilated the carcass of a lamb. On the strength of *Cut Piece*, the modish gallerist John Dunbar, husband of Marianne Faithfull, offered Yoko an exhibition at his Indica Gallery. The works she assembled for it included *Hammer and Nail Piece*, consisting of a hammer chained to a block of wood, with a small jar of gold-plated nails alongside it, and *Apple Piece*, a fresh apple on a Plexiglas stand, on offer for £200. *Ladder Piece* had a stepladder which led up to a card pasted onto the ceiling, with a magnifying glass dangling beside it. Viewed through the magnifying glass, the word on the card read 'Yes'.

For decades afterwards, Yoko Ono would be credited as a pioneer of conceptual art, even though Duchamp's idea that anything humdrum may be transformed into art simply by placing it in a gallery was by then half a century old. The eagle-eyed also detected a strangely hand-me-down quality to her instructional poems. 'Composition 1960 #10', by La Monte Young, reads: 'Draw a straight line and follow it.' 'Piano Piece for David Tudor # 1', also written by La Monte Young in 1960, reads: 'Bring a bale of hay and a bucket of water onto the stage for the piano to eat and drink. The performer may then feed the piano or leave it to eat by itself . . .' They might easily have been written by Yoko; yet they weren't. Her first book of poems, *Grapefruit*, was published four years later, in 1964.

These days, the meeting of John and Yoko at Indica has become as much a part of our island story as the meeting of Stanley and Livingstone at Ujiji, and subject to as many contradictory accounts.

Yoko has insisted that she had no idea who John was: 'I knew the name Beatles and I knew Ringo, because Ringo's easy to remember.* I never read pop magazines or pop newspapers or turned on a pop programme on the TV, you know. It's just that it never occurred to me,' she told one

---

* Incidentally, and coincidentally, 'Ringo' is Japanese for 'apple'.

interviewer. When John arrived at the gallery the night before the private view, 'I thought, "What's he doing? Didn't I tell him I didn't want anyone to come until the opening?" I felt a bit angry about it, but I was too busy to complain or make a fuss . . . I didn't realise then who John was.' Over the years, Yoko has persisted in stating how very unimpressed she was by John's supposed status: 'When I found out I didn't care. I mean, in the art world a Beatle is, well, you know. Also he was in a suit. He looked so ordinary.' To John's biographer Philip Norman, she even claimed to have discovered John's identity only after he had left the building: 'I went downstairs, where there were several art students who were helping us. And one said, "That was John Lennon . . . one of the *Beatles*." I said, "Oh, really? I didn't know that."'

Others recall events rather differently. The clear-headed Beatles historian Jonathan Gould writes: 'Few things she ever said would inspire such widespread disbelief as her insistence that she didn't know John Lennon from Adam when she was introduced to him by John Dunbar.' Albert Goldman was, as one might expect, more rabid in his scepticism: 'John Lennon and Yoko Ono . . . were brought together not by chance but by the Coxes' relentless efforts to advance their shared career.'

Allan Kaprow remembered being surprised at how much Yoko knew about the Beatles before she left for London, which suggests she would certainly have recognised the group's leader. Tony Bramwell remembered Yoko telling Dunbar, 'John Lennon said he might come to the exhibition. Why not ask him to a private preview? He's a millionaire, he might buy something.' Dunbar said that though Yoko hadn't encouraged John to be there, she certainly knew he was coming: 'Yoko didn't want anyone to see it before it was totally finished. But we said, "He's a Beatle. He's got lots of money. He might buy something."'

It seems probable that John himself liked to believe that Yoko had no idea who he was. After three years of being lionised by one and all, he clearly found her show of indifference as bracing as a chill wind on a muggy day: 'So, I'm looking for action, you know, and I see this thing called *Hammer and Nail*. It's a board with a chain and a hammer hanging on it, and a bunch of nails at the bottom. I said, "Well, can I hammer a nail in?" and she said, "No." So John Dunbar whisks her away. He takes her in a corner and says, "That's a millionaire, you know. You know who

that is?" She didn't know who I was. Anyway, she came over and said,
"Five shillings, please!" So I said, "I'll give you an imaginary five shillings
and hammer in an imaginary nail." She said, "All right."'

It was similar, in its way, to the meeting of the Duke and Duchess of
Windsor three decades earlier. In his memoirs, the duke remembered turning to Wallis Simpson at a dinner party and, by way of conversation, asking her whether, as an American living in England, she missed the central
heating.

'I am sorry, sir, but you have disappointed me.'

'In what way?'

'Every American woman who comes to your country is always asked
the same question. I had hoped for something more original from the
Prince of Wales.'

As accustomed to sycophancy as John was, this twice-married American's abrasiveness must have made his heart skip a beat. From that moment on, he was hers. These two sentences are as applicable to John as
they are to the duke: 'From the day I met her,' he said, 'she demanded
equal time, equal space, equal rights.' He continued: 'She showed me
what it was to be Elvis Beatle and to be surrounded by sycophants and
slaves who were only interested in keeping the situation as it was. She
said to me, "You've got no clothes on." Nobody had dared tell me that
before. With us, it's a teacher–pupil relationship . . . She's the teacher and
I'm the pupil.'

Barry Miles witnessed what happened next at the Indica Gallery.
'Throughout the viewing, Yoko had linked her arm around John's as she
explained the works, and when he made a move to go, she asked him to
take her with him, even though Tony Cox was there. John had been up
three days and was on his way back to Kenwood. He politely declined,
climbed in the back of his black-glass chauffeur-driven SS Cooper Mini
and sped off.'

John's chauffeur, Les Anthony, was waiting outside, but this didn't stop
him offering an X-ray-vision panorama to Albert Goldman: 'Yoko took
one look at John and attached herself to him like a limpet mine . . . She
clung to his arm while he went around the exhibition, talking away to him
in her funny little high-pitched voice until he fled.'

In the days and weeks that followed, Yoko Ono was the beneficiary of the trusting nature of the British media. She convinced them that she was a major artist in New York and Japan; that it was she, not her first husband, who had studied with John Cage; and that she had performed at Carnegie Hall, rather than the little recital theatre attached to it. They were happy to repeat whatever she told them, because it made for better headlines and juicier copy. No one seemed to mind that her work carried eerie echoes of other artists: like Christo, she wrapped tarpaulin around the lions in Trafalgar Square; like Warhol, she produced a film of 360 bare bottoms (giving it the po-faced title *Unfinished Film # 4*). On top of all this, she affected to be upset by the extent of her own renown. 'I despised myself for being too respected for my work, for being so highly unusual and unique,' she recalled.

Soon after her Indica Gallery exhibition, Yoko arrived at the Beatles' office, but found John absent. By chance, Ringo was in the building, so she directed herself at him instead, and began to recount her philosophy of life and art. Unfortunately, Ringo couldn't decipher a word she was saying, and exited as fast as his legs could carry him. Who knows? If she had spoken more clearly, and on more down-to-earth issues, we might now be talking of Ringo and Yoko, and it might have been not John but Ringo who posed naked on the cover of *Two Virgins*. Or would Ringo have insisted on the two of them remaining fully clothed? His influence might have been felt in her poetry, too:

Carry a heavy object up a hill. But not for too long, or it'll do your back in.

Sit at the dock. Watch the seagulls dance. If they come near your chips, give them a good whack.

Carry a bag of peas. Pour it into boiling water. Leave for two minutes. Drain and serve.

Some have related Yoko's pursuit of John in terms of a Hammer horror, with her little black-clad figure rearing up out of the fog at any time, day or night. Tony Bramwell writes of her arriving at Kenwood uninvited, claiming to have an appointment with John. Cynthia, who had no idea who she was, told her that John wasn't there. Yoko seemed to be leaving, but 'when

Cynthia glanced out of a window, she saw Yoko standing at the end of the drive . . . She gazed steadfastly at the house, as if willing the gates to swing open and admit her. Hours later, Cynthia looked again, and Yoko was still there . . . waiting for John to return. Eventually, as darkness fell, she disappeared. That was the thing about Yoko: she would appear from nowhere and then disappear . . . The strange visitations to Kenwood continued in all weathers.'

Once, when Yoko took up her position at the end of the drive in the pouring rain, Cynthia's mother took pity on her, and let her indoors to use the phone to call a taxi. 'Later, Mrs Powell noticed that Yoko had left her ring in the cloakroom. "I think she'll be back," she said.'

Bramwell says that letters and cards from Yoko arrived through the post daily, 'mysterious little notes with minuscule black drawings or incomprehensible one-liners'. According to him, one such parcel contained a broken white cup smeared with red paint inside a tampon box.

Cynthia herself paints a slightly less Gothic portrait, though she agrees that Yoko was no stranger to the pillarbox, posting letters to John at a furious rate. By Cynthia's account, the first time she set eyes on Yoko was at a meeting between the Beatles and the Maharishi's assistant, arranged to finalise the details of their forthcoming trip to Rishikesh. 'As we entered the main room I saw, seated in a corner armchair, dressed in black, a small Japanese woman. I guessed immediately that this was Yoko Ono, but what on earth was she doing there? Had John invited her, and, if so, why?'

Yoko sat still, saying nothing. When John and Cynthia came to leave, John's chauffeur opened the car door, 'and to my astonishment, Yoko climbed in ahead of us. John gave me a look that intimated he didn't know what the hell was going on, shrugging, palms upturned, nonplussed.' Yoko asked if they could give her a lift somewhere. She gave her address – 25 Hanover Gate – and they drove there, without another word spoken.

'What was all that about?' asked Cynthia after they had dropped her off. 'Search me, Cyn,' replied John.

Some compared Cynthia to an ostrich, but she was far from daft: 'He insisted he hadn't invited Yoko, and knew nothing of her being there, but common sense dictated that it had to have been John who had asked her to come.'

Amidst a pile of fan mail, Cynthia came across a letter from Yoko to John in which Yoko apologised for talking about herself so much, thanked John for his patience, said she always thought about him, and expressed an ongoing fear that, whenever they said goodbye, she would never see him again. Cynthia confronted John about it. 'She's crackers, just a weirdo artist who wants me to sponsor her,' he insisted. 'Another nutter wanting money for all that avant-garde bullshit. It's not important.'

109.

In February 1968 the Beatles flew to the Maharishi's camp in Rishikesh, John and George ten days before the more tentative Paul and Ringo. 'They do not want publicity, fans or press,' Mal Evans informed the swarm of reporters outside the gates. 'They want to be left alone to meditate and take a holy dip in the Ganges . . . They are here to meditate for three months, and there is no doubt they will remain here until the end of the course.'

The next day, the Maharishi Mahesh Yogi, no shrinking violet, boasted that 'within three months, I promise to turn Harrison, Lennon, McCartney and Starr into fully qualified teachers or semi-Gurus of Hindu meditation. George and John have progressed fantastically in the few days since they arrived here. I am not pushing them too hard at first, only a few hours of meditation a day. I am feeding them high-level philosophy in simple words.'

At first glance, it might be a school photograph. The headmaster sits in the centre, with the head prefects and the sports stars with him on the rostrum. As your eye drifts away from the bigwigs, the sitters become increasingly small-fry: the school juniors, the supply teachers, the under-matrons; the balding, the plain, the elderly, the inconsequential. These are the odd-bod civilians who had booked onto the course before the Beatles. Among them are Gunther, a Lufthansa pilot, Tony, a blackjack dealer from Las Vegas, and Nancy, the wife of a news analyst.

Only Mia Farrow is missing. From the start, the Maharishi made a great fuss of her, placing a crown on her head, strewing garlands over her shoulders and asking her to pose for photographs morning, noon and night. Eventually she decided that enough was enough, and set off on a five-day tiger hunt instead. 'Stuff like this, it reminded her of studio calls on the coast,' explained her friend the TV actor Tom Simcox, veteran of *Bonanza* and *Gunsmoke*.

The Maharishi himself had masterminded the group shot and supervised

the building of the platform, telling two of his monks exactly where to put the flowers and the potted plants and the painting of Guru Dev. He had also worked out the unapologetically stratified *placement*, with the biggest fishes to the fore. As the meditators drifted over, all in their best clothes, they were told precisely where to sit.

While the juniors took their prescribed places in the sun, the Maharishi preferred to sit in the shade of a grove of trees along with the Beatles, their partners, Pattie Boyd's sister Jenny, Mike Love of the Beach Boys and 'Magic Alex' Mardas. It was the ashramic equivalent of the Royal Box at Ascot. At last the elderly photographer, the proprietor of a small shop in Rishikesh, who had lugged his heavy, old-fashioned wood and brass 8-by-10-plate camera up the hill, announced that he was ready, and the Maharishi and his group finally joined the others in the heat of the sun.

The photographer ducked his head under a black cloth to frame and focus. Every now and then he would emerge, call, 'Ready! Everyone look happy!' and press the button in his right hand. But the Maharishi remained in sole charge, bossing the photographer about – 'You must shout one, two, three before you snap . . . Any snap, you must shout!' and bellowing, 'Up higher! You don't get good scenes from there!' when he felt the camera's position was too low.

The strict order of precedence was maintained in the evenings, when everyone would adjourn to the lecture hall, described by one participant as 'a damp and hangar-like building with whitewashed walls and a floor of compressed cow dung'. The Beatles and their spouses sat on wicker chairs in front, with everyone else gathered in neat rows behind them.

'The Maharishi invariably turned up at least an hour late, nodding and murmuring praises to the Guru Dev,' recalled one participant. 'An almost coquettish smile straying across his face, he sat cross-legged on his antelope skin, often toying with a flower or a strand of beads. When he spoke to us, his voice remained gentle and soothing, as if he were speaking from some-place far away, where everything, somehow, was much simpler.'

Life at Rishikesh was far from spartan. The ashram had been built in 1963, with a $100,000 donation from the tobacco heiress Doris Duke. It is strange to think that, had Americans smoked Lucky Strike cigarettes with less gusto, the Maharishi would never have entertained the Beatles at Rishikesh, and most of *The White Album* might not have been written. Set within fourteen acres of forest, the property consisted of six large bunga-lows, each with half a dozen double bedrooms, plus a post office, lecture theatre and swimming pool. Peacocks wandered the grounds, squawking. The Maharishi employed a staff of forty, including cooks, cleaners and a masseuse. Before the arrival of the Beatles, new mattresses were delivered, along with new curtains and mirrors. The Beatles' rooms were equipped with four-poster beds and electric fires. 'It was back to Butlin's,' said Paul. 'You all had your own chalet.'

Every now and then a tailor would appear, to measure guests for Indian clothes. 'We all wore pyjama trousers and big baggy shirts, and the boys grew beards,' recalled Pattie Boyd.

Breakfast was served between 7 and 11 a.m., with a choice of porridge, puffed wheat or cornflakes, fruit juice and coffee, plus toast with marma-lade or jam. Ninety-minute lectures took place at 3.30 and 8.30 p.m., but there was no roll-call or penalties for any absentees. These lectures covered a mixed bag of topics, including reincarnation, meditation, the nature of creativity, how to live life to the fullest and astral travelling.

Even Ringo, who enjoyed his time at Rishikesh least of the Beatles, had no complaints about its pace of life. Burdened with a weak stomach from his childhood illnesses, he had prepared for the onset of spicy, unfamiliar food by packing a suitcase full of Heinz baked beans. His foresight left him with few complaints. 'We would walk about a bit and meditate or bathe,' he recalled. 'Of course, there were lectures or things all the time, but it was very much like a holiday. The Maharishi did everything he could to make us comfortable.' He was less satisfied, however, with the sanitary arrangements. 'You'd have to fight off the scorpions and tarantulas to try to get into a bath, so there used to be amazing noise in the bathroom. To have a bath, you'd start shouting – "OH YES, WELL, I THINK I'LL BE HAVING A BATH NOW" – and banging your feet. You'd keep shouting in the bath – "WHAT A TIME I'M HAVING, YES, IT'S WONDER-FUL." Then you'd get out of the bath, get dry and get out of the room before all the insects came back in.' Ringo's wife Maureen, who nursed an extreme dislike of creepy-crawlies, was particularly unnerved. John was impressed by the ferocity of Maureen's hatred of insects: he claimed that she once gave the flies in her bedroom such a thunderous black look that a second later they all dropped down dead.

As the weather turned warmer, the fly population multiplied and then settled on the food. Ringo and Maureen expressed their misgivings to the Maharishi. 'To those lost in meditation, the flies no longer matter,' he replied. Ringo was quick to spot the limitations of this aphorism.

'But that doesn't zap the flies, does it?' he replied.

110.

On 25 February 1968 the Rishikesh community threw a party for George's twenty-fifth birthday. The Maharishi made his usual fuss over the Beatles and their wives, inviting them up onstage to sit on special cushions at his feet. His monks went down on their knees, ready to smudge yellow splodges on their guests' foreheads. From time to time the Maharishi stroked George's head. Meanwhile, as a monk chanted, a woman called Edna, dressed in leopardskin-print pyjamas, paraded through the audience handing out garlands of fresh marigolds. As the chanting came to an end, they all queued to hang these garlands around George's neck. At the end of this process, one observer thought George looked 'like a man in a lifejacket'.

The Maharishi launched into one of his bubbly soliloquies, gushing forth like the Ganges. Hope is alive in the world, he said: the moment he met George Harrison and his 'blessed friends' the Beatles, he knew his movement would succeed and that mankind would suffer no more. George was, he added, 'a sublime soul for whom God and all the angels give thanks'. Even for a Beatle, this was flattery on a scale unknown; just six years earlier, on the night before George's nineteenth birthday, the Beatles had been booed offstage at the YMCA in Hoylake.

The Western well-wishers of Rishikesh joined in a rousing chorus of 'Happy Birthday to You' as the Maharishi presented George with a cake topped by two candles. He also gave him a plastic globe, turned upside down. 'George, the globe I am giving you symbolises the world today,' he explained. 'As you see, it needs to be corrected. I hope you will help us all in the task of putting it right.'

Cynthia Lennon felt that Rishikesh marked a turning point in George's life. Having been, in her words, 'the most tactless, blunt and often pig-headed of the Beatles', the combination of his experiences with LSD and his time in

India meant that 'He grew up very quickly, changing from a tactless youth into a sensitive, thinking individual. The rough edges were smoothed down and self-discipline became the cornerstone of his character.'

But, given time, sanctity can elongate into sanctimony; Rishikesh also brought out George's more solemn and po-faced, disapproving side. One day, when Paul casually told him that he had been thinking about their next album, George snapped, 'We're not fucking here to do the next album, we're here to meditate!' Paul was taken aback. 'It was like, "Ohh, excuse me for breathing!"'

While Pattie loved frolicking around in the Ganges, George thought it frivolous, and told her so. On the other hand, he never felt any conflict between his spirituality and his libido. Quite the opposite: in time, he came to regard them as operating in tandem, the one the handmaiden to the other. Over the course of their stay in India, Pattie noticed that George became 'fascinated by the god Krishna, who was always surrounded by young maidens'. She felt he returned to Britain 'wanting to be some kind of Krishna figure, a spiritual being with lots of concubines. He actually said so. And no woman was out of bounds.'

Paul looked back on his time in Rishikesh with a mixture of contentment and scepticism. He had meditated, but in a very English way. Whereas George extolled the benefits of meditation with evangelistic fervour – 'There's high and there's *high*, and to get really high – I mean so high that you can walk on water, *that* high – that's where I'm going. The answer's not pot, but yoga and meditation and working and discipline, working out your karma' – Paul approached it more matter-of-factly. One of his aids to meditation was, he said, to imagine someone leaning over a farm gate with a straw hanging out of his mouth – 'that feeling of being very, very calm'. Throughout it all, he hung on to the Beatles' natural sense of the ridiculous, coupled with their instinctive aversion to authority. 'Quick lads, fags out – here comes Teach!' he would say whenever he spotted the Maharishi approaching. He was even amused by the Maharishi's interest in the material world, and admired his pragmatism: one day he had asked for the Beatles' advice on the best new car. 'We said, "Well, a Merc, Maharishi. Mercedes, very good car." "Practical? Long-running? Good works?" "Yes." "Well, we should get a Mercedes then."'

John was, as usual, the most conflicted of the four, embracing or reject-ing the aura of Rishikesh as the mood took him. Free of hard drugs – none were allowed or available in the ashram – he threw himself into medita-tion. To a fan who wrote asking him what Transcendental Meditation was all about, he replied across two pages, signing off 'jai guru dev', explaining that 'It takes the mind down to that level of consciousness which is Abso-lute Bliss (Heaven).' In line with this, one of the many songs he wrote in India was called 'Child of Nature'. Its hippy-dippy lyrics ('I'm just a child of nature/I don't need much to set me free') are as un-John as can be, with no trace of bite. But when he came to record the song three years later, he kept the tune but junked the lyrics. Its new title was 'Jealous Guy', and the new lyrics made it all about insecurity, loss of control, pain, spite, jealousy and remorse.

At first, Cynthia loved India – 'just peace, quiet and sweet mountain air filled with the scent of flowers. Best of all, John and I could be to-gether for much of the time.' But after a week, others noticed that, though the other Beatles were affectionate and tactile with their partners, and John was perfectly pleasant to everyone else, he could be very offhand with Cynthia.

'They were bright and friendly with me, but distinctly distant and cool with each other,' noted the photographer Paul Saltzman. It was not until later that Cynthia learned that John's solitary morning walks had taken him straight to the post office, to pick up daily cards from a Japanese fan he had once described to Cynthia as 'off her rocker'.

'I felt so sorry for Cynthia,' remembered Pattie. 'He received notes from Yoko in the post almost every day saying things like, "If you look up at the sky and see a cloud, it's me sending you love."' These cards were being for-warded from a Delhi hotel by the Beatle apparatchik Tony Bramwell, who was in on their secret: 'To save problems, I put these open cards in a plain manila envelope so Cynthia wouldn't be upset.'

John remembered his Indian sojourn as, above all, a time of self-doubt. 'It was that period when I was really going through a "What's it all about? Songwriting is nothing. It's pointless and I'm not talented, and I'm a shit, and I couldn't do anything but be a Beatle and what am I going to do about it?"' Was he dreading the choice he would have to make on his return?

Yet the songs poured out of him, possibly because there was not much else to do, and no drugs, or at least hard drugs, to hand: 'Julia', 'Dear

Prudence', 'Bungalow Bill', 'Across the Universe', 'Cry Baby Cry', 'Polythene Pam', 'Mean Mr Mustard', 'I'm So Tired'. Some of these songs are cheerful, but filtered through John's memory they turned to gloom. 'The funny thing about the camp was that although it was very beautiful and I was meditating about eight hours a day, I was writing the most miserable songs on earth,' he recalled. 'In "Yer Blues", when I wrote, "I'm so lonely I want to die", I'm not kidding. Up there trying to reach God and feeling suicidal.'

Ringo and Maureen were the first to leave, chased away by flies and creepy-crawlies. 'The Maharishi's a nice man, but he's not for me,' Ringo informed the press. He and Maureen had nothing against meditation, but they were missing their children. 'It is not a gigantic hoax . . . If everyone in the world started meditating, then the world would be a much happier place.' Back home at Sunny Heights, Ringo received a postcard from John: 'Just a little vibration from India. We've got two LPs worth of songs now so get your drums out.'

Paul and Jane left after six weeks, declaring it 'a very rewarding experience'. It had certainly been fruitful for Paul musically: 'Blackbird', 'Rocky Racoon', 'Back in the USSR', 'I Will', 'Mother Nature's Son' and 'Ob-La-Di, Ob-La-Da', as well as the brief and bullish 'Why Don't We Do it in the Road?', inspired by the sight of a couple of monkeys copulating *en plein air*.

For John and Cynthia and George and Pattie, it all ended in tears. On a whim, John told the Maharishi he had a friend who could build a radio station in Rishikesh that would beam the message of Transcendental Meditation all over the world. Any spare energy could be used to light up the ashram and all the neighbouring villages. This wizard was, of course, his new Greek friend 'Magic' Alex Mardas, for whom no job was ever too large to be started or too small to leave unfinished. Mardas arrived in Rishikesh equipped with a small rucksack containing a selection of screwdrivers and a few wires. He can be spotted in the group photograph, two back from Ringo, unsmiling in dark glasses and staring directly at the camera, in a manner reminiscent of the vengeful Bruno at the tennis tournament in Hitchcock's *Strangers on a Train*.

For some reason, Mardas seems to have taken against the Maharishi.

Perhaps he was jealous of the way his own shamanic place in the Beatles' hearts had been usurped by this leathery old guru with his easy promises of levitation. Or was he fearful that he himself would be unmasked as a fraud? Tony Bramwell heard it rumoured that the Maharishi, the holder of a physics degree, was asking too many questions as to how exactly Magic Alex proposed to create an international radio station out of a handful of wires and fuses: 'He asked many searching questions that Alex was unable to answer, and the young Greek panicked.'

Iago had wheedled his way into Shangri-La. Two weeks before John and George were due to leave, Mardas began pouring malice into their ears, saying that the Maharashi had made advances to a young woman, first asking to hold her hand, then suggesting an inappropriate place to put it. Not only that, but this self-styled vegetarian had been spotted scoffing chicken behind their backs. 'He seemed convinced that Maharishi was evil,' remembered Pattie. 'He kept saying, "It's black magic."'

Cynthia looked on powerless as Magic Alex's gossip took root in the minds of John and George: 'Alexis's statements about how the Maharishi had been indiscreet with a certain lady, and what a blackguard he had turned out to be, gathered momentum. All, may I say, without a single shred of evidence or justification. It was obvious to me that Alexis wanted out, and more than anything he wanted the Beatles out as well.'

Soon, John and George were coming round to the idea that their guru was up to no good. 'Why would the Maharishi want a double four-poster bed?' asked Magic Alex, and George seemed to agree, with John following suit: 'When George started thinking it might be true, I thought, "Well, it must be true, because if George started thinking it might be true, there must be something in it."'

By the end of the night they had made up their minds. By chance, Pattie had what she described as 'a horrid dream' about the Maharishi, and was now keen to leave too. 'Out of confusion and accusation came anger and aggression,' recalled Cynthia.

The next morning Magic Alex ordered taxis, and John and George and their gang approached the Maharishi. 'I was the spokesman,' recalled John, 'and I said, "We're leaving." "Why?" he asked, and I said, "Well, if you're so cosmic, you'll know why!" . . . He said, "I don't know why. You must tell me," and I just kept saying, "You ought to know," and he gave me a look like, "I'll kill you, you bastard." I knew then that I had called his bluff and I was a bit rough to him.'

But Cynthia saw it differently: 'I felt that what we were doing was very, very wrong. To sit in judgement on a man who had given us nothing but happiness.'

As they waited by the outside tables for their taxis, the Maharishi emerged from his bungalow and went to sit a hundred yards away, in a little wooden shelter. One of his monks walked over to the Lennons and Harrisons with a message from the Maharishi. 'He said he was very sad and wanted desperately to put things right and to convince us that we should stay,' recalled Cynthia. 'I wanted to cry. It was so sad.'

When the taxis arrived, everyone stood up and filed past the Maharishi without a glance in his direction or saying a word. It reminded Cynthia of the biblical scene in which Jesus is denied by his disciples.

By taking them on their trip to India, George had, for the first time, assumed leadership of the Beatles. In the manner of his leaving, he had allowed himself to succumb once more to the more forceful character of John. Even as they were driving away, he began to regret siding with John against his old friend and guru. On the road to Delhi, John started singing, 'Maharishi, what have you done? You made a fool of everyone.' But George objected: 'You can't say that, it's ridiculous.' To appease him, John changed 'Maharishi' to 'Sexy Sadie'.

George later came to believe that John had wanted to leave, and had seized on Magic Alex's fabrications as a perfect excuse. 'This whole piece of bullshit was invented. There were a lot of flakes there; the whole place was full of flaky people. Some of them were us.'

On their arrival back in Britain, the Beatles remained surprisingly tight-lipped over any reservations they had concerning the Maharishi. Any admission of disillusionment would have required an acknowledgement of gullibility, so perhaps they felt it best to stay silent.

For his part, the Maharishi made the most of his connection. In May of that year he embarked on a concert tour of the USA with the Beach Boys. Billed as 'the Most Exciting Event of the Decade', it consisted of a set by the Beach Boys followed by a lecture on Transcendental Meditation by the

Maharishi, with time for questions and answers. Sadly, audiences tended to shout '"California Girls"!' or '"Barbara Ann"!' just as the Maharishi was explaining the more ethereal business of chakras and mantras. Following disappointing ticket sales, the final twenty-four dates of the twenty-nine-date tour were cancelled. Nonetheless, the Maharishi continued to thrive, attracting a wealth of celebrities to his Transcendental Meditation workshops, among them Kurt Vonnegut, the Rolling Stones, Major-General Franklin M. Davis, head of the United States Army War College, and, perhaps inevitably, the actress Shirley MacLaine.

The Maharishi went on to head a twenty-four-hour global satellite television channel, beaming Transcendental Meditation in twenty-two languages to 144 countries on a subscription basis. A complex network of related companies dealt in TM-related merchandise – books, CDs, spiritual consultations, massage oils. He also controlled new-age health centres, universities and charitable trusts, as well as the Heaven on Earth property company, and founded the Natural Law Party, which stood in British general elections of the 1990s on a platform of low taxes, yogic flying and a herb village in every town. He died in 2008, on an ashram in a former monastery in a small town on the Dutch–German border with the surprisingly down-to-earth name of Vlodorp.

III.

Whatever happened to the Beatles? Compare their first and last press conferences in America. In the first, they are outgoing and full of joie-de-vivre; in the last, self-absorbed and world-weary. Yet barely four years separate the two.

On 7 February 1964 they arrive at Kennedy Airport looking wide awake and happy, and are whisked into a noisy press room, where cameramen jostle for pictures. Their press officer has to shout at the top of his voice for quiet. Standing behind a dozen microphones, the four Beatles remain bright and chirpy, bantering away, undaunted by the barrage of questions. They are full of fun and enthusiasm, and clearly the best of friends, delighting in each other's company, laughing at each other's jokes and finishing off each other's answers.

REPORTER: What do you think of Beethoven?

RINGO: Great, especially his poems.

REPORTER: Can you explain your strange English accents?

GEORGE: It's not English. It's Liverpudlian.

REPORTER: In Detroit, there's people handing out car stickers saying, 'Stamp Out the Beatles'.

PAUL: Yeah, well, we've got two answers to that. First of all, we're bringing out a Stamp Out Detroit campaign.

REPORTER: What do you think of the comment that you're nothing but a bunch of British Elvis Presleys?

RINGO: (imitating Elvis's gait and voice) It's not true! It's not true!

REPORTER: How many of you are bald, so that you have to wear those wigs?

RINGO: All of us.

PAUL: I'm bald! Don't tell anyone, please!

JOHN: Oh, we're all bald, yeah . . . And deaf and dumb too.

REPORTER: Are you for real?

JOHN: Come and have a feel.

On 10 February, the morning after their American debut on *The Ed Sullivan Show*, they give another press conference, this time in the Baroque Room of the Plaza Hotel:

FEMALE REPORTER: Who chooses your clothes?

JOHN: We choose our own. Who chooses yours?

FEMALE REPORTER: My husband. Now tell me, are there any subjects
   you prefer not to discuss?

JOHN: Yes. Your husband.

REPORTER: Which do you consider is the greatest danger to your
   careers: nuclear bombs or dandruff?

RINGO: Bombs. We've already got dandruff.

Four years later, on 11 May 1968, John and Paul are back in America, this time to launch their new organisation, Apple. Even now, in this more laid-back era, they are greeted by screaming fans at Kennedy Airport. On 14 May they sit down for a press conference in the Versailles Room of the Americana Hotel.

John never smiles. His answers are tinged with aggression. Every now and then a sprinkling of polite laughter greets one of his offhand replies. Is the laughter prompted by wishful thinking? Are these journalists hoping to be transported back to those carefree days of 1964? Sitting to John's left, Paul looks bored and distracted, and hardly joins in. Jane Asher left him a few days ago; could this be the cause of his despondency? Whatever their reasons, neither Paul nor John shows a trace of excitement at the launch of this new venture.

REPORTER: Why are you here today?

JOHN: To do this. What's it look like? What are you doing here?

. . .

REPORTER: Could you tell us about your newest corporate business
   venture?

JOHN: It's a business concerning records, films and electronics, and
   as a sideline, whatever it's called, manufacturing, or whatever. We

want to set up a system whereby people who just want to make a film about anything don't have to go on their knees in somebody's office, probably yours.

. . .

REPORTER: Could you give us some idea about the capitalisation of this new corporation?

JOHN: No. We'll do it short-term, and we'll make sure we get what we want, y'know. Otherwise we won't do it. So we'll make sure.

. . .

REPORTER: How will you run your company?

JOHN: There's people we can get to do that. We don't know anything about business.

REPORTER: How will you set about film financing?

JOHN: We don't plan. Now we don't have any manager, there's no planning at all.

REPORTER: Tell us about your electronics division of Apple. What will it do?

PAUL: There won't be any gimmicks. But we won't say what it is until it's out.

The most complete, or least incomplete, statement of the aims of the new organisation comes from Paul: 'We're in the happy position of not needing any more money. So for the first time the bosses aren't in it for the profit. If you come to me and say, "I've had such and such a dream," I will say, "Here's so much money. Go away and do it."' Their aim, he says, is to create 'a beautiful place where you can buy beautiful things, a controlled weirdness, a kind of Western communism'.

But his tone – offhand and morose – is at odds with his message. The devil-may-care optimism and camaraderie of 1964 have disappeared. A trailer for Apple insists that the organisation will place 'EMPHASIS ON ENJOYMENT', but there is little evidence of that here today, in the Versailles Room of the Americana Hotel.

112.

Throughout John and Paul's press conference at the Americana, Magic Alex sat at John's right hand, toying with a bunch of flowers. Long-haired and bearded, he looked much like any other hippy, but he was now head of Apple's Electronics Division.

A month later, he was filmed for an Apple promotional film to be screened at a Los Angeles sales convention later the same day. The film begins with heavy guitar music, and a voiceover says: 'The concept of Apple is to bring together the artists of today with the methods and media of tomorrow.'

For the next three minutes Mary Hopkin plays guitar beneath a tree and sings sweetly, while Paul's dog Martha potters around. When she finishes, Paul walks on, and crouches beside her on the grass. 'That was Mary Hopkin – and this is Alex.'

The scene switches to a room full of boxes and machines. Magic Alex wears a white shirt and trousers beneath a white technician's coat. He is seen 'fiddling with a pile of junk', as the director of the film, Tony Bramwell, put it.

Against an insistent background clamour of *Dr Who*-ish bleepy-bloppy noises, Magic Alex walks towards the camera, picks up a microphone and says, in his heavy Greek accent, 'Hullo. Arm Alexis vrum Abul Elegtronigs. Ar, I vood like to say hullo to vall my bruzzers around the world and to all the gells around the world and to all the electronic people around the world er und er –' (points to the machines and boxes behind him) '– thad is Abull Elegronigs.'

The wacky noises continue as a blue light trails up and down across a screen, as in a low-budget sci-fi movie, or an amateur heart monitor.

The film cuts to an office. John passes a phone to Paul. Music seems to be coming out of it. Paul holds the phone to the ear of the unApple-ish figure of the Beatles' music publisher Dick James, bald and heavily bespectacled. 'Fair enough,' he says, with the tired curiosity of an exhausted parent. 'Where's that come from? Whassat? Oh, it's a radio built in.'

'Wrong,' says Paul, with a laugh. 'It's a phone. Just a little thing we have up our sleeves.'

Those of Mardas's ideas that worked were not his own, and those that were his own failed to work. In all, Apple applied for one hundred different patents for Mardas's inventions, not one of which was accepted. The telephone in the promotional video might well be the one he claimed to have invented, which had voice-recognition, and could display the number of the incoming call. But Apple lawyers were soon to discover that both of these had been patented by the Bell company some time before.

Other inventions by Magic Alex included:

a) an X-ray camera that could see through walls
b) a force-field that envelops any building in coloured air, rendering it invisible
c) a solar-powered electric guitar
d) paint that makes objects invisible
e) a house that hovers in the air, suspended on an invisible beam
f) a home heating system that runs on ordinary household batteries
g) a device for preventing records being taped off the radio by sending out a series of high-pitched squeals
h) special paint that changes colour at the flick of a switch

One of his more audacious inventions was 'loudpaper', an audible form of wallpaper. Paul listened wide-eyed as the electronics guru described it: 'He would sit and tell us of how it would be possible to have wallpapers which were speakers, so you would wallpaper your room with some sort of substance and then it could be plugged into and the whole wall would vibrate and work as a loudspeaker – "loud-paper". And we said, "Well, if you could do that, we'd like one." It was always, "We'd like one."'

But George Martin, older and wiser, was less easily impressed. 'Of all the army of hangers-on, the one I recall most vividly . . . was Magic Alex . . . who was so preposterous that it would have been funny had he not caused so much embarrassment and difficulty with me in the recording studio.' His irritation increased after he overheard Mardas boasting that he could do Martin's job so much better. 'I found it very difficult to chuck him out, because the boys liked him so much. Since it was very obvious that I didn't, a schism developed.'

Martin remained studiously undeceived. 'I confess that I tended to laugh myself silly when they came and announced the latest brainchild of Alex's fertile imagination. Their reaction was always the same: "You'll laugh on the other side of your face when Alex comes up with it." But of course he never did.'

Persuaded by Magic Alex, Apple bought two huge computers for £20,000 each. But no one could make them work, least of all Magic Alex. Before long they were moved to Ringo's garage, where they remained for years to come.

Of all Mardas's visions, the one that impressed the Beatles most, and George Martin least, was the Sonic Screen. 'I was informed of this work of inventive genius by the boys one day. "Why do you have to put Ringo with his drums behind all those terrible screens?" they asked. "We can't see him. We know it makes a good drum sound, and it cuts out all the spill to our guitars and things, but damn it, with those bloody great screens locking him in, it makes him feel claustrophobic."

'I waited silently, knowing that the problem would have been solved by a flash of Greek inspiration. And so it had. "Alex has got a brilliant idea! He's come up with something really great: a sonic screen! He's going to place these ultra-high-frequency beams round Ringo, and when they're switched on he won't be able to hear anything, because the beams will form a wall of silence." Words, I fully admit, failed me.'

Mardas started work on a flying saucer, built around two V12 engines, one borrowed from George's Ferrari, the other from John's Rolls-Royce. The Beatles also financed his scheme to create an artificial sun to light up the sky above the new Apple Boutique in Baker Street. But on opening night – 7 December 1967 – the sun failed to appear. This was, of course, not Mardas's fault: it all came down to a lack of 'energy'. Other inventions had, he insisted, been days from completion when, as luck would have it, a fire swept through his workshop, ensuring that their due date had to be postponed.

He somehow persuaded the Beatles to let him design them a new studio, the best in the world, equipped with recording consoles that were not just four-track, as at EMI, or eight-track, as in America, but seventy-two-track. For months he pretended to be busying away, constructing a studio in the basement of the Apple headquarters at 3 Savile Row, and regularly asking for more money for the task.

As autumn turned to winter, the Beatles, already fractious, began to find their Twickenham studios too cold and draughty. Their patience was ebbing away; they demanded to move into the swish, state-of-the-art new studio as soon as possible.

Magic Alex finally let them into their new studio late in 1969. It immediately proved unusable, with no studio desk or any form of soundproofing. Conversations from neighbouring rooms and footsteps from upstairs could easily be heard, while every time the building's central heating was fired up a great whooshy noise filled the studio. Geoff Emerick was unimpressed: 'Alex basically did not know what he was doing. The studio he built for them was a complete and utter disaster.' George Martin realised at once that there was no space in the wall for the cables between the studio and the control room; the only solution was to open the doors so the cables could snake along the corridor. Far from being revolutionary, the mixing console was just a sheet of plywood with sixteen faders and an oscilloscope stuck in the middle. 'It looked like the control panel of a B-52 bomber,' complained the sound engineer Dave Harries. 'They actually tried a session on this desk, they did a take, but when they played back the tape it was all hum and hiss. Terrible. The Beatles walked out, that was the end of it.' George Martin made a frantic call to Abbey Road: 'For God's sake get some decent equipment down here!'

'He'd charged them thousands, and bought the stuff second-hand,' said John Dunbar, who had grown disillusioned with his former wunderkind. George Harrison, too, suffered a crisis of faith: 'Alex's recording studio at Apple was the biggest disaster of all time. He was walking around with a white coat on like some sort of chemist, but didn't have a clue about what he was doing.' Alan Parsons, a junior EMI tape operator, arrived with equipment borrowed from Abbey Road. He too was disappointed by Mardas's efforts: 'It had obviously been done with a hammer and chisel instead of being properly designed and machined.' But their recordings struggled on, creating what John later called, in his undainty way, 'the shittiest load of badly recorded shit with a lousy feeling to it ever'. Finally, when Allen Klein took over the management of the Beatles' affairs in 1969, he wound up Apple Electronics, and stopped all payments to Magic Alex. In the end, the famous cutting-edge mixing console was sold as scrap metal to a second-hand electronics shop in the Edgware Road for £5.

Magic Alex came to personify the hippy-dippy gullibilities of the Beatles' later years. He spent the rest of his life in Greece, selling bulletproof cars and security devices to the wealthy and paranoid. He also made a fortune selling all the Beatles memorabilia he had managed to accumulate: in 2011 he was paid $408,000 for a custom-made Vox Kensington guitar with a plaque reading:

TO MAGIC ALEX
ALEXI THANK YOU
FOR BEEN [sic] A FRIEND
2-5-1967 JOHN

In 2008, after an article in the *New York Times* described him as a 'charlatan', he threatened to take the newspaper to court. Following two years of protracted negotiations, he agreed to drop his action on condition that the paper made it clear that by calling him a charlatan, it did not intend to mean that he was also a conman.

On his death in 2017, his obituarist in *The Times* calculated that, in today's money, Alex Mardas's projects had cost the Beatles £4 million, with no tangible return.

113.

At Quarry Bank, the boys would indulge in saucy group sessions in the bushes after school. At that time they would have been thirteen or fourteen years old. 'Our fantasies, at least, were strictly heterosexual,' recalled Pete Shotton, a little priggishly. '"Right boys," someone would venture, "who should we do it to today?"' They would then take it in turns to call out the names of famous pin-ups, 'each name spurring us on to new heights of ecstasy'.

When it came to John's turn, he liked to enlist the vision of Brigitte Bardot, for whom the term 'sex kitten' had recently been coined. The French actress shot to fame in Britain after posing in a bikini at the Cannes Film Festival to publicise her relatively minor role in *Act of Love* (1953). Her career blossomed during John's adolescent years: she starred opposite Dirk Bogarde and James Robertson Justice in *Doctor at Sea* (1955), before going on to play the title role in *Naughty Girl* (1956), and then 'a demon driven temptress' in *And God Created Woman* (also 1956).*

During one of their unabashed sessions, John suddenly switched his regular call from 'Brigitte Bardot!' to 'Winston Churchill!' which had the instant effect of pouring cold water on their shared fantasies.†

Around this time, he started collecting a new series of photographs in *Weekend* magazine. In weekly instalments, the magazine offered a new piece of what would eventually grow into a life-size pin up of Brigitte

---

* 'A role that will make you gasp and never forget', according to the trailer.

† Though Shotton failed to mention Paul's participation in this game, Paul certainly included himself when he shared roughly the same story with readers of *GQ* magazine in 2018: 'It was just a group of us, and instead of just getting roaring drunk and partying – I don't even know if we were staying over or anything – we were all just in these chairs, and the lights were out, and somebody started masturbating, so we all did. We were just, "Brigitte Bardot! Whoo!" and then everyone would thrash a bit more. I think it was John who sort of said, "Winston Churchill!" . . . It was quite raunchy when you think about it. There's so many things like that from when you're a kid that you look back on and you're, "Did we do that?" But it was good harmless fun. It didn't hurt anyone. Not even Brigitte Bardot.'

Bardot in a swimsuit. Having collected the full set, he taped the composite poster onto the ceiling above his bed.

Paul shared John's passion for the sultry French actress. 'She was it, she was the first, she was one of the first ones you ever saw nude or semi-nude,' he recalled. 'She was a great looker, and she was French, so Brigitte for us, with the long blonde hair and the great figure and the little pouty lips, was the epitome of female beauty . . . It was the fact that she was thought to have loose morals; we could fantasise that she did anyway.'

John was still entertaining these fantasies about Brigitte Bardot in 1957, when he left school to enrol at the Liverpool College of Art. There he had caught the eye of Cynthia Powell, who had by chance overheard him compare one of their fellow students approvingly to Bardot. Determined to win John's heart, Cynthia dyed her hair blonde, and started wearing false eyelashes, tight black trousers and clingy sweaters. Sure enough, John began to take an interest, and they soon became a couple.

Just before the Beatles set off on their first trip to Hamburg, Cynthia received a telephone call from John telling her to come over as fast as she could. Aunt Mimi had left to visit her sister Nanny in Birkenhead: the house was free. John's first impulse was to borrow a camera. 'He insisted I try out various seductive poses while he snapped away, so I put my hair up, let it down, hitched up my skirt and thrust out my chest in an attempt to do my best Brigitte Bardot. After the photo session, we made love, then lit a fire and lay on the sofa in front of the television, eating anything we could find in the fridge. It was all the more exciting for being so illicit.'

John took these photographs with him to Hamburg. When Cynthia and Paul's girlfriend Dot visited them there, John and Paul persuaded them both to wear leather skirts, just like Bardot. Many years later, Paul remembered John saying, 'Yeah, well, the more they look like Brigitte, the better off we are, mate!' Tony Barrow once went so far as to claim that during John's marriage to Cynthia 'John admitted to me that he would metaphorically shut his eyes and think of some movie star, probably Brigitte Bardot.'

Paul and John's fidelity to Brigitte survived money and fame. An early version of the *Sgt. Pepper* cover, drafted in pen and ink by Paul, shows the Beatles in their colourful uniforms standing in front of a wall of framed photographs of their idols. To their left is a pin-up of Brigitte Bardot kneeling with her hands behind her head, ten times the size of anyone else. But for reasons lost to time, she failed to make the final cover, her place being filled by Mae West and Diana Dors.

In June 1968, fantasy collided with reality when Brigitte Bardot arrived in London, and sent word to Apple that she would like to meet one or more of the Beatles. John was the sole volunteer. He boasted to Pete Shotton that he would soon be meeting the girl of their schoolboy dreams. 'Naturally, I begged John to let me tag along, but since Brigitte had specified she wasn't prepared to meet a crowd of strangers, only Derek [Taylor] was permitted to accompany him.'

Before the big meeting, John popped round to see Taylor at the Apple offices in Wigmore Street, and asked him for some marijuana to calm him down. Taylor only had LSD, so they both took that instead. The two of them then climbed into John's Rolls-Royce and were driven the short distance to the Mayfair Hotel, where Bardot was staying. Suffering an attack of nerves, John sent Taylor into the hotel while he remained crouched on the floor of the car.

Taylor found Brigitte Bardot dressed all in black leather, surrounded by female companions. When he told her that John Lennon was in the car outside she seemed disappointed that no other Beatles had come. By this time, Taylor's tabs of LSD were kicking in, causing great waves of paranoia. He and John were in danger, he told Bardot, and they were being watched by mysterious people. Bardot didn't understand what he was saying, but suggested he ask John to come up.

John duly came to the room, but the twin traumas of LSD and Brigitte Bardot in leather rendered him speechless. With some effort he managed to say 'Hello,' but little else. Bardot said that she had booked a table in the hotel restaurant, but neither John nor Taylor were sure they could walk that far. Taylor was nonplussed: 'Suddenly everyone was standing up, ready to go. This was terrible! For a start, neither of us was capable of eating anything at all; we weren't even sure we could stand up . . . "Please don't think us bourgeois," we begged, "but we are both married and this is getting out of hand and" . . . oh Christ! What a mess!'

Brigitte, in Taylor's words, 'was not best pleased'. She and her female companions stomped off to the restaurant downstairs, leaving John and Taylor in the hotel suite. When Bardot and her entourage returned from dinner, they were surprised to find the two men still there, Taylor slumped on Bardot's bed, and John strumming a guitar, playing a selection of songs he had composed in India. Bardot's indifference quickly turned to irritation; before long she asked them to leave.

John returned to Kenwood, where Pete Shotton was staying. '"What happened, what happened?" I said breathlessly. "I can't bear the suspense another minute!"

'"Fucking *nothing* happened," said John. "I was so fucking nervous that I dropped some acid before we went in and got completely out of me head. The only thing I said to her all night was hello, when we went to shake hands with her. Then she spent the whole time talking in French with her friends, and I could never think of anything to say."'

It had been, he concluded, 'a fucking terrible evening'.

114.

THE TURDS

The explosive truth

The atmosphere at the Bond Street offices of Rubbish Ltd. is of intense boredom enlivened by occasional surrealistic hyper-symmetry. A Turd drifts by wearing an Oriental bell-bottomed pull-over with rubberised attachments. A thin spotty girl at reception is saying, 'It's the Official Receiver. Shall I say you're out?'

Already under construction at Bond Street are the biggest television aerial in the world, eighty-nine magic lanterns and some eight patented inventions by a life-long friend of the Turds, 'Mad Sid' Saint-Beuve.

These inventions include an electric blotting-paper liquidiser, a toilet roll which plays the national anthem and a car with no wheels.

A South Croydon firm has already offered the Turds £2 to take the car away.

Turd Spiggy Topes became worried last year over the decline in sales of Turd records in the USA. With the growth of miniature tape recorders fans were taping records from the radio and not buying the records. Under Turd sponsorship, a service has been patented to prevent this happening. All Turd records will in future emit a loud wailing noise so excruciating to the naked ear that no one will listen to them ever again.

For the Turds the wailing noise makes a new departure. Their latest LP, *A Day in the Life of Ex-King Zog of Albania*, took over five years to make and includes combs and paper, the sound of the Cornish Riviera Express leaving Paddington, two million zithers, an electric hydrofoil, and the massed strings of the Tel Aviv Police Band.

Says Spiggy: 'I was always terrified of classical music. I mean to say Mendelssohn and that and all those long names. And then the other day I met this taxi driver who was reading this Mozart sheet music. "You won't like this," he frankly admitted to me, "it's highbrow." And that's what I used to think. But it's not, you know. I mean, it's exactly what's happening in pop today. We are Mozart. I mean to say Christ. We're also him, that reminds me.'

Private Eye, 13 September 1968

115.

In Rishikesh, Cynthia had felt that John was avoiding her: 'I was not having the second honeymoon I'd hoped for. John was becoming increasingly cold and aloof towards me. He would get up very early and leave our room. He spoke to me very little, and after a week or two he announced that he wanted to move into a separate room to give himself more space. From then on, he virtually ignored me, both in private and in public.' Little did she know that John was receiving letters from Yoko Ono almost every day.

Two weeks after they got back from India, John suggested to Cynthia that she should join Donovan, his manager Gypsy Dave, Pattie Boyd's sister Jenny and Magic Alex on a fortnight's holiday in Greece. She and John rarely holidayed separately, so Cynthia was reluctant. 'I've got a lot on at the moment and I can't go, but you should. It might cheer you up,' said John.

On her return from holiday, Cynthia drove to Kenwood with Jenny Boyd and Magic Alex, arriving at 4 p.m. She straight away knew something was wrong: 'The porch light was on, the curtains were still drawn and everything was silent.' Normally her housekeeper, Dot, would have come out to greet her with Julian. Instead, there was silence.

The front door was unlocked. 'Where are you all?' she shouted. Were they hiding behind a door?

'As I put my hand on the sunroom door I felt a sudden frisson of fear. I hesitated for a second, then opened it. Inside, the curtains were closed and the room was dimly lit, so it took me a moment to focus. When I did, I froze. John and Yoko were sitting on the floor, cross-legged and facing each other, beside a table covered with dirty dishes. They were wearing the towelling robes we kept in the poolhouse, so I imagined they had been for a swim. John was facing me. He looked at me, expressionless, and said, "Oh, hi." Yoko didn't turn round.'

It was clear to Cynthia that they wanted her to find them like that. She found the cruelty of John's act hard to fathom. She was so taken aback that she went into a state of emotional paralysis, behaving as if nothing were out of order, and asking him if he'd like to come out to dinner with them.

'No thanks,' replied John.

Cynthia rushed out of the room. Jenny was hovering awkwardly in the kitchen, so she asked if she could stay with her. Then she went upstairs to pack a bag. On the landing she stumbled across a pair of small Japanese slippers, placed neatly outside the guest bedroom. She looked inside. The bed was untouched.

116.

Pete Shotton found himself in overall charge of the Apple Boutique, which was to be stocked with psychedelic clothes, Oriental bric-à-brac, hand-painted furniture and inflatable chairs. The three young Dutch designers collectively known as The Fool were hired to design the shopfront and provide the stock, having already applied their swirly, curly, lava-lampy decorations to George's bungalow, John's grand piano and the set for 'All You Need is Love'. Like many of those who fluttered around the Beatles, they dressed in gypsy head-dresses, great bundles of necklaces, bell-sleeved shirts splashed with stars and moons, Elizabethan jerkins and low-slung satin belts snaking around velvet 'loons'. Their dreamy personas neverthe-less concealed a shrewd instinct for money – or bread, as they preferred to call it – and how best to extract it from their utopian employers. On top of their regular wages, they gently asked for a bonus on signature of contract of £40,000, or £675,000 in today's money. The Beatles' startled accoun-tant advised the group strongly against handing it over, but they ignored him. Once this deal was done and dusted, The Fool embarked on a ten-day 'research' trip to Morocco, with all expenses paid.

The clothes they designed, all rainbows and flowers and dreamy landscapes, were poorly executed, their shapes ungainly, their seams frail, their sleeves lopsided. 'We had to find people to *make* these clothes,' sighed Pete Shotton. 'And when we finally did, the clothes were shit.'

Over a weekend – the same weekend the Beatles were recording their starry-eyed video for 'Hello, Goodbye' – The Fool gathered art students to paint the exterior of the Apple townhouse in Savile Row. The mu-ral featured moons and shooting stars and an androgynous wide-eyed hippy figure, stretching across four storeys. The launch party – 'Come at 7.46. Fashion Show at 8.16' – attracted a mixed bag of celebrities, includ-ing John and George, Cilla Black, Eric Clapton, Victor Spinetti, Twiggy, Keith Moon and Richard Lester. A circus clown handed out apples, while a conga line of hippies played finger-cymbals and tambourines. Towards the end of the evening, rather too many people tried to squeeze into rather too small a space; as partygoers clambered outside for air, trampling half the stock underfoot, a man from the BBC fainted from lack of oxygen.

Within days the Westminster planning department were insisting on the removal of the mural, for which they had never granted permission. Further Apple money was spent on contesting the decision, but to no avail: down it went.

Pete Shotton never felt at ease in the boutique he had been hired to manage: 'Every time I caught one of the blow-up chairs with my cigarette, I would collapse in a heap on the floor.'

In the spirit of the age, clothes flew off the rails and out of the door, with no intervening trip to the counter. The staff, being cool, didn't like to insist on payment, though they themselves were happy to exit each evening carrying armfuls of bell-bottoms and Nehru jackets, with little attempt at concealment. Within seven months the Apple Boutique had lost £20,000, or £340,000 in today's money.

At the end of July 1968 the Beatles decided to close it down. The night before it shut for the last time, the four of them arrived with friends and took what they fancied. John raced around, gleefully grabbing whatever he could, apparently unaware that he was purloining from himself. The next day, shoppers piled in, attracted by the idea that there was now no need to shoplift. In under twenty-four hours Apple offloaded £10,000 worth of clothes. But this left a fresh debt with which to deal: in their haste, the management forgot that all the stock was subject to purchase tax at 12½ per cent, even if it had been given away for nothing.

Having closed the boutique, the Beatles moved Apple's headquarters to 3 Savile Row, losing their tax records along the way. Their new headquarters was turned into a free-for-all, with guests and employees alike vying to see who could charge most to Apple. Whenever John and Yoko dropped by, Yoko would order a pot of caviar costing £60; Barry Miles calculated that this was 'about five weeks' wages for one of the cooks who served it'.

The Apple phone bill came to roughly £4,000 a quarter. 'Every time you turn around there are at least half a dozen people on the phone who don't even work in the building,' noted Richard DiLello, who perused the bills with astonishment. 'Since when is there an Apple office in Katmandu? Or in Sausalito? Or Acapulco?'

Visitors and employees alike walked off with all sorts of stuff: televisions, electric typewriters, speakers, cases of wine, fan heaters. One employee removed the lead from the roof on a daily basis, soon creating leaks that caused thousands of pounds' worth of damage. Musicians and artists and film-makers sponsored by Apple refused to acknowledge any distinction between loans and gifts. 'We were giving out all that money and the cameras and equipment and half of the people we never saw again – they just went off with it,' observed Ringo.

Once in a while, management made a half-hearted attempted to rein everyone in. On 2 June 1968, Neil Aspinall sent a memo to department heads:

> Please ensure that your staff are prompt each morning. Recently, a number of people have been getting very tardy. There's no excuse. Ten o'clock should be within everybody's reach. Also, please don't put joss sticks in the typewriter carriages, please keep drunken Irishmen out of our board meetings, please tell the girl hiding in the lavatory that Paul never uses that one [and] please don't try to play jam butties on the hi-fi equipment.

Apple was a runaway horse. For a year the company employed a full-time mystic called Caleb, whose role was to steer the business with regular readings of tarot cards and the *I Ching*. 'The weirdness was not controlled at the start,' noted Derek Taylor. 'You can't control weirdness, anyway; weirdness is weirdness.' He was one to talk: in the space of a fortnight, his own press office clocked up a bill for six hundred Benson & Hedges cigarettes, eight dozen Cokes, eight bottles of J&B whisky, four bottles of Courvoisier brandy, three bottles of vodka, two dozen ginger ales, one dozen tonic waters, two dozen bitter lemons, one dozen tomato juices, three bottles of lime and four dozen lagers. Having studied the invoice, another Apple employee commented, 'Oh, they've cut back a bit then.' In an editorial in the Apple house magazine Derek Taylor said, 'We've had many guests at Apple, friends. Can't remember any of them. Very stoned, you see. Affects the memory.'

George, once so beady about money and so wary of the taxman, succumbed to the anti-materialism in the air. Only when the clouds had lifted could he see the Beatles' big mistake. 'We've been giving away too much to the wrong people,' he told Pattie. 'This place has become a haven for dropouts. The trouble is, some of our best friends are dropouts.'

In this barmy army, it didn't help that the top brass were, more often than not, out of their heads. When the Beatles finally heard the sirens wail, they had no idea which way to run. 'It's really like Vietnam,' said George, with a touch of hyperbole. 'It's escalated. It's got so big, but we can't really see the way out.'

Having woken up to what was happening, John went from stupor to panic, with nothing in between, pointing an accusing finger at everyone but himself: 'People were robbing us and living on us . . . Eighteen or twenty thousand pounds a week was rolling out of Apple and nobody was doing anything about it. All our buddies that had worked for us for fifty years were all just living and drinking and eating like fuckin' Rome! And I suddenly realised it. We were losing money at such a rate that we would have been broke, really broke. We didn't have anything in the bank really, none of us did. Paul and I could probably have floated, but we were sinking fast. It was just hell, and it had to stop.'

Dismayed at all the money pouring out of their money-saving scheme, John met Derek Taylor and Neil Aspinall to work out a plan of action. The three men kicked off their business meeting by taking LSD, before deciding – quite reasonably, given the circumstances – that all Apple's problems could be solved by walking down Weybridge High Street and knocking on the doors of the local bank manager and the local solicitor. 'Listen,' they planned to say, 'Apple is in a mess, but we need a simple solution: a simple bank manager who is reliable and a simple solicitor who can see his way through all this mess.'

John, according to Paul – or Paul, according to John – then called in the very same big businessmen that Apple had been founded to oppose. Sir Joseph Lockwood of EMI suggested they hire the former Conservative Party chairman Lord Poole, who in turn suggested Lord Beeching, whose 1963 report into the future of the British rail network had resulted in the axing of a third of all railway stations. Beeching examined Apple's financial records, before advising the Beatles to stick to music.

On 21 March 1969, John, George and Ringo asked the New Jersey bruiser Allen Klein, a man characterised by Alistair Taylor as having 'the charm of a broken lavatory seat', to be their business manager. In a series of deft manoeuvres, Klein had managed to persuade John that he was just the man to take charge of their affairs. He won Yoko over by promising to arrange a major show of her work in the US.* Ringo had been even more easily wooed: 'All I wanted was to be looked after. I would get off the plane or the *QE2* in New York and there'd be a guy there: a pretty stocky guy who would get me through, get me in a limo, give me a pack of money, get me a suite in a hotel – and that was it. That was cool for me. I was easily pleased. Just get me to the place on time!'

A bull in this most higgledy-piggledy of china shops, Klein charged about upsetting almost everyone at Apple, including the diligent Geoff Emerick, who was perturbed by his habit of saying 'Ker-ching!' whenever a Beatles song came on the radio. Derek Taylor compared this period to 'the last days of Pompeii, when the boiling shit hit the fan and sprayed over leaders and followers alike, leaving us all feeling grubby and ugly and useless'. Within days, Klein had fired most of the Apple staff, including the general manager, Alistair Taylor, who had worked for the Beatles since the day they were first signed by Brian Epstein. Taylor rang each of the four Beatles in turn to tell them what had happened, but none of them was able to come to the phone.

Many unrealised ideas, at various stages of development or undevelopment, died with Apple. John had championed Apple Limousines, a fleet of psychedelic Rolls-Royces. Paul planned to open a store selling only white products: 'You can never get anything white, like cups and all that. I've been looking for a decent set of white cups for five years.' All four Beatles envisaged opening an Apple School, offering carefree education to the children of the Beatles and their staff. Other unrealised projects included an Apple Entertainment and Shopping Centre on Regent Street, with a cinema, sauna and restaurant; Apple Cosmetics, offering a range of perfumes, lipsticks and lotions in apple-shaped containers; and an international franchise of Sgt. Pepper discothèques.

In a sense, the spirit of Apple lived on in John and Yoko. Throughout

---

* This finally took place on 9 October 1971. As Yoko had not completed enough work to fill the available space, a team of workers was hired to construct further installations. Cost overruns meant that all four Beatles were left with a bill for $80,000.

the rest of 1969 they initiated a variety of schemes more impractical and improbable than any they had just abandoned. Most came to nothing. In the autumn they wrote a long letter to Eric Clapton suggesting what they called 'a kind of "Easy Rider" at sea': a ship for thirty people, including musicians and crew, plus 'doctors, etc, in case of any kind of bother', cruising from Los Angeles to Tahiti, all being filmed and financed by EMI or a film company. 'The whole trip would take 3–4–5–6 months, depending how we all felt – all families, children whatever are welcome etc.'

Generally, John's ideas would come and go. Paul developed a technique for letting them float away on air, like bubbles. One day John suggested the two of them undergo joint trepanning: 'It's an ancient Roman thing – you have a hole drilled in your skull.' Paul ummed and erred before saying, 'You have it done, and if it's fine we'll all have it done as well.' These vaguely encouraging noises were, he had worked out, the best way to ensure that nothing happened. 'Otherwise he would have had us all with holes in our heads the next morning.'

117.

One day, shortly after John had run off with Yoko, Paul drove to Wey-bridge to see Cynthia. He thought she might need cheering up. 'Paul was the only member of the Beatles family who'd had the courage to defy John – who had apparently made it quite clear that he expected everyone to follow his lead in cutting me off. But Paul was his own man and not afraid of John,' Cynthia remembered. She had heard nothing from Ringo or George, or either of their wives: 'They didn't want to bring John's fury on themselves, and probably didn't know what to say to me anyway.'

Julian was then five, the same age John had been when his own father left home. Paul had always been close to Julian. He had a rapport with children that was lost on John: when the Beatles went to Greece to buy their island, John spent his time reading the newspapers while Paul played Cowboys and Indians with Julian. 'He'd been like an uncle to him,' John admitted years later. 'Paul was always good with kids.'

In this respect, Paul felt sorry for John. 'I remember John coming up to me once and he took me aside and said, "How do you do it?" I said, "What do you mean?" He said, "With Julian. How do you play with kids like that?" I remember feeling a wave of sorrow coming over me . . . I tried to give the potted version, you know, "Play, pretend you're a kid. Play with him." But John never got it. Never got the hang of it.' Now in late middle age, Julian remembers seeing more of Paul than of his father: 'We had a great friendship going, and there seem to be far more pictures of me and Paul playing together at that age than there are pictures of me and my dad.'

Driving down to Weybridge in his Aston Martin, Paul was thinking about the consequences of the split on Julian: 'I knew it was not going to be easy for him. I always feel sorry for kids in divorces.' From out of no-where, a song came into his head. 'Hey Jules,' it began, 'don't make it bad. Take a sad song, and make it better.'

118.

In August 1968 the Rolling Stones had much to celebrate. They had completed their new album, *Beggars Banquet*, Mick Jagger had just turned twenty-five, and the Vesuvio Club, part owned by Jagger and Keith Richards, was reopening.

The party they threw at the Vesuvio was a suitably wild celebration of these three events. Moroccan tapestries draped the walls, along with giant photographs of the Stones. A helium-filled zeppelin floated up and down, vast silver bowls were filled with a mixture of punch and mescaline, and tables groaned with plates piled with hash cakes. Hubble pipes were provided, along with dainty dishes of hash, for those who preferred inhaling to ingesting.

'My only fear,' recalled the club's manager Tony Sanchez,* 'was the club's proximity to Tottenham Court Road police station. It was only three hundred yards away, and a couple of inquisitive cops would have been able to arrest just about every superstar in Britain if they had decided on a raid that night.'

Jagger arrived early, having flown from Ireland with the first advance pressing of *Beggars Banquet*. Sanchez, acting as disc jockey, proceeded to play it. It was an instant success: everyone present seemed either to be dancing to it or saying how amazing it was, or both at the same time. On top of all this, John Lennon and Yoko Ono dropped by, the summer of '68's progressive equivalent of a visit from the Queen and the Duke of Edinburgh.

Arriving a little later than most of the other partygoers was Paul McCartney, fresh from Trident Studios, a short walk away in Soho, bringing

---

* Sanchez was the 'personal assistant' of Keith Richards, and has also been credited with the no less onerous role of preferred drug dealer to the Rolling Stones, Robert Fraser and, from time to time, the Beatles.

with him the acetate disc of the Beatles' next single. Having greeted his hosts, he walked through the dancers to the turntables, and discreetly handed the disc to Tony Sanchez, saying, 'See what you think of it, Tony. It's our new one.'

Once *Beggars Banquet* had come to an end, and Mick and Keith were milling about, garnering praise from their guests, Sanchez slipped the new Beatles single onto the turntable.

'Hey Jude, don't make it bad, take a –'

Everyone stopped talking. For the next seven minutes eleven seconds, they remained completely silent.

'It just went – boom! – straight to the chest,' recalls Marianne Faithfull. 'It was the first time anyone had heard it, and we were all just blown away . . . We had a sense of everyone being in the right place, at the right time, with the right people.'

Tony Sanchez felt Mick Jagger's mood changing: 'When it was over, I noticed that Mick looked peeved.' Paul remembers Mick coming up to him and saying, 'Fuckin' 'ell! Fuckin' 'ell! That's something else, innit? It's like two songs. It's got the song and then the whole "na na na" at the end. Yeah.'

Later that night, John staggered over to Sanchez, 'looking as though his eyes were about to pop out of his head', and asked him to call a cab. All three doormen went outside to hail one, but they failed to come back. Sanchez was later to discover that the interaction of the fresh air with the mescaline and the hash had rendered the three of them insensible: they completely forgot who they were, where they were, and what they were supposed to be doing. Jagger saved the day by volunteering the use of his own Aston Martin DB6, and Tony Sanchez's cousin, acting as chauffeur, successfully drove John and Yoko all the way back to Ascot, Surrey.

119.

It was late afternoon on a perfect English summer's day, 30 June 1968. Paul was in his Rolls-Royce, being driven back to London from Yorkshire, where he had been recording 'Thingumybob' with the Black Dyke Mills Band. Derek Taylor, Peter Asher and a journalist from the *NME* were also in the car. As they travelled down the M1 they decided to stop off somewhere. But where? Derek, high on LSD, suggested that Peter should take a look at the AA map of Bedfordshire, and pick the village with the most beautiful name.

After a very long time, Peter made an unlikely choice: Harrold. The chauffeur obediently wended his way along minor roads until they arrived at the village of that name. For Derek, it was like a dream come true: 'Thrushes and blackbirds sang and swallows dived into thatches and a little old mower wheezed as we walked down the only street there was.'

In the garden of Mulberry Lodge, his home on the High Street, Gordon Mitchell, a mustachioed dentist, was out in his shorts, clipping a hedge. He looked up to see three men led by Paul McCartney, who asked him the way to the river. Mitchell gave him the directions, and they went on their way. Mitchell nipped inside to tell his wife Pat what had happened: Paul McCartney had just asked him the way to the river. Together, they beetled off in the same direction, hoping to bump into Paul and his friends.

Sure enough, they found them in the Magpie pub, and fell into conversation with them. Soon they were all feeling peckish, and Pat suggested that if they came back to Mulberry Lodge she could rustle something up. 'Paul showed his humanity by visiting Pat's father, at that time an invalid in bed, and had a long chat with him,' recalled Gordon Mitchell forty years later.

They tucked into ham and rice. Gordon told Paul of the raffle he was organising for the Playing Fields Association the following weekend. Mitchell's daughter Shuna brought out a child-sized guitar and handed it to Paul, who immediately started tuning it, putting two coins under the bridge. Paul wondered if they'd care to hear a song he had just composed, and they all said yes. 'Hey Jude, don't make it bad,' he began.

'Why can't life always be like this?' sighed Pat Mitchell.

According to Gordon Mitchell, 'They were all the nicest people one could wish to meet, and great fun, and it was a very special evening.'

Around 11 p.m. someone arrived to say that though the Oakley Arms was officially closed, the landlord had agreed to reopen it, 'in your honour, Paul'. So off they went to the Oakley Arms, which, according to Derek, was packed: 'The whole village was there. Paul played the piano, including another rendition of "Hey Jude", until at three o'clock a woman stood and sang "The Fool on the Hill" and he left the piano to dance with her and kiss her on the cheek.'

In the early hours of the morning Paul and his gang set off back to London in his Rolls-Royce. A few days later, Gordon and Pat Mitchell received a thank-you letter, along with two bottles of champagne for the raffle.

120.

Possibly so as to avoid wounding John's fragile self-esteem, Paul changed 'Hey Jules' to 'Hey Jude' before singing it to him for the first time. John took the song to be about him, and his need for Yoko: 'If you think about it, Yoko's just coming into the picture. He's saying, "Hey, Jude – hey, John." I know I'm sounding like one of those fans who reads things into it, but you CAN hear it as a song to me. The words "go out and get her" – subconsciously he was saying, "Go ahead, leave me." But on a conscious level, he didn't want me to go ahead. The angel inside him was saying, "Bless you." The devil in him didn't like it at all, because he didn't want to lose his partner.'

John was not alone in his solipsism. Many Beatles songs have a vague, fluid quality that pulls the listener towards a personal interpretation. The lyric of 'Hey Jude' is at one and the same time pliable and precise. On its release, some took it to be directed at Bob Dylan, who had become a recluse at his farm in Woodstock. *Time* magazine thought it was a call for commitment; *Rolling Stone* felt it was a plea for John to end his negative attitude towards women.

Aged sixteen, Douglas Adams* was queuing outside a gym when the word went round that one of his schoolmates had heard the Beatles' latest single. 'We basically held him against the wall and made him hum it to us.'

John Updike, thirty-six, flush from the success of his novel *Couples*, was enjoying an extended break in London with his family. That late summer, the Beatles 'were very much around'. Sitting in a double-decker bus, Updike looked out of the window and there was Paul walking along the street, 'looking quite unshaven'.

---

* Douglas Adams (1952–2001), author of *The Hitchhiker's Guide to the Galaxy*.

In retrospect, Updike saw 'Hey Jude' as 'a great song of farewell . . . farewell to London, farewell to the Beatles, as it turns out. And it mounts in a way as most of this music does to a kind of ecstasy. It really is a thrilling piece, showing the Beatles at their most adventurous and offhand at the same time.'

Aged seventeen, Gordon Brown* was in hospital, recovering from an operation to save his right eye, having already lost the sight in his left. Forever after, he would associate being in hospital with 'Hey Jude' being played over the air. For him, its message was both melancholy and optimistic: 'It's sad to start with, but actually very positive by the time it ends.'

The philosopher Raymond Tallis was twenty-one, and completing a medical degree at Oxford. More than any other tune, 'Hey Jude' made him feel the spirit of 'infinite possibility you have when you're young'.

This blank canvas of meaning was evident from the start. The first time Paul played the song to John, he was embarrassed by the ricketiness of a particular line: 'the movement you need is on your shoulder'.

'I'll fix that bit,' he assured him.

'You won't, you know,' said John. 'That's the best line in the song. I know what it means – it's great.'

But what exactly, or even inexactly, *does* it mean? Paul, something of a stickler for clarity, had two immediate objections to the line: first, he had already used the word 'shoulders' earlier in the song; and second, 'It's a stupid expression, it sounds like a parrot.' Both are true; yet for some reason, when bound to the music it does make a kind of sense. Until I started writing this book, I had always thought he was singing 'the *moment* you need is on your shoulder', which obviously means something quite different to 'the *movement* you need is on your shoulder'. Yet when I realised that I had been making a mistake for fifty years, I was surprised to find that it made no real difference to the meaning. One makes more sense than the other, but without the music, neither of them makes much sense at all.

Sung to the music, there is something very moving about those words: in fact, they become the key lines of the verse, speaking of kindness, consolation and the need to keep going. We tend to regard music as abstract,

* Gordon Brown (1951–), prime minister 2007–10.

and lyrics as concrete. But in a good song, they are indivisible. Lyrics removed from music are like fish removed from water, or butterflies pinned
to a card.

You could almost say that the more sense lyrics make in print, the less
power they have in song: rock works most powerfully when it is like a
native chant, or a Latin hymn, its scattered meanings transformed into
abstract sound, floating free of specificity. This is why the valiant attempts
of Professor Sir Christopher Ricks to bolster the significance of Bob Dylan
by interpreting his lyrics with the solemnity of academia are doomed. It is
as though a fan of balloons tried to convey his enthusiasm by taking out
a sharp pin and piercing them. Allotting three pages of his five-hundred-
page book *Dylan's Visions of Sin* to the song 'All I Really Want to Do',
Ricks urges the reader to 'notice Dylan's dexterity with "knock you up":

> I ain't lookin' to block you up
> Shock or knock or lock you up.

'The cunning propriety tactfully, pregnantly, separates "knock" from "you
up"; for a couple of words; after all, the preceding "shock" would more
suggest "shock you" than "shock you *up*".'

Under the professor's keen eye, the line 'Why wait any longer for the
one you love' becomes unfathomably complex. 'It is as though "longer"
were a longer form of the word "long", and so it is, but not of this yearning meaning of the word. The feeling of longing is evoked, of longing and
waiting. But how much longer?'

Explaining the end of 'If Not for You', Ricks writes: 'How does the end
of "If Not for You" succeed in ringing true? The inescapable acknowledgement that even gratitude cannot be expressed for ever is brought home by
Dylan's decision to depart from the song with the words "If not for you"
repeated and repeated – in their beautiful simplicity – as if they, though
they have got to go, could go on ad infinitum.' Hang on, Professor, you
want to shout: it's called a fade-out, and is often employed in pop songs
when a producer can't come up with anything better.

Do 'Hey Jude's' words really matter? After all, over the years, many
listeners have misheard them, converting 'Hey Jude' to 'Hey dude', or even
'Hay chewed'. There are those who have spent their whole lives hearing
'The minute you let her under your skin' as 'Remember, there's lettuce un-

der your skin'. Who knows? Perhaps this Rorschach method has increased the impact of the song, each listener unknowingly crafting lyrics appropriate to the particular demands of his or her own existence. Small wonder, in a way, that John thought it was all about him. These days, when Paul sings the song at concerts, he finds the line 'The movement you need is on your shoulder' particularly poignant: 'When I play that song, that's the line when I think of John, and I sometimes get a little emotional during that moment.' So John's suspicion has, to this extent, been proved right: in the mind of its composer and performer, during those few seconds, 'Hey Jude' is indeed a song about John.

The last four minutes of 'Hey Jude' are, of course, virtually wordless, all meaning subsumed by chant. The na-na-na-nanananas are a mantra, its force born of endless repetition. 'Hey Jude' was originally intended as a message of hope for the five-year-old Julian Lennon, but it soon turned into a message of hope for the world. For John Updike, the Beatles were like 'the sun coming up on Easter morning'.

121.

Joel Soroka was twenty-one in 1968. Having grown up in New York, he spent that summer travelling around Europe. It was the first time he had ever left North America. 'In early September, I found myself in a B&B off the Edgware Road. There were no showers or central heating, and we ate rare bacon for breakfast. It was all new to me.'

On 3 September he caught a bus from the Edgware Road to Piccadilly, in order to pick up mail from home. Still new to the complexities of London Transport, he caught the wrong bus back. By chance, an attractive woman sat next to him. 'We got chatting. Then, out of the blue, she asked, "Would you like to meet the Beatles?" I said something like, "Give me a break."' She told him she worked for Apple, and that the Beatles were filming a promotional film for their new single the following night. 'They were looking for a crowd, and she liked my face.'

Handing him what he describes as 'an unofficial-looking piece of paper', she told him to be at Victoria station the next day at 4 p.m: a bus would be waiting.

Joel didn't believe a word of it, but he turned up on the off-chance. Sure enough, a bus was waiting, and, along with many others, he boarded it. 'We were a mixed bag of people and ages, everyone chatting excitedly, but there was a sense that no one believed we were actually going to meet the Beatles.'

They were dropped off at Twickenham Studios, which he thought looked like a hangar, and then led into a brightly lit area, with technical people milling around a platform on which drums and other instruments had been arranged. A group of about a hundred people waited around expectantly, under the gaze of the director Michael Lindsay-Hogg. Suddenly the door opened, and in trooped the Beatles. 'I thought, "Is this really happening?" We were told to hang out while they warmed up. I was in a state of total glee. Despite being a Beatlemaniac, I'd never seen them live.'

The Beatles played 'Hey Jude' three or four times. The coachload of randomers were told to surround the stage and sing along with the chorus. Joel noted that most of them 'were so quiet and British, but I was determined to make my mark'. He wheedled himself into a strategic position close to the platform. At one point Ringo placed his tambourine on the floor and, quick off the mark, Joel seized the opportunity to climb onstage and pick it up.

'I was hoping they'd go with that take, but they did about a dozen. Each time, more and more people joined me onstage. With each take, I was obsessed with getting my hands on the tambourine. I must have been a bit of a bore.'

In between takes, he introduced himself to each of the Beatles. 'Paul was charming. John was sarcastic. I recall him saying, "You're from New York? Did you come to our concerts there?" In the spirit of sarcasm, I replied, "What, pay money to see the Beatles?" I think he liked my reply. George was silent. And Ringo was a sweetheart. "Call me Ritchie," he said.' Joel went around inviting each of the Beatles back to his bed-and-breakfast, but when filming finished they were all whisked away in a limousine.

On Joel's arrival back in New York, no one believed his story, 'but soon after, the film appeared on the Smothers Brothers' show, as well as on *Top of the Pops* in the UK. And there I was.'

In 2020, Joel turned seventy-three. 'They are just people to me now, but in 1968 the Beatles were gods. Other than my children being born, it's the most amazing thing that's happened to me.'

Tom Topping was eleven in 1968, on a month's holiday in London with his parents and his twelve-year-old sister. As they were queuing to see the film of *Yellow Submarine* in Leicester Square, a man with a clipboard approached his father and invited them all to catch a bus from Victoria station to Twickenham the next day. 'For two kids from Los Angeles who loved the Beatles, it was an amazing adventure.'

On one of the takes, Tom managed to nip up onstage and sit next to Paul and his piano. 'I reached over and touched the red velvet dinner jacket like it was the cloak of Turin. Several young women were crowded around, and one was pinching my leg so I would get out of her way. OUCH! She meant business.'

———

Margaret Morel had an American pen-friend, on holiday in London, who tipped off Margaret and her flatmate Coral about the trip to Twickenham. Margaret arrived at Victoria station in a bright yellow dress. When their coach drew up outside the studios, the girls peered out and saw the Beatles watching them through a window, 'giving us smiles and waves. Everyone was very excited and happy, of course.'

Inside the studio, they were told to gather round the Beatles the second the chorus began. 'Paul helped by saying "Now" when it was time to join in.' Coral and Margaret were quick off the mark: 'My friend Coral and I got up onto the stage each time and stood next to George Harrison. I don't know how we managed to do that with all the people who were scrambling to get as near as they could to the Beatles . . . They filmed lots of takes of "Hey Jude" all day. We seemed to sing our na na nas dozens of times. If I remember correctly, they began filming during the morning and we finished about 10 p.m. or later. My friend's parents came to collect us with their car. We were exhausted but very happy, our heads full of all that had taken place that day.'

Unfortunately, when the film was premiered four days later, on David Frost's show, Margaret's boss happened to be watching, so he spotted Margaret in her yellow dress standing next to George. 'I was supposed to be ill that day and had taken the day off,' recalls Margaret. 'I swore it wasn't me.' Her boss graciously accepted her denial. 'He was a lovely man and just let me think he believed me.'

In the finished film, the Beatles appear to be alone in the studio until Paul leads into the chorus, at which point lots of people flood in to join them, including a man in a purple turban, a woman in a large white dress, a black man in a fancy waistcoat and a heavily-made-up blonde sporting an elaborate hairdo. They all race to grab a prominent spot beside Paul. Despite jockeying for position, they look relaxed and delighted to be there. Two young boys, one in a tweed jacket and tie and horn-rimmed specs, the other in a more groovy military jacket, secure themselves places on either side of Ringo, who gives them a broad grin. Not for the first time, he seems the happiest of all the Beatles.

Six minutes in, a toothless old geezer appears, a hippy Albert Steptoe, with large flowers tucked behind both ears. Just as bizarrely, he is holding a flat brown package of some sort. He introduces a note of jeopardy into the proceedings. Every now and then, he sees it as his duty to turn around and conduct all the others. At one point he nudges up very close to Paul, and touches him on his shoulder. For a second Paul shows a flash of irritation – the movement he doesn't need is on his shoulder – and brushes him off.

As the years have rolled by, this batty old geezer has become an object of fascination in online discussion groups.

'Does anyone know who the strange old guy at the end of Hey Jude annoying Paul is?'

'I don't remember his name . . . He was a local drunkard and possibly homeless man who was hanging out nearby, so they brought him in. He kind of ruins the video but at the same time makes it better.'

'He looks like a man who used to wander the streets of London's Soho back then (1968). We all called him "Rosie" in reference to his penchant for floral adornments, although I think he usually wore carnations as in the video. Not sure how he made it out to Twickenham though.'

'His name was Bill and he helped the Beatles with Magical Mystery Tour.'

'Where does he come from and why is there a piece of cardboard pinched under his right armpit? And what is the black object that he is raising in the air with his left hand at 6:31 and again at 6:50? Is it a bottle? Why is he showing this? This object is gone at 7:14.'

The more one looks at the 'Hey Jude' video, the more mesmerising this batty old codger becomes. Like everybody else, he is in the right place at the right time, but unlike the others, he is the wrong person in the right place at the right time. Yet he doesn't hesitate to make the most of it. Bursting with self-confidence, he edges closer and closer to Paul, orchestrating the crowd, bursting with joie-de-vivre, proudly convinced of his own indispensability.

Beatle-watchers devote an inordinate amount of time to identifying this oddball. He is, in his way, the British equivalent of the umbrella man in Dealey Plaza.

'Is there a connection with the red carnations and left-handed guitar made of white carnations on the cover of Sgt Pepper? What is the connection to the carnations in the booklet accompanying the Magical Mystery Tour album?'

'What puzzles me most is that he touches the right shoulder of Paul twice. First at 7:26 and again at 7:36 . . . And then at 7:46 he looks upwards and points his left hand forefinger to the ceiling.'

The Beatles shone so brightly that anyone caught in their beam, no matter how briefly, became part of their myth.

122.

In Beatles mythology, Detective Sergeant Norman Clement 'Nobby' Pilcher looms like a bumbling avenging angel. He is Tom trying to trap Jerry, Jaws snapping at innocent bathers, Cruella de Vil sizing up dalmatians for the slaughter, or – perhaps closer to the reality – a Keystone Kop balancing a bucket of water on top of a door then forgetting all about it and getting soaked himself.

Five years older than John and Ringo, Norman Pilcher joined the Metropolitan Police in 1955, moving from the Flying Squad to the Drugs Squad in 1966, the very same year the Beatles were urging the young to turn off their minds, relax and float downstream. Pastimes such as these were far from Pilcher's agenda: he wanted to bring criminals to justice, by whatever means possible.

One of Pilcher's earliest victims, Eric Clapton, described him, not inaccurately, as 'a kind of police groupie'. He was an autograph-hunter with handcuffs at the ready. He would keep an eye out for glassy-eyed singers and musicians, then target them for immediate investigation. As a consequence, his own fame began to rise commensurately.

Det. Sgt Pilcher conducted his first celebrity raid on 11 June 1966. Some weeks previously he had taken a keen interest in *A Boy Called Donovan*, a TV documentary about the hippy lifestyle of the fey, self-styled 'troubadour', in whose most recent single, 'Sunshine Superman', he had detected clear references to blowing minds. Its B-side, 'The Trip', was even more explicit.

In the documentary, louche long-haired young men and groovy women were seen lying around on cushions, playing guitars, handing around cigarettes shaped like barrage balloons and talking about freedom and love and ending all wars. It ended with two policemen entering one of these free-and-easy gatherings, apparently hosted by Donovan, searching about, finding nothing and leaving empty-handed. At this point Donovan gave

a big, bleary wink to the camera, brazenly signalling that he himself was under the influence and couldn't care less who knew it.

Pilcher had found his next target. A few weeks later, he led nine Drugs Squad officers on a raid of Donovan's flat in the Edgware Road. There, in the bedroom of the singer's friend 'Gypsy Dave' Mills, they found a block of cannabis resin. Donovan, Gypsy Dave and a lady friend were immediately arrested and charged with possession.

George and Paul rallied around, hiring their lawyer, David Jacobs, to represent the accused. But they were found guilty, and fined £250. Eight months later, in February 1967, Pilcher sanctioned a raid on Keith Richards's house, 'Redlands', in West Wittering, narrowly missing George and Pattie Harrison, who had left just a few minutes before.

And so it continued. On 19 August 1968, Pilcher successfully raided the flat of the jazz musician Tubby Hayes, charging him with possession of diamorphine and heroin. Later that month Donovan received an urgent call from John, who said: 'I just got a call from a friend. I'm going to be busted.' Donovan and Gypsy Dave drove down to Surrey, where they found John 'swaggering like a sailor, his long hair flying, angry and ready to fight'. Donovan tried to calm him down: 'Leave it to Gyp, he knows what to do.'

On a long glass coffee table were what Donovan recognised straight away as 'three pyramids of sinsemilla', a highly psychoactive variety of cannabis, the latest of a batch delivered to John every three months by a wealthy American admirer, hidden in the wings of a Mercedes. John sat back and played a Howlin' Wolf song on his jukebox while Gypsy Dave and Donovan took charge of flushing the pyramids down the loo.

According to Donovan, they had just concluded another round of vigorous flushing when Det. Sgt Pilcher arrived. Finding nothing, he 'assembled his men in the hall and said, "Next time we will get you, Lennon, mark my words."' Donovan looked on askance. 'I thought John was going to nut him then and there, but Gyp held him back. As the cops filed out of the door John held it open for them, then crashed it shut with a "Good bloody riddance. Fuck off you bastards!" And they were gone.'

John's actor friend Victor Spinetti remembers the incident slightly differently. In his version Donovan was already at John's house, getting ready to show a film, when someone phoned with a tip-off. 'Oh God,' said John, 'there's going to be a police raid.' He scooted around the house, picking up the cannabis, throwing it down the loo and attempting to flush it: 'It took forever to float away, but then it was a silly place to put it.' John then spotted something in a box, snatched it up and buried it in the garden. 'At that moment, the police barged in, went upstairs, woke Julian, John's son, and shook out his bed, this child's bed! There was nothing hidden in it. After that they went right through the house, ransacking the place. We just sat there.' According to Spinetti the police left the house empty-handed, but not before asking John for an autograph.

Two months later John and Yoko were living in Ringo's flat in Montagu Square. One Friday Pete Shotton dropped by, only to find John hard at work with the vacuum cleaner.

'Oh Christ, Pete! Am I glad to see you! The Drug Squad's on the way!'

This time John had been tipped off by Don Short, the showbusiness correspondent of the *Daily Mirror*, who had himself been tipped off by the police. Before embarking on a raid, Pilcher liked to be sure of publicity.

John grew ever more frantic with his cleaning. 'Jimi fucking Hendrix used to live here!' he yelled as he rammed the Hoover back and forth against the walls. 'Christ knows what the fuck is in these carpets!'

While Pete and John bustled about looking for anything incriminat-
ing, John disappeared into the bedroom. Through the door, Pete heard
him arguing with Yoko. It soon dawned on Pete that they were arguing
about him. 'I don't want him here! I just don't want him here!' screeched
Yoko. The two of them had never got along.

'Well, I fucking want him here!' replied John. 'We can use a bit of fucking help right now, and Pete just wants to help us!'

'We can handle this ourselves, John, we don't need HIM around! I
don't *want* him around!'

Tactfully, Pete let himself out, taking the vacuum-cleaner bag with
him. Just before midnight, six policemen and one policewoman arrived on
the doorstep. Yoko opened the door for just long enough to hear the policewoman say they had a search warrant. Then, in the measured words of
Det. Sgt Pilcher, 'Upon being informed that we were police officers and the
reason for our visit, she ran back along the passage into the flat and slammed
and locked the door.'

At the same time, an officer nipped round to the back of the building,
and attempted to open the bedroom window while John held it shut, shouting, 'I don't care who you are, you're not bloody coming in here!' Then
Yoko took over window duty while John got dressed.

'Just open the window! You'll only make it worse for yourself!' shouted
the officer.

'I want to see the warrant!' John shouted back. The police pressed the
warrant to the window, and he pretended to read it. The police then tried
to force the front door. Grudgingly, John let them in.

The police contingent included two dog handlers, but for some reason
they had neglected to bring their dogs. In the half-hour it took for them to
arrive John rang Neil Aspinall, who in turn rang Peter Brown, who was
busy shepherding Paul's latest discovery, the innocent Welsh songstress
Mary Hopkin, between her various appointments. Brown raced round to
find John and Yoko being formally charged with possession: the sniffer
dogs, blessed with the inappropriately happy-go-lucky names of Yogi and
Boo-Boo,* had apparently uncovered cannabis in a leather binocular case
and a suitcase. John was mystified – in his words, 'I'm not stupid. I went
through the whole damn house.'

---

* Or were they pseudonyms?

By now, the press had assembled in force outside the building. They watched John and Yoko being taken to Paddington Green police station, where they were each bailed for £100, and booked to appear in court the next morning.

Their hearing lasted five minutes. Det. Sgt Pilcher read out the two charges against them, one for possession of a dangerous drug, the other for 'wilfully obstructing Norman Pilcher, a constable of the Metropolitan Police Force . . .' The case was adjourned until 28 November. On leaving the courtroom, John and Yoko were forced to wait in a scrum of journalists and photographers for their car to arrive. Never slow to turn a mishap to their advantage, they included one of these photographs on the back cover of their next album, *Unfinished Music No 2: Life with the Lions*.

Two days after their court appearance, a Labour MP tabled a written question to the Home Secretary, James Callaghan, drawing attention to the excessive use of manpower in the raid. In his defence, hand-delivered to the Home Secretary, Det. Sgt Pilcher explained that 'at least five officers were required because of the difficulty in gaining entry to the premises and the fact that the premises consisted of two floors with numerous rooms that were in a very untidy condition'. He had needed extra manpower, he said, because 'it is not unusual when executing search warrants for premises occupied by members of the entertainment world to find that there are large numbers of people present taking part in unusual parties. In this case it was found that only two persons were present, and both were in a state of undress.'

Two days later, Mr Callaghan was asked 'to what extent the Metropolitan Police notified the press and publicity services of their intention to raid the private residence of John Lennon'. Det. Sgt Pilcher denied he had leaked news of the forthcoming raid, suggesting that a neighbour might have been responsible. However, an internal police report later concluded that 'One thing is certain as far as this incident is concerned, and that is the press was informed by somebody.'

Five months later, Pilcher struck again. This time he chose the day of Paul and Linda's wedding to raid George's home in Esher, imagining no one would be in. But, unknown to Pilcher, Paul had decided against inviting the other Beatles and their partners. This meant that Pattie was at home, waiting for George to drop by later to take her to a party in London: 'Suddenly I heard a lot of cars on the gravel in the drive – far too many for it to be just George. My first thought was that maybe Paul and Linda wanted to party after the wedding. Then the bell rang. I opened the door to find a crowd of uniformed policemen, one policewoman and a dog.'

The senior policeman introduced himself as Detective Sergeant Pilcher, and showed her his search warrant. 'In they came, about eight policemen through the front, another five or six through the back, and there were more in the greenhouse.' Yogi and Boo-Boo came too. George was later to suspect that Pilcher named Yogi after the Maharishi – not unlikely, given Pilcher's peculiarly needy relationship with those he sought to prosecute.

Pattie rang George at Apple. Calmly, George said he would sort something out. Soon the ever-faithful Pete Shotton, who lived around the corner, arrived. As the police scoured the bungalow, Pattie poured herself and Pete a vodka and tonic. Pete pulled out a packet of Rothmans, only to remember with a start that among the cigarettes were a couple of joints. Suddenly Det. Sgt Pilcher appeared. 'Look what Yogi has found!' he said to Pattie, brandishing a block of hash.

'Are you mad?' said Pattie. 'You brought that with you.'

Pilcher denied it: 'Yogi found it in one of your husband's shoes.'

'This is a joke,' retorted Pattie, adding, with beguiling honesty, 'If we had a lump of hash like that we certainly wouldn't keep it in George's shoes. If you'd said at the start you were looking for cannabis, I would have told you it's in the sitting room on the table in a pot. But you said you were looking for drugs. I thought you meant heroin or something dangerous . . .'

Pilcher was not amused. 'I want to save you from the evils and peril of heroin,' he said, or she said he said.

Pattie replied that she'd never touch heroin. She then accused Pilcher once again of planting the lump of hash. There was silence.

'Now what are you all going to do?' she asked.

'Any chance of a cup of tea?' asked Pilcher.

'Well, I'm not going to make it.'

To this day, the correct etiquette in such a situation remains hazy. As it was, a policewoman boiled the kettle and handed out the mugs. The various policemen then stood around looking awkward. One asked if they could watch the television. Another tried to break the ice with a polite question: 'Have the Beatles been doing any new music?'

'Yes,' snapped Pattie, 'but you're not going to hear it.'

Pete asked them about life in the Drugs Squad. Had they ever taken drugs, just so they'd know what they were after? One of them said he'd run his finger along someone's mantelpiece and then licked it, only to find himself embarking on an acid trip.

In a while, George arrived, together with Derek Taylor and a lawyer. Taylor noted how much the police were in awe of George: at the tender age of twenty-five he was, after all, one of the four most famous men in the world: 'They stood to attention and were almost elbowing each other out of the way to get closer to him.' Calm in the face of adversity, George ascended to a higher plain. 'Birds have their nests and animals have their holes,' he said, 'but the son of man hath nowhere to lay his head.' Perhaps not catching the biblical allusion, Det. Sgt Pilcher arrested him.

George was scornful of the two pieces of evidence produced by Pilcher and his officers. His defence was both novel and, within its own limits, persuasive: one piece of dope was indeed his, 'but I've never seen this one before in my fucking life! You don't have to bring your own dope to my house, I've got plenty myself! I could have shown you where the stuff was if you'd asked me.'

Later, he explained that he was exceptionally tidy by nature: 'I keep records in the record rack, tea in the tea caddy, pot in the pot box. This was the biggest stick of hashish I've ever seen, and something I'd obviously know about if I had seen it before.'

As George and Pattie were leaving for the police station, a press photographer appeared and started snapping away, causing George to lose his cool. 'What the fuck do you think you're doing on my property? I'm going to fucking kill you, you bastard!' He chased the photographer around the garden, followed, hot on his heels, by the Drug Squad. 'I couldn't help but laugh,' recalled Pete – it reminded him of a Marx Brothers chase.

At the police station, George and Pattie were fingerprinted and charged. 'We got home feeling gloomy,' recalled Pattie, 'so George said, "Come on, let's go to the party."'

The party in question was being thrown by the talented Old Etonian painter and musician Rory McEwen. As they entered, George and Pattie bumped into Lord Snowdon and Princess Margaret. 'You can't believe what happened,' said George. 'We got busted.'

'What a shame,' said Princess Margaret.

'Can you help us?' asked George. 'Can you use your influence?'

'Oh, I don't think so!' replied the princess, with a look of alarm.

Pattie's youngest sister Paula, who was also present, failed to pick up the signs. Instead, she lit a joint, took a puff and offered it to the princess, who abruptly turned on her heels and left, taking her baffled husband with her.

At Esher and Walton magistrates' court the following March, George and Pattie Harrison were found guilty of possession of cannabis and fined £250 each, plus ten guineas each in costs. 'I hope the police will leave us alone now,' George said as they left court.

The next month, George and Eric Clapton dropped in on an early-evening party given by the drug charity Release, but they didn't stay long. Soon after their departure, Det. Sgt Pilcher arrived with his band of officers from the Drugs Squad, demanding to know the whereabouts of Harrison and Clapton. Told that they were on their way to a B.B. King concert at the Royal Albert Hall, he sighed and left.

Like so many who bobbed along in the wake of the Beatles, Det. Sgt Norman Pilcher tried to keep up with them, but ended up lost at sea. In 1972 he resigned from the Metropolitan Police in shadowy circumstances. Towards the end of that year he boarded a liner bound for Australia, where he planned to start a new life; but on his arrival at Fremantle he was arrested on charges of perjury and conspiracy to pervert the course of justice, and extradited back to Britain.

In September 1973, Pilcher was sentenced to four years in custody. The tables had turned. 'You poisoned the wells of criminal justice and set about it deliberately,' said Justice Melford Stevenson, never chummy. 'What is equally bad is that you have betrayed your comrades in the Metropolitan Police Force, which enjoys the respect of the civilised world – what remains of it.'

Thereafter, Norman Pilcher disappears from view, though some say he retired to Kent. But his legend lives on. Time has made a pantomime figure of him: the clodhopping, evidence-planting copper, mesmerised by those he yearns to bring down, rapping on the door after his prey has skedaddled. Yet he has achieved a form of immortality. In one *Monty Python* sketch he was immortalised as a giant hedgehog called Spiny Norman, 'twelve feet from snout to tail', who sleeps in an aeroplane hangar at Luton

Airport and spies on the notorious gangsters the Piranha Brothers. In another he is Police Constable Pan-Am, bent on arresting everyone, including witnesses and victims: 'I must warn you that anything you may say will be ignored . . . One more peep out of you and I'll do you for heresy . . . I'm charging you with illegal possession of whatever we happen to have down there.' In Eric Idle and Neil Innes's spoof Beatles documentary *The Rutles*, he is Detective Inspector Brian Plant, who plants Indian tea and biscuits on a member of the Rutles.

Norman Pilcher is also often credited as the 'semolina pilchard' in 'I am the Walrus', though the dates don't support it: the song was recorded in September 1967, just over a year before Det. Sgt Pilcher first turned up uninvited on the doorstep of Montagu Square.

123.

On 26 August 1968, the first four Apple singles – 'Hey Jude' by the Beatles, 'Those Were the Days' by Mary Hopkin, 'Sour Milk Sea' by Jackie Lomax, and 'Thingumybob' by the Black Dyke Mills Band – were delivered by chauffeur-driven Mercedes to HM the Queen at Buckingham Palace, HM the Queen Mother at St James's Palace, and HRH Princess Margaret and Lord Snowdon at Kensington Palace. A few days later, this letter was received:

Dear Sir:

I am commanded by Queen Elizabeth the Queen Mother to send Her Majesty's thanks for so kindly sending the four new records recently made by the Apple Corps. Her Majesty is greatly touched by this kind thought from the Beatles and their new company, and has much enjoyed listening to these recordings.

Yours faithfully,

Jean Rankin, Lady-in-waiting,

Birkhall, Ballater

124.

On Saturday, 23 October 2010, a small crowd of people, among them a handful of dignitaries from English Heritage, gathered for a ceremony outside 34 Montagu Square, just five doors away from where Anthony Trollope once lived. Yoko Ono delivered a brief speech, in the precise, businesslike manner of her near-contemporary, Queen Elizabeth II.

'I am very honoured to unveil this blue plaque, and thank English Heritage for honouring John in this way. This particular flat has many memories for me and is a very interesting part of our history. In what would have been John's seventieth year, I am grateful to you all for commemorating John and this particular part of his London life, one which spawned so much of his great music and great art.'

To a smattering of polite applause, she pulled a cord, causing two red velvet curtains to swing apart and reveal London's latest blue plaque:

JOHN LENNON

1940–1980

MUSICIAN

AND SONGWRITER

LIVED HERE IN

1968

In February 1965, Ringo had signed a rental agreement on Flat 1, 34 Montagu Square, shortly before his marriage to Maureen Cox. The residents did their best to take it in their stride. 'We're a very distinguished square,' Lord Mancroft, a former Conservative minister, told a journalist, 'and I'm sure we'll welcome such a distinguished gentleman and his lady.'

The flat consisted of two bedrooms and a living room on the ground floor, with a further living room and a kitchen in the basement. 'The flat was small and impractical,' was the snooty verdict of Brian Epstein's assistant Peter Brown, 'but Ringo and Maureen insisted on it.'

Ringo and Maureen contracted Brian's designer, Ken Partridge, to decorate it. They wanted him to complete the task within a month, while the Beatles were off shooting *Help!*. Ringo returned to find the first-floor living room covered with blue silk wallpaper and furnished with the streamlined white ultra-modern chairs, tables and sofas that were all the rage. Silk curtains and lead-streaked mirrors abounded, and the fashionable picture was completed by a sunken bath in the ground floor's en suite pink bathroom.

Ringo's passion for electronic gadgets was also well represented, with a wide selection of televisions, burglar alarms and record players. Visitors recall telephones 'every four or five feet'– a bright red phone in the principal bedroom had a direct line to Mr Epstein.

Within days of the Starrs' arrival, Beatles fans were flocking to gaze at no. 34, causing much neighbourly upset. By August, complaints were coming from the Swiss embassy, which backed onto no. 34; inconsiderate fans had apparently been defacing the back wall with graffiti, much of it lewd. 'It is now very unsightly,' explained an embassy spokesman. 'Our chauffeur, who is French and took part in the First World War, says the language some of these young people use is worse than anything he ever heard in the trenches.'

In July the Starrs moved away, to 'Sunny Heights' in Weybridge, renting their Montagu Square flat to Paul, who was living with the Ashers in Wimpole Street but needed a studio. Paul immediately converted the basement room into a makeshift studio, and let his electronics technician Ian Sommerville live in the bedroom.

In those carefree days the flat fast became a fashionable hang-out, with modish figures like John Dunbar, Christopher Gibbs, Barry Miles and Robert Fraser regularly dropping by. One of the more unbudgeable visitors was Sommerville's boyfriend William S. Burroughs, the spindly avant-garde American author of *Junky* and *The Naked Lunch*. Burroughs was still notorious, and in some circles celebrated, for a drunken party trick that went horribly awry. One evening in Mexico in 1951, he had encouraged his wife Joan to balance a glass on the top of her head. Saying, 'It's time for our William Tell act,' he then fired his .380 automatic at it. Sadly, his aim was skew-whiff, and Joan slumped forward, dead. Silence ensued. 'Bill, I think you hit her,' observed a guest.

Joan's death was no hindrance to Burroughs's renown; in fact it proved a boon, sealing his reputation as a literary daredevil. From then on, he could expound uninterrupted on his mescaline-fuelled dreams, while retaining the interest of the hip and the cool.

Burroughs favoured 'the cut-up', a method of writing involving cutting words and phrases out of books and newspapers, then lining them up at random to, in the words of one enthusiast, 'create entirely new texts . . . to reveal the secret meaning of things'. In reality, it resulted in free-floating gibberish: 'Old Mother Hubbard show business went to the cupboard to get the cowboy boots dog in the family he was known when he said that blackout falaling Christmas day slithery hood bar for the dog boots a drunk policeman.' Burroughs's influence on John was considerable, particularly in songs like 'I am the Walrus' and 'Happiness is a Warm Gun'. In return, the Beatles honoured him with a place on the cover of *Sgt. Pepper*.

He spent hours in Montagu Square experimenting on a Uher tape-recorder with 'musical cut-ups' and 'sleep recordings'. Paul was happy to allow him to use the flat in this way, even if he never felt entirely on Burroughs's wavelength. For his part, Burroughs described Paul as 'very pleasant and prepossessing. Nice-looking young man, fairly hardworking.'

After Paul bought his own home in Cavendish Avenue, Ringo, the most easy-going of landlords, let Jimi Hendrix move into the Montagu Square flat with Chas Chandler of the Animals and their respective girlfriends,

Kathy Etchingham and Lotta Null. Fresh from an argument with Kathy, Hendrix composed 'The Wind Cries Mary'. On another occasion, high on acid, he hurled paint over Ringo's prized silk wallpaper. In the end, Ringo asked him to leave; after Hendrix's departure, he had the flat repainted white.

In June 1968, Cynthia and Julian retreated to Montagu Square after Yoko moved into Kenwood. Three months later they switched places with John and Yoko, who complained that they found life in the country boring.

John and Yoko proved barely more houseproud than Jimi Hendrix. In the words of one visitor, 'They existed on a diet of champagne, caviar and heroin.' Hoovering and washing up were out of the question.

One day John asked his dogsbody Tony Bramwell to set up a camera with a timer, and to teach him how to operate it. The following day he furtively handed Bramwell the film for developing: 'They're a bit risqué, you know. Don't let anyone see them, know what I mean?'

When the developed photographs arrived at Apple, Peter Brown thought they were a sick joke. 'They were so scandalous that I locked them away in my desk drawer and didn't share them with anyone.' In his fastidious fashion, he wanted to look neither at Yoko, 'smiling coyly, her breasts sagging towards the floor', nor at John, 'glassy-eyed and heroin-stoned . . . grinning idiotically, so proud to be exposing to the world his shrivelled, uncircumcised penis'. He was almost more upset by the state of the flat. 'The bedroom is a pigsty, a junkie's haven of rumpled sheets, dirty clothes, newspapers and magazines heaped all over the floor.'

A few days later John announced that one of these photographs, of himself and Yoko stark naked, staring at the camera, was to be the cover of their new album, *Two Virgins*. According to Bramwell, on hearing the news everyone in the office 'fell about laughing . . . Yoko was not a pretty sight, but she and John in the buff together were plain embarrassing. None of us thought they would go through with it.'

Up until then, John had exhibited a decidedly prim attitude towards nudity. Entering a birthday party for Allen Ginsberg in June 1965, he and Cynthia had been greeted by the hairy Beat poet wearing nothing but boxer shorts on his head and a 'Do Not Disturb' sign on his penis. John was not amused: 'You don't do that in front of the birds.'

In a strange way, John also tried to disassociate himself from the naked figure on the cover of *Two Virgins*. In a rambling interview with *Rolling Stone* later that year, he said: 'When we got the pictures back, I admit that I was a bit shocked. Of course, I've never seen my prick on an album or on a photo before. I thought, "Hello! What on earth? There's a fellow with his prick out" . . . You're not used to it, being naked.'

When John and Yoko showed their proposed cover to Ringo, he didn't know where to look. Searching for something to say, he pointed at a copy of *The Times* in the photograph, lying on the floor beside John's feet, and remarked, 'Oh, you've even got *The Times* in it.' But he then grew less bashful. 'I said, "Ah, come on, John. You're doing all this stuff, and it may be cool for you, but you know we all have to answer for it."'

Paul was more vehemently opposed. Peter Brown recalled that he 'hated the cover beyond words', while Bramwell saw him having 'seven thousand kinds of fits. He thought it was disgusting, and was absolutely appalled that John was seriously intending to go through with it.' According to Bramwell, Paul put the blame on Yoko: 'John had been very prudish before he met Yoko. Now, Paul argued, she had released his inhibitions, to disastrous effect. "Doesn't John realise that we're all in this together? . . . It might be him and Yoko, but people will say it's the Beatles who are out of their tree and getting into straight porn."'

Paul called a meeting with John and Yoko and Sir Joseph Lockwood, the chairman of EMI. Sir Joseph kicked off the discussion by saying that he didn't find the pictures obscene. It was a clever tactic, undermining John and Yoko's desire to be seen as *enfants terribles*.

> JOHN: Well, aren't you shocked?
> SIR JOSEPH: No, I've seen worse than this.
> JOHN: So, it's all right then, is it?
> SIR JOSEPH: No, it's not all right. I'm not worried about the rich
>   people, the duchesses and those people who follow you. But your
>   mums and dads and girl fans will object strongly. You will be
>   damaged, and what will you gain? What's the purpose of it?
> YOKO: It's art.
> SIR JOSEPH: Well then, why not show Paul in the nude? He's so much
>   prettier!

In the end, Sir Joseph declared that EMI would not distribute the album with the naked cover, though they would manufacture the record itself for their usual fee. It was eventually released on the Apple label and distributed by the Who's label, Track. It was sold in record shops wrapped in a plain brown wrapper. Inevitably, many people bought *Two Virgins* for the cover alone: for some of the Beatles' younger fans, it was to be their first ever glimpse of grown-ups in the nude.

125.

Around the age of seven, I realised that the Beatles were watching me. I would become aware, every so often, that there were four heads lined up alongside my bedroom door or peering around the wall. The tops of torsos would be just visible, reassuringly constrained in jackets, white collars and black ties. They would make their presence felt at an awkward moment – when I was getting dressed, for instance. I would hastily rearrange my clothes, pulling pyjamas off and on through underwear, so that at no point was any flesh exposed. I thought the Beatles might be rather impressed, both by my modesty and dexterity.

Generally though, like the black mammies in old films, they were there for the big moments. When I finished a race on sports day, they were there at the touchline, clapping their hands. If I sustained an injury in the playground, they would be there, peering round nurse's door, shaking their heads and clicking their tongues, doubtless noting how brave I was being.

I wanted to contain the Beatles within my thoughts; there they would stay the same, protected from the vicissitudes of reality. Unfortunately, the real Beatles endlessly changed. The Beatles of my thoughts were usually about two changes behind. No sooner had I grown accustomed to them in casual clothes (*Revolver*) than I had to learn to visualise them in weird silk soldiers' uniforms (*Sgt. Pepper*).

I first heard *Sgt. Pepper* with my friend Fiona. My dislike of change meant I was always the last to hear new albums. And my conviction that the Beatles should have been frozen in time in 1964 was borne out by what seemed to me a downward spiral of sex and drugs. I was told of allusions to drugs in several songs; I myself came across shocking allusions to sex such as 'Girl, you let your knickers down' in 'I am the Walrus'. I was in Fiona's playroom when I examined with horror a poster of John in the nude. So that was what John *really* looked like; what he had really looked like all along. For a moment I felt duped.

I began a Lett's schoolgirl diary in 1969. After months of 'nothing much happened today', I introduced a mysterious new character, an older brother, 'Alicky'. I savoured imaginary conversations in which I revealed to my friends, under appropriate duress, the real identity of Alicky – Paul McCartney.

I pictured their expressions of amazement and admiration. Alas, despite months of intriguing entries – 'Went to Abbey Road', 'Saw John today' – nobody other than myself ever saw the diary.

When the Beatles broke up in 1970, I had a small sense of heartbreak. Noting that my friends had moved on and were indifferent, I snatched up the mantle of grief with righteous relish. I can't recall to what extent I was pretending. I know I would get a drawing ache in the chest and then remember, with a slight pang of anguish, what had gone wrong. I know I felt amazed that this change had happened without my having the least intimation of it.

But I didn't cry. This was awkward, as I felt that in order to serve honour I ought to shed tears every night. Instead, I had to lie in bed imagining certain songs in my head – 'And I Love Her' or 'Let it Be' – in order to squeeze a tear from each eye. As the long-awaited drops finally trickled over the bridge of my nose I felt sure the Beatles would be moved by my devotion.

By the time I was thirty, I wanted to embrace classical music but found the Beatles endlessly impinging. Jumbles of lyrics continued to flow through my head like so many unruly, uninvited guests: like 'rain into a paper cup'. And whenever I heard the date 18 June, I would try to prevent the association springing up – but I was never quick enough to quell the tiny, jubilant voice: 'It's Paul's birthday!'

126.

Of all the intellectuals who disliked the Beatles, none did so for so long, or with such passion, as Anthony Burgess.

'I have normally only to see a photograph of the Beatles to start shivering with ague,' he wrote in *The Listener* on October 1963. '. . . Obviously the phenomenon will last as long as the money: there's certainly plenty of that to be made. But what, in God's name, are we going to do about these children, with their screechings as in orgasm, their distorted faces, their cutting-off of the higher centres?'

In 1968 Burgess was interviewed by Tony Palmer for his celebrated documentary about contemporary pop music, *All My Loving*. In the Crush Bar of the Royal Opera House, Burgess railed against youth culture in general, and the Beatles in particular:

'I remember an old proverb which says: "Youth thinks itself wise, just as drunk men think themselves sober." Youth is not wise; youth knows nothing about life. Youth knows nothing about anything except a mass of clichés which, for the most part, through the media of pop songs, are just foisted on them by middle-aged entrepreneurs and exploiters who should know better.'

The same year, at the age of fifty-one, Burgess published a novel, *Enderby Outside*, in which his anarchist hero Enderby nurses a hatred for Yod Crewsy, of Yod Crewsy and the Fixers, who has just made a movie in the Bahamas, and received an MBE in the Birthday Honours. Crewsy is now being enrolled as a Fellow of the Royal Society of Literature: 'There were cheers. The guests of honour had come at last, embraced and worshipped from their very entrance. Hogg stopped mixing to have a good look at them. They were, he thought, about as horrible in appearance as it was possible any four young men to be.' The four of them 'were vulgarly at home, punching each other in glee and then doing a kind of ring-a-roses round the prime minister'.

Crewsy is a plagiarist, fraud and solipsist, as well as a terrible poet. To an adoring audience, he reads a few lines of one of his poems, adding, 'Don't ask me what it means; I only wrote it. No, serious like, I feel very humble. But I put them poems together in this book just like to show. You know, show that we do like think a bit and the kvadrats, or squares which is what some of you squares here would like call yourselves, can't have it all their own way.'

Burgess's loathing of the Beatles continued long after they disbanded. 'The words of their songs, pathetic when compared with Cole Porter, are so vapid that psychedelic meanings have to be imposed on them,' he complained. He particularly scorned those of the intelligentsia, like Kenneth Tynan, who promoted their 'twanging nonsense' over Wagner and Beethoven: 'Do they merit vitriol, even a drop of it? Yes, because they corrupt the young, persuading them that the mature world, which produced Beethoven and Schweitzer, sets an even higher value on the transient anodynes of youth than does youth itself. For this they stink to heaven.'

As he grew older, Burgess prayed that there would be a special circle of hell set aside for the Beatles, in which they would be bound to 'a white-hot turntable (45rpm for ever and ever) stuck all over with blunt and rusty acoustic needles, each tooth hollowed to the raw nerve and filled with a micro-transistor (thirty-two pop stations blaring through all eternity thirty-two worn flip-sides into their sinuses), an eternal Ringo battering the tympanic membrane'.

127.

Others let their resentment simmer.

A year after the death of Joe Orton, the Beatles were still searching around for material for their next feature film. Might *The Lord of the Rings* be suitable? In February 1968 Donovan had brought Tolkien's trilogy out to Rishikesh, giving John, Paul and George each a volume to read; Ringo was no bookworm, preferring comics.

Soon after the Beatles' return to England, there were rumours in the music press that they would be starring in an adaptation of *The Lord of the Rings*. Paul would play the lovable Frodo Baggins, Ringo his loyal sidekick Sam Gamgee, and George the wizard Gandalf. John was to play Gollum. His casting might have channelled a secret empathy, as his feelings towards his group were akin to Gollum's towards the ring: 'He loved it and hated it, just as he hated and loved himself.'

With its elves, quests and magic, *The Lord of the Rings* attracted a strong hippy following. Though forged in the trenches of the First World War, it would be possible to overlay it with a dreamy, psychedelic vision derived from the recent songs of the Beatles.

As the year progressed, the talk turned to the director. Who should it be? David Lean? Antonioni? John's favourite film of 1968 was *2001: A Space Odyssey*; he said he planned to watch it every week. One day he called on the film's director, Stanley Kubrick, hoping to spark his interest. But he came away disappointed: Kubrick told him it was too large and complex ever to be adapted for the screen. John complained to Pete Shotton about Kubrick's negativity. How, he grumbled, could the guy who directed *2001* be so 'nowhere'?

Soon afterwards, Victor Spinetti, a mainstay of *A Hard Day's Night* and *Help!*, was sitting in bed at home when the doorbell rang. It was the postman, with a parcel from Apple Corps. There were four books: *The Hobbit*

and the *Lord of the Rings* trilogy. He started to read them, but found the process effortful. Before he had got very far, the telephone rang.

It was John. 'Have you got the books? They're going to do a film. We'll be the hobbits and you'll be Gandalf.'

Spinetti agreed to press on, but 'it was no use. I found them turgid and twee.'

He phoned John back. 'What do you think?' asked John.

'Oh, John,' sighed Spinetti. 'I couldn't finish –'

'That's all right, neither could I. Forget it.'

Nevertheless, the Beatles persisted with the project, the only barrier being Professor Tolkien himself. Fifty years their senior, and by nature a traditionalist, he nursed a particular dislike of pop music, born of bitter experience. In 1964, at the height of Beatlemania, a local band used to re-hearse in a garage close to Tolkien's home on Oxford's Sandfield Road. He had detested the racket. 'In a house three doors away dwells a member of a group of young men who are evidently aiming to turn them into a Beatle Group,' he wrote to a friend. '. . . The noise is indescribable.'

Four years later, when the Beatles approached him to turn his trilogy into a film, Professor Tolkien's mind drifted back to the hullaballoo that had assailed him from that garage down the road. Thinking no more about it, he turned them down without further ado.

128.

I ended my first term of boarding at Farleigh House in July 1965. The headmaster and founder of the school was Jocelyn Trappes-Lomax, a tubby man in his early sixties who was in the habit of wearing the same uniform as his pupils (grey flannel shorts, Boy Scout belt, short-sleeved shirt, Start-Rite sandals). Towards the end of those long, hot summer holidays, we were informed that Mr Trappes-Lomax had died of a heart attack in his bath.

He was replaced by a more go-ahead geography and art teacher, known as 'CJ', who must have been in his thirties. One of CJ's early acts as headmaster was to convert a disused underground cellar beneath the chapel into a club for boys in their last two years at the school, the youngest of whom would have been eleven and the oldest thirteen. It was called the Cavern, presumably in a nod to the Beatles, and consisted of three dark, slightly dank chambers, enlivened by psychedelic murals of underwater scenes painted by CJ and the senior boys. One of the chambers had a ping-pong table, another a billiard table, and the third was furnished with armchairs, a beanbag and a record player.

The Beatles' *White Album* was released on 22 November 1968, when I was exactly eleven and a half years old. It was a double album, so doubly expensive – £3.12s.6d. My parents gave it to me for Christmas, and I spent the next few months luxuriating in its pure white cover, so sleek and so shiny, studying its four-colour headshots of the freshly unsmiling Beatles, and, above all else, examining every detail of its full-length poster, which came pre-folded so it could fit into the package.

On one side of the poster were the words to all but one of the songs, from the first track on side one, 'Back in the USSR', to the last on side four, 'Good Night'. I liked following the words with my finger as the record spun round, imagining that I was somehow directing the words as they flowed off the paper and into the air.

Many of the lyrics seemed to raise more questions than they answered. What is a stupid get? How could an onion be glass? Why don't we do *what* in the road?

On the other side of the lyrics sheet was a collage of photographs, some large, others so small you could scarcely see them. Again, smiles were few and far between, and mainly on snapshots from long ago: the Beatles with Harold Wilson in March 1964, or a beaming Brian Epstein looking calm and relaxed in shirt and tie around that same time.

But generally speaking, the four of them looked sullen. If you compared the moody scowls of *The White Album* to the cheery grins on the cover of *Please Please Me*, just five years before, you would come away with a poor impression of fame and fortune. The only truly happy photograph on *The White Album* was also the most formal: the bearded Ringo Starr, spruce in black tie and dinner jacket, dancing arm in arm with a visibly delighted Elizabeth Taylor against a posh background of a chandelier and ruched curtains.

At that time, I was used to family photographs of everyone looking cheerful, or at least making an effort, which meant roughly the same. We would dress smartly, and smile when the photographer told us to ('Say cheese!'). But one of the largest photographs in the Beatles collage, top right, was of Paul lying in a murky, soap-sodden bath, with his chin stubbly and his eyes shut, rather like poor Mr Trappes-Lomax. He certainly wasn't making an effort. Towards the bottom left of the poster was a black-and-white photograph of John, naked but for his spectacles and necklace, sitting cross-legged on a bed, talking on the phone while Yoko slept, or at least pretended to sleep (her head was set at an uncomfortable angle). Nude adults abounded. Close to the centre, just along from Elizabeth Taylor, was a small photograph of Paul, also naked, standing in a bathroom with a towel around his shoulders. The shot was taken through a window: the central frame covered his private parts, but only just. Up a bit and left a bit was one of John's squiggly cartoons of himself and Yoko. They too were in the nude.

Other photographs were mysteriously shoddy: it was almost as though the Beatles had plundered their rejects box for snaps that were out of focus, or dingy, or showed them at their worst: a smudgy Polaroid of John looking as if he was about to pick a fight with the photographer; a large photograph of George – the largest of the lot – with half his face lost in an overexposed blaze of white; a blurred picture of Ringo on the drums, bored stiff.

The collage was scrappy but mesmerising – or scrappy *and* mesmerising, like *The White Album* itself. And like *The White Album* it seemed modern and cutting-edge and devil-may-care, but at the same time it came steeped in a sense of nostalgia. I now see that half the photographs are from happier days – in Rishikesh, or on the set of *Help!*, or at the Variety Club awards. Two date back to John's carefree twenty-first-birthday trip to Paris with Paul, before they were famous. In one of them – presumably taken by Paul – John is sitting up in bed wearing a black T-shirt and a bowler hat. In the other, the two of them are leaning moodily against a wall plastered with concert posters, their hands half-in, half-out of the pockets of their black jeans. The photograph itself is wonky: half of each head is cut off, and, for no reason, the camera is slanted towards their winkle-pickers.

In fancy italic lettering, a message reads: '*Order of the British Empire to our trusty and well beloved Ringo Starr (Richard Starkey Esquire).*' This too is a throwback to more innocent days.

The only other words on the poster are hand-written in red biro over the imprint of pink lips:

I love you

Who was the I and who was the you? No clue was provided. Could I be the you? I found the thought sinister.

129.

With my schoolfriend Charlie Miller I would sit in the Cavern, listening to *The White Album* over and over again, reading the lyrics, staring at the collage on the poster almost as though, if we stared at it for long enough, it might yield clues to the adult world. Though much of the album was strange or threatening – the weird, screechy little 'Wild Honey Pie', the gloomy 'I'm So Tired' and 'Yer Blues' ('I'm lonely wanna die') – nothing struck us as nearly so creepy as 'Revolution 9', the only track for which the lyrics were not printed. At some point during the Easter term, Charlie and I set each other a dare: would either of us be able to sit in the Cavern by himself with the lights off, in the pitch-dark, and listen to 'Revolution 9' *all the way through*? We both tried a number of times – coming in at 8 minutes 12 seconds, 'Revolution 9' is the longest Beatles track ever recorded – but we never got to the end before flicking the lights on and rushing for the exit.

'Number 9, number 9, number 9, number 9, number 9 . . .' It sounded rather like James Callaghan, the then Home Secretary, but in fact it belonged to a man whose voice John had plundered from the examination tapes for the Royal Academy of Music, which for some reason were stored at the EMI studios.

The track rapidly turns into a cacophony of meaningless jabber and screeches – cars tooting, crowds chanting, machine-guns firing, instruments played backwards, people moaning and yelling – with random words spoken by anonymous human beings, culled from goodness knows where: 'Every one of them knew that as time went by they'd get a little bit older and a little bit slower.' 'Only to find the nightwatchman unaware of his presence in the building.' 'Take this brother, may it serve you well.' No slave to melody, Yoko regularly emits intermittent high-pitched hums, moans, howls and screeches, as well as the spoken words 'You become naked.'

Rolling Stone called the song 'an aural litmus of unfocused paranoia'. Less indulgently, the *New Musical Express* described it as 'a pretentious piece of old codswallop'. In his masterly book *Revolution in the Head*, Ian MacDonald at first suggests that it was somehow prophetic: 'Here, in the random interaction of scores of tape fragments – some looped, others spun backwards – is a representation of the half-sceptical, half-awake, channel-hopping state of mind he [John] liked to relax in (and which, twenty-five years on, has become characteristic of a generation).' But in the end he loosely agrees with those two eleven-year-old boys who listened to it as they sat in the dark for a dare: 'the actual experience of listening to this track, where not merely boring or baffling, often inclines to the sinister'.

Yet John remained convinced of its genius. Pete Shotton remembers him declaring, 'This is the music of the future. You can forget all the rest of the shit we've done – this is *it*! Everybody will be making this stuff one day – you don't even have to know how to play a musical instrument to do it!'

Over the course of four days, John and Yoko had raided the archives of EMI for snippets of classical music, speech, chants and random noises. On Thursday, 20 June 1968, with Paul and Ringo away, John booked all three studios at Abbey Road. While all the available maintenance engineers stood around in their regulation white coats spooling loops onto tape machines with their pencils, John and Yoko sat at the console fading the sounds in and out. Geoff Emerick was unimpressed: 'There was a good deal of resentment among the staff because the session was running quite late – well past midnight – and they wanted to go home. Many of them had been there since nine in the morning.' The track was finally completed at 3.30 a.m. on 21 June.

When Paul returned from New York, John played him 'Revolution 9'. Geoff Emerick watched his reaction: 'I could see from the dark cloud that came over Paul's face that he was totally underwhelmed . . . and there was an awkward silence after the track faded out. John looked at Paul expectantly, but Paul's only comment was "Not bad," which I knew was a diplomatic way of saying that he didn't like it. Ringo and George Harrison had nothing to say about the track at all. They looked distinctly embarrassed, and you could tell that neither one of them wanted to get caught in the middle of this. "Not bad?" Lennon said derisively to Paul. "You have no idea what you're talking about. In fact, this should be our bloody next single! This is the direction the Beatles should be going from now on.'"

Yoko took John's side: 'I agree with John. I think it's great.'

John and Yoko added '9' to the word 'Revolution' because they were both adherents of numerology. John had been born on 9 October 1940. His first home was 9 Newcastle Road, Wavertree, Liverpool: all three place names in that address contain nine letters, as does 'McCartney'. And 'Revolution 9' appeared on the Beatles' ninth album.

Yoko once offered a further explanation for their choice: 'It turns out to be the highest number in the one, two, et cetera. Up to nine.'

130.

For Charles Manson, the Beatles' *White Album* joined all the remaining dots together. Even the pure whiteness of the sleeve served as a signal that his time had come. In Canoga Park, California, at his rented house in Gresham Street, which he painted yellow and nicknamed 'The Yellow Submarine', Manson held seminars on the album. He wanted his followers to understand that what might seem a disparate group of unrelated songs was in fact a coherent call to arms, specially encoded for his own, uniquely privileged, Family.

Manson convinced the Family that the black people of America were arming themselves, ready to rise up and kill millions of their wealthy white oppressors. This insurrection would be followed by a civil war between whites and blacks. As the slaughter took place, the Manson Family would shelter in a mystic hole in Death Valley. 'People are going to be slaughtered, they'll be lying on their lawns dead,' he promised. Then the triumphant blacks would employ their 'super awareness' to find their true leader: Charles Manson.

These prophecies were all to be found in the lyrics of the Beatles. Paul's song 'Blackbird' was an incitement to a race war. George's 'Piggies' required little interpretation: life for all the little piggies was getting worse, while the bigger piggies 'always have clean shirts . . . clutching forks and knives to eat their bacon'. As Ian MacDonald points out, even without misinterpretation, this is a lyric that shows 'the misanthropy at the heart of so much spiritual piousness'.

George began writing the song in 1966, and was still struggling with the lyrics while staying with his parents in Liverpool in 1968. Never a fluent lyricist, he couldn't think of a rhyme for 'backing' other than 'lacking', which he had already used. From out of nowhere his mother came up with the lyric 'What they need's a damn good whacking!' Might Louise Harrison's sole foray into lyric-writing have inadvertently contributed to the death of Leno LaBianca, who was found with a fork in his stomach, and 'Death to Pigs' daubed in blood on his living-room wall?

The Beatles themselves were the four angels charged with bringing death to mankind; the buggies on which the Manson Family rode would be their horses. From the Book of Revelation, Manson discovered that locusts would arrive 'with scales like iron breastplates' – these locusts of course being 'beetles', and their scales guitars. The Beatles would one day have a fifth member, or 'angel', who would be 'given the key to the bottomless pit': this was obviously Manson himself. Together they would wreak righteous havoc: 'Neither repented they of their murders, nor of their sorceries, nor of their fornication, nor of their thefts.'

Words conjured up as playful nonsense by the Beatles metamorphosed, in Manson's mind, into rallying cries for a battle to the death. In Britain, a helter skelter is a brightly coloured fairground slide that spirals around a central column. But it is one of those English expressions that has never made the journey across the Atlantic. Ignorant of its meaning, Manson convinced himself that it was a call to insurrection: one of his followers said that he employed the term 'Helter Skelter' as shorthand for the forthcoming race war. 'What it meant was the Negroes were going to come down and rip the cities all apart.' In *My Life with Charles Manson*, one of his followers, Paul Watkins, wrote, 'Before Helter Skelter came along, all Charlie cared about was orgies.'

At the conclusion of his murder trial in November 1970, Manson stated: 'Helter Skelter is confusion. Confusion coming down fast. If you don't see the confusion coming down fast, you can call it what you wish. It's not my conspiracy. It's not my music. I hear what it relates. It says "Rise!" It says "Kill!" Why blame it on me? I didn't write the music. I am not the person who projected it into your social consciousness.' Lyrics born of whimsy had become as menacing as machetes. Later, Manson explained that the Beatles' music was 'bringing on the revolution, the unorganized overthrow of the Establishment. The Beatles know in the sense that the subconscious knows.'

Even the lightest, fluffiest song was code for something much more ominous. In a merry mood, Paul had written 'Honey Pie', a tinkly pastiche of 1920s ragtime, as a present for his jazz-loving father. But for Manson it was all about the apocalypse, the lines 'sail across the Atlantic/back where you belong' a clear indication that the Beatles would soon be joining the

Family at their ranch in Death Valley. Accused at his trial of ordering the murders, Manson replied, 'It's the Beatles, the music they're putting out. They're talking about war. These kids listen to this music and pick up the message. It's subliminal.' His followers scrawled the words 'RISE' and 'DEATH TO PIGS' in blood on the wall of their victims' home, and 'HEALTER SKELTER' on the fridge.

Listening on headphones to 'Revolution 9', Manson was sure he could hear the Beatles saying, 'Charlie, Charlie, send us a telegram.' Peter Brown and Derek Taylor later remembered getting a stream of phone calls from Los Angeles from a woman who called herself Squeaky Fromme. She kept burbling on about a guy called Charlie.

As he listened to 'Revolution 9', Charlie took to screaming 'Rise! Rise! Rise!' For him, it was just like Revelation, Chapter 9:

And out of the smoke locusts came down on the earth and were given power like that of scorpions of the earth. They were told not to harm the grass of the earth or any plant or tree, but only those people who did not have the seal of God on their foreheads. They were not allowed to kill them but only to torture them for five months.

After Manson's arrest, Family members couldn't work out why the Beatles hadn't come to Charlie's rescue, just like Charlie said they would. 'Tell them to call. Give them our number,' they told two writers from *Rolling Stone*. Manson himself instructed his attorneys to call the Beatles as witnesses: he knew they would support him. His attorneys obeyed his instruction; but their letters went unanswered.

131.

Apple Christmas Party
3 Savile Row, London W1
23 December 1968

On 4 December 1968, George circulated the following memo to all the Apple staff:

> Hell's Angels will be in London within the next week on the way to straighten out Czechoslovakia. There will be twelve in number complete with black leather jackets and motorcycles. They will undoubtedly arrive at Apple and I have heard that they might try to make full use of Apple's facilities. They may look as if they are going to do you in but are very straight and do good things, so don't fear them or uptight them. Try to assist them without neglecting your Apple business and without letting them take control of Savile Row.

A close reading of this breezy text might have sounded alarms – *'I have heard that they might try to make full use of Apple's facilities'* . . . *'They may look as if they are going to do you in'* . . . *'don't fear them or uptight them'*. But the mood in Apple during that prelapsarian period, before the entrance of Allen Klein, was determinedly, almost compulsorily, free and easy.

The arrival of the Hell's Angels was preceded by a call from Customs and Excise to Derek Taylor. 'Is this right? We've got two Harley-Davidsons that you're going to pay the freight duty on?'

Obeying George's order to assist the Hell's Angels, Taylor nodded it through, and also paid £250 for shipping. Presently, two Angels – Frisco Pete and Billy Tumbleweed – showed up at 3 Savile Row, along with the author Ken Kesey, a hippy called Spider, and twelve hangers-on: 'zonked, wired', in the words of Taylor's assistant Richard DiLello, 'smelly, stoned' according to Peter Brown.

DiLello witnessed this mixed bag of people 'in all their splendor, sprawled across the reception lounge; laughing, smoking and reeking of patchouli oil. There were men and women and babes in arms; leather, suede, headbands, cowboy hats, bells, sleeping bags, backpacks, beads, mountain boots, sticks of incense, flutes and guitars.' Collectively, they came to be known by the Apple staff as the California Pleasure Crew.

Snippets of the Hell's Angels' conversation recorded by DiLello mix entitlement with bullishness:

'Hey, where are the Beatles?'

'How much is ten shillings in American money?'

'I've gotta take a piss!'

'Who's got Mick Jagger's phone number?'

'Where can we dump all our shit?'

On their arrival at reception, Taylor came down to greet them, and proceeded to introduce them to everyone else as though they were visiting dignitaries, which is, in a way, what they were. DiLello transcribed Taylor's meandering greeting:

'Well, you are here and so are we and this is Sally who has just joined us and that is Carol who has always been with us and Richard you know, and if you would like a cup of tea then a cup of tea it is, but if you would rather have a glass of beer or a bottle of wine or a Scotch and Coke or a gin and tonic or a vodka and lime, then that it is because it is all here and if it is not then we will come up with something, but have a seat or have a cigarette or have a joint, and I will be back in three minutes so please don't go away because there is a lot to talk about and more to find out and stranger days to come.'

'Beer!' came their reply.

Their demanding attitude soon prompted Taylor to despatch another memo to staff:

Watch out, don't let them take over. You have to keep doing what you're doing, but just be nice to them. And don't upset them because they could kill you.

During the same period, the lounge at Apple was occupied by two American hippies, Frank and Emily, and their five little hippy children.* They had originally entered Apple explaining that, while undergoing an acid trip, Emily had received a psychic message telling her to take John and Yoko to Fiji. Consequently, she and the rest of the family were allowed to camp out at Apple until John and Yoko could spare the time to see her. No stickler for formality, Emily remained naked most of the time, which meant that Apple's two kitchen ladies, Shirley and Janet, refused to enter the room. Within days the guest lounge at Apple had developed its own distinctive aroma, a pungent mix of hashish, patchouli oil and sweat.

Meanwhile, the Hell's Angels occupied their leisure hours racing their Harley-Davidsons to the West End Central police station at the top of Savile Row, screeching to a halt, turning round, and whizzing back again. 'They knew it was a police station,' recalled Debbie Wellum, an Apple receptionist. 'I told them. But they didn't care. They tried to get me to go on the back of a motorbike with them and I wouldn't go.'

The Hell's Angels were still living at Apple on 23 December, the date set aside for the company's first Christmas party. Everything had been meticulously planned. For instance, a turkey weighing forty-three pounds – billed by the butcher as the largest in the UK – had been ordered, and invitations had been posted well in advance, a typically quirky mixture of formal, casual and long-winded:

The Apple Christmas party will be held on December 23 at 2:30 in the afternoon and will go on until evening. In the middle of the party, we

---

* On the day Taylor later referred to as 'Black Friday', other visitors to Apple included the managers of the Grateful Dead, the Beach Boys, the Radha Krishna Temple, two Transcendental Meditators from Rishikesh, Yoko Ono, a German television producer and the poet Tambi Muttu, as well as the Hell's Angels and their party and the homeless family. Recollections of the homeless family differ. Taylor thought they were called Mick and Annie, had four children, not five, and had travelled to Britain in order to persuade Paul, not John, to finance their purchase of an island near Fiji 'where the sun shines all the time'. They were convinced that their case for Paul's sponsorship was good: after all, 'Annie WAS the Lady Madonna of the song, wasn't she?' An easy touch, Taylor let them live in the third-floor waiting room until they found a home. Eventually John let them live on an island he had accidentally bought off the coast of Ireland. 'Determination pays off,' he concluded. He might have added, 'And so does money.' Chris O'Dell, working at Apple at the time, recalled that 'they set up camp on the fourth floor, ate our food and walked our hallways as if they owned the place'. On top of all this, their fifteen-year-old daughter 'kept asking Derek if she could ball George'.

will be visited by Ernest Castro and April,* entertainers to the Queen and Duke of Cornwall and the late Sir Winston Churchill, McDonald Hobley,† and others. Mr Castro is a conjuror, ventriloquist and children's entertainer. April is his assistant and also his wife, and she plays guitar. So the idea is that all of us at Apple will bring our children and those of us who have no children are invited to bring a couple unless they can arrange to have one of their own in the meantime. Immaculate conceptions will not be accepted. There will be a party with food and wine and children and a Christmas tree, and it will be very good. I would be glad if today you will write your name on this memorandum together with the number of children you will be bringing and hand it to Carol Paddon. It goes without saying that wives, husbands, boy and girl friends are welcome, but no more than one per person unless bigamists wish to plead a special case.

By 9 a.m. on the big day preparations were well under way, with Prudence and Primrose, Apple's two *cordon bleu* cooks, already hard at work. By 11 a.m. the press office was filled with journalists and assorted figures from the music business, already slurping champagne. By 11.30 a.m. the Black Room was, in Richard DiLello's words, 'swollen to standing-room-only proportions with hashish smokers puffing their brains out'. Meanwhile, the front office catered for the more traditional 'Scotch and Coke' brigade.

---

* That very same year, Ernest and April Castro – veteran entertainers of children throughout London and the Home Counties – travelled down to Westcott, near Dorking in Surrey, to entertain the Brown family. I imagine we must have welcomed them into our house first, as the Beatles' party was so close to Christmas. In our navy-blue shorts and with well-brushed hair, we were doubtless more like the Castros' usual audiences. Ernest was one of the old school. He wore a dinner jacket and black tie, while his wife April wore a glamorous, sparkly, broad-rimmed pink dress of the type often seen at the time on *Come Dancing*. I remember Mr Castro producing a doll called Lettice Leefe from a black case, and then engaging her in jaunty dialogue while we all shouted 'I can see your lips moving!' Lettice Leefe and the Castros encouraged us to sing along to a song they performed together called 'The Lettice Leefe Hop' – quite a remove from the Beatles' tracks of the time, such as 'Why Don't We Do it in the Road' and 'I'm So Tired'. Before he departed, Mr Castro gave the Brown family a glossy black-and-white brochure full of pictures of his act, as well as six copies of 'The Lettice Leefe Hop', recorded on a shiny red disc. We found it irritating, but for some reason we used to play it quite often.

† McDonald Hobley (1917–87), pioneering BBC TV continuity announcer and panel-show favourite, voted 'TV Personality of the Year' in 1954. Serving with the Royal Artillery in the Second World War, Hobley (pronounced 'nobly') had been involved in a plan to abduct Adolf Hitler and bring him to Britain. The plan was later abandoned. His post-war TV career met with only one hiccup: he once introduced Sir Stafford Cripps, the Chancellor of the Exchequer, as 'Sir Stifford Crapps'.

By noon, the music had been turned up loud, and the two different strands of party – drink and drugs – had merged into one.

The first gaggle of the anticipated forty children arrived at 2.15 p.m., to be ushered into Peter Brown's office, where the party was scheduled to take place. By three o'clock, according to DiLello, 'Peter Brown's office was a scene of unparalleled frenzy as more than a hundred children screamed and smashed their way through a mountain of ice cream, cake and sausage rolls, impatiently clamoring to be entertained by the ventriloquist and conjuror they had been promised.'

Ernest and April Castro launched into their splendid routine of magic, ventriloquism and barnyard imitations ('With a moo-moo here, and a moo-moo there . . .') with their usual gusto, finishing the show with their trademark tune, 'The Lettice Leefe Hop'. DiLello recalled hearing 'eardrum-shattering squeals of delight' from the assembled children.

Next, less than a month since their naked appearance on the cover of *Two Virgins*, John and Yoko entered the room dressed as Father and Mother Christmas. Pete Shotton felt that John was low on seasonal cheer: 'He made for the most miserable-looking Santa I'd ever seen in my life.' Nonetheless, he managed to mutter 'Ho ho ho' while he and Yoko handed out presents, the two of them assisted by the more Christmassy Mary Hopkin.

As the children unwrapped their parcels, the sound of barracking came from the back of the room. 'Hey man! We want some food! GIVE US THE FUCKING FOOD, MAN!' It was the Hell's Angel Frisco Pete, at his most peckish.

'They're arranging it right now,' said John. 'It should be out very soon.'

'What the fuck is goin' on in this place!?! We wanna eat! What's all this shit about HAVIN' TO WAIT?'

At this point Alan Smith, a journalist with the *New Musical Express*, stepped in, politely asking for a little consideration. Frisco Pete promptly punched him in the face, then shouted at John, 'You got more fuckin' food in that kitchen than there are people and it's all locked up and those two fuckin' broads upstairs tell me I've gotta wait until seven o'clock just like everybody else! There's a forty-three-pound turkey in that fuckin' kitchen and I fuckin' want some of it NOW!!!'

John looked non-committal.

'I don't know where those fuckin' heads of yours are at,' continued Frisco Pete, 'but where *I* come from when we got food we feed people, not starve them!'

Peter Brown intervened: 'We have every intention of feeding you and I apologise for the delay, but I was hoping you could appreciate that the kitchen staff have been working since nine o'clock and they've been under considerable pressure. We're waiting for the caterers to finish laying the tables and it shouldn't take more than another ten minutes and then we can all go downstairs and gorge ourselves to death, but please, I beg you, be patient.'

In response, Frisco Pete shook his head and stomped out of the room.

Ten minutes later the doors to Neil Aspinall's office were thrown open, revealing tables groaning with hors d'oeuvres, cold meat, jellied fish, salads, cheese and biscuits, cakes, fruit and boiled sweets. Resplendent in the centre of the table sat the largest turkey in the country, roasted to perfection by Prudence and Primrose.

Hurtling past everybody else – staff and children, hippies, journalists, hangers-on – came Frisco Pete, who picked up the turkey, ripped off its left leg and started to gnaw on it. 'It easily weighed four pounds, and more closely resembled a caveman's hunting club than a turkey leg,' recalled DiLello.

By early January, George was starting to regret his open-house policy. Throughout the building things had been going missing, among them television sets, electric typewriters, adding machines, three hundred copies of *Two Virgins*, a movie camera, three secretarial pay packets, half a dozen speaker cones from the studio, six fan heaters, an electric skillet, several cases of wine and all the lead from the roof. George now plotted to disinvite the California Pleasure Crew. At first he issued a directive to Derek Taylor that he didn't want them round any more. 'What am I supposed to say?' asked Derek, remembering the punches that had flown at the Christmas party, and how close Peter Brown and John had come to being beaten up.

In the end it was George, stubborn George, who finally gave the Hell's Angels their marching orders. Once, when he had been in his teens, a man had come knocking at the door of his family home, trying to sell them something. George's mother, Louise, instinctively knew what to do. She went to the upstairs bedroom with a tub of water and poured it over the poor man, yelling, 'Go away!'

'I think George got his toughness from her . . .' reflected Paul years later. 'She didn't suffer fools gladly – and neither did George.'

If his recent embrace of hippy mysticism sometimes led George down the wrong path, there was still a more steely part of him that knew how to get back on track. So one evening he walked into the guest lounge of Apple and simply announced, 'Hello everyone! Well, are you moving all of your stuff out of here tonight?'

In turn, the California Pleasure Crew were struck mute, astonished to be addressed in such a manner by George himself.

Spider was the first to speak. 'Hey, man. I just wanna ask you one question. Do you dig us or don't you?'

'Yin and yang, heads and tails, yes and no,' replied George, enigmatically.

DiLello noticed an immediate change in the atmosphere. 'The answer to that question completely *fucked* everyone's mind. No one knew quite what to say or how to say it.'

Eventually, it was Spider who spoke up.

'All right, man, I can dig it. We'll be outta here in ten minutes.'

132.

On 30 January 1969, shortly after midday, Police Constable Ken Wharfe noticed that the blue light was flashing on the police phonebox at the corner of Piccadilly Circus. He walked over and picked up the Bakelite receiver.

It was the duty sergeant.

'Can you hear that awful noise?'

'What noise?'

'Get your men over there and go and turn it down.'

PC Wharfe replaced the handset, and turned to his colleague. 'OK, listen. Old Sarge there wants us to go and turn the noise down.'

The two of them walked down Regent Street, where they found a crowd – 'Mainly of women, I have to say' – rushing down Vigo Street. It turned out that the noise was coming from the roof of 3 Savile Row, the headquarters of the Beatles.

At the chartered accountants Auberbach Hope, on Regent Street, a junior employee called Sidney Ruback was eating a sandwich at his desk when the music started playing: 'We went to the window and we could see people playing instruments on the roof, but from that distance we couldn't make out who they were.' Together with a few young colleagues, Sidney climbed out of the window, 'and we scampered over the roof and went up a fire escape to the roof opposite, which was Savile Row. We used a drainpipe as well . . . We walked along and suddenly found ourselves standing about fifteen feet away from the Beatles.'

Working, or at least trying to work, at Wain, Shiell & Son Wool Merchants at 2 Savile Row, Stanley Davis was a good deal less delighted. Within minutes of the music starting, he telephoned West End Central police station to complain that the company's switchboard operators couldn't hear to put the calls through. 'It's disgraceful!' he said. 'I want this bloody music stopped!'

PC Wharfe – still only a probationary officer – duly knocked at the front door of the Apple building, and was let in, only to discover that several other policemen were already there. There seemed to be too many to deal with a minor noise infringement, but none were prepared to leave. 'We chatted among ourselves: should we stay or should we go? But we said that we were never going to see the likes of this again, so we stayed. The fact is that nobody was going to call anybody off, because this was a unique occasion.'

Most of the police gathered that day in the Apple hallway were the same age as the Beatles or younger, and so, almost necessarily, Beatles fans. At nineteen, Ken Wharfe was nearly seven years George's junior. Small wonder, then, that they were unsure what to do. 'In fact, we were effectively trespassing there, because we hadn't been invited, not properly, so it's possible that they could have asked us to leave.'

Wharfe's colleague PC Ray Shayler tried to work out the legal situation. 'We were scratching on the subject. We were thinking that it was a breach of the peace, because while the property may be private, the effect was public. And that's how we worked it out – that's how we were going to deal with it if we needed to.'

They approached the receptionist, Debbie Wellum, and asked to see the person in charge. Debbie went to get Mal Evans, who tried to stall the police for as long as possible by sauntering down the stairs rather than taking the lift. When he finally arrived in the hall 'about ten minutes later', Debbie was all ears: 'He talked to the police. They were saying, "You can't do this," and "It's too noisy, we're getting complaints, and charges will be pressed." Mal said it would be over pretty soon, but the police insisted they go up. I remember Mal telling them that they couldn't go up, because the roof was unstable and there were already people up there. We were thinking that if they all went up there, they might have arrested a Beatle each.'

In the streets outside, traffic had ground to a standstill. 'The taxi drivers weren't happy – they were shouting and hollering,' recalls one bystander, Paula Marshall. Meanwhile, more and more office workers were scrambling up ladders and scaling fire escapes to get onto adjacent roofs, though not Paula. 'I was wearing a miniskirt, so I didn't think it would have been a good idea.'

Jimmy, the Apple doorman, finally escorted all the police upstairs. Ken

Wharfe remembers arriving on the roof near the lift shaft, and finding himself next to Ringo. 'I was completely starstruck with the fact that I, like most people that age a real fan of the Beatles, had this free concert on the roof in Savile Row. Nobody from the police could work out what to do. Nobody wanted to do anything. I remember John Lennon throwing out lots of quips about being arrested or whatever, but there was a real party atmosphere.'

While the Beatles continued to play, police officers negotiated with Peter Brown. 'They said, "You can't do this," and I said, "*Why* can't we do it?" "Well, you just can't do this." And I said, "I don't see why we can't do it," and they said, "Well, does your landlord know?" And I said, "We are our own landlords. We *own* the place. So why can't we do this on the roof of our own property?" And they didn't have any answer.'

Mal Evans told PC Shayler that the Beatles had to record just one more track, and then they would be finished, and the noise would stop. 'And so I said, "If you do that, that's fine. But if you try and play beyond that, then we'll have to take action."' Hearing their conversation, one of the Beatles' technicians, Dave Harries, noticed George Martin blanching at the possibility of arrest. On the other hand, he himself couldn't help thinking, 'This is great! We're all going to be arrested with the Beatles!'

'One, two, three, four . . .' said George, and they launched into 'Get Back', the last song they would ever play together live. When it came to an end, the four Beatles behaved according to character: Paul apologised to the police officers; John and George refused to speak to them; and Ringo fooled around: 'I'll go quietly – don't use the handcuffs!' Later, Ringo expressed disappointment that the police had been so discreet: the film would have been so much more dramatic, he felt, if he had been hauled off his drums and clapped in irons.

When Ken Wharfe* reported back to West End Central police station, the sergeant who had phoned to alert him earlier that morning said, 'You got that music turned down, then?'

'Hey Sarge, it was amazing,' Ken replied. 'It was the Beatles on the roof down at the Apple building.'

'Let me tell you something, lad,' replied the sergeant, who was in his

---

* Eighteen years later, Inspector Ken Wharfe was appointed a Personal Protection Officer to Diana, Princess of Wales.

late forties. 'When I came to London, I was dating a girl in Holborn. Every Wednesday afternoon, duties permitting, we used to go and have afternoon tea at the Waldorf Hotel in the Aldwych and listen to music from a *proper* band. Any group of musicians that is forced to play on the roof of their office has got no future.'

133.

At Farleigh House, the morning's post was distributed during breakfast in the dining room, an out-building of recent construction, its walls lined with grey, pleasingly crumbly asbestos, easily extractable for playing with.

Once a week I would receive a chatty letter from my mother, talking about goings-on at home and ending 'Not long now until half-term!', or 'Not long now until the holidays!'

Parcels were a rarity, largely restricted to my birthday, early in the summer term, but in the holidays I had pre-ordered *Abbey Road* from a record shop in my home town of Dorking. For a little bit extra, to cover postage and packing, they agreed to send it to me at Farleigh House. I can now date its arrival to 27 September 1969, the day after its national release. I remember my excitement as I took it out of its stiff brown cardboard envelope with the other boys looking on, not so much amazed as bemused. Only a handful had any interest in pop music – most of them preferred football, yo-yos, the *Beezer* or the *Eagle*, making dodecahedrons out of card, or constructing Airfix models of Spitfires and Lancaster bombers.

'What's that then?' asked the Latin master, Mr Needham, as I sat there, perusing the cover of *Abbey Road*. 'Top of the Flops?' He liked speaking in puns: he called the Everett brothers 'Ever Wet', and the Brown brothers 'Hovis', after the brown-bread slogan: 'Don't Say Brown, Say Hovis'.

During the summer term I had attempted to get myself into Mr Needham's good books by pointing out that both Status Quo and Procul Harum had Latin names. Misreading my level of interest, he went on at tedious length about the meaning of *status quo*, and pedantically pointed out that if *procul harum* meant anything at all, it meant 'at this', which meant nothing at all. I wished I'd never mentioned it.

On first setting eyes on the cover of *Abbey Road*, I felt a keen sense of disappointment. The shiny white sleeve of *The White Album* had looked grand and luxurious, and came with all those bits and pieces inside – the

colour photos, the poster which opened to reveal yet more photos and all the lyrics on the other side. *Sgt. Pepper*, too, had all those different characters standing as if for a sort of school photograph on the front, and the gatefold sleeve, and the cut-outs, and the lyrics in rivetingly small print on the back. But the front cover of *Abbey Road* just seemed dull – the four Beatles walking over a zebra crossing as though it were a bit of a chore, not even bothering to smile or look at the camera or lark about, and generally looking as if they couldn't be arsed. And the back was even duller: a dreary road sign saying ABBEY ROAD, plus something out of focus and blue swishing past. Furthermore, it was just a single sleeve, with no extras tucked inside: no lyrics, no cut-outs, no photos. Surely, with all their money, the Beatles could have come up with something better than *this*?*

---

* Little did I know it at the time, but they had in fact been planning something much more ambitious. After toying with the titles 'Four in the Bar' or 'All Good Children Go to Heaven', they had decided to call the album 'Everest', with a cover photo of the four Beatles climbing the highest mountain in the world. Paul was excited by the idea of a trip to Tibet, but John and George kept changing their minds, and Ringo was dead against it, as foreign food disagreed with him. With the deadline approaching, John and George sided with Ringo. According to Geoff Emerick, a frustrated Paul said, 'Well, if we're

But posterity can't be second-guessed. As with the *Mona Lisa* and the Eiffel Tower and Her Majesty, time can render the dull iconic. In 2010 the British government awarded Grade II listed status to the zebra crossing on Abbey Road, on account of its 'cultural and historical importance'. And the markets took it seriously too: in 2014 a limited edition of six prints of the various Beatles/Abbey Road photographs, numbered and signed by the photographer, sold at auction for £180,000.

It is hard to think of an album cover more frequently imitated. Booker T and the MGs, Benny Hill, George Benson, *Sesame Street*, the Community of St Saviour's Monastery Jerusalem, Ivor Biggun, the King's Singers, the Red Hot Chilli Peppers, Jive Bunny, Blur and many more have released albums with cod–*Abbey Road* covers. The only time the Simpsons were featured on the cover of *Rolling Stone* it was with Lisa (as George), Bart (Paul), Marge (Ringo) and Homer (John) on the Abbey Road zebra crossing.* Paul McCartney parodied the *Abbey Road* cover for his 1993 solo album *Paul is Live*, on the cover of which he is pictured with one leg high in the air, crossing the road with his Old English sheepdog Arrow.†

At first, the basic details of the shoot appear relatively straightforward. At 11.35 a.m. on Friday, 8 August 1969 the four Beatles spent ten minutes being photographed walking across the Abbey Road zebra crossing by Iain Macmillan. But like virtually everything to do with the Beatles, even this is open to question. There are, for instance, ongoing arguments as to the exact time of the shoot: Mark Lewisohn and Barry Miles pin it to 11.35 a.m., but *The Beatles Bible* says it was 10 a.m., and Bob Spitz says it was 'some time after 10.00 a.m.'.

Most online discussion revolves around the people visible in the background, comparing the different photographs taken by Macmillan over the ten-minute period. The website of The Daily Beatle ('News and articles about the Beatles since 2008') features a long discussion about who they were, or who they might have been. The webmaster devotes a lot of attention

---

not going to name it "Everest" and pose for the cover in Tibet, where are we going to go?' To which Ringo replied, half-jokingly, 'Fuck it. Let's just step outside and call it "Abbey Road".'

* Indeed, the cover of my own little book *1966 and All That* (2005), an update of the classic *1066 and All That*, featured a Ken Pyne pastiche of *Abbey Road*, with the parts of John, Ringo, Paul and George being taken, respectively, by Bobby Charlton, the Queen Mother (on a Zimmer frame), Sid Vicious and Winston Churchill.

† Offspring of the more famous Martha.

to what he calls 'Mystery man' in a brown jacket, standing on the right, with his arms crossed. In another photo 'Mystery man' is still there, but has moved further away, and now shares the pavement with a woman in a red sweater who is looking directly at the camera.

'Here's where it gets interesting,' says the webmaster, optimistically. 'You have to look very, very carefully on the left pavement to spot her, but in the closest gateway, just behind the Beetle, is a young woman in a purple top. This is her first appearance, but she is present in three of the six frames – just one fewer appearances than "Mystery man".' In a fourth photograph 'There's no sign of "Mystery man" but there is another man in a white shirt, striding with some purpose, walking towards the camera.'

And so to photograph number five, picked for the cover because it was the only one which had the Beatles walking in step. 'On the left pavement, further back, stand three decorators, subsequently identified as Alan Flanagan, Steve Millwood and Derek Seagrove . . . There is no sign of the mysterious girl in the purple top.' A Mrs N.C. Seagrove writes that Derek is her husband; together with Flanagan and Millwood he was coming back from a lunch break when the picture was taken. 'They hung around just to be nosy. Derek thought if it was used, he and his mates would be edited out.'

More controversy centres around the 'Mystery man', who stands next to a police van. 'In February 2008, news was that Florida resident Paul Cole, the man beside the police van, had died, aged ninety-three. But was he really that man? I don't think so, and here's why.' In 2004 Paul Cole claimed to have been in that spot, waiting for his wife, who was visiting a nearby museum. He said he had been starting a conversation with the driver of the police van when he spotted the Beatles. 'A bunch of kooks, I called them, because they were rather radical-looking at that time. You didn't walk around in London barefoot.' A year later, his wife, a church organist, had been given *Abbey Road* to play at a wedding. 'I saw it resting against her keyboard and I said, "Hey! It's those four kooks! That's me in there!"' Cole had never listened to the album, though he had heard one or two Beatles songs. 'It's not my kind of thing. I prefer classical music.'

But the webmaster casts doubt on Cole's claims: 'There's no museum in that part of Abbey Road. The police van was a late arrival to the photo session, as evidenced by the previous photos, so Paul Cole can't have had a conversation prior to the Beatles arriving at the scene.' He concludes that

Paul Cole was a fraud. But is he wrong? There certainly was a museum nearby – the Ben Uri Gallery, dedicated to the work of émigré artists. Furthermore, Cole only claimed to have been *starting* a conversation with the police driver when his attention was caught by the Beatles crossing the road. And he was remembering events from thirty-five years before: there were bound to be inconsistencies.

'I have heard stories about people claiming to be or to know "the man on the cover" for as long as I have been a Beatles fan,' writes the webmaster. 'One of them supposedly was a gay man who died in the seventies.' He then quotes someone called Jo Pool, who writes, 'As soon as I saw the cover, I shouted, "That's my brother, Tony." Tony Staples was thirty-three and six foot four inches tall. On the day in question he was on his way to work as an administrative secretary for the National Farmers' Union.' But is this true? To my mind he looks older than thirty-three, and it seems unlikely that a secretary at the NFU would be leaning quite so nonchalantly against a wall at ten or eleven in the morning while 'on his way to work'.

The mysteries do not end there. Who is the woman in the blue dress on the back cover? Some bloggers seem convinced it is Jane Asher, though they offer no evidence. Others, tired of debating the figures on the front or back covers, seek to extend the parameters of their inquiries to those who were somewhere else. 'Does anyone know the name of the police officer who held up traffic while the photo was taken, or know anything about him?' asks Randy Ervin. But his question draws a blank.

134.

A few weeks after the release of *Abbey Road*, the Apple press office began to receive calls from around the world wanting to know if Paul was dead. This type of rumour was by no means a rarity – as early as 1961, a reader of *Mersey Beat* had written in to ask whether one of the Beatles had just died in a car crash – but this one took on a life of its own, each denial acting as further confirmation of a cover-up.

The rumour of Paul's death appears to have started on 12 October 1969, when Russ Gibb, a disc jockey on the Detroit station WLNR-FM, took a call from a listener who said that Paul McCartney had died in a car accident. Tom drew Gibb's attention to the voice on 'Revolution 9' that repeated 'number nine, number nine' over and over again. The listener claimed that if you played the message backwards it said: 'Turn me on, dead man.'

Gibb broadcast it backwards. It sounded more like 'tunmyondenmum', but for anyone predisposed to believe, it offered proof galore. And so the rumour mushroomed, with everyone joining the scramble for fresh proof that Paul was indeed dead. According to one listener, at the end of 'Strawberry Fields Forever' John confesses, 'I buried Paul.' Another listened hard to the mumbles between the tracks 'I'm So Tired' and 'Blackbird' on *The White Album* and heard 'Paul is dead, man, miss him, miss him.' And so on.

On 14 October a student newspaper called the *Michigan Daily* produced a satirical spoof of these crazy rumours, illustrated with a photo of Paul's head separated from his body. Under the headline 'McCartney is Dead: New Evidence Brought to Light', the report concentrated on the cover of *Abbey Road*. The four Beatles were clearly in funeral procession, argued the author Fred LaBour. But spoofs are often mistaken for the truth – in fact, that is partly their purpose. Sure enough, the parody served only to reinforce the rumour it had set out to debunk.

Before long it seemed that virtually everything in the universe was pointing to the fact that Paul had died:

1. Paul – or rather, the man impersonating Paul – is the only Beatle to be walking barefoot on the cover of *Abbey Road*. His eyes appear to be closed, and he is out of step with the others.

2. The white VW Beetle parked on the left has the licence number LMW 28IF. LMW stands for 'Linda McCartney Weeps', and 28IF signifies that Paul would have been twenty-eight *if* he had not died. Strictly speaking, this is not so (he would have been twenty-seven) but – let's not forget! – Indian mystics date a person's real age from their conception.

3. John, dressed in white, is the preacher. Ringo, in black, is the pallbearer. George, in denim, is the gravedigger. 'Paul' is pictured with a cigarette in his right hand, but the real Paul was left-handed.

4. To the left of the road stand three men dressed in white. A single person, dressed in dark clothes, stands alone on the other side.

5. If you trace a line from the bottom of the VW Beetle through the three cars behind it, the line goes through Paul's head. Paul died of a head injury.

6. On the Australian cover there is a red stain on the road just behind Ringo and John, indicating a traffic accident.

7. On the back cover, eight dots on the wall to the left of the words 'THE BEATLES' can be joined together to form a 3 – the number of Beatles remaining after Paul's death.

8. If you turn the back cover 45 degrees anticlockwise, the shadow on the wall creates the clear image of a skull with a black gown.

9. On the night of the fatal crash, Paul gave a lift to a fan. The woman in blue on the back cover is that same fan, either fleeing the scene or running for help.

10. The signs saying 'BEATLES' and 'ABBEY ROAD' on the back cover appear to be divided into BE AT LES ABBEY RO AD. 'R' and 'O' are the eighteenth and fifteenth letters of the alphabet. Added together they make 33, which is the numerical equivalent of 'CC'. Paul is therefore buried at St Cecilia's Abbey on the Isle of Wight. Thirty-three multiplied by two, which is the number of letters, is sixty-six. Paul died in 1966.

11. On 'Come Together' John sings 'One and one and one is three'. This indicates that only three Beatles remain.

12. *Sgt. Pepper* holds almost as many clues. On the front cover, the man immediately behind 'Paul' – the music-hall comedian Issy Bonn – is holding his right hand over Paul's head. This is a symbol of death, as is the black musical instrument held by Paul. The entire cover is a depiction of Paul's funeral, with the Beatles standing around a freshly dug grave.

13. On the inside of the gatefold, 'Paul' is wearing a black armband with the letters 'OPD'. This is the Canadian acronym for Officially Pronounced Dead.

14. On the back cover, Paul is the only Beatle whose back is turned to the camera.

15. 'A Day in the Life' contains the line 'He blew his mind out in a car.'

16. At the end of 'While My Guitar Gently Weeps', George wails 'Paul, Paul.'

17. The poster included with *The White Album* also contains a number of opaque references to Paul's death. The photograph of Paul in the bath – eyes closed, head floating as though separate from his body – shows what he would have looked like after the fatal crash. To the bottom right of the poster there is a small photo of Paul in white trousers, clapping and dancing. Behind him there is something blurry and unexplained. Is it the hands of a skeleton reaching out for him?

18. On 'Glass Onion' John sings: 'And here's another clue for you all – the Walrus was Paul.' In many cultures a walrus symbolises death – even if no one is quite sure exactly which cultures these are.

19. 'I am the Walrus' is John's coded account of the fatal accident, which took place after Paul left the Abbey Road studio in a temper on a 'stupid bloody Tuesday'. John sings 'I'm crying' over and over again. It's an expression of grief.

20. At the beginning of the same song, two notes are repeated, making a sound similar to an ambulance siren. The 'pretty little policemen waiting for the van to come' are the police who arrived at the site of the accident. They were paid to keep quiet. 'Yellow matter custard dripping from a dead dog's eye' is a description of

Paul's horrific facial injuries. 'I am he as you are he and we are all together' is an admission that the other three Beatles were involved in a conspiracy of silence. On page 557 of James Joyce's *Finnegans Wake* the words 'googoo goosth' are in the same sentence as 'them four hoarsemen on their apolkaloops'.

21. The fake Paul grew a moustache to cover up the scars of the plastic surgery he had undergone. Once the scars had healed, the powers that be let him remove it.

22. The fake Paul protested that what John was really saying at the end of 'Strawberry Fields Forever' is not 'I buried Paul,' but 'Cranberry sauce.' This is part of the cover-up.

23. On the cover of *Magical Mystery Tour*, the title is written in stars. If you turn the cover upside down, the stars form a phone number. If you call this number, you will be told the details of Paul's death.

24. In the lavish 'Your Mother Would Know' sequence of the *Magical Mystery Tour* film, 'Paul' is wearing a black carnation. The others wear white carnations.

All these signs pointed to just one conclusion: three years earlier, on 6 November 1966, Paul had died in a car crash. From then on his place had been taken by a lookalike. After all, there was no photograph of Paul for eighteen days from 6 November, and then he had been pictured with new facial hair – clearly there to cover up the scars from the plastic surgery on his lookalike. And who was the lookalike? An actor called William Shears Campbell, otherwise known as 'Billy Shears', who had won a Paul McCartney lookalike competition and had never been seen again. Until now.

Heartbroken fans jammed the Apple switchboard. Derek Taylor contacted Paul in Scotland, and asked what he wanted to do about it. 'Nothing,' replied Paul. 'Just let it go.'

Unable to field the real Paul, Taylor's sidekick Tony Bramwell came up with a fiendish plan to scotch the rumours. Putting his own Liverpudlian accent to good use, he phoned the DJ Richie York on CING-FM in Burlington, Ontario. 'This is Paul McCartney,' he said. 'As you can hear, I'm alive and kicking.'

This aroused suspicions in two other radio stations. They immediately submitted the tape to two experts in voice recognition. Having compared Bramwell's voice with a recording of the known voice of Paul McCartney, Professor Oscar Tossey* of Michigan State University and Dr Henry M. Truby of Miami University both testified to the fact that they were not the same. This was further proof of a cover-up: Paul McCartney was, indeed, dead.

Paul was obliged to issue a written statement through the Apple press office: 'I am alive and well and concerned about the rumours of my death, but if I were dead, I would be the last to know.' This half-hearted message served only to fuel the fire. Now Derek Taylor was driven to issue a press release: 'Paul refuses to say anything more than that. Even if he appeared in public, it wouldn't do any good. If people want to believe he's dead, then they'll believe it. The truth is not at all persuasive.' Once again, the denial was taken as proof positive of a cover-up.

Two of the other Beatles stated that Paul was not dead. 'It's the most stupid rumour I've ever heard,' John said on WLNR. 'Sure, you can play anything backwards and you're going to get different connotations, 'cause it's backwards.' Ringo also pitched in, though only to explain why he wasn't pitching in. 'I'm not going to say anything,' he said, 'because nobody believes me when I do.'

At this stage, even some of Paul's friends began to entertain suspicions. One day Peter Blake, the designer of the *Sgt. Pepper* cover, bumped into the real, living Paul McCartney. 'He said to me, "Yes, it's true. I'm not actually Paul McCartney. You know Paul McCartney, he didn't have a scar on his mouth. I'm very like him, but I'm actually not him." I looked, and indeed there was a scar, but Paul didn't have a scar. What had happened was that he had fallen off his bike and had got a scar since I last saw him. Of course, it was Paul, and he did kid me for two minutes. And for three minutes I did believe him.'

Meanwhile the celebrated defence attorney F. Lee Bailey† had been hired by RKO to conduct a mock trial for a television special in which he cross-questioned 'expert witnesses', including Allen Klein and Peter Asher. Those defending the allegations included Fred LaBour, whose joky piece in

---

* His real name.

† Legal representative of celebrity defendants including Albert DeSalvo ('The Boston Strangler') and, later, Patty Hearst and O.J. Simpson.

the *Michigan Daily* had set the ball rolling. Before he took the stand, La-Bour confessed to Bailey that he had perpetrated the hoax. 'Well,' replied Bailey, 'we have an hour of television to do, so you're going to have to go along with this.'

By now, four different singles on the Paul is Dead theme had been released: 'Brother Paul' by Billy Shears and the All-Americans, 'We're All Paul Bearers' by Zacherias and the Tree People, 'Saint Paul' by Terry Knight, and 'So Long Paul' by Werbley Finster,* which contained the somewhat pedestrian chorus:

So long Paul, we hate to see you go,
So long Paul, after making all that dough.

Later the same month, *Life* magazine sent a team of photographers and reporters to Scotland to track Paul down. Having walked four miles over marshy land to his farmhouse, they were confronted by Martha, Paul's Old English sheepdog. Alerted by Martha's barking, an irate Paul emerged from his house and told them to get off his land, before throwing a bucket of water over them, an act caught by one of the photographers. As they left, Paul, ever conscious of his public image, and feeling he had gone too far, chased after them, offering an interview and photos in return for the offending photo.

Under the heading 'THE CASE OF THE MISSING BEATLE: Paul is Still With Us', the photograph on the cover of the November 1969 issue of *Life* showed the McCartney family – Paul, Linda, Heather and baby Mary – in rural bliss. In the accompanying interview Paul said, 'It is all bloody stupid. I picked up that OPD badge in Canada. It was a police badge. Perhaps it means Ontario Police Department or something. I was wearing a black flower because they ran out of red ones. It is John, not me, dressed in black on the cover and inside of *Magical Mystery Tour*. On *Abbey Road* we were wearing our ordinary clothes. I was walking barefoot because it was a hot day. The Volkswagen just happened to be parked there . . . The people who are making up these rumors should look to themselves a little more. There

---

* Later revealed as a pseudonym of José Feliciano, the blind Puerto Rican singer still probably best known for his 1968 rendition of 'Light My Fire'.

is not enough time in life. They should worry about themselves instead of worrying whether I am dead or not.'

To coincide with the interview, Apple released a triumphant and characteristically long-winded press release.

> Paul McCartney is alive. He says so. His wife says so, his children show he is. The recent photos confirm it, the new songs make it concrete, and the very fact that he is alive should be enough. If in doubt, read *Life* magazine. If still in doubt, there is nothing we can do. The Paul McCartney who wrote 'And I Love Her' still loves you, and is still alive, and has a lot to write. There are a thousand songs unwritten and much to do. Have faith and believe. He is alive and well and hopes to remain so as long as possible. If that doesn't work, then we'll start our own rumour that the public is dead from the neck up and they've been using a stand-in facsimile of a brain for the past three and a half years and then sit back and see who denies it.

Fifty years on, there are still those who believe that Paul died in 1966, and that his part is being played by a gifted impostor. In 2009 the Italian edition of *Wired* magazine published a nine-page article in which a forensic pathologist called Gabriella Carlesi and a computer scientist called Francesco Gavazenni went to great lengths to test before and after photographs of Paul, measuring differences in his teeth, lips, jaws and ears. They concluded that they were not of the same man.

A book by Tina Foster called *Plastic Macca: The Secret Death and Replacement of Beatle Paul McCartney* (2019) presents yet more evidence, including the revelation that 'the remaining Beatles and their business representatives made a pact with Paul's relatives, for a large sum of money, to keep Paul's death a secret, and hired a replacement to protect the group's image, career, popularity, and finances'.

Foster suggests that one of the initial motives for the fraud was the fear that fans would be so distraught over Paul's death that they would be driven to suicide. 'There is a precedent for this theory,' she writes. 'Shortly before Christmas 1962, a puppy named "Petra" appeared on the children's TV show, *Blue Peter*. Sadly, the dog died of distemper two days later. Rather than traumatise millions of children by revealing the puppy's tragic fate, the show's bosses found a lookalike black and brown puppy to replace the original Petra. Not a single viewer noticed.'

The book's blurb states that 'Attorney and author Tina Foster has devoted years of her life to unearthing what happened to James Paul McCartney . . . Recognised as an authority on the subject, Tina has been invited to speak on radio shows in the USA, UK, Canada and Australia.'

Oddly enough, Foster never explains why the remaining Beatles and their co-conspirators were so keen to give away their own secret by offering quite so many tell-tale clues to its unlocking.

135.

There was lunacy in the air. Soon after the stage adaptation of John's books, *In His Own Write*, opened at the Old Vic in June 1968, Yoko Ono summoned Victor Spinetti, its director. Spinetti kept a note of their conversation.

'"Ah," she said. "I want you to direct *my* play."

'"Oh," I said. "What is it? Let me see the script."

'"No, no. No script. All audience get in bus. And allowed to go to house. Then all people in bus allowed to come and open door to symbolise awareness. Then everyone get back in bus. Then they go to other house. All allowed to come out. This time allowed to meet one person. Symbolise beginning communication. Then audience get back on bus –"'

Spinetti interrupted her monologue. 'Now wait a minute, Yoko. What's the big finish? I mean, what happens?'

'Oh, everyone go into Hyde Park and wait for something to happen.'

'Like what?'

'Like chair falling out of sky.'

At this point Spinetti glanced at John, whose face was radiating love and wonder.

'Ooh, that's fookin' great, that is, Vic, "chair falling out of sky".'

Spinetti couldn't work out whether or not John was joking. Thinking it was time to leave, he said, 'You don't want me to direct it, darling. You want to get Cook's Tours. They're great with buses.'

Yoko was not amused. 'She didn't speak to me for months,' he recalled.

Around the same time, an ambitious eighteen-year-old called Richard Branson secured a promise from John and Yoko to provide the first issue of his new magazine, *Student*, with a flexidisc recording to be attached to the front cover. On the strength of this promise, Branson had ordered an ambitious print run of 100,000 copies, commissioning the self-styled 'Man with Kaleidoscope Eyes', Alan Aldridge, to create one of his psychedelic pictures for the cover.

But as the print date drew closer, the promised recording failed to appear. In desperation, Branson instructed a lawyer to threaten to sue Apple and the Lennons for £100,000, on the grounds of breach of promise.

The threat seemed to work wonders. A few days later, Branson received a telephone call from Derek Taylor. 'Come round to Apple, Richard. We've got something for you.'

Branson was led into the basement studio at Savile Row, where he sat with John and Yoko as Taylor switched on a tape recording. Branson was all ears.

'The hiss of the tape recorder was followed by a steady, metronomic beat, like the sound of a human heart.

'"What is it?" I asked.

'"It's the heartbeat of our baby," said John.

'No sooner had he spoken than the sound stopped. Yoko burst into floods of tears and hugged John. I didn't understand what was going on, but before I could speak John looked over Yoko's shoulder straight into my eyes.

'"The baby died," he told me. "That's the silence of our dead baby."'

Taylor reassured him that it was 'conceptual art', but Branson was flummoxed. What should he do? A free recording of a baby dying was unlikely to send his magazine flying off the shelves.

'I felt unable to release this private moment as a record,' wrote Branson, with due solemnity, in his autobiography decades later. Instead, he scrapped the cover, redesigned the magazine and reduced the print order. For their part, John and Yoko had successfully sidestepped legal action. A few weeks later, the genial Taylor wrote Branson a note of apology for any trouble caused, signing off 'All you need is love'.

After Yoko's miscarriage, John stayed with her at Queen Charlotte's Hospital while she recuperated.

One morning he phoned Victor Spinetti and asked him to pay them a visit. Spinetti found Yoko sitting up in bed, typing, while John lay on the floor, looking dreadful.

'My God,' he said. 'Which one's had the miscarriage?'

John laughed; Yoko continued typing. 'I'm writing to my little daughter,' she said. 'I'm sending her a poem.' She then read out the poem: 'Do not worry, Kyoko. Mummy is only looking for her hand in the snow.'

Spinetti was taken aback. 'How old is she?'

'Five.'

'And when did you last see her?'

'Four years ago.'

'Darling – send her a doll's house,' said Spinetti.

On Spinetti's next visit, Yoko filled him in on her next venture. 'I have bought ten thousand cups. John and I take hammer. Smash cup. We sell broken cup and people all over the world will buy it and stick broken cup that John and I break, stick it together, because, you see, now we are married, we are more famous than the Burtons.' This time, Spinetti felt it expedient to keep quiet.

136.

On Saturday, 14 June 1969, John and Yoko were interviewed by David Frost in London. They kicked off the show by throwing acorns to the audience, explaining that it was 'Acorns for Peace' week. Yoko then presented Frost with what she called a 'box of smile'. Upon opening it, Frost found a small mirror. He then asked them about Bagism.

JOHN: What's Bagism? It's like a tag for what we all do, we're all in a bag, you know, and we realised that we came from two bags – I was in this pop bag going round and round in my little clique and she was in her little avant-garde clique going round and round and you're in your little telly clique and they're in their . . . you know? And we all sort of come out and look at each other every now and then, but we don't communicate. We all intellectualise about how there is no barrier between art, music, poetry . . . but we're still all – 'I'm a rock and roller.' 'He's a poet.' So we just came up with the word so you would ask us what bagism is – and we'd say We're all in a bag, baby!

FROST: Well now, you've got in a bag, you've got in a sack . . .

JOHN: Well, we got out of one bag and into the next, you just keep moving from bag to bag.

FROST: You've got a bag there with you, what do you do with it?

JOHN: Well sometimes we get in it and sometimes other people get in it.

YOKO: You know, this life is speeded up so much and the whole world is getting tenser and tenser because things are just going so fast, you know, so it's so nice to slow down the rhythm of the whole world, just to make it peaceful. So like the bag, when you get in, you see that it's very peaceful and your movements are sort of limited. You can walk around on the street in a bag.

FROST: Can you?

JOHN: If people did interviews for jobs in a bag they wouldn't get turned away because they were black or green or long hair, you know, it's total communication.

FROST: They'd get turned away because they were in a bag. (Audience laughter)

YOKO: Well no, if that was specified that when you interviewed the people that you wanted to employ – and you had this prejudice – and the people had to wear a bag, then you'd only judge them on what they communicated to you and you wouldn't have to think 'Oh, he's wearing black suede is he? Don't like it.'

137.

FROM THE DIARY OF KENNETH WILLIAMS, 15 JUNE 1969

The Beatle who is married to an Asiatic lady was on The Frost Programme. The man is long-haired & unprepossessing, with tin spectacles and this curious nasal Liverpudlian delivery: the appearance is either grotesque or quaint & the overall impression is one of great foolishness. He and his wife are often 'interviewed' from inside bags to achieve 'objectivity' and they have 'lie-ins' whereby they stay in bed for long periods & allow a certain number of people into the room. I think this man's name is Ringo Starr or something (no – it's John Lennon) but he began as a 'singer' and instrumentalist with this group called the Beatles and one searches in vain for any valid reason for his being interviewed *at all*. What this ex-pop-singer is doing pontificating about the state of humanity, I cannot imagine. It's mind-bending to listen to.

138.

In September 1969, on a visit to Aunt Mimi, John stealthily removed his MBE from the mantelpiece upon which it had sat for the past four years and took it back to London without a word. He then asked his staff to enquire about the correct way of returning it to HM the Queen. Bill Oakes, Peter Brown's personal assistant at Apple, pursued the matter, and wrote this formal memo:

> The medal, with a brief explanation, should be sent to – The Secretary of the Central Chancery, 8 Buckingham Gate, London, SW1
>> Two optional letters should be sent to:
>
> a) Harold Wilson. The main protest should be lodged here – presumably this letter would become public?
>
> b) H.M. The Queen. Solicitors advise no more than a respectful, regretful note.

On 25 November 1969, John wrote the following single-sentence letter:

```
Your Majesty,
    I am returning this MBE in protest against Britain's involvement
in the Nigeria – Biafra thing, against our support of America in
Vietnam and against Cold Turkey slipping down the charts.
    with love
    John Lennon
```

He then instructed his chauffeur, Les Anthony, to deliver it to Buckingham Palace, also giving him letters to deliver to the prime minister and the secretary of the Central Chancery.

Calling a press conference at the Apple headquarters, John claimed he was always uneasy about his MBE. The Beatles had, he said, been pressured into accepting their awards by Brian Epstein: 'I always squirmed when I saw "MBE" on my letters. I didn't really belong to that sort of world. I think the Establishment bought the Beatles with it. Now I am giving it back, thank you very much . . .

'I had been mulling it over for a few years. Even as I received it, I was mulling it over. I gave it to my auntie who proudly had it over the mantelpiece, which is understandable – she was very proud of it. But I can't not do it because of my auntie's feelings. So I took it a few months back and didn't tell her what I was going to do with it – no doubt she knows now. And I'm sorry Mimi, but that's the way it goes.'

When Mimi found out what had happened, she was extremely upset: 'If I knew what John wanted it for, I never would have given it to him.' She clearly felt too humiliated to admit that he had taken it without asking.

139.

A Party:
Chelsea Town Hall
King's Road, London SW3
3 July 1969

On the Monday, Apple Records send out an invitation:

Apple Peace/Postcard/Communication/John and Yoko and Apple Records invite you to join them on Thursday this week, July 3, to meet the Plastic Ono Band in Chelsea Town Hall, Kings Road.

But on the Tuesday, driving in the Scottish Highlands, John swerves into a ditch. The front of his car is crushed, and John, Julian, Yoko and her daughter Kyoko are all taken to hospital. John is given seventeen stitches, Yoko fourteen and Kyoko four. Julian is treated for shock, but released. 'John isn't a driving man, hasn't driven for years,' explains Derek Taylor.

John is adamant, however, that the proposed launch party for the Plastic Ono Band's 'Give Peace a Chance' should go ahead. As he and Yoko will now be unable to attend, he instructs Taylor to send a film crew to Scotland to 'tape a greeting from the hospital bed'.

On the day before the party, Taylor receives a phone call from the head of the film crew, who tells him that John and Yoko would not agree to see them; they were apparently feeling 'shitty'. So he is on his way back to London, without any film.

But the party goes ahead, with no expense spared. Chelsea Town Hall is lavishly decorated with floral arrangements and vast white banners declaring 'LOVE AND PEACE'. Tables groan with enough food and drink for five hundred guests, even though only three hundred have been invited.

They start arriving at 5.30 p.m., to be welcomed by Derek Taylor, who apologises for the absence of the hosts. 'Give Peace a Chance' is played on a loop through the loudspeakers. Hours later, after what Taylor describes as 'gargantuan amounts of alcohol' have been drunk, a conga line forms, and everyone dances out onto the street. This is the last party ever to be thrown by a Beatle, and not one of the Beatles was there.

140.

The American journalist Gloria Emerson interviewed John and Yoko at the Apple headquarters on 3 December 1969. Having begun her career as a foreign correspondent in Saigon in the 1950s, she knew what she was talking about. The heated argument between Emerson and John and Yoko – notable, because Emerson was clearly no establishment reactionary – was broadcast by BBC Radio 2 a fortnight later.

> JOHN: If I'm gonna get on the front page I might as well get on the front page with the word 'peace'.
> GLORIA EMERSON: But you made yourself ridiculous!
> JOHN: To some people, but I don't care, if it *saves lives*!
> GLORIA: You don't think you – ? Oh, my dear boy! You're living in a never-never land! You don't think you've saved a single life?!
> JOHN: Maybe we'll save some in the future!

Eleven years older than John, and three years older than Yoko, Emerson sounds exasperated, like an adult confronted by unrepentant children.

> GLORIA: What do you know about a protest movement anyway? It consists of a lot more than sending your chauffeur in your car back to Buckingham Palace!
> JOHN: You're just a snob about it. The only way to make –
> GLORIA: You're a fake! I mean, I know in England it's kind of smart not to be serious about everything –

Silent up to now, suddenly Yoko pipes up.

> YOKO: Everything needs a smile, you know.

GLORIA: I see. The Pinkville massacre,* ha ha ha! Can't you give up
something else if it –

There is an awkward silence. John looks daggers at Gloria, and starts to
chew his gum much more vigorously. She, in turn, puffs on a cigarette.

JOHN: It's not the sacrifice. You can't get that into your head, can you?
You've stated half a dozen times the MBE is irrelevant. I agree, it
was no sacrifice to get rid of the MBE, because it was embarrassing.
GLORIA: But what kind of a protest did you make?
JOHN: (raising his voice) I did an ADVERTISING CAMPAIGN FOR
PEACE! DO YOU UNDERSTAND THAT?
GLORIA: No, I can't.
JOHN: – a very big advertising campaign for peace!
GLORIA: I think it shouts of self-aggrandisement! Are you advertising
John Lennon or peace?

John begins shouting at her. If she is treating him like a child, he is treating
her as a bourgeois flibbertigibbet. Perhaps he doesn't know that she is a war
correspondent; if he does, he seems to have forgotten.

JOHN: If you want nice middle-class gestures for peace and intellectual
manifestos written by a lot of half-witted intellectuals and nobody
reads them! That's the trouble with the peace movement!
GLORIA: Well, it just seems a never-never land. I mean, I can't think
of anyone who seems more remote from the ugliness of what's
happening than you. I do see you getting up on a Tuesday morning
and thinking, 'Let's see, what shall we do today, what war is on?'
YOKO: But that's your imagination!
JOHN: Why don't you make a film while you're at it?
GLORIA: I'm someone who admired you very much.
JOHN: Well, I'm sorry you liked the old moptops, dear, and you

---

* The notorious My Lai massacre (March 1968) was originally known as the Pinkville massacre,
'Pinkville' being the US Army's name for the area in which it took place.

thought I was very satirical and witty and you liked *Hard Day's Night*, love. But I've grown up, and you obviously haven't.

GLORIA: What have you grown up to?

JOHN: Twenty-nine.

GLORIA: Yes.

At this point she becomes quieter, more conciliatory. Perhaps she has only just realised quite how young he is, so finds his naïvety more forgivable.

GLORIA: How was Greece?

YOKO: Beautiful.

JOHN: We did a nice war protest on the army TV while we were there. I suppose you didn't like us going to Greece, eh? You think we shouldn't go to a fascist country like Greece where it's all right to live in a fascist country like Britain or America, is it?

Emerson is unruffled, looking to the ceiling for a second and taking stock before continuing.

GLORIA: I think America's a good place to live right now because I mean if you were interested or committed OR not too cowardly you might conceivably make a difference by what you did.

JOHN: Well, we've been trying to go to America to do something for the last seven or eight months, but I can't get in.

GLORIA: You don't understand how they protest, my dear –

JOHN: Tell me, what were they singing at the moratorium, the recent big one? They were singing 'Give Peace a Chance'! And it was written specifically for them!

GLORIA: Where are we and what is this and what do you have to do with the moratorium? So they sang one of your songs! Great song, sure. But is that all you can say about that?

John wags his finger at her.

JOHN: You were saying that in America (starts imitating her accent) 'they're so serious about the protest movement but they were so flippant that they were singing a happy-go-lucky song' which happens to be one I wrote and I'm glad they sang it and when I get there I'll sing it with them, when I get in, and that was a message from me to America or to anywhere that I use my songwriting ability to write a song that we could all sing together and I'm PROUD that they sang it at the moratorium. I wouldn't have cared if they'd sang 'We Shall Overcome' but it just so happens they sang that and I'm PROUD of it and I'll be glad to go there and sing with 'em!

GLORIA: Make it jolly.

JOHN: I WILL make it jolly.

Yoko now gives her only long speech. She speaks in a peculiarly childish voice, almost as though reading a children's book.

YOKO: We have to make it jolly because if we make it jolly maybe we might stop the war because the thing is when you're happy and when you're smiling you don't want to kill someone, do you, you know, it's when you're very serious you start to think about violence and death and killing. I mean, have you ever seen a person killing somebody with a smile on his face and being happy? No! Killers are unhappy people and they're violent because they're so unhappy and so damn serious.

Emerson picks up her bag.

GLORIA: Mr and Mrs Lennon, we're boring each other, so I'll go away. Thank you. Goodbye!

JOHN: Well, I think that's what you wanted!

Emerson leaves the room, without another word.

YOKO: (to John) The last point was a good point and she didn't want to respond to it.

JOHN: She didn't hear anything.

The following year Gloria Emerson returned to Saigon, saying she 'wanted to go back to write about the Vietnamese people and the immense un-happy changes in their lives, not a subject widely covered by the huge press corps who were preoccupied with covering the military story'. In her first reports she exposed the false American body counts, and the use of hard drugs by GIs. Years later she said that, by the end of her time there, she had lost count of the number of young American soldiers she had comforted in their final moments.

Nineteen years later, in the December 1988 issue of Q magazine, Yoko spoke to the journalist Tom Hibbert about the legacy of the bed-ins, in which she and John had stayed in bed 'for peace'.

HIBBERT: Are those bed-ins something you look back on with pride?
YOKO: Oh yes. Pride and great joy. Those things we did were blessings.
At the time we were doing it people used to sort of laugh at us – we
were hoping that they would laugh *with* us but it didn't work out
that way. But in the end, you see, it did have an effect. Last year
when Reagan and Gorbachev had their summit and shook hands, I
sort of felt, well, John and I did have an effect.

141.

On 6 December 1969 my father was about to enter the Bull Hotel in Long Melford, Suffolk, when he found his way blocked by John and Yoko, who were trying to exit.

To a child – I was twelve at the time – the difference in age between my father and John Lennon was a century or more. It's odd to think that in reality only twenty years separated them: my father (b.1920) was then forty-nine, and John (b.1940) was twenty-nine. Oddly enough, my mother (b.1930) was, and remains, only three years older than Yoko Ono (b.1933).

My father had come to Suffolk to shoot pigeons. John and Yoko had come to Suffolk to shoot a film, *Apotheosis no. 2*. It involved a hot-air balloon rising from the square of the pretty medieval village of Lavenham. As often happened in those days when they were the centre of attention, John and Yoko were also being filmed while filming, on this occasion for a BBC documentary called *24 Hours: The World of John and Yoko*.

You can still see them on YouTube, checking into the Bull Hotel (as 'Mr and Mrs Smith'), then having tea in bed, before being driven through the snow from Long Melford to Lavenham in their white Rolls-Royce. Eerily, at the beginning of the film, lying in another hotel bed, John reads out a letter to Yoko:

Dear Mr Lennon,
    From information I received while using a Ouiji [*sic*] Board, I believe that there will be an attempt to assassinate you. The spirit that gave me this information was Brian Epstein.

John and Yoko both laugh.

In Lavenham, they sit on a bench in the snow, staring into space, shrouded in black, with only their eyes and noses visible. A vast orange hot-air balloon floats up into the air as they look on. I remember seeing a video of them and their balloon on the BBC's *Top of the Pops*, as a back-drop to their single 'Instant Karma'.

The doorway of the Bull Hotel was broad enough to allow my father to enter, or John and Yoko to exit, but not all three at the same time. 'I stood my ground,' my father told me when he got home. In the end, John and Yoko had moved to one side – but, his triumphant tone implied, not without a struggle.

In those days the generation gap was often an issue, especially when the talk turned to John and Yoko. The older generation knew they were up to no good: they were getting away with something, though no one knew quite what. In the *Daily Telegraph*, my future father-in-law, Colin Welch (b.1924), attempted to articulate these suspicions. 'It was as if the Beatles and the young had in common a secret language, incomprehensible to oth-ers, yet full of dark meaning to them,' he wrote years later. For him, by the end of the sixties the Beatles had turned into 'not just entertainers but avatars and prophets, heroes and philosophers of a whole generation, exem-plary in their meretricious triumphs, political posturings, shallow "think-ing" and sentimental feeling'. They were, he said, Pied Pipers leading children away from their parents. 'From this world, certain boring virtues are completely missing. All the military and marital virtues, all fidelity, re-straint, thrift, sobriety, taste and discipline, all the virtues associated with work, with the painful acquisition of knowledge, skill and qualifications. All these give place to a decadent self-expression, in which nothing is ex-pressed because nothing has been cultivated to be expressed.'

The great divide was, of course, the Second World War. At the age of nineteen, John was having fun playing skiffle with the Quarrymen in the Casbah. At the same age, my father had enlisted in the Cameron High-landers. For the next six years he had been off at war, wounded at Nor-mandy, losing his only brother at Salerno. Aged twenty, Colin was also fighting in Normandy: his battalion of the Royal Warwickshire Regiment lost a staggering 170 per cent of its original complement in the ten months after D-Day. 'The smell of Normandy was death . . . a gigantic abattoir, bodies everywhere, human, animal, theirs, ours, French, no chance to bury them, all stiff and hideously swollen, covered with white dust or mud, faces blown away or dreadfully distorted, crawling with flies, rotting, giving off that terrible sweet-sour stench which, once smelt, is not forgotten.'

The war affected both men deeply; how could it not? 'The fragility and preciousness of civil society, as also the dire consequences of its collapse, were indelibly impressed on us,' wrote Colin. 'In a way, we all became profoundly conservative, keenly aware of what had been lost, desperately anxious to preserve what remained.'

Aged twenty, John was playing the Cavern, set to embark on a life of phenomenal freedom, singing and playing to adoring audiences all over the world, rewarded with every luxury and indulgence life can offer. Small wonder, then, that so many of those of the war generation viewed his life with a mixture of bemusement, frustration and – who knows? – perhaps a little envy.

142.

It must have been hard, too, for the generation in between. Ross Mac-Manus* was thirty-five in January 1963, and singing with the Joe Loss Orchestra. At that time an arrangement existed between the BBC and the Musicians' Union that only five hours of recorded music could be played on the radio each day: beyond that, everything had to be performed live. The Joe Loss Orchestra plugged this gap, learning the latest hits by other artistes in a matter of days, then replicating them over the air.

MacManus's nine-year-old son Declan listened as his father learned the latest hits by playing them time after time, and singing along. 'I was used to my father's voice coming from the front room where he was practising new songs. It rattled the pane of frosted glass in the door to the hallway.'

In January, MacManus had been told to learn a song called 'Please Please Me', by a new group, the Beatles. Young Declan listened intently to the disc as his father played it over and over again. He was startled by the vocal harmony line: the second singer seemed to be singing the same note repeatedly against the lead singer. 'I knew that my dad's colleagues, Rose and Larry, would be answering his "C'mon" and probably find the whole thing a bit daft, but I couldn't hear enough of that crescendo, especially when it broke into the title line, with a little falsetto jump on the first "Please".'

Declan asked his father if he could have the record when he'd finished with it. 'He laughed and handed the record to me.' As the year went by, and the fame of the Beatles increased, Declan looked forward to his father bringing home each new Beatles single, knowing that it would soon be

---

* Ross MacManus (1927–2011). On YouTube you can see him and the Joe Loss Orchestra performing 'Please Please Me' in 1963. MacManus looks very like his son, and wears the same uncompromising spectacles. His dancing to the Latin-American rhythms is remarkably free-form, almost experimental, and makes the Beatles' stolid jigging seem a little creaky. In 1970 his version of 'The Long and Winding Road' reached number 16 in the Australian charts.

his. They arrived hot off the press: many had a label printed in red reading 'DEMO DISC' and 'DICK JAMES MUSIC LIMITED'.

At the beginning of November, Ross MacManus was booked to sing 'If I Had a Hammer' with the Joe Loss Orchestra at the Royal Variety Show. To Declan, the idea that his dad would be sharing a bill with the Beatles was infinitely more exciting than performing before royalty.

The morning after the big day, Declan tried to play it cool, asking matter-of-fact questions.

'Did you see Steptoe and son? . . . And Dickie Valentine?'

But before long he could hold out no longer.

'Did you actually meet the Beatles?'

His father mumbled that yes, he did, and very nice lads they were too. 'Then he reached into a jacket slung over the back of his chair and pulled out a sheet of thin airmail paper and handed it to me. I unfolded it, and there were the signatures of all four of the Beatles on one page . . . The ink seemed barely dry.'

Declan's autograph book was too small to hold the entire sheet of paper, so he cut around each signature, lopped the 'e' off the 'The' in 'The Beatles', and pasted in the four severed scraps.

Ten years later, when Declan was embarking on a career in music, Ross advised him never to tell a soul that his dad had sung with the Joe Loss Orchestra, or they wouldn't take him seriously. Declan MacManus added to the subterfuge by changing his name to Elvis Costello. 'When I think about it, he was thirty-five. It must have been tough for him to go up to these twenty-two-year-olds and say "I want an autograph for my boy."'

143.

Every Christmas Day throughout her reign, Queen Elizabeth II has broadcast a Christmas message to the people of Great Britain and the Commonwealth. She delivered her first Christmas message in 1952, ten months after she acceded to the throne. She was twenty-six years old.

'Each Christmas, at this time, my beloved father broadcast a message to his people in all parts of the world,' she began. 'Today I am doing this to you, who are now *my* people.'

She went on to ask her subjects 'to keep alive that courageous spirit of adventure that is the finest quality of youth'. Looking towards her coronation, she concluded her broadcast by saying, 'I want to ask you all, whatever your religion may be, to pray for me on that day – to pray that God may give me wisdom and strength to carry out the solemn promises I shall be making, and that I may faithfully serve Him and you, all the days of my life.'

Among the many millions who heard her words over the wireless that Christmas was the ten-year-old Paul McCartney, who had passed his 11-Plus exam earlier in the year. A few months later, he entered Liverpool's Coronation essay competition. Sure enough, he won a prize, which was presented to him at a special ceremony in the city's Picton Hall.

'On the Coronation Day of William the Conqueror, senseless Saxon folk gathered round Westminster Abbey to cheer their Norman king as he walked down the aisle,' began the neatly-written essay by 'Paul McCartney, age 10 years, 10 months'. 'The Normans thinking this was an insult turned upon the Saxons killing nearly all of them.' It continued on a more reassuring note: 'But on the Coronation of our lovely young queen, Queen Elizabeth II, no rioting nor killing will take place because present day royalty rule with affection rather than force.'

Eleven years later, Paul and his fellow Beatles gathered at the EMI studios for the recording of the first of their own Christmas messages, to be

posted on flexible discs to members of their fan club. This was to become a tradition, continuing up to Christmas 1969, just before the four members of the group went their different ways.

Each of their seven Christmas recordings can now be seen as a strange sort of counterbalance to the stiffer, rather more traditional form of message delivered by Her Majesty.

1963

QUEEN'S CHRISTMAS MESSAGE

'Since my last message of Christmas greetings to you all, the world has witnessed many great events and sweeping changes, but they are already part of the long record of history' (an oblique reference to the assassination of President Kennedy in November). 'Now, as ever, the important time for mankind is the future.

'Humanity can only progress if we

BEATLES' CHRISTMAS MESSAGE

'Good King Wenceslas' is sung by all four Beatles, complete with larky variations on the original words, e.g. 'Brightly shone the boot that night, on the mossy cru-el . . .'

John: 'Hello, this is John speaking, with his voice. We're all very happy to be able to talk to you, on this little bit of plastic . . . This time last year we were really chuffed because "Love are truly ambitious for what is good and honourable.

'We know the reward is peace on earth, good will towards men . . .' The Queen closes by reminding her subjects that 'much has been achieved, but there is still much to do', adding that 'All my family joins me in sending, every one of you best wishes for Christmas, and may God's blessing be with you in the coming year.'

Me Do" had got into the top 20 and we can't really believe that so many things have happened in between already.' (Sings: 'Gary Chrimble to you, Gary Nimble to you!')

Paul: 'Everything John said goes for me too.' (Halfway through thanking the fans for their cards and parcels, he is pinched by somebody – presumably John – and yelps 'Ow!' before bursting into laughter.) Paul goes on to say that, having once mentioned that the Beatles loved jelly babies, 'We've been getting them in boxes and crates and anyway we've gone right off jelly babies.' However, 'we still like peppermint creams and chocolate drops and dolly mixtures'.

The Beatles end by singing 'Happy Christmas' in a loose version of German, but with confident accents, a reminder of their many months in Hamburg. They then sing 'Ringo the Red-Nosed Reindeer'.

1964

QUEEN'S CHRISTMAS MESSAGE

'All of us who have been blessed with young families know from long experience that when one's house is at its noisiest, there is often less cause for anxiety . . .' The Queen makes a direct appeal to young people: 'Upon you rests our hope for the future. You young people are needed; there is a great task ahead of you – the building

BEATLES' CHRISTMAS MESSAGE

The music is 'Jingle Bells', and then they all chorus, 'I don't know where we'd be without you!' to which John adds, 'In the army, perhaps.'

Even at this early stage, they are showing signs of nostalgia. 'We are taping this little message in Number Two studio at EMI,' says Paul. 'The same studio we've used all along since of a new world. You have brains and courage, imagination and humanity; direct them to the things that have to be achieved in this century, if mankind is to live together in peace and prosperity.'

She ends by saying, 'God bless you and a very, very happy Christmas to you all.'

the old days of "Love Me Do", many years ago, it seems.' 'Oh, those were the days,' adds John.

John mentions his new book – 'the usual rubbish but it won't cost much. That's the bargain we're going to strike up.'

The Beatles end by singing 'Oh, You Can Wash Your Father's Shirt', before shouting 'Happy Christmas' over and over again.

1965

QUEEN'S CHRISTMAS MESSAGE

'There is overwhelming evidence that those who cannot experience a full and happy family life for some reason or another are deprived of a great stabilising influence in their lives . . . Cynics may shrug off the Christmas message as a waste of time, but that is only the gloomy side of the picture; there are also brighter and more hopeful signs.'

She finishes: 'To each one of you I wish a very happy Christmas, and if throughout the Commonwealth we can all make a sustained effort, perhaps Christmas next year will be a much happier one for many more people.'

BEATLES' CHRISTMAS MESSAGE

Each year the Beatles' message becomes looser and more impromptu. 1965's starts with an ad-hoc rendition of 'Yesterday', sung off-key, followed by banter.

John employs a rapid succession of accents, including broad Scottish – 'We be-lang to Edinburgh! Bannie Christmas!' At one point he slips into singing the Four Tops' number 'It's the Same Old Song', until he is cautioned by Ringo: 'Copyright, Johnny!'

1966

QUEEN'S CHRISTMAS MESSAGE

A new stridency creeps into Her Majesty's tone: 'This year, I should like to speak especially to women . . . It is difficult to realise that it was less than fifty years ago that women in Britain were first given the vote.' It has been women, she says, who have 'breathed gentleness and care into the harsh progress of mankind'. She ends with: 'God be with you, and a very happy Christmas to you all.'

BEATLES' CHRISTMAS MESSAGE

It opens with Paul improvising a song on the piano: 'Everywhere it's Christmas!'

This year the Beatles take a day off recording their epic 'Strawberry Fields Forever' to broadcast a makeshift Goon-style pantomime.

The storyline is hard to fathom. 'Our story opens in Corsica,' says John. 'Meanwhile, high up in the Swiss Alps, two elderly Scotsmen munch upon a Swiss cheese . . .'

The Beatles bring their message to an end with a song called 'Please Don't Bring Your Banjo Back, I Don't Know Where it's Been'.

1967

QUEEN'S CHRISTMAS MESSAGE

Her Majesty celebrates Canada's centenary: 'Canada has every reason to feel proud.'

She also pays tribute to the 'great feat of seamanship' of Sir Francis Chichester, who has sailed *Gypsy Moth* single-handed around the world.

Closer to home, she says, 'Let there be no doubt that Britain is faced with formidable problems, but let there also be no doubt she will overcome them.' In the end, 'determined and well-directed effort by a people

BEATLES' CHRISTMAS MESSAGE

This is their last to be recorded all together as a group: their final couple of messages will be spliced together from individual recordings. Things have become more fragmented since Brian Epstein's death in August. On Boxing Day, *Magical Mystery Tour* is broadcast, leading to much bemusement among viewers.

In this message, a linking song, 'Christmas Time is Here Again', links a bizarre melange of Goonish voices, orchestral breaks, applause, sound who for centuries have given ample evidence of their resources of character and initiative, must bring its own reward'.

She ends: 'I hope and pray that, with God's help, this Christmas spirit of family unity will spread and grow among our Commonwealth family of nations.'

effects, mock advertisements, quiz-show banter ('And what prize have you got your eyes on?') and greetings delivered in a sarcastic tone ('We'd like to thank you for a wonderful year'). The effect is psychedelic, hallucinogenic, meaningless and disquieting, to some extent a prototype for 'Revolution 9', recorded a year later.

1968

QUEEN'S CHRISTMAS MESSAGE

The theme this year is the brotherhood of man, words that 'have a splendid ring about them'. However, 'this should not remain a vague thought nor an abstract idea. Each of us can put it into practice by treating one another with kindness and consideration at all times and in spite of every kind of provocation.'

Unlike the Beatles, Her Majesty speaks of peace. In a foretaste of John Lennon's song 'Imagine', she says: 'Philosophers and prophets have concluded that peace is better than war, love is better than hate, and that mankind can only find progress in friendship and cooperation . . . We should not be obsessed by material problems.'

She ends: 'Christmas is the festival of peace. It is God's will that it should be our constant endeavour to establish "Peace on Earth, Goodwill towards Men". I hope you all have a

BEATLES' CHRISTMAS MESSAGE

Of the four Beatles, the closest in character to Her Majesty is the stolid Ringo, whose voice is the first to be heard. 'Hi, this is a big hi and a sincere merry Christmas from yours truly, Ringo Starr.'

He is followed by a burst of 'Ob-La-Di, Ob-La-Da' from the recently-released *White Album*, a speeded-up snatch of 'Helter Skelter', and bursts of opera, telephone pips and random screams ('I think it's insAAAne!'), all unevenly stitched together by John, celebrating his recent romance with freewheeling gobbledegook. 'Once upon a time there were two balloons called Jack and Yono, they were strictly in love bound to happen in a million years they were together man unfortunatimetable they seemed to . . .'

More traditionally, George offers greetings 'to all our faithful beloved very happy Christmas and every good fortune in the New Year.'

Finally, George announces, 'We have a special guest here, Mr Tiny Tim.' The high-pitched Tiny Tim then sings 'Nowhere Man' to a ukulele accompaniment.

fans all over the world', and Paul sings a little.

1969

QUEEN'S CHRISTMAS MESSAGE

'In a short time, the 1960s will be over, but not out of our memories.'

This is not the Beatles talking, but the Queen. She, at least, is keeping it together. She reminds everyone that in July the first men 'reached beyond our own planet and set foot on the moon, but each one of us will have our own special triumphs or tragedies to look back on'.

She says that her own thoughts 'are with my older children who are entering the service of the people of this country and the Commonwealth. It is a great satisfaction and comfort to me and my husband to know that they have won a place in your affections.

'We are all looking forward to our visit to Australia and New Zealand for the Cook bicentenary celebrations, and also to Fiji and Tonga. Later next year we hope to see something of the fascinating development of Northern Canada . . .'

BEATLES' CHRISTMAS MESSAGE

It may seem peculiar that in the closing weeks of 1969, in their advanced stage of disintegration, the Beatles should have recorded any sort of Christmas message for their fan club – or indeed that in those hippy times they still ran a fan club. Yet the Official Beatles Fan Club not only survived, but outlasted them by nearly two years.

Once again, their contributions are recorded individually. John is walking around his garden, chatting with his new wife, who steers him. 'You are strolling in Ascot garden with your wife Yoko,' she reminds him helpfully. 'But do you have any special thoughts for Christmas?'

'Well, Yoko, it is Christmas, and my special thoughts tend towards eating . . .'

Yoko emits a girlish giggle. 'So what do you like to eat?'

'I like cornflakes prepared by Parisian hands and I'd like it blessed by Hare Krishna mantra.'

She adds that 'It is only natural that we should all be dazzled and impressed by the triumphs of technology, but Christmas is a festival of the spirit.'

Her Majesty concludes by saying that 'At this time our concern is particularly for the lonely, the sick, and the elderly. I hope they will all feel the warmth and comfort of companionship and that all of you will enjoy a very happy Christmas with your families and friends. God bless you all.'

George wishes everyone a simple happy Christmas; Ringo sings 'Good evening to you gentlemen, happy to be here', Paul sings in a high voice, 'This is to wish you a merry new year,' and says that he wishes everyone 'a good fortunate, happy new year'. John asks Yoko about the new decade. 'Everyone will just be flying around,' she says.

'I'd like a big teddy!' says John. 'Oh, thank you, mommy!'

'You're a good boy, John,' says Yoko.

144.

DAILY MIRROR FRONT PAGE, FRIDAY, 10 APRIL 1970

THE END FOR THE LENNON–MCCARTNEY SONG TEAM

PAUL IS QUITTING THE BEATLES

by Don Short

Paul McCartney has quit the Beatles. The shock news must mean the end of Britain's most famous pop group, which has been idolised by millions the world over for nearly ten years.

Today, 27-year-old McCartney will announce his decision, and the reasons for it, in a no-holds-barred statement.

It follows months of strife over policy in Apple, the Beatles' controlling organisation, and an ever-growing rift between McCartney and his songwriting partner, John Lennon.

In his statement, which consists of a series of answers to questions, McCartney says:

'I have no future plans to record or appear with the Beatles again. Or to write any more music with John.'

Last night, the statement was locked up in a safe at Apple headquarters in Savile Row, Mayfair – in the very rooms where the Beatles' breakup began.

The Beatles decided to appoint a 'business adviser'. Eventually they settled for American Allen Klein.

His appointment was strongly resisted by Paul, who sought the job for his father-in-law, American attorney Lee Eastman.

After a meeting in London Paul was out-voted 3–1 by John, and the other Beatles, George Harrison and Ringo Starr.

Since the Klein appointment, Paul has refused to go to the Apple offices to work daily.

He kept silent and stayed at his St John's Wood home with his photographer wife Linda, her daughter Heather, and their own baby, Mary.

Close friends tried to pacify John and Paul. But August last year was the last time they were to work together – when they collaborated on the *Abbey Road* album.

Films

There were other elements that hastened Paul's decision to quit. John Lennon, on his marriage to Yoko Ono, set out on projects of his own, Ringo went into films, and George stepped in as a record producer.

Today McCartney will reveal his own plans for a solo programme.

Early today an Apple spokesman denied reports that Paul McCartney had left the Beatles.

But he said that there were no plans 'at the moment' for any more recordings.

145.

It was John who first said, 'I want a divorce.'

In the autumn of 1969, Paul began to feel nostalgic for the days when the Beatles were at their happiest. He felt that the only way to restore their lost sense of camaraderie was to go back on the road, turning up unannounced to play small halls in out-of-the-way places: 'I thought, "That's what I miss, and what they miss too – playing."'

He mentioned his plan to Ringo and John. Ringo appeared to go along with it, but John replied, 'You're daft,' adding, 'Anyway, I'm leaving the group. I want a divorce.'

John had in fact been talking about the end of the Beatles, on and off, ever since the days of 'I Want to Hold Your Hand'. 'Sometimes I feel I'd like to try something completely different, like film directing,' he told a journalist from *Rave* magazine in February 1964, just as they were conquering America. '. . . There'd be less of the limelight, but I wouldn't mind.' Two years later, he gloomily told Maureen Cleave: 'We can't go on holding hands forever. We have been Beatles as best as we ever will be – those four jolly lads. But we're not those people any more. We are old men.' At that time he was twenty-five years old.

Yet for all their hyperbole, John's words contained a bizarre truth: the Beatles had aged with an almost macabre rapidity. In the five years from 1964 to 1969 they matured at a rate of knots, not only in the range and depth of their music, but also physically. Look at the two photos of them on the following page – the top taken in 1964 and the bottom in 1969.

Comparing these photographs, just five years apart, it's as though they have been crushed by the weight of the world's adulation. Such talent, so many dreams, such joy – and now they just looked trapped and bruised. Within the space of those five years they went from innocence to experience, from hope to *weltschmerz*. It reminds me of the terrifying climax to Rider Haggard's *She*:

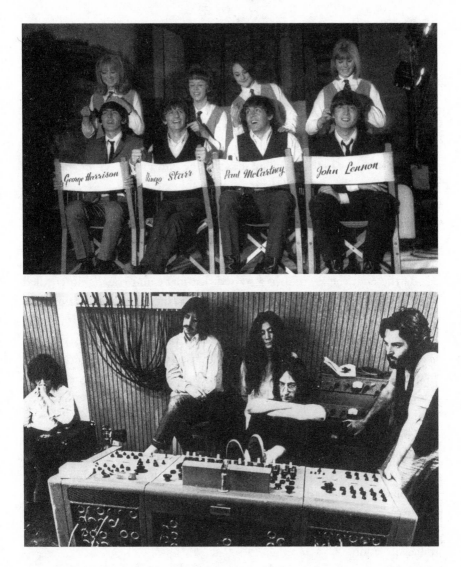

Oh, how beautiful she looked there in the flame! No angel out of heaven could have worn a greater loveliness. Even now my heart faints before the recollection of it, as she stood and smiled at our awed faces, and I would give half my remaining time upon this earth to see her once like that again.

But suddenly — more suddenly than I can describe — a kind of change came over her face, a change which I could not define or explain, but none the less a change. The smile vanished, and in its place there came a dry, hard look; the rounded face seemed to grow pinched, as though some great anxiety were leaving its impress upon it. The glorious eyes, too, lost their light, and, as I thought, the form its perfect shape and erectness . . . And her face – by Heaven! – *her face was growing old before my eyes!*

. . . 'Oh, *look! – look! – look!*' shrieked Job, in a shrill falsetto of terror, his eyes nearly dropping out of his head, and foam upon his lips. '*Look! – look! – look!* she's shrivelling up! she's turning into a monkey!' and down he fell upon the ground, foaming and gnashing in a fit.

Pictures of them around this time could almost accompany cautionary tales, or act as illustrations of the famous observation by St Teresa of Ávila: 'More tears are shed over answered prayers than unanswered prayers.'

By the end, their world had soured. Intimacy and friendship curdled into irritation and recrimination. Despite his increasing reputation as a songwriter, George felt that John and Paul were still treating him as the little boy who tagged along. 'John and Paul did allow him the occasional track on the Beatles' albums – but only in the same grudging spirit as one might throw a dog a bone to keep him quiet,' observed Geoff Emerick. He remembered George snapping, 'Look, I don't have to listen to you!' when Paul offered him advice on 'Here Comes the Sun'.

John also resented being bossed around by Paul; in turn, Paul was frustrated by John's inertia, his sneery refusal to join in.

Meanwhile, Yoko's continued presence in the studio, crouching silently, all in black, set them all on edge, not least the prickly John, on red alert for any tremors of antipathy towards her: as Paul sang 'Get back to where you once belonged', John convinced himself that he was shooting nasty looks in her direction.

John's paranoia on this score was not entirely delusional. Paul, George and Ringo resented Yoko being in the studio. 'John's in love with Yoko and he's no longer in love with the three of us,' Paul confided to a journalist at the time. George later recalled, 'The vibe I picked up was that she was a wedge that was trying to drive itself deeper and deeper between him and us.'

Tony Barrow witnessed Yoko's early days in the studio. 'The first time Yoko spoke out at full volume during a recording session it was to convey some relatively trivial word of advice to John about whatever he was singing at the moment. The other Beatles looked around, straight-faced, startled, stunned. There was a moment's dead silence that was broken by Paul: "Fuck me! Did somebody speak? Who the fuck was that?" Of course he knew full well who had spoken. The others joined in: "Did you say something, George? Your lips didn't move!" "Have we got a new producer?"'

Regardless of Yoko, the atmosphere between the four had grown fractious and scratchy. Whenever they could, they worked separately from each other. Harmonies were few and far between. At different times, George and Ringo both stormed out of the studio in reaction to perceived slights and stayed away for several days.

As it happens, this was Ringo's second day back at work: two weeks before, while they were recording 'Back in the USSR', he had walked out, saying, 'I'm going on holiday.' Everything had come to a head: like Paul and George, Ringo resented Yoko's presence in the studio; he worried that his drumming wasn't up to scratch; and he felt that the other three were treating him as an outsider. The final straw came when Paul, at his most bossy, ticked him off for fluffing the tom-toms. In Sardinia, Ringo received a telegram saying 'YOU'RE THE BEST DRUMMER IN THE WORLD. COME ON HOME. WE LOVE YOU.' When he finally reappeared, they had decorated the whole studio with thousands of flowers to welcome him back. 'And that was a beautiful moment for me.'

Ringo had come to believe that the others looked down on him: 'I . . . felt that the other three were really happy and I was an outsider. I went to see John . . . I said, "I'm leaving the group because I'm not playing well and I feel unloved and out of it, and you three are really close." And John said, "I thought it was you three!" So then I went over to Paul's and knocked on his door. I said the same thing: "I'm leaving the band. I feel you three guys are really close and I'm out of it." And Paul said, "I thought it was you three!"'

Working as an assistant engineer on *Abbey Road*, the eighteen-year-old John Kurlander noticed how hard the group found it to be in a room together: 'When just one of the Beatles was on a session it would be absolutely great; with two of them it would be OK; with three of them the atmosphere would get a bit tense; and when the four of them were together it would occasionally be unbearable.'

And they were at war over money: after they split up, their multitudes of legal actions went on almost as long as the group itself. For his part, George Martin considered it odd that they lasted as long as they did: 'They were in each other's pockets as prisoners, virtually, for eight years, and they didn't lead individual lives. They just wanted to lead their own normal lives, with wives and families, and they were eventually able to do that, and I think it was quite right that they should do.' But he acknowledged that their split was also caused by more worldly struggles: 'Money gets in the way of things . . . There's bound to be differences when there's so much money involved. And it was more than that. It was a question of control, too.'

The day after Paul's announcement, Derek Taylor gave an interview to the *Daily Sketch*. 'It is almost as if they have divorced each other,' he said.

146.

CRESSIDA CONNOLLY'S TALE

I was born in 1960 and the Beatles were an integral part of my childhood. They were never not on the turntable of my older half-siblings' record players, so that their songs really did seem to be the soundtrack to life itself. The gaps between the release of their records – in some cases as little as only months apart – seemed interminable, as distant and as longed-for as the beginning of the school holidays appeared to be, on the first day of a new term.

I was the sort of child who had an imaginary friend. This perhaps explains why I thought of Paul and John as essentially a second mum and dad. Or it could be a case of extreme narcissism. In any case, my real-life father was a bespectacled writer and could be difficult, preoccupied and a bit grumpy: John shared these characteristics. Paul, though, was cosy and round-faced and chipper; all qualities you'd want in a mother. I felt that, if Paul was my mum, all the children in my class would want to come back to mine for tea. He'd whistle along with the kettle and flash his cheeky grin and everyone would think my family were the nicest, happiest family.

All children long for their parents to love each other, and so it was with me and Paul and John. When they came on the telly, I was hungry for evidence of their mutual affection – and there it was: the complicit smirking, the suppressed giggles; like Dud and Pete with guitars. Dad/John was cleverer than Mum/Paul, and even a bit sarky sometimes; but Mum/Paul could handle him, coax him towards good humour.

I didn't really know that they wrote songs separately until *The White Album* came out and my half-brother told me that John had written 'Julia' about his own, dead mother. This brought up feelings too complicated to be easily managed. How was it possible that there were things about John/Dad I didn't know? In real life, too, there was a paternal grandmother I had never known, so this was at least feasible. But why had I never seen a photograph of John's mother, when she was, in a sense, my own grandmother?

My main concern was how it could be possible that Paul and John wrote songs apart when they were indivisible. Lennon/McCartney: one entity. On the other hand, this revelation did make sense of quite a lot of their output. Clearly, Paul/Mum was thinking of the family when composing such child-friendly tunes as 'The Fool on the Hill', 'I Will', 'Martha, My Dear' and – of course – 'Your Mother Should Know'. Whereas John/Dad had obviously gone off to sulk in his writing room and compose peculiar stuff like 'I Am the Walrus'. This had its equivalent in real life, where my actual father would be in the library thinking about the Cantos of Ezra Pound while my mother was in the kitchen tapping her foot to Fred Astaire singing Cole Porter.

The news of their split, which came in April 1970, was cataclysmic. (Decades later, my own daughters would take the news of Geri's departure from the Spice Girls with the same horror and disbelief.) A divorce! Breaking up the family! It wasn't possible, surely? Could it be legal, even? Someone would stop them and bang their heads together and tell them to think of the kids – wouldn't they?

And then, with a sickening inevitability, came the step-families. At least Linda had a kind face and obviously made Paul/Mum happy. But she did bring her daughter, Heather, into the new family; which meant that Paul/Mum now lived with an actual little girl of his own. Competition, a usurper. Whereas Yoko . . . well, John/Dad didn't look at all OK. He was pale and unshaven and remote. (The fact that Yoko had a daughter too didn't register until I was a grown-up.) Also, why did she have to be around, ALL THE TIME? How would I ever get a minute alone with him, now? These puzzles and resentments and sorrows went on for at least two years, possibly three. Then in time I became a teenager and forgot all about my parents and only thought about the Jackson Five and the Bay City Rollers and how to style my hair like Suzi Quatro.

147.

Theme park, wheeler-dealer and the *beehive* hairdo entered the language in 1960, the year the Silver Beetles changed their name to the Beatles and set off for Hamburg.

The next three years saw the arrival of *life-style, Purple Heart, Chelsea boots, trendy, no problem* and *mind-expanding.* New trends gave rise to new words: *flares,* for bell-bottomed trousers, first appeared in 1964, along with *gonk* and *disco. Swinger, topless* and the phrase *beautiful people* heralded a less hidebound age.

In 1964, the Liverpudlian writer Alun Owen coined the adjective *grotty* in his script for *A Hard Day's Night.* Owen peppered the dialogue of the film with a number of words he thought the Beatles might use, such as *dig, fab* and *drag.* He had been under the impression that *grotty* was standard Liverpool slang, so was surprised to find that none of the Beatles had ever heard of it. 'We thought the word was really weird,' recalled John. 'And George curled up with embarrassment every time he had to say it.' But the film's popularity ensured that by the end of the year *grotty* had become part of the language.

Mini-skirt arrived in 1965, together with *go-go dancer, teeny bopper, loon, zit, downer, women's liberation* and *chat show,* as well as the injunctions *freak out* and *turn on.* They were joined in 1966 by *freaky, peacenik, centrefold, suss out* and *blow-dry. Transcendental Meditation* was mentioned in print for the first time that same year, though it was not until 1967, when the Beatles first met the Maharishi Mahesh Yogi, that it came into common parlance, along with *love-in, rave, encounter group, hype, groupie, generation gap, mind-blowing* (a late companion for *mind-expanding*), *flower power* and *flower people.*

Vibes also first appeared in 1967, though its first recorded use by a Beatle came the following year, when George caught Yoko eating one of his ginger biscuits without asking and snapped, 'You give off bad vibes.' 1968 also gave the English language *paparazzi, druggy, permissive society, granny glasses, phone-in, love beads, tank top, unisex* and *no way*, in its meaning of 'Can't be done.'

1969 gave birth to *ego trip, one-parent family, alternative society, jet lag, bovver boot, missionary position* and *roadie*; four years too late, *turn on* was joined by its antonym, *turn off*. On 25 March that year, at the Hilton Hotel in Amsterdam, John and Yoko simultaneously coined and demonstrated the neologism *bed-in*, a horizontal variation on *sit-in* (which had, perhaps surprisingly, already been around for forty years). A week later, at a press conference in Vienna, they introduced *bagism*.

The Beatles disbanded in April 1970, just as *hot pants, counter-culture, right on, lava lamp, upfront, pop festival, full-frontal* and *let it all hang out* were coming into being. By the end of the year these words and expressions had been joined by *noise pollution, microprocessor, property developer* and *chicken brick*, each one the harbinger of a drabber, more prosaic age.

148.

The most successful pop group of the twentieth century was formed in Liverpool in 1959 by Gerry Marsden and his brother Fred. Together with Les Chadwick and Arthur McMahon, Gerry and the Pacemakers built up a huge local following in their home city, while fine-tuning their talents in Hamburg, West Germany.

Many books have been written about Gerry and the Pacemakers, their origins, their influence, and their sociological and artistic impact on the 1960s. Different periods of their lives – from their early days rehearsing at the Cammell Laird shipyard at Birkenhead to their eventual break-up – have been turned into movies, the most recent starring Ryan Gosling as Gerry Marsden.

Why did Gerry and the Pacemakers succeed in overtaking musical rivals like the Dave Clark Five, the Searchers, the Beatles and the Swinging Blue Jeans to become four of the best-known faces in the world of pop?

For a start, their repertoire was broader than their rivals': by 1960 they had built up a repertoire of 250 songs, from rockers like 'What'd I Say' to ballads such as 'Will You Love Me Tomorrow?' Contemporary Merseybeat groups like the Beatles, who met with similar success in the early years, never possessed quite the same range. Moreover, the Beatles lacked a front man, so had no focal point. It's hard to imagine, but had things gone differently, the world might now be talking of John, Paul, George and Ringo (the first names of the Beatles) instead of Gerry, Fred, Les and Arthur.

Their success was rapid. In January 1962 Gerry and the Pacemakers were voted number 2 in the *Mersey Beat* readers' poll when the Beatles were number 1, but this proved a blip. Historians now see the Beatles' decision to turn down the hit song 'How Do You Do It?' as their greatest mistake. It had been offered to them by record producer George Martin, but instead they insisted on releasing one of their own songs, 'Love Me Do'. This left 'How Do You Do It?' to be snapped up by Gerry and the Pacemakers. And

the rest is history: the song reached number 1 in the national charts, leaving 'Love Me Do' languishing at number 2. Gerry and the Pacemakers'
next couple of singles, 'I Like It' and 'You'll Never Walk Alone', also went
to number 1. To this day, they remain the only artists to have achieved the
number 1 slot with each of their first three singles.

For some reason, Gerry and the Pacemakers managed to catch the sixties zeitgeist in a way that no other group could. Nevertheless, the Searchers, the Beatles and the Swinging Blue Jeans enjoyed perfectly lucrative
careers as mainstays in sixties revival tours throughout the 1980s and
1990s. Their surviving members still regularly appear in documentaries
about Gerry and the Pacemakers, and are happy to make personal appearances at Gerry and the Pacemakers conventions.

In the second half of the 1960s, Gerry and the Pacemakers became
strongly identified with the hippy movement. In 1968, having fallen under
the spell of the Maharishi Mahesh Yogi, they spent several weeks studying
Transcendental Meditation in Rishikesh, India. They returned to Britain
with many new songs, which they included on their famous *Black Album*,
released on their own Orange label. Around this time, Gerry Marsden was
taken up by the Japanese conceptual artist Yoko Ono, and went to live
with her in New York. In 1980 he was shot dead outside their apartment
by a deranged fan.

But what became of the Fab Four's early rivals, the Beatles? George
Harrison died of cancer in 2001, following a successful career as a session
musician. John Lennon and Paul McCartney toured Britain last year with

their 'Tribute to Gerry and the Pacemakers' show, thrilling audiences up and down the country with their exact rendition of 'You'll Never Walk Alone'. Touchingly, they still perform one or two of their own numbers – 'Yesterday' and 'A Hard Day's Night' – in each set. 'We sneak 'em in, even if no one wants to hear 'em!' quips John.

Ringo Starr retired from the music business in 1966 to pursue an earlier ambition. He now owns and manages a successful chain of hairdressing salons throughout the North-East.

149.

Eleanor Roosevelt once said that the only two hotels worth staying in outside the USA were the George V in Paris and the Adelphi in Liverpool. In its heyday, Noël Coward, Frank Sinatra, Winston Churchill and FDR all came to stay at the Adelphi. On one occasion, Roy Rogers rode his horse Trigger down the Adelphi stairs.* Throughout his time as leader of the opposition and prime minister, Harold Wilson – MP for the Liverpool constituency of Huyton – used it as his campaign base.

These days, the Adelphi is past its prime. The carpets and curtains are dank. The mock-Grecian swimming pool in the basement displays a sign saying 'No Knives'. What was once an elegant cocktail bar now advertises two-for-one deals on lager during Happy Hour. In 2019 an American couple, Jane and Cliff Maugham, complained to the *Liverpool Echo* of vomit stains in the corridor outside their room, the ceiling of which was so riddled with damp that 'it looked like it could come down at any minute. The bathroom was filthy and the beds in the bedroom were awful. You couldn't open the windows as they were filthy and the curtains were half hanging off.'

Despite it all, the vast hall of the Adelphi was pullulating when I arrived at mid-morning on the Sunday of the annual International Beatleweek. Hundreds of memorabilia stores were crammed in, with more spilling out into neighbouring rooms. Most items were on sale for roughly 150 times their original price. A bath towel (US 1964) decorated with unrecognisable drawings of the Fab Four in Edwardian bathing suits was £140; a tin of Beatles talcum powder (UK 1964) £210; a 'Mega Rare Nearly New' Beatles pencil case (Germany 1965) £920; a *Hard Day's Night* bubblegum box 'with one original uncut wax bubblegum wrapper' £420; a 1967 Beatles jigsaw puzzle £250; a Beatles calendar (UK 1965) £360; a Ringo Starr

---

* And presumably up them, too. Or did Trigger use the lift?

bubblebath (USA 1964) £140; a Paul McCartney bubblebath (USA 1964) £240; a *Yellow Submarine* lunchbox (USA 1968) £235; a Beatles wallet (UK 60s, 'excellent condition') £175; a Beatles reversible headband ('suits all head sizes') in original plastic bag £45; a red Beatles coinholder £85. And so on.

At a stall towards the back, I came across a small sheet of George V Hotel notepaper. Next to it stood a typed letter headed 'BEATLES AUTOGRAPHS'.

To Whom It May Concern

The purpose of this letter is to serve as an authentification of the signatures of John Lennon, Paul McCartney and George Harrison. These signatures are found on a sheet of note paper from the Hotel George V in Paris, France. The Beatles were in Paris for several weeks just prior to their first visit to America, performing a residency at The Olympia Theatre, playing 18 days of concerts, ending on February 4th – just 4 days before they flew to America for their first historic visit. While there in Paris, they stayed at the Hotel George V. All three have autographed a sheet of George V note paper beautifully, with John and George using a red felt tip marker while Paul has signed in black felt tip, additionally adding 'Best wishes from the Beatles'. It is also signed for Ringo Starr in his absence.

It is my professional opinion that the aforementioned sheet of signed hotel note paper is authentic, as described. I base this opinion on over 31 years of study and experience with Beatles signed and handwritten material.

Sincerely,

Frank Caiazzo

The asking price for what turned out to be the autographs of just three of the four Beatles was £6,000.*

* A snip, compared to some of the items offered by Frank Caiazzo at his New Jersey base. These include a brief letter written by John to a fan in early 1963, beginning 'Dear Dawn, Thanks for your letter, glad you liked the show,' and signed 'Cherrio [*sic*] love John Lennon X', which is selling for $19,500, and a 'Rare Important and Revealing John Lennon Handwritten Letter' from Rishikesh to a fan called Beth in February 1968, signed 'God Bless You – jai guru dev. with love John Lennon', which is selling for $75,000. In an introductory message to his online store, Mr Caiazzo notes that 'handwritten material represents a very special intimate part of the Beatles' lives that were seldom imparted to the

At another stall, I chanced upon what seemed like a bargain: the 45 rpm single 'That's My Life' recorded by Freddie Lennon, with backing vocals by the Ladybirds, in mint condition. It was selling for £10, which was about £100 cheaper than the next cheapest item. I handed over my £10, half-expecting the dealer to say 'There's been some mistake,' but he took it with a smile. It was only later that I noticed the small print:

> This track has been digitally remastered from an original 1965 single kindly supplied by Freddie's manager, Tony Cartwright.

This meant that I had just paid £10 for a brand-new single.

The man behind one stall was raising money for the Brian Epstein Statue Project. 'Our vision is to realise a world first: a statue of Brian, the Fifth Beatle, and one of the world's great creative individuals,' read the flyer. 'He united the world in the most powerfully sustaining way, and his impact is overwhelmingly positive. His legacy is also largely unseen, even though his impact on popular culture is incalculable. Yet his smiling face is unknown to so many around the world. This is why we need this memorial in his honour. He needs to stay amongst us and will be a truly collaborative work [*sic*]. By the people, for the people. WE will make Brian, together . . .'

I wandered in and out of the various neighbouring rooms. The Bluebeetles from Brazil were playing 'For the Benefit of Mr Kite' in Crompton's Bar, where Noël Coward might once have sipped a dry martini. In the Wave Bar a Finnish group called She's Leaving Home were playing 'Lovely Rita'. In the Crosby Suite, I half expected to find a group called Lovely Rita playing 'She's Leaving Home'. Instead, Abbey Road from Spain were singing 'Come Together', and in the American Bar the Fab Twins, an acoustic duo from Bristol, were singing 'Here, There and Everywhere'.

I began to feel engulfed by so many Beatles collectors and vendors and lookalike musicians, almost to the point of claustrophobia. Was I going to pass out from Beatlemania? Looking for somewhere to take a breather, I darted up a staircase off the main hall. To my surprise, halfway up the stairs I heard a voice cry, 'Craig!' An elderly man, sitting on one of the

---

public in any way. To acquire even one of these treasures is indeed quite an accomplishment for any fan or collector.'

steps, was beckoning me over. I had no idea who he was, or how he knew who I was.

'Stevie T told me to look out for you!' he said. 'Bill Smith!'

As we shook hands, I remembered that Stevie T, the tour guide from the day before, had told me to keep an eye out for Bill Smith, who was one of the original Quarrymen.

'You know the history, right?' said Bill. I said yes, but of course I was bluffing. I find it hard to get to grips with the Quarrymen. Their endless comings and goings seem to me as demanding as the Wars of the Roses, or the Schleswig-Holstein question. As far as I can work out, there were at least nine different line-ups from summer 1956 (when Bill was with them) to October 1959 (when Paul and George and someone called Ken Brown had joined, and all the others had left, apart from John). Around that time – are you still with me? – the Quarrymen changed their name to Johnny and the Moondogs, then to the Beatals, then to the Nerk Twins, then to the Silver Beetles, and finally, on 12 August 1960, to the Beatles. But even this list is incomplete: at various other stages, they were also the Silver Beats, the Beetles and Long John and the Silver Beatles.

And that is only Module One on the beginners' course. A real Beatles buff could rattle off at least two thousand words on each incarnation of the Quarrymen, and would happily sit up all night arguing over whether the young George Harrison first met the Quarrymen at the Wilson Hall on 7 December 1957, as Barry Miles says, or at the same venue on 6 February 1958, as Mark Lewisohn says, or at the Morgue Skiffle Cellar on 13 March 1958, as the Quarrymen drummer Colin Hanton says, or at a local chip shop on an unknown date, as George's mother Louise always maintained.

Encountering Bill Smith on that Adelphi staircase transported me back into another age. I might just as well have bumped into a junior member of Mr Gladstone's cabinet. What should I ask him? Happily, Bill was keen to talk unprompted. He said that he and John had been at Quarry Bank School together. 'We were always mucking about. For instance, one of us would whistle when the teacher's back was turned. And he'd turn round, but wouldn't know who'd done it. Then someone else would whistle, and he'd turn round again. Still nothing. And so it would go on. We sent him mad! And then John landed Pete Shotton in it by saying out loud, but as if it were under his breath, "Hey! Pete! You'd better stop now! I think he suspects!" And so thanks to John, Pete took the blame!'

John had the idea of forming a group in 1956. He persuaded his best friend Pete Shotton to be a member, and together they started trying to make instruments. Pete found a washboard in his father's shed, and thought playing it looked easy. Then John invited Bill, who stole a tea chest from the school woodwork room, rode away with it on his bike and turned it into a bass by putting a broom handle through it. Together with their classmates Eric Griffiths (guitar) and Rod Davis (banjo), they formed a group to play skiffle songs. What to call them? 'I came up with the Quarrymen, because we all went to Quarry Bank. John didn't like the name. He said, "No, I don't think that's much good." He probably thought it was too "Establishment", but Pete said, "No, it's good," and Eric agreed, and John couldn't think of anything else, so the Quarrymen it was.'

I found Bill very genial. Unlike so many who have rubbed shoulders with the Beatles, he was a man with no illusions. He didn't try to big himself up. He told me he hadn't been a Quarryman for long: 'My father wanted me to get on in life. We had exams to pass. Then two of us Quarrymen joined the merchant navy, and Pete joined the police. Of course, John had no father, so when he left school he idled away his time at art school.'

He said he had no regrets about leaving the group, and oddly enough, I believed him. 'I've had a good life, ups and downs of course, like anyone, but it's been a good life.' But then one regret did come to mind. 'When I left the group, I took my tea chest with me. I put it in my dad's garage. But John and Len Garry stole it. So I went and stole it back. And when I stole it back I found John had drawn all over it, cartoons and things. I sometimes wonder what it would be worth now. But my dad only went and threw it out!'

Bill had a book in his hand. I spotted that it had the word 'Beatles' in the title, so I asked what it was. 'Don't ask!' he said. He told me he had just bought it at one of the stalls. He passed it to me: *John, Paul & Me Before the Beatles: The True Story of the Very Early Days*, by Len Garry. Before long, I wished I hadn't mentioned it.

'True story, indeed! True story! Absolute CODSWALLOP! It's not as if I even wanted to buy it! I saw Len's wife the other day, and she said, "Have you read Len's book yet?" and I said, "No, I'm not a reader," and she said, "Oh, but you must," and she went on and on at me, so I bought one off her daughter, who was sitting behind one of those desks over there, with a big pile of them. It was £15, so I gave her a twenty and she said she didn't have any change. So she kept the twenty and gave me a free CD, which I never even wanted in the first place! And I was browsing through Len's book just now, and look where the page opened – just look!'

He flicked through to page 75, which was headed:

Chapter Five
Pete Shotton, John Lennon and the Tea Chest Bass
Thursday 11th November 1956: Time – 3:30

I obediently read the offending passage:

John Lennon and Pete Shotton, the two members of the newly formed Quarrymen Skiffle Group collected their respective bicycles from the shed at Quarrybank School. It was a relatively warm afternoon for mid November and so they took their time.

'Listen John, why did you let Bill Smith join the group? He never turns up to any of the rehearsals and I can't stand the guy anyway.'

'Well, Pete, he was keen enough to join in the first place, but perhaps we should be looking to replace him because he's so unreliable.'

'What about Len Garry? You know he can sing, and he has a good sense of humour.'

'Yeah, Len sounds like just the man.'

Sixty-three years on, Bill was seething. He thought it an appalling misrepresentation of what had happened. 'Load of crap! Utter rubbish! He wasn't even there, so how does he know what they said? I left the group of my own accord! I had other things to do! And Len came much later! He wasn't even in our class! Complete and utter codswallop! And to think he's charging £15 for this load of crap!'

Bill hadn't intended to come to the Beatles Convention, and had only turned up because Stevie T told him he owed it to history. I got up to go. 'Stevie T told me not to mention Brexit to you!' I said as a parting shot. His eyes lit up. Half an hour later, Bill Smith, founder member of the Quarrymen, was still holding forth about the iniquities of the European Union.

150.

Later, after the funeral and the inquest, Brian's secretary, Joanne Newfield, goes to his house in Belgravia. His brother Clive has asked her to clear out some of Brian's papers. She doesn't want to, but she feels it is her duty.

The house is empty. She goes up to Brian's bedroom, where she found him. It is eerie: she somehow feels his presence.

She wants to pick everything up, throw it all into bags, and get out of the house. She comes across a large book in which she used to leave letters for Brian to sign. Inside it, she comes across two suicide notes, one to his mother, Queenie, the other to Clive. Curiously, they are both dated several weeks before his death.

They are very short, covering barely a page. Later, she remembers them saying something along the lines of: 'Don't be sad. Don't be unhappy. I'm OK. Take good care of yourself. I love you.'

Maybe Brian had forgotten they were there.

8 SEPTEMBER 1967

At the inquest, Dr R. Donald Teare, consultant pathologist, reports that there were 168 milligrams of bromide in the blood of the deceased. Bromide is contained in the sedative Carbrital, but such a large figure could only have been reached by taking Carbrital over a long period. 'The stomach saturation suggests six capsules. The blood concentration about nine capsules, but not taken as a single dose.' Dr Teare says that Mr Epstein was 'approaching a state of bromide intoxication. To achieve the blood bromide figure would have taken weeks rather than days.' He adds that raised blood bromide might result in a man becoming careless and injudicious.

Dr Flood, Brian's psychiatrist, tells the inquest that 'With regard to drugs, the patient had for at least five years been taking amphetamines in large doses and he had also been regularly smoking marijuana. He had also experimented with heroin but was not addicted. At times, and in particular over the last two years, he drank excessively and had a tendency to take excessive doses of any drug.' He adds that the patient, who had 'always shown some signs of emotional instability', was also homosexual, and 'had been unable to come to terms with this problem'.

29 AUGUST 1967

They bury Brian close to his father in the Jewish Cemetery at Aintree. His father died just six weeks ago. Brian had sobbed uncontrollably in the car on the way home. Now it is Brian's turn to have others grieve.

Fearful that the crowds would get out of hand, Brian's mother Queenie has asked George and the other Beatles to stay away, so it is relatively quiet. Brian's business partner Nat Weiss disregards the Jewish rule of no flowers at funerals, and drops a single sunflower on top of Brian's grave. It is what George asked him to do.

At the synagogue in Greenbank Drive, Liverpool, the officiating rabbi, Dr Norman Solomon, suggests that Brian's death is 'symbolic of the malaise of a generation'. This strikes many in the congregation, including Nat Weiss, as unjust: 'How can a man who filled stadiums, who literally was the catalyst for the greatest musical event of the twentieth century, be treated as a malaise?'

Cilla Black is so overcome with grief that Queenie Epstein gives her a Valium.

28 AUGUST 1967

John, Paul, George and Ringo go to Chapel Street to pay their respects to Queenie Epstein. She thinks they are 'like four lost children'. In fact, she is not far out: Ringo, the oldest, has just turned twenty-seven. George, the youngest, is twenty-four. They are all very distressed. They tell her they will do anything she wants about the funeral. She tells them she would prefer it if they didn't come: she dreads it turning into a circus.

John says, 'Come to India with us and meditate.'

What, she asks, do they actually *do* when they meditate?

'Well, you think of something – like, say, a carrot,' replies John.

Queenie's reply is characteristically straightforward. 'Whenever I think of a carrot, I think of tomorrow's lunch.'

The obituaries are full of praise. 'In all his dealings, he was completely honest and trustworthy,' says *The Times*. 'By his presence and success in the pop world, he not only transformed its power and stature, he made it more respectable.'

27 AUGUST 1967

In the late afternoon, Paul has taken a break from the Transcendental Meditation gathering in Bangor, Wales, organised by the Maharishi Mahesh Yogi. He is chatting to a friendly reporter from the *Liverpool Echo*. In the background, a telephone won't stop ringing. Paul says he'd better go and see who it is. The reporter watches him pick up the receiver. He hears Paul saying, 'Oh no. Oh God, no. Oh no. Oh no'. Paul puts down the receiver and runs upstairs to where John, George and Ringo are. Some time later, he arrives back downstairs and says to the reporter, 'Brian was found dead in his bed this morning. It's an overdose of sleeping tablets or something. I don't know anything really. We've got to get back to London right away.'

John is scared. 'I knew that we were in trouble then. I didn't really have any misconceptions about our ability to do anything other than play music . . . I thought, "We've had it now."'

Early on the Sunday afternoon of that bank holiday weekend, Alistair Taylor has just arrived home from California when the phone rings. It is Brian Epstein's secretary, Joanne. She is with Antonio and Maria, Brian's household staff in Belgravia. They are worried: Brian hasn't appeared since late on Friday, and his bedroom door is locked. They have knocked on it, but he hasn't responded. Joanne says she is afraid to go in alone.

Alistair takes a cab to Chapel Street. Twice in the past, both times on a Sunday, Brian has phoned him to say he is going to commit suicide. 'Oh, Alistair, I've had enough now. I am just ringing to say goodbye.' Both times, Alistair has rushed over, to be greeted by an indignant Brian: 'Oh, don't be stupid. I was just a bit down. Leave me alone.'

On his arrival at Chapel Street, Alistair finds that Joanne has already summoned a doctor. The doctor forces the door open with his shoulder. Alistair follows him in. Brian is in bed. 'He looked as though he was asleep, but I knew straight away that he was dead. A wave of almost indescribable pain swept over me.'

The doctor says, 'I'm afraid he's dead.'

Alistair feels numb. He has a sense of everything, including himself, existing in slow motion.

He looks around. On one side of the bed sits a pile of correspondence, on the other a plate with three chocolate digestive biscuits. A glass and a half-empty bottle of bitter lemon are on the floor. Eight bottles of pills are on the bedside table. 'He lived on pills – pills to wake him up, pills to send him to sleep, pills to keep him lively, pills to quieten him down, pills to cure his indigestion.' All the bottles are full, and have their caps on. None of them are empty.

Together with the doctor, Alistair searches the room. There is no note, no sign of disturbance. In a drawer, Alistair finds an enormous ready-rolled joint. He slips it quietly into his trouser pocket. The two of them go downstairs. Alistair tells Joanne that Brian is dead. The doctor rings the coroner's office. Alistair braces himself and rings Brian's brother Clive.

'You're *lying*. You're *lying*,' says Clive, and hangs up.

13 MAY 1967

After his psychiatrist, Dr John Flood, diagnoses 'insomnia, agitation, anxiety and depression', Brian checks himself into the Priory hospital in Roehampton. They keep him in an induced sleep for just under a week.

Upon waking, he receives a stream of visitors. They find him crotchety and slightly paranoid, but he has the odd moment of emotional release. In the middle of a business visit from Robert Stigwood and Nat Weiss, an enormous bouquet of flowers arrives. He opens the note, and reads it out. It is from John. 'You know I love you, I really do.' Brian breaks down in tears. His two visitors retreat to the hallway. 'He's not in his right mind,' says Stigwood.

Paul writes Brian a four-page letter, a sweet but uneasy mix of admonishment and encouragement: 'Your BIGGEST TROUBLE IS YOU TAKE IT ALL TOO SERIOUSLY!' He cuts a headline – 'WHO CARES?' – out of a newspaper and sticks it to the third page, adding, in his own writing, 'Some people do, friends, and the time has come to listen to them.' He ends the letter, 'THINK FINE, keep your pecker up, and speedy recovery.'

The Beatles ask Peter Brown to bring a portable record player and an early copy of their new album to the Priory. Brian sits up in bed and listens to *Sgt. Pepper's Lonely Hearts Club Band* for the very first time.

SPRING 1967

Brian's behaviour is becoming increasingly erratic. Once so prompt, he is seldom on time. He cancels appointments at the last minute. At business meetings, he fails to make any general sense, but will latch on to some little detail, and make a terrible scene about it, shouting and screaming, 'Why hasn't this been done??!!'

28 FEBRUARY 1967

Brian is staying at the Waldorf Towers hotel in Manhattan. He is about to set off for a radio interview with Murray 'The K' Kaufman at WOR-FM when Nat Weiss drops by, and finds him slurring his words. It emerges that he has taken a handful of Nembutal barbiturates, and is set to take more. Weiss wrestles him to the floor, and throws the bottle out of the window. He then plies him with coffee and, on Brian's insistence, drives him to the interview.

Weiss sits close to him in the studio, to prevent him from slumping over. For the first few minutes Brian mumbles incoherently while Murray The K fills in with DJ babble. But soon the stimulants kick in, and Brian springs back to life.

Whenever he is in Manhattan, Brian's favourite pastime is to sit by himself in the back of a chauffeur-driven limousine. Then he likes to dip into his silver cigarette case for a joint, pre-rolled by one of his staff, while being driven around Central Park. He always asks for the same music to be played over and over again on the car's stereo system: 'It's the Same Old Song' by the Four Tops.

LATE JANUARY 1967

In a reversal of the usual order of things, the Beatles are concerned about Brian. 'Eppy seems to be in a terrible state,' John tells his friend Pete. 'The guy's head's a total mess, and we're really worried about him.' His concern is as much professional as personal: 'We just don't know what the fuck we can do about it. It's time for us to go off in our own direction, and that's that.'

John puts on a tape recording, which Pete later describes as 'barely recognisable as that of a human voice, alternately groaning, grunting, and shrieking – and occasionally mumbling words which, even when decipherable, made no apparent sense whatsoever'.

Pete asks who it is.

'That's Brian,' replies John. 'He made this tape for me in his house. I don't know why he sent it, but he's trying to tell me something, fuck knows what. He just can't seem to communicate with us in the usual way any more.'

MID-JANUARY 1967

Brian asks Paddy Chambers, a Liverpool musician, to Chapel Street. 'I've got a surprise for you,' he says.

Paddy finds the four Beatles there with their wives and girlfriends. Brian vanishes, and returns carrying a big silver tray with a little sugar cube on it. 'I've got to see someone tripping for the first time,' says John. It emerges that everyone else has already taken one.

Within two hours, everyone is ripping up newspapers and flinging them around. Brian produces more and more newspapers until they are knee-deep in them.

LATE NOVEMBER–DECEMBER 1966

Now that the Beatles have stopped touring, they have less need of Brian, and less time for him too. Their studio engineer, Geoff Emerick, senses that they don't really like him hanging around in the studio. Brian misses his daily contact with them. With less and less to do, his flight from boredom grows more and more reckless.

29 AUGUST 1966

In San Francisco, just hours before the Beatles play Candlestick Park, Brian seems dejected. He has decided not to attend the concert himself. Instead, he stays in his suite in the Beverly Hills Hotel in Los Angeles. He says to Nat Weiss, 'This will be the last Beatles concert ever.'

He tells Nat that his old lover John 'Dizz' Gillespie has popped by; in fact, they spent the afternoon in and around the hotel swimming pool. 'He's changed,' says Brian.

'He hasn't changed,' says Weiss. 'Get rid of him.'

'Oh, you don't understand . . . he really loves me.'

Brian insists that the Beatles like Gillespie. Weiss knows this to be untrue: they have made their dislike known. Brian appears to be sexually excited by insolence and aggression, though in everyday life there is nothing that upsets him more. While the Beatles are playing what will, indeed, be their final concert, Brian and Nat go out to dinner. They return to find that Gillespie has run off with their briefcases. Brian's black Samsonite briefcase contained contracts for the Beatles tour, a bottle of illegal Seconal barbiturates and $20,000 in cash.

Later, Gillespie sends them a blackmail-cum-ransom note, demanding $10,000 for the return of their cases. Brian tells Nat to 'let it go', but by now Weiss's dislike of Gillespie has curdled to hatred. Once Brian is back in England, Weiss hires a private detective to meet Gillespie at a railway station. He has set a trap for him. Gillespie is arrested, and Brian is reunited with his briefcase and half the money it contained.*

But Brian regards Nat's action not as heroic or sensible but as a breach of trust: he had instructed him to leave Gillespie alone, and Nat had dis-

---

* Fifty-three years later the briefcase was sold at auction in Los Angeles, 'accompanied by a letter of authenticity from Epstein's nephew, Henry Epstein', for £3,437.50.

obeyed him. 'He was very depressed by the whole thing,' reflects Weiss years later. 'The whole betrayal is what really destroyed him.'

7 AUGUST 1966

Brian is in New York, trying to calm the furore that has greeted the news that, earlier in the year, John said the Beatles were 'bigger than Jesus'. By chance, Nat Weiss notices that Brian has a row of tiny little pockets tailored into the inside of his jacket. Brian explains that these are his 'pill pockets', stocked with amphetamines and tranquillisers in ascending order of strength.

6 APRIL 1966

After a party to celebrate Cilla Black's opening night of a three-week residency in the Persian Room of the Plaza Hotel, Brian tells Weiss that he has a problem. Dizz Gillespie is in New York, and has been in touch. He says he wants to see Brian again. Brian feels powerless to resist, but at the same time he lives in fear that Dizz will do something to embarrass the Beatles.

Nat agrees to help, and invites Gillespie to his office. The moment he walks through the door he recognises his type: 'the garden-variety hustler'.

Gillespie insists he loves Brian. 'I don't want anything from him. I just want to see him.'

'Good. Because you're not going to get anything from him, and you're not going to see him. I want you to stay away from him.'

'Well, then. Brian's got lots of money. If he wants me to stay away . . . well, if I had a car I could go away.'

Weiss relays Gillespie's demands to Brian, but advises him against agreeing to them, saying, 'He'll only come back for more.' But Brian tells him to give Gillespie $3,000 for a car. Before he hands over the money, Weiss tells Gillespie he must agree to remain locked in a room at the Warwick Hotel, under guard, until Brian and the Beatles have left town.

1965–66

Brian frequently dines with the *NME* journalist Chris Hutchins at Overton's restaurant in St James's. He seldom eats much. Instead, he spends time poring over the menu, choosing his dish with great care, telling the waiter exactly how he wants his vegetables cooked, and so on. Then he swallows a handful of pills, before passing some to Hutchins, insisting he joins him in enjoying what he calls 'our little helpers'. These are uppers, which have the effect of suppressing the appetite. By the time the food arrives, neither of them wants it. Time after time, the lobster and fillet steak dishes are sent back to the kitchen with 'Mr Epstein's compliments to the chef'.

17 AUGUST 1965

The American journalist Larry Kane, who has grown close to the Beatles after travelling with them throughout their first US tour, observes a notable change in Brian. He has become volatile. One minute his face is beaming, the next it bears 'a look of outright depression'.

MARCH 1965

Brian's new boyfriend, Dizz Gillespie, has a capacity for violence. Brian and Dizz spend their evenings ingesting uppers washed down with cognac. These evenings often end in fierce arguments, involving smashed vases and mirrors. One night, Gillespie gets in such a rage that Brian orders him to leave the flat. Gillespie grabs a kitchen knife, holds it to Brian's jugular and extracts money from Brian's wallet.

SPRING 1965

Paddy Chambers visits Brian in his Knightsbridge flat. Chaos confronts him: 'He just totally wrecked the whole, very expensive flat, ripped all the drapes down, smashed the cocktail cabinet to bits . . . For some strange reason, and I suppose it had to be drugs, he was "off his cake".'

FEBRUARY 1965

Someone gouges the word 'QUEER' with a key onto the door of Brian's Bentley, parked in the mews behind his new house in Chapel Street.

JANUARY 1965

On the telephone to his parents, Brian sounds so peculiar that they rush over to his house. They find him heavily hung over, unable to face the day. He confesses his love of Gillespie. His mother, Queenie, insists that he try to forget about him by taking a holiday in the south of France with Peter Brown. That afternoon, Brian and Peter set off for a hotel in Cap d'Antibes. On his return, Brian sells the flat that has been the scene of so much unhappiness and buys a five-storey Georgian house in Chapel Street, Belgravia.

DECEMBER 1964

Brian Epstein is now the most successful manager and impresario in Britain, perhaps the world. Earlier this year the Beatles occupied the top five positions on the *Billboard* Hot 100.

Other artists under his management have also achieved extraordinary success. In March, Gerry and the Pacemakers reached number 1 with their debut single, 'How Do You Do It?'. In June, Billy J. Kramer and the Dakotas reached number 1 with their debut single, 'Do You Want to Know a Secret', written by Lennon and McCartney. And so it goes on: Gerry and the Pacemakers back at the top in July with 'I Like It', followed by Billy J. Kramer in August with 'Bad to Me', and Gerry and the Pacemakers back again in November with 'You'll Never Walk Alone'. By the end of the year his various artists have had eight number ones.

Brian's staff are surprised when he adds an actor to the agency's roster of talent: John 'Dizz' Gillespie.

6 NOVEMBER 1964

Brian appears on BBC radio's prestigious *Desert Island Discs*. Apart from a version of 'All My Loving' by the George Martin Orchestra and 'She's a Woman' by the Beatles, his choices are broadly classical: Bach's Brandenburg Concerto Number 5, Sibelius's 2nd Symphony, Bruch's Violin Concerto. Asked to choose one book for his desert island, he picks *Elected Silence*, the autobiography of the Trappist monk Thomas Merton.*

With hindsight, this unexpected choice seems peculiarly significant. 'What can we gain by sailing to the moon if we are not able to cross the abyss that separates us from ourselves?' asks Merton in one memorable passage. 'This is the most important of all voyages of discovery, and without it, all the rest are not only useless, but disastrous.'

OCTOBER 1964

Brian meets Dizz Gillespie, a young American in his early twenties with, in the words of one associate, 'dark hair, mischievous eyes and an impish, upturned nose'. Gillespie is keen to become an actor or a singer, or both. 'There's something special about him,' says Brian. 'Something I can't name.'

Brian pays off Gillespie's debts, gives him an allowance from his personal account, signs him to NEMS on a £50 a week retainer, and buys him a new wardrobe. The newspapers announce that he is Brian's latest discovery.

15 SEPTEMBER 1964

The Beatles appear at the Public Auditorium in Cleveland, Ohio. Their fans have never been more fervent. A police cordon encircles the Sheraton Hotel where they are staying. A young boy is discovered hiding in a packing case, hoping to be smuggled into the hotel. A young girl pretends to faint outside in the street, then refuses to receive first aid unless she is taken inside.

During the show, the local disc jockey Jim Staggs climbs a two-hundred-foot lighting scaffold, hoping to get a better view. Halfway up he looks over his shoulder, only to see Brian Epstein climbing up behind him. 'Jim!' he shouts. 'You wouldn't be taping this performance, would you?'

Larry Kane, covering the tour for the Miami radio station WFUN, is impressed by such tenacity: 'The fact that he put himself at risk to make the climb was proof positive that Brian Epstein would do anything to protect the artistic sanctity – and profitability – of his Beatles.'

---

* First published in America in 1948 under the title *The Seven Storey Mountain*.

JULY 1964

The British Clothing Manufacturers' Federation presents Brian Epstein with a silver plaque, citing his 'exemplary standards in the choice and wearing of clothes', and adding that 'His sartorial taste hits the mark as surely as his eye for talent.'

Brian favours made-to-measure suits, Burberry raincoats, polkadot cravats, Christian Dior silk ties and gold cufflinks. His personal valet keeps everything in pristine order. Brian's client Cilla Black thinks he cuts quite a dash: 'He was immaculate from head to toe, like Cary Grant . . . He was everything you wanted a posh fella to look like.'

'He always looked as if he'd just stepped out of the bath,' says his Liverpool tailor George Hayes. 'He would always be polite and appreciative, but also demanding.'

17 MAY 1964

Brian is interviewed by the *Observer*'s star interviewer, Kenneth Harris, who asks him how long he thinks the Beatles will go on. 'Indefinitely,' he replies. 'They are bound to. There's so much talent there. Each one is a remarkable man.' Asked what they have got that other people haven't, he says: 'They've got this astonishing naturalness, this freedom from *un*naturalness. In private they are unspoiled, unaffected, sincere – themselves all the time, and to *everybody*, regardless.'

Brian talks about his shyness, and his unhappiness at school. Harris asks, 'So the Beatles solved your problem for you?'

Brian replies: 'Yes, it's a funny thing, and I've never thought about it that way before. But it's quite true. Everything about the Beatles was right for me. Their kind of attitude to life, the attitude that comes out in their music and their rhythm and their lyrics, and their humour, and their personal way of behaving – it was all just what I wanted. They represented the direct, unselfconscious, good-natured, uninhibited human relationships which I hadn't found and had wanted and felt deprived of. My own sense of inferiority evaporated with the Beatles because I knew I could help them, and that they wanted me to help them, and trusted me to help them. Then the success I registered in social and money terms was important. It didn't matter much to me in myself, but it mattered to other people. My

parents were impressed that I had shown good judgement and initiative, so I felt I hadn't let them down. So my tensions and frustrations all went. I've got plenty of problems. But I'm not pulled down by them any more.'

14 JANUARY 1964

The Beatles begin a series of eighteen concerts at the Olympia Theatre in Paris. After one of the shows Brian says, 'They didn't know it but I cried tonight, I really did. They never noticed, but I cried.'

DECEMBER 1963

The Beatles end the year as the most famous pop group in Britain, having had three number 1 hits – 'From Me to You', 'She Loves You' and 'I Want to Hold Your Hand'. Brian is now carefully plotting their arrival in America, where they remain an unknown quantity.

JANUARY 1963

In the *NME* annual readers' survey, the Beatles finish in joint 111th place. They share their position with Mike Berry,* the Clyde Valley

---

* Mike Berry (1942–), singer. His single 'Don't You Think it's Time' reached number 6 in January 1963. In 1981 he was cast as Bert Spooner in the eighth season of *Are You Being Served?*, remaining with the show until 1985.

Stompers* and Norman Vaughan.† In the 'British Small Group' category, they gain 743 votes compared to the Shadows' 45,951. They end up in eighth position, between the Temperance Seven‡ at number 7 and Sounds Incorporated§ at number 9.

7 JUNE 1962

Having listened to their demo disc, George Martin from EMI calls the Beatles in for a test recording, but without much enthusiasm: during their session he pops out for tea and biscuits in the canteen. He sees no reason to pay special attention to 'four berks from Liverpool'. Once their audition is over he remains sceptical, particularly about their self-written songs. He is 'quite certain that their songwriting ability had no saleable future'.

But chatting to them afterwards in a café, he is struck by their magic: their quick wits, their cock-snooking banter, their devil-may-care energy.

'The next fifteen to twenty minutes was pure entertainment. When they left I just sat there saying, "Phew! What do you think of that lot then?" I had tears running down my face.'

Broadly speaking, it is on the strength of their personalities, rather than their music, that he decides to offer the Beatles a contract.

8 MAY 1962

Brian has been to so many record companies that he has run out of demos, so he goes into the HMV shop in Oxford Street with a tape of the Beatles'

---

* The Clyde Valley Stompers, trad jazz band, formed in Glasgow in the 1950s. 'Before Beatlemania erupted, there was Stompermania' – *The Scotsman*. The Clyde Valley Stompers reached number 25 in August 1962 with their jazzed-up version of 'Peter and the Wolf', but achieved no subsequent chart success.

† Norman Vaughan (1923–2002), all-round family entertainer, actor (*No Sex Please, We're British*) and game-show host (*The Golden Shot*, 1972–73).

‡ The Temperance Seven, trad jazz band known for their zany humour. Their 1960 hit with Peter Sellers, 'Ukulele Lady', was produced by George Martin. Their song 'You're Driving Me Crazy' reached number 1 in 1961.

§ Sounds Incorporated, instrumental group. They signed to Brian Epstein's NEMS in 1963, and reached number 30 in the charts with 'The Spartans' in April 1964, and number 35 with 'Spanish Harlem'. They achieved more success in Australia with their version of 'The William Tell Overture', which reached number 2. They were the Beatles' opening act at Shea Stadium in August 1965, and broke up a year after the Beatles, in 1971.

rejected Decca recordings, and pays £1 to transfer it to disc. The disc-cutter, Jim Foy, tells him that the group sounds 'not at all bad', and asks if they have a contract. 'No, I've been trying everywhere and everyone,' says Brian.

Foy takes him upstairs, and introduces him to EMI's music publisher, Sid Coleman. Sid asks him if he's tried EMI, and Brian says he has: 'I was told no go.' Sid asks him if he saw George Martin.

'Who's he?'

'He runs Parlophone.'

Brian feels that he has now really hit rock bottom: for him, Parlophone is a non-event, a dustbin for comedy and jazz.

MAY 1962-DECEMBER 1961

Brian keeps taking time off work to go up to London, travelling from record company to record company with the Beatles' demo.

He doesn't want his father to know about these trips. 'Don't tell Daddy,' he says to his assistant Alistair Taylor whenever he sets off. 'If he comes in the shop, don't tell him where I've gone.'

Waiting for him to return from each trip, Paul and John always sit in the same coffee shop in Lime Street station. As Brian walks towards them, they look at his face to see if it's good news or bad. It's always bad.

Touting the demo around, Brian always carries a brief explanatory note about the Beatles. It reads: 'These four boys, who are superb instrumentalists, also produce some exciting and pulsating vocals. This is a group of exceptional talents and appealing personalities.'

He tells everyone he meets that the Beatles will be bigger than Elvis. He continues to say it even after he has been turned down countless times. Deep down, observes a friend, Brian thinks of himself as a man of destiny.

FOUR

FEBRUARY 1962

Fans at the Cavern are struck by the change in the Beatles' appearances and general demeanour. What has happened? A fifteen-year-old schoolgirl,

Shelagh Carney, is 'hit like a brick' when she sees them. 'They had looked so rough until then. Suddenly they looked steam-cleaned, from their skin and shiny hair to their fingernails and their clothes.'

Nobody can understand how Brian Epstein has managed to get them to conform. 'How Epstein ever persuaded Lennon to put on a suit I shall never know,' says a local musician, Rod Pont.

THREE

I FEBRUARY 1962

For a fee of £18, minus Brian's commission of 10 per cent, Brian's new group plays the Thistle Café in West Kirby, ten miles from Liverpool. This is the first booking he has made for them.

Earlier that same day, the Beatles sign a contract with Brian Epstein for a five-year period. Brian is to receive 10 per cent of the group's income up to £1,500 a year each, increasing to 15 per cent thereafter.

TWO

29 JANUARY 1962

Brian pays off the Beatles' £200 debt, accumulated from hire-purchase agreements for guitars and amplifiers. He takes the boys to Beno Dorn, his tailor, who kits them out in smart dark-blue mohair suits with narrow lapels. They keep insisting that they want their trousers narrower. Brian bargains Dorn down from 28 guineas to 23, telling him that the Beatles will be big, and so he'll get more orders.

Brian's assistant, Alistair Taylor, comes too: 'Brian embarked on a total clean-up job on the four boys. Haircuts followed the suits, and complete new wardrobes of shirts, ties, shoes, everything followed. Brian asked them face-to-face if they had any objections to his plans, and there wasn't even a murmur of dissent. Just as Brian believed in the Beatles, it was clear from the very start that the Beatles believed in Brian.'

Brian insists that they smarten themselves up. He gives them each firm directives, typed on top-quality paper: 'Onstage, there must be no drinking, no smoking, no chewing gum, and especially no swearing. The audience is not there to talk to you so don't chat to the pretty girls while you're onstage. Be punctual. If you're scheduled to arrive at a certain time, make sure you arrive when you are meant to. Remember that you are professionals now, with a reputation to keep up.'

The most troublesome member of the group, John Lennon, is impressed. Later, he recalls how 'Brian put all our instructions down on paper and it made it all seem real. We were in a daydream 'til he came along . . . We stopped chomping at cheese rolls and jam butties onstage.'

ONE

9 NOVEMBER 1961

One.

    Two.

        Three.

            Four.

In their neat black suits and ties, Brian Epstein and his personal assistant Alistair Taylor make their way down the eighteen steep steps into the sweaty basement on Mathew Street. Brian finds it 'as black as a deep grave, dank and damp and smelly'. He wishes he hadn't come. Both he and Taylor would prefer to be attending a classical concert at the Philharmonic, but curiosity got the better of them. Four young musicians saunter onto the stage. Brian recognises them from the family record shop he manages: they are the ones who lounge around in the booths, listening to the latest discs and chatting to the girls, with absolutely no intention whatsoever of buying a record.

Between songs, the three yobs with guitars start yelling and swearing, turning their backs on the audience and pretending to hit one another. Taylor notices Brian's eyes widen with amazement. Taylor himself is undergoing one of the most shocking experiences of his life – 'like someone thumping you' – and he is pretty sure Brian feels the same.

After the show, Taylor says, 'They're just AWFUL.'

'They ARE awful,' agrees Brian. 'But I also think they're fabulous. Let's just go and say hello.'

George is the first of the Beatles to spot the man from the record shop approaching.

'Hello there,' he says. 'What brings Mr Epstein here?'

'Does anyone seriously believe that Beatles music will be an unthinkingly accepted part of daily life all over the world in the 2000s?'

—*Bryan Magee, philosopher and politician, article in* The Listener, *February 1967*

SOURCES

Many good books have been written about the Beatles: in fact, the general standard is much higher in terms of style and honesty than those dealing with my last subject, the royal family. For a microscopic account of their early lives, *The Beatles: All These Years – Tune In Special Extended Edition Volumes 1 and 2* by Mark Lewisohn is indispensable. I have also relied on *The Beatles* by Hunter Davies; *Beatles '66: The Revolutionary Year* by Steve Turner; *The Beatles: The Biography* by Bob Spitz; *Shout!: The True Story of the Beatles* by Philip Norman; *Can't Buy Me Love: The Beatles, Britain and America* by Jonathan Gould; *The Beatles Anthology* by the Beatles; *The Complete Beatles Chronicle* by Mark Lewisohn; *The Complete Beatles Recording Sessions: The Official Story of the Abbey Road Years 1962–1970* by Mark Lewisohn; *The Beatles Diary: An Intimate Day by Day History* by Barry Miles; *Love Me Do: The Beatles' Progress* by Michael Braun; *The Beatles Off the Record* by Keith Badman; *The Beatles: Paperback Writer – Forty Years of Classic Writing* edited by Mike Evans; *The Beatles in Their Own Words* compiled by Barry Miles; *The Beatles: A Day in the Life* compiled by Tom Schultheiss; *Ticket to Ride: Inside the Beatles' 1964 and 1965 Tours that Changed the World* by Larry Kane; *The Rough Guide to the Beatles* by Chris Ingham; *The Beatles Encyclopaedia* by Bill Harry; and the ever-thrilling *Revolution in the Head: The Beatles' Records and the Sixties* by Ian MacDonald.

Particularly useful have been two works dealing with more specialist aspects of the Beatles: *You Never Give Me Your Money: The Battle for the Soul of the Beatles* by Peter Doggett, a wonderfully clear survey of their complicated finances; and *Riding So High: The Beatles and Drugs* by Joe Goodden, an equally clear survey of their equally complicated drug lives. Other specialist books include: *The Beatles and the Historians* by Erin Torkelson Weber; *The Beatles on the Roof* by Tony Barrell; *The Beatles Lyrics: The Unseen Story Behind Their Music* by Hunter Davies; *The Walrus Was Ringo: 101 Beatles Myths Debunked* by Alan Clayson and Spencer Leigh; *How the Beatles Rocked the Kremlin: The Untold Story of a Noisy Revolution* by Leslie Woodhead; *The Beatles Are Here!* by Penelope Rowlands; *The Beatles Sent to Coventry* by Pete Chambers; *Dear Beatles* compiled by Bill Adler; *Dreaming the Beatles* by Rob Sheffield; *The Greatest Beatles Stories Ever Told* edited by Luis Miguel; *Beatles Hamburg: A Tour Guide*

to Beatles Sites in Hamburg by Mark A. Schneegurt; *The Beatles in India* by Paul
Saltzman; *The Beatles' Gear: All the Fab Four's Instruments, from Stage to Studio*
by Andy Babiuk; *A Day in the Life of the Beatles* by Don McCullin; *Get Back:
The Unauthorized Chronicle of the Beatles' Let It Be Disaster* by Doug Sulpy and
Ray Schweighardt; *John, Paul & Me Before the Beatles: The True Story of the
Very Early Days* by Len Garry; *The Quarrymen* by Hunter Davies; *The Beatles
in Hamburg* by Ian Inglis; *The Beatles' Liverpool* by Ron Jones; *Plastic Macca:
The Secret Death and Replacement of Beatle Paul McCartney* by Tina Foster;
and *Beatlemania! The Real Story of the Beatles' UK Tours 1963–1965* by Martin
Creasy.

Many books by and about individual members of the Beatles have come in
very useful, among them *Paul McCartney: The Biography* by Philip Norman;
Paul McCartney: Many Years from Now by Barry Miles; *Paul McCartney* by
Alan Clayson; *Conversations With McCartney* by Paul du Noyer; *Sixties: Por-
trait of an Era* by Linda McCartney; *George Harrison* by Alan Clayson; *I Me
Mine* by George Harrison; *Ringo Starr* by Alan Clayson; *Lennon and McCartney*
by Malcolm Doney; *Being John Lennon: A Restless Life* by Ray Connolly; *John
Lennon: The Life* by Philip Norman; *John Lennon* by Alan Clayson; *John Lennon
in His Own Words* compiled by Barry Miles; *The Lives of John Lennon* by Albert
Goldman; *John Lennon: One Day at a Time* by Anthony Fawcett; *Memories of
John Lennon* introduced and edited by Yoko Ono; *The Penguin John Lennon*;
and *The John Lennon Letters* edited and with an introduction by Hunter Davies.

Works by family members include Cynthia Lennon's two interesting if
sometimes contradictory biographies of John: *A Twist of Lennon* (1978) and
John (2005); *Imagine This: Growing Up With My Brother John Lennon* by Julia
Baird; *Thank U Very Much: Mike McCartney's Family Album*; *George Harrison:
Living in the Material World* by Olivia Harrison; *Wonderful Today* by Pattie
Boyd with Penny Junor; and *Daddy, Come Home: The True Story of John Lennon
and His Father* by Pauline Lennon.

Virtually everyone who ever worked in any capacity for the Beatles seems to
have put pen to paper, or to have had others put pen to paper on their behalf.
Many of these books are full of fascinating bits and pieces, among them my
favourite, *The Beatles, Lennon and Me* by Pete Shotton and Nicholas Schaffner;
but also *As Time Goes By* by Derek Taylor; *The Love You Make: An Insider's Story
of the Beatles* by Peter Brown and Steven Gaines; *All You Need is Ears* by George
Martin with Jeremy Hornsby; *Magical Mystery Tours: My Life With the Beatles*
by Tony Bramwell with Rosemary Kingsland; *With the Beatles* by Alistair Taylor; *The Man Who Gave the Beatles Away* by Alan Williams and William Marshall; *The Cutting Edge: The Story of the Beatles' Hairdresser Who Defined an Era*
by Leslie Cavendish; *The Longest Cocktail Party* by Richard DiLello; *Here, There
and Everywhere: My Life Recording the Music of the Beatles* by Geoff Emerick

and Howard Massey; and *John Paul George Ringo and Me* by Tony Barrow. Particular mentions should be made of *Beatle!: The Pete Best Story* by Pete Best and Patrick Doncaster, and a biography of the ill-fated Jimmie Nicol, *The Beatle Who Vanished* by Jim Berkenstadt.

I particularly enjoyed two fine biographies of the troubled, enigmatic figure of Brian Epstein: *In My Life: The Brian Epstein Story* by Debbie Geller, edited by Anthony Wall; and *Brian Epstein: The Man Who Made the Beatles* by Ray Coleman.

Part of the fun of writing a book about the Beatles lies in the extraordinary number of colourful characters who surrounded them. Biographies and memoirs of these figures include: *Tearing Down the Wall of Sound: The Rise and Fall of Phil Spector* by Mick Brown; *Miss O'Dell* by Chris O'Dell with Katherine Ketcham; *I'm With the Band* by Pamela Des Barres; *Walking Back to Happiness* by Helen Shapiro; *I Read the News Today, Oh Boy* by Paul Howard; *Groovy Bob: The Life and Times of Robert Fraser* by Harriet Vyner; *Allen Klein* by Fred Goodman; *The Day Elvis Met Nixon* by Egil 'Bud' Krogh; *Victor Spinetti Up Front* by Victor Spinetti; *King of Clubs* by Peter Stringfellow; *Freddie Starr Unwrapped* by Freddie Starr; *Christine Keeler: The Truth at Last* by Christine Keeler and Douglas Thompson; *Me* by Elton John; *The Hurdy Gurdy Man* by Donovan; *Be My Baby: How I Survived Mascara, Miniskirts and Madness* by Ronnie Spector with Vince Waldron; *King of the World: Muhammad Ali and the Rise of an American Hero* by David Remnick; *Can You Tell What it is Yet?: My Autobiography* by Rolf Harris; *I Am Brian Wilson: A Memoir* by Brian Wilson with Ben Greenman; *Catch a Wave: The Rise, Fall and Redemption of the Beach Boys* by Brian Wilson; *An Affectionate Punch* by Justin de Villeneuve; *House of Nutter: The Rebel Tailor of Savile Row* by Lance Richardson; *East End, West End: An Autobiography* by Bernard Delfont; *Faithfull* by Marianne Faithfull; *Memories, Dreams and Reflections* by Marianne Faithfull; *What's it All About?* by Cilla Black; *Eric Clapton: The Autobiography* by Eric Clapton with Christopher Simon Sykes; *Don't Let Me Be Misunderstood* by Eric Burdon with J. Marshall Craig; *Careless Love: The Unmaking of Elvis Presley* by Peter Guralnick; *Elvis Meets the Beatles* by Chris Hutchins and Peter Thompson; *Sinatra: The Life* by Anthony Summers and Robbyn Swan; *Frank: The Making of a Legend* by James Kaplan; *My Father's Daughter: A Memoir* by Tina Sinatra and Jeff Coplon; *Parcel Arrived Safely: Tied With String* by Michael Crawford; *Tom Jones: A Biography* by Stafford Hildren and David Gritten; *Redeeming Features: A Memoir* by Nicholas Haslam; *Long Drawn Out Trip: A Memoir* by Gerald Scarfe; *Wild Tales* by Graham Nash; *Losing My Virginity* by Richard Branson; *The Harder Path* by John Birt; *Grapefruit* by Yoko Ono; *Chronicles: Volume One* by Bob Dylan; *Mick and Keith* by Chris Salewicz; *The Stones* by Philip Norman; *Life* by Keith Richards; *Stoned* by Andrew Loog Oldham; *Brian Jones* by Laura

Jackson; *Sympathy for the Devil* by Paul Trynka; *Up Against It: A Screenplay for the Beatles* by Joe Orton; *The Orton Diaries* edited by John Lahr; and *Prick Up Your Ears: The Biography of Joe Orton* by John Lahr. Rereading, and re-rereading, *The Pillowbook of Eleanor Bron* has been a particular delight.

Other works from which I have drawn include: *Wondrous Strange: The Life and Art of Glenn Gould* by Kevin Bazzana; *The Odd Thing About the Colonel and Other Pieces* by Colin Welch; *The Virgin's Baby: The Battle of the Ampthill Succession* by Bevis Hillier; *A King's Story* by The Duke of Windsor; *The Mountbattens: Their Lives and Loves* by Andrew Lownie; *Shirley Temple: American Princess* by Anne Edwards; *R.V.W.: A Biography of Ralph Vaughan Williams* by Ursula Vaughan Williams; *Born to Run* by Bruce Springsteen; *Unfaithful Music and Disappearing Ink* by Elvis Costello; *This Boy* by Alan Johnson; *My Life, Our Times* by Gordon Brown; *Let Me Take You Down: Inside the Mind of Mark David Chapman* by Jack Jones; *Manson: The Life and Times of Charles Manson* by Jeff Guinn; *My Life With Charles Manson* by Paul Watkins; *It Could Have Been Yours* by Jolyon Fenwick and Marcus Husselby; *The People's Music* by Ian MacDonald; *Uncommon People: The Rise and Fall of the Rock Stars* by David Hepworth; *Revolt Into Style: The Pop Arts in Britain* by George Melly; *The People's Songs: The Story of Modern Britain in Fifty Songs* by Stuart Maconie; *Stardust Memories: Talking About My Generation* by Ray Connolly; *Hunting People: Thirty Years of Interviews With the Famous* by Hunter Davies; and *Who the Hell . . . ?* by the remarkable Tom Hibbert. The first book I ever read about pop remains one of the best, even though its author is not a wholehearted fan of the Beatles: *Awopbopaloobop Alopbambboom: Pop from the Beginning* by Nik Cohn.

Diaries and letters are always my favourite sources. I greatly enjoyed plundering: *Philip Larkin: Letters to Monica* edited by Anthony Thwaite; *The Letters of Kingsley Amis* edited by Zachary Leader; *The Letters of Noël Coward* edited by Barry Day; *The Noël Coward Diaries* edited by Graham Payn and Sheridan Morley; *The Kenneth Williams Letters* edited by Russell Davies; *The Kenneth Williams Diaries* edited by Russell Davies; *Like it Was: The Diaries of Malcolm Muggeridge*; *Rub Out the Words: The Letters of William S. Burroughs, 1959–1974* edited by Bill Morgan; *The Kenneth Tynan Letters* edited by Kathleen Tynan; *The Kenneth Tynan Diaries* edited by John Lahr; *Out of the Wilderness: Diaries 1963–67* by Tony Benn; *The Castle Diaries 1964–1976* by Barbara Castle; and *The Macmillan Diaries Vol. II* edited by Peter Catterall. Also: *All What Jazz* by Philip Larkin; *Philip Larkin: Collected Poems*; and *Philip Larkin: A Writer's Life* by Andrew Motion.

Books I have raided for intriguing information about other movements, personalities and events in the sixties include: *Modernity Britain: Opening the Box, 1957–59* by David Kynaston; *Modernity Britain: A Shake of the Dice,*

1959–62 by David Kynaston; *The People: The Rise and Fall of the Working Class 1910–2010* by Selina Todd; *Never Had it So Good: A History of Britain from Suez to the Beatles* by Dominic Sandbrook; *White Heat: A History of Britain in the Swinging Sixties* by Dominic Sandbrook; *The Great British Dream Factory: The Strange History of Our National Imagination* by Dominic Sandbrook; *The Sixties* by Francis Wheen; *1966: The Year the Decade Exploded* by Jon Savage; *1963: Five Hundred Days* by John Lawton; *Our Times: The Age of Elizabeth II* by A.N. Wilson; *The Bad Trip: Dark Omens, New Worlds and the End of the Sixties* by James Riley; *The Neophiliacs* by Christopher Booker; and *The White Album* by Joan Didion. For the chapter comparing the Christmas messages of the Beatles and the Queen, *Voices Out of the Air: The Royal Christmas Broadcasts 1932–1981* was invaluable.

Random works mentioned in *150 Glimpses of the Beatles* include: *Through the Looking-Glass* by Lewis Carroll; *Aspects of Alice: Lewis Carroll's Dreamchild as Seen Through the Critics' Looking-Glasses* edited by Robert Phillips; *The Lore and Language of Schoolchildren* by Iona and Peter Opie; the *Just William* books by Richmal Crompton; *She* by H. Rider Haggard; *A Word Child* by Iris Murdoch; *Iris Murdoch as I Knew Her* by A.N. Wilson; *1066 and All That* by W.C. Sellar and R.J. Yeatman; *The Goon Show Scripts* by Spike Milligan; *Enderby Outside* by Anthony Burgess; *20th Century Words* by John Ayto; *Dylan's Visions of Sin* by Christopher Ricks; and the lovely *A Complete Book of Aunts* by Rupert Christiansen.

The world of pop music continues to amass a library of reference books that now seem to be outpacing those about religion or politics. I have spent many enjoyable hours consulting: *The Guinness Book of British Hit Singles*; *The Sound and the Fury: Forty Years of Classic Rock Journalism* edited by Barney Hoskyns; *The* Rolling Stone *Encyclopaedia of Rock & Roll* edited by Jon Pareles and Patricia Romanowski; *The* Rolling Stone *Interviews 1967–1980*; *The Book of Rock Lists* by Dave Marsh and Kevin Stein; Time Out *Interviews, 1968–1998* edited by Frank Boughton; *Teenage Idols* by Frank Clews; *The Faber Companion to Twentieth-Century Music* by Phil Hardy and Dave Laing; *Whatever Happened to . . . ?* by Bill Harry; *The Faber Book of Pop* edited by Hanif Kureishi and Jon Savage; and *The Best of* Rolling Stone edited by Robert Love.

Online reference works are equally valuable, perhaps more so, as they are so up-to-date. Billboard.com offers an omniscient view of the American charts; rocksbackpages.com gives access to the best music papers; and The Beatles Bible strikes me as the single best source of information on all aspects of the Beatles: often, after I had patted myself on the back for discovering some particularly arcane fact, I found to my irritation that it had been in The Beatles Bible all along. My book has also benefited from research in the archives of the *New York Times*; *Los Angeles Times*; *New Yorker*; *British Medical Journal*; the

Margaret Thatcher Foundation; *The Listener*; *Private Eye*; *Desert Island Discs*; *Daily Telegraph* obituaries; *Daily Mirror*; *Liverpool Echo*; *Saturday Evening Post*; *National Review*; *Seattle Times*; *GQ*; *Life*; *New Statesman*; Britishnewspaper archive.co.uk; rollingstone.com; Omega Auctions; *Queen*; *Independent* obituaries; thisamericanlife.org; and beatlesinterviews.org.

I have spent many hundreds of hours on YouTube, watching old interviews, videos, press conferences, news footage and documentaries, such as *24 Hours: The World of John and Yoko* from the BBC, and *A Boy Called Donovan*. My chapter on the rooftop concert was greatly helped by a BBC Radio 4 documentary, *The Beatles' Final Concert*. Finally, a word of thanks to virtually everyone to whom I have spoken over the past year or two: rare is the person who does not have a favourite Beatle, or a favourite Beatles album, or an anecdote about meeting one Beatle or another, or strong opinions on the Maharishi, or the Rolling Stones, or the sixties in general.

ACKNOWLEDGEMENTS

Thanks to: Stephen Bayley, Antony Beevor, Vicky Bippart, Eleanor Bron, Alistair Brown, Jack Chalmers, Cressida Connolly, Seraphina D'Arby, Cathy Drysdale and everyone at *Desert Island Discs*, Cecily Engle, Edel Eustace, Ian Hislop, David Jenkins, Mary Killen, Robert Lacey, Naomi Mantin, Charles Miller, Sheila Molnar, Omega Auctions, Nicholas Pearson, John Preston, Zoe Shine, Maxine Sibihwana, Bill Smith, Jack Smyth, Robin and Liz Summers, Hugo Vickers, Francis Wheen, Felix White, and, most of all, my wife, Frances Welch.

ILLUSTRATION CREDITS

A NOTE ABOUT THE AUTHOR

Craig Brown is a prolific journalist and author. His column in *Private Eye* magazine has been running for more than thirty years. His awards include the Sony Radio Academy Gold Award for Comedy, the Glenfiddich Food and Drink Award, and Press Awards for best humorist, best columnist, and best critic. He has written for many publications, including *Vanity Fair*, *The Guardian*, the *Daily Mail*, *New York*, *The Sunday Times* (London), *The Times Literary Supplement*, and *The New York Review of Books*. His last book, *Ninety-Nine Glimpses of Princess Margaret*, won the James Tait Black Prize for best biography and the South Bank Sky Arts Award for Literature, and was short-listed for the National Book Critics Circle Award. He lives in Aldeburgh, Suffolk, with his wife, Frances Welch; they have two children, both writers.